Secretary of the Treasury

Secretary of the Treasury

Annual Report, 1868

Secretary of the Treasury

Secretary of the Treasury
Annual Report, 1868

ISBN/EAN: 9783741136504

Manufactured in Europe, USA, Canada, Australia, Japa

Cover: Foto ©Thomas Meinert / pixelio.de

Manufactured and distributed by brebook publishing software
(www.brebook.com)

Secretary of the Treasury

Secretary of the Treasury

40TH CONGRESS, 3d *Session.* } HOUSE OF REPRESENTATIVES. { EX. DOC. No. 2.

SECRETARY OF THE TREASURY

ON THE

STATE OF THE FINANCES

FOR

THE YEAR 1868.

WASHINGTON:
GOVERNMENT PRINTING OFFICE.
1868.

INDEX.

REPORT

OF

THE SECRETARY OF THE TREASURY.

TREASURY DEPARTMENT,
December 1, 1868.

In compliance with the requirements of law, the Secretary of the Treasury has the honor to make to Congress the following report:

In his former communications, the Secretary has expressed so fully his views upon the great subjects of the currency, the revenues, and the public debt, that it may be thought quite unnecessary for him again to press them upon the attention of Congress. These subjects, however, have lost none of their importance; on the contrary, the public mind during the past year has been turned to their consideration with more absorbing interest than at any former period. The Secretary will, therefore, he trusts, be pardoned for restating some of the views heretofore presented by him.

If there is any question in finance or political economy which can be pronounced settled by argument and trial, it is, that inconvertible and depreciated paper money is injurious to public and private interests, a positive political and financial evil, for which there can be but one justification or excuse, to wit: a temporary necessity arising from an unexpected and pressing emergency; and it follows, consequently, that such a circulation should only be tolerated until, without a financial shock, it can be withdrawn or made convertible into specie. If an irredeemable bank-note circulation is an evidence of bankrupt or badly managed banking institutions, which should be deprived of their franchises, or compelled to husband and make available their resources in order that they may be prepared at the earliest day practicable to take up their dishonored obligations, why should not an irredeemable government currency be regarded as an evidence of bad management of the national finances, if not of national bankruptcy? And why should not such wise and equal revenue laws be enacted, and such economy in the use of the public moneys be enforced, as will enable the government either judiciously to fund or promptly to redeem its broken promises? The United States notes, although declared by law to be lawful money, are, nevertheless, a dishonored and disreputable currency. The fact that they are a legal tender, possessing such attributes of money as the statute can give them, adds nothing to their real value, but makes them all the more dishonorable to the government, and subversive of good morals. The people are compelled to take as money what is not money; and becoming demoralized by its constantly changing value, they are in danger of losing that sense of honor in their dealings with the government and with each other which is necessary for the well-being of society. It is vain to expect on the part of the people a faithful fulfilment of their duties to the government as long as the government is faithless to its own obligations; nor will those who do not hesitate to defraud the public revenues long continue to be scrupulous in their private business. Justifiable and necessary as the measure was then regarded, it is now apparent that an unfortunate step was taken when irredeemable promises were issued as lawful money; and especially when they were made a valid tender in payment of debts contracted when specie was the legal as well as the commercial standard of value. The legal-tender notes enabled debtors to pay their debts in a currency largely inferior to that which was alone recognized as money at the time they were incurred, and thus the validity of contracts was virtually impaired. If all creditors had been compelled by law to pay into the public treasury fifty per cent. or ten per cent., or, indeed, any portion of the amounts received by them from their debtors, such a law would have been condemned as unequal and unjust; and yet the effect of it would have been to lessen, to the extent of the receipts from this source, the necessity for other kinds of taxation, and thus to relieve in some measure the class unjustly, because unequally, taxed. By the legal-tender acts a portion of the property of one class of citizens was virtually confiscated for the benefit of another, without an increase thereby of the public revenues, and, consequently, without any compensation to the injured class. There can be no doubt that these acts have tended to blunt and deaden the public conscience, nor that they are chargeable in no small degree with the demoralization which so generally prevails.

The economical objections to these notes as lawful money—stated at length in previous reports of the Secretary—may be thus briefly restated. They increased immensely the cost of the war, and they have added largely to the expenses of the government since the restoration of peace; they have caused instability in prices, unsteadiness in trade, and put a check upon judicious enterprises; they have driven specie from circulation and made it merchandise; they have sent to foreign countries the product of our mines, at the same time that our European debt has been steadily increasing, and has now reached such magnitude as to be a heavy drain upon the national resources and a serious obstacle in the way of a return to specie payments; they have shaken the public credit by raising dangerous questions in regard to the payment of the public debt; in connection with high taxes, (to the necessity for which they have largely contributed,) they are preventing ship-building, and thereby the restoration of the commerce which was destroyed by the war; they are an excuse for (if indeed they do not necessitate) protective tariffs, and yet fail, by their fluctuating value, to protect the American manufacturer against his foreign competitor; they are filling the coffers of the rich, but, by reason of the high prices which they create and sustain, they are almost intolerable to persons of limited incomes. The language of one of the greatest men of modern times, so often, but not too often, quoted, is none too strong in its descriptions of the injustice and the evils of an inconvertible currency:

Of all the contrivances for cheating the laboring classes of mankind, none has been more effectual than that which deludes them with paper money. Ordinary tyranny, oppression, excessive taxation—these bear lightly on the happiness of the mass of the community compared with a fraudulent currency and the robberies committed by depreciated paper. Our own history has recorded for our instruction enough and more than enough of the demoralizing tendency, the injustice, and the intolerable oppression, on the virtuous and well-disposed, of a degraded paper currency authorized or in any way countenanced by government.

The experience of all nations that have tried the experiment of inconvertible paper money has proved the truth of the eloquent words of Mr. Webster. If our country is in a measure prosperous with such an incubus upon it, it is because it is so magnificent in extent, so diversified in climate, so rich in soil, so abundant in minerals, with a people so full of energy, that even a debased currency can only retard but not put a stop to its progress.

The Secretary still adheres to the opinion so frequently expressed by him, that a reduction of the paper circulation of the country until it appreciated to the specie standard was the true solution of our financial problem. But as this policy was emphatically condemned by Congress, and it is now too late to return to it, he recommends the following measures as the next best calculated to effect the desired result.

Agreements for the payment of coin seem to be the only ones, not contrary to good morals, the performance of which cannot be enforced in the courts. "Coin contracts" executed before the passage of the legal-tender acts, as well as those executed since, are satisfied in all the States except California by the payment of the amounts called for, in depreciated notes. This shackle upon commerce, this check upon our national progress, this restriction upon individual rights, should no longer be continued. If it be admitted that the condition of the country during the war, and for a time after its close, created a necessity for laws and decisions making promissory notes (fluctuating in value according to the result of battles and of speculative combinations) the medium in which contracts should be discharged, this necessity no longer exists. Steps should now be taken to give stability to business and security to enterprise; and to this end, *specific contracts to be executed in coin* should at once be legalized. Perhaps no law could be passed which would be productive of better results, with so little private or public inconvenience. Such a law would simply enable the citizen to do what the government is doing in its receipts for customs, and in the payment of its bonded debt; it would merely authorize the enforcement of contracts voluntarily entered into, according to their letter. The effect of such a law would be to check the outflow of specie to other countries, by creating a necessity for the use of it at home; to encourage enterprise extending into the future, by removing all uncertainty in regard to the value of the currency with which they are to be carried on. Such a law would remove a formidable embarrassment in our foreign trade, would familiarize our people again with specie as the standard of value, and show how groundless is the apprehension so generally existing, that a withdrawal of depreciated notes, or the appreciation of these notes to par, would produce a scarcity of money, by proving that specie, expelled from the country by an inferior circulating medium, will return again when it is made the basis of contracts, and is needed in their performance. Business is now necessarily speculative because the basis is unreliable. Currency, by reason of its uncertain future value, although usually plentiful in the cities, and readily obtained there at low rates on short time, with ample collaterals, is comparatively scarce and dear in the agricultural districts, where longer loans on commercial paper are required. Prudent men hesitate both to lend or to borrow for any considerable period by reason of their inability to determine the value of the medium in which the loans are to be paid. With currency now worth 70 cents on the dollar, and which within six months may advance to 80, or decline to 60, is it strange that the flow is to the business centres, where it can be loaned "on call," leaving the interior without proper supplies, at reasonable rates, for moving the crops and conducting other legitimate business? Is it strange that, in such an unsettled condition of the currency, gambling is active while enterprise halts, trade stagnates, and distrust and apprehension exist in regard to the future? It is not supposed that such a measure as is recommended will cure the financial evils which now afflict the country, but it will be a decided movement in the right direction, and the Secretary indulges the hope that it will receive the early and favorable consideration of Congress.

The legal-tender acts were war measures. By reference to the debates upon their passage, it will be perceived that, by all who advocated them, they were expected to be temporary only. It was feared that irredeemable government notes, in the unfortunate condition of the country, could only be saved from great depreciation by being made a legal tender —the great fact not being sufficiently considered that, by possessing this character, their depreciation would not be prevented, but merely disguised. Hence it was declared that they should be "lawful money and a legal tender in payment of all debts, public or private, within the United States, except duties on imports and interest on the public debt." They were issued in an emergency, for which it then seemed that no other provision could be made. They were, in fact, a forced loan, justified only by the condition of the country, and they were so recognized by Congress and the people. By no member of Congress and by no public journal was the issue of these notes as lawful money advocated on any other ground than that of necessity; and the question arises, should they not now, or at an early day, be divested of the character which was conferred upon them in a condition of the country so different from the present? The Secretary believes that they should, and he therefore recommends, in addition to the enactment by which contracts for the payment of coin can be enforced, that it be declared, *that after the first day of January*, 1870, *United States notes shall cease to be a legal tender in payment of all private debts subsequently contracted; and that after the first day of January*, 1871, *they shall cease to be a legal tender on any contract, or for any purpose whatever, except government dues, for which they are now receivable.* The law should also authorize the conversion of these notes, at the pleasure of the holders, into bonds, bearing such rate of interest as may be authorized by Congress on the debt into which the present outstanding bonds may be funded. The period for which they would continue to be a legal tender would be sufficient to enable the people and the banks to prepare for the contemplated change, and the privilege of their conversion would save them from depreciation. What has been said by the Secretary in his previous reports on the pernicious effects upon business and the public morals of inconvertible legal-tender notes, and what is said in this report upon the advantages which would result from legalizing coin contracts, sustain this recommendation. It may not be improper, however, to suggest another reason for divesting these notes of their legal-tender character by legislative action. Although the decisions of the courts have been generally favorable to the constitutionality of the acts by which they were authorized, grave doubts are entertained by many of the ablest lawyers of the country as to the correctness of these decisions; and it is to be borne in mind that they have not yet been sustaind by the Supreme Court of the United States.

The illustrious lawyer and statesman, whose language upon the subject of irredeemable paper money has been quoted, in the Senate of the United States, on the 21st day of December, 1836, expressed the following opinion:

> Most unquestionably there is no legal tender in this country, under the authority of this government or any other, but gold and silver, either the coinage of our own mints or foreign coins, at rates regulated by Congress. This is a constitutional principle, perfectly plain, and of the very highest importance. The States are expressly prohibited from making anything but gold and silver a legal tender in payment of debts, and although no such express prohibition is applied to Congress, yet, as Congress has no power granted to it in this respect but to coin money and to regulate the value of foreign coins, it clearly has no power to substitute paper or anything else for coin as a tender in payment of debts and in discharge of contracts. Congress has exercised this power fully in both its branches. It has coined money, and still coins it; it has regulated the value of foreign coins, and still regulates their value. The legal tender, therefore, the constitutional standard of value, is established, and cannot be overthrown. To overthrow it would shake the whole system.

It is by no means certain that the Supreme Court will differ from Mr. Webster upon this question, and no one can fail to perceive how important it is that the legislation recommended should precede a decision (from which there can be no appeal) that United States notes are not, under the federal Constitution, a legal tender.

The receipts from customs for the last three years have been as follows:

For the fiscal year ending June 30, 1866............. $179,046,651 58
For the fiscal year ending June 30, 1867............. 176,417,810 88
For the fiscal year ending June 30, 1868............. 164,464,599 56

While it appears from these figures that the customs receipts since the commencement of the fiscal year 1865 have been, in a revenue point of view, entirely satisfactory, the question naturally arises, what do these large receipts, under a high tariff, indicate in regard to our foreign trade and to our financial relations with foreign nations?

It is impossible to ascertain with precision the amount of our securities held in Europe, nor is there any perfectly reliable data for ascertaining even what amount has gone there annually since the first bonds were issued for the prosecution of the late war. In his report of 1866, the Secretary estimated the amount of United States securities of different kinds, including railroad and other stock, held in Europe, at $600,000,000. He soon after became satisfied that this estimate was too low, by from $100,000,000 to $150,000,000. It would be safe to put the amount so held at the present time, exclusive of stocks, at $850,000,000, of which not less than $600,000,000 are United States bonds, nearly all of which have left the United States within the last six years. The amount is formidable; and little satisfaction is derived from the consideration that these securities have been transferred in payment of interest and for foreign commodities; and just as little from the consideration that probably not over $500,000,000 in gold values have been received for these $850,000,000 of debt. In this estimate of our foreign indebtedness, railroad and other *stocks* are not included, as they are not a debt, but the evidence merely of the ownership of property in the United States. Fortunately, for some years past, individual credits have been curtailed, and our foreign and domestic trade, in this particular, has not been unsatisfactory. In addition, then, to the stocks referred to and the individual indebtedness, of the amount of which no accurate estimate can be made, Europe holds not less than $850,000,000 of American securities, on nearly all of which interest, and on the greater part of which interest in gold, is being paid. Nor, under the present revenue systems, and with a depreciated paper currency, is the increase of our foreign debt likely to be stayed. With an abundant harvest and a large surplus of agricultural products of all descriptions, United States bonds are still creating, to no small extent, the exchange with which our foreign balances are being adjusted. We are even now increasing our debt to Europe at the rate of $60,000,000 or $70,000,000 per annum in the form of gold-bearing bonds.

The gold and silver product of California and the Territories, since 1848, has been upwards of $1,300,000,000. Allowing that $100,000,000 have been used in manufactures, and that the coin in the country has been increased to an equal amount, the balance of this immense sum, $1,100,000,000, has gone to other countries in exchange for their productions. Within a period of twenty years, in addition to our agricultural products, and to our manufactures which have been exported in large quantities, we have parted with $1,100,000,000 of the precious metals; and are, nevertheless, confronted with a foreign debt of some $850,000,000, which is steadily increasing; and all this has occurred under tariffs in a good degree framed with the view of protecting American against foreign manufacturers. But this is not all. During the recent war, most of our vessels engaged in the foreign trade were either destroyed by rebel cruisers or transferred to foreigners. Our exports as well as our imports are now chiefly in foreign bottoms. The carrying trade between the United States and Europe is almost literally in the hands of Europeans. Were it not for the remnant of ships still employed in the China trade, and the stand we are making by the establishment of a line of steamers on the Pacific, the coastwise trade, which is retained by the exclusion of foreign competition, would seem to be about all that can, under existing legislation, be relied upon for the employment of American shipping.

There are many intelligent persons who entertain the opinion that the country has been benefited by the transfer of our bonds to Europe, on the ground that capital has been received in exchange for them, which has been profitably employed in the development of our national resources: and that it matters little whether the interest upon the debt is received by our own people or by the people of other countries. This opinion is the result of misapprehension of facts, and is unsound in principle. It is not to a large extent true that capital, which is being used in developing the national resources, has been received in exchange for the bonds which are held in Europe. While many articles, such as railroad iron, machinery and raw materials, used in manufacturing—the value of which to the country is acknowledged—have been so received, a large proportion of the receipts have been of a different description. Our bonds have been largely paid for in articles for which no nation can afford to run in debt—for articles which have neither stimulated industry nor increased the productive power of the country, which have, in fact, added nothing to the national wealth. A reference to the custom-house entries will substantiate the correctness of these statements. Two-thirds of the importations of the United States consist of articles which, in economical times, would be pronounced luxuries. The war and a redundant currency have brought about unexampled extravagance, which can only be satisfied by the most costly products of foreign countries. No exception could be taken to such importations if they were paid for in our own productions. This unfortunately is not the fact. They are annually swelling our foreign debt, without increasing our ability to pay it. How disastrous such a course of trade, if long

Nor is it an unimportant matter that the interest upon a large portion of our securities is received by citizens of other countries instead of our own. If the interest upon a public debt is paid out where the taxes to provide for it are collected, the debt, although a burden upon the mass of tax-payers who are not holders of securities, may be so managed as not to be a severe burden upon the nation. The money which goes into the treasury by means of taxes, will flow out again into the same community in the payment of interest; and were it not for the expenses attending it, the process would not, in a purely economical view, be an exhausting one. If the bonds of the United States were equally distributed among the people of the different States, there would be less complaint of the debt than is now heard. Anti-tax parties will attain strength only in those States in which few bonds are held. If the people of the west are more sensible of the burdens of federal taxation than are those of the eastern States, it is because they are not holders to the same extent of national securities. This inequality cannot of course be prevented by legal or artificial processes. The securities will be most largely held where capital is the most abundant; and they will be more equally distributed among the respective States—if not among the people—as the new States approach the older ones in wealth.

These manifest truths indicate how important it is that the debt of the United States should be a home debt, so that the money which is collected for taxes may be paid to our own people in the way of interest. In fact, a large national debt to be tolerable, must of necessity be a home debt. A nation that owes heavily must have its own people for creditors. If it does not, the debt will be a dead weight upon its industry, and will be quite likely to force it eventually into bankruptcy. The United States are not only able to pay the interest on their debt, but to set a good example to other nations by steadily and rapidly reducing that debt. What is now required, as has been already intimated, are measures which will tend only to prevent further exportation of our bonds, and in the regular course of trade to bring back to the country those that have been exported, but which will also tend to restore those important interests that are now languishing, as the result of the war and adverse legislation. The first and most important of these measures are those which shall bring about, without unnecessary delay, the restoration of the specie standard. The financial difficulties under which the country is laboring may be traced directly to the issue, and continuance in circulation, of irredeemable promises as lawful money. The country will not be really and reliably prosperous until there is a return to specie payments. The question of a solvent, convertible currency, underlies all other financial and economical questions. It is, in fact, a fundamental question; and until it is settled, and settled in accordance with the teachings of experience, all attempts at other financial and economical reforms will either fail absolutely or be but partially successful. A sound currency is the life-blood of a commercial nation. If this is debased the whole current of its commercial life must be disordered and irregular. The starting point in reformatory legislation must be here. Our debased currency must be retired or raised to the par of specie, or cease to be lawful money, before substantial progress can be made with other reforms.

Next in importance to the subject of the currency is that of the revenues. Taxes are indispensable for the support of the government, for the maintenance of the public credit, and the payment of the public debt. To tax heavily, not only without impoverishing the people, but without checking enterprise or putting shackles upon industry, requires the most careful study, not only of the resources of the country and its relations with other nations, but also of the character of the people as affected by the nature of their institutions. While much may be learned by the study of the revenue systems of European nations, which have been perfected by years of experience and the employment of the highest talent, it must be obvious that these systems must undergo very considerable modifications before they will be fitted to the political and physical condition of the United States. In a popular government like ours, where the people virtually assess the taxes, as well as pay them, the popular will, if not the popular prejudice, must be listened to in the preparation of revenue laws. Justice must, in some instances, yield to expediency; and some legitimate sources of revenue may be unavailable because a resort to them might be odious to a majority of tax-payers. The people of the United States are enterprising and self-reliant. Most of them are the "architects of their own fortunes;" few the inheritors of wealth. Engaged in various enterprises, with constantly varying results, and in sharp competition with each other, they submit reluctantly to inquisitions of tax-gatherers, which might not be obnoxious to people less independent and living under less liberal institutions. Then, too, the United States are a new country, of large extent and diversified interests; with great natural resources, in the early process of development. Not only may systems of revenue which are suited to England, or Germany, or France, be unsuited to this country, but careful and judicious observation and study are indispensable to the preparation of tax bills suited to the peculiar interests of its different sections. It was with a view of supplying Congress with such information as was needed to secure the passage of equal and wise excise and tariff laws, which would yield the largest revenue with the least oppression and inconvenience to the people, that a revenue commission was created in 1865. The creation of this commission was the first practical movement towards a careful examination of the business and resources of the country, with a view to the adoption of a judicious revenue system. The reports of this commission were interesting and valuable, and they exhibited so clearly the necessity for further and more complete investigations, that by the act of July 13, 1866, the Secretary of the Treasury was authorized to appoint an officer in his department, to be styled the special commissioner of revenue, whose duty it should be to "inquire into all the sources of national revenue, and the best method of collecting the revenue; the relation of foreign trade to domestic industry; the mutual adjustment of the systems of taxation by customs and excise, with a view of insuring the requisite revenue with the least disturbance or inconvenience to the progress of industry, and the development of the resources of the country," &c. Under this act Mr. David A. Wells was appointed special commissioner of the revenue. With what energy and ability he has undertaken the very difficult duties devolved upon him has been manifested by the reports which he has already submitted to Congress. That which accompanies, or will soon follow this communication, will prove more fully than those which have preceded it have done the importance of the investigations in which he is engaged, and the judicious labor which he is bestowing upon them. The facts which he presents, and the recommendations based upon them, are entitled to the most careful consideration of Congress. These reports of the commissioner are so complete that they relieve the Secretary from discussing elaborately the questions of which they treat His remaks, therefore, upon the internal revenues and the tariff will be general and brief.

The following is a statement of receipts from internal revenues for the last three fiscal years:

For the year ending June 30, 1866	$309, 226, 813 42
For the year ending June 30, 1867	266, 027, 537 43
For the year ending June 30, 1868	191, 087, 589 41

It thus appears that the internal revenue receipts for the year ending June 30, 1867, fell below the receipts for the year ending June 30, 1866, $43,199,275 99, and that the receipts for the year ending June 30, 1868, fell short of the receipts for 1867, $74,939,948 02. The receipts for the first four months of the present fiscal year were $48,736,348 33. If the receipts for these months are an index of those for the remaining eight, the receipts for the present fiscal year will be $146,209,044.

This large reduction of internal revenue receipts is attributable both to inefficient collections and to a reduction of taxes. It is quite obvious that the receipts from customs cannot be maintained without an increase of exports or of our foreign debt. If the receipts from customs should be diminished, even with a large reduction of the expenses of the government, our internal revenues must necessarily be increased. The first thing to be done is to introduce economy into all branches of the public service, not by reduced appropriations to be made good by "deficiency bills," but by putting a stop to all unnecessary demands upon the treasury. There is no department of the government which is conducted with proper economy. The habits formed during the war are still strong, and will only yield to the requirements of inexorable law. The average expenses of the next ten years for the civil service ought not to exceed $40,000,000 per annum. Those of the War Department, after the bounties are paid, should be brought down to $35,000,000, and those of the Navy to $20,000,000. The outlays for pensions and Indians cannot for some years be considerably reduced, but they can doubtless be brought within $30,000,000. The interest on the public debt when the whole debt shall be funded, at an average rate of interest of five per cent., will amount to $125,000,000, which will be reduced with the annual reduction of the principal.

When the internal revenue and tariff laws shall be revised so as to be made to harmonize with each other, it is supposed that $300,000,000 can annually be realized from these sources without burdensome taxation. How much shall be raised from each, can be determined when the whole subject of revenue shall be thoroughly investigated by Congress, with the light shed upon it by Commissioner Wells in his exhaustive report of the present year. The Secretary does not doubt, however, that the best interests of the country will be subserved by a reduction of the tariff and an increase of excise duties.

According to this estimate the account would stand as follows:

Receipts from customs and internal revenues	$300,000,000
Expenditures for the civil service	$40,000,000
Expenditures by the War Department	35,000,000
Expenditures by the Navy Department	20,000,000
Expenditures for pensions and Indians	30,000,000
Expenditures for interest on the public debt	125,000,000
Total	250,000,000

Leaving as an excess of receipts $50,000,000 to be applied to the payment of the principal of the debt. If the growth of the country should make an increase of expenditures necessary, this increase will, by the same cause, be provided for by increased receipts under the same rate of taxation; and as it is to be hoped that the regular increase of the revenues, without an increase of taxation, resulting from the advance of the country in wealth and population, will be greater than the necessary increase of expenses, there will be a constantly increasing amount in addition to that arising from a decrease of interest, to be annually applied to the payment of the debt. If large additional expenditures should be unavoidable, they should at once be provided for by additional taxes. What is required, then, at the present time, is a positive limitation of the annual outlays to $300,000,000, including $50,000,000 to be applied to the payment of the principal of the debt, and such modifications of the revenue laws as will secure this amount, without unwise restrictions upon commerce, and with the least possible oppression and inconvenience to the tax-payers. In the foregoing estimates of resources, miscellaneous receipts and receipts for sales of public lands are omitted. The miscellaneous receipts heretofore have been derived from sales of gold and of property purchased by the War and Navy Departments during the war, and no longer needed. On a return to specie payments there will be no premiums on coin; very little government property will hereafter be sold; and under the homestead law, and with liberal donations of the public domain, which are likely to be made as heretofore, no considerable amount can be expected from lands. Whatever may be received from these sources will doubtless be covered by miscellaneous expenses, of which no estimate can be made.

The act of March 31, 1868, exempting from taxes nearly all the manufactures of the country other than distilled spirits, fermented liquors, and tobacco, was sudden and unexpected. It not only deprived the treasury of an immense revenue, but the reduction was so great as to leave an impression on the public mind that it would be only temporary, and that a tax in some degree equivalent to that which was removed would of necessity soon be resorted to. It is, perhaps, for this reason that this measure has failed to give relief to the public by a diminution of prices, and has benefited manufacturers rather than consumers. The frequent and important changes which have been made in the internal revenue laws, the ease with which exemptions from taxation have been obtained, and the suddenness with which taxes have been greatly augmented or reduced, have constituted one of the greatest evils of the system. Sudden changes in the revenue laws are not only destructive of all business calculations, but they excite—not unreasonably—a feeling of discontent and a sense of injustice among the people most unfavorable to an efficient collection of taxes. While it is admitted that, in a new and growing country like ours, modifications of the taxes will be frequently necessary, some definite policy should at once be inaugurated in regard to our internal revenues, the general principles of which should be regarded as finally established.

Assuming that the receipts from customs will be reduced by a reduction of duties, or by the effects of a return to specie payments upon importations under the present tariff, and that, consequently, there must be an increase of internal taxes, there are three sources of revenue which are likely to be considered.

First. An increase of taxes upon distilled spirits.

The idea of deriving the bulk of the revenue from this article is a very popular one; and even our unfortunate experience has only partially convinced the public of its impossibility. The late exorbitant tax on

The objections to the restoration of this tax are, that it would indicate vacillation on the part of Congress, and that this tax, principally on account of numerous exemptions, was partial and unjust. It is also apparent that, if restored, it would fail to be permanent by reason of the persistent and united hostility of a class of citizens influential and powerful, and whose influence and power are rapidly increasing.

Third. An increased and uniform tax on sales; and this the Secretary respectfully recommends.

Under the present law wholesale and retail dealers in goods, wares, and merchandise of foreign or domestic production, wholesale and retail dealers in liquors, and dealers in tobacco, are subject to a similar but unequal tax on sales. This inequality should be removed, and a tax levied upon all sales sufficient, with the revenues from other sources, to meet the wants of the government. The reasons in favor of a tax upon sales are, that it could be levied generally throughout the country, and would not be liable to the imputation of class legislation; that it would be so equally distributed as not to bear so oppressively as other taxes upon individuals or sections; and that no depression of one branch of industry, which did not injuriously affect the business of the entire country, could greatly lessen its productiveness.

As has been already stated, the receipts from customs for the fiscal year ending June 30, 1866, were $179,046,651 58; for the year ending June 30, 1867, $176,417,810 88; and for the last fiscal year, $164,464,599 56. These figures show that the tariff has produced large revenues, although it is in no just sense a revenue tariff. In this respect it has exceeded the expectations of its friends, if, indeed, it has not disappointed them. It has not checked importations, and complaint is made that it has not given the anticipated protection to home manufactures, not because it was not skillfully framed to this end, but because an inflated currency—the effect of which upon importations was not fully comprehended—has, in a measure, defeated its object. It has advanced the prices of dutiable articles, and, by adding to the cost of living, has been oppressive to consumers without being of decided benefit to those industries in whose interest it is regarded as having been prepared. In his last report, the Secretary recommended the extension of specific duties, but did not recommend a complete revision of the tariff, on the ground that this work could not be intelligently done as long as business was subject to constant derangement by an irredeemable currency. The same difficulty still exists, but as decided action upon the subject of the currency ought not to be longer postponed, the present may not be an unfavorable time for a thorough examination of the tariff. It is obvious that a revision of it is required, not only to relieve it of incongruities and obscurity, and to harmonize it with excise taxes and with our agricultural and commercial interests, but also to adapt it to the very decided change which must take place in the business of the country upon the restoration of the specie standard. Large revenues are now derived from customs, because a redundant currency produces extravagance, which stimulates importations. If the currency were convertible, and business were regular and healthy, the tariff would be severely protective, if not in many instances prohibitory. Indeed, of some valuable articles it is prohibitory already.

There will be in the future, as there have been in the past, widely different opinions upon this long-vexed and very important subject, but the indications are decided that the more enlightened sentiment of the country demands that the tariff shall hereafter be a tariff for revenue and not for protection, and that the revenues to be derived from it shall be no larger than, in connection with those received from other sources, will be required for the economical administration of the government, the maintenance of the public faith, and the gradual extinguishment of the public debt. While the country is not at present, and may not be for many years to come, prepared for the abrogation of all restrictions upon foreign commerce, it is unquestionably prepared for a revenue tariff. The public debt is an incumbrance upon the property of the nation, and the taxes, the necessity for which it creates, by whatever mode and from whatever sources collected, are at last a charge upon the consumers. Taxes should not, therefore, be increased, nor will the tax-payers permit them to be permanently increased, for the benefit of any interest or section. Fortunately, or unfortunately, as the question may be regarded from different standpoints, the necessities of the government will be such for many years, that large revenues must be derived from customs, so that a strictly revenue tariff must incidentally benefit our home manufactures. According to the estimate made by the Secretary, an annual revenue of three hundred millions will be required to meet the necessary demands upon the treasury, and for a satisfactory reduction of the public debt. How much of this amount shall be derived from customs it will be for Congress to determine. In examining this difficult question, the magnitude of our foreign debt, and the necessity not only of preventing its increase but of rapidly reducing it, must be kept steadily in view. It may be necessary that a large portion of our bonds now held in Europe be taken up with bonds bearing a lower rate of interest, payable in some European city, in order that they may be less likely to be returned to the United States at unpropitious times. Whether this is accomplished or not, it is of the last importance that our tax laws, and especially the tariff, should be so framed as to encourage exports and enlarge our commerce with foreign nations, so that balances may be in our favor, and the interest, and in due time the principal, of our foreign debt may be paid by our surplus productions. Many of the investigations of the revenue commissioner have been made with the view of furnishing Congress with the data necessary for a thorough examination and a wise determination of this most important question, and it is fortunate that the subsidence of political excitement removes many of the difficulties heretofore in the way of an impartial consideration of it.

ERRATA.

On page XVII, 23d line from bottom, "November, 1857," should read "November, 1867."

The public debt on the first day of November, 1867, amounted to $2,491,504,450, and consisted of the following items:

Debt bearing coin interest	$1,778,110,991 80
Debt bearing currency interest	426,768,640 00
Matured debt not presented for payment	18,237,538 83
Debt bearing no interest	402,385,677 39
Total	2,625,502,848 02
Cash in the treasury	133,998,398 02
Amount of debt less cash in the treasury	2,491,504,450 00

On the first day of November, 1868, it amounted to $2,527,129,552 82, and consisted of the following items:

Debt bearing coin interest	$2,107,577,950 00
Debt bearing currency interest	114,519,000 00
Matured debt not presented for payment	9,753,723 64
Debt bearing no interest	409,151,898 42
Total	2,641,002,572 06
Cash in the treasury	113,873,019 24
Amount of debt less cash in the treasury	2,527,129,552 82

By a comparison of these statements it appears that the debt, between the first day of November, 1857, and the first day of November, 1868, increased $35,625,102 82. Of this increase $24,152,000 is chargeable to the Pacific railroads, and $7,200,000 to the purchase of Russian America. Within the same period, there was paid for bounties $44,060,515, and at least $4,000,000 for interest, on compound and seven three-tenth notes, which had accrued prior to the first of November, 1867. If these extraordinary advances and payments had not been made, the receipts would have exceeded the expenditures $43,787,412 18. Considering the heavy reduction of internal taxes, made at the last session of Congress, and the large expenditures which have attended the military operations against the Indians on the frontier, and the maintenance of large forces at expensive points in the southern States, this statement of the amount of the debt cannot be regarded an unsatisfactory one. The bounties will, it is expected, be entirely paid within the next three months, and very little interest, except that which accrues upon the funded debt, is hereafter to be provided for. Should there be henceforth no extraordinary expenditures, and no further donations of public moneys in the form of bounties or of additional subsidies to railroad companies, with proper economy in the administration of the general government, and with judicious amendments of the revenue laws, and proper enforcement thereof, the public debt, without oppressive taxation, can be rapidly diminished and easily extinguished within the period heretofore named

The ability of the United States to maintain their integrity against insurrection as well as against a foreign enemy can no longer be doubted. The question of their ability, under democratic institutions, to sustain a large national debt, is still to be decided. That this question should be affirmatively settled, it is, in the opinion of the Secretary, of the highest importance that the tax-paying voters should be encouraged by the fact that the debt is in the progress of rapid extinguishment, and is not to be a permanent burden upon them and their posterity. If it be understood that this debt is to be a perpetual incumbrance upon the property and industry of the nation, it is certainly to be feared that the collection of taxes necessary to pay the interest upon it may require the exercise of power by the central government, inconsistent with republicanism, and dangerous to the liberties of the people. The debt must be paid. Direct repudiation is an impossibility; indirect repudiation, by further issues of legal-tender notes, would be madness. To insure its payment without a change in the essential character of the government, every year should witness a reduction of its amount and a diminution of its burdens. The Secretary is confident that he expressed the sentiments of the intelligent tax-payers of the country when he said in his report of 1865:

> The debt is large, but if kept at home, as it is desirable it should be, with a judicious system of taxation, it need not be oppressive. It is, however, a debt. While it is capital to the holders of the securities, it is still a national debt, and an encumbrance upon the national estate. Neither its advantages nor its burdens are or can be shared or borne equally by the people. Its influences are anti-republican. It adds to the power of the Executive by increasing federal patronage; it must be distasteful to the people, because it fills the country with informers and tax-gatherers. It is dangerous to the public virtue, because it involves the collection and disbursement of vast sums of money, and renders rigid national economy almost impracticable. It is, in a word, a national burden, and the work of removing it, no matter how desirable it may be for individual investment, should not long be postponed.
>
> As all true men desire to leave to their heirs unincumbered estates, so should it be the ambition of the people of the United States to relieve their descendants of this national mortgage. We need not be anxious that future generations shall share the burden with us. Wars are not at an end, and posterity will have enough to do to take care of the debts of their own creation.
>
> The Secretary respectfully suggests that on this subject the expression of Congress should be decided and emphatic. It is of the greatest importance in the management of a matter of so surpassing interest that the right start should be made. Nothing but revenue will sustain the national credit, and nothing less than a fixed policy for the reduction of the public debt will be likely to prevent its increase.

And in his report of 1867, when he remarked:

> Old debts are hard debts to pay; the longer they are continued the more odious they become. If the present generation should throw the burden of this debt upon the next, it will be quite likely to be handed down from one generation to another, a perpetual if not a constantly increasing burden upon the people. Our country is full of enterprise and resources. The debt will be lightened every year with great rapidity by the increase of wealth and population. With a proper reduction in the expenses of the government, and with a revenue system adapted to the industry of the country, and not oppressing it, the debt may be paid before the expiration of the present century. The wisdom of a policy which shall bring about such a result is vindicated, in advance, by the history of nations whose people are burdened with inherited debts and with no prospect of relief for themselves or their posterity.

In his last report the Secretary referred to the condition of the treasury at the close of the war, and at some subsequent periods, alluding especially to the emergency in the spring of 1865, arising from the very large requisitions which were waiting for payment, and the still larger requisitions that were to be provided for, to enable the War Department to pay arrearages due to the army, and other expenses which had already been incurred in the suppression of the rebellion. In briefly reviewing the administration of the treasury from April, 1865, he did not think it necessary to state how much of the large revenue receipts had been expended in the payment of debts incurred during the war; and he would not undertake to do it now did not misapprehension exist in the public mind in regard to the expenditures of the government since the conclusion of hostilities, prejudicial to both the law-making and law-executing branches of the government.

The war was virtually closed in April, 1865. On the first day of that month the public debt amounted, according to the books and accounts of the department, to $2,366,955,077 34. On the first day of September following it amounted to $2,757,689,571 43, having increased in four months $390,734,494 09. From that period it continued to decline until November 1, 1867, when it had fallen to $2,491,504,450. On the first day of November last, it had risen to $2,527,129,552 82. By this statement it appears that between the first day of April, 1865, and the first day of September of the same year the debt increased $390,734,494 09, and that between the first day of September, 1865, and the first day of November, 1868, it decreased $230,560,018 61; and that on the last day mentioned it was $160,174,475 48 larger than it was on the first day of April, 1865. Since then the Treasurer's receipts from all sources of revenue have been as follows:

For April, May, and June, 1865	$83, 519, 164 13
For the year ending June 30, 1866	558, 032, 620 06
For the year ending June 30, 1867	490, 634, 010 27
For the year ending June 30, 1868	405, 638, 083 32
June 30 to November 1, 1868	124, 652, 184 42
Total of receipts	1, 662, 476, 062 20
To which should be added the increase of the debt between the first day of April, 1865, and the first day of November, 1868	160, 174, 475 48
	1, 822, 650, 537 68

This exhibit shows that the large sum of $1,822,650,537 68 was expended in the payment of the interest and of other demands upon the treasury in three years and seven months, being an average annual

If the statement of the public debt on the first day of April, 1865, had included all debts due at that time, and $1,822,650,537 68 had really been expended in payment of the interest on the public debt, and the current expenses of the government between that day and the first day of November last, there would have been a profligacy and a recklessness in the expenditures of the public moneys discreditable to the government and disheartening to tax-payers. Fortunately this is not the fact. That statement, (as is true of all other monthly statements of the treasury,) exhibited only the adjusted debt, according to the books of the treasury, and did not, and could not, include the large sums due to the soldiers of the great Union army (numbering at that time little less than a million of men) for "pay" and for "bounties," or on claims of various kinds which must of necessity have been unsettled. For the purpose of putting this matter right, the Secretary has endeavored to ascertain from the War and Navy Departments how much of their respective disbursements, since the close of the war, has been in payment of debts properly chargeable to the expenses of the war. The following is the result of his inquiries:

By the War Department..............................	$595,431,125 90
By the Navy Department..............................	35,000,000 00

It has been impossible to obtain an exact statement of the amount of such debts paid by the Navy Department, but sufficient information has been received to justify the Secretary in estimating it in round numbers at thirty-five millions, which is probably an under rather than over-estimate. The expenditures of the War Department have been furnished in detail, and are believed to be substantially correct.

These figures show that the money expended by the War and Navy Departments, between the first day of April, 1865, and the first day of November, 1868, on claims justly chargeable to the expenses of the war,

amounted to..	$630,431,125 90
To which should be added amount advanced to the Pacific roads..	42,194,000 00
Amount paid for Alaska..	7,200,000 00
	679,825,125 90

Deducting this sum from the amount of the revenues, $1,662,476,062 20, and $160,174,475 48, the increase of the public debt—the remainder, $1,142,825,411 78, or an average of $318,928,021 89 per annum, is the amount actually expended in the payment of current expenses and interest.

books of the treasury on the first day of April, 1865, it appears that the debt of the United States at that time was $2,997,386,203 24, and that the actual reduction has been $470,256,650 42; and but for the advances to the Pacific roads, and the amount paid for Alaska, would have been $519,650,650 42.

Nothing can better exhibit the greatness of the resources of this young nation than this statement, or show more clearly its ability to make "short work" of the extinguishment of the public debt. It will be borne in mind that these immense revenues have been collected while one-third part of the country was in a state of great destitution, resulting from its terrible struggle to separate itself from the Union, with its political condition unsettled, and its industry in a great degree paralyzed; and while also the other two-thirds were slowly recovering from the drain upon their productive labor and resources—a necessary accompaniment of a gigantic and protracted war.

The Secretary has noticed with deep regret indications of a growing entiment in Congress—notwithstanding the favorable exhibits which have been from time to time made of the debt-paying power of the country—in favor of a postponement of the payment of any part of the principal of the debt, until the national resources shall be so increased as to make the payment of it more easy. If this sentiment shall so prevail as to give direction to the action of the government, he would feel that a very great error had been committed, which could hardly fail to be a severe misfortune to the country. The people of the United States will never be so willing to be taxed for the purpose of reducing the debt as at the present time. Now, the necessity for its creation is better understood and appreciated than it can be at a future day. Now, it is regarded by a large majority of tax-payers as a part of the great price paid for the maintenance of the government, and, therefore, a sacred debt. The longer the reduction of it is postponed the greater will be the difficulties in the way of accomplishing it, and the more intolerable will seem to be the burden of taxation. The Secretary, therefore, renews the recommendations made in his first report, that a certain definite sum be annually applied to the payment of the interest and the principal of the debt. The amount suggested was two hundred millions of dollars. As the debt is considerably smaller than its maximum was estimated at, the amount to be so applied annually might now safely be fixed at one hundred and seventy-five millions of dollars, according to the estimate already made in this report.

The subject of the currency in which the five-twenty bonds may be paid—agitated for some time past—was freely discussed during the recent political canvass, and made a question upon which parties, to some extent, were divided. The premature and unfortunate agitation and discussion of this question have been damaging to the credit of the government, both at home and abroad, by exciting apprehensions that the good faith of the nation might not be maintained, and have thus prevented our bonds from advancing in price, as they otherwise would have advanced, after it was perceived that the maximum of the debt had been reached, and have rendered funding at a low rate of interest too unpromising to be undertaken. In his report in 1865, the Secretary used the following language:

Before concluding his remarks upon the national debt, the Secretary would suggest that the credit of the five-twenty bonds, issued under the acts of February 25, 1862, and June 30, 1864, would be improved in Europe, and consequently their market value advanced at home, if Congress should declare that the principal as well as the interest of these bonds is to be paid in coin. The policy of the government in regard to its funded debt is well understood in the United States, but the absence of a provision in these acts that the principal of the bonds issued under them should be paid in coin, while such a provision is contained in the act under which the ten-forties were issued, has created some apprehension in Europe that the five-twenty bonds might be called in at the expiration of five years, and paid in United States notes. Although it is not desirable that our securities should be held out of the United States, it is desirable that they should be of good credit in foreign markets on account of the influence which those markets exert upon our own. It is, therefore, important that all misapprehension on these points should be removed by an explicit declaration of Congress, that these bonds are to be paid in coin.

Without intending to criticise the inaction of Congress in regard to a matter of so great importance, the Secretary does not hesitate to say that, if his recommendations had been adopted, that the public debt would have been much less than it is; and that the reduction of the rate of interest would ere this have been in rapid progress. The Secretary does not think it necessary to discuss the question in this report. His opinions upon it are well known to Congress and the people. They were definitely presented in his report for 1867, and they remain unchanged. He begs leave merely to suggest, as he has substantially done before, that alleviation of the burden of the public debt is to be obtained—not in a decrial of the national credit—not in threats of repudiation—not in a further issue of irredeemable notes—not in arguments addressed to the fears of the bondholders—but in a clear and explicit declaration by Congress, that the national faith, in letter and spirit, shall be inviolably maintained, that the bonds of the United States, intended to be negotiated abroad as well as at home, are to be paid, when the time of payment arrives, in that currency which is alone recognized as money in the dealings of nation with nation. Let Congress say this promptly, and there can be but little doubt that the credit of the government will so advance that within the next two years the interest on the larger portion of the debt can be reduced to a satisfactory rate. He therefore earnestly recommends that it be declared, without delay, by joint resolution, that the principal of all bonds of the United States is to be paid in coin.

to exceed the rate of five per cent.; provided that the Secretary may, in his discretion, make the principal and interest of $500,000,000 of these bonds payable at such city or cities in Europe as he may deem best.

The fact that, according to the recommendation, $50,000,000 of the bonds to be issued are to become due each year for ten consecutive years (at the expiration of which time all of the bonds would be under the control of the government) would insure an annual reduction of $50,000,000 of the public debt, and impart a credit to the other bonds which would insure the negotiation of them on favorable terms.

Of the expediency of an issue of bonds corresponding, to some extent, in amount with those held in Europe, the interest and principal of which shall be paid in the countries where they are to be negotiated, there can be but little doubt. On this point the Secretary used the following language in his report of 1866:

> The question now to be considered is not how shall our bonds be prevented from going abroad, for a large amount has already gone, and others will follow as long as our credit is good and we continue to buy more than we can pay for in any other way, but how shall they be prevented from being thrown upon the home market, to thwart our efforts in restoring the specie standard? The Secretary sees no practicable method of doing this at an early day, but by substituting for them bonds which, being payable principal and interest in Europe, will be less likely to be returned when their return is the least to be desired. The holders of our securities in Europe are now subject to great inconvenience and not a little expense in collecting their coupons; and it is supposed that five per cent., or, perhaps, four and a half per cent. bonds, payable in London or Frankfort, could be substituted for our six per cents., without any other expense to the United States than the trifling commissions to the agents through whom the exchanges might be made. The saving of interest to be thus effected would be no inconsiderable item; and the advantages of having our bonds in Europe placed in the hands of actual investors, is too important to be disregarded.

The Secretary has nothing further to say on this point than that careful reflection has only strengthened his convictions of the correctness of the views expressed in the foregoing extract

In recommending the issue of bonds bearing a lower rate of interest, to be exchanged for the outstanding six per cents., the Secretary must not be understood as having changed his opinion in regard to the expediency or the wisdom of the recommendation in his last report—

> That the act of March 3, 1865, be so amended as to authorize the Secretary of the Treasury to issue six per cent. gold-bearing bonds, to be known as the consolidated debt of the United States, having 20 years to run, and redeemable, if it may be thought advisable, at an earlier day, to be exchanged at par for any and all other obligations of the government, one-sixth part of the interest on which, in lieu of all other taxes, at each semi-annual payment, shall be reserved by the government, and paid over to the States according to population.

He refers to what he then said in advocacy of that recommendation as an expression of his well-considered opinions at the present time, and he is only prevented from repeating the recommendation, by the fact that it met with little approval at the last session, and has not grown into favor since. He sincerely hopes that the future history of the debt will vindicate the wisdom of those who are unable to approve the proposition.

The following is a statement of the public debt on the 1st of July, 1868:

DEBT BEARING COIN INTEREST.		
5 per cent. bonds	$221,588,400 00	
6 per cent. bonds of 1867 and 1868	6,893,441 80	
6 per cent. bonds, 1881	283,677,200 00	
6 per cent. 5-20 bonds	1,557,844,600 00	
Navy pension fund	13,000,000 00	
		$2,083,003,641 80
DEBT BEARING CURRENCY INTEREST.		
6 per cent. bonds	$29,089,000 00	
3-year compound interest notes	21,604,890 00	
3-year 7.30 notes	25,534,900 00	
3 per cent. certificates	50,000,000 00	
		126,228,790 00
MATURED DEBT NOT PRESENTED FOR PAYMENT.		
3-year 7.30 notes, due August 15, 1867, and June 15 and July 15, 1868	$12,182,750 00	
Compound-interest notes, matured June 10, July 15, August 15, October 15, and December 15, 1867, and May 15, 1868	6,556,920 00	
Bonds, Texas indemnity	256,000 00	
Treasury notes, acts July 17, 1861, and prior thereto	155,111 64	
Bonds, April 15, 1842	6,000 00	
Treasury notes, March 3, 1863	555,492 00	
Temporary loan	797,029 00	
Certificates of indebtedness	18,000 00	
		20,527,302 64
DEBT BEARING NO INTEREST.		
United States notes	$356,141,723 00	
Fractional currency	32,626,951 75	
Gold certificates of deposit	17,678,640 00	
		406,447,314 75
Total debt		2,636,207,049 19
Amount in treasury, coin	$100,500,561 28	
Amount in treasury, currency	30,505,970 97	
		131,006,532 25
Amount of debt less cash in treasury		2,505,200,516 94

The following is a statement of receipts and expenditures for the fiscal year ending June 30, 1868:

Receipts from customs	$164,464,599 56
Receipts from lands	1,348,715 41
Receipts from direct tax	1,788,145 85
Receipts from internal revenue	191,087,589 41
Receipts from miscellaneous sources (of which amount there was received for premium on bonds sold to redeem treasury notes, the sum of $7,078,203 42)	46,949,033 09
Total receipts, exclusive of loans	$405,638,083 32

Expenditures for the civil service, (of which amount there was paid for premium on purchase of treasury notes prior to maturity, $7,001,151 04)	$60,011,018 71
Expenditures for pensions and Indians	27,883,069 10
Expenditures by War Department	123,246,648 62
Expenditures by Navy Department	25,775,502 72
Expenditures for interest on the public debt	140,424,045 71
Total expenditures, exclusive of principal of public debt	$377,340,284 86

The following is a statement of receipts and expenditures for the quarter ending September 30, 1868:

The receipts from customs	$49,676,594 67
The receipts from lands	714,895 03
The receipts from direct tax	15,536 02
The receipts from internal revenue	38,735,863 08
The receipts from miscellaneous sources (of which amount there was received from premium on bonds sold to redeem Treasury notes the sum of $587,725 12	6,249,979 97
Total receipts, exclusive of loans	95,392,868 77

Expenditures for the civil service, (of which amount there was paid as premium on purchase of treasury notes prior to maturity $300,000,)	$21,227,106 33
Expenditures for pensions and Indians	12,358,647 70
Expenditures for War Department	27,219,117 02
Expenditures for Navy Department	5,604,785 33
Expenditures for interest on public debt	38,742,814 37
Total expenditures, exclusive of principal of public debt	105,152,470 75

The Secretary estimates that, under existing laws, the receipts and expenditures for the three quarters ending June 30, 1869, will be as follows:

From customs	$125,000,000 00
From lands	1,000,000 00
From internal revenue	100,000,000 00
From miscellaneous sources	20,000,000 00
Receipts	246,000,000 00

And that the expenditures for the same period, if there be no reduction of the army, will be—

For the civil service	$40 000,000 00
For pensions and Indians	18,000,000 00
For War Department, including $6,000,000 bounties	66,000,000 00
For Navy Department	16,000,000 00
For interest on public debt	91,000,000 00
Expenditures	231,000,000 00

The receipts and expenditures under existing laws for the fiscal year ending June 30, 1870, are estimated as follows:

From customs	$160,000,000 00
From internal revenue	140,000,000 00
From lands	2,000,000 00
From miscellaneous sources	25,000,000 00
Receipts	327,000,000 00

The expenditures for the same period, if the expenses of the army should be kept up to about the present average, will be as follows:

For the civil service	$50,000,000 00
For pensions and Indians	30,000,000 00
For War Department	75,000,000 00
For Navy Department	20,000,000 00
For interest on public debt	128,000,000 00
Expenditures	303,000,000 00

The accompanying report of the Commissioner of Internal Revenue gives the necessary information in regard to the bureau, and contains many very judicious recommendations and suggestions which are worthy the careful consideration of Congress.

The internal branch of the revenue service is the one in which the people feel the deepest interest. The customs duties are collected at a few points, and although paid eventually by the consumers, they are felt only by the great mass of the people in the increased cost of the articles consumed. Not so with the internal taxes. These are collected in every part of the Union; and their burdens fall, to a large extent, directly upon the tax-payers. Assessors, collectors, inspectors, detectives—necessary instruments in the colllection of the revenues—are found in every part of the country. There is no village or rural district where their faces are not seen, and where collections are not made. The eyes of the whole people are therefore directed to this system, and it is of the greatest importance that its administration should be such as to entitle it to pubic respect. Unfortunately this is not the case. Its demoralization is admitted; and the question arises, where is the remedy? The Secretary is of the opinion that it is to be found in such amendments to the act as will equalize the burdens of taxation, and in an elevation of the standard of qualification for revenue offices.

Upon the subject of internal taxes the Secretary has already spoken. In regard to the character of the revenue officers he has only to say, that there must be a decided change for the better in this respect if the system is to be rescued from its demoralized condition. After careful reflection, the Secretary has come to the conclusion that this change would follow the passage of the bill reported by Mr. Jencks, from the Joint Committee on Retrenchment and Reform, on the 14th of May last, entitled "A bill to regulate the civil service and promote the efficiency thereof." The Secretary gives to this bill his hearty approval, and refers to the speech which was made, upon its introduction, by the gentleman who reported it, for an able and lucid exposition of its provisions, and for a truthful and graphic description of the evils of the present system of appointments to office.

On the 5th day of October last, the day for their regular quarterly reports, the number of national banks was 1,644, 17 of which were in voluntary liquidation. Their capital was $420,634,511; their discounts, $655,875,277 35; their circulation, $295,684,244; and their deposits, $601,830,278 40.

In no other country was so large a capital ever invested in banking, under a single system, as is now invested in the national banks; never before were the interests of a people so interwoven with a system of banking, as are the interests of the people of the United States with their national banking system. It is not strange, therefore, that the condition and management of the national banks should be, to them and to their representatives, a matter of the deepest concern. That the national banking system is a perfect one is not asserted by its friends; that it is a very decided improvement, as far as circulation is regarded, upon the systems which it has superseded, must be admitted by its opponents. Before it was established, the several States, whether in conformity with the Constitution or not—jointly with the general government, during the existence of the charter of the United States Bank, and solely after the expiration of that charter—excercised the power of issuing bills of credit, in the form of bank notes, through institutions of their own creation, and thus controlled the paper money, and thereby, in no small degree, the business and commerce of the country. In May, 1863, when the National Currency Bureau was established in Washington, some 1,500 banks organized under State laws, furnished the people of the United States with a bank-note currency. In some of the States, banks were compelled to protect—partially at least—the holders of their notes against loss, by deposits of securities with the proper authorities. In other States, the capital of the banks (that capital being wholly under the control of their managers) was the only security for the redemption of their notes. In some States there was no limit to the amount of notes that might be issued, if secured according to the requirements of their statutes, nor any necessary relation of circulation to capital. In others, while notes could be issued only in certain proportions to capital, there was no restriction upon the number of banks that might be organized. The notes of a few banks, being payable or redeemable at commercial centres, were current in most of the States, while the notes of other banks (perhaps just as solvent) were uncurrent beyond the limits of the States by whose authority they were issued. How valueless were the notes of many of the State banks is still keenly remembered by the thousands who suffered by their insolvency. The direct losses sustained

losses to the country resulting from the deranged exchanges, caused by a local currency constantly subject to the manipulations of money changers, and from the utter unsuitableness of such a currency to the circumstances of the country, can be counted by millions. It is only necessary to compare the circulation of the State banks with that furnished by the national banks, to vindicate the superiority of the present system. Under the national banking system, the government which authorizes the issue of bank notes, and compels the people to receive them as money, assumes its just responsibility and guarantees their payment. This is the feature which especially distinguishes it from others and gives to it its greatest value.

The object of the Secretary, however, in referring to the national banks is not to extol them, but to call the attention of Congress to the accompanying instructive report of the Comptroller of the Currency, especially to that part of it which exhibits the condition and management of the banks in the commercial metropolis, and to the amendments proposed by him to the act.

On the 5th day of October last, the loans or discounts of the banks in the city of New York amounted to $163,634,070 23, only $90,000,000 of which consisted of commercial paper, the balance being chiefly made up of what are known as loans on call, that is to say, of loans on collaterals, subject to be called in at the pleasure of the banks. Merchants or manufacturers cannot, of course, borrow on such terms, and it is understood that these loans are confined mainly to persons dealing, or rather speculating, in stocks or coin. This statement shows to what extent the business of the banks in New York has been diverted from legitimate channels, and how deeply involved the banks have become in the uncertain and dangerous speculations of the street.

The deposits of these institutions on the day mentioned amounted to $226,645,655 80, and of their assets $113,332,689 20 consisted of certain cash items which were in fact mainly certified checks, which had been passed to the credit of depositors, and constituted a part of the $226,645,655 80 of deposits, although the banks always deduct such checks from their deposits in making up their statement for the payment of interest, and their estimates for reserves. It is understood to be the practice of a number of the banks (perhaps the practice exists to a limited extent in all) to certify the checks of their customers in advance of the deposits out of which they are expected to be paid; in other words, to certify checks to be good, under an agreement between the banks and the drawers that the money to protect them shall be deposited during the day, or at least before the checks, which go through the clearing-house, can be presented for payment. The Secretary has learned with great surprise that a number of banks—generally regarded as being under judicious management—certify in a single day the checks of stock and gold brokers to many times the amount of their capitals, with no money actually on deposit for the protection of the checks at the

inconsistent with prudent, not to say honest banking, cannot be conceived. It is unauthorized by the act, and should be prohibited by severe penalties. Aside from the risk incurred by this reckless method of banking, the effect of such practices is to foster speculation by creating inflation. It is, in fact, part and parcel of that fictitious credit which is so injurious to the regular business of the city, and to the business of all parts of the country, which feel and are affected by the pulsation of the commercial centre. It is this very dangerous practice, combined with the more general practice of making loans "on call," which leads to unsafe extensions of credits, and makes many of the banks in New York helpless when the money market is stringent. Can anything be more discreditable to the banks of the great emporium of the country, or afford more conclusive evidence of their imprudent management, than the fact, that with a capital—including their surplus and their undivided profits—of one hundred millions of dollars, the withdrawal from circulation of ten or fifteen millions of legal-tender notes, by combinations for speculative purposes, can create a money stringency, by which not only the stock market is broken down, but the entire business of the city, and to some extent the business of the country is injuriously affected. If the banks were no more extended than they ought to be, or had proper control over their customers, no such combinations would be likely to be formed, or if formed, they would utterly fail of their object.

These remarks do not, of course, apply to all of the banks in New York, for some of them are strictly commercial institutions, and are under the control of men who are distinguished alike for their talents and their conservatism. They are, however, applicable to them as a class, and they undoubtedly apply in some measure to many banks in other cities.

The recommendation of the Comptroller that all national banks be prohibited by law from certifying checks which are not drawn upon deposits actually existing at the time the checks are certified to be good, is heartily concurred in.

The Secretary has long entertained the opinion that the practice of paying interest on deposits—tending, as it does, to keep the banks constantly extended in their discounts—is injudicious and unsafe. He therefore approves of the recommendation of the Comptroller that national banks be prohibited from paying interest on bank or individual balances.

The Secretary also agrees with the Comptroller in his recommendation that authority be given to him to call upon the banks for reports on days to be fixed by himself. If a reserve is necessary, it should be kept constantly on hand, and the business of the country ought not to be disturbed by the preparation of the banks for the quarterly reports.

The views of the Secretary in regard to the necessity of a central redeeming agency for the national banks have been frequently presented, and it is not necessary for him to repeat them.

There are other suggestions in the Comptroller's report deserving the attention of Congress, which the Secretary lacks the time to consider. There is one subject, however, not discussed by the Comptroller, to which the Secretary invites special attention.

Although the national banking system should be relieved from the limitation now imposed upon the aggregate amount of notes that may be issued, this cannot safely be done as long as the suspension of specie payments continues. Nevertheless, measures should at once be adopted to remedy, as far as practicable, the inequality which exists in the distribution of the circulation. As the government has, by the tax upon the notes of State banks, deprived the States of the power of furnishing facilities to their citizens, it is obviously just that those States which are thus deprived of these facilities, or which do not share equally with other States in the benefits of the national banking system, should be supplied with both banks and notes. There are two modes by which this may be accomplished: One by reducing the circulation of the banks of large capital only; the other by limiting the amount of notes to be furnished to all the banks—say to 70 per cent. of their respective capitals. The latter mode is preferable, as by it no discrimination would be made between the banks, and all would be strengthened by a reduction of their liabilities, and by a release of a part of their means now deposited with the Treasurer, which would be of material service to them in the preparation they must make for a return to specie payments. If a redeeming agency should be established, the reduction of the circulation of the existing banks could be effected as rapidly as new banks can be organized in the western and southern States where they are needed.

The new Territory of Alaska has been the object of much attention during the past year, but its distance and the uncertainty and infrequency of communication with it, and our imperfect knowledge of its condition, have somewhat embarrassed the department in organizing therein a satisfactory revenue system.

Under the authority of the act of the last session, the administration, by special agency, (which, in the absence of the regular machinery, was of necessity resorted to,) has been superseded by the appointment of a collector, to reside at Sitka, who left for his post in September last, and has probably, ere this, entered upon the discharge of his duties.

A gentleman from this department accompanied him to assist in establishing the collection service on a proper foundation, and in perfecting arrangements for the prevention of smuggling.

Recognizing also the vast importance of reliable information on matters not immediately connected with these objects, but having nevertheless a most important bearing upon them more or less direct, another agent, long familiar with that country, was, at the same time, despatched with directions to apply himself to the ascertainment of its natural resources, the inducements and probable channels of trade, and the needs of commerce in the way of lights and other aids to navigation. He was also particularly intrusted with a supervision of the fur interests, and the enforcement of the law prohibiting the killing of the most valuable fur-bearing animals.

The existence of coal at numerous points has been known for years, and some of the beds were worked by the Russians, with indifferent success; none, however, has been hitherto procured on the North American Pacific coast equal to that from the Nanaimo mines, on Vancouver's island; and this, though raised from a considerable depth, is not of superior quality. The officers of the cutters were therefore instructed to explore the coast as far as practicable, for the purpose of ascertaining the supply and the quality of coal in the Territory. A number of localities producing coal were visited, including the abandoned Russian mines, but at none did the outcroppings exhibit any flattering promise except on the coast of Cook's inlet. There, near Fort Kenay, about 700 miles from Sitka, were found upon the cliffs numerous parallel veins extending many miles along the shore. Some of the coal taken from them proved to be superior to that taken from the Nanaimo mines. The indications are that the supply is abundant and the quality fair.

The protection of the fur-bearing animals is a matter of importance hardly to be overrated. In consequence of information received last spring, the captain of the "Wayanda" was directed to visit, as early in the season as practicable, the islands in Behring's sea, where the fur seal chiefly abounds. On his arrival at St. Paul's and St. George's islands, he found there several large parties engaged in hunting the animals indiscriminately, and in traffic with the natives in ardent spirits and other forbidden articles. Quarrels had arisen, and the natives complained that the reckless and unskilful movements of the new hunters had already driven the animals from some of their usual haunts. The captain of the cutter instituted such measures as he felt authorized to institute for the maintenance of the peace and the protection of the animals from indiscriminate slaughter.

The preservation of these animals, by the observance of strict regulations in hunting them, is not only a matter of the highest importance in an economical view, but a matter of life or death to the natives. Hitherto, seals have been hunted under the supervision of the Russian company, and exclusively by the natives, who are trained from children to that occupation, and derive from it their clothing and subsistence. They have been governed by exact and stringent rules as to the time of hunting, and the number and kind of seals to be taken. It is recommended that these rules be continued by legal enactment, and that the existing law prohibiting absolutely the killing of the fur seal and sea otter be repealed, as starvation of the people would result from its strict enforcement. The natives (with the exception of the Indians in the southern part of the Territory, who are fierce and warlike) are a gentle, harmless race, easy to govern, but of great enterprise and daring in the pursuit of game—many of them passing annually in their skin canoes from the main land and Aleutian islands to the islands of St. Paul and St. George, a distance of about 150 miles, through a strong sea, and returning with the proceeds of their hunt.

The seals are extremely timid and cautious. They approach their accustomed grounds each year with the greatest circumspection, sending advance parties to reconnoitre, and at once forsaking places where they are alarmed by unusual or unwelcome visitors. They have been in this way driven from point to point, and have taken refuge in these remote islands, whence, if they are now driven, they must resort to the Asiatic coast. There can be no doubt that, without proper regulations for hunting, these valuable animals, and the more valuable but less numerous sea otters, a very profitable trade will very soon be entirely destroyed.

The United States cannot of course administer such a trade as a government monopoly, and the only alternative seems to be to grant the exclusive privilege of taking these animals to a responsible company for a series of years, limiting the number of skins to be taken annually by stringent provisions. A royalty or tax might be imposed upon each skin taken, and a revenue be thus secured sufficient to pay a large part of the expenses of the Territory.

Our relations with the Hudson Bay Company, and the regulation of the transit of merchandise between their interior trading posts and the sea-coast, by way of Stikine river, will doubtless require early attention, but at present the Secretary is not sufficiently advised to offer any recommendations upon the subject.

The recent political changes in Spain, and the indications of a more liberal commercial policy on her part, before the revolution took place, add force to the remarks and recommendation of the Secretary in his last report, in regard to our commercial relations with that country. He again strongly recommends the repeal of the acts of July 13, 1832, and June 30, 1834, so that Spanish vessels may be subject to our general laws, which are ample to afford protection against unfriendly Spanish legislation, and are free from the innumerable difficulties of administration which exist under these special enactments.

The Secretary asks attention to the necessity of more exact and stringent laws respecting the carriage of passengers, and also of such legislation as shall settle, so far as they can be settled in this manner, some of the vexed questions arising under steamboat laws.

It is necessary merely to repeat what has been at other times stated, in regard to the insufficiency of the tax fund to meet the necessary expenses of the marine hospitals, notwithstanding the economy which, during the past year, has reduced the expenditures more than $12,000. It is impossible to ignore the fact that these hospitals are and must be, unless the rate of the tax is largely increased, a constant drain upon the treasury.

The revenue cutter service now comprises 25 steamers, and 17 sailing vessels. Of the six steamers on the lakes, all but one are at present, agreeably to the views of Congress, out of commission, the "Sherman" alone being in active service.

Five of the steamers on the sea-coast are small tugs, from 40 to 60 tons burden, the utility and efficiency of which at the leading ports—as substitutes for ordinary row-boats on the one hand, and for the light cutters on the other, both in the harbor duties of inspection and police, and in the prevention and detection of smuggling—have been so thoroughly tested by experience, that it is thought they should be employed still more extensively than they now are. Upon the lakes, in particular, they would be of the greatest value, and they should be substituted for the large steamers now there, which should, with one exception, be sold, as they are depreciating in value and are a useless expense. The exception is the "S. P. Chase," which is of such dimensions that she might be brought to the sea-coast, where she could be used to advantage. This would probably be preferable to a sale of her where she lies. The schooner "Black," being old and not fit for further service, has been sold. The "Morris" also is about to be disposed of for the same reason. The steamer "Nemaha," stationed at Norfolk, has been destroyed by accidental fire.

On the Pacific coast are the "Wayanda" in Alaska, and the "Lincoln" at San Francisco, both in excellent condition; the schooner "Reliance," recently ordered to Sitka, is also in good order. The schooner "Lane," at Puget sound, is old and unfit for the requirements of that station.

The addition of several thousand miles of sea-coast, by the purchase of Alaska, renders the cutter force in the Pacific inadequate for even the ordinary duties pertaining to the service, without regard to the additional demands upon it for the protection of the fur-bearing animals. The recommendation heretofore made that two first-class steamers be built or purchased for the western coast is therefore renewed. A steam cutter is also needed for Charleston, and one for the coast of Texas.

In his report for the year 1866, the Secretary called the attention of Congress especially to the condition of the shipping interest of the United States. In his report of last year he again referred to it in the following language:

The shipping interest of the United States, to a great degree prostrated by the war, has not revived during the past year. Our ship-yards are, with rare exceptions, inactive. Our surplus products are being chiefly transported to foreign countries in foreign vessels. The Secretary is still forced to admit, in the language of his last report, "that with unequalled facilities for obtaining the materials, and with acknowledged skill in ship-building, with thousands of miles of sea-coast, indented with the finest harbors in the world, with surplus products that require in their transportation a large and increasing tonnage, we can neither profitably build ships nor successfully compete with English ships in the transportation of our own productions.

No change for the better has taken place since that report was made. On the contrary, the indications are that the great ship-building interest of the eastern and middle States has been steadily declining, and that consequently the United States is gradually ceasing to be a great maritime power. A return to specie payments will do much, but will not be sufficient to avert this declension and give activity to our ship-yards. The materials which enter into the construction of vessels should be relieved from taxation by means of drawbacks; or if this may be regarded as impracticable, subsidies might be allowed as an offset to taxation. If subsidies are objectionable, then it is recommended that all restrictions upon the registration of foreign-built vessels be removed, so that the people of the United States, who cannot profitably build vessels, may be permitted to purchase them in the cheapest market. It is certainly unwise to retain upon the statute-books a law restrictive upon commerce when it no longer accomplishes the object for which it was enacted.

What was said by the Secretary in 1866 and 1867, upon this subject, is true at the present time, and he therefore feels it to be his duty to repeat his recommendations. The shipping interest was not only prostrated by the war, but its continued depression is attributable to the financial legislation, and the high taxes consequent upon the war. The honor and the welfare of the country demand its restoration.

Accompanying this report there is a very accurate and instructive chart, prepared by Mr. S. Nimmo, jr., a clerk in this department, which presents, in a condensed form, the progress of ship-building in the United States from 1817 to 1868.

Since the abrogation of the treaty of June 4, 1854, between the United States and Canada, no favorable opportunity for a reconsideration of the commercial relations of the two countries has been presented. Canada has yet to consolidate a political confederation with the other English colonies and possessions on this continent, and until the hostility of Nova Scotia to that measure is removed, and the concurrence of Northwest British America is secured, the authorities at Ottawa are in no situation to make an adequate proposition to the United States, in exchange for the great concession of an exceptional tariff, on our northern frontier, in favor of the leading Canadian staples. On the other hand, until the United States shall have fully matured a satisfactory system of duties, external as well as internal, the Secretary would be indisposed to favor any special arrangement which would remove any material branch of the revenue system from legislative control. Meanwhile, a Canadian policy for the enlargement of the Welland and St. Lawrence canals to dimensions adequate to pass vessels of one thousand tons burden from the upper lakes to the Atlantic, will doubtless be regarded as indispensable to any substantial renewal, by treaty or legislation, of the former arrangement. The discussions and experience of the last twelve months are regarded, by the Secretary, as warranting an authoritative comparison of views between the representatives of Great Britain and Canada and the government of the United States, and in that event this department will cheerfully contribute, by all appropriate means, to comprehensive measures which shall assimilate the revenue systems of the respective countries, make their markets mutually available, and for all commercial or social purposes render the frontier as nearly an imaginary line as possible. There certainly seems no just reason why all the communities on the American continent might not imitate the example of the Zollverein of the German states.

The progress of the coast survey has been satisfactory and commensurate with the appropriations, as will be seen from the annual report of the superintendent of that work. During the past year, surveys have been in progress in the following localities, named in geographical order, viz: On the coast of Maine, in Penobscot bay and on the islands lying within its entrance; on the shores of St. George's and Medomak rivers; in Muscongus bay; on the estuaries of Quohog bay, and in the vicinity of Portland; completing all the in-shore work between the Penobscot and Cape Elizabeth. In Massachusetts, between Barnstable and Monomoy, completing the survey of Cape Cod. In Rhode Island, on the western part of Narraganset bay. In New York, at Rondout and in the bay of New York. In New Jersey, on the coast near the head of Barnegat bay. In Maryland and Virginia, on the Potomac river and the southern part of Chesapeake bay. In North Carolina, in Pamlico sound and on its western shore, including Neuse and Bay rivers, and off the coast north of Hatteras. In South Carolina, on the estuaries of Port Royal sound. In Georgia, on St. Catherine's, Doboy, and St. Andrew's sounds; in the Florida straits and in the bay between the keys and main shore of Florida. On the coast between Pensacola and Mobile entrances. At the passes of the Mississippi, and in Galveston, Matagorda, and Corpus Christi bays, on the coast of Texas. In California, surveying parties have been at work on the coast between Buenaventura and Santa Barbara, at Point Sal, and on the peninsula of San Francisco. In Oregon, on Yaquina bay, Columbia and Malheur rivers. In Washington Territory, on Fuca straits and in Puget sound.

In the Coast Survey office, 48 charts have been entirely or partially engraved during the year, of which 19 have been published. Regular observations of the tides at seven principal stations have been kept up, and tide tables for all parts of the United States for the ensuing year have been published. A new edition of the Directory or Coast Pilot for the western coast has been prepared, and a preliminary guide for the northwestern coast has been compiled.

This brief glance at the operations of the coast survey during the past year shows the great scope of that work, which has justly earned a large measure of public favor. Its importance to the commerce and navigation of the country are now well understood, nor can its incidental contributions to science fail to be appreciated by the representatives of the people. The work should be pressed steadily forward, with means sufficient for the most effective working of the existing organization, so that it may embrace, at no distant period, the whole of our extended coast line within its operations, including the principal harbors in our newly-acquired Territory of Alaska.

The report of the Light-house Board is as usual an interesting one. No bureau of the Treasury Department is conducted with more ability or with a more strict regard to the public interests than this.

In view of the extension of the light-house system, consequent upon the increase of the commerce of the country and the acquisition of sea-coast territory, it is respectfully submitted that some authoritative definition of the limit to which aids to navigation shall be extended by the general government should be established.

It may well be doubted whether the general government should be called upon to do more than to thoroughly provide the sea and lake coasts with lights of high order, both stationary and floating, and so to place lights of inferior order as to enable vessels to reach secure anchorages at any season of the year.

The act of Congress, approved August 31, 1852, establishing the Light-house Board, directs that the coasts of the United States shall be divided into twelve districts. It is recommended that authority be given to increase the number of districts to fourteen.

The business of the bureau would be facilitated if Congress should confer the franking privilege upon the Light-house Board in the same manner and upon the same terms as it is now exercised by the several bureaus of the Treasury Department.

The attention of Congress is called to the annual report of the director of the mint, which contains the usual statistics of the coinage of the country, and various suggestions and recommendations, which are worthy of consideration.

The total value of the bullion deposited at the mint and branches during the fiscal year was $27,166,318 70, of which $25,472,894 82 was in gold, and $1,693,423 88 in silver. Deducting there deposit, the amount of actual deposit was $24,591,325 84.

The coinage for the year was in gold coin, $18,114,425; gold bars, $6,026,810 06; silver coin, $1,136,750; silver bars, $456,236 40; nickel, copper, and bronze coinage, (one, two, three, and five-cent pieces,) $1,713,385; total coinage, $20,964,560; total bars stamped, $6,483,046 54.

The gold deposits of domestic production were: at Philadelphia, $1,300,338 53; at San Francisco, $14,850,117 84; at New York, $5,409,996 55; at Denver, $357,935 11. The silver deposits were at Philadelphia, $67,700 78; at San Francisco, $651,239 05; at New York, $262,312 96; at Denver, $5,082 67.

The gold and silver deposits of foreign production were $1,686,602 35. The amount of gold coined at Philadelphia was $3,864,425; at San Francisco, $14,979,558 52; of silver at Philadelphia, $314,750; at San Francisco, $822,000; of nickel, copper, and bronze at Philadelphia, $1,713,385. Total number of pieces struck, 49,735,840.

The mint at Philadelphia and the branch mint at San Francisco have the confidence of the people and of the government, and when the new mint building in San Francisco is erected, these mints will be of ample capacity to supply coinage for the whole country. The business of coinage requires large and expensive establishments, under charge of men of science and of undoubted integrity; and such can be successfully maintained only at commercial centres, where bullion of different degrees of fineness is continually offered for manipulation. The establishment of additional branch mints is, therefore, unnecessary, and would be injudicious.

The entire deposits at the branch mint in San Francisco were formerly in unparted bullion; now nearly two-thirds of the amount is deposited in bars, refined by private establishments. The law requires that the parting charge shall equal the actual cost of the process; but the experience of the past four years shows that not less than $30,000 annually may be saved to the government by discontinuing the busines of refining upon the Pacific coast; and it is, therefore, recommended that the Secretary be authorized to exchange the unparted bullion deposited at the mint for refined bars whenever, in his opinion, it may be for the public interest to do so.

It is also recommended that authority be given for the redemption of the one and two-cent pieces by the Treasurer, under such rules and regulations as may be prescribed by the department.

On the first day of April last Mr. R. W. Raymond was appointed Commissioner of Mining Statistics, in place of Mr. J. Ross Browne, now commissioner to China.

Mr. Raymond was instructed to continue the work so ably commenced by his predecessor, and his report will show with what diligence and ability he is performing the duties assigned to him. The Secretary invites the attention of Congress to this report, and asks for the recommendations which it contains due consideration.

The following extract from the Secretary's report of 1867 presents, in language which he cannot make more explicit, his present views:

The Secretary respectfully recommends the reorganization of the accounting offices of the Treasury Department, so as to place this branch of the public service under one responsible head, according to what seems to have been designed in the original organization of the department, and followed until the increase of business led to the creation of the office of Second Comptroller, and subsequently to that of Commissioner of Customs. There are now three officers controlling the settlements of accounts, each independent of the others, and, as

warrants on the treasury, and of collecting debts due the government, now constituting a part of the duties of the First Comptroller; and that the adjustment of accounts pertaining to the customs be restored to the latter office.

The Secretary also renews the recommendation contained in his last annual report, of a reorganization of the bureaus of the department, and most respectfully and earnestly solicits for it the favorable action of Congress. The compensation now paid is inadequate to the services performed, and simple justice to gentlemen of the ability and character of those employed in the department, requires a liberal addition to their present compensation. Since the rates of compensation now allowed were established, the duties, labors, and responsibilities of the bureaus have been largely increased, and the necessary expenses of living in Washington have been more than doubled.

The Secretary also again recommends that a change be made in regard to the adjustment and settlement of accounts in the office of the Third Auditor; that a period be fixed within which war claims shall be presented, and that measures be adopted to perpetuate testimony in cases of claims that are disallowed.

The able report of the Treasurer gives a detailed account of the operations of the treasury during the last fiscal year, and contains many valuable suggestions for the consideration of Congress.

The report of the supervising architect gives full and detailed accounts of the progress that has been made in the construction of public buildings.

The reports of the heads of all the respective bureaus will be found to be of unusual interest—containing, as they do, accurate information in regard to the affairs of the government in this interesting period of its history.

Mr. S. M. Clark having resigned the office of superintendent of the Bureau of Engraving and Printing, Mr. G. B. McCartee has been placed temporarily in charge of it. As the past management and present condition of this bureau are now under investigation by the Joint Committee on Retrenchment and Reform, the Secretary feels at liberty only to say, at this time, that, from the examinations which he has caused to be made by officers and clerks of this department, he feels justified in remarking, that the reports which have been at various times put in circulation in regard to over-issues of notes or securities, and of dishonesty in the administration of the bureau, are unfounded.

A systematic effort is being made to reduce the expenses of the administration of the customs service, and with considerable success. The process is necessarily slow and beset with difficulties; but material reduction has been already made, and still greater is in progress.

During the war the business of the Treasury Department was so largely and rapidly increased, and so many inexperienced men were necessarily employed, that perfect order and system could not be enforced. Many accounts were unsettled, and some branches of business had fallen into confusion. Much attention has been given by the Secretary to "straightening up" the affairs of the department. He is now gratified in being able to say, that order and system have been introduced where they

and that the "machinery" of the department is in as satisfactory condition as perhaps it can be, under existing laws. The result of the examinations which he has caused to be made has excited his admiration of the wisdom displayed by Mr. Hamilton in the system of accounting which he introduced, and most favorably impressed him with the value of the services of the men, who, poorly paid, and little known beyond the walls of the treasury building, have, for years, conducted, with unfaltering fidelity, the details of a business, larger and more complicated than was ever devolved upon a single department by any government in the world.

In concluding this communication it may not be inappropriate for the Secretary, in a few brief words, to review some points in the general policy of the administration of the treasury for the past four years.

The following statement—published in the last treasury report—exhibits the condition of the treasury on the 1st of April, 1865:

Funded debt	$1,100,361,241 80
Matured debt	349,420 09
Temporary loan certificates	52,452,328 29
Certificates of indebtedness	171,790,000 00
Interest-bearing notes	526,812,800 00
Suspended or unpaid requisitions	114,256,548 93
United States notes, legal tenders	433,160,569 00
Fractional currency	24,254,094 07
	2,423,437,002 18
Cash in the treasury	56,481,924 84
Total	2,366,955,077 34

By this statement it appears that, with $56,481,924 84 in the treasury, there were requisitions waiting for payment (the delay in the payment of which was greatly discrediting the government) to the amount of $114,256,548 93, that there were $52,452,328 29 of temporary loan certificates liable to be presented in from ten to thirty days' notice, and $171,790,000 of certificates of indebtedness which had been issued to contractors, for want of the money to pay the requisitions in their favor and which were maturing daily. At the same time the efforts to negotiate securities were not being attended with the usual success, while the expenses of the war were not less than $2,000,000 per day. The vouchers issued to contractors for the necessary supplies of the army and navy, payable one-half in certificates of indebtedness and the other half in money, were being sold at a discount of from 10 to 20 per cent., indicating by their depreciation how low was the credit of the government, and how uncertain was the time of payment.

The fall of Richmond and the surrender of the army of Virginia under

General Lee, (which virtually closed the war,) had not the effect of relieving the treasury. On the contrary, its embarrassments were increased thereby, inasmuch as it seemed to leave the government without excuse for not paying its debts, at the same time that popular appeals for subscriptions to the public loans were divested of much of their strength. As long as the government was in danger, by the continuation of hostilities, the patriotism of the people could be successfully appealed to for the purpose of raising money and sustaining the public credit, without which the war could not be vigorously prosecuted. When hostilities ceased, and the safety and unity of the government were assured, self-interest became again the controlling power. It will be remembered that it was then generally supposed that the country was already fully supplied with securities, and that there was also throughout the Union a prevailing apprehension that financial disaster would speedily follow the termination of the war. The greatness of the emergency gave the Secretary no time to try experiments for borrowing on a new security of long time and lower interest, and removed from his mind all doubts or hesitation in regard to the course to be pursued. It was estimated that at least $700,000,000 should be raised, in addition to the revenue receipts, for the payment of the requisitions already drawn, and those that must soon follow—preparatory to the disbandment of the great Union army—and of other demands upon the treasury. The anxious inquiries then were, By what means can this large amount of money be raised? and not what will be the cost of raising it. How can the soldiers be paid, and the army be disbanded, so that the extraordinary expenses of the War Department may be stopped? and not what rate of interest shall be paid for the money. These were the inquiries pressed upon the Secretary. He answered them by calling to his aid the well-tried agent who had been employed by his immediate predecessors, and by offering the seven and three-tenths notes—the most popular loan ever offered to the people—in every city and village, and by securing the advocacy of the press, throughout the length and breadth of the land. In less than four months from the time the work of obtaining subscriptions was actively commenced, the treasury was in a condition to meet every demand upon it.

But while the treasury was thus relieved, the character of the debt was by no means satisfactory. On the first day of September it consisted of the following items:

Funded debt	$1,109,568,191 80
Matured debt	1,503,020 09
Temporary loan	107,148,713 16
Certificates of indebtedness	85,093,000 00
Five per cent. legal-tender notes	33,954,230 00
Compound interest legal-tender notes	217,024,160 00
Seven-thirty notes	830,000,000 00
United States notes, legal tenders	433,160,569 00

Fractional currency	$26, 344, 742 51
Suspended requisitions uncalled for	2, 111, 000 00
Total	2, 845, 907, 626 56
Deduct cash in treasury	88, 218, 055 13
Balance	2, 757, 689, 571 43

From this statement it will be perceived that $1,276,834,123 25 of the public debt consisted of various forms of temporary securities; $433,160,569 of United States notes—the excess of which over $400,000,000 having been put into circulation in payment of temporary loans—and $26,344,782 of fractional currency. Portions of this temporary debt were maturing daily, and all of it, including $18,415,000 of the funded debt, was to be provided for within a period of three years. The seven-thirty notes were, by law and the terms of the loan, convertible at maturity, at the will of the holder, into five-twenty bonds, or payable like the rest of these temporary obligations in lawful money.

It was of course necessary to make provision for the daily maturing debt, and also for taking up, from time to time, such portions of it as could be advantageously converted into bonds, or paid in currency, before maturity, for the purpose of avoiding the necessity of accumulating large sums of money, and of relieving the treasury from the danger it would be exposed to if a very considerable portion of the debt were permitted to mature, with no other means for paying it than that afforded by sales of bonds, in a market too uncertain to be confidently relied upon in an emergency. In addition to the temporary loan, payment of which could be demanded on so short a notice as to make it virtually a debt payable on demand—the certificates of indebtedness which were maturing at the rate of from fifteen to twenty millions per month—the five per cent. notes which matured in January following, and the compound-interest notes, which were payable at various times within a period of three years—there were $830,000,000 of seven-thirty notes which would become due as follows, viz:

August 15, 1867	$300, 000, 000
June 15, 1868	300, 000, 000
July 15, 1868	230, 000, 000

As the option of conversion was with the holders of these notes, it depended upon the condition of the market, whether they would be presented for payment in lawful money, or be exchanged for bonds. No prudent man, intrusted with the care of the nation's interest and credit, would permit two or three hundred millions of debt to mature without making provision for its payment; nor would he, if it could be avoided, accumulate large sums of money in the treasury which would not be called for, if the price of bonds should be such as to make the conversion of the notes preferable to their payment in lawful money. The policy of the Secretary was therefore, as he remarked in a former report, determined by the condition of the treasury and the country, and by the character of the debt. It was simply, first, to put and keep the Treasury in such condition as not only to be prepared to pay all claims upon presentation, but also to be strong enough to prevent the success of any combinations that might be formed to control its management; and, second, to take up quietly, in advance of their maturity, by payment or conversion, such portions of the temporary debt as would obviate the necessity of accumulating large currency balances in the Treasury, and at the same time relieve it from the danger of being forced to a further issue of legal-tender notes, or to a sale of bonds, at whatever price they might command. In carrying out this policy, it seemed also to be the duty of the Secretary to have due regard to the interests of the people, and to prevent, as far as possible, the work of funding from disturbing legitimate business. As financial trouble has almost invariably followed closely upon the termination of protracted wars, it was generally feared, as has been already remarked, that such trouble would be unavoidable at the close of the great and expensive war in which the United States had been for four years engaged. This, of course, it was important to avoid, as its occurrence might not only render funding difficult, but might prostrate those great interests upon which the government depended for its revenues. It was, and constantly has been, therefore, the aim of the Secretary so to administer the treasury, while borrowing money and funding the temporary obligations, as to prevent a commercial crisis, and to keep the business of the country as steady as was possible on the basis of an irredeemable and constantly fluctuating currency. Whether his efforts have contributed to this end or not, he does not undertake to say; but the fact is unquestioned, that a great war has been closed—large loans have been effected—heavy revenues have been collected, and some thirteen hundred millions of dollars of temporary obligations have been paid or funded, and a great debt brought into manageable shape, not only without a financial crisis, but without any disturbance to the ordinary business of the country. To accomplish these things successfully, the Secretary deemed it necessary, as has been before stated, that the treasury should be kept constantly in a strong condition, with power to prevent the credit of the government and the great interests of the people from being placed at the mercy of adverse influences. Notwithstanding the magnitude and character of the debt, this power the treasury has, for the last three years, possessed; and it has been the well known existence, rather than the exercise of it, which has, in repeated instances, saved the country from panic and disaster. The gold reserve, the maintenance of which has subjected the Secretary to constant and bitter criticism, has given a confidence to the holders of our securities, at home and abroad, by the constant evidence which it exhibited of the ability of the government, without depending upon purchases in the market, to pay the interest upon the public debt, and a steadiness to trade, by preventing violent fluctuations in the convertible value of the currency, which have been a more than ample compensation to the country for any loss of interest that may have been sustained thereby. If the gold in the treasury had been sold down to what was absolutely needed for the payment of the interest on the public debt, not only would the public credit have been endangered, but the currency; and, consequently, the entire business of the country would have been constantly subject to the dangerous power of speculative combinations.

Of the unavailing effort that was made by the Secretary to contract the currency, with the view of appreciating it to the specie standard, he forbears to speak. His action in respect to contraction, although authorized, and for a time sustained, was subsequently disapproved (as he thinks unwisely) by Congress. This is a question, however, that can be better determined hereafter than now.

Complaint has been made that, in the administration of the Treasury Department since the war, there has been too much of interference with the stock and money market. This complaint, when honestly made, has been the result of a want of reflection, or of imperfect knowledge of the financial condition of the government. The transactions of the treasury have, from necessity, been connected with the stock and money market of New York. If the debt after the close of the war had been a funded debt, with nothing to be done in relation to it but to pay the accruing interest, or if business had been conducted on a specie basis, and consequently been free from the constant changes to which it has been and must be subject—as long as there is any considerable difference between the legal and commercial standard of value—the treasury could have been managed with entire independence of the stock exchange or the gold room. Such, however, was not the fact. More than one-half of the national debt, according to the foregoing exhibits, consisted of temporary obligations, which were to be paid in lawful money or converted into bonds; and there was in circulation a large amount of irredeemable promises constantly changing in their convertible value. The Secretary, therefore, could not be indifferent to the condition of the market, nor avoid connection with it, for it was in fact with the market he had to deal. He would have been happy had it been otherwise. If bonds had to be sold to provide the means for paying the debts that were payable in lawful money, it was a matter of great importance to the treasury that the price of bonds should not be depressed by artificial

influences that controlled it, or had hesitated to exercise the power with which Congress had clothed him, for successfully funding the temporary debt by conversions or sales, he would have been false to his trust. The task of converting a thousand millions of temporary obligations into a funded debt, on a market constantly subject to natural and artificial fluctuations, without depressing the prices of bonds, and without disturbing the business of the country, however it may be regarded now, when the work has been accomplished, was, while it was being performed, an exceedingly delicate one. It is but simple justice to say that its successful accomplishment is, in a great measure, attributable to the judicious action of the Assistant Treasurer at New York, Mr. Van Dyck.

Similar complaint has also been made of the manner in which gold and bonds have been disposed of, by what has been styled "secret sales;" and yet precisely the same course has been pursued in these sales that careful and prudent men pursue who sell on their own account. The sales have been made when currency was needed, and prices were satisfactory. It was not considered wise or prudent to advise the dealers precisely when and to what amount sales were to be made, (no sane man operating on his own account would have done this,) but all sales of gold have been made in the open market, and of bonds by agents or the Assistant Treasurer in New York, in the ordinary way, with a view of obtaining the very best prices, and with the least possible disturbance of business. In the large transactions of the treasury, agents have been indispensable, but none have been employed when the work could be done equally well by the officers of the department. Whether done by agents or officers, the Secretary has no reason to suppose that it has not been done skilfully and honestly, as well as economically. He is now gratified in being able to say, that unless a very stringent market, such as was produced a few weeks ago by powerful combinations in New York, should send to the treasury large amounts of the three per cent. certificates for redemption, no further sales of bonds are likely to be necessary. Until, however, the receipts from internal revenues are increased, the necessities of the government will require that the sales of gold shall be continued. These sales are now being made by advertisements for sealed bids, instead of the agencies heretofore employed. The result, so far, has not been entirely satisfactory, but a proper respect for what, according to the tone of the press, appeared to be the public sentiment seemed to require it. The new mode will be fairly tested and continued if it can be without a sacrifice of the public interest.

earnestly presented his own views without seeking popular favor. It has been his good fortune to have had for his immediate predecessors two of the ablest men in the country, to whose judicious labors he has been greatly indebted for any success that may have attended his administration of the treasury. Nor is he under less obligation to his associates, the officers and leading clerks of the department, whose ability and whose devotion to the public service have commanded his respect and admiration.

HUGH McCULLOCH,
Secretary of the Treasury.

Hon. SCHUYLER COLFAX,
Speaker of the House of Representatives.

No. 1.

Statement of the receipts and expenditures of the United States during the fiscal year ending June 30, 1868, agreeably to warrants issued.

The receipts into the treasury were as follows:

From customs, viz:		
During the quarter ending September 30, 1867	$48,081,907 61	
December 31, 1867	32,983,305 08	
March 31, 1868	40,143,161 68	
June 30, 1868	43,256,225 19	
		$164,464,599 56
From sales of public lands, viz:		
During the quarter ending September 30, 1867	287,460 07	
December 31, 1867	379,059 62	
March 31, 1868	199,817 62	
June 30, 1868	482,378 10	
		1,348,715 41
From direct tax, viz:		
During the quarter ending September 30, 1867	647,070 83	
December 31, 1867	382,614 83	
March 31, 1868	384,274 80	
June 30, 1868	374,185 39	
		1,788,145 85
From internal revenue, viz:		
During the quarter ending September 30, 1867	53,784,027 49	
December 31, 1867	45,398,204 84	
March 31, 1868	41,504,194 11	
June 30, 868	50,401,162 97	
		191,087,589 41
From incidental and miscellaneous sources, viz:		
During the quarter ending September 30, 1867	18,361,462 62	
December 31, 1867	6,916,304 89	
March 31, 1868	9,550,495 05	
June 30, 1868	12,120,750 53	
		46,949,033 09
Total receipts, exclusive of loans		405,638,083 32
From loans, &c.:		
From 6 per cent 20-year bonds, per act July 17, 1861	1,800 00	
United States notes, per act February 25, 1862	10,071,559 20	
temporary loans, per act February 25, 1862	3,260,000 00	
postage and other stamps, per act July 17, 1862	1,800 00	
fractional currency, per act March 3, 1863	25,022,624 00	
certificates of gold coin deposits, per act March 3, 1863	77,939,900 00	
7.30 3-year coupon bonds, per act June 30, 1864	600 00	
5 per cent. 10-40-year bonds, per act March 3, 1864	23,052,750 00	
6 per cent. 5-20-year bonds, per act March 3, 1865	435,760,400 00	
3 per cent. certificates, per act March 2, 1867	50,000,000 00	
		625,111,433 20
Total receipts		1,030,749,516 52
Balance in the treasury, July 1, 1867		170,146,986 47
Total means		1,200,896,502 99

The expenditures for the year were as follows:

CIVIL.

For Congress, including books	$3,609 135 00	
executive	6,757 402 45	
judiciary	723,378 57	
government in the Territories	282 064 80	
assistant treasurers and their clerks	260,113 88	
officers of the mint and branches and assay office at New York	112,960 15	
supervising and local inspectors, &c	109,891 98	
surveyors general and their clerks	95,209 75	
Total civil list		$11,950,156 58

FOREIGN INTERCOURSE.

For salaries of ministers, &c	291,300 92	
contingent expenses of all missions abroad	51,559 63	
contingent expenses of foreign intercourse	147,923 99	
expenses incident to carrying into effect the convention with the republic of Venezuela, &c	1,975 58	
salaries of secretaries and assistant secretaries of legation, &c	56,185 30	
compensation of commissioners and consuls general to Hayti, Dominica, and Liberia	5,747 53	
salaries of interpreters, &c., at Constantinople and China	8,441,98	
mail steamship service between the United States and Brazil	150,000 00	
expenses of rescuing citizens of the United States from shipwreck	5,297 61	
expenses of the neutrality act	25,000 00	
bringing home from foreign countries persons charged with crime	23,902 58	
salaries of marshals of consular courts in Japan, China, Siam, and Turkey	12,676 18	
rent of prisons for American convicts in Japan, China, Siam, and Turkey	13,515 26	
compensation of secretary and commissioner to run and mark the boundary line between the United States and British possessions in Washington Territory	28,070 00	
an act to encourage immigration	14,115 75	
expenses of the Universal Exposition at Paris	38,305 24	
blank books, &c., for United States consuls, &c.	65,104 96	
office rent for United States consuls, &c	35,597 78	
expenses, &c., of the Hudson Bay and Puget Sound Agricultural Companies	18,667 18	
relief and protection of American seamen	82,425 88	
salaries of consuls general, &c., including loss of exchange	362,646 49	
sundry miscellaneous items	2,884 21	
Total foreign intercourse		1,441,344 05

MISCELLANEOUS.

For mint establishment	694,682 76	
building court-houses, post offices, &c	733,397 27	
overland mail transportation	1,125,000 00	
mail steamship between San Francisco and Japan.	41,666 66	
carrying the mails upon the post roads established by Congress during the first session of the 39th Congress	486,525 00	
further payment, &c., for mail service performed for the two houses of Congress	2,400,000 00	
deficiencies in the proceeds of the money-order system	92,952 03	
facilitating communication between the Atlantic and Pacific States by electric telegraph	39,999 99	
expenses of the Smithsonian Institution	37,330 82	
extension of the treasury building	331,201 33	

For survey of the Atlantic and Gulf coasts	$249,635 43
publishing observations on the surveys of the coasts of the United States	4,090 53
survey of the Florida reefs and keys	22,230 19
repairs of steamers used in the coast survey	28,000 00
pay and rations for engineers of seven steamers, &c	9,082 01
surveys of western coasts of the United States	142,662 56
contingent expenses under the act for the safe-keeping of the public revenue	170,958 63
expenses, &c., of a national loan	2,017,822 43
resolution in relation to national banking associations	2,283 58
plates, paper, special dies, &c., the printing of circulating notes, &c	33,241 46
detection and bringing to trial persons charged with crime	152,804 41
consular receipts	3,609 85
building vaults in United States depositories	22,420 00
return of proceeds of captured and abandoned property	642,948 91
compensation of watchmen, gardener, gate keepers, &c	37,779 87
alteration and repairs of public buildings in Washington, improvement of grounds, &c	440,715 78
completion of the Washington aqueduct	53,245 14
support of transient paupers in the District of Columbia	12,000 00
lighting the President's House, Capitol, &c	55,014 01
annual repairs, fuel, &c, for the President's House	31,750 00
refunding duties erroneously or illegally collected, &c	696,155 25
allowance or drawback on articles on which internal tax has been paid	1,375,940 11
expenses incident to the assessment and collection of the internal revenue	8,730,357 65
sundry miscellaneous accounts	49,494 86
expenses of collecting the revenue from customs	7,615,675 45
payment of debentures, drawbacks, bounties or allowance	792,766 30
refunding duties to extend the warehouse system	26,156 00
repayment to importers of excess of deposit, &c	2,279,377 54
debentures and other charges	22,226 07
salaries of special examiners of drugs	3,179 88
additional compensation to collectors and naval officers	1,356 29
the light-house establishment	2,613,739 45
the marine hospital establishment	506,842 35
repairs and preservation of custom-houses, marine hospitals, &c	153,669 70
unclaimed merchandise	37,115 43
proceeds of sales of goods, wares, &c	31,118 24
furniture and repairs of public buildings, &c	40,089 74
construction of fire-proof appraiser's store, Philadelphia Bank building	50,000 00
distributive shares of fines, penalties, and forfeitures	229,426 98
expenses, &c., in regard to quarantine and health laws	50,018 18
expenses incurred in collection of abandoned property	14,123 50
janitors of the Treasury Department	7,869 22
building custom-houses, &c., including repairs	296,988 34
rents, &c., of office of surveyors general, &c	22,101 64
patent fund	714,528 68
Patent Office building	102,607 91
support, &c., of hospital for insane	127,603 75
five per cent. fund in Michigan	11,747 33
five per cent. fund in Oregon	3,566 79
five per cent. fund in Kansas	924 67

For five per cent. fund in Wisconsin	$5,674 11	
five per cent. fund in Minnesota	2,475 67	
indemnity for swamp land purchased by individuals	13,187 85	
expenses of United States courts	1,768,358 47	
repayments for lands erroneously sold	11,485 47	
surveying the public lands, &c	373,252 30	
suppression of the slave trade	17,478 12	
deposits of individuals for expenses of survey of public lands	10,373 46	
expenses of the eighth census of United States, &c.	26,701 49	
salaries and expenses of the Metropolitan police	208,850 00	
Columbia Institute for the Deaf, Dumb, and Blind in the District of Columbia	92,048 34	
support, &c., of convicts transferred from the District of Columbia	12,226 89	
packing and distributing congressional documents	5,933 10	
reliefs of sundry individuals	348,503 77	
Total miscellaneous		$30,618,367 04

UNDER DIRECTION OF THE INTERIOR DEPARTMENT.

For the Indian department	$3,988,353 59	
pensions, military	23,423,651 35	
pensions, naval	358,735 43	
reliefs	112,328 73	
Total for Interior Department		27,883,069 10

UNDER DIRECTION OF THE WAR DEPARTMENT.

For the pay department	57,347,589 60	
the commissary department	7,254,195 87	
the quartermasters' department	28,953,113 20	
the ordnance department	1,702,959 41	
the engineer department	5,334,897 28	
the Inspector General	174,368 94	
the Adjutant General	6,741,777 27	
the Surgeon General	1,028,146 34	
For the Secretary's office, (army expenditures)	14,308,659 25	
reliefs and miscellaneous	400,941 46	
Total for the War Department		123,246,648 62

UNDER DIRECTION OF THE NAVY DEPARTMENT.

For the Secretary's bureau	$8,949,477 46	
the marine corps	1,493,192 15	
the Bureau of Yards and Docks	2,389,780 64	
the Bureau of Equipment and Recruiting	2,492,754 82	
the Bureau of Navigation	553,355 27	
the Bureau of Ordnance	1,272,140 21	
the Bureau of Construction and Repair	2,123,191 52	
the Bureau of Steam Engineering	4,796,492 17	
the Bureau of Provisions and Clothing	1,527,781 23	
the Bureau of Medicine and Surgery	134,605 11	
reliefs	42,732 15	
Total for Navy Department		25,775,502 72
To which add—		
Interest on the public debt		140,424,045 71
Premium on treasury notes, per acts June 30, 1864, and March 3, 1865.		7,001,151 04
Total expenditures, exclusive of principal of the public debt		377,340,284 86
Principal of the public debt:		
Redemption of the loan of 1842	$51,561 64	
1847	6,431,850 00	
1848	226,350 00	

Reimbursement of treasury notes issued prior to July 22, 1846	$50 00	
Reimbursement of treasury notes, per act July 22, 1846	100 00	
Redemption of Texan indemnity stock, per act September 9, 1850	11,000 00	
Payment of treasury notes, per act December 23, 1857	200 00	
Payment of treasury notes, per act December 17, 1860	500 00	
Payment of treasury notes, per act March 2, 1861	150 00	
Redemption of 7.30 three-year coupon bonds, per act July 17, 1861	13,800 00	
Redemption of treasury notes, per act July 17, 1861	25,690 50	
Redemption of treasury notes, per act February 25, 1862	33,529,643 20	
Redemption of temporary loan, per acts February 25 and March 17, 1862	7,197,664 45	
Redemption of certificates of indebtedness, per act March 17, 1862	15,000 00	
Redemption of postage and other stamps, per act July 17, 1862	691,187 43	
Redemption of fractional currency, per act March 3, 1863	19,576,640 66	
Redemption of gold certificates, per act March 3, 1863	79,029,040 00	
Redemption of 2-year 5 per cent. interest-bearing treasury notes, per act March 3, 1863	568,338 00	
Redemption of 3-year 6 per cent. compound interest notes, per act March 3, 1863	94,232,670 00	
Redemption of 3-year 7.30 coupon treasury notes, per acts June 30, 1864, and March 3, 1865	450,948,250 00	
Total principal of public debt		$692,549,685 88
		1,069,889,970 74
Balance in the treasury on July 1, 1868, agreeably to warrants		131,006,532 25
		1,200,896,502 99

No. 2.

Statement of receipts and expenditures of the United States during the quarter ending September 30, 1868.

RECEIPTS.

From customs		$49,676,594 67
sales of public lands		714,895 03
direct tax		15,536 02
internal revenue		38,735,863 08
miscellaneous and incidental sources		6,249,979 97
Total receipts, exclusive of loans		95,392,868 77
From loans:		
6 per cent. 5-20 bonds, act March 3, 1865	$32,538,850 00	
7.30 treasury notes, acts June 30, 1864, and March 3, 1865	300,932 93	
Legal-tender U. S. notes, act February 25, 1862	1,833,859 20	
3 per cent. certificates, act March 2, 1867	17,865,000 00	
6 per cent. 20-year bonds, act July 17, 1861	2,000 00	
1881 bonds, act March 3, 1863	537,473 94	
5-20 bonds, act June 30, 1864	52,645 75	
10-40 bonds, act March 3, 1864	2,114 99	
Certificates of gold coin deposits, act March 3, 1863	19,982,280 00	
Fractional currency, act March 3, 1863	6,204,179 00	
		79,319,335 81
Total receipts		174,712,204 58

EXPENDITURES.

Civil, foreign intercourse, and miscellaneous		$21,227,106 33
Interior, (pensions and Indians)		12 358,647 70
War		27,219,117 02
Navy		5,604,785 33
Interest on the public debt		38,742,814 37
Expenditures, exclusive of principal of the public debt		105,152,470 75
Redemption of treasury notes, acts 17th July and 5th August, 1861	$4,168 25	
Redemption of treasury notes, act 25th February, 1862	1,000,000 00	
Redemption of certificates of indebtedness	5,000 00	
Redemption of 7.30 3-year coupon bonds, act 17th July, 1861	700 00	
Redemption of postage and other stamps, act 17th July, 1862	69,692 98	
Redemption of fractional currency, act 3d March, 1863	5,861,576 74	
Redemption of 5 per cent. 2-year notes, act 3d March, 1863	110,000 00	
Redemption of 7.30 3-year treasury notes, acts June 30, 1864, and 3d March, 1865	34,256,850 00	
Redemption of gold certificates, act 3d March, 1863	17,424,520 00	
Redemption of loan of 1847	485,500 00	
Redemption of loan of 1848	6,720,850 00	
Redemption of 3-year 6 per cent. compound interest notes, act 3d March, 1863	16,593,890 00	
Redemption of 3 per cent. certificates, act 2d March, 1867	2,580,000 00	
Reimbursement of temporary loan, acts February 25, 1862, and March 17, 1862	208,771 00	
		85,326,518 97
Total expenditures		190,478,989 72

No. 3.—*Statement of the indebtedness*

	Acts authorizing loans, and synopsis of same.
Acts of July 21, 1841, and April 15, 1842.	Authorized a loan of $12,000,000, bearing interest at a rate not exceeding 6 per cent. per annum, and reimbursable at the will of the Secretary, after six month's notice, or at any time after three years from January 1, 1842. The act of April 15, 1842, authorized the loan of an additional sum of $5,000,000, and made the amount obtained on the loan after the passage of this act reimbursable after six months' notice, or at any time not exceeding twenty years from January 1, 1843. This loan was made for the purpose of redeeming outstanding treasury notes, and to defray any of the public expenses.
Act of Jan. 28, 1847...	Authorized the issue of $23,000,000 in treasury notes, bearing interest at a rate not exceeding 6 per cent. per annum, with authority to borrow any portion of the amount, and issue bonds therefor, bearing interest at a rate not exceeding 6 per cent., and redeemable after December 31, 1867. The 13th section authorized the funding of these notes into bonds of the same description. The act limited the amount to be borrowed or issued in treasury notes and funded as aforesaid to $23,000,000, but authorized the funding of treasury notes issued under former acts beyond that amount. The excess of the $23,000,000 is made up of treasury notes funded under the 14th section.
Act of March 31, 1848.	Authorized a loan of $16,000,000, bearing interest at a rate not exceeding 6 per cent. per annum, and reimbursable at any time after twenty years from July 1, 1848. Authority was given to the Secretary to purchase the stock at any time.
Act of Sept. 9, 1850...	Authorized the issue of $10,000,000 in bonds, bearing 5 per cent. interest, and redeemable at the end of fourteen years, to indemnify the State of Texas for her relinquishment of all claims upon the United States for liability of the debts of Texas, and for compensation for the surrender to the United States of her ships, forts, arsenals, custom-houses, &c., which became the property of the United States at the time of annexation.
Old funded and unfunded debts.	Consisting of unclaimed dividends upon stocks issued before the year 1800, and those issued during the war of 1812.
Acts prior to 1857.....	Different issues of treasury notes..
Act of Dec. 23, 1857..	Authorized an issue of $20,000,000 in treasury notes, bearing interest at a rate not exceeding 6 per cent. per annum, and receivable in payment of all public dues, and to be redeemed after the expiration of one year from date of said notes
Act of June 14, 1858...	Authorized a loan of $20,000,000, bearing interest at a rate not exceeding 5 per cent. per annum, and reimbursable at the option of the government at any time after the expiration of fifteen years from January 1, 1859.
Act of June 22, 1860..	Authorized a loan of $21,000,000, bearing interest at a rate not exceeding 6 per cent. per annum, and reimbursable within a period not beyond twenty years, and not less than ten years, for the redemption of outstanding treasury notes, and for no other purpose.
Act of Dec. 17, 1860...	Authorized an issue of $10,000,000 in treasury notes, to be redeemed after the expiration of one year from the date of issue, and bearing such a rate of interest as may be offered by the lowest bidders. Authority was given to issue these notes in payment of warrants in favor of public creditors, at their par value, bearing 6 per cent. interest per annum.
Act of Feb. 8, 1861....	Authorized a loan of $25,000,000, bearing interest at a rate not exceeding 6 per cent. per annum, and reimbursable within a period not beyond twenty years, nor less than ten years. This loan was made for the payment of the current expenses, and was to be awarded to the most favorable bidders.
Act of March 2, 1861..	Authorized a loan of $10,000,000. bearing interest at a rate not exceeding 6 per cent. per annum, and reimbursable after the expiration of ten years from July 1, 1861. In case proposals for the loan were not acceptable, authority was given to issue the whole amount in treasury notes bearing interest at a rate not exceeding 6 per cent. per annum. Authority was also given to substitute treasury notes for the whole or any part of the loans for which the Secretary was by law authorized to contract and issue bonds at the time of the passage of this act, and such treasury notes were to be made receivable in payment of all public dues, and redeemable at any time within two years from March 2, 1861.
Act of March 2, 1861..	Authorized an issue, should the Secretary of the Treasury deem it expedient, of $2,800,000, in coupon bonds, bearing interest at the rate of 6 per cent. per annum, and redeemable in twenty years, for the payment of expenses incurred by the Territories of Washington and Oregon in the suppression of Indian hostilities during the years 1855 and 1856.
Acts of July 17, 1861, and August 5, 1861.	Authorized a loan of $250,000,000, for which could be issued bonds bearing interest at a rate not exceeding 7 per cent. per annum, irredeemable for twenty years, and after that redeemable at the pleasure of the United States; treasury notes bearing interest at the rate of 7.30 per cent. per annum, payable three years after date, and United States notes without interest, payable on demand, to the extent of $50,000,000, (increased by act of February 12, 1862, to $60,000,000,) to bonds and treasury notes to be issued in such proportions of each as the Secretary may deem advisable. The supplementary act of August 5, 1861, authorized an issue of bonds bearing 6 per cent. interest per annum, and payable at the pleasure of the United States after twenty years from date, which may be issued in exchange for 7.30 treasury notes, but no such bonds to be issued for a less sum than $500; and the whole amount of such bonds not to exceed the whole amount of 7.30 treasury notes

of the United States, June 30, 1868.

Title.	Length of loan.	When redeemable.	Rate of interest.	Price of emission.	Amount authorized.	Amount issued.	Amount outstanding.
Loan of 1842....	20 years	After Dec. 31, 1862.	6 per ct. per annum.	Par..	$17, 000, 000	$8, 000, 000	$6, 000 00
Loan of 1847....	20 years	After Dec. 31, 1867.	6 per ct. per annum.	Par..	23, 000, 000	28, 207, 000	742, 250 00
Loan of 1848....	20 years	After July 1, '68.	6 per ct. per annum.	Par..	16, 000, 000	16, 000, 000	6, 151, 191 80
Texas indemnity	15 years	After Dec. 31, 1864.	5 per ct. per annum.	Par..	10, 000, 000	5, 000, 000	256, 000 00
Old funded debt.	Demand.	On demand.....	5 and 6 per ct.	Par..	....	....	113, 915 48
Treasury notes.	....	On demand.....	1 m. to 6 p. ct.	Par..	....	....	104, 511 64
Treasury notes.	1 year..	1 year after date	5 to $5\frac{1}{2}$ per ct..	Par..	20, 000, 000	....	2, 600 00
Loan of 1858....	15 years	Dec. 31, 1873 ...	5 per ct. per annum.	Par..	20, 000, 000	20, 000, 000	20, 000, 000 00
Loan of 1860....	10 years	After Dec. 31, 1870.	5 per ct. per annum.	Par..	21, 000, 000	7, 022, 000	7, 022, 000 00
Treasury notes.	1 year..	1 year after date	6 and 12 per ct. per annum.	Par..	10, 000, 000	10, 000, 000	500 00
Loan of Feb. 8, 1861.	10 or 20 years.	After June 1, '71.	6 per ct. per annum.	Par..	25, 000, 000	18, 415, 000	18, 415, 000 00
Treasury notes.	2 years.	2 years after date.	6 per ct. per annum.	Par..	22, 468, 100	22, 468, 100	3, 550 60
	60 days.	60 days after date.			12, 896, 350	12, 896, 350	
Oregon war	20 years	After July 1, '81.	6 per ct. per annum.	Par..	2, 800, 000	1, 090, 850	945, 050 00

No. 3.—*Statement of the indebtedness*

	Acts authorizing loans, and synopsis of same.
Act of Feb. 25, 1862...	Authorized the issue of $500,000,000 in 6 per cent. bonds, redeemable after five years, and payable twenty years from date, which may be exchanged for United States notes. Also, on
March 3, 1864.........	Authorized the issue of not over $11,000,000 additional of similar bonds, to meet subscriptions already made and paid for.
June 30, 1864....... } January 28, 1865.... }	On hand unsold in the United States or Europe ....
Act of Feb. 25, 1862...	Authorized the issue of $150,000,000 in legal-tender U. S. notes, $50,000,000 of which to be in lieu of demand notes issued under act of July 17, 1861.
Act of July 11, 1862...	Authorized an additional issue of $150,000,000 legal-tender notes, $35,000,000 of which might be in denominations less than five dollars; $50,000,000 of this issue to be reserved to pay temporary loans promptly in case of emergency.
Resolution of Congress, January 17, 1863.	Authorized the issue of $100,000,000 in United States notes, for the immediate payment of the army and navy, such notes to be a part of the amount provided for in any bill that may hereafter be passed by this Congress. (The amount in this resolution is included in act of March 3, 1863.)
Act of March 3, 1863..	A further issue of $150,000,000 in United States notes, for the purpose of converting the treasury notes which may be issued under this act, and for no other purpose. And a further issue, if necessary, for the payment of the army and navy, and other creditors of the government, of $150,000,000 in United States notes, which amount includes the $100,000,000 authorized by the joint resolution of Congress, January 17, 1863.
Act of April 12, 1866..	*Provided*, That of United States notes, not more than ten millions of dollars may be retired and cancelled within six months from the passage of this act, and thereafter not more than four millions of dollars in any one month: *And provided further*, That the act to which this is an amendment shall continue in full force in all its provisions, except as modified by this act.
Act of Feb. 25, 1862...	Authorized a temporary loan of $25,000,000 in United States notes, for not less than thirty days, payable after ten days' notice, at 5 per cent. interest per annum. (This was increased to $100,000,000 by the following acts.)
March 17, 1862........	Authorized an increase of temporary loans of $25,000,000, bearing interest at a rate not exceeding 5 per cent. per annum.
July 11, 1862	Authorized a further increase of temporary loans of $50,000,000, making the whole amount authorized $100,000,000.
Act of June 30, 1864 ..	Authorized the increase of temporary loans to not exceeding $150,000,000, at a rate not exceeding 6 per cent.
Act of March 3, 1863 ..	Authorized a loan of $300,000,000 for this, and $600,000,000 for the next fiscal year, for which could be issued bonds running not less than ten, nor more than forty years, principal and interest payable in coin, bearing interest at a rate not exceeding 6 per cent. per annum, payable in bonds not exceeding $100 annually, and on all others semi-annually, the whole amount of bonds, treasury notes, and United States notes, issued under this act, not to exceed the sum of
Act of June 30, 1864...	$900,000,000. And so much of this act as limits the loan to the current fiscal year is repealed by act of June 30, 1864, which also repeals the authority to borrow money conferred by section 1, except so far as it may affect $75,000,000 of bonds already advertised.
Act of March 3, 1863..	And treasury notes to the amount of $400,000,000, not exceeding three years to run, with interest at not over 6 per cent. per annum, principal and interest payable in lawful money, which may be made a legal-tender for their face value, excluding interest or convertible into United States notes. Secretary may receive gold on deposit and issue certificates therefor, in sums not less than twenty dollars.
Act of March 3, 1864..	Authorizes the issue of bonds not exceeding $200,000,000, bearing date March 1, 1864, or any subsequent period, redeemable at the pleasure of the government after any period not less than five years, and payable at any period not more than forty years from date, in coin, bearing interest not exceeding 6 per cent. yearly, payable on bonds not over one hundred dollars annually, and on all other bonds semi-annually, in coin.
Act of March 1, 1862..	Authorized an issue of certificates of indebtedness, payable one year from date, in settlement of audited claims against the government. Interest 6 per cent. per annum, payable in gold; and by
Act of March 3, 1863..	Payable in lawful currency on those issued after that date. Amount of issue not specified.
Act of July 17, 1862...	Authorized an issue of notes of the fractional parts of one dollar, receivable in payment of all dues, except customs, less than five dollars, and exchangeable for United States notes in sums not less than five dollars. Amount of issue not specified.
Act of March 3, 1863..	Authorized an issue not exceeding $50,000,000 in fractional currency, (in lieu of postage or other stamps,) exchangeable for United States notes in sums not less than three dollars, and receivable for any dues to the United States less than five dollars, except duties on imports. The whole amount issued, including postage and other stamps issued as currency, not to exceed $50,000,000. Authority was given to prepare it in the Treasury Department, under the supervision of the

of the United States, &c.—Continued.

Title.	Length of loan.	When redeemable.	Rate of interest.	Price of emission.	Amount authorized.	Amount issued.	Amount outstanding.
Five-twenties.	5 or 20 years.	After April 30, 1867.	6 per cent	Par..	$515, 000, 000	$514, 780, 500	$514, 780, 500 00
United States notes, new issue.	....	....	None.........	Par ..	450, 000, 000	....	356, 000, 000 00
Temp'y loan..	Not less than 30 days.	After 10 days' notice.	4, 5, and 6 per cent.	Par ..	150, 000, 000	....	13, 797, 029 00
Loan of 1863..	....	After June 30, 1881.	6 per cent	Pre'm 4.13 p. cent.	75, 000, 000	75, 000, 000	75, 000, 000 00
Treasury notes.	2 years.	2 years after date	5 per cent	Par ..	.... } 400, 000, 000 }	211, 000, 000	555, 492 00
	1 year..	1 year after date	5 per cent	Par ..			
Gold certificates.	....	On demand	....	Par ..	Not specified.	....	17, 678, 640 00
Ten-forties ...	10 or 40 years.	After Feb. 28, 1874.	5 per cent	Par ..	200, 000, 000	172, 770, 100	194, 566, 400 00
Five-twenties	5 or 20 years.	After October 31, 1869.	6 per cent	Par ..	....	....	3, 882, 500 00
Certificates of indebtedness.	1 year..	1 year after date	6 per cent	Par ..	Not specified.	....	18, 000 00
Postal currency.	....	....	....	Par ..	Not specified.	....	4, 881, 091 27
Fractional currency.	....	....	....	Par ..	500, 000, 000	....	27, 745, 860 48

No. 3.—*Statement of the indebtedness*

	Acts authorizing loans, and synopsis of same.
Act of June 30, 1864..	Authorized the issue of $400,000,000 of bonds redeemable at the pleasure of the government after any period not less than five nor more than thirty years, or, if deemed expedient, made payable at any period not more than forty years from date. And said bonds shall bear an annual interest not exceeding six per centum, payable semi-annually in coin. And the Secretary of the Treasury may dispose of such bonds, or any part thereof, and of any bonds commonly known as five-twenties, remaining unsold, on such terms as he may deem most advisable, for lawful money of the United States, or, at his discretion, for treasury notes, certificates of indebtedness, or certificates of deposit, issued under any act of Congress.
Act of March 3, 1863..	Authorizes an issue of treasury notes, not exceeding three years to run, interest at not over six per cent. per annum, principal and interest payable in lawful money.
Act of June 30, 1864..	Also authorizes the issue of and in lieu of an equal amount of bonds authorized by the first section, and as a part of said loan, not exceeding $200,000,000 in treasury notes of any denomination not less than $10, payable at any time not exceeding three years from date, or, if thought more expedient, redeemable at any time after three years from date, and bearing interest not exceeding the rate of 7 3-10 per centum, payable in lawful money at maturity, or, at the discretion of the Secretary, semi-annually; and such of them as shall be made payable, principal and interest, at maturity, shall be a legal tender to the same extent as United States notes, for their face value, excluding interest, and may be paid to any creditor of the United States, at their face value, excluding interest, or to any creditor willing to receive them at par, including interest; and any treasury notes issued under the authority of this act may be made convertible, at the discretion of the Secretary of the Treasury, into any bonds issued under the authority of this act, and the Secretary may redeem and cause to be cancelled and destroyed any treasury notes or United States notes heretofore issued under authority of previous acts of Congress, and substitute in lieu thereof an equal amount of treasury notes, such as are authorized by this act, or of other United States notes; nor shall any treasury note bearing interest issued under this act be a legal tender in payment or redemption of any notes issued by any bank, banking association, or banker, calculated or intended to circulate as money.
Act of Jan 28, 1865....	Whole amount may be issued in bonds or treasury notes, at the discretion of the Secretary.
Act of March 3, 1865..	Authorized an issue of $600,000,000 in bonds or treasury notes; bonds may be made payable at any period not more than forty years from the date of issue, or may be made redeemable at the pleasure of the government, at or after any period not less than five years nor more than forty years from date, or may be made redeemable and payable as aforesaid, as may be expressed upon their face, and so much thereof as may be issued in treasury notes may be made convertible into any bonds authorized by this act, and be of such denominations, not less than fifty dollars, and bear such dates, and be made redeemable or payable at such periods as the Secretary of the Treasury may deem expedient. The interest on the bonds payable semi-annually; on treasury notes semi-annually, or annually, or at maturity thereof; and the principal or interest, or both, be made payable in coin or other lawful money; if in coin, not to exceed 6 per cent. per annum; when not payable in coin, not to exceed 7 3-10 per cent. per annum. Rate and character to be expressed on bonds or treasury notes.
Act of April 12, 1866, amendment to act of March 3, 1865.	Authorizes the Secretary of the Treasury, at his discretion, to receive any treasury notes or other obligations issued under any act of Congress, whether bearing interest or not, in exchange for any description of bonds authorized by the act to which this is an amendment; and also to dispose of any description of bonds authorized by said act, either in the United States or elsewhere, to such an amount, in such manner, and at such rates as he may think advisable, for lawful money of the United States, or for any treasury notes, certificates of indebtedness, or certificates of deposit, or other representatives of value, which have been or which may be issued under any act of Congress, the proceeds thereof to be used only for retiring treasury notes or other obligations issued under any act of Congress; but nothing herein contained shall be construed to authorize any increase of the public debt.
Acts of July 1, 1862, and July 2, 1864.	Bonds issued to the Union Pacific Railroad Company in accordance with these acts.
Act of March 2, 1867..	For the purpose of redeeming and retiring any compound interest notes outstanding, the Secretary of the Treasury is authorized and directed to issue temporary loan certificates in the manner prescribed by section four of the act entitled "An act to authorize the issue of United States notes and for the redemption or funding thereof, and for funding the floating debt of the United States," approved February twenty-fifth, eighteen hundred and sixty-two, bearing interest at a rate not exceeding 3 per centum per annum, principal and interest payable in lawful money on demand; and said certificates of temporary loan may constitute and be held by any national bank holding or owning the same, as a part of the reserve provided

of the United States, &c.—Continued.

Title.	Length of loan.	When redeemable.	Rate of interest.	Price of emission.	Amount authorized.	Amount issued.	Amount outstanding.
Five-twenties...	5 or 20 years.	After Oct. 31, 1869.	6 per cent...	......	....	....	$125, 561, 300 00
Treas'y notes.	3 years.	3 yrs. after date.	6 p. ct. comp. interest.	Par...	....	$17, 250, 000	28, 161, 810 00
Treas'y notes.	3 years.	3 yrs. after date.	6 p. ct. comp. interest.	......	Substitute redeemed 5 p. ct. notes.	177, 045, 770	
Treas'y notes.	3 years.	3 yrs. after date.	6 p. ct. comp. interest.	......	....	22, 728, 390	
....	......	....	....	......	$400, 000, 000	....	....
7.30 treasury notes.	3 years.	3 yrs. after Aug. 15, 1864.	7.30 per cent.	Par...	....	234, 400, 000	....
7.30 treasury notes, three issues.	3 yrs.	After Aug. 14, 1867. After June 14, 1868. After July 14, 1868.	7 3-10 p. ct..	Par...	600, 000, 000	....	37, 717, 650 00
Five-twenties	5 or 20 years.	After Oct. 31, 1870.	6 per cent...	Par...	....	....	197, 794, 250 00
Five-twenties...	5 or 20 years.	After June 30, 1870.	6 per cent...	Par...	....	....	332, 998, 950 00
Five-twenties...	5 or 20 years.	After June 30, 1872.	6 per cent...	Par...	....	....	365, 248, 150 00
Five twenties...	5 or 20 years.	After June 30, 1873.	6 per cent...	Par...	....	....	17, 648, 950 00
Union Pacific R. R. Co. bonds.	30 yrs..	After Jan. 15, 1895.	6 per cent...	Par...	....	....	29, 089, 000 00

No. 3.—*Statement of the indebtedness*

Acts authorizing loans, and synopsis of same.	
Act of March 2, 1867—*Continued.*	for in sections thirty-one and thirty-two of the act entitled "An act to provide a national currency secured by a pledge of United States bonds, and to provide for the circulation and redemption thereof," approved June three, eighteen hundred and sixty-four: *Provided*, That not less than two-fifths of the entire reserve of such bank shall consist of lawful money of the United States: *And provided further*, That the amount of such temporary certificates at any time outstanding shall not exceed fifty millions of dollars.
Act July 25, 1868	Twenty-five millions additional ....

of the United States, &c.—Continued.

Title.	Length of loan.	When redeemable.	Rate of interest.	Price of emission.	Amount authorized.	Amount issued.	Amount outstanding.
3 p. ct. certs ..	....	On demand	3 per cent. ..	Par..	$75, 000, 000	$50, 000, 000	$50, 000, 000 00
							2,636,320,964 67

REPORT

OF THE

COMPTROLLER OF THE CURRENCY.

OFFICE OF THE COMPTROLLER OF THE CURRENCY,
Washington, November 10, 1868.

SIR: In compliance with the provisions of section 61 of the national currency act, I have the honor to present, through you, to the Congress of the United States the following report:

Since the last annual report 12 national banks have been organized, of which five are new associations. One was organized to take the place of an existing State bank, and six were organized to take the place of national banks previously organized but now in liquidation and winding up, making the total number organized up to October, 1685.

Table exhibiting the number of banks, with the amount of capital, bonds deposited, and circulation, in each State and Territory, September 30, 1868.

States and Territories.	Organization.			Capital paid in.	Bonds on deposit.	Circulation issued.	In actual circulation.
	Organized.	Closed or closing.	In operation.				
Maine	61	......	61	$9, 085, 000 00	$8, 497, 250	$7, 569, 166	$7. 510, 066
New Hampshire	40	......	40	4, 785, 000 00	4, 839, 000	4, 328, 195	4, 281, 695
Vermont	40	......	40	6, 560, 012 50	6, 517, 000	5, 802, 960	5, 737, 560
Massachusetts	209	2	207	80, 032, 000 00	64, 718, 400	58, 561, 030	57, 084, 640
Rhode Island	62	......	62	20, 364, 800 00	14, 185, 600	12, 676, 630	12, 491, 480
Connecticut	83	2	81	24, 684, 220 00	19, 768, 000	17, 800, 625	17, 443, 793
New York	314	15	299	116, 544, 941 00	79, 442, 500	73, 823, 505	68, 853, 726
New Jersey	55	1	54	11, 583, 350 00	10, 678, 650	9, 520, 485	9, 397, 985
Pennsylvania	205	8	197	50, 247, 390 00	44, 303, 350	39, 940, 700	38, 772, 102
Maryland	32	......	32	12, 790, 202 50	10, 065, 750	9, 150, 800	8, 904, 800
Delaware	11	......	11	1, 428, 185 00	1, 348, 200	1, 217, 225	1, 198, 825
District of Columbia	6	2	4	1, 550, 000 00	1, 398, 000	1, 278, 000	1, 137, 700
Virginia	20	2	18	2, 500, 000 00	2, 429, 800	2, 157, 930	2, 146, 670
West Virginia	15	......	15	2, 216, 400 00	2, 243, 250	2, 020, 350	1, 988, 550
Ohio	137	4	133	22, 404, 700 00	20, 763, 800	18, 667, 750	18, 410, 425
Indiana	71	3	68	12, 867, 000 00	12, 532, 500	11, 169, 055	11, 018, 735
Illinois	83	......	83	12, 070, 000 00	11, 047, 950	9, 777, 650	9, 648, 150
Michigan	43	1	42	5, 210, 010 00	4, 357, 700	3, 872, 955	3, 826, 455
Wisconsin	37	3	34	2, 960, 000 00	2, 768, 050	2, 583, 950	2, 541, 410
Iowa	48	4	44	4, 057, 000 00	3, 763, 750	3, 349, 805	3, 252, 228
Minnesota	16	1	15	1, 710, 000 00	1, 712, 200	1, 501, 900	1, 476, 800
Kansas	5	......	5	400, 000 00	382, 000	354, 600	341, 000
Missouri	20	2	18	7, 810, 300 00	4, 724, 050	4, 305, 550	4, 129, 310
Kentucky	15	......	15	2, 885, 000 00	2, 665, 900	2, 367, 270	2, 338, 620
Tennessee	13	1	12	2, 025, 300 00	1, 492, 700	1, 270, 220	1, 204, 755
Louisiana	3	1	2	1, 800, 000 00	1, 308, 000	1, 245, 000	1, 131, 415
Mississippi	2	2	......	150, 000 00	75, 000	66, 000	64, 035
Nebraska	4	......	4	350, 000 00	235, 000	170, 000	170, 000
Colorado	3	......	3	350, 000 00	297, 000	254, 500	254, 000
Georgia	9	1	8	1, 600, 000 00	1, 383, 500	1, 235, 400	1, 234, 000
North Carolina	6	......	6	653, 300 00	399, 500	317, 600	316, 000
South Carolina	3	......	3	685, 000 00	204, 000	153, 000	135, 000
Alabama	3	1	2	500, 000 00	370, 500	353, 025	304, 900
Nevada	1	......	1	155, 000 00	155, 000	131, 700	131, 700
Oregon	1	......	1	100, 000 00	100, 000	88, 500	88, 500
Texas	4	......	4	525, 000 00	472, 100	417, 635	407, 535
Arkansas	2	......	2	200, 000 00	200, 000	179, 500	179, 500
Utah	1	......	1	150, 000 00	150, 000	135, 500	135, 000
Montana	1	......	1	100, 000 00	40, 000	36, 000	36, 000
Idaho	1	......	1	100, 000 00	75, 000	63, 500	63, 500
Total	1, 685	56	1, 629	426, 189, 111 00	342, 010, 950	309, 915, 166	299, 806, 565

From the number of banks organized, heretofore stated to be 1,685, should be deducted 56, leaving the number in active operation 1,629.

The banks to be excluded are the following:

NEVER COMPLETED THEIR ORGANIZATION SO AS TO COMMENCE BUSINESS.

The First National Bank of Lansing, Michigan, No. 232.
The First National Bank of Penn Yan, New York, No. 169.
The Second National Bank of Canton, Ohio, No. 463.
The Second National Bank of Ottumwa, Iowa, No. 195.

SUPERSEDED BY SUBSEQUENT ORGANIZATION WITH THE SAME TITLES.

The First National Bank of Norwich, Connecticut, original No. 65; present No. 458.

The First National Bank of Utica, New York, original No. 120; present No. 1,395.

IN VOLUNTARY LIQUIDATION.

The First National Bank of Columbia, Missouri.
The First National Bank of Carondelet, Missouri.
The National Union Bank of Rochester, New York.
The National Bank of the Metropolis, Washington, D. C.
The First National Bank of Leonardsville, New York.
The Farmers' National Bank of Richmond, Virginia.
The Farmers' National Bank of Waukesha, Wisconsin.
The City National Bank of Savannah, Georgia.
The National Bank of Crawford County, Meadville, Pennsylvania.
The First National Bank of Elkhart, Indiana.
The First National Bank of New Ulm, Minnesota.
The Pittston National Bank, Pennsylvania.
The Berkshire National Bank of Adams, Massachusetts.
The Fourth National Bank of Indianapolis, Indiana.
The Kittanning National Bank, Kittanning, Pennsylvania.
The First National Bank of Providence, Pennsylvania.
The National State Bank of Dubuque, Iowa.
The Ohio National Bank of Cincinnati, Ohio.

Since October 1, 1867:

The First National Bank of Kingston, New York.
The First National Bank of Bluffton, Indiana.
The First National Bank of Skaneateles, New York.
The First National Bank of Jackson, Mississippi.
The First National Bank of Downingtown, Pennsylvania.
The National Exchange Bank of Richmond, Virginia.
The Appleton National Bank, Appleton, Wisconsin.
The National Bank of Whitestown, New York.
The First National Bank of New Brunswick, New Jersey.
The First National Bank of Titusville, Pennsylvania.
The First National Bank of Cuyahoga Falls, Ohio.
The First National Bank of Cedarburg, Wisconsin.
The Commercial National Bank of Cincinnati, Ohio.
The Second National Bank of Watertown, New York.
The Second National Bank of Des Moines, Iowa.

The First National Bank of South Worcester, New York.
The National Mechanics and Farmers' Bank of Albany, New York.
The First National Bank of Plumer, Pennsylvania.

Of the banks in liquidation, the following are winding up for the purpose of consolidating with other banks:

The Pittston National Bank, Pittston, Pennsylvania, with the First National Bank of Pittston.

The Berkshire National Bank of Adams, Massachusetts, with the First National Bank of Berkshire.

The Fourth National Bank of Indianapolis, Indiana, with the Citizens' National Bank of Indianapolis.

The Kittanning National Bank, Kittanning, Pennsylvania, with the First National Bank of Kittanning.

The First National Bank of Providence, Pennsylvania, with the Second National Bank of Scranton, Pennsylvania.

The National State Bank of Dubuque, Iowa, with the First National Bank of Dubuque.

The Ohio National Bank of Cincinnati, Ohio, with the Merchants' National Bank of Cincinnati.

The First National Bank of Titusville, Pennsylvania, with the Second National Bank of Titusville.

The National Exchange Bank of Richmond, Virginia, with the First National Bank of Richmond.

The Second National Bank of Watertown, New York, with the First National Bank of Watertown.

The following banks in liquidation are succeeded by new organizations, which are to take their circulation as fast as it is redeemed; this being the only process by which a change of location can be effected.

The First National Bank of Downington, Pennsylvania, succeeded by the First National Bank of Honeybrook, Pennsylvania.

The First National Bank of New Brunswick, New Jersey, succeeded by the Princeton National Bank, Princeton, New Jersey.

The Second National Bank of Des Moines, Iowa, succeeded by the Pacific National Bank of Council Bluffs, Iowa.

The First National Bank of Plumer, Pennsylvania, succeeded by the First National Bank of Sharon, Pennsylvania.

Statement showing the national banks in liquidation for the purpose of closing up and going out of existence, their capital, bonds deposited to secure circulation, circulation delivered, circulation redeemed, and circulation outstanding, October 1, 1868.

Name of bank.	Capital.	U. S. bonds on deposit.	Legal Tenders deposited.	Circulation delivered.	Circulation returned and destroyed.	Circulation outstanding.
The First National Bank of Columbia, Mo	$100,000	....	$90,000	$90,000	$6,910	$83,090
The First National Bank of Carondelet, Mo	30,000	....	25,500	25,500	16,640	8,860
The National Union Bank of Rochester, N. Y	400,000	$220,000	....	192,500	....	192,500
The National Bank of the Metropolis, Washington, D. C.	200,000	202,000	....	180,000	....	180,000
The First National Bank of Leonardsville, N. Y	50,000	50,500	....	45,000	....	45,000
The Farmers' National Bank of Richmond, Va	100,000	100,000	....	85,000	....	85,000
The Farmers' National Bank of Waukesha, Wis	100,000	....	90,000	90,000	140	89,860
The City National Bank of Savannah, Ga	100,000	....	....	(*)	....	....
The National Bank of Crawford County, Meadville, Pa.	300,000	....	....	(*)	....	....
The First National Bank of Elkhart, Ind	100,000	100,000	....	88,150	1,000	87,150
The First National Bank of New Ulm, Minn	60,000	60,000	....	54,000	....	54,000
The First National Bank of Kingston, N. Y	200,000	200,000	....	180,000	....	180,000
The First National Bank of Bluffton, Ind	50,000	50,000	....	45,000	....	45,000
The First National Bank of Skaneateles, N. Y	150,000	153,000	....	135,000	....	135,000
The First National Bank of Jackson, Miss	100,000	45,000	....	40,500	....	40,500
The Appleton National Bank, Appleton, Wis	50,000	50,000	....	45,000	....	45,000
The National Bank of Whitestown, N. Y	120,000	50,000	....	44,500	....	44,500
The First National Bank of Cuyahoga Falls, Ohio	50,000	50,000	....	45,000	....	45,000
The First National Bank of Cedarburg, Wis	100,000	80,000	....	90,000	18,000	72,000
The Commercial National Bank of Cincinnati, Ohio	500,000	407,000	....	345,950	....	345,950
The First National Bank of South Worcester, N. Y.	175,000	177,700	....	157,400	....	157,400
The National Mechanics and Farmers' Bank of Albany, N. Y.	350,000	350,000	....	314,950	3,520	311,430

* No circulation.

Statement showing the national banks in liquidation for the purpose of consolidating with other banks, their capital, bonds, and circulation.

Name of bank.	Capital.	U. S. bonds on deposit.	Circulation delivered.	Circulation returned and destroyed.	Circulation outstanding.
The Pittston National Bank, Pittston, Pa	$200,000	....	(*)	....	....
The Berkshire National Bank of Adams, Mass	100,000	....	(*)	....	....
The Fourth National Bank of Indianapolis, Ind	100,000	$94,000	$85,700	$1,100	$84,600
The First National Bank of Providence, Pa	100,000	101,550	90,000	1,000	89,000
The Kittanning National Bank, Kittanning, Pa	200,000	....	(*)	....	....
The Ohio National Bank of Cincinnati, Ohio	500,000	530,000	450,000	2,500	447,500
The National State Bank of Dubuque, Iowa	150,000	146,000	127,500	3,400	124,100
The National Exchange Bank of Richmond, Va	200,000	206,300	180,000	....	180,000
The First National Bank of Titusville, Pa	100,000	100,000	86,750	1,505	85,245
The Second National Bank of Watertown, N. Y	100,000	100,000	90,000	....	90,000

* No circulation.

Statement showing the national banks in liquidation for the purpose of changing their location, their capital, bonds, and circulation.

Name of bank.	Capital.	U. S. bonds on deposit.	Circulation delivered.	Circulation returned and destroyed.	Circulation outstanding.
The First National Bank of Downingtown, Pa	$100,000	$100,000	$89,500	$1,400	$88,100
The First National Bank of New Brunswick, N. J	100,000	100,000	90,000	500	89,500
The Second National Bank of Des Moines, Iowa	50,000	50,000	42,500	....	42,500
The First National Bank of Plumer, Pa	100,000	100,000	87,500	....	87,500

NATIONAL BANKS WHICH HAVE FAILED TO REDEEM THEIR CIRCULATING NOTES, AND FOR WHICH RECEIVERS HAVE BEEN APPOINTED.

The First National Bank of Attica, New York, Leonidas Doty, receiver.

The Venango National Bank of Franklin, Pennsylvania, Harvey Henderson, receiver.

The Merchants' National Bank of Washington, D. C., James C. Kennedy, receiver.

The First National Bank of Medina, New York, Edwin P. Healey, receiver.

The Tennessee National Bank of Memphis, Tennessee, William A. Hill, receiver.

The First National Bank of Newton, Newtonville, Massachusetts, D. Wayland Jones, receiver.

The First National Bank of Selma, Alabama, Cornelius Cadle, jr., receiver.

The First National Bank of New Orleans, Louisiana, Charles Case, receiver.

The National Unadilla Bank, Unadilla, New York, Lewis Kingsley, receiver.

The Farmers and Citizens' National Bank of Brooklyn, New York, Frederick A. Platt, receiver.

The Croton National Bank of the city of New York, C. P. Bailey, receiver.

The National Bank of Vicksburg, Mississippi, Edwin F. Brown, receiver.

The First National Bank of Keokuk, Iowa, H. W. Sample, receiver.

The First National Bank of Bethel, Connecticut, E. S. Tweedy, receiver.

The affairs of the First National Bank of Attica have been finally closed, and a dividend paid to the creditors of forty-eight per cent.

The affairs of the First National Bank of Newton have been finally closed. The government claims were paid in full, and a dividend of forty per cent. paid to the general creditors.

A partial dividend has been declared to the creditors of the Farmers and Citizens' National Bank of Brooklyn, New York, of fifty-five per cent., and to the creditors of the Croton National Bank of the city of New York of fifty per cent. upon all claims approved or adjudicated.

Statement showing the national banks in the hands of receivers, their capital, amount of United States bonds deposited to secure circulation, amount of circulation delivered, the amount of circulation redeemed at the treasury of the United States, and the amount outstanding on the 1st day of October, 1868.

Name and location of bank.	Capital.	U. S. bonds on deposit.	Legal Tenders on deposit, realiz'd from sale of bonds.	Circulation delivered.	Circulation redeemed.	Circulation outstanding.
The First National Bank of Attica, N. Y.	$50,000	....	$44,000 00	$44,000	$32,750	$11,250
The Venango National Bank of Franklin, Pa	300,000	$40,000	61,871 00	85,000	64,030	20,970
The Merchants' National Bank of Washington, D. C	200,000	80,000	127,741 00	180,000	125,800	54,200
The First National Bank of Newton, Mass.	150,000	146,000	....	130,000	6,500	123,500
The First National Bank of Medina, N. Y.	50,000	20,000	27,329 25	40,000	26,210	13,790
The Tennessee Nat'l B'k of Memphis, Tenn	100,000	50,000	53,372 00	90,000	59,465	30,535
The First National Bank of Selma, Ala.	100,000	60,000	41,247 20	85,000	48,125	36,875
The First National Bank of New Orleans, La	500,000	100,000	104,742 00	180,000	113,585	66,415
The National Unadilla Bank, Unadilla, N. Y	120,000	61,200	53,183 50	100,000	64,880	35,120
The Farmers and Citizens' National Bank of Brooklyn, N. Y	300,000	185,500	106,504 10	253,900	137,920	115,980
The Croton National B'k of the city of New York, N. Y	200,000	142,000	72,181 90	180,000	105,111	74,889
The First National Bank of Bethel, Conn.	60,000	30,000	....	26,300	2,020	24,280
The First National Bank of Keokuk, Iowa.	100,000	100,000	....	90,000	28,780	61,220
The First National Bank of Vicksburg, Miss	50,000	30,000	....	25,500	1,965	23,535

The following statement exhibits the number and amount of notes issued, redeemed and outstanding, October 5, 1868:

ONES.

	Notes.	
Issued	8,896,576	$8,896,576
Redeemed	254,754	254,754
Outstanding	8,641,822	8,641,822

TWOS.

Issued	2,978,160	$5,956,320
Redeemed	73,176	146,352
Outstanding	2,904,984	5,809,968

FIVES.

Issued	23,106,728	$115,533,640
Redeemed	482,132	2,410,660
Outstanding	22,624,596	113,122,980

TENS.

Issued	7,915,914	$79,159,140
Redeemed	142,359	1,423,590
Outstanding	7,773,555	77,735,550

TWENTIES.

Issued	2,219,322	$44,386,440
Redeemed	36,355	727,100
Outstanding	2,182,967	43,659,340

FIFTIES.

Issued	355,181	$17,759,050
Redeemed	17,256	862,800
Outstanding	337,925	16,896,250

ONE HUNDREDS.

Issued	267,350	$26,735,000
Redeemed	15,583	1,558,300
Outstanding	251,767	25,176,700

FIVE HUNDREDS.

Issued	13,486	$6,743,000
Redeemed	1,759	879,500
Outstanding	11,727	5,863,500

ONE THOUSANDS.

Issued	4,746	4,746,000
Redeemed	1,846	1,846,000
Outstanding	2,900	2,900,000

Total of all denominations outstanding on the first Monday of October, 1868	$299,806,110
Add for fragments of notes outstanding, lost or destroyed, portions of which have been redeemed	455
	$299,806,565

Table of the state of the lawful money reserve (required by sections 31 and 32 of the national currency act) of the National Banking Associations of the United States, as shown by the quarterly reports of their condition on the morning of the first Monday in JANUARY, 1868, *before the commencement of business.*

States and territories.	Number of banks reporting.	Liabilities to be protected by a reserve of fifteen per cent. of the amount.	Amount required as reserve.	Items of reserve.				Amount of available reserve.	Percentage of available reserve to liabilities.
				Legal Tenders.	Specie.	Compound int'st notes and three per cent. temporary loan certificates.	Amount due from approved associations in the redemption cities, available for the redemption of circulating notes.		
Maine	61	$12, 840, 497	$1, 926, 075	$895, 735	$57, 279	$243, 490	$1, 828, 556	$3, 025, 060	23 6-10
New Hampshire	40	6, 735, 456	1, 010, 318	482, 809	33, 137	164, 220	1, 259, 407	1, 939, 573	28 8-10
Vermont	40	7, 985, 866	1, 197, 880	593, 553	38, 424	200, 690	836, 047	1, 668, 714	20 9-10
Massachusetts	161	52, 216, 507	7, 832, 476	3, 336, 586	391, 480	2, 027, 840	7, 020, 862	12, 776, 768	24 5-10
Rhode Island	62	19, 434, 289	2, 915, 143	1, 330, 472	35, 132	637, 800	2, 174, 936	4, 178, 340	21 5-10
Connecticut	82	30, 232, 869	4, 534, 930	1, 872, 686	149, 624	1, 132, 520	3, 766, 403	6, 921, 233	22 9-10
New York	239	78, 438, 272	11, 765, 741	5, 035, 167	345, 410	3, 305, 020	9, 352, 191	18, 037, 788	23
New Jersey	54	24, 028, 436	3, 604, 265	1, 728, 999	111, 737	956, 270	3, 649, 085	6, 446, 091	26 8-10
Pennsylvania	153	45, 923, 862	6, 888, 579	4, 551, 074	134, 224	1, 867, 680	3, 939, 386	10, 492, 364	22 8-10
Delaware	11	2, 585, 326	387, 799	163, 678	6, 305	120, 990	312, 244	603, 217	23 3-10
Maryland	19	4, 406, 632	660, 995	506, 280	58, 285	182, 640	366, 627	1, 113, 832	25 3-10
District of Columbia	1	206, 528	30, 979	13, 525	4, 863	8, 620	12, 443	39, 451	19 1-10
Virginia	19	5, 451, 793	817, 769	573, 710	109, 685	97, 600	267, 727	1, 048, 722	19 2-10
West Virginia	15	4, 686, 394	702, 959	517, 628	30, 837	137, 100	326, 423	1, 011, 988	21 6-10
North Carolina	5	950, 996	142, 649	119, 806	19, 469	1, 750	122, 463	263, 488	27 7-10
South Carolina	2	1, 018, 807	152, 821	224, 243	7, 752	4, 160	416, 152	652, 307	64
Georgia	8	3, 618, 992	542, 849	882, 979	23, 298	111, 850	353, 911	1, 372, 038	37 9-10
Alabama	2	720, 532	108, 080	105, 900	19, 040	....	136, 067	261, 007	36 2-10
Mississippi	1	144, 685	21, 703	27, 741	3, 394	....	4, 810	35, 945	24 8-10
Texas	4	1, 414, 486	212, 173	126, 187	245, 580	65, 220	227, 794	664, 781	47
Arkansas	2	765, 683	114, 852	86, 856	15, 718	370	60, 398	163, 342	21 3-10
Kentucky	11	2, 937, 055	440, 558	316, 064	8, 753	74, 230	322, 067	721, 114	24 6-10
Tennessee	12	4, 511, 938	676, 790	563, 013	47, 776	97, 450	285, 859	994, 098	22
Ohio	123	30, 541, 249	4, 581, 187	3, 699, 798	120, 828	939, 280	2, 243, 885	7, 003, 791	22 9-10
Indiana	70	18, 093, 231	2, 713, 985	2, 282, 507	119, 826	735, 040	888, 759	4, 026, 132	22 2-10
Illinois	69	14, 437, 742	2, 165, 661	1, 811, 577	145, 609	346, 140	1, 287, 406	3, 590, 732	24 9-10
Michigan	37	6, 478, 351	971, 753	774, 454	20, 759	274, 860	575, 102	1, 645, 175	25 4-10
Wisconsin	32	5, 460, 371	819, 056	820, 932	39, 384	135, 200	536, 063	1, 531, 579	28
Iowa	45	9, 060, 552	1, 359, 083	1, 459, 404	54, 650	216, 140	652, 504	2, 382, 698	26 3-10
Minnesota	15	3, 411, 488	511, 723	455, 177	28, 520	93, 940	168, 050	745, 687	21 9-10
Missouri	9	2, 282, 845	342, 427	252, 117	37, 678	41, 620	221, 007	552, 422	24 2-10
Kansas	3	358, 821	53, 823	23, 843	2, 083	4, 930	24, 905	55, 761	15 5-10

Nebraska	3	1,998,130	299,720	160,048	19,340	130,549	34,767	344,695	17 3-10
Nevada	1	233,964	35,095	27,904	28,220	130	....	56,254	24
Oregon	1	240,812	36,122	44,624	10,343	17,270	19,858	92,095	38 2-10
Colorado	3	1,103,308	165,496	233,666	7,239	800	90,348	332,053	30-1-10
Montana	1	94,436	14,165	9,060	24,508	150	6,366	40,084	42 4-10
Utah	1	191,859	28,779	25,571	2,642	....	4,600	32,813	17 1-10
Idaho	1	79,306	11,895	3,428	6,390	....	....	9,818	12 3-10
Total	1,418	405,322,366	60,798,353	36,138,801	2,565,221	14,373,550	43,795,478	96,873,050	23 9-10

Table of the state of the lawful money reserve—Continued. CITIES, *for quarter ending on the first Monday in* JANUARY, 1868.

Redemption cities.	Number of banks reporting.	Liabilities to be protected by a reserve of twenty-five per cent. of the amount.	Amount required as reserve.	Items of reserve.				Amount of available reserve.	Percentage of available reserve to liabilities.
				Legal Tenders.	Specie.	Compound int'st notes and three per cent. temporary loan certificates.	Amount due from approved associations in New York city, available for the redemption of circulating notes.		
Boston	46	$73,257,147	$18,314,287	$10,092,748	$1,868,307	$5,262,310	$6,312,171	$23,535,536	32 1-10
Albany	8	12,447,347	3,111,837	675,217	30,209	1,268,850	2,527,622	4,501,898	36 2-10
Philadelphia	30	52,815,841	13,203,960	13,204,015	308,485	4,116,520	1,879,357	19,508,377	36 9-10
Pittsburgh	16	14,570,911	3,642,728	1,998,682	115,682	796,380	1,340,558	4,251,302	29 2-10
Baltimore	13	19,075,727	4,768,932	3,208,347	388,862	1,089,770	1,486,342	6,173,321	32 4-10
Washington	4	4,484,242	1,121,061	136,116	51,345	677,180	338,670	1,203,311	26 8-10
New Orleans	2	2,279,632	569,908	646,127	136,482	....	44,487	827,096	36 3-10
Louisville	4	1,342,116	335,529	230,559	6,165	94,660	68,200	399,584	29 8-10
Cincinnati	7	11,096,509	2,774,127	1,595,232	89,219	446,280	470,858	2,601,589	23 4-10
Cleveland	5	5,303,844	1,325,961	529,352	43,743	393,290	607,575	1,573,960	29 2-10
Chicago	13	14,619,215	3,654,804	2,646,716	54,934	481,500	1,588,605	4,771,755	32 6-10
Detroit	4	3,678,374	919,594	490,585	296	188,040	854,196	1,533,117	41 7-10
Milwaukee	5	2,699,237	674,809	390,644	15,780	132,160	353,120	891,704	33
St. Louis	8	10,969,942	2,742,485	1,874,639	160,365	355,270	513,656	2,903,930	26 5-10
Leavenworth	2	991,713	247,928	156,015	2,234	38,300	81,393	277,942	28
Total	167	229,631,797	57,407,950	37,874,994	3,272,108	15,340,510	18,466,810	74,954,422	32 6-10
New York	57	$210,021,541	$52,505,385	$40,292,696	$12,266,650	$18,527,970	....	$71,087,316	33 8-10

Table of the state of the lawful money reserve—Continued. STATES, *for quarter ending on the first Monday in* APRIL, 1868.

States and Territories.	Number of banks reporting.	Liabilities to be protected by a reserve of fifteen per cent. of the amount.	Amount required as reserve.	Items of reserve.				Amount of available reserve.	Percentage of available reserve to liabilities.
				Legal Tenders.	Specie.	Compound int'st notes and three per cent. temporary loan certificates.	Amount due from approved associations in the redemption cities available for the redemption of circulating notes.		
Maine	61	$12,789,225	$1,918,383	$941,083	$19,119	$251,180	$1,675,338	$2,886,720	22 6-10
New Hampshire	40	6,532,909	979,936	383,316	4,329	227,310	956,376	1,571,331	24 1-10
Vermont	40	8,057,002	1,208,550	547,142	19,553	238,060	889,581	1,694,336	21
Massachusetts	161	52,155,797	7,823,369	3,009,465	223,271	2,024,800	6,638,702	11,896,238	22 8-10
Rhode Island	62	19,226,135	2,883,920	1,189,251	28,973	607,570	1,823,947	3,649,741	19
Connecticut	81	30,349,531	4,552,430	1,657,834	124,993	1,109,490	3,415,410	6,307,727	20 8-10
New York	239	77,622,416	11,643,362	4,846,767	288,763	3,553,100	8,589,989	17,278,619	22 3-10
New Jersey	54	24,818,458	3,722,768	1,666,272	65,716	999,070	3,309,098	6,040,156	24 3-10
Pennsylvania	153	49,927,044	7,489,057	5,413,437	96,129	1,968,180	4,368,532	11,846,278	23 7-10
Delaware	11	2,658,986	398,848	167,379	4,883	119,810	313,330	605,402	22 8-10
Maryland	19	4,476,108	671,416	446,592	52,240	186,400	353,857	1,039,089	23 2-10
District of Columbia	1	169,620	25,443	14,272	951	540	9,281	25,043	14 8-10
Virginia	19	5,575,223	836,284	414,611	83,235	93,960	460,604	1,052,410	18 9-10
West Virginia	15	4,548,232	682,240	384,734	48,176	130,900	315,036	878,846	19 3-10
North Carolina	5	1,044,869	156,730	113,985	24,390	690	122,878	261,943	25 1-10
South Carolina	2	1,483,658	222,548	313,700	9,948	4,160	633,321	961,129	64 8-10
Georgia	8	4,094,260	614,139	907,723	21,215	111,770	389,879	1,430,587	34 9-10
Alabama	2	801,898	120,283	226,074	28,783	....	38,269	293,066	36 5-10
Mississippi	1	98,273	14,741	21,751	8,019	....	1,190	30,960	31 5-10
Texas	4	1,522,415	228,362	245,211	149,871	350	436,515	831,947	54 6-10
Arkansas	2	808,601	121,290	37,380	3,957	....	33,911	75,248	9 3-10
Kentucky	11	2,894,461	434,169	358,184	18,129	68,460	234,480	679,253	23 5-10
Tennessee	12	4,788,536	718,280	674,737	28,674	102,860	399,637	1,205,908	25 2-10
Ohio	123	29,853,314	4,477,997	3,124,639	49,013	1,015,230	2,097,370	6,286,252	21 1-10
Indiana	70	19,314,425	2,897,164	2,101,438	72,280	729,620	1,399,550	4,302,888	22 3-10
Illinois	69	14,995,290	2,249,293	1,714,886	106,742	340,560	1,414,808	3,576,996	23 9-10
Michigan	38	6,729,558	1,009,433	672,028	20,104	285,090	661,059	1,638,281	24 3-10
Wisconsin	32	4,892,225	733,834	535,452	15,109	163,960	469,784	1,184,305	24 2-10
Iowa	44	9,110,696	1,366,604	1,390,602	47,482	198,940	572,079	2,209,103	24 2-10
Minnesota	15	3,191,928	478,789	297,853	5,546	90,330	232,150	625,879	19 6-10
Missouri	10	2,627,801	394,170	332,120	39,763	42,400	232,643	646,926	24 6-10
Kansas	3	401,990	60,299	58,518	456	4,740	67,623	131,337	32 7-10
Nebraska	3	2,823,916	423,587	284,358	19,891	23,280	248,551	576,080	20 4-10

Nevada	1	228, 209	34, 231	23, 888	30, 072	130	6, 469	60, 559	26 5-10
Oregon	1	267, 225	40, 084	61, 701	3, 166	17, 380	17, 411	99, 658	37 3-10
Colorado	3	980, 351	147, 053	108, 065	9, 606	550	58, 447	176, 668	18
Montana	1	108, 151	16, 223	10, 000	29, 755	170	5, 389	45, 314	41 9-10
Utah	1	209, 917	31, 487	25, 613	972	....	481	27, 066	12 9-10
Idado	1	72, 718	10, 907	13, 640	743	....	....	14, 383	19 8-10
Total	1, 418	412, 251, 361	61, 837, 703	34, 735, 700	1, 804, 017	14, 711, 040	42, 892, 915	94, 143, 672	22 8-10

Table of the state of the lawful money reserve—Continued. CITIES, *for quarter ending on the first Monday in* APRIL, 1868.

Redemption cities.	Number of banks reporting.	Liabilities to be protected by a reserve of fifteen per cent. of the amount.	Amount required as reserve.	Items of reserve.				Amount of available reserve.	Percentage of available reserve to liabilities.
				Legal Tenders.	Specie.	Compound int'st notes and three per cent. temporary loan certificates.	Amount due from approved associations in New York city available for the redemption of circulating notes.		
Boston	46	$74, 880, 262	$18, 720, 066	$6, 021, 514	$865, 475	$6, 791, 370	$6, 007, 653	$19, 686, 012	26 3-10
Albany	8	14, 418, 449	3, 604, 612	778, 489	16, 679	1, 341, 090	2, 814, 645	4, 950, 903	34 3-10
Philadelphia	30	47, 961, 651	11, 990, 413	6, 870, 066	238, 116	6, 736, 570	1, 659, 074	15, 503, 826	32 3-10
Pittsburg	16	14, 938, 897	3, 734, 724	2, 096, 454	53, 161	891, 240	1, 529, 329	4, 570, 184	30 6-10
Baltimore	13	18, 622, 877	4, 655, 719	2, 367, 862	310, 509	1, 494, 780	1, 012, 535	5, 185, 686	27 8-10
Washington	4	4, 076, 456	1, 019, 114	192, 638	30, 958	552, 610	210, 581	986, 787	24 2-10
New Orleans	2	3, 045, 229	761, 307	962, 986	243, 380	....	88, 468	1, 294, 834	42 5-10
Louisville	4	1, 477, 973	369, 493	310, 941	8, 675	114, 710	98, 053	532, 379	36
Cincinnati	7	11, 502, 020	2, 875, 505	1, 473, 341	32, 911	705, 030	579, 908	2, 791, 190	24 3-10
Cleveland	5	4, 919, 177	1, 229, 794	404, 483	9, 113	329, 660	556, 145	1, 299, 401	26 4-10
Chicago	14	18, 407, 363	4, 601, 841	3, 137, 751	51, 124	611, 740	1, 837, 361	5, 637, 976	30 6-10
Detroit	4	3, 663, 691	915, 923	366, 887	3, 748	189, 420	723, 686	1, 283, 741	35
Milwaukee	5	2, 556, 951	639, 238	339, 873	6, 002	99, 390	336, 370	781, 635	30 6-10
St. Louis	8	11, 755, 002	2, 938, 750	1, 481, 596	81, 359	654, 420	929, 993	3, 147, 368	26 8-10
Leavenworth	2	1, 494, 449	373, 612	135, 440	1, 210	35, 990	72, 936	245, 576	16 5-10
Total	168	233, 720, 447	58, 430, 111	26, 940, 321	1, 952, 420	20, 548, 020	18, 456, 737	67, 897, 498	29 1-10
New York	57	195, 364, 482	48, 841, 120	22, 714, 198	11, 623, 221	27, 913, 430	....	62, 250, 849	31 9-10

Table of the state of the lawful money reserve—Continued. STATES, *for quarter ending on the first Monday in* JULY, 1868.

States and Territories.	Number of banks reporting.	Liabilities to be protected by a reserve of fifteen per cent. of the amount.	Amount required as reserve.	Items of reserve.				Amount of available reserve.	Percentage of available reserve to liabilities.
				Legal Tenders.	Specie.	Compound int'st notes and three per cent. temporary loan certificates.	Amount due from approved associations in the redemption cities, available for the redemption of circulating notes.		
Maine	60	$13,422,108	$2,013,316	$927,822	$41,227	$125,430	$1,796,980	$2,891,459	21 5-10
New Hampshire	40	6,717,111	1,007,567	459,749	6,598	169,970	946,002	1,582,319	23 6-10
Vermont	40	8,401,725	1,260,259	617,780	48,126	169,090	970,236	1,805,232	21 4-10
Massachusetts	161	54,159,991	8,123,999	3,451,371	232,259	1,518,790	8,060,107	13,262,527	24 5-10
Rhode Island	62	19,938,531	2,990,780	1,231,074	32,727	517,660	2,604,589	4,386,050	22
Connecticut	81	32,223,020	4,833,453	2,058,950	79,459	727,030	4,492,831	7,358,270	22 8-10
New York	239	78,419,924	11,762,989	4,853,220	336,123	2,687,720	9,951,662	17,828,725	22 7-10
New Jersey	54	23,943,390	3,591,508	1,722,567	58,587	763,430	3,437,081	5,981,665	24 9-10
Pennsylvania	152	47,826,271	7,173,941	4,393,767	93,059	1,687,660	4,781,690	10,956,176	22 9-10
Delaware	11	2,667,485	400,123	192,431	10,258	118,230	327,613	648,532	24 3-10
Maryland	19	4,523,845	678,577	465,895	51,841	135,090	408,704	1,061,530	23 4-10
District of Columbia	1	158,192	23,729	15,782	369	200	10,893	27,244	17 2-10
Virginia	19	6,141,220	921,183	533,877	112,026	72,820	560,964	1,279,687	20 8-10
West Virginia	15	4,644,386	696,658	441,402	38,403	106,220	349,987	936,012	20 1-10
North Carolina	5	1,127,358	169,104	180,206	17,202	2,880	72,126	272,414	24 2-10
South Carolina	3	1,671,537	250,730	486,045	17,391	4,160	511,949	1,019,545	61
Georgia	8	4,085,662	612,849	1,018,653	28,442	123,060	319,784	1,489,939	36 4-10
Alabama	2	646,226	96,934	125,599	61,746		82,283	269,628	41 6-10
Mississippi	1	40,500	6,075	17,880			525	18,405	45 4-10
Texas	4	1,479,353	221,903	210,884	255,952		291,983	758,819	51 2-10
Arkansas	2	871,668	130,750	86,087	2,709		78,849	167,645	19 2-10
Kentucky	11	2,867,252	430,088	382,271	5,057	46,400	220,409	654,137	22 8-10
Tennessee	11	4,207,963	631,194	611,080	31,259	65,070	341,936	1,049,345	24 9-10
Ohio	123	30,695,041	4,604,256	3,172,545	64,099	648,670	2,829,875	6,715,189	21 9-10
Indiana	70	19,587,040	2,938,056	2,318,088	66,902	326,060	1,453,189	4,164,239	21 2-10
Illinois	69	15,741,642	2,361,246	1,841,666	94,091	266,960	1,907,708	4,110,425	26 1-10
Michigan	37	6,903,431	1,035,515	796,478	23,566	140,120	871,202	1,831,366	26 5-10
Wisconsin	31	5,022,811	753,422	641,617	23,213	99,530	621,737	1,386,097	27 5-10
Iowa	44	10,793,436	1,619,015	1,536,233	64,268	116,310	1,785,428	3,502,239	32 4-10

Nevada	1	217, 866	32, 680	26, 785	31, 391	....	13, 044	71, 220	28
Oregon	1	294, 690	44, 204	80, 122	2, 829	17, 470	18, 912	119, 333	40 5-10
Colorado	3	1, 083, 019	162, 453	157, 645	28, 926	500	125, 685	312, 756	28 9-10
Montana	1	95, 168	14, 275	11, 357	11, 362	190	6, 589	29, 498	31
Utah	1	206, 450	30, 968	20, 680	2, 009	....	15, 570	38, 259	18 4-10
Idaho	1	73, 421	11, 013	22, 055	9, 051	....	1, 759	32, 865	44 8-10
Total	1, 414	419, 787, 829	62, 968, 177	36, 247, 168	2, 058, 989	10, 743, 600	51, 732, 763	100, 782, 520	24

Table of the state of the lawful money reserve—Continued. CITIES, *for quarter ending on the first Monday in* JULY, 1868.

Redemption cities.	Number of banks reporting.	Liabilities to be protected by a reserve of twenty-five per cent. of the amount.	Amount required as reserve.	Items of reserve.				Amount of available reserve.	Percentage of available reserve to liabilities.
				Legal Tenders.	Specie.	Compound int'st notes and three per cent. temporary loan certificates.	Amount due from approved associations in New York city, available for the redemption of circulating notes.		
Boston	46	$77, 593, 925	$19, 398, 481	$9, 354, 456	$2, 261, 301	$6, 416, 450	$9, 020, 112	$27, 052, 329	34 8-10
Albany	8	14, 025, 196	3, 506, 299	885, 215	40, 380	1, 204, 840	2, 241, 747	4, 372, 182	31 1-10
Philadelphia	30	53, 596, 743	13, 399, 186	10, 118, 245	233, 714	6, 668, 200	2, 774, 787	19, 794, 946	36 8-10
Pittsburg	16	17, 197, 502	4, 299, 375	2, 234, 157	41, 521	894, 470	1, 645, 202	4, 815, 350	27 9-10
Baltimore	13	19, 687, 011	4, 921, 753	3, 011, 497	430, 196	1, 414, 660	1, 304, 198	6, 160, 551	31 2-10
Washington	4	3, 940, 517	985, 129	146, 653	61, 804	559, 540	317, 371	1, 085, 368	27 5-10
New Orleans	2	2, 103, 463	525, 866	471, 315	102, 683	....	160, 533	734, 531	34 8-10
Louisville	4	1, 249, 750	312, 438	237, 077	340	83, 270	68, 415	389, 102	31
Cincinnati	7	10, 610, 077	2, 652, 519	1, 165, 595	84, 664	770, 400	809, 492	2, 830, 151	26 6-10
Cleveland	5	5, 821, 847	1, 455, 462	337, 980	14, 529	373, 960	527, 801	1, 254, 270	21 5-10
Chicago	14	18, 975, 436	4, 743, 859	3, 177, 557	46, 162	846, 720	2, 417, 924	6, 488, 363	34 2-10
Detroit	4	5, 131, 882	1, 282, 970	506, 208	1, 687	198, 540	828, 890	1, 535, 325	29 9-10
Milwaukee	5	3, 144, 081	786, 020	374, 977	10, 534	100, 750	530, 435	1, 016, 696	32 2-10
St. Louis	8	11, 992, 281	2, 998, 070	1, 364, 513	67, 412	647, 470	1, 393, 342	3, 472, 737	28 9-10
Leavenworth	2	1, 040, 340	260, 085	109, 665	2, 029	28, 160	61, 347	201, 201	19 3-10
Total	168	246, 110, 049	61, 527, 512	33, 495, 110	3, 398, 956	20, 207, 430	24, 101, 596	81, 203, 092	32 9-10
New York	57	247, 703, 974	61, 925, 993	30, 423, 822	15, 297, 976	33, 427, 190	....	79, 148, 988	31 9-10

Table of the state of the lawful money reserve—Continued. STATES, *for quarter ending on the first Monday in* OCTOBER, 1868.

States and Territories.	Number of banks reporting.	Liabilities to be protected by a reserve of fifteen per cent. of the amount.	Amount required as reserve.	Items of reserve.				Amount of available reserve.	Percentage of available reserve to liabilities.
				Legal Tenders.	Specie.	Compound int'st notes and three per cent. temporary loan certificates.	Amount due from approved associations in the redemption cities available for the redemption of circulating notes.		
Maine	61	$13, 150, 366	$1, 972, 555	$1, 090, 129	$23, 532	$80, 350	$1, 792, 123	$2, 986, 134	22 7-10
New Hampshire	40	6, 650, 149	997, 522	458, 066	4, 442	122, 960	1, 118, 479	1, 703, 947	25 6-10
Vermont	40	8, 414, 338	1, 262, 151	691, 468	15, 087	142, 330	927, 925	1, 776, 830	21 1-10
Massachusetts	161	55, 073, 216	8, 260, 981	4, 213, 071	188, 482	731, 950	7, 638, 472	12, 771, 975	23 2-10
Rhode Island	62	19, 240, 527	2, 886, 079	1, 412, 625	25, 982	289, 910	2, 289, 973	4, 018, 490	20 9-10
Connecticut	81	30, 295, 938	4, 544, 391	2, 182, 190	91, 917	531, 330	3, 688, 105	6, 493, 542	21 4-10
New York	240	78, 352, 552	11, 752, 883	5, 692, 860	264, 228	2, 015, 920	9, 644, 501	17, 617, 509	22 5-10
New Jersey	55	24, 164, 877	3, 624, 732	1, 896, 575	68, 349	491, 020	3, 459, 199	5, 915, 143	24 5-10
Pennsylvania	152	46, 019, 920	6, 902, 988	4, 609, 730	60, 295	1, 314, 310	4, 501, 592	10, 485, 927	22 8-10
Delaware	11	2, 778, 110	416, 717	205, 713	4, 773	106, 680	339, 123	656, 289	23 6-10
Maryland	19	4, 332, 839	649, 926	551, 721	42, 517	79, 850	372, 517	1, 046, 605	24 2-10
District of Columbia	1	139, 720	20, 958	14, 392	322	250	14, 065	29, 029	20 8-10
Virginia	19	5, 955, 479	893, 322	576, 903	83, 106	66, 920	418, 521	1, 145, 450	19 3-10
West Virginia	15	4, 676, 224	701, 434	440, 909	43, 477	85, 310	358, 911	928, 607	19 9-10
North Carolina	6	1, 433, 259	214, 989	216, 064	36, 376	460	81, 129	334, 029	23 3-10
South Carolina	3	1, 352, 131	202, 820	279, 343	26, 438	3, 460	117, 915	427, 156	31 6-10
Georgia	8	3, 624, 672	543, 701	791, 778	36, 901	127, 460	425, 975	1, 382, 114	38 1-10
Alabama	2	588, 736	88, 310	157, 534	36, 803		9, 844	204, 181	34 7-10
Mississippi	1	40, 500	6, 075	17, 450			659	18, 109	44 7-10
Texas	4	1, 262, 815	189, 422	185, 192	217, 903		99, 036	502, 121	39 8-10
Arkansas	2	751, 668	112, 750	85, 611	2, 427		38, 209	126, 247	16 8-10
Kentucky	11	2, 812, 531	421, 890	371, 131	6, 482	26, 020	248, 185	651, 818	23 2-10
Tennessee	12	4, 559, 839	683, 976	597, 856	30, 371	53, 590	294, 128	975, 945	21 4-10
Ohio	123	30, 331, 143	4, 549, 671	3, 440, 905	33, 632	541, 760	2, 395, 084	6, 411, 381	21 1-10
Indiana	70	19, 496, 571	2, 924, 486	2, 478, 047	71, 156	193, 980	1, 298, 872	4, 042, 055	20 7-10
Illinois	70	15, 468, 811	2, 320, 322	1, 833, 982	104, 039	152, 250	1, 712, 510	3, 802, 781	24 6-10
Michigan	38	7, 194, 969	1, 079, 245	890, 921	19, 934	79, 830	803, 320	1, 794, 005	24 9-10
Wisconsin	31	4, 934, 557	740, 184	661, 841	17, 286	64, 510	396, 610	1, 140, 247	23 1-10
Iowa	44	9, 987, 718	1, 498, 158	1, 370, 525	43, 525	35, 540	737, 406	2, 186, 996	21 9-10
Minnesota	15	3, 816, 459	572, 469	550, 928	11, 992	10, 950	314, 799	887, 669	23 5-10
Missouri	10	2, 724, 280	408, 642	360, 515	51, 125	17, 620	261, 952	691, 212	25 4-10
Kansas	3	562, 856	84, 428	83, 964	1, 155	3, 260	71, 922	160, 301	28 5-10
Nebraska	4	2, 514, 649	377, 197	261, 789	26, 232	6, 240	975, 572	1, 269, 833	50 5-10

Nevada	1	253, 367	38, 005	16, 165	51, 593	....	13, 163	80, 921	31 9-10
Oregon	1	261, 812	39, 271	57, 761	1, 598	....	19, 418	78, 777	30 1-10
Colorado	3	1, 127, 886	169, 183	192, 994	20, 390	....	168, 709	382, 093	33 9-10
Montana	1	136, 894	20, 534	33, 500	16, 200	....	6, 612	56, 312	41 1-10
Utah	1	212, 019	31, 803	32, 000	1, 013	....	2, 420	35, 433	16 7-10
Idaho	1	82, 031	12, 305	21, 402	237	....	3, 596	25, 235	30 8-10
Total	1, 422	414, 776, 428	62, 216, 475	39, 034, 570	1, 781, 317	7, 376, 020	47, 060, 541	95, 252, 448	22 9-10

Table of the state of the lawful money reserve—Continued. CITIES, *for quarter ending on the first Monday in* OCTOBER, 1868.

Redemption cities.	Number of banks reporting.	Liabilities to be protected by a reserve of twenty-five per cent. of the amount.	Amount required as reserve.	Items of reserve.				Amount of available reserve.	Percentage of available reserve to liabilities.
				Legal Tenders.	Specie.	Compound int'st notes and three per cent. temporary loan certificates.	Amount due from approved associations in New York city available for the redemption of circulating notes.		
Boston	46	$72, 159, 413	$18, 039, 853	$7, 761, 879	$777, 703	$6, 345, 010	$6, 992, 376	$21, 876, 968	30 3-10
Albany	8	13, 073, 716	3, 268, 429	1, 028, 154	16, 329	944, 490	2, 706, 129	4, 695, 102	35 9-10
Philadelphia	30	52, 395, 965	13, 098, 991	7, 951, 090	186, 065	7, 485, 220	1, 099, 173	16, 721, 548	31 9-10
Pittsburg	16	15, 548, 966	3, 887, 242	2, 259, 766	103, 281	900, 570	1, 309, 227	4, 572, 844	29 4-10
Baltimore	13	18, 423, 410	4, 605, 853	2, 241, 071	277, 973	1, 356, 410	1, 315, 709	5, 191, 163	28 2-10
Washington	4	4, 060, 082	1, 015, 021	133, 028	18, 010	655, 730	253, 066	1, 059, 834	26 1-10
New Orleans	2	1, 927, 261	481, 815	596, 600	99, 599	....	52, 714	748, 913	38 9-10
Louisville	4	1, 370, 396	342, 599	276, 054	2, 900	55, 870	67, 959	402, 783	29 4-10
Cincinnati	7	10, 644, 031	2, 661, 008	1, 244, 965	5, 594	609, 290	813, 687	2, 673, 536	25 1-10
Cleveland	5	5, 581, 144	1, 395, 286	458, 812	1, 786	427, 290	660, 731	1, 548, 619	27 7-10
Chicago	13	19, 089, 874	4, 772, 469	3, 420, 730	41, 522	857, 540	2, 427, 647	6, 747, 439	35 3-10
Detroit	4	4, 657, 468	1, 164, 367	471, 720	338	202, 910	1, 036, 417	1, 711, 385	36 7-10
Milwaukee	5	2, 698, 345	674, 586	499, 354	9, 935	50, 000	341, 624	900, 913	33 4-10
St. Louis	8	11, 333, 468	2, 833, 367	1, 450, 155	55, 779	617, 250	700, 684	2, 823, 868	24 9-10
Leavenworth	2	1, 042, 210	260, 553	107, 273	467	10, 660	127, 594	245, 994	23 6-10
Total	167	234, 005, 749	58, 501, 439	29, 900, 651	1, 597, 281	20, 518, 240	19, 904, 737	71, 920, 909	30 7-10
New York	56	206, 164, 901	51, 541, 225	23, 518, 254	8, 370, 846	35, 699, 470	....	67, 588, 570	32 8-10

STATEMENT OF LOANS AND DISCOUNTS MADE BY NATIONAL BANKING ASSOCIATIONS, 1867.

States and Territories.	Number of distinct loans and discounts.	Aggregate amount of loans and discounts.	Average amount of each loan and discount.	Average time of each loan and discount.
				Days.
Maine	37, 838	$50, 703, 349 37	$1, 340 00	95
New Hampshire	13, 329	11, 030, 942 20	827 00	95
Vermont	30, 652	19, 085, 570 80	623 00	69
Massachusetts	182, 300	392, 562, 183 16	2, 153 00	90
Rhode Island	27, 058	67, 036, 311 10	2, 477 00	102
Connecticut	83, 200	105, 467, 506 31	1, 268 00	86
New York	545, 322	1, 668, 141, 362 30	3, 059 00	62
New Jersey	111, 830	84, 098, 828 11	752 00	75
Pennsylvania	274, 182	352, 138, 245 20	1, 284 00	71
Delaware	13, 439	10, 256, 133 14	763 00	72
Maryland	45, 396	59, 094, 941 02	1, 302 00	54
District of Columbia	7, 814	4, 689, 302 09	600 00	64
Virginia	23, 667	18, 757, 303 36	793 00	66
West Virginia	9, 363	7, 810, 086 91	834 00	77
North Carolina	4, 169	3, 967, 136 21	951 00	54
Georgia	8, 174	18, 156, 271 47	2, 221 00	39
Alabama	728	1, 638, 463 50	2, 250 00	60
Texas	851	1, 615, 071 89	1, 898 00	50
Arkansas	1, 765	1, 795, 782 11	1, 017 00	49
Kentucky	7, 114	11, 427, 829 62	1, 606 00	91
Tennessee	7, 810	14, 116, 503 32	1, 807 00	50
Ohio	75, 454	147, 287, 568 46	1, 952 00	70
Indiana	43, 880	48, 674, 671 07	1, 109 00	74
Illinois	65, 395	105, 645, 384 90	1, 615 00	65
Michigan	35, 518	33, 606, 901 10	946 00	65
Wisconsin	30, 279	22, 491, 388 40	742 00	62
Minnesota	13, 810	9, 906, 349 58	717 00	66
Iowa	29, 008	21, 785, 700 45	751 00	74
Missouri	14, 669	39, 660, 096 85	2, 704 00	72
Kansas	1, 650	1, 471, 809 63	892 00	55
Nebraska	3, 251	2, 737, 775 35	842 00	70
Oregon	252	178, 659 31	708 00	72
Colorado Territory	1, 755	1, 715, 399 94	977 00	89
Utah Territory	220	592, 275 30	2, 694 00	90
Montana Territory	85	240, 646 00	2, 831 00	60
Idaho Territory	65	96, 327 19	1, 482 00	55
Louisiana	3, 991	11, 322, 588 36	2, 837 00	60
Total	1, 755, 283	3, 351, 004, 665 08	1, 909 00	71

NOTE.—The banks in Mississippi, (2,) South Carolina, (2,) and Nevada, (1,) in all five banks, not having reported, are not included in above.

STATEMENT SHOWING THE AMOUNT AND RATE OF TAXATION, (UNITED STATES AND STATE,) OF THE NATIONAL BANKING ASSOCIATIONS FOR THE YEAR ENDING DECEMBER 31, 1867.

States and Territories.	Capital.	Amount of taxes paid to United States.	Rate per ct. of United States taxation.	Amount of taxes paid to and assessed by State authorities.	Rate per cent. of State taxation.	Total amount of taxes paid to the United States and State authorities.	Rate per ct. of United States and State taxation on capital.
Maine	$9, 085, 000 00	$180, 119 00	.02	$141, 225 64	.015	$321, 344 64	.035
New Hampshire	4, 735, 000 00	88, 772 90	.019	93, 178 83	.019	181, 951 73	.038
Vermont	6, 510, 012 50	122, 213 57	.019	144, 163 50	.022	266, 377 07	.041
Massachusetts	79, 932, 000 00	1, 616, 824 50	.0202	1, 562, 128 10	.02	3, 178, 952 60	.0402
Rhode Island	20, 364, 800 00	324, 844 25	.015	195, 355 32	.01	520, 199 57	.025
Connecticut	24, 584, 220 00	434, 440 35	.017	387, 146 26	.016	821, 586 61	.033
New York	116, 494, 941 00	3, 022, 662 16	.0261	4, 058, 706 11	.0348	7, 081, 368 27	.0609
New Jersey	11, 333, 350 00	253, 359 31	.022	223, 106 28	.02	476, 465 59	.042
Pennsylvania	50, 277, 795 00	1, 242, 037 40	.0247	278, 268 04	.0055	1, 520, 305 44	.0302
Maryland	12, 590, 202 50	260, 261 25	.0206	166, 054 11	.0131	426, 315 36	.0337
Delaware	1, 428, 185 00	32, 620 68	.0228	1, 260 61	.0008	33, 881 29	.0236
District of Columbia	1, 350, 000 00	15, 329 45	.0133	3, 285 94	.0028	18, 615 39	.0161
Virginia	2, 500, 000 00	48, 344 81	.0193	13, 925 66	.0055	62, 270 47	.0248
West Virginia	2, 216, 400 00	46, 966 34	.021	51, 457 38	.023	98, 423 72	.044
Ohio	22, 404, 700 00	514, 681 46	.0229	520, 951 20	.0232	1, 035, 632 66	.0461
Indiana	12, 867, 000 00	278, 797 60	.0216	200, 372 29	.0155	479, 169 89	.0371
Illinois	11, 620, 000 00	321, 406 24	.0276	231, 917 00	.02	553, 323 24	.0476
Michigan	5, 070, 010 00	111, 789 56	.022	68, 061 41	.0134	179, 850 97	.0354
Wisconsin	2, 935, 000 00	76, 583 25	.0261	62, 011 51	.021	138, 594 76	.0471
Iowa	3, 992, 000 00	106, 349 34	.0266	88, 281 27	.0221	194, 630 61	.0487
Minnesota	1, 660, 000 00	39, 132 43	.02	29, 522 20	.013	68, 654 63	.033
Kansas	400, 000 00	10, 229 23	.025	7, 801 08	.02	18, 030 31	.045
Missouri	7, 559, 300 00	133, 141 77	.014	189, 247 69	.02	322, 389 46	.034
Kentucky	2, 885, 000 00	59, 816 01	.021	17, 466 77	.006	77, 282 78	.027
Tennessee	2, 100, 000 00	52, 459 82	.027	27, 974 80	.014	80, 434 62	.041
Louisiana	1, 300, 000 00	35, 894 28	.0276	20, 041 58	.0154	55, 935 86	.043
Nebraska	250, 000 00	10, 734 67	.0429	7, 014 39	.028	17, 749 06	.0709
Colorado	350, 000 00	9, 701 72	.0277	1, 615 00	.0046	11, 316 72	.0323
Georgia	1, 700, 000 00	40, 844 75	.025	6, 050 46	.004	46, 895 21	.029
North Carolina	583, 300 00	9, 048 71	.0155	5, 144 31	.0088	14, 193 02	.0243
Alabama	500, 000 00	8, 762 52	.0175	3, 829 49	.0095	12, 592 01	.027
Oregon	100, 000 00	1, 623 86	.024	....	....	1, 623 86	.024
Texas	576, 450 00	6, 865 36	.0119	2, 149 34	.0037	9, 014 70	.0156
Arkansas	200, 000 00	5, 745 38	.0287	1, 350 99	.0068	7, 096 37	.0355
Utah	150, 000 00	1, 887 42	.0125	1, 097 00	.0073	2, 984 42	.0198
Montana	100, 000 00	837 31	.0083	560 00	.0056	1, 397 31	.0139
Idaho	100, 000 00	478 65	.0047	1, 405 36	.014	1, 884 01	.0187
Total	422, 804 666 00	9, 525, 607 31	2¼	8, 813, 126 92	2. 082	18, 338, 734 23	4. 332

Statement showing the amounts and kinds of United States bonds held by the Treasurer of the United States to secure the redemption of the circulating notes of national banks on the 30th day of September, 1868.

Description of securities.	Amounts.
Registered bonds—Act of June 14, 1858	$805, 000
Registered bonds—Act of June 22, 1860	59, 000
Registered bonds—Act of February 8, 1861	3, 487, 000
Coupon bonds—Act of February 8, 1861	1, 000
Coupon bonds—Act of March 2, 1861	16, 000
Registered bonds—Acts of July 17 and August 5, 1861	58, 611, 000
Coupon bonds—Acts of July 17 and August 5, 1861	9, 000
Registered bonds—Act of February 25, 1862	65, 063, 300
Coupon bonds—Acts of February 25, 1862	4, 200
Registered bonds—Act of March 3, 1863	34, 142, 050
Registered bonds—Act of March 3, 1864, 5 per cent	88, 596, 150
Coupon bonds—Act of March 3, 1864, 5 per cent	10, 000
Registered bonds—Act of June 30, 1864	38, 045, 000
Registered bonds—Acts of July 1, 1862, and July 2, 1864	9, 263, 000

Registered bonds—Act of March 3, 1864, 6 per cent......	$3,503,500
Registered bonds—Act of March 3, 1865, first series......	27,218,100
Registered bonds—Act of March 3, 1865, second series....	10,714,100
Registered bonds—Act of March 3, 1865, third series.....	2,287,550
Registered bonds—Act of March 3, 1865, fourth series....	185,000
Total..	342,019,950

REPORTS.

The national currency act requires every association to make a report, exhibiting in detail its resources and liabilities on the first Monday of January, April, July and October, of each year. In addition to this, every association is required on the first Tuesday of each month to make a statement, exhibiting the average amount of loans and discounts, specie and other lawful money, deposits, and circulation; and banks not located in the cities named in section 31 of the act are required also to return the amount due them available for the redemption of their circulation.

The quarterly reports, coming, as they do, upon a certain specified day, known in advance, and for which the amplest preparation may be made, can hardly be expected to present the actual working condition of the banks. They are, of course, careful to exhibit the full amount of reserve required, and otherwise a full compliance with all the important provisions of the law. But it is in the large cities, especially in New York, that this plan proves most objectionable. Gold and stock speculators, knowing that at a certain time the banks will make it a point to have a full supply of lawful money in their vaults, get up combinations for the purpose of producing a scarcity of legal-tender notes, and a stringent money market, so as to depress the market for government, State, railroad, and other securities. National banks, held firmly to the requirements of the law, are seriously embarrassed by such trickery. Their necessities compel them to have the lawful money at any hazard. Besides the damage resulting from an unnecessary and forced depression of public securities, regular commercial transactions are impeded, suspended, or forced to be carried on at ruinous rates, owing to the artificial stringency thus produced. It is becoming more manifest, as one quarter succeeds another, that the evil is becoming more and more intolerable. Honest industry, regular trade, and legitimate business of every kind, which depend upon the banks for their usual facilities, are subjected to great inconvenience, hardship, and loss, through the abuses thus practiced.

This state of things calls for a prompt and efficient remedy. This may be found in an amendment to section 34 of the act, authorizing the Comptroller of the Currency to call upon the banks for five detailed statements or reports during each year, fixing upon some day that is past for the date of the report. In this way the condition of the banks may be ascertained at irregular intervals, without previous preparation on their part; and the precise period when the reports will be called for being unknown to the public, outside operators will be prevented from conspiring against the banks and the honest trade of the country.

This subject is commended to the early attention of Congress.

BANKS IN VOLUNTARY LIQUIDATION.

thirds of its stock; that due notice of such action shall be published, &c.; and at any time after the expiration of one year from the publication of such notice, the said association may pay over to the Treasurer of the United States the amount of its outstanding notes in lawful money of the United States, and take up the bonds which it has on deposit with the Treasurer as security for such circulating notes—leaving it optional with the bank or its representatives to take up the bonds, or not.

Under this provision a bank may go into liquidation, pay off its depositors and other creditors, do no business, have no existence as a bank of discount and deposit, and yet reap all the benefits of a circulation guarantied by the government. In some cases the ownership has been concentrated in the hands of two or three individuals, who continue to do business as private bankers, avoid taxation, evade the requirements of the currency act, and still retain the most profitable feature of a national bank.

To correct abuse of this kind, it is suggested that national banking associations which go into voluntary liquidation be required to provide for their outstanding circulation in lawful money, and take up their bonds within three or six months; in default of which, the Comptroller shall have power to sell their bonds at public auction in New York city, and, after paying to the Treasurer the amount of the outstanding circulation of the bank in lawful money, to pay over any excess realized from the sale of the bonds to the association or its legal representatives.

Banks that are winding up for the purpose of consolidating with other banks, or for the purpose of reorganizing at some other and more desirable points, should be excepted from the foregoing requirements.

A CENTRAL REDEEMING AGENCY.

The opinion was expressed in the last annual report from this office that it was important that a system of redemptions for national bank notes should be established as early as practicable, by means of which they should be made convertible into the lawful money of the country, whether it be paper or gold, at the principal centre of trade. Without repeating the argument then made, the conviction is again expressed that only by rigid, unfailing redemptions at a central point, can the bank currency of the country be kept at a uniform par value.

A prevalent objection to this doctrine is, that it would render the country banks tributary to New York. While there is strong reason to believe this objection would prove to be unfounded, yet it may be entirely removed by authorizing the national banks of the country to take the whole matter into their own hands. If Congress should provide by law for the organization of a national bank in New York city, without circulation, in which every national bank should be required to become a stockholder in proportion to its surplus fund, a bank with a capital of from ten to fifteen or twenty millions could be established, which would become the redeeming agency of the whole country, and the clearing-house of all national bank

place the bank circulation of the country at once upon the soundest footing, and demonstrate practically the fact that the banks stand ready to make their issues not only redeemable, but actually convertible at all times in the great markets of the Union.

Moreover, such an agency, by becoming a place of deposit for that portion of the reserves kept in New York, would remedy the evils adverted to in my last report, growing out of the payment of interest on the balances of the country banks, and their consequent use by the New York city banks. The reserves, instead of being loaned on call to speculators and brokers, as is largely done at present, would be held exactly where they would be needed, and would be applied to just the purpose for which they were intended. They would be actual reserves, and at all times available as such; thus adding to the safety and the credit of the currency of the country, and carrying into practical operation the spirit and intent of the law on this subject.

This suggestion is earnestly commended to the consideration of Congress, as tending to reconcile the interests of all sections on the question of redemptions.

THE PERIODICAL STRINGENCY IN NEW YORK CITY.

A careful study of the bank statements of New York taken separately, and the application of the facts so obtained to the aggregate statement or abstract of the whole, affords valuable and instructive information.

The abstract shows the total of loans to be $163,634,000.

An examination of the statements in detail shows the character of the loan to be substantially as follows:

Commercial or business paper	$90,000,000
Demand loans	68,500,000
Accommodation loans	3,500,000
Suspended loans	1,500,000
Total	163,500,000

Nine-sixteenths, or rather more than half the loan, is legitimate business paper; the balance is upon call, or for accommodation. The amount loaned on call for commercial purposes is not stated; but reliable information leads to the belief that it is very small. The customs and necessities of trade are of such a character as to preclude loans of this kind. The merchant, with his capital invested in trade, must know when his liabilities are to mature, in order that he may be prepared to meet them. It would be unsafe for him to use money in his business which he is liable to be called on to pay at any moment. Consequently, merchants and others in business where the profits are regular and legitimate, yielding a fair return to skill and industry, cannot afford to borrow money on call. Dealers in money, stocks, and gold, constitute almost the only class of business men whose transactions are of such a nature as to make call loans desirable or profitable; and it is scarcely possible to avoid the inference that nearly one-half of the available resources of the national banks in the city of New York are used in the operations of the stock and gold exchange; that they are loaned upon the security of stocks which are bought and sold largely on speculation, and which are manipulated by cliques and combinations, according as the bulls or bears are, for the moment, in the ascendency.

In addition to this direct loan of $70,000,000, they furnish facilities by means of certified checks to the same class of operators to an amount ranging from $110,000,000 to $120,000,000 daily, (on the 5th of October the amount was $112,800,000,) and these checks are made to swell the amount of individual deposits. They are credited to depositors as money, and are circulated and treated as money by the banks and by their customers; yet, when ascertaining the amount of deposits upon which they must hold a reserve, or upon which they must pay taxes, the banks invariably deduct all such checks on hand. For instance, on the 1st Monday of October they reported:

Individual deposits	$224, 170, 000
But deducting checks on hand	112, 800, 000
They had actual deposits of	111, 370, 000

Taking the call loans and the certified checks together, the somewhat startling fact is developed, that the New York national banks furnish $70,000,000 of capital and $112,000,000 of credit, for speculation.

The use of certified checks is a direct inflation to that extent; which stimulates the stock market, and keeps the price of a large class of miscellaneous securities much above their actual value, so that the market is feverish and fluctuating, and a slight stringency reduces the prices. Taking advantage of an active demand for money to move the crops, west and south, shrewd operators form their combinations to depress the market by "locking up" money—withdrawing all they can control or borrow from the common fund; money becomes scarce, the rate of interest advances, and stocks decline. The legitimate demand for money continues; and, fearful of trenching on their reserve, the banks are straitened for means. They dare not call in their demand loans, for that would compel their customers to sell securities on a falling market, which would make matters worse. Habitually lending their means to the utmost limit of prudence, and their credit much beyond that limit, to brokers and speculators, they are powerless to afford relief. Their customers, by the force of circumstances, become their masters. The banks cannot hold back or withdraw from the dilemma in which their mode of doing business has placed them. They must carry the load to save their margins. A panic, which should greatly reduce the price of securities, would occasion serious if not fatal results to the banks most extensively engaged in such operations, and would produce a feeling of insecurity which would be very dangerous to the entire banking interest of the country.

The fact that a banking interest with capital and surplus of $100,000,000 can be, and has been repeatedly, placed at the mercy of a few shrewd, though bold and unscrupulous men, is evidence of some inherent defect in its management, and the foregoing statement may serve in some degree to show where the error lies:

1st. In demand or call loans to brokers and speculators, on collateral security, by which nearly one-half the active resources of the banks are used directly to foster and promote speculative operations.

2d. Certified checks or loans of credit to the same class of men, whereby stocks are inflated and immense operations are carried on daily upon fictitious capital.

3d. The payment of interest on bank balances; which, being payable on demand, must be loaned on call in order to avoid loss.

The necessity for making call loans is, in part, owing to the fact that a large fund, belonging to country banks, is held by the New York city banks, subject to the payment of interest. This fund is liable to be demanded at any time. But, bearing interest, it cannot be suffered to lie unemployed, and so *must* be loaned on call. It may be merely a coincidence; but on the first Monday of October, the bank deposits held by the New York city banks were $68,529,417, and the call loans reported were $68,500,000. These loans, as before stated, are made to brokers, stock and gold operators, on collateral security, and constitute a large portion of the capital used in speculation. Thus, by a vicious practice, the reserve fund of the country is handed over to the tender mercies of Wall street and its purlieus.

Not content with the $70,000,000 so absorbed, a fictitious capital of $120,000,000 is created by means of certified checks, which, by an ingenious arrangement, after being traded on the street, are finally traded back to the banks that issue them, without materially increasing or diminishing the cash deposits. Many of the largest and best managed national banks in New York deprecate the practice herein set forth, and look with anxiety and alarm toward the final issue; but they are all involved in the danger. The failure of one or more institutions, through reckless management, would endanger the whole. If all bankers were wise and prudent, no law would be required to restrain them; but they are in the position of trustees—trustees for their stockholders, trustees for their depositors, and trustees for the public. If they habitually engage in practices dangerous to stockholders, depositors and the public, the law may be invoked to provide a remedy. It is not becoming that institutions organized under an act of Congress for the public good, should so far pervert their corporate powers and privileges as to work detriment to the public interests. If they regard legislative interference as arbitrary and tyrannical, they may have the option of conforming to the requirements of law, or of withdrawing from a system to which they add no strength.

A return to specie payments would be the best remedy for speculation; as every departure from specie value is the signal and incentive for its rise and reign. As a present corrective, however, it is recommended that national banks be prohibited by law from paying interest on bank balances, and also from certifying checks to be good which are not drawn against actually existing cash deposits standing to the credit of the drawer when the checks are made and presented.

PANICS.

Notwithstanding the fact, however, that the troubles to which the banking interest is liable are caused primarily by the disregard of sound principles on the part of the banks themselves, it is nevertheless true that they do recur from time to time, and that they are usually the cause of wide-spread disaster—disaster reaching far beyond the immediate circle in which the trouble originated, and extending into every branch of trade, and into every section of the country.

When money is abundant, the temptation is very great to find employment for as much of it as possible; and though the danger of too great extension is palpable, and has been demonstrated by experience, yet the majority of bankers are prone to go on, carrying full sail, until they find themselves in the breakers, repeating the same mistakes and suffering the same retributions which they themselves, or their predecessors, have before made and suffered. The facts must be taken as they are found to exist. Panics come; and while it would be wise to learn lessons of wisdom from experience, so as to avoid their recurrence, the fact that we are, and will probably continue to be, liable to panics as long as men make mistakes, or act in reckless disregard of established principles, should be duly considered. Recognizing this fact, it may not be without profit to ascertain the nature of the trouble that prevails in a time of financial pressure.

If banks habitually lend all their available means when times are easy, or when there is no extraneous demand for money, it is evident that when an extra demand arises, it can be met only by withdrawing or calling in loans previously made. For instance, during the summer months there is but little demand for money throughout the country generally, beyond the ordinary wants of regular trade, and a large surplus is accumulated in the large cities, principally in New York. The banks in New York, with their coffers full to overflowing, seek employment for their money, and loan freely as far as they can find borrowers, and at low rates. Their funds are thus absorbed, and to a considerable extent form the basis upon which a large amount of business is transacted. Abundance of money at low rates stimulates and builds up a certain kind of business, which comes to depend upon the banks for its activity and support. Meantime the grain crops of the West, and the cotton crops of the South, are gathered, and are made ready for shipment to market. Both are prime necessities to the country at large. They must go forward, and money is required to buy them and to move them. The demand is paramount and must be answered; but it can be met only by withdrawing money that has been absorbed and become the very life blood of a business built up and supported by its use.

The banks contract their loans, and murmurs are heard of stringency. The crops require all the money in the country to pay for them; but Wall street demands its share, insisting, and not without reason, that the banks encouraged its speculative operations by tendering means in abundance, and now to withdraw the accustomed support will be ruinous to its interests. The banks, interested so largely in the operations of their customers, cannot afford to call in their loans, or to cut off supplies; their own safety is at stake, and they must carry their customers through, or suffer with them the consequences of a dangerous convulsion, possibly of a fatal collapse.

This is substantially the history of a panic under the present order of things. Possibly it might be prevented by a proper conservatism exercised in season; but prudence is not the most distinguishing trait of the times. The important question, therefore, is how to relieve the public? There is not money enough in the country to meet all the demands at once. A suspicion that a financial institution is unable to respond to all demands, is almost fatal to its stability; and when confidence is unsettled, judgment loses its sway, and unreasoning panic follows.

THE REMEDY.

If the treasury of the United States could hold in reserve a certain amount of legal tender notes in excess of the amount of money in regular circulation, to be advanced to banking institutions at a specified rate of interest upon the deposit of United States bonds as collateral security, a source of relief would be established which would effectually prevent a monetary pressure from being carried to any ruinous extent.

This proposition is not anomalous or without precedent. In time of severe pressure, the Bank of England has been authorized by the Chancellor of the Exchequer to issue its notes in excess of the limitations prescribed in its charter. This was done in violation, or without authority, of law, upon the pledge by the government of an act of indemnity. In our government no power to make such pledges exists; and, therefore, any extraordinary provision of the character suggested must be authorized by law.

The measure is one of relief and protection to the interests of the public at large, and therefore justifiable. If the consequences of overtrading, speculation, and otherwise reckless conduct could be confined to the parties or institutions so overtrading or speculating, they might well be left to their own resources; but immense interests are involved which are in no way responsible for the trouble. A financial panic generally extends to commercial circles, and in several instances has damaged the trade and industry of the country to such an extent that its effects have been felt for years. Any measure that would mitigate or prevent such calamities would be a measure of national importance and a proper subject for congressional legislation.

SPECIE PAYMENTS.

The subject of specie payments naturally comes up whenever the currency question is discussed, and much ingenuity has been exercised in devising plans for an early resumption.

The principal obstacle to specie payments may be found in the statement of the public debt of the United States for the 1st of October, 1868, under the head of "Debt bearing no interest," as follows:

United States notes	$356,021,073 00
Fractional currency	32,933,614 17
Making together	388,954,687 17

of government notes circulating as money, and designed to take the place of gold and silver by being made "a legal tender for all debts, public and private, except duties on imports" and interest on the bonded debt. As long as the people prefer an inferior currency—inferior because irredeemable and inconvertible except at a heavy discount—they will have it to the entire exclusion of the precious metals. Whenever the people conclude that it is more economical to conduct the business of the country on a specie basis, they can ordain specie payments by making provision through their representatives in Congress for the payment or withdrawal of the present depreciated paper currency issued and kept in circulation by the government. And whenever the people wish to restore the credit of the nation, they can do it through their representatives in Congress, by removing the only embarrassment that stands in the way—by directing that provision shall be made for the payment of a floating indebtedness amounting to $388,000,000, consisting of promises to pay that are never paid—and so establish the fact that the United States is a solvent debtor, able and willing to pay every debt as it becomes due. Specie payments and the restoration of public credit are within the reach, and depend upon the will, of the people of the United States.

FREE BANKING.

Whenever Congress shall inaugurate measures looking to the appreciation of United States notes to a gold standard, the effect of such measures will probably be to diminish the volume of such notes in circulation. To what extent the reduction would have to be carried in order to place them permanently on a specie basis, would at present be mere matter of speculation. Doubtless a large amount might be carried, with profit to the government and with benefit to the public.

As soon as the effect of such measures becomes apparent, by the gradual approach of legal tender notes to a par with gold, the restrictions imposed upon the issue of circulating notes by national banks may be safely removed, provided the establishment of a central redeeming agency in the city of New York, at which all national bank notes are redeemable at par, shall be required by law. Any inconvenience resulting from a reduction of legal tenders may thus be remedied, and the remedy will be in the hands of the only competent judge of the necessities of the case—the business public of the United States.

Respectfully submitted:

H. R. HULBURD,
Comptroller of the Currency.

Hon. HUGH McCULLOCH,
Secretary of the Treasury.

List of clerks, messengers, &c., employed in the office of the Comptroller of the Currency.

Names.	Class.	Salary per year.
Hiland R. Hulburd	Comptroller	$5,000
John Jay Knox	Deputy Comptroller	2,500
Linus M. Price	Fourth class	1,800
J. Franklin Bates	do	1,800
Edward Wolcott	do	1,800
George C. Williams	do	1,800
John D. Patten, jr	do	1,800
L. P. Hulburd	do	1,800
George W. Martin	do	1,800
John W. Magruder	do	1,800
John W. Griffin	do	1,800
John Burroughs	Third class	1,600
David Lewis	do	1,600
Henry H. Smith	do	1,600
Charles H. Norton	do	1,600
Gurden Perkins	do	1,600
Edward Myers	do	1,600
Charles D. F. Kasson	do	1,600
Edward S. Peck	do	1,600
Derrick F. Hamlink	do	1,600
George Wood	do	1,600
Aaron Johns	do	1,600
Fernando C. Cate	do	1,600
Edwin C. Denig	do	1,600
John Joy Edson	Second class	1,400
Charles H. Cherry	do	1,400
Henry W. Berthrong	do	1,400
William A. Page	do	1,400
Charles A. Jewett	do	1,400
Charles Scott	do	1,400
William Cruikshank	do	1,400
J. C. Langworthy	do	1,400
J. A. Kayser	First class	1,200
Horatio Nater	do	1,200
J. M. Hughes, jr	do	1,200

List of clerks, messengers, &c.—Contined.

Name.	Class.	Salary per year.
William H. Barton	First class	$1,200
A. C. Lansing, jr	do	1,200
J. A. Corwin	do	1,200
George Sage	do	1,200
Philo Burr	Night watchman	900
Ozro N. Hubbard	Assistant messenger	840
Michael C. Weaver	do	840
John H. Kaufman	do	840
William E. Hughes	do	840
James B. Tirney	do	840
Edmund E. Schreiner	Laborer	720
Henry Sanders	do	720
Mrs. Sarah F. Fitzgerald	Copyist	900
Mrs. Etha E. Poole	do	900
Mrs. Mary G. Smith	do	900
Mrs. M. H. Sherwin	do	900
Mrs. H. A. Peters	do	900
Mrs. E. C. Woodbridge	do	900
Mrs. M. C. Ringgold	do	900
Miss Kate E. Anderson	do	900
Miss Celia N. French	do	900
Miss Eliza R. Hyde	do	900
Miss A. C. Ingersoll	do	900
Miss L. W. Knowlton	do	900
Miss Annie W. Story	do	900
Miss Julia M. Baldwin	do	900
Miss Virginia Miller	do	900
Miss M L. Simpson	do	900
Mrs. Louise A. Hodges	Counter	900
Mrs. Mary M. Blossom	do	900
Mrs. Sophie C. Harrison	do	900
Miss Elizabeth C. Berthrong	do	900
Miss Agnes C. Bielaski	do	000
Miss A. M. Donaldson	do	900
Miss M. M. Redwood	do	900
Miss M. M. Stockton	do	900
Miss Minta Watkins	do	900
Miss C. Hinde	do	900
Miss A. A. McKenney	do	900

Expenditures of the office of the Comptroller of the Currency for the fiscal year ending June 30, 1868.

Special dies, paper, printing, &c	$33,241 46
Salaries	89,335 20
Contingent	6,668 03
Total	129,244 69

REPORT OF THE FIRST COMPTROLLER.

TREASURY DEPARTMENT,
Comptroller's Office, November 5, 1868.

SIR: The business operations of this office during the fiscal year ending June 30, 1868, may be summed up as follows:

Warrants of the Secretary of the Treasury have been countersigned, entered in blotters, and posted, to wit:

Public debt warrants	560
Quarterly salary warrants	1,155
Treasury proper warrants	1,500
Treasury (Interior) warrants	2,457
Treasury, customs warrants	3,325
Treasury, internal revenue warrants	11,116
War, pay warrants	4,168
War, repay warrants	638
Navy, pay warrants	1,502
Navy, repay warrants	305
Interior, pay warrants	2,363
Interior, repay warrants	145
Diplomatic warrants	2,017
War, civil warrants	61
Treasury appropriation warrants	26
Customs appropriation warrants	11
Interior appropriation warrants	42
War and Navy appropriation warrants	14
Land covering warrants	414
Customs covering warrants	1,560
Internal revenue appropriation warrants	3,400
Miscellaneous warrants	3,636
Aggregate number of warrants	40,415

The accounts described as follows, which are reported to this office by the First and Fifth Auditors, and by the Commissioner of the General Land Office, have been duly entered, revised, and the balances found thereon certified to the Register of the Treasury, viz:

Judiciary.—Embracing accounts of the United States marshals for their fees, and the expenses of the United States courts in their respective districts; of the United States district attorneys; and of the clerks and the commissioners of United States courts	1,363
Public debt.—Embracing accounts for the redemption of United States stock and notes; interest on the public debt; United States Treasurer's accounts; United States assistant treasurer's accounts; and matters pertinent thereto	1,163
Mint and its branches.—Embracing accounts of gold, silver and cent bullion; of salaries of the officers; of ordinary expenses, &c.	71
Public printing.—Embracing the accounts for the public printing, for binding, and for paper	101
Territorial printing.—Embracing accounts for the paper, printing, and binding of the territorial legislatures	57

Congressional.—Embracing the accounts for the contingent expenses of the Senate and the House of Representatives	55
Land.—Embracing accounts of registers and receivers of land offices; surveyors general nd their deputies; and of land erroneously sold	1868
Inspectors of steamboats.—Embracing accounts for their salaries and incidental expenses	475
Diplomatic and consular.—Embracing accounts arising from our intercourse with foreign nations; expenses of consuls for sick and disabled seamen; and of our commercial agents in foreign countries	1, 573
Collectors of internal revenue.—Embracing their accounts for the collection of the internal tax and the necessary disbursements which are connected therewith	2, 678
Commissioner of internal revenue.—Accounts for the refunding of imposts illegally collected, &c	91
Agents and inspectors of internal revenue.—Accounts for expenses and disbursements	4, 286
Assessors of the internal revenue.—Accounts for their commissions and expenses in levying the internal tax	1, 050
Drawbacks.—Accounts arising from drawbacks connected with internal revenue	3, 167
Miscellaneous.—Embracing accounts of disbursing agents for the contingent expenses of the executive departments and public offices at Washington; the salaries of judges and officers of United States courts; of informers' shares under the internal revenue laws, &c., &c	2, 573
Letters written on official business	9, 816
Receipts of collectors of internal revenue examined, entered, and filed	3, 635
The following requisitions have been duly examined and reported on, viz:	
Diplomatic and consular	544
United States marshals	201
Collectors internal revenue	2, 938

During the past year the work of this office has increased beyond any demand heretofore made upon its resources, and it is believed that this increase will continue. It is only by the most assiduous and constant attention on the part of the clerks and other persons connected with the office that the daily work can be kept up, and no arrears detrimental to the public service suffered to exist; and I take pleasure in commending their general efficiency.

I beg leave to repeat the recommendations and suggestions contained in my last annual report. The experience of the past year has confirmed and strengthened my convictions as then expressed.

Respectfully submitted:

R. W. TAYLER, *Comptroller.*

Hon. HUGH MCCULLOCH,
Secretary of the Treasury.

REPORT OF THE SECOND COMPTROLLER.

TREASURY DEPARTMENT,
SECOND COMPTROLLER'S OFFICE,
Washington, October 8, 1868.

SIR: I have the honor to submit herewith a statement of the operations of this bureau for the fiscal year that ended with the 30th of June, 1868.

The aggregate number of disbursing officers' accounts received from the Second, Third, and Fourth Auditors during that time, and also the number revised in this office are as follows:

	Received.	Revised.	Amount involved.
From the Second Auditor	2,718	3,225	$216,236,574
From the Third Auditor	7,098	6,626	979,324,609
From the Fourth Auditor	430	403	78,106,424
Totals	10,246	10,254	1,273,667,607

These are made up of the following classes:

FROM THE SECOND AUDITOR.

	Received.	Revised.	Amount involved.
Collecting, organizing, and drilling accounts	158	174	$11,076,833
Paymasters' accounts	1,123	1,540	178,502,707
Recruiting accounts	303	391	1,850,803
Ordnance accounts	129	124	8,746,986
Indian accounts	519	508	6,854,644
Medical accounts	339	341	6,264,788
Military asylum accounts	28	28	29,160
Contingent of the army	119	119	2,910,653
Totals	2,718	3,225	216,236,574

FROM THE THIRD AUDITOR.

	Received.	Revised.	Amount involved.
Quartermasters' accounts	3,390	3,509	$944,293,703
Subsistence, army, accounts	2,268	1,721	12,866,880
Pension, army, accounts	1,207	1,189	5,426,761
Engineering accounts	92	85	13,434,140
Bureau of Freedmen's accounts	141	122	3,305,125
Totals	7,098	6,626	979,324,609

FROM THE FOURTH AUDITOR.

	Received.	Revised.	Amount involved.
Marine corps accounts	24	24	$1,703,231
Navy paymasters' accounts	237	242	19,066,573
Navy yard paymasters' accounts	18	17	3,457,150
Navy agents' accounts	51	54	53,518,334
Navy pension agents' accounts	70	66	361,136
Totals	430	403	78,106,424

The claims revised in this office during the year are as follows:

	Received.	Revised.	Amount involved.
Soldiers' pay and bounty claims	160,874	158,504	$18,433,562
Sailors' prize claims	7,134	6,589	548,557
Sailors' pay claims	2,390	2,279	221,302
Contract surgeons' claims	193	193	31,455
Lost property claims	805	789	77,257
Oregon and Washington war claims	71	71	12,485
State claims	26	33	8,568,080
Totals	171,493	170,458	27,892,698

For the purpose of comparing the work of the year in question with that of the preceding year the work of both is collated:

Official accounts from Second Auditor, 1867	2,944
Official accounts from Second Auditor, 1868	3,225
Excess in 1868	281
Official accounts from Third Auditor, 1867	9,460
Official accounts from Third Auditor, 1868	6,626
Excess in 1867	2,834
Official accounts from Fourth Auditor, 1867	531
Official accounts from Fourth Auditor, 1868	403
Excess in 1867	128
The number of claims revised in 1867 was	82,483
The number of claims revised in 1868 was	170,458
Excess in 1868	89,975

The respective amounts involved in the settlements of the two years were:

In 1867	$1,384,169,835
In 1868	1,301,560,307
Excess in 1867	82,609,528

The number of requisitions made upon the Secretary of the Treasury by the Secretaries of the War, Navy, and Interior Departments, and countersigned in this office during the fiscal year that ended June 30, 1868, were 9,636, distributed as follows:

	War.	Navy.	Interior.
Accountable	1,177	1,170	690
Refunding	573	666	139
Settlement	2,591	95	1,560
Transfer	397	475	103
Totals	4,738	2,406	2,492

selves, but, as precedents, involving large amounts; and these require much and careful investigation, as well of the common law and their bearing upon the treasury and the public welfare, as of the acts of Congress and the departmental precedents and regulations. As the period of the war recedes, the claims arising out of it become more intricate, and the evidence in support of them more difficult to obtain. They are still very numerous, and much time, labor, and money will yet be required for the settlement even of those over which the laws have given the executive department jurisdiction.

Respectfully submitted:

J. M. BRODHEAD,
Comptroller.

Hon. HUGH MCCULLOCH,
Secretary of the Treasury.

REPORT OF THE COMMISSIONER OF CUSTOMS.

TREASURY DEPARTMENT,
OFFICE OF COMMISSIONER OF CUSTOMS,
October 28, 1868.

SIR: In compliance with the law and the regulations of the department, I have the honor to present to you my annual report of the operations of this bureau, and such remarks and suggestions as I deem proper on the occasion.

The following is a statement of the ordinary business performed in the office of Commissioner of Customs from June 30, 1867, to July 1, 1868:

Statement of customs accounts received and disposed of during the year ending June 30, 1868.

Period.	Accounts received.	Accounts adjusted.	Accounts returned to the Auditor.	Letters recorded.	Letters received.	Letters written.	Returns received and examined.	Requisitions.	Amount of requisitions.
July, 1867	417	488	3	1,443	376	1,332	334	205	$1,548,014 06
August, 1867	291	284	3	1,310	219	692	209	165	911,705 57
September, 1867	351	296	6	880	249	775	214	228	1,086,292 59
October, 1867	408	476	5	863	246	1,006	218	184	849,171 54
November, 1867	402	393	8	1,117	422	980	289	235	1,228,521 40
December, 1867	328	332	6	918	327	747	335	249	1,251,590 75
January, 1868	381	384	3	880	325	1,140	318	291	1,169,337 54
February, 1868	473	445	10	983	366	759	417	155	668,545 96
March, 1868	401	441	4	991	907	1,047	381	258	1,159,307 62
April, 1868	469	479	3	1,176	901	824	419	179	953,416 32
May, 1868	442	414	6	1,215	901	809	364	138	1,087,485 63
June, 1868	523	504	8	1,016	809	957	417	244	1,425,403 67
Totals	4,886	4,936	65	12,792	6,048	11,068	3,915	2,531	13,339,792 65
On hand July 1, 1867	284								
Total	5,170								

DUTIES REFUNDED.

The amount of duties refunded during the fiscal year ending June 30, 1868, was $154,854 67.

CAPTURED AND ABANDONED PROPERTY AND INTERNAL AND COASTWISE COMMERCIAL INTERCOURSE ACCOUNTS.

In the division of captured and abandoned property and internal and coastwise commercial intercourse, the number of accounts received and adjusted was as follows: Accounts received, 92; accounts adjusted, 95; amount, $2,861,648 55; accounts returned to Auditor, 5; letters received, 238: letters written, 225; letters recorded, 818; requisitions, 156; amount of requisitions, $311,776 99.

In addition to the ordinary current work of the division during the six months ending on the 30th of June last there was performed the following: Reports written, 35; papers copied, 197; papers transmitted, 420; papers filed, 5, 673. These accounts are many of them very complicated, and owing to the fact of the transfer of a large amount of property and money from one agent of the department to another, and the peculiar relation of the military commanders in many districts to the treasury agents, it is often necessary in the examination of one account to partially examine several others. The very imperfect condition in which many of these accounts reach the office, arising doubtless in a great measure from the unfavorable exigency in which the agents were often placed and the length of time which has elapsed since the service was rendered, adds very much to the perplexity and labor.

In several cases agents have failed to render any account, or have done so in such an imperfect manner that it has hitherto been impossible for the Auditor to state an account. In some instances this has occurred where it is believed considerable amounts are involved.

WAREHOUSE ACCOUNTS.

By your direction a division was organized in this bureau in the month of September, 1867, for the purpose of adjusting and keeping accounts with collectors of all merchandise warehoused and withdrawn for consumption, transportation, or exportation, and of the bonds taken in pursuance of law and the regulations.

Previous to that time many collectors had failed to render any account of their warehouse transactions, while others rendered their accounts so imperfectly as to render them of little or no value. To insure a strict accountability on the part of collectors, as well as to trace merchandise from the time of importation to the final payment of the duties or its exportation without the limits of the United States, and the taking and cancelling of bonds, a circular was issued with your approval prescribing to collectors a uniform mode of rendering their accounts monthly. Blank forms were printed and distributed to collectors and surveyors.

Great difficulty has been encountered in obtaining the proper accounts from collectors, owing to the defective manner in which their books were kept and the want of knowledge and skill in the art of bookkeeping.

Books have been opened in this office dating from the 1st of July, 1867, in which collectors and surveyors are charged with the duty on all

has been taken by visiting various custom-houses to instruct collectors as well as to cause proper books and registers to be kept; and although it was difficult, in some instances, for collectors and their clerks to comprehend the system of keeping the accounts, that task has been fully accomplished, and the system is working in a most satisfactory manner. By this system every bale of goods bonded for transportation or exportation is kept, as it were, under the eye of this office until it is finally disposed of and the duties thereon paid, if delivered for consumption, or the merchandise is landed abroad.

As a general rule accounts are well kept and promptly rendered by collectors of customs; and this is owing in no small degree to the fact that a large portion of the collectors of customs, their deputies and clerks, in what may be termed the loyal States, have acquired experience and a knowledge of their duties by having been in their performance during a longer period than has, for some forty years past, been permitted by the mutation of parties and the demoralizing rule of "rotation in office" even among those of the same political affiliation. In some few collection districts petty and disgraceful personal and political squabbles —a desire on the part of an aspiring politician to attain or retain a high position by the aid of government patronage dispensed by him through the hands of a pliant friend—have caused changes in custom-house officers which in scarcely any instance have improved the condition of the office, but in most cases proved injurious to the interests of the government, and, if I may use the expression, have *demoralized* the accounts as well as the force employed in and about the custom-house. Still, as a general rule, it is the opinion of those who have long been familiar with customs affairs, as well as my own—and I take great pleasure in expressing it—that there has been no time within the past thirty or forty years when the duties devolving on collectors, naval officers, surveyors, deputy collectors, &c., &c., have been more faithfully and efficiently performed than they now are.

This tribute from me is justly due to that highly meritorious class of public servants through whose hands come the revenue with which to pay the interest on our sacred public debt, and maintain untarnished the honor of the nation. But there are, unfortunately, exceptions to this rule, of which I shall have occasion to speak hereafter.

In regard to the accounts coming from officers of customs in the States lately in rebellion, I can only say that in most cases they are quite satisfactory; in some admirably well kept and promptly returned; in others less satisfactory, but everywhere an improvement is perceptible where the collector has been long enough in office to acquire a knowledge of his duties, or has a deputy who has had experience enough to become familiar with the revenue laws and the mode of keeping the accounts.

The accounts of collectors in the States lately in rebellion, previous and up to the moment of the rebellion, have been a source of no little perplexity. In some cases they have been rendered up to March, 1861; in others the collectors ceased to consider themselves as officers of the

dollars due him from the United States, which accrued previous to the rebellion. In strict justice this ought to be paid; but the payment is prohibited by the joint resolution of Congress of March 2, 1867.

Is it the duty of this office to take the proper steps to have all balances standing in favor of the government in those States at the breaking out of the rebellion collected by process of law, while payment of balances in favor of collectors is to be refused? Another question also arises: up to what time shall collectors in those States be held responsible to the United States; and, further, where such collectors were compelled to pay moneys in their hands belonging to the United States to the States in which they respectively resided or to the confederate government, can they be compelled to pay such moneys to this government? I put the latter question, because it has in one case been decided by Judge Bryan, of the United States district court of South Carolina, in the negative, the court holding that the defendant was compelled by a power which he could not resist and against which the United States were unable to protect him.

If these balances are to be collected, proceedings should be instituted soon; otherwise the bondsmen, in most cases, will be found to be poor security, as they are now in some instances, and the principals no better.

I have again, as heretofore, respectfully to call your attention to the complexity of the laws relating to the revenue from customs. The acts passed by Congress in 1799 relating to this subject were, it is understood, drawn up with much care by some one or more fully conversant with the subject, and were, for the circumstances of the country and the condition of our commerce and navigation, as perfect a system as could be devised. But a long period of time has elapsed since then, and most remarkable changes have come over the country, demanding from time to time changes and amendments which have again and again, perhaps, been changed and amended, until what was once a complete and admirable system, working most harmoniously, has become such a piece of complex and mended machinery as to make it very difficult to comprehend its various parts and much more to reconcile their incongruities.

To amend these would seem to be but putting patch upon patch without improving them. The task of adapting them to the present condition of the country by amendments is a hopeless one; the whole should be recast in a new code, and this could only be properly done by men who have had much experience in administering these laws, and who have had opportunities to observe and most sensibly to feel their defects, and who have the ability, natural and acquired, to perform the task in a manner creditable and beneficial to a nation second to none in commercial importance and the extent of its navigation. If not thus performed, they had better remain as they are, much as they need codifying.

At the time these laws were chiefly enacted, the channels of commerce were confined to bodies or streams of water, and ports were established where vessels arrived; now, commerce breaks away from these channels and sweeps over plains, mountains and valleys, wherever it listeth;

general rule, the offices of collector, naval officer and surveyor, where the two latter existed, should be self-supporting; that is to say, that such officers should be paid by the fees and commissions, fines, penalties and forfeitures received. In cases where it was supposed that these sources of emolument would not furnish an adequate compensation, a small salary was added; but there was no limitation or maximum of compensation fixed. The collector took all the fees and his commissions, no matter what they might amount to, and paid all the expenses of the custom-house, except the compensation of inspectors, which was then, as now, payable out of the revenues.

This act was materially altered by the act of 7th May, 1822, by which the compensation of collectors was limited, and they were required to render an account of all the fees received. Various acts have since been passed in regard to compensation, not regulating it by any uniform rule, but making it almost as multiform as the number of officers employed. The compensation of nearly all the collectors was established at a period when the dollar of our currency bore a very different relationship to a bushel of wheat, corn, rye and potatoes, and a day's labor from what it does now. The fees, too, which furnished an important portion of the compensation of collectors, were established in 1799, when one dollar, for all exchangeable purposes, was worth as much as four are now. This depreciation in the value of our money, even gold and silver, has rendered it necessary to resort to expedients from time to time to carry on the business at some ports where all the sources of emolument were wholly inadequate to defray the necessary incidental expenses of the office.

These expedients have had a tendency to throw the whole system into confusion, and to render it extremely perplexing and difficult to keep the accounts in a proper condition; and furthermore, they have substituted to some extent the discretion of the Secretary for a fixed rule of law.

You are aware that in the act of 7th May, 1822, deputy collectors at all other than certain enumerated ports were allowed a compensation not exceeding $1,000 per annum; the act declaring that such deputy should not receive more than that sum in any one year "for any services he may perform for the United States in any office or capacity." And yet, as our currency depreciated, it became impossible to obtain the services of any man competent to perform the duties of a deputy collector for that compensation, and so, in spite of this law, deputy collectors were also appointed inspectors of customs, and thus paid two salaries, amounting in several cases to more than twice the compensation fixed by law. The only justification of this, in my judgment, is that "necessity knows no law." Such cases imperiously demand legislation; and legislation is needed to re-establish system and proper rates of compensation to every grade of customs officers. In some cases the compensation of the collector is a fixed sum, exclusive of fees, all of which he is to pay into the treasury; but the compensation thus allowed is scarcely sufficient to pay the simple board of a single person, and no inducement to any competent individual to accept the office, as, if honest, he must leave it poorer than when he went into it, whether he holds it one year or ten.

COMPENSATION OF NAVAL OFFICERS AND SURVEYORS.

negative. The subject, with my decision, was, however, referred to the Secretary of the Treasury, who referred it to the Solicitor of the Treasury for his opinion. The Solicitor concurred with me, and the Secretary took the same view of the law, but soon after sent an order suspending the carrying of that decision into effect.

Since then the question has again been considered, and a similar decision made here. It was then referred to the Attorney General for his opinion, which was given sustaining my own. These officers are now allowed only the compensation provided by the act of 7th May, 1822. With this they are, and have reason to be, dissatisfied, as by that act the salary of the surveyor at New York and Boston is less than that of a deputy collector, and less than that of some of the clerks. It is my duty, however, as it is the duty of all executive officers, to execute the laws as we find them; it is for Congress in its wisdom to say whether the laws shall be altered or not. I respectfully suggest that so much of the 5th section of the act of the 3d March, 1841, as relates to the compensation of collectors, naval officers, and surveyors be repealed, and an act passed regulating the whole subject of compensation.

The per diem of inspectors of customs is limited by law to four dollars a day; in some localities two and a half or three dollars a day is a fair compensation; but in others, New Orleans and other extreme southern ports, four dollars is an inadequate remuneration for the services of men of sufficient capacity, probity, and activity to perform the duties of an inspector as they should be performed, in a climate where out-door duties such as those performed by inspectors are almost certain, during the summer months, to subject the officer to serious, expensive, and, in many cases, fatal sickness. Besides, officers inadequately paid can hardly be expected to show that zeal, vigilance, and alacrity in the performance of their duties which is desirable and even necessary for the protection of the revenue, and may at times be strongly tempted to make up deficiencies by convenient blindness, to the great loss of the government. If an officer is expected to be above temptation he must be kept above want, though unfortunately this does not always secure the government against indifference and unfaithfulness.

SURVEYORS OF CUSTOMS.

At each of the ports of Boston, New York, Philadelphia, Baltimore, New Orleans, and San Francisco a large force of inspectors is employed under the general superintendence of the surveyor.

The 21st section of the act of 2d March, 1799, declares that "the surveyor shall superintend and direct all inspectors, weighers, measurers, and gaugers within his port, and shall, once every week, report to the collector the name or names of such inspectors, weighers, gaugers, and measurers as may be absent from, or neglect to do, their duty," &c. Though one of the three most important officers of customs, the surveyor is little more than a subordinate of the collector. Though he has charge of the inspectors, and is responsible for the faithful performance of their

lector, and that he shall have exclusive jurisdiction over all matters of inspection, weighing, gauging, and measuring; in short, over all the out-door business of the custom-house, or that which is performed by inspectors, weighers, gaugers, and measurers.

The in-door business at these several ports is quite as much as any man can properly perform; and to relieve the collectors of all responsibility in regard to inspecting, weighing, gauging, and measuring will enable them to give more attention to their own proper duties.

SMUGGLING.

The contest with smugglers has been carried on during the past year with such success that it has in a great measure ceased on some portions of the northern frontier; and along the remainder it has been upon a diminished scale. Since the passage of the internal revenue act, reducing the tax on whiskey, all inducement to smuggle that article into the United States has been removed; indeed, the only articles which can now be clandestinely introduced with a profit sufficient to warrant the risk of detection are silks, velvets, ribbons, gloves, opium, or morphine, jewelry, laces, and other small, light articles of great value; all these can be put up in packages of small bulk and introduced in such a manner as to elude the vigilance of the local customs officers, who make few or no seizures at the present day, nearly all being made through information obtained by secret means.

And it may be proper here to remark that a force of 20 or 25 men under the control of one man will accomplish more in the way of preventing and detecting frauds upon the revenue than the whole local force upon that frontier; and the same remark is equally applicable to every other portion of our frontier, coast and inland. In the language of one of my agents, who has had large experience and great success in detecting frauds, "The men now engaged in the contraband trade are the equals in wealth, shrewdness, and cunning to any of the best business men in the country. Their plans are laid to secure the safe introduction of their property before it leaves the foreign territory. Let a merchant of known pecuniary responsibility from any one of our cities visit Montreal or Liverpool, and he will find men who will contract to deliver goods at his own door without the payment of duties." Can the government expect to successfully combat this warfare upon the revenue without the aid of shrewd, sagacious, vigilant men acting in concert and unison, though stationed at distant points from each other? As obstacles to success to such men, our local, inexperienced, and easily deceived local inspectors are scarcely worth consideration. I do not wish to impugn the probity of this class of officers; generally they are honest and faithful, but at such large ports as New York, Philadelphia, Baltimore, Charleston, and New Orleans it is almost certain that among the subordinate officers, appointed as they are, there will be some who cannot, or have no desire to, resist temptation, and who are therefore used by

large scale. In most of these cases the guilty parties were merchants of good standing in the community, men who would have spurned and perhaps resented the charge of dishonesty, had any of their neighbors been so inconsiderate as to make it.

Their alarm and anxiety on learning that "a chiel was among them taking notes," and that there was great probability that they would have to answer for their deeds done in the dark, in open court, may well be imagined. To have transactions which they had fondly hoped were buried in oblivion rise up to stare them in the face like Banquo's ghost, was well calculated to disturb their equanimity. The bringing to light such old cases and compelling such *respectable* men and *highly esteemed* citizens to disgorge their ill-gotten gains, has had more effect in intimidating them and others than the detection in the act of a dozen cases of smuggling.

A few such cases have been ferreted out at Philadelphia and New York, and more, it is hoped, will be brought to light and their authors to justice.

Along the southern coast from Charleston, South Carolina, to the Rio Grande, but more especially from Key West to the latter place, smuggling has been prosecuted with as much activity and success, probably, during the past year and up to the present moment as at any former period; and such is the character of the coast, the facilities offered by the many convenient and out-of-the-way bays, bayous, inlets, and rivers accessible to small vessels, the disposition of the inhabitants to favor illicit trade, and the indisposition of juries as well as some of the judges to convict any one charged with violating the revenue laws, even upon the most positive testimony, that the task of stopping this contraband trade is an exceedingly perplexing and arduous one. But in reference to this I refer to the report of Captain J. C. Dutch, hereafter given.

REPORTS OF SPECIAL AGENTS.

The following extracts from the annual reports made to me by special agents F. Carlisle, General N. M. Curtis, N. W. Bingham, Davis, Hartley, Godwin, and Dutch, acting under my instructions, will show, not the work that they have performed during the past year, for that would be impossible, but the results of their labors:

Extract from Mr. Carlisle's report. (*Mr. Carlisle has charge of the frontier from Niagara to Lake Superior.*)

As preliminary I would state: that since the first of March last a portion of the expenses charged to and paid by the customs department were incurred through my investigations (under special instructions) relative to certain frauds upon the revenue of the Post Office Department. It would seem proper, therefore, that in this comparison of "results and expenses" the customs should either receive credit into so much as this portion of expenses amount to, or of a part of the results obtained from this investigation in the "matter of frauds upon the Post Office Department." I, however, give the actual results and expenses on account of customs, making the frauds on the Post Office Department a subject of a special report, showing the results and expenses which have been paid by the customs.

The "results" given include only those obtained in cases worked up by myself or the officers acting with me.

RESULTS.

Persons arrested 115; of this number ninety-three (93) have been convicted and paid fines from $50 to $3,000; 16 are under indictment, and six (6) have been discharged; and were made in the States of New York, Vermont, Illinois, Wisconsin, and Michigan.

The net amount paid as fines was	$18,938 34
Net proceeds of seizures	2,264 88
Total moneys realized	21,203 22

We have now in court waiting adjudication claims amounting to $31,500.

The officers detailed to act under my directions from time to time during this period, and the compensation paid them while so employed, including travelling expenses, were as follows, viz:

Wm. Hutchinson, 9 months' expenses and compensation	$1,815 00
D. E. Mosely, 8 months' expenses and compensation	1,573 00
George W. Smith, 12 months' expenses and compensation	2,540 00
George W. Smith, 8 months' expenses and compensation	1,615 90
General J. G. Parkhurst, 3 months' expenses and compensation	679 59
Add my own during this period	5,432 86
Total expenses	13,656 35

RECAPITULATION OF RESULTS AND EXPENSES.

Moneys paid into the treasury	$21,203 22
Claims in court	31,500 00
Total	52,703 22
Deduct expenses	13,656 35
Difference	39,046 87

You will readily understand that the foregoing results have been obtained only by the expenditure of much time and labor, and that the "offences" producing them occurred (some of them at least) three years ago, and have required a good deal of manipulation to bring them to light.

Extract from General Curtis's report. (General Curtis has charge of the frontier from Niagara to Rouse's Point.)

Number of seizures made by me during the year ending June 30, 1868: Two (2) horses at Cape Vincent; settled for $400; expenses $6.

Ninety-three (93) head of stock cattle at Plattsburg district; "in court;" $2,421 currency value. Other seizures were made by collectors on my information, of which I am not able to make a specific report.

The number of suits instituted and their result: Suits, six; result not yet known. These cases are instituted for fraudulent entries of lumber for large sums, and the evidence is most complete and conclusive against all parties.

General Curtis enumerates seventeen (17) cases compromised for various sums from $28 up to $2,600 each, chiefly for fraudulent undervaluation of hoops, pease, lumber, &c., and states the aggregate settled in currency to be $8,611 66; the aggregate settled in gold to be $1,143 10; the aggregate value of seizures, $2,821.

Compensation for services for the year ending June 30, 1868	$2,190 00
Expenses for same period	2,443 02
	4,633 02

Report of N. W. Bingham. (Mr. Bingham has charge of the frontier from Rouse's Point, to and including the coast of Maine.)

I have the honor to submit the following report, setting forth the result of the labors of our force in the detection of smuggling, for the year ending June 30, 1868:

Whole number of seizures during the year, 50.

Number of criminal prosecutions during the year, 23.

Fines and penalties received on submissions to the department, and recovered in court during the year, 144.

Imprisonments and convictions during the year, 6.

Amounts already received as fines, penalties, and forfeitures from the above	$83,910 15
Less the costs	1,500 25
Net amount	82,409 90
Moiety accruing to the United States	$41,204 95
Estimated safe value to the government of suits now pending	20,000 00

Expenses of the force employed—N. W. Bingham, salary and mileage	$3,998 30	
Rent of room	300 00	
Salary and expense account of officers Kimball, Burnham, Davis, Morehouse, Toole, Peaslee, Ames, and Hutchins	14,500 00	
Total expense of force		$18,798 30
Deduct from total amount accruing to the government		42 406 65
Net profit to the United States on money already received		$22,406 65
Add safe estimate for suits now pending, of the above		20,000 00
Total		42,406 64

In addition to the above is the extra duty of 10 per cent. that was paid upon 33 pipes of gin, exported from warehouse to St. John's and returned to Boston without having been unladen from the vessel, and which instead of being seized was admitted again to warehouse at Boston by paying said additional duty. Of the amount received as above, there has been distributed to collectors and informers only about $10,366 77, the residue remaining either in the treasury or with the collectors.

I beg to add that the ad damnum in the writs in suits now pending amounts to several hundred thousand dollars.

As to what we have been able to accomplish by way of the prevention of smuggling, and thereby adding to the revenue, of course no proximate estimate can be made, but I think it fair to say that the revenue cannot have been increased; in the matter of duties, less than the amount of money that we have collected, viz., about $84,000; to which, if we add the net profit, as above stated, we shall have the sum of $126,406 65.

Much embarrassment has been experienced on account of the provisions of the act of March 2, 1867, by which the government, from the net proceeds of seizures of a greater value than $500, receives a sum equivalent to the duties, which in the case of spirits and drugs, in nine cases out of ten, results in leaving nothing for the informer. This is not only a great injustice to him who risks his property, reputation, and perhaps life, to give valuable information to the government, but is actually, in a financial point of view, bad policy for the government. And since it has become known that such is the law, I have found it almost impossible to induce persons to give me information.

At the best, with the existing public sentiment upon the coast and frontier, men are very loth to aid the government at the expense of their neighbors, and, therefore, instead of lessening the inducements for them to aid the customs officers in the discharge of their duties for the collection and protection of the revenue, it clearly seems to me that they should be materially increased.

Report of T. Davis.

Mr. T. Davis, located at Boston, reports the following sums as paid in to the custom-house through him, namely:

1867.	
September 12, fine (settled February 7, 1868)	$193 00
September 16, fine (settled February 7, 1868)	275 00
September 16, fine (settled February 7, 1868)	258 00
September 25, fine (settled February 3, 1868)	1,392 00
September 25, fine (settled February 3, 1868)	5,300 00
September 26, fine (settled February 7, 1868)	547 50
September 26, fine (settled February 7, 1868)	182 50
November 21, fine (settled May 2, 1868)	353 00
November 21, fine (settled May 2, 1868)	400 00
1868.	
January 18, seizure, (appraised value, cigars)	1,300 00
March 20, seizure, (appraised value)	168 00
May 6, seizure, (appraised value, silk)	400 00
Total	10,769 00

A suit is pending in the United States district court against Messrs. Thayer & Lincoln, merchants, of Boston, charging them with purchasing smuggled goods, knowing them to be smuggled. At first trial the jury disagreed. There is also seizure of the schooner Martha Anna, at Portland, Maine, not yet disposed of.

The number of seizures which occurred in September, 1867, may be attributed to the return of passengers from the Paris Exposition, by steamer.

Report of Edward Hartley, special agent, in charge of the collection districts on the seaboard of the middle States and Chesapeake bay.

During the last fiscal year, Mr. Hartley reports, as the total collection made by himself and assistant from all sources as $31,029 63, and that there are before the courts in his district property awaiting adjudication for frauds on the revenue valued at $60,000. Through his efforts smuggling on the Delaware and Chesapeake bays has diminished, and at the port of Philadelphia it has nearly ceased. He has also done much to break up the fraudulent importation of so-called free lumber from the St. Croix river to the Atlantic ports south of New England.

Mr. Hartley is, however, principally employed under your direct orders in the examination of government offices and other special business, and is reported to have effected considerable reduction of expenses by the discharge of unnecessary and incompetent officials, and the correction of abuses at ports visited. He reports the following:

Schedule of collections made by E. Hartley, Special Agent of the Treasury, for the year ending June 30, 1868.

Amount of collections of fines, penalties, and forfeitures	$16,029 63
By correction of entries, and collection of unpaid duties	15,000 00
Total	31,029 63
Deduct estimated expenses of force	5,000 00
	26,029 63

Cases in court, two; value of property, $60,000.
Criminal cases pending, one.
Cases settled, one: amount of decree, $639 25.

Extract from the report of W. N. I. Godwin, stationed at Norfolk, Virginia.

By reference to the foregoing statement it will be observed that I have, during the year ending June 30, 1868, besides attending to various other duties, been instrumental in causing to be paid into the treasury about eighteen hundred dollars ($1,800) in currency, and over fifteen thousand dollars ($15,000) in gold, which it would probably not otherwise have received. I have, also, been enabled to save to the government two thousand three hundred and thirty-five dollars ($2,335) in other ways.

At present, whatever smuggling is carried on, I feel sure is done by vessels trading from the south, coastwise north, who get the goods, &c., from vessels coming on the coast from the West Indies. This can be only guarded against by examining these vessels on their arrival north, which is not often done, hence the undertaking.

Extract from report of Captain J. C. Dutch, having charge of the coast from North Carolina to Pensacola.

The actual results of my year's work show as follows:

Moneys received on compromises, in gold	$14,189 06
Fines, penalties, forfeitures, and currency	9,150 00
By decree of court	3,500 00
Amounts claimed in suits instituted on goods smuggled	28,353 40
Penalties in suits instituted	50,000 00

During the year I have travelled on the South Atlantic and Gulf coast 10,650 miles.

Owing to the lack of transportation much of my travel has been performed in small boats, canoes, and on horseback, which, in the hot and sickly climate, makes the labor very hard and uncomfortable.

From personal observation I find smuggling is done principally, and in large amounts, in

and open coast of the southern States offers the best of facilities. The great distance between ports where officers are stationed, and the hundreds of bays, rivers, creeks, and inlets, make detection almost impossible; and, if discovered, a small fee from the smuggler silences every tongue upon the subject, as under existing laws there are no inducements for private citizens to give information to officers of the government, as there is seldom any moiety for the informer after costs and duties are paid.

The first of these causes can only be remedied by greater care and watchfulness on the part of consuls and consular agents in certifying to invoices which are undervalued, or which are short in weight or gauge, "as by connivance with the weighers and gaugers any amount can be smuggled and accounted for as leakage, wastage, &c.," thus cheating, at the same time, the government of its duties, and the underwriters on the cargo.

The second difficulty can be overcome by filling the subordinate offices with honest, active, and capable men.

The third can only be successfully obviated by placing a sufficient number of small light-draught, cruising, or patrolling boats on the various bays, rivers, and inlets, "with a good officer in each;" only a man who, by his tastes and habits, is familiar with boating is fit for this service.

That smuggling is carried on pretty extensively on the southern coast I have good reason to know, and the mode has been in part described by Captain Dutch. Another agent, stationed at New Orleans, says:

Smuggling on the southern coast has become a profession, principally followed by Spaniards, Sicilians, and Italians; they use small schooners which they own. With these they enter shallow bays, bayous, or inlets, and land their goods in out-of-the-way places, from whence they are immediately taken to New Orleans; or, if not convenient to thus dispose of their merchandise, it is often transferred to a coasting vessel and carried direct to the city, these vessels never being inspected.

As an inducement for persons to act as detectives to prevent this illegal traffic the agent urges the necessity of giving the informer a larger share of the proceeds of forfeited merchandise. It is very certain that, unless the government offer greater inducements for the detection of fraud upon the revenue, there will be few detections or convictions in that section of the country, as the informer's life is in constant peril from the shrewd, sharp and unscrupulous fellows whom he watches, and who, upon mere suspicion, would not hesitate to put him where he could never testify against them.

The most effectual mode of putting a stop to this way of smuggling would be the use of several small boats, manned with resolute fellows, and armed with a small swivel and fire-arms. Very few of the revenue cutters now on the coast are fit for this service, or can do any good whatever. The boats used should be able to pursue the smuggler into any bayou, inlet, or stream which the latter can enter, as the ferret pursues the rat, and catches him in his own hole.

Until quite lately agents have been stationed on the Isthmus of Panama to look after our transit trade and prevent smuggling, but it being found impracticable to prevent in that manner the clandestine introduction of foreign goods into San Francisco and New York by means of the steamers plying from those places, respectively, to Aspinwall and Panama, it has been deemed advisable to withdraw these agents from the isthmus and station them at New York and San Francisco, respectively, to carry into effect a system of cording and sealing goods destined from one place to the other, and of inspecting all goods arriving from either place not corded and sealed at the place of departure. This plan has hardly got into working order, but I have strong hopes that, in the hands of those who have the execution of it, it will prove effectual; if so, it will put a stop to a large amount of fraud.

The following table will show that some of the officers of customs have not been wholly inattentive to their duties:

Statement showing the amount of money received from fines, penalties, and forfeitures.

Districts.	Periods.	Amount.
Bangor, Me	June 30, 1867, to April 30, 1868	$5,605 84
Bath, Me	do do	8,175 27
Belfast, Me	June 30, 1867, to December 31, 1867	1,491 50
Castine, Me	do do	19,698 45
Frenchman's Bay, Me	do do	1,141 52
Kennebunk, Me		
Machias, Me	June 30, 1867, to March 31, 1868	5,259 52
Passamaquoddy, Me	June 30, 1867, to July 31, 1868	14,000 53
Portland and Falmouth, Me	June 30, 1867, to January 19, 1868	12,576 64
Saco, Me		
Waldoborough, Me	June 3', 1867, to December 31, 1867	3,371 50
Wiscasset, Me		
York, Me		
Portsmouth, N. H	June 30, 1867, to January 31, 1868	1,748 62
Vermont	March 2, 1867, to June 30, 1868	24,149 76
Bristol and Warren, R. I		
Newport, R. I		
Providence, R. I	September, 1867	142 21
Fairfield, Conn	June 30, 1867, to September 30, 1867	20 00
Middletown, Conn	June 30, 1867, to August 31, 1867	220 00
New Haven, Conn	June 30, 1867, to May 31, 1868	260 87
New London, Conn	June 30, 1867, to September 30, 1868	60 00
Stonington, Conn	March 2, 1867, to December 31, 1867	60 00
Barnstable, Mass	June 30, 1867, to September 30, 1867	368 85
Boston and Charlestown, Mass	June 30, 1867, to June 30, 1868	30,687 80
Edgartown, Mass	June 30, 1867, to May 31, 1868	650 00
Fall River, Mass		
Gloucester, Mass	June 30, 1867, to March 31, 1868	709 43
Marblehead, Mass		
Nantucket, Mass		
New Bedford, Mass	June 30, 1867, to December 31, 1867	537 60
Newburyport, Mass		
Plymouth, Mass		
Salem and Beverly, Mass	March 2 to September, 1867	60 00
Buffalo Creek, N. Y	June 1 to November 30, 1867	938 54
Cape Vincent, N. Y	June 30, 1867, to March 31, 1868	4,473 30
Champlain, N. Y	do do	8,218 26
Dunkirk, N. Y	March 1, 1867, to December 31, 1867	117 52
Genesee, N. Y	May 1, 1867, to March 31, 1868	3,794 11
New York, N. Y	June 30, 1867, to June 30, 1868	253,338 22
Niagara, N. Y	do do	2,905 62
Oswegatchie, N. Y	April 1, 1867, to May 31, 1868	5,279 49
Oswego, N. Y	June 30, 1867, to November 30, 1867	4,665 00
Sag Harbor, N. Y		
Bridgetown, N. J		
Burlington, N. J		
Great Egg Harbor, N. J		
Little Egg Harbor, N. J		
Newark, N. J		
Perth Amboy, N. J		
Erie, Pa	June 30 to September 30, 1867	100 00
Philadelphia, Pa	June 30, 1867, to June 30, 1868	9,652 90
Pittsburg, Pa		
Delaware		
Georgetown, D. C	June 30, 1867, to June 30, 1868	790 00
Annapolis, Md	March 1, 1866, to June 30, 1868	23 00
Baltimore, Md	June 30, 1867, to March 31, 1868	20,383 94
Eastern District, Md	June 30, 1867, to January 31, 1868	20 00
Alexandria, Va		
Cherrystone, Va	June 30, 1867, to September 30, 1867	50 00
Norfolk and Portsmouth, Va	June 30, 1867, to June 30, 1868	1,453 34
Petersburg, Va		

Statement showing the amount of money received, &c.—Continued.

Districts.	Periods.	Amount.
Richmond, Va	June 30, 1867, to June 30, 1868	$95 72
Tappahannock, Va		
Yorktown, Va		
Beaufort, N. C	June 30, 1867, to July 31, 1867	50 00
Pamlico, N. C		
Albemarle, N. C		
Wilmington, N. C	June 30, 1867, to March 31, 1868	1,014 82
Beaufort, S. C	November 1, 1867, to February 29, 1868	1,020 00
Charleston, S. C		
Georgetown, S. C		
Brunswick, Ga		
Savannah, Ga		
St. Mary's, Ga		
Mobile, Ala	June 30, 1867, to February 29, 1868	314 90
Pearl River, Miss		
Natchez, Miss		
Vicksburg, Miss		
New Orleans, La	June 30, 1867, to April 30, 1868	10,803 12
Teche, La		
Appalachicola, Fla		
Fernandina, Fla	June 30, 1867, to June 30, 1868	297 26
Key West, Fla		
Pensacola, Fla		
St. Augustine, Fla		
St. John's, Fla		
St. Mark's, Fla	June 30, 1867, to April 30, 1868	843 86
Brazos de Santiago, Tex		
Saluria, Tex	June 30, 1867, to March 31, 1868	410 30
Texas, Tex	November 1, 1867, to February 29, 1868	777 96
Paso del Norte, Tex		
Corpus Christi, Tex		
Cuyahoga, Ohio	June 30, 1867, to June 30, 1868	1,638 65
Miami, Ohio	June 30, 1867, to October 31, 1867	100 00
Sandusky, Ohio	January 1, 1867, to June 30, 1868	10 2
Detroit, Mich	June 30, 1867, to March 31, 1868	24,961 29
Huron, Mich	June 30, 1867, to June 30, 1868	8,646 28
Superior, Mich	June 30, 1867, to July 31, 1867	255 97
Michigan, Mich	June 30, 1867, to September 30, 1868	818 85
Chicago, Ill	June 30, 1867, to June 30, 1868	5,614 39
Milwaukee, Wis		
Minnesota	February 1, 1867, to June 30, 1868	96 92
San Francisco, Cal	June 30, 1867, to October 31, 1867	17,935 23
Oregon		
Puget sound, W. T		
Montana and Idaho		
St. Louis, Mo	June 30, 1867, to January 31, 1868	700 00
Total		503,704 69

VALUABLE WEARING APPAREL INTRODUCED WITHOUT PAYING DUTIES.

I have good reason to believe that no inconsiderable amount of foreign merchandise is clandestinely brought into some of our large ports as, or concealed in what is claimed to be, "ordinary wearing apparel," chiefly by persons arriving from Europe.

Strenuous efforts have been made to prevent this, but thus far, since 1865–'66, they have not been eminently successful. A rule has been adopted, if I am correctly informed, that such an amount of wearing apparel, new or worn, shall be admitted as such, duty free, as the social position of the owner seems to render necessary and proper. That is to say, if the owner be a gentleman or lady of wealth and high social position, he or she shall be allowed to bring into the country from abroad a very much larger quantity of clothing, and of superior quality and value too, than a person not so wealthy and whose position in social life is less elevated. Under this rule the millionaire comes from Paris or London with from 15 to 30 large trunks, well packed with the most expensive dresses, laces, ribbons, velvets, gloves, shoes, &c., which may have cost five, ten, or fifteen thousand dollars in gold in Paris, all of which being considered appropriate to the wealth and station of the individual, is allowed to pass as "ordinary wearing apparel," although never yet worn; while if the wife of an immigrant farmer or mechanic, or a woman in an humble sphere of life, who comes as a passenger in the same ship, shall have even one trunk full of rich, unworn clothing, she must pay duty thereon, because such apparel does not comport with her station in life, and is not her "*ordinary* wearing apparel."

Can anything be more contrary to justice than the practical working of this rule? Is it right that, because one has been more favored by fortune than another, the more fortunate should be allowed privileges which are denied to the less? To state the case, it seems to me, is to suggest the answer.

There are comparatively few in the United States who can afford to visit Paris once or twice a year for the purpose of purchasing a stock of wearing apparel for the season; yet the millionaire lady may do this on the score of *economy* as well as pleasure, since the amount she saves on her importations exceeds the cost of the trip across the Atlantic and a residence of a few weeks in Paris. Whether this is done or not, I will not affirm; but I know that there are those who have exulted that they had brought from Europe rich dresses enough to last them for years, on which they were required to pay nothing. By the operation of this rule some of those who are most able to pay obtain large amounts of foreign goods duty free. It is for Congress to say whether this is right and just.

DECADENCE OF OUR SHIPPING.

The great decadence of our shipping interest, especially of our vessels engaged in foreign trade, within four or five years past, is a subject which it appears to me deserves the immediate consideration of Congress. The time was when much the largest portion of the carrying trade of the world was confined to American bottoms, and the proportion of foreign vessels seen in our ports was small. Now, much the largest portion of merchandise imported into the United States, at least from England and France, comes in foreign bottoms. With the proverbial energy and enterprise of American merchants this ought not to be, and would not be, unless there was some cause for it. This cause should be removed by Congress.

CONDITION OF BUSINESS AT SOME OF THE CUSTOM-HOUSES.

I have felt it my duty to speak of the general efficiency of the officers of customs, and the satisfactory manner in which their duties are performed, but it is proper that I should say that this commendation does not apply to all. Wherever these officers have been retained for a number of years, five, six, or seven, it is noticeable that the business is done with commendable accuracy, promptitude, and fidelity; accounts are correctly kept and seasonably returned to the Auditor or to this office; money received promptly paid, and few or no causes of complaint given. But, on the other hand, where the officers have been frequently changed; where some aspiring and influential politician has determined to use and succeeds in using the custom-house as a motive power for his political car, and causes removals to be made with that view, and perhaps has been succeeded by one who has been able to unhorse him and is no less determined to use the patronage of the custom-house to promote his own personal interest, in such cases, as might be expected, the accounts are badly kept, the business of the office is performed in an unsatisfactory manner, and there is a want of vigilance and zeal, as well as of knowledge and experience on the part of all employed, from the collector, perhaps the most incompetent of all, down to the night watchman.

The corrollary is, that if an office is run in the interest of individuals, it will not be conducted in the interest of the government.

I have the honor to be, very respectfully, your obedient servant,

N. SARGENT, *Commissioner.*

Hon. HUGH MCCULLOCH,
Secretary of the Treasury.

REPORT OF THE FIRST AUDITOR.

TREASURY DEPARTMENT,
First Auditor's Office, October —, 1868.

SIR: I have the honor to submit the following report of the operations of this office for the fiscal year ending June 30, 1868:

Accounts adjusted.	Number of accounts.	Amounts.
RECEIPTS.		
Collectors of customs	1,405	$192,308,122 66
Collectors under steamboat act	534	226,257 21
Internal and coastwise intercourse	8	47,882 34
Captured and abandoned property	77	346,840 73
Mints and assay offices	9	21,884,946 81
Fines, penalties, and forfeitures	308	646,361 80
Seamen's wages forfeited, &c	13	1,149 59
Lading fees	10	36,368 09
	2,364	215,497,955 23
DISBURSEMENTS.		
Collectors as disbursing agents of the treasury	1,163	$6,497,929 17
Official emoluments of collectors, naval officers, and surveyors	936	1,358,725 02
Excess of deposits for unascertained duties	105	2,088,959 70
Debentures, drawbacks, bounties, and allowances	80	741,079 35
Special examiners of drugs	28	2,463 94
Superintendents of lights	389	1,099,678 97
Agents of marine hospitals	465	482,076 43
Accounts for duties illegally exacted, fines remitted, judgments satisfied, and net proceeds of unclaimed merchandise paid	290	192,648 79
Judiciary accounts	1,471	1,827,759 70
Redemption of the public debt and the payment of interest thereon	1,174	733,212,194 93
Inspectors of steam vessels for travelling expenses, &c	278	42,339 76
Public printing	84	1,272,630 02

Statement—Continued.

Accounts adjusted.	Number of accounts.	Amounts.
Columbia Institution for the Deaf and Dumb	11	$89,156 80
Columbia Hospital for Women	2	6,542 00
Designated depositaries for additional compensation	1	920 91
Designated depositaries for contingent expenses	20	3,797 10
Construction and repairs of public buildings	759	2,263,357 90
Life-saving stations	20	13,226 28
Timber agents	6	2,420 68
Compensation and mileage of the members of the Senate and House of Representatives	3	3,068,855 67
Contingent expenses of the Senate and House of Representatives and of the several departments of the government	461	3,156,919 00
Mints and assay offices	76	19,412,230 47
Territorial accounts	30	228,716 78
Captured and abandoned property	77	221,419 67
Salaries of the civil list paid directly from the treasury	1,192	492,317 35
Coast survey	23	452,080 71
Disbursing clerks for paying salaries	347	6,060,240 56
Withdrawals of applications for patents	5	260 00
Treasurer of the United States for general receipts and expenditures	4	1,154,776,962 18
Distribution of fines, penalties, and forfeitures	164	58,882 45
Commissioner of Public Buildings	111	372,916 58
Commissioner of Agriculture	46	347,148 56
Capitol extension, new dome, and Patent Office building	33	445,028 54
Warehouse and bond accounts examined, stated, and transmitted to Commissioner of Customs	400	
Internal and coastwise intercourse	6	45,638 19
Miscellaneous	1,133	8,872,154 32
Total	11,396	1,949,304,257 09

Reports and certificates recorded	10,160
Letters written	1,737
Letters recorded	1,737
Powers of attorney registered and filed	5,022
Acknowledgments of accounts written	7,431
Requisitions answered	273
Judiciary emolument accounts entered and referred	374
	26,734

I deem it not inappropriate, in conclusion, to use the language of my official report for 1866, which is in all respects applicable to this:

"This report is presented in a condensed form, comprising the specific heads of each branch of the business of the office, and the aggregate of each, with their total.

"To have gone into an exhibit in detail of the vast work from which the report is drawn would have made it voluminous, without giving anything that was essential to be brought to your notice, or to add value to a public document."

T. L. SMITH, *Auditor.*

Hon. HUGH McCULLOCH,
Secretary of the Treasury.

REPORT OF THE SECOND AUDITOR.

TREASURY DEPARTMENT, SECOND AUDITOR'S OFFICE,
Washington, November 9, 1868.

SIR: I have the honor to submit herewith the annual report of this office for the fiscal year ending June 30, 1868.

Statement of the operations of the Second Auditor's office during the fiscal year ending June 30, 1868, *showing the number of accounts settled and the expenditures embraced therein, and in general the other duties pertaining to the business of the office, prepared in accordance with instructions from the Secretary of the Treasury.*

The whole number of accounts settled during the year is 210,293, embracing an expenditure of $196,952,639 67, under the following heads, viz:

PAYMASTERS' DIVISION.

Paymasters' accounts	$145,016,696 72	
Amount of fines, forfeitures, &c., for support of the national asylum for disabled volunteer soldiers, found to have accrued from all sources, to and including June 30, 1868, and paid to said asylum by requisitions on the treasury, in accordance with act of Congress of March 21, 1866	838,824 93	
Amount of fines, forfeitures, stoppages, &c., against soldiers of the regular army, paid to the treasurer of the Soldiers' Home, in accordance with act of Congress of March 3, 1859	179,839 36	
Amount transferred to the credit of the Commissioner of Internal Revenue on the books of this office and turned over to him by requisitions for the tax on salaries withheld from officers of the army	270,167 13	
		$146,305,528 14

ORDNANCE, MEDICAL, AND MISCELLANEOUS DIVISION.

Ordnance disbursing officers' accounts	16,266,063 77
Ordnance private claims	234,941 27
Medical disbursing officers' accounts	1,841,980 12
Expended by disbursing officers out of quartermasters' funds, not chargeable to said funds, but to certain appropriations on the books of this office	623,801 27
Medical private claims	59,121 95
Miscellaneous, viz:	
Contingencies of the army	1,334,864 01
Pay and supplies of hundred-days volunteers	55,571 08

Medical and surgical history and statistics	$32,246 66	
Sick and wounded soldiers' fund	18,086 44	
Twenty per cent. additional compensation—joint resolution, February 28, 1867	6,654 15	
Expenses of the commanding general's office	4,860 82	
Secret service	3,248 34	
Providing for the comfort of sick and wounded soldiers	1,422 44	
Contingent expenses of Adjutant General's department	639 15	
Keeping and transporting and supplying prisoners of war	286 66	
Relief of certain musicians and soldiers at Fort Sumter, in South Carolina, act July 24, 1861	14 00	
Joint resolution for relief of William D. Nelson, January 31, 1867	1,000 00	
		$20,484,802 13
RECRUITING DIVISION.		
Recruiting officers' accounts—regular army	359,965 96	
Disbursing officers' accounts, under appropriations, viz:		
Collecting, drilling, and organizing volunteers	2,373,418 41	
Draft and substitute fund	1,683,279 48	
Pay of bounty to volunteers and regulars	759,319 39	
Pay of two and three years' volunteers,	29,522 32	
Relief of drafted men	51,300 00	
Twenty per cent. extra compensation	5,335 07	
		5,262,140 63
INDIAN DIVISION.		
Superintendents' and agents' accounts and private claims	5,301,722 89	5,301,722 89
PAY AND BOUNTY DIVISION.		
Claims for arrears of pay and bounty to discharged and deceased officers and soldiers	19,569,282 27	
Amount paid to Soldiers' Home from stoppages and fines adjudged against soldiers of the regular army, forfeitures on account of desertion, and moneys belonging to the estate of deceased soldiers unclaimed for three years, the same being set apart by act of Congress for the support of said Home	29,163 61	
		19,598,445 88
Total expenditures		196,952,639 67

Property accounts examined and adjusted	129,463
Letters written, recorded, and mailed	603,698
Claims, &c., received, briefed, and registered	220,209
Requisitions registered and posted, amounting to $78,314,486 21	1,868
Certificates and answers to inquiries given to various offices, involving an examination of muster and pay rolls and other records of the office, viz:	
To the Commissioner of Pensions	6,509
To the Paymaster General's office	3,559
To the division of referred claims	304,035
To the Adjutant General's office	5,399
To the Quartermaster General's office	247
To the Third Auditor's office	485
To the Fourth Auditor's office	174
Corrections and endorsements made by request	5,949
Claims for arrears of pay and bounty rejected	41,219

In addition to the foregoing, various statements and reports have been prepared and transmitted from the office, as follows:

Annual statement of disbursements in the department of Indian affairs for the fiscal year ending June 30, 1867, prepared for Congress.

Annual statement of the recruiting fund, prepared for the Adjutant General of the army.

Annual statement of the contingencies of the army, prepared in duplicate for the Secretary of War.

Annual statement of the contingent expenses of this office, transmitted to the Secretary of the Treasury.

Annual statement of the clerks and other persons employed in this office during the year 1867, or any part thereof, showing the amount paid to each on account of salary, with place of residence, &c., in pursuance of the 11th section of the act of 26th August, 1842, and resolution of the House of Representatives of the 13th January, 1846; transmitted to the Secretary of the Treasury.

Annual report of balances on the books of this office remaining unaccounted for more than one year, transmitted to the First Comptroller.

Annual statement of balances on the books of this office remaining unaccounted for more than three years, transmitted to the First Comptroller.

Statement, showing the name, place of birth, residence, when appointed, and annual salary of each person employed in this office on the 30th day of September, 1867, transmitted to the Register of the Treasury.

Monthly reports of the clerks in this office, submitted each month to the Secretary of the Treasury, with a tabular statement, showing the amount of business transacted in the office during the month, and the number of accounts remaining unsettled at the close of the month.

Monthly reports of absences from duty of employés in this office, with reasons for such absence.

All claims that have been presented by heirs of deceased soldiers for bounty under the act of July 28, 1866, have been disposed of except a small number which are suspended awaiting further testimony. Certificates have also been furnished to the Paymaster General, after an examination of the rolls and other vouchers in this office, in reply to all inquiries made by him for information upon which to settle the additional bounty to discharged soldiers.

A very large proportion of the unsettled claims of white soldiers or their heirs for arrears of pay and bounty are not in a condition to be settled at present, being suspended for various causes of which the claimants or their attorneys have been informed.

Many thousands of the claims of colored soldiers, or their heirs, for the bounty granted by the resolutions of June 15 and July 26, 1866, remain unsettled.

The peculiar condition of this class of claimants, their ignorance and defencelessness, and the difficulty of so identifying each as to secure the faithful execution of the law and at the same time to protect the government against fraudulent claims, suggested the resolution of March 30, 1867, directing the payment of the certificates issued in these cases by this office, to be made through the Commissioner of the Freedmen's Bureau, who can successfully meet these difficulties through the aid of his subordinates.

Being satisfied that without such a system, the government has little if any security against the successful prosecution of fraudulent claims and no sufficient guarantee that rightful claimants shall receive what is granted to them, it seemed to be imperative that this class of claims should be settled while that bureau is in a condition to execute the trust imposed upon it. By reason of the diminution of other work in this office, seven or eight thousand could be settled monthly, if the necessary information could be obtained.

The law makes a distinction between colored soldiers, who were free on the 19th of April, 1861, and those who were not, in the amount of bounty to be paid, but provides that "where nothing appears on the muster-roll or of record to show that a colored soldier was not a freeman at the date aforesaid, under the provisions of the fourth section of the act making appropriations for the support of the army for the year ending the 30th of June, 1865, the presumption shall be that the person was free at the time of his enlistment."

To ascertain the military history of the soldier and what appears upon "the muster-roll, or of record," it has been deemed necessary to address an inquiry in each case to the Adjutant General. About 14,000 of these inquiries are now unanswered, and while this office is sending about 100 daily, only about 80 replies are received, which he assures me are all that can be furnished, in consequence of the small force of clerks employed in that office.

During a portion of the past year 100 temporary clerks have been employed in addition to the regular force, to expedite examinations of the rolls and vouchers and to furnish replies to the inquiries from the Paymaster General. That work having been accomplished, the clerical force has been reduced to 382, and in consequence of the diminishing demand upon other branches of the office, a further large reduction should be made at an early day. It is believed that after July 1, 1869, it will not be necessary to employ the services of more than 200 clerks.

Notwithstanding that in each annual report a statistical summary of the transactions of the office has been given, I have thought that a condensed statement in figures, of the work (so far as it can be reduced to figures) that has been accomplished since July 1, 1861, would be not only proper, but interesting. I therefore present the following table, which has been compiled from the reports of seven years. It shows that the number of claims and accounts examined and allowed, paid or rejected, is 1,371,243, and if to that number is added the examination and reports to the Paymaster General, that 1,938,924 have been disposed of during the seven years; but the wearisome details, the anxious, patient and faithful clerical labor necessary to accomplish this, can only be imagined.

Statement of accounts settled and amounts involved from June 30, 1861, to June 30, 1868

For the year ending—	Paymasters' accounts.		Ordnance, medical, and miscellaneous accounts.		Indian agents' accounts.		Bounty, arrears of pay, &c., accounts.		Recruiting service, &c., accounts.		Total.	
	No.	Amount.	No.	Amount.	No.	Amount.	No.	Amount.	No.	Amount.	No.	Amount.
June 30, 1862	141	$4,181,276 33	4,017	$29,128,526 30	616	$3,335,885 23	3,328	$249,180 64	1,504	$217,088 97	9,606	$37,111,957 47
June 30, 1863	645	47,875,231 36	11,802	38,847,899 20	590	2,099,257 87	19,191	2,443,293 39	1,356	398,785 94	33,584	91,664,467 76
June 30, 1864	773	88,944,415 39	15,988	55,539,537 64	501	2,242,154 74	80,756	10,970,528 91	1,880	2,229,744 15	99,898	159,917,380 83
June 30, 1865	738	90,094,847 46	22,059	42,647,077 68	866	3,231,449 00	81,517	14,047,599 35	2,594	8,019,331 56	110,774	158,040,305 05
June 30, 1866	981	110,209,718 62	7,228	26,902,784 54	448	2,881,256 33	78,335	16,189,247 17	4,317	21,353,127 68	91,309	177,536,134 34
June 30, 1867	1,451	183,041,476 09	3,206	23,050,181 18	821	4,273,268 91	59,121	10,638,762 78	3,765	19,891,437 59	68,364	240,895,026 55
June 30, 1868	1,038	146,305,528 14	1,897	20,484,802 13	962	5,301,722 89	203,980	19,598,445 88	2,416	5,262,140 63	210,293	196,952,639 67
Total	5,767	670,652,493 39	66,197	236,600,808 67	4,804	23,364,934 97	529,228	74,137,078 12	17,832	57,362,656 52	623,828	1,662,117,971 67

Statement of property accounts and miscellaneous work performed in connection with the settlement of above accounts.

For the year ending—	Number of—					
	Property acts examined and adjusted.	Back pay and bounty claims rejected.	Letters written.	Letters, claims, &c., received, briefed, and registered.	Requisitions registered and posted.	Certificates from rolls furnished Pay'r Gen'l.
June 30, 1862	5,021	822	14,584	37,473	5,589	....
June 30, 1863	7,368	1,470	40,651	134,816	5,144	....
June 30, 1864	29,745	2,374	108,373	254,690	5,410	....
June 30, 1865	163,429	2,210	126,569	170,340	5,995	38,904
June 30, 1866	176,263	19,099	370,020	245,903	2,698	74,041
June 30, 1867	141,698	27,236	478,477	486,305	2,401	134,328
June 30, 1868	129,463	11,217	603,698	220,209	1,868	320,408
Total	652,987	94,428	1,742,372	1,549,736	29,105	567,681

In the settlement of such a vast number and variety of claims, where much of the evidence is presented in the form of affidavits, it is not surprising that frequent instances of fraud have occurred. Every method that care and experience could suggest has been adopted to protect the interests of the government and of honest claimants. Many and probably by far the largest number of these attempted frauds have been discovered and frustrated, but quite a large number have been successfully prosecuted through perjury and forgery. As the law is now, in consequence of the lapse of time between their perpetration and discovery, but few of these offences can be criminally punished, and the civil remedy furnished by the act of March 2, 1863, is comparatively valueless, in claims for pay and bounty, in consequence of the poverty of the fraudulent claimants.

Through the active co-operation of the United States district officers, about $50,000 have been recovered which had been paid in fraudulent cases, and occasionally criminals have been convicted and punished. The division in charge of this work has now about 400 cases under investigation. To prosecute such cases successfully, it is necessary that authority should be given for the appointment of clerks for detective service, to be employed in the same manner as is now done by the Pension Office. This measure is especially recommended and also an appropriation of $10,000 for the purpose of defraying the necessary expenses of such service. I cannot doubt that it would be a valuable and economical expenditure for the discovery and prevention of such frauds and to secure the repayment of money fraudulently obtained.

I am, sir, very respectfully, your obedient servant,

EZRA B. FRENCH, *Auditor.*

Hon. HUGH MCCULLOCH,
Secretary of the Treasury.

REPORT OF THE THIRD AUDITOR.

TREASURY DEPARTMENT,
Third Auditor's Office, October 29, 1868.

SIR: I have the honor to submit the following report of the operations of this office for the fiscal year ending 30th June, 1868, and for the first quarter of the current fiscal year, with such suggestions as seem proper to promote the prompt and efficient disposition of public business.

During the past fiscal year the following amounts were drawn from the treasury, to wit:

Amount drawn out of the treasury in the fiscal year ending 30th June, 1868	$101,552,446 48
As follows:	
Amount advanced same period	$96,916,296 70
Amount of claims paid	4,636,149 78
	101,552,446 48
Amount of counter-requisitions drawn on sundry persons same period, in favor of the Treasurer of the United States	$21,689,574 04

As follows:

Third Auditor's transfers	$14,012,215 15
Second Auditor's transfers	123,621 94
Adjutant General, War Office	1,065 53
Drafts cancelled	64,898 00
Deposits	7,487,773 42
	21,689,574 04

Amount of accounts settled, of advances made to the disbursing officers, agents, and States, prior to and in the fiscal year ending 30th of June, 1868	$434,577,597 74
Amount of claims settled and paid	4,636,149 78
Total	439,213,747 52

First quarter, ending 30th September, 1868.

Amount drawn out of the treasury for the quarter ending 30th September, 1868	$25,686,711 18

As follows, to wit:

Amount advanced	$25,051,972 86
Amount of claims paid	634,738 32
	25,686,711 18

Amount of counter-requisitions drawn on sundry persons in favor of the Treasurer of the United States	$4,488,945 24

As follows, to wit:

Third Auditor's transfers	$3,071,886 59
Second Auditor's transfers	694,529 10
Deposits	722,529 55
	4,488,945 24

Amount of accounts settled in the quarter ending 30th September, 1868	$72,787,864 92
Amount of claims paid	634,738 32
	73,422,603 24

SUMMARY OF SETTLEMENTS.

Amount settled for fiscal year	$439,213,747 52
Amount settled for first quarter	73,422,603 24
Aggregate	512,636,350 76

The following is a statement of the amount drawn out of the treasury, under the several heads of appropriations for the fiscal year ending 30th June, 1868, to wit:

Quartermasters' department	$58,579,901 80	
Subsistence of the army	4,120,816 28	
Engineer department	6,107,538 35	
Pensions	28,660,116 75	
Horses and other property lost	178,677 12	
Freedmen's Bureau	3,905,396 18	
		$101,552,446 48
And for the first quarter of the current fiscal year there were drawn—		
Quartermasters' department	$10,522,477 66	
Subsistence of the army	1,931,555 13	
Engineer department	1,570,536 37	
Pensions	11,073,486 75	
Horses and other property lost	88,655 27	
Freedmen's Bureau	500,000 00	
		25,686,711 18
Total		127,239,157 66

Report of the operations of the quartermasters' division for the fiscal year ending June 30, 1868.

	Money accounts.		Property returns.	Supplemental settlem'ts.			Signal accounts.			Total.		Number of letters sent out.
	Number.	Amount involved.		Property.	Money.	Amount involved.	Property.	Money.	Amount involved.	Number.	Amount involved.	
On hand June 30, 1867	1,909	$170,087,515 73	37,620	......	......	......	......	1	$358 19	39,530	$170,087,873 92	......
Received during the month of July, 1867	158	10,328,996 06	218	173	25	$20,875 31	1	1	445 05	576	10,350,316 42	......
August, 1867	117	11,669,840 11	429	135	49	1,060 82	1	......	......	731	11,670,900 93	......
September, 1867	43	8,111,767 40	884	143	30	......	......	2	702 35	1,102	8,112,469 75	......
October, 1867	88	8,609,805 39	769	149	41	10,191 15	2	1	533 24	1,050	8,620,529 78	......
November, 1867	103	9,860,986 15	723	154	48	1,800 64	......	......	......	1,028	9,862,786 79	......
December, 1867	107	9,763,672 30	816	189	25	......	......	......	......	1,137	9,763,672 30	......
January, 1868	94	2,612,653 45	535	328	85	820,442 51	......	......	......	1,042	3,433,095 96	......
February, 1868	77	21,989,080 89	383	265	87	24,315 91	......	......	......	812	22,013,396 80	......
March, 1868	126	7,749,854 31	425	287	59	12,097 09	......	......	......	897	7,761,951 40	......
April, 1868	122	5,150,503 20	286	201	39	19,899 33	6	6	3,835 20	660	5,174,237 73	......
May, 1868	79	5,262,408 83	172	268	97	42,600 03	1	1	1,142 72	618	5,306,151 58	......
June, 1868	78	5,253,762 41	486	217	51	20,190 63	......	......	......	832	5,273,953 04	......
Total	3,101	276,450,846 23	43,746	2,509	636	973,473 42	11	12	7,016 75	50,015	277,431,336 40	......
Reported during the month of July, 1867	263	$7,558,835 33	1,219	173	25	$20,875 31	......	......	......	1,680	$7,579,710 64	1,369
August, 1867	200	17,039,588 21	718	135	49	1,060 82	2	......	......	1,104	17,040,649 03	798
September, 1867	226	18,728,720 94	1,028	143	30	......	......	......	......	1,427	18,728,720 94	1,151
October, 1867	221	7,623,215 25	1,033	149	41	10,191 15	......	......	......	1,444	7,633,406 40	1,226
November, 1867	199	4,992,089 67	895	154	48	1,800 64	......	......	......	1,296	4,993,890 31	1,564
December, 1867	243	7,023,696 98	818	189	25	......	......	......	......	1,275	7,023,696 98	904
January, 1868	224	11,201,645 26	1,151	328	85	820,442 51	......	......	......	1,788	12,022,087 77	2,036
February, 1868	170	4,056,604 43	1,000	265	87	24,315 91	......	......	......	1,522	4,080,920 34	2,026
March, 1868	140	6,249,038 67	1,145	287	59	12,097 09	......	......	......	1,631	6,261,135 76	3,756
April, 1868	185	11,673,071 29	940	201	39	19,899 33	......	......	......	1,365	11,692,970 62	3,786
May, 1868	150	3,148,236 34	979	268	97	42,600 03	......	......	......	1,494	3,190,836 37	4,005
June, 1868	276	61,357,813 79	1,086	217	51	20,190 63	......	......	......	1,630	61,378,004 42	4,011
Total	2,497	160,652,556 16	12,012	2,509	636	973,473 42	2	......	......	17,656	161,626,029 58	26,632
Remaining unsettled June 30, 1868	604	115,798,290 07	31,734	......	......	......	9	12	......	32,359	115,805,306 82	......
Total	3,101	276,450,846 23	43,746	2,509	636	973,473 42	11	12	......	50,015	277,431,336 40	26,632

Report of the operations of the quartermasters' division for the first quarter of the fiscal year ending June 30, 1869.

	Money accounts.		Prop'ty returns.	Supplemental settlements.			Signal accounts.			Total.		No. of letters sent out.
	No.	Am't involved.		Prop'ty.	Money.	Am't involved.	Prop'ty.	Money.	Am't involved.	No.	Am't involved.	
On hand June 30, 1868	604	$115, 798, 290 07	31, 734				9	12	$7, 016 75	32, 359	$115, 805, 306 82	
Received during the month of July, 1868	50	3, 442, 186 99	222	384	57	$9, 093 67				713	3, 451, 280 66	
Received during the month of August, 1868	29	6, 837, 624 54	117	224	81	8, 629 11				451	6, 846, 253 65	
Received during the month of Sept., 1868	41	3, 493, 719 91	118	253	92		9	3	19, 412 95	516	3, 513, 132 86	
Total	724	129, 571, 821 51	32, 191	861	230	17, 722 78	18	15	26, 429 70	34, 039	129, 615, 973 99	
Reported during the month of July, 1868	138	$1, 315, 812 62	972	384	57	$9, 093 67				1, 551	$1, 324, 906 29	3, 689
Reported during the month of August, 1868	83	2, 560, 000 68	989	224	81	8, 629 11				1, 377	2, 574, 629 79	2, 151
Reported during the month of Sept., 1868	57	482, 361 74	1, 077	253	92					1, 479	482, 361 74	3, 299
Total	278	4, 364, 175 04	3, 038	861	230	17, 722 78				4, 407	4, 381, 897 82	9, 139
Remaining unsettled September 30, 1868	446	125, 207, 646 47	29, 153				18	15	$26, 429 70	29, 632	125, 234, 076 17	
Total	724	129, 571, 821 51	32, 191	861	230	17, 722 78	18	15	26, 429 70	34, 039	129, 615, 973 99	9, 139

NOTE.—Of the accounts stated as "remaining unsettled" in this report, the greater number are under examination, in various stages of settlement; the examination of vouchers connected therewith amounting to $55,598,756 89, being complete, and the cases nearly ready to be reported to the Comptroller.

SUBSISTENCE DIVISION.

The following is a report of the business transacted in the subsistence division during the fiscal year ending June 30, 1868:

There have been received and registered during the year 3,627 money accounts of officers disbursing in the subsistence department, involving the expenditure of $11,276,166 91.

During the same period 3,776 accounts (containing 64,696 vouchers) were audited and reported to the Second Comptroller of the Treasury, involving the expenditure of $12,249,009 77.

In connection with the above, there were received and registered during the year 2,528 provision returns, and within the same period 2,704 provision returns (containing 62,662 vouchers) were examined and adjusted.

The total number of vouchers contained in the accounts examined was 127,358.

During the year 1,354 official letters were written, 1,245 pages of differences written and copied, and 3,427 queries received and answered.

Recapitulation.

No. of accounts.		Amount involved.
1,374	Remaining on hand June 30, 1867	$2,908,699 55
3,627	Received during the year ending June 30, 1868	11,276,166 91
5,001	Total	14,184,866 46
3,776	Audited and reported to the Second Comptroller during the year	12,249,009 77
1,225	Remaining unsettled June 30, 1868	1,935,856 69

Provision returns on hand June 30, 1867		1,338
Provision returns received during the fiscal year		2,528
Total		3,866
Provision returns examined during the year		2,704
Provision returns remaining on hand June 30, 1868		1,162
Number of money accounts on hand June 30, 1867	1,374	
Number of provision returns on hand June 30, 1867	1,338	
		2,712
Number of money accounts received during the fiscal year	3,627	
Number of provision returns received during the fiscal year	2,528	
		6,155
Total		8,867
Number of money accounts audited during the year	3,776	
Number of provision returns examined during the year	2,704	
		6,480
Total number of accounts on hand June 30, 1868		2,387

During the quarter ending September 30, 1868, there were received and registered 806 money accounts, involving an expenditure of $2,419,441 12, to which add 1,225 accounts, involving an expenditure of $1,935,856 69, on hand June 30, 1868, making a total of 2,031 accounts, involving $4,355,297 81, of which 647 accounts, involving $2,526,778 09, were audited and reported to the Second Comptroller during the quarter, leaving unsettled 1,384 accounts, involving $1,828,519 72, as recapitulated below.

No. of accounts.		Amount involved.
1,225	Accounts unsettled June 30, 1868	$1,935,856 69
856	Accounts received during the quarter	2,419,441 12
2,031	Total	4,355,297 81
647	Accounts audited during the quarter	2,526,778 09
1,384	Accounts on hand unsettled September 30, 1868	1,828,519 72

Provision returns on hand June 30, 1868	1,162
Provision returns received during the quarter	653
Total	1,815
Provision returns examined during the quarter	620
Provision returns remaining on hand September 30, 1868	1,195

Number of letters written during the quarter, 261; number of vouchers in money accounts examined, 12,281; number of vouchers in provision returns examined, 13,401; total vouchers, 15,682.

ENGINEER DIVISION.

Statement of business transacted in the engineer division during the year ending June 30, 1868.

Referring to quarterly and monthly accounts.	Number of accounts.		Amount involved per officers' statements.
	Quarterly.	Monthly.	
Remaining on file unadjusted June 30, 1867	21	269	$4,446,891 07
Received during the year ending June 30, 1868	9	550	6,365,977 95
Total to be accounted for	30	819	10,812,869 02
Adjusted and otherwise accounted for.			
Adjusted	14	488	$6,550,320 87
Returned to engineer department	7	12	36,816 21
Referred to the Second Comptroller		2	15,070 48
Aggregate	21	502	6,602,207 56
Remaining on file unadjusted June 30, 1868	9	317	$4,210,661 46

The amount of disbursements credited to disbursing officers in the accounts adjusted during the year is	$5,106,888 67
And the amount so credited in nineteen special settlements is	72,151 23
Aggregate	5,179,039 90

Statement of business transacted in the engineer division during the first quarter of the fiscal year ending the 30th of June, 1868.

Referring to quarterly and monthly accounts.	Number of accounts.		Amount involved per officers' statements.
	Quarterly.	Monthly.	
On file unadjusted at the commencement of the quarter	9	317	$4,210,661 46
Received during the quarter	30	47	571,111 25
Total to be accounted for	39	364	4,781,772 71
Adjusted during the quarter	12	169	2,227,126 60
Remaining on file at the close of the quarter, September 30, 1868	27	195	2,554,646 11

The amount of disbursements credited to disbursing officers in the accounts adjusted during the quarter is	$2,288,789 38
And the amount so credited in six special settlements is	44,202 48
Aggregate	2,332,991 86

STATE WAR CLAIMS.

Statement showing the operations of the State war claims division for the year ending June 30, 1868.

	Original accounts.		Special settlements.	
	No.	Amount.	No.	Amount.
On hand June 30, 1867	1	$3,427,392 43		
Received during fiscal year	39	2,583,872 64	25	$3,623,433 33
Total	40	6,011,265 07	25	3,623,433 33
Reported during the fiscal year	33	$4,339,576 44	25	$3,623,433 33
On hand June 30, 1868	7	1,671,688 63		
Total	40	6,011,265 07	25	3,623,433 33

Letters received from July 1, 1867, to June 30, 1868, inclusive, 236.
Letters written from July 1, 1867, to June 30, 1868, inclusive, 248.

Statement showing the operations of the State war claims division for the quarter ending September 30, 1868.

	Original accounts.		Special settlements.	
	No.	Amount.	No.	Amount.
On hand June 30, 1868	7	$1,671,688 63		
Received during the months of July, August, and September, 1868	12	557,580 44	10	$3,341,261 45
Total	19	2,229,269 07	10	3,341,261 45
Reported during the months of July, August, and September, 1868	7	$1,126,284 40	10	$3,341,261 45
On hand September 30, 1868	12	1,102,984 67		
Total	19	2,229,269 07	10	3,341,261 45

The several State authorities have been more prompt and energetic during the last year than during any previous year in supplying deficiencies, filing additional evidences, explanations, &c., and the result is seen in the satisfactory condition and nearness to final settlement of the accounts on file in the division.

CLAIMS DIVISION.

The following statement exhibits the operations of the division of claims during the fiscal year ending June 30, 1868, and also the condition of its business at that date.

The duties of this division embrace the settlement of claims of a miscellaneous character arising in various branches of service in the War Department under current appropriations, and also under special acts of Congress; of claims for compensation for horses and other property lost or destroyed in the military service of the United States, under act of March 3, 1849; of claims for value of steamboats and other vessels and railroad engines and cars lost or destroyed while in same service, as provided for in same act; and also claims growing out of the Oregon and Washington Indian war of 1855 and 1856, under act of March 2, 1861.

1. *Miscellaneous claims.*

The number of this class of claims received and docketed during the year is 2,868, in 2,759 of which the aggregate amount claimed was $3,213,385 37. In the remaining 109 no sums were stated.

The number of claims (including those received prior to, as well as during the year) audited and otherwise disposed of within the same period is 2,725, in which the aggregate amount claimed was $3,203,943 34, and the aggregate allowed $2,782,760 03.

During the year there have been 1,890 letters written relative to this class of claims and 2,130 letters received and docketed. Special reports in 93 cases have also been made to the Second Comptroller during the year.

The following table exhibits the state of the business of this division at the commencement of the year, its progress through the year, and its condition at the end thereof:

	No.	Am't claimed.	Amount allowed.
A. Claims undisposed of and remaining on hand June 30, 1867	3,388	$1,381,452 73	
B. Claims received during the year ending June 30, 1868	2,868	3,213,385 37	
C. Claims audited and otherwise disposed of during the year ending June 30, 1868	2,725	3,203,943 34	$2,782,760 03
D. Claims undisposed of and remaining on hand June 30, 1868	3,531	1,390,894 76	

A. The above is the aggregate claimed in 2,342 of the cases; in the remaining 1,046 no sums are stated.

B. These figures show the aggregate claimed in 2,759 cases, no amounts being stated in the remaining 109.

C. In 63 of the cases disposed of amounts were not specified; the above shows the aggregate claimed in 2,662 cases.

D. The above sum exhibits the aggregate claimed in 2,398 claims; in the other 1,133 no amounts were stated.

2. *Horse claims.*

The number of horse claims, &c., received and docketed during the year ending June 30, 1868, is 656, in which the aggregate amount claimed was $254,744 74.

The number settled and finally disposed of during the same period (including those received prior to, as well as during the year) was 848, in which the aggregate amount claimed was $173,226 39, and on which the aggregate amount allowed was $79,895 91.

There have been during the year 13,471 letters written relative to this class of claims and 4,620 letters have been received and docketed, 9,400 claims have been examined and suspended and 2,650 briefs made.

The following table presents the condition of the business in this branch of the division both at the commencement and close of the year as well as its progress through the year.

	No.	Amount claimed.	Am't allowed.
Claims on hand undisposed of June 30, 1867...	6,481	$1,071,142 70	....
Claims received during the year ending June 30, 1868..................................	656	254,744 74	....
*Claims settled and otherwise disposed of during the year ending June 30, 1868..........	848	173,226 39	$79,895 91
Claims on hand undisposed of June 30, 1868...	6,289	1,152,661 05	....

*Of this number 515 were allowed and 333 disallowed.

3. *Claims for value of lost steamboats, &c.*

The number of this class of claims received and docketed during the year ending June 30, 1868, is 11, in which was claimed an aggregate of $114,423.

The number settled and otherwise disposed of during the year is 25, involving an aggregate of $189,007 09; the aggregate amount awarded on these cases was $116,254 21.

During the year 152 letters have been written and 60 received and docketed relative to this class of claims.

The subjoined table shows the condition of the business in this branch of the division at the beginning of the year, its progress through the year, and likewise its condition at the end thereof.

	No.	Amount claimed.	Am't allowed.
Claims on hand undisposed of June 30, 1867...	97	$956,425 20	....
Claims received during the year ending June 30, 1868..................................	11	114,423 00	....
Claims settled and otherwise disposed of during the year ending June 30, 1868..............	25	189,007 09	$116,254 21
Claims on hand undisposed of June 30, 1868 ..	83	881,841 11	....

4. *Oregon and Washington Indian war claims.*

The number of these claims received and docketed during the year is 128, in which the aggregate amount claimed was $15,095 56.

The number settled and otherwise disposed of during the year is 110, on which an aggregate amount of $24,328 54 was claimed, and an aggregate amount of $11,938 85 allowed.

178 letters relative to this class of claims have been written during the year, and 145 received and registered.

The following table exhibits the condition of the business in this branch of the division:

	No.	Amount claimed.	Am't allowed.
Claims on hand undisposed of June 30, 1867...	876	$117,606 30	....
Claims received during the year ending June 30, 1868..........................	128	15,095 56	....
Claims settled and otherwise disposed of during the year ending June 30, 1868.............	110	24,328 54	$11,938 85
Claims undisposed of and remaining on hand June 30, 1868	894	108,373 32	....

The following tabular statements show the condition of the business in the various branches of the division of claims both at the commencement and close of the quarter ending September 30, 1868, and also its progress during that period:

1. *Miscellaneous claims.*

	No.	Amount claimed.	Am't allowed.
A. Claims on hand undisposed of June 30, 1868.	3,531	$1,390,894 76	....
B. Claims received during the quarter ending September 30, 1868..........................	874	495,611 91	....
C. Claims settled and otherwise disposed of during the quarter ending September 30, 1868.	479	500,168 98	$399,810 17
D. Claims on hand undisposed of September 30, 1868..................................	3,926	1,386,337 69	....

A. This amount is the aggregate claimed in 2,398 claims, the amounts claimed in the other 1,133 not being stated.

B. This amount is the aggregate claimed in 861 cases; in the other 13 no amounts were stated.

C. This number and amount includes 82 claims referred elsewhere for adjudication, the aggregate claimed therein being $7,557 73.

D. This amount is the aggregate claimed in 2,780 claims, no amounts being stated in the other 1,146.

2. *Horse claims.*

	No.	Amount claimed.	Am't allowed.
Claims on hand undisposed of June 30, 1868...	6,289	$1,152,661 06	....
Claims received during the quarter ending September 30, 1868..........................	115	18,783 16	....
*Claims settled and otherwise disposed of during the quarter ending September 30, 1868...	143	22,887 77	$14,504 74
Claims undisposed of and remaining on hand September 30, 1868..........................	6,261	1,148,556 44	....

* Of this number 112 were allowed and 31 rejected, transferred, &c.

3. *Claims for lost steamboats, &c.*

	No.	Amount claimed.	Am't allowed.
Claims on hand undisposed of June 30, 1868	83	$881,841 11	....
Claims settled and otherwise disposed of during the quarter ending September 30, 1868	3	42 000 00	$29,350 32
Claims undisposed of and remaining on hand September 30, 1868	80	839,841 11	....

4. *Oregon and Washington Indian war claims.*

	No.	Amount claimed.	Am't allowed.
Claims on hand undisposed of June 30, 1868	894	$108,373 32	....
Claims received during the quarter ending September 30, 1868	34	3,642 12	....
Claims settled and otherwise disposed of during the quarter ending September 30, 1868	30	8,599 03	$5,218 94
Claims on hand undisposed of September 30, 1868	898	103,416 41	....

Report of the Bureau of Refugees, Freedmen, and Abandoned Lands division.

The following is a report of the operations of the division engaged in the settlement of the accounts appertaining to the Bureau of Refugees, Freedmen, and Abandoned Lands, for the fiscal year ending the 30th June, 1868, and also for the quarter ending 30th September, 1868.

	Money accounts.		Property returns.	Provision returns.
	No.	Amount involved.		
On hand 30th June, 1867	380	$1,870,990 30	608	....
Received during the fiscal year, per detailed statement	187	3,545,760 17	2,402	513
	567	5,416,750 47	3,010	513
Reported during the fiscal year, per detailed statement	563	$5,370,574 12	2,960	513
On hand 30th June, 1868	4	$46,176 35	50	....
Received from June 30 to September 30, 1868	61	970,352 01	542	....
	65	1,016,528 36	592	....
Reported from June 30 to September 30, 1868	28	527,620 75	440	....
	37	488,907 61	152	....

Detailed statement.

	Money accounts.	Involving.	Property returns.
Received in July, 1867	26	$381,443 69	107
Received in August, 1867	21	465,604 52	186
Received in September, 1867			323
Received in October, 1867	32	629,579 85	208
Received in November, 1867	14	239,906 36	182
Received in December, 1867	21	405,666 28	103
Received in January, 1868	20	305,488 18	246
Received in February, 1868	16	248,884 78	194
Received in March, 1868	3	182,820 67	247
Received in April, 1868	13	170,210 57	167
Received in May, 1868	19	469,978 92	172
Received in June, 1868	2	46,176 35	202
	187	3,545,760 17	2,402
Reported in July, 1867	21	162,600 11	140
Reported in August, 1867	91	217,240 38	195
Reported in September, 1867	105	630,943 80	134
Reported in October, 1867	109	417,768 60	43
Reported in November, 1867	9	107,177 16	92
Reported in December, 1867	55	1,633,031 27	135
Reported in January, 1868	64	822,633 37	224
Reported in February, 1868	23	105,563 87	351
Reported in March, 1868	32	519,575 14	383
Reported in April, 1868	17	240,537 13	284
Reported in May, 1868	12	237,583 43	483
Reported in June, 1868	25	275,919 86	496
	563	5,370,574 12	2,960

PENSION DIVISION.

General report of the business of the pension division for the fiscal year ending 30th June, 1868.

	Number of accounts.	Amount involved.	Letters.	
			Received.	Written.
Accounts of agents on hand 1st July, 1867	401	$16,094,239 71		
Accounts received during the year	728	23,822,743 16		
Total	1,129	39,916,982 87	5,573	6,716
Accounts reported to Second Comptroller, as settled during the year	482	12,204,728 00		
Remaining unsettled 1st July, 1868	647	27,712,254 87		
Pension claims settled during the fiscal year	1,093	67,970 11		

Number of pensioners' names recorded and transferred, including those whose pensions have been increased during the year, 47,833.

General report of the business of the pension division for the quarter ending 30th September, 1868.

	Number of accounts.	Amount involved.	Letters.	
			Received.	Written.
Accounts of agents on hand July 1, 1868.	647	$27,712,254 87	....	....
Accounts of agents received during the quarter............................	172	1,799,630 60	....	....
Total..........................	819	29,511,885 47	1,011	1,292
Accounts reported to Second Comptroller during the quarter................	156	4,137,363 71	....	....
Remaining unsettled 1st October, 1868..	663	25,374,521 76	....	....
Pension claims settled during the quarter.	133	12,280 57	....	....

Number of pensioners' names recorded and transferred, including those whose pensions have been increased during the quarter, 47,139.

BOUNTY LAND DIVISION.

Report for the fiscal year ending June 30, 1868, of the "soldiers' claims and bounty land division."

During the fiscal year ending June 30, 1868, 915 bounty land claims, under the acts of Congress of September 28, 1850, and March 3, 1855, have been examined and returned to the Commissioner of Pensions under proper certificates.

Thirty-five invalid pension claims have been reported to the Commissioner of Pensions for his action.

A settlement was made in favor of the Soldiers' Home, or Military Asylum, for $21,294 50, being for arrears due and unpaid to deceased soldiers of the war of 1812, as appears by the records of this office.

Two hundred and fifteen letters were written on matters relating to the war of 1812 and the war of the Revolution.

The following is a report of the bounty land division of this office for the quarter ending 30th September, 1868, viz:

Two hundred and thirty-six bounty land claims examined and returned to the Commissioner of Pensions under proper certificates.

Nine invalid pension claims reported to the Commissioner of Pensions for his action.

Seventy-five letters written on subjects relating to the war of the Revolution and the war of 1812.

From the foregoing statements it will be perceived that the vast amount of business that accumulated in this office during the rebellion is being rapidly disposed of.

In the division of quartermasters' accounts, all the money accounts for 1865 and preceding years; all for 1866, except 18; all for 1867, except 122; and all for 1868, except 306, have been settled and disposed of.

There are, however, about 27,000 property accounts unsettled; but the clerks now in charge of the money accounts can soon be employed on the property accounts, when the latter will in like manner be rapidly disposed of.

All the accounts of the commissaries' division, except three for 1867, and

1,381 for 1868, have also been settled and disposed of. This division, in fact, is now about up to the peace standard.

In the engineers' division all the accounts have also been settled, except 16 for 1867, and 206 for 1868.

The State war claims division is progressing rapidly and satisfactorily in the settlement of the claims of the several States for money advanced and liabilities incurred in furnishing men and munitions of war to aid in suppressing the rebellion.

Much delay has arisen in disposing of this business by the peculiar and anomalous claims that have been presented.

At the breaking out of the rebellion but little was known among the authorities and people of the loyal States of military matters. When appeals were made by the lamented President Lincoln to those States for men and munitions of war, to save the very life of the nation, those appeals were responded to in the most prompt and patriotic manner, without reference or care for cost, so that the great object should be attained of preserving the Constitution and the Union. Being unacquainted, as already stated, with the laws and regulations of the War Department on such subjects, disbursements were made and liabilities incurred, to large amounts, that were not sanctioned by those laws and regulations; and as the accounting officers of the treasury are properly controlled and directed by these laws and regulations, they are compelled to disallow many such items of expenditure. It would seem but just, however, that the States should be refunded all moneys advanced by them, or for which they have become responsible, where such expenditures were pertinent to the great object of saving the nation in the day of its darkest and heaviest trial.

The business of the pension division of this office is already very heavy, and is rapidly increasing. There are now on the rolls of this office the following pensioners, viz:

Revolutionary—act of 4th July, 1836	1
" " 2d February, 1848	55
" " 29th July, 1848	45
" " 3d February, 1853	787
War of 1812, Florida war, Mexican war, and Indian and other wars	1,303
Invalid pensions—rebellion	74,782
Widows' pensions "	90,052
Making an aggregate of	167,025

And requiring for their payment the enormous sum of $23,658,598.

Large as the number is, and great the amount necessary to their payment, the numbers are constantly increasing, as 94,890, including children, were added to the list during the fiscal year ending 30th June, 1868.

While every patriotic heart earnestly desires that those who have been disabled in the service of their country shall be provided for, and the families also of those who laid down their lives a noble sacrifice on the altar of liberty, a just regard to the true interests of those beneficiaries and to the rest of our fellow-citizens requires that this just bounty of our country should not be abused. There can be but little doubt that many frauds have been and are being practiced upon the government under color of the pension laws, and effectual measures should be adopted to expose, punish and prevent those frauds. To this end the pension lists should first be purged; and when there is reason to believe that one person is drawing two or more pensions on wounds received at different times, or in different grades of service, such pensioner should be graded according to his highest rank, and greatest amount of disability, and no more. Where persons have been drawing pensions for different grades of disability, who have entirely recovered from their wounds, such persons should be stricken from the pension roll. When the rolls are thus purged, a commutation system might be introduced, especially with reference to the small pensions. In very many cases the few dollars paid biennially can be of but little benefit to the recipients, and, in fact, much of those small stipends is absorbed by agents. In such cases a reasonable sum in hand, calculated on the basis of life annuities, would be a substantial benefit, enabling the recipients to engage in small business, and relieving the country from a constantly accruing and onerous tax. When the list is thus reduced, the rest could be paid direct from the treasury, without the intervention of agents for the government or for the pensioners. Of course this process would require the employment of reliable and disinterested persons, and such legislation is recommended as will authorize their employment, and the whole proceedings herein suggested.

I would again respectfully renew the recommendation heretofore made, for the establishment of a Bureau or Commissioner of Claims, with authority to receive all that may be offered, and restricting the time in which those that arose under the recent rebellion should be presented. Such restriction should be accompanied with a provision forever barring those not presented within that time.

All claims thus presented should be docketed and arranged in classes. Those that can be disposed of under existing laws, to be settled and paid, or rejected. And here I would suggest that provision should be made that claims rejected on a fair hearing should not again be entertained by the executive officers, but should be left to the action of the Court of Claims, or of Congress. Where parties have had full opportunity to furnish all their testimony, and the case is taken up, examined and disposed of at their earnest instance, that should terminate the matter. But as matters now are, it is but the commencement; and it seems that some, if not many, persons only need to know what is required to prove the whole matter. It will be remembered that the testimony generally in these cases is *ex parte*, without an opportunity for government officers to cross-examine the witnesses. In many cases the testimony is evidently written out to meet the objections and carry the cases through, with blanks for names, dates, &c., and thus such claims are finally sustained. In others, witnesses flatly contradict their previous testimony, and frequently great anxiety is manifested to get copies of the testimony previously given, that the new evidence may not entirely controvert it. For these reasons the doctrine of *stare decisis* should be established and maintained. No apprehension need be entertained that meritorious cases would be rejected under such rule. When cases have merit, and claimants do not present them properly, the fullest opportunity is given to amend their record and complete their cases, so that justice may be done.

Where cases are presented that are not embraced by existing laws, but are meritorious, they should be docketed in like manner and reported to Congress, with the testimony; a brief accompanying each case, setting forth the facts in the case; the opinion of the examining office, and the reasons for that opinion.

Where cases are presented not embraced by existing laws, and are not meritorious, reports should in like manner be made to Congress, the cases being docketed, giving the reasons for the unfavorable action, with all the testimony. In this way the facts in the cases will be perpetuated, and the country be saved in the future hundreds of millions of dollars.

The experience of the past fully justifies the necessity and propriety of a statute of limitation to all claims against the government, and of securing the testimony in relation to all such as exist within a reasonable time, and while the facts are attainable. Even now claims for services, &c., in the revolutionary war are frequently arising, where from lapse of time, destruction or decay of records, or total want of knowledge where to look for the facts, effectually prevent the refutation of any statement that may be made. When, in like manner, years shall have elapsed, and by no means the number that have passed since the Revolution, claims will be brought forward for property taken or destroyed during the recent rebellion, and in all probability the least worthy will be the best sustained and first paid. The experience of over the third of a century, in the examination of claims, causes me to urge this matter on your serious attention.

The law division of this office has charge of the settlement or collection of outstanding balances reported to be due on a final statement of their accounts, from quartermasters, commissaries, pension agents, officers of the engineer corps acting as disbursing agents of the government, who, on ceasing to disburse public moneys, are found in default on such statements of their accounts, as also of contractors who have failed to fulfil their contracts for army supplies, &c.

In such cases the operations of this division involve chiefly a correspondence with the delinquent officer, or sureties to his official bond, with a view to an amicable adjustment of the claims of the United States, and also the preparation of transcripts and briefs for suits, when so ordered by the Second Comptroller of the Treasury.

The number of letters embraced in such correspondence during the past year was 157 written and 83 received. The number of bonds notified, registered and filed, 23. The number of cases referred here for special action amounted to 85.

The balances charged as outstanding in these cases when they were thus referred amounted in the aggregate to the sum of $1,003,769 67. Of these, 19 have been reported "closed," covering an aggregate of $305,610 27. In 20 of them further special statements have been made on corrected vouchers and explanations of "disallowances," and the reduction of indebtedness amounted in the aggregate to the sum of $249,716 22, making in the whole a reduction of the indebtedness in the sum of $555,326 49; thus leaving an aggregate of balances unsettled of $448,443 18.

Most of the cases in which these balances occur are now either with the accounting divisions of this bureau for special statement, on further papers and explanations furnished, or with the Second Comptroller on such statements reported to him, and I am informed will be largely reduced, if not entirely closed on such statements.

Two of the 85 cases above enumerated are before Congress, one before the Court of Claims, one reported for suit, and five, parties "not found."

In February, 1868, a claim was referred here from the War Department for suit against John C. Reeside, of Baltimore, Maryland, contractor, for non-fulfilment of his contract, amounting to $106,877 30. It was referred from this to the claims division for special statement, preliminary to a call upon the sureties to his bond for its adjustment. Since then it is understood that an application had been made by the contractor and his sureties to Congress for relief in the premises, and that the papers had all been sent to "the committee" having it in charge. Proceedings here were in consequence suspended.

The tabular form of the foregoing statements may be rendered thus, viz:

Number of letters written		157
Number of letters received		83
Bonds notified, registered, and filed		23
Cases referred here and acted upon		85
Amount charged as outstanding when referred		$1,003,769 67
Cases closed, amount	$305,610 27	
Cases reduced on settlements, amount	249,716 22	
		555,326 49
Balances unsettled, aggregate		448,443 18

I beg leave to call your attention to the suggestions heretofore made, of a modification of the manner of liquidating the obligations of the government.

By the present mode of advancing large amounts to disbursing officers very considerable portions of the funds of the government must lie dormant in the hands of those officers, or in the depositories wherein they are placed, while the temptation is ever present of using those funds, resulting sooner or later in some defalcations. To obviate these evils provision could be made by law that all purchases for government use should be made by officers designated for that purpose, either by contracts, after due public notice, or in the open market, as now provided by law. These purchasing officers should report the accounts for the articles purchased, with duplicates of the contracts or agreement, to another class of officers, also specially designated as receiving officers, who should certify on those accounts that the articles therein designated of the quality and quantity specified had been received. The accounts thus certified should be transmitted to the department on whose account the articles were purchased; and after receiving the administrative examination of that department, should be transmitted to the proper auditing officer. After receiving the necessary examination by such auditing office they should be referred to the proper Comptroller, and on being admitted and certified by him, should be sent to the Treasurer, by whom a draft should be sent to the creditor of the government. The Auditor, Comptroller, and Treasurer could make up their accounts quarterly of the money thus paid out, submit them to the First Comptroller, and on his certificate the amounts could be entered by the Register.

This would obviate the necessity of keeping any money accounts, except against the appropriations; and as the property purchased would be charged against the receiving officers, their accounts for property would be all that would require subsequent adjustment, and in those there is but little risk of loss. The manner of relieving this objection in pension accounts has already been considered.

The following statements, marked A, B, and C, have been prepared with much care, showing the operations of this office by calendar years from 1820 to 1860, both inclusive, the latter being about the beginning of the rebellion; and from 1861 to the 30th September, 1868.

—*Statement of fiscal operations of Third Auditor's office from January 1, 1820, to January 1, 1861; also amounts of accounts settled during said period.*

Year.	Amount drawn out of the treasury in each year.	Amount advanced to disbursing officers, agents, and States in each year.	Amount of claims paid in each year.	Amount of counter requisitions issued in favor of Treasurer of the United States during each year.	Amount of transfers in settlements in each year.	Amount of deposits in each year.	Amount of requisitions and treasury drafts cancelled in each year.	Amount of accounts settled of advances made to disbursing officers, agents, and States in each year.	Am't of accounts settled of advances made to disbursing officers, agents, and States under the provisions of the act of May 1, 1820, settled under the general head of "arrearages" in each year	Amount of accounts settled under the provisions of the act of March 2, 1855, on account of civil fund of California.	Amount of accounts settled under the provisions of the act of March 3, 1849, on account of military contributions in Mexico.	Amount of accounts settled of claims allowed and paid out of the appropriation pertaining thereto.
1820	$3,752,527 78	$3,585,487 62	$167,040 16					$4,567,699 11	$8,680,190 83			$167,040 16
1821	2,971,240 49	2,830,675 55	140,564 94					4,356,271 72	7,615,737 24			140,564 94
1822	3,496,635 76	3,392,532 47	104,103 29	$62,209 34				3,504,181 28	2,504,034 99			104,103 29
1823	3,108,101 12	3,007,888 37	100,212 75	166,056 69				2,537,098 98	2,118,509 86			100,212 75
1824	2,913,613 61	2,831,519 25	82,094 36	63,930 63				3,438,545 93	283,280 45			82,094 36
1825	3,487,091 99	3,410,600 87	76,491 12	404,985 98	$100,330 80	$304,655 18		3,359,777 27	107,916 19			76,491 12
1826	3,558,052 16	3,427,502 23	130,549 93	128,938 88	33,443 67	95,495 21		3,225,524 02	146,345 37			130,549 93
1827	2,920,829 84	2,871,393 80	49,436 04	95,406 28	80,649 06	14,737 22		3,702,070 27	94,123 53			49,436 04
1828	2,786,496 68	2,743,402 09	41,094 59	89,137 98	58,699 66	30,438 32		2,822,182 22	33,728 48			41,094 59
1829	3,401,822 24	3,362,476 02	39,346 22	112,756 61	41,093 45	71,663 16		3,608,630 64	28,646 86			39,346 22
1830	4,031,580 44	3,897,491 70	134,088 74	32,703 87	25,276 43	7,427 44		3,083,130 73	46,464 92			134,088 74
1831	4,014,144 40	3,988,898 15	25,246 25	136,468 45	115,718 22	20,750 23		4,658,610 45	45,128 67			25,246 25
1832	4,070,836 27	4,002,509 83	68,326 44	115,356 31	96,631 47	18,724 84		3,506,297 28	52,844 28			68,326 44
1833	8,288,739 94	8,251,135 64	37,604 30	292,005 56	262,145 00	29,860 56		4,944,648 16	61,632 69			37,604 30
1834	6,560,246 57	6,495,846 13	64,400 44	126,705 51	102,691 04	24,014 47		5,652,843 81	65,678 87			60,400 44
1835	5,263,364 84	5,213,914 95	49,449 89	149,450 94	136,617 28	12,833 66		6,969,538 56	20,165 07			49,449 89
1836	10,081,515 96	9,972,672 04	108,843 88	316,952 89	299,186 07	17,766 82		6,535,253 74	8,844 03			107,843 88
1837	11,939,359 56	11,847,530 48	91,829 08	713,678 90	644,065 43	69,613 47		9,270,056 94	40,397 96			91,829 08
1838	11,655,932 34	11,360,151 64	295,780 70	1,224,025 68	1,160,695 52	63,330 16		11,888,567 17	20,617 25			295,780 70
1839	9,649,046 92	9,288,261 67	360,785 25	1,123,422 29	947,434 07	175,988 22		10,113,979 06	6,344 34			360,785 25
1840	6,033,667 57	5,897,181 46	136,486 11	682,895 44	630,678 93	52,216 51		8,559,130 53	2,275 64			136,486 11
1841	7,675,509 37	7,514,140 52	161,368 85	676,451 23	655,110 76	21,340 47		7,222,605 46	861 17			161,368 85
1842	4,467,795 28	4,321,325 20	146,470 08	396,774 86	383,667 25	13,107 61		5,000,790 71	10,953 32			146,470 08
1843	5,389,491 86	5,279,721 41	109,770 45	774,130 45	732,242 84	41,887 61		7,776,813 23	147 58			109,770 45
1844	4,782,116 11	4,701,608 17	80,507 94	516,417 42	511,196 07	5,221 35		5,165,361 32				80,507 94
1845	5,888,575 89	5,719,098 56	169,477 33	483,414 38	441,852 21	41,562 17		5,373,733 05	90 00			169,477 33
1846	15,342,829 14	15,245,311 59	97,517 55	404,018 97	376,644 83	27,374 14		5,589,579 20				97,517 55
1847	25,181,061 22	24,942,637 04	238,424 18	646,957 02	613,455 02	33,502 00		11,204,746 86				238,424 18
1848	15,328,858 62	15,059,860 06	268,998 56	2,050,994 10	2,014,330 34	36,663 76		9,063,493 63				268,998 56
1849	7,411,947 96	7,053,205 46	358,742 50	1,254,715 35	1,247,514 04	7,201 31		8,745,513 45	1,323 28		$1,887,482 46	358,742 50
1850	9,061,275 13	8,701,622 91	359,652 22	2,070,172 96	2,056,905 13	13,267 83		12,398,178 35			211,101 21	359,652 22
1851	13,119,113 81	12,943,498 11	175,615 70	686,114 65	208,203 11	477,911 54		11,639,127 50	447 20		369,812 44	175,615 70

Statement of fiscal operations of Third Auditor's office from January 1, 1820, &c.—Continued.

Year.	Amount drawn out of the treasury in each year.	Amount advanced to disbursing officers, agents, and States in each year.	Amount of claims paid in each year.	Amount of counter requisitions issued in favor of Treasurer of the United States during each year.	Amount of transfers in settlements in each year.	Amount of deposits in each year.	Amount of requisitions and treasury drafts cancelled in each year.	Amount of accounts settled of advances made to disbursing officers, agents, and States in each year.	Am't of accounts settled of advances made to disbursing officers, ag'ts, & States under the provisions of the act of May 1, 1820, settled under the general head of "arrearages" in each year.	Amount of accounts settled under the provisions of the act of March 2, 1853, on account of civil fund of California.	Amount of accounts settled under the provisions of the act of March 3, 1849, on account of military contributions in Mexico.	Amount of accounts settled of claims allowed and paid out of the appropriation pertaining thereto.
1852	$6,058,073 60	$5,903,823 89	$154,249 11	$4,590,655 44	$4,553,984 24	$36,671 20	....	$7,453,925 23	....	....	$286,774 18	$154,249 11
1853	14,681,533 88	14,400,626 28	280,907 60	674,256 68	605,539 75	68,716 93	....	14,661,044 33	$137 80	....	160,808 09	280,907 60
1854	12,802,262 94	12,544,189 80	258,073 14	8,657,404 73	8,615,403 84	42,000 89	....	19,474,148 90	147 75	....	261,570 52	258,073 14
1855	17,083,529 28	16,704,147 00	379,382 28	3,975,832 67	3,780,528 94	195,303 73	....	13,359,300 93	14,279 58	$623,057 35	98,141 68	379,382 28
1856	14,102,031 70	13,120,758 32	981,273 38	2,630,785 23	2,544,642 66	86,142 57	....	16,440,291 89	68,392 78	4,659 44	331,300 21	981,273 38
1857	17,569,858 66	17,242,766 42	327,092 24	1,935,805 56	1,794,685 73	141,119 83	....	14,606,563 16	5,385 00	420 75	190,659 10	327,092 24
1858	23,110,381 57	22,584,503 19	525,878 38	1,080,068 94	973,684 81	106,384 13	....	15,382,245 13	....	525 00	15,937 27	525,878 38
1859	14,109,003 88	13,927,118 34	181,885 54	1,748,351 81	1,716,220 18	32,131 63	....	20,535,395 48	....	715 19	98,038 28	181,885 54
1860	10,539,647 25	10,352,388 88	187,258 37	1,115,718 57	942,819 00	172,899 57	....	15,578,738 07	....	55	13,076 80	187,358 37
	357,689,742 99	349,943,423 11	7,746,319 88	42,406,129 25	39,503,886 85	2,609,945 74	....	337,015,633 75	22,085,092 98	629,378 26	3,924,702 24	7,746,319 88

B.—*From January 1, 1861, to September 30, 1868.*

Year.	Amount drawn out of the treasury in each year.	Amount advanced to disbursing officers, agents, and States in each year.	Amount of claims paid in each year.	Amount of counter requisitions issued in favor of Treasurer of the United States during each year.	Amount of transfers in settlements in each year.	Amount of deposits in each year.	Amount of requisitions and treasury drafts cancelled in each year.	Amount of accounts settled of advances made to disbursing officers, agents, and States in each year.	Am't of accounts settled of advances made to disbursing officers, ag'ts, & States under the provisions of the act of May 1, 1820, settled under the general head of "arrearages" in each year.	Amount of accounts settled under the provisions of the act of March 2, 1853, on account of civil fund of California.	Amount of accounts settled under the provisions of the act of March 3, 1849, on account of military contributions in Mexico.	Amount of accounts settled of claims allowed and paid out of the appropriation pertaining thereto.
1861	$12,223,347 81	$12,183,724 49	$39,623 32	$1,965,108 68	$1,126,616 15	$838,492 53	....	$12,657,121 87	....	....	$432 41	$39,623 32
1862	232,655,673 35	227,259,721 34	5,395,952 01	1,448,216 28	588,829 83	38,365 90	$821,021 25	16,944,573 84	....	....	....	5,395,952 01
1863	319,718,985 76	317,265,409 14	2,453,576 62	606,807 53	202,336 11	203,656 42	200,815 00	29,286,842 57	....	....	....	2,453,576 62
1864	432,270,588 96	431,025,998 32	1,244,590 64	572,546 57	198,083 21	218,779 55	155,683 81	94,814,773 53	....	....	....	1,244,590 64
1865	607,769,067 74	604,546,485 34	3,222,582 40	2,120,023 80	201,961 64	482,487 16	1,435,575 00	237,935,303 03	....	....	....	3,222,582 40
1866	90,200,402 40	87,771,416 66	2,428,985 74	17,594,592 93	7,846,127 99	9,316,830 19	431,634 84	377,355,469 01	....	....	....	2,428,985 74
1867	97,843,931 34	93,377,241 55	4,466,689 79	16,707,893 68	13,412,651 70	3,284,057 98	11,184 00	295,907,387 99	....	....	....	4,466,689 79
1868	101,552,446 48	96,916,296 70	4,636,149 78	21,689,574 04	14,136,902 62	7,487,773 42	64,898 00	434,577,597 74	....	....	....	4,636,149 78
(*)	25,686,711 18	25,051,972 86	634,738 32	4,498,945 24	3,766,416 14	722,529 55	....	73,422,603 24	....	....	....	634,738 32
	1,919,921,155 02	1,895,398,266 40	24,522,888 62	67,193,709 45	40,479,925 30	22,592,972 70	3,120,791 90	1,672,901,672 82	....	....	432 41	24,522,888 62

* From July 1 to September 30, 1868.

C.—*Comparative statement of amount of business done in Third Auditor's office during the incumbency of present Auditor and previously.*

In the following table the results of the forty-one years are placed in one column, and of the seven years and nine months opposite, that the proportion of the business done in the two periods may be apparent, as follows, to wit:

	From 1820 to 1860, both inclusive, a period of 41 years.	From January 1861, to September 30, 1868, a period of seven years and nine months.
Amount of accounts settled of advances made to disbursing officers, agents, and States	$337,015,633 75	$1,672,901,672 82
Amount drawn out of the treasury	357,689,742 99	1,919 921,155 02
Amount advanced to disbursing officers, agents, and States	349,943,423 11	1,895,398,266 40
Amount of claims	7,746,319 88	24,522,888 62
Amount of counter requisitions issued in favor of the Treasurer of the United States	42,406,129 25	67,193,709 45
Amount of transfers in settlements	39,503,886 85	40,479,925 30
Amount of deposits	2,609,945 74	22,592,972 70
Amount of requisitions and treasury drafts cancelled	....	3,120,791 90
Amount of accounts settled of advances made to disbursing officers, agents, and States under the provisions of the act of May 1, 1820, settled under the head of "Arrearages"	22,085,092 98	....
Amount of accounts settled under the provisions of the act of March 2, 1855, on account of civil fund of California	629,378 28	....
Amount of accounts settled under the provisions of the act of March 3, 1849, on account of military contributions in Mexico	3,924,702 24	432 41
Amount of accounts settled of claims allowed and paid out of the appropriations pertaining thereto.	7,746,319 88	24,522,888 62

From the last table, which in fact is but a condensation of the two preceding statements, it will be perceived that nearly five times the amount of accounts have been settled of advances made to disbursing officers since the commencement of the rebellion that were settled in 41 years prior thereto. More than five times the amount of money has been drawn out of the treasury and advanced to disbursing officers, and more than three times the amount of claims has been settled and paid, &c. In fact, since the commencement of the fourth quarter of the calendar year 1864, when I took charge of this office, nearly $1,443,000,000 of accounts have been settled of advances made to disbursing agents and States, against $467,000,000 previously settled, running back to 1820. $15,700,000 of claims have been settled and paid, against $16,561,000 previously settled and paid; and $1,031,120,000 have been drawn out of the treasury, against $1,246,390,000 previously drawn out, also running back to 1820.

This vast amount of business has been transacted by the intelligence, ability, and industry of the clerks in this office. It is but justice to these gentlemen to say that with few exceptions they labor with as much zeal, take as much pride in the prompt and efficient discharge of their duties, and manifest as much talent as if the public business was their own private matters, and by the prompt and efficient discharge of it they would realize fortunes. All this, too, for compensations, wholly inadequate in many cases, should not continue; and I most earnestly and respectfully recommend that the reorganization measures now before Congress be pressed upon the attention of that body, that some little better compensation be made them for their noble and able efforts, though the salaries therein specified are far below their just deserts.

Since the passage of the act of 30th March, 1868, to amend the act entitled "An act to provide for the prompt settlement of public accounts," approved March 3, 1817, the provisions of that amendatory law have been fully carried out by this department. The accounting officers of the treasury have faithfully discharged the duties confided to them, and in each case have reported the amount found justly due by the government to claimants, according to their best judgment. I am aware, however, that where a difference of opinion has existed at the War Department in some of these cases, though requisitions have been promptly issued, as directed by that amendatory law, they were so issued as a matter of duty, and with that reluctance that always springs from compulsory action against one's judgment. It is the earnest wish and desire of this office that the utmost harmony shall exist among all the offices and departments charged with this duty, as we are all influenced by the single desire to pay all just demands against the government, and to prevent the recognition of fraudulent and erroneous claims. In performing this duty a difference of opinion will almost necessarily spring up in some cases. The accounting officers of the treasury, acting on their best judgments, may allow a claim. The Secretary of War, who is charged with the custody of the appropriations from which such claim is to be paid, may differ in opinion from the accounting officers, and yet, under the amendatory act of 1868, he must pay it. This is in direct conflict with the spirit and intent of the decision of the Supreme Court of the United States at the December term of 1855, in the case of the United States *vs.* Jones. (Howard's Reports, vol. 18, page 92.) In that case the court awarded very high and broad powers to the Secretary of the Navy, to the extent, indeed, of placing the appropriations at his discretion, independent of the accounting officers. On the other hand, in the case of Kendall *vs.* The United States, decided at the December term of 1838, (12 Curtis, p. 834,) and of Kendall *vs.* Stockton and Stokes, (3 Howard, p. 87,) the court held that the executive act was performed by the Solicitor of the Treasury, and the payment of the money by the Postmaster General was a mere ministerial act, and therefore subject to the mandamus by which Mr. Kendall was required to pay the amount. There can be no doubt that Congress had the power to pass the act of 1868, but I would respectfully and earnestly suggest that measures be adopted to remove this cause of difficulty, by relieving the Secretary of War of the responsibility of the care and custody of the money in such cases, or that all such cases be referred to the Court of Claims for adjudication before payment.

I beg leave to submit the accompanying statement of balances that have remained on the books of this office since 1st July, 1815, and which had been accruing previous thereto as far back as May, 1792. As far as I can ascertain, there is not the slightest probability that any of this money will ever be recovered, and I respectfully recommend that the books of this office be closed, so far as those balances are concerned, and that the list be filed in the office of the Solicitor of the Treasury for such action from time to time hereafter as that officer may direct.

Respectfully submitted:

JOHN WILSON, *Auditor.*

Hon. HUGH MCCULLOCH,

Statement of balances standing at the debit of the following persons on the books of the Third Auditor, arising out of advances made between May, 1792, and July 1, 1815, and in pursuance of the act of May 1, 1820, brought down under the head of arrearages, and when collected to be carried to the surplus fund in the treasury.

Pages.	Name.	Rank.	Amount.	Remarks.
				Arrearages:
185	David Allison		$4,236 37	Transferred from treasury June 30, 1822.
189	Presley Neville	Lieutenant	46 81	Do. do.
193	James Collins	do	1,600 00	Do. do.
220	John Sevier	Brigadier general	1,602 73	Balance November 25, 1792.
221	Richard Butler	do	200 00	Amount transferred from treasury June 30, 1822.
228	John Clarke	Major	11 08	Balance May 13, 1803.
230	John McMickle	Ensign	20 00	Balance January 1, 1820.
236	Robert Thompson	Lieutenant infantry	170 00	Balance December 1, 1803.
247	Wm. Davidson	Lieutenant cavalry	155 95	Transferred from treasury June 30, 1822.
248	Wm. A. Lee	do	430 33	Transferred from treasury September 17, 1816.
251	I. F. Hamtramck	Major	430 69	Transferred from treasury June 30, 1822.
253	Ballard Smith	Captain	107 38	Do. do.
254	Archibald Gray	Ensign	211 69	Do. do.
257	Wm. Buchanan	Captain	300 59	Do. do.
261	John Steele	Lieutenant	28 36	Do. do.
261	Samuel Drake	Ensign	50 00	Do. do.
263	Ebenezer Massey	Lieutenant artillery	671 41	Do. do.
265	James Wells	Captain	293 60	Do. do.
273	Jacob Melcher	Lieutenant	138 92	Do. do.
274	Thosas Hughes	Captain	31 36	Balance January 1, 1820.
275	Wm. Miller	Ensign	70 00	Do. do.
283	Howell Lewis	Captain	188 03	Transferred from treasury June 30, 1822.
283	John Tillinghast	Ensign	34 11	Do. do.
288	John Guthrie	Captain	91 89	Do. do.
290	John Rucastle	do	460 10	Do. do.
292	John Cumming	Lieutenant rifles	255 11	Balance January 1, 1820.
297	Joseph Brock	Captain	320 80	Transferred from treasury June 30, 1822.
300	John Paine	Ensign	1,013 15	Do. do.
329	Joseph Strong	Surgeon	31 66	Do. do.
356	Charles Wright	Ensign	13,706 19	Do. do.
368	George Baynton		45 05	Do. do.

				Arrearages:
392	John Edwards	Lieutenant	$528 07	Transferred from treasury June 30, 1822.
393	Thomas Bodley	Ensign	500 00	Do. do.
398	Robert Semple	do	300 00	Do. do.
417	George Taylor	Captain	320 00	Do. do.
424	Wm. A. Lee	do	500 00	Balance January 1, 1820.
426	Yelverton Peyton	Ensign	45 39	Transferred from treasury June 30, 1822.
437	Wm. Lawton	Surgeon	301 00	Do. do.
438	John Toomy	Sergt. major	5 41	Balance January 1, 1820.
453	Wm. Nicholson	Deputy paymaster	1,506 60	Transferred from treasury June 30, 1822.
460	Benjamin Rand	Ensign	160 00	Balance January 1, 1820.
479	James Dunham	Major	2,432 94	Do. do.
503	Paul McDermott	Cornet	272 00	Transferred from treasury June 30, 1822.
506	Wm. A. McCrea	Surgeon's mate	80 95	Do do.
512	Wm. Rickard	Captain	1,016 70	Do. do.
518	John W. Thompson	Ensign	16 87	Balance January 1, 1820.
706	Isaac Craig	Deputy paymaster	1,857 89	Amount advanced by Jno. Wilkins in 1842.
713	Samuel Lewis, senior	Clerk War Office	2,565 55	Balance January 1, 1820, dead and insolvent.
763	John Wilkins, jr	Quartermaster General	17 21	Balance November 12, 1842.
817	Stephen Hillis	Deputy paymaster	243 45	Transferred from treasury June 30, 1822.
828	John Armstrong	Captain	10 36	Balance January 1, 1820.
829	Thomas Doyle	Captain	91 57	Do. do.
834	James Lanier	Paymaster	212 31	Transferred from treasury June 30, 1822.
835	Joseph Dickinson	Lieutenant	360 19	Do. do
838	Wm. P. Smith	Ensign	454 66	Do. do.
840	Hamilton Armstrong	do	56 00	Balance January 1, 1820.
840	Thomas Pasteur	Lieutenant	661 22	Transferred from treasury June 30, 1822,
844	Robert Parkisen	do	334 22	Do. do.
854	Samuel Tinsley	do	13 00	Do. do.
856	John McClary	Ensign	623 94	Do. do.
865	Larkin Dickinson	do	88 67	Do. do.
871	Resin Webster	Lieutenant	256 01	Balance January 1, 1820.
876	Stephen G. Simmons	do	1,129 13	Transferred from treasury June 30, 1822.

907	James Read	Captain	248 00	Do. do.
924	Henry Glen	Agent	3,350 30	Transferred from treasury June 30, 1822.
927	Jno. Furgus	Lieutenant	39 72	Balance January 1, 1820.
955	Lewis Landais		56 00	Do. do.
965	Garrett Pendergrast	Surgeon's mate	3 82	Do. do.
969	Daniel Newman	Lieutenant 4th infantry	149 50	Transferred from treasury June 30, 1822.
974	Samuel Seton	Quartermaster	26 33	Do. do.
974	John Leybourn	Lieutenant artillery	141 56	Balance January 1, 1820.
975	Benj. Williamson	Captain cavalry	2,515 56	Transferred from treasury June 30, 1822.
995	Samuel Bent	Lieutenant	3,172 53	Balance October 30, 1823.
1004	Leonard Williams	do	211 17	Balance January 1, 1820.
1008	Wm. Yates	do	555 00	Transferred from treasury June 30, 1822.
1029	Wm. A. Rogers	Contractor	77 88	Do. do.
1041	Rufus Graves	Lieutenant	39 90	Do. do.
1049	James Taylor	Captain	341 50	Do. do.
1051	Samuel Allenson	Ensign	96 75	Do. do.
1056	Philemon C. Blake	Lieutenant	4 00	Balance January 1, 1820.
1058	Samuel McGuire	do	145 50	Do. do.
1058	Thomas Lee	do	612 00	Do. do.
1062	Archibald Crary	Agent	10 57	Balance June 30, 1856.
1065	Archibald Lee	do	47 50	Balance June 7, 1825.
1069	Abner Prior	Captain	41 60	Balance January 1, 1820.
1073	Aaron Gregg	Lieutenant	477 49	Transferred from treasury June 30, 1822.
1074	George Strother	Ensign	180 00	Do. do.
1079	Jno. B. Armistead	Captain	100 00	Balance January 1, 1820.
1081	Jno. F. Powell	Lieutenant	10 52	Do. do.
1088	J. W. Hocker		20 84	Transferred from treasury June 30, 1822.
1354	Owen Evans	Contractor	3 34	Do. do.
1361	Samuel Clinton	Lieutenant	120 00	Do. do.
1364	Cornelius Lyman	Captain	312 75	Do. do.
1369	George Salmon	Lieutenant	286 90	Do. do.
1372	Michael McKewan & Co	Contractors	623 89	Do. do.
1377	Michael McKewan & Co.	do	276 87	Do. do.
1380	John B. Barnes	Lieutenant	1,609 67	Balance June 11, 1827.
1386	Seymour Rennut	do	68 00	Balance January 1, 1820.
1393	Edward Milton	Captain	10 97	Transferred from treasury June 30, 1822.
1396	Enos Noland	Lieutenant	35 23	Balance January 1, 1820.
1406	Dodridge Crocker		163 34	Do. do.
1417	John A. Davidson		197 47	Transferred from treasury June 30, 1822.
1429	George Y. Ross	Ensign	2 00	Do. do.
1434	Ephraim Emery	Lieutenant	120 12	Balance January 1, 1820.

Statement of balances standing at the debit of the following persons on the books of the Third Auditor, &c.—Continued.

	Name.	Rank.	Amount.	Remarks.
				Arrearages:
1445	Benjamin Price	Captain	$3,192 53	Transferred from treasury June 30, 1822.
1447	Jacob Blount		750 00	Balance January 1, 1820.
1451	John Saxon	Lieutenant	121 00	Do. do.
1451	John Horton	do	18 00	Do. do.
1455	Hannibal M. Allen	Cadet	15 21	Do. do.
1457	George Waterbouse	Lieutenant	260 28	Do. do.
1470	John Frantz		100 00	Transferred from treasury June 30, 1822.
1472	Cord N. Daniell	Surgeon's mate	45 75	Balance January 1, 1820.
1477	John Wade	Captain	5,905 88	Transferred from treasury June 30, 1822.
1485	Joseph Cross	Lieutenant	88 72	Balance January 1, 1820.
1487	Peter Lamkin	do	208 00	Do. do.
1492	Ferdinand S. Claiborne		500 00	Do. do.
1500	Matthew Lyon	Contractor	28 61	Transferred from treasury June 30, 1822.
1504	Thomas Davis	do	300 00	Do. do.
1507	John Smith	do	21,869 38	Do. do.
1512	Charles M. Taylor	Lieutenant	39 00	Balance January 1, 1820.
1517	Barth Homistead	do	337 94	Transferred from treasury June 30, 1822.
1518	Carey Clarke	do	32 32	Balance January 1, 1820.
1518	Michael Kalteison		123 40	Do. do.
1528	George Salmon	Paymaster	22,797 85	Do. do.
1531	Adrian Hunn	do militia	346 44	Transferred from treasury June 30, 1822.
1532	Paul McDermott	do	11,641 72	Balance January 1, 1820.
1544	Thomas Lawrence	do	7,795 69	Do. do.
1544	William Dayton	do	12,021 06	Do. do.
1546	Thomas Robinson	do	7,625 32	Do. do.
1546	Joseph March	do	3,045 60	Do. do.
1551	John C. Symes	Ensign	38 91	Do. do.
1559	James Logan	do	353 45	Do. do.
1562	John Glasco		300 00	Do. do.
1567	John Smith	Contractor	224 86	Transferred from treasury June 30, 1822.
1570	James McKellar	Lieutenant	569 93	Do do.
1578	Abner Woodruff	Paymaster	16,731 87	Balance January 1, 1820.

1595	Robert Ritchie	Lieutenant	3,622 03	Transferred from treasury June 30, 1822.
1597	John Smith	Contractor	1,766 00	Do. do.
1604	William Hall	....do	3,000 00	Do. do.
1612	James Bludworth	Lieutenant	68 88	Balance January 1, 1820.
1614	John V. Duforest	Ensign	8 60	Do. do.
1619	Joseph Kimball	Lieutenant	1,624 30	Do. do.
1622	Thomas Clements	Ensign	6 06	Do. do.
1625	Robert Williams	Governor	324 12	Do. do.
1636	John Smith	Contractor	1,892 93	Transferred from treasury June 30, 1822.
1940	Charles Magnan	Ensign	31 09	Balance January 1, 1820.
1949	James S. Smith	Lieutenant	1,803 55	Do. do.
1949	Alfred Sebastian	....do	300 00	Do. do.
1951	Robert W. Osborne	....do	158 79	Do. do.
1950	Francis Newman	....do	12 00	Do. do.
1955	William C. Mead	Ensign	196 11	Do. do.
1959	William F. Ware	....do	4 50	Do. do.
1961	John Milliken	Express	100 00	Do. do.
1961	Jacob Jackson	Lieutenant	24 53	Do. do.
1962	Josiah Taylor	Lieut. and asst. military agent.	34,425 66	Transferred from treasury June 30, 1822.
1963	Robert Peyton	Ensign	50 00	Do. do.
1964	John Roney	....do	500 00	Balance January 1, 1820.
2000	Hugh Philips	Colonel Virginia militia	934 64	Transferred from treasury June 30, 1822.
2008	A. B. Armistead	Captain	48 00	Balance January 1, 1820.
2008	Jonathan Robeson	....do	54 64	Transferred from treasury June 30, 1822.
2027	William C. Baen	....do	486 00	Balance January 1, 1820.
2030	David Byres	....do	619 20	Transferred from treasury, June 30, 1822.
2031	William Hutchins	....do	19 48	Balance January 1, 1820.
2034	William N. Irvine	....do	330 49	Do. do.
2035	Richard Dale	....do	21 41	Do. do.
2035	Alex. F. Rose	....do	105 60	Do. do.
2036	Solomon D. Townsend	....do	447 65	Do. do.
2037	Thomas Anderson	....do	1,600 82	Transferred from treasury June 30, 1822.
2037	John Ragan	....do	232 82	Balance January 1, 1820.
2042	Thomas Made	....do	900 28	Do. do.
2042	Nathan N. Wright	....do	908 00	Transferred from treasury June 30, 1822.
2043	William P. Bennet	....do	2,176 10	Do. do.
2045	Samuel Cherry	....do	2,144 24	Balance January 1, 1820.
2049	James T. Bowie	Lieutenant	600 00	Do. do.
2054	Mosman Houstoun	Captain	668 50	Do. do.
2057	Edward Taylor	....do	801 70	Do. do.
2058	James Hanna	Lieutenant colonel militia	6,050 25	Do. do.

				Arrearages:
2058	Maurice Beesby	Captain	$873 02	Balance January 1, 1820.
2059	Walter Evans	Paymaster	7,388 64	Do. do.
2060	Daniel May	Lieutenant colonel militia	4,789 05	Do. do.
2061	Ebenezer Finley	Paymaster militia	2,686 30	Do. do.
2062	Thomas Foster	do	6,086 46	Do. do.
2063	John Greer	do	2,791 96	Do. do.
2064	Jeremiah Mosher	Lieutenant colonel militia	4,425 53	Do. do.
2064	Edward Duffield	Paymaster militia	10,576 92	Do. do.
2065	Stephen Stevenson	Lieutenant colonel militia	1,402 61	Do. do.
2065	Kearney Wharton	Paymaster militia	15,971 14	Do. do.
2066	John Light	Major militia	1,835 10	Do. do.
2066	George Eddy	Paymaster militia	6,949 13	Do. do.
2067	William Henderson	Captain militia	243 03	Do. do.
2067	William Harris	Paymaster militia	9,544 37	Do. do.
2068	Samuel Everitt	Major militia	2,105 21	Do. do.
2068	George Fisher	do	1,221 66	Do. do.
2069	Thomas Elder	Paymaster militia	2,211 15	Do. do.
2072	James R. Peyton	Lieutenant	2 00	Do. do.
2074	Isaiah Doane	Captain	35 73	Do. do.
2075	Elijah Craig	do	476 00	Transferred from treasury June 30, 1822.
2078	Thomas Van Dyke	do	872 64	Do. do.
2079	George W. Prescott	do	882 14	Balance January 1, 1820.
2080	Moses Whitney	do	846 33	Do. do.
2081	David Findley	do	179 43	Do. do.
2082	Prentis Law	do	146 00	Do. do.
2084	Benj. Walton	do	715 19	Do. do.
2085	John Saunders		3,877 66	Transferred from treasury June 30, 1822.
2089	Ross Bird	Captain	151 63	Balance January 1, 1820.
2089	Arthur Morgan	do	600 00	Transferred from treasury June 30, 1822.
2090	Alexander S. Lyle	Lieutenant	960 00	Do. do.
2101	Thomas Davis	Captain	20	Balance January 1, 1820.
2111	Le Roy Opie	Lieutenant	205 62	Do. do.

2121	Fielder Ridgway	Captain	137 40	Do.	do.
2127	Joseph Constant	Lieutenant colonel	224 90	Do.	do.
2135	The Sufferers Conn. Land Co		932 12	Do.	do.
2132	John C. Carter	Ensign	109 67	Do.	do.
2139	Thomas Hubbard	Captain	540 82	Do.	do.
2139	James Clarke	do	699 83	Do.	do.
2143	Alden G. Cashman	Lieutenant	36 00	Do.	do.
2146	James Chambers		471 88	Do.	do.
2148	Edward L. Lomax	Ensign	200 00	Do.	do.
2157	Thomas Sumpter		50 00	Do.	do.
2160	Wm. M. Lithgow	Lieutenant	65 25	Do.	do.
2162	John Smith	Lieutenant colonel	1 00	Do.	do.
2163	Robert Purdy	do	150 00	Do.	do.
2164	Samuel Price	Lieutenant artillery	200 00	Do.	do.
2170	William Johnston	Lieutenant	42 00	Do.	do.
2174	Samuel Marsh		118 75	Do.	do.
2179	Benjamin Harvey	Ensign	50 00	Do.	do.
2183	Samuel B. Rathburn	Lieutenant	18 00	Do.	do.
2185	William H. Wooldridge		140 00	Do.	do.
2187	Gad Humphreys	Lieutenant	150 00	Do.	do.

6 T

The foregoing balances will be found on the old books of this office arising out of advances between May, 1792, and March 3, 1809.

The following balances will be found on the books of the Third Auditor arising out of advances between March 4, 1809, and July 1, 1815, and, in pursuance of the third section of the act May 1, 1820, carried down under the general head of arrearages, and when collected will revert to the surplus fund in the treasury, as follows:

Pages.	Names.	Rank.	Amount.	Remarks.
				Arrearages:
5	Jeremiah R. Munson	Major 27th infantry	$17,585 00	Balance May 8, 1822.
8	Daniel Connor	Lieutenant 28th infantry	40 41	Balance January 1, 1820.
10	James Campbell	Major 43d infantry	245 09	Do. do.
11	James McDonald	Captain 14th infantry	100 00	Balance March 31, 1821.
12	David McMillan	Lieutenant	900 00	Balance January 1, 1820.

				Arrearages:
12	Benjamin Duncan	Lieutenant 39th infantry	$10 00	Balance January 1, 1820.
13	Wm. O. Butler	Captain 44th infantry	20 00	Do. do.
14	James H. Campbell	Captain 24th infantry	60 00	Balance April 3, 1826.
14	Israel Smith	Lieutenant 30th	02	Balance January 1, 1820.
15	Randolph Quarles	Lieutenant 39th infantry	4 00	Do. do.
17	Peter Berry	Lieutenant colonel	54 08	Balance February 9, 1828.
18	Mathew N. Sanbourn	Captain 40th infantry	23 66	Balance February 1, 1820.
21	E. B. Baskerville	Ensign	421 00	Balance November 24, 1820.
22	Philip P. Price	Lieutenant 39th infantry	409 74	Do. do.
22	James Gray	do	188 00	Balance January 1, 1820.
23	Andrew Greer	Lieutenant	778 00	Balance January 18, 1820.
23	Leonard Ross	Captain 40th infantry	49 82	Balance January 1, 1820.
24	Elias Beall	Captain 43d infantry	66 35	Do. do.
24	Thomas Hyde	do	248 95	Do. do.
25	John Tyler	Lieutenant 25th infantry	85 00	Do. do.
26	Daniel L. Scott	Quartermaster	239 01	Do. do.
30	James McCloskey	A. D. quartermaster general	5,054 55	Balance August 19, 1822.
34	Joseph H. Vanderslice	Lieutenant 22d	220 79	Balance April 12, 1824.
35	Obadiah Crawford	Lieutenant	195 00	Balance January 1, 1820.
36	Thomas C. Porter	do	115 00	Do. do.
36	Mosman Housten	Major	3,303 00	Do. do.
36	Philip Cook	Major 8th	133 24	Balance February 23, 1820.
39	Harbaugh & Potter	Contractors	7 38	Balance January 1, 1820.
40	Charles West	Lieutenant 27th	192 00	Do. do.
41	William Walker	Captain 39th	298 34	Balance March 15, 1821.
43	John C. Payne	A. D. Q. M. general	2,219 77	Balance January 1, 1820.
44	James H. Audrain	Captain	4,495 21	Balance August 1, 1820.
46	Joseph J. Miles	Captain 44th	98 00	Balance January 1, 1820.
46	Waters Clark	Major 44th	379 00	Do. do.
46	Paul G. Hoit	Ensign	32 36	Do. do.
47	John Bluker	D. Q. M. general	2,721 35	Balance January 16, 1821.
49	E. M. Giles	Lieutenant and Q. M	236 40	Balance January 1, 1820.

51	Rodolphus Simons	Lieutenant 23d	50 56	Do. do.
51	R. M. Malcolm	Major 13th	2,714 32	Balance April 22, 1824.
52	Edward Olmstead	Lieutenant 6th	471 65	Balance January 1, 1820.
53	Joseph Kenny	Captain 25th	389 34	Do. do
55	George Dunham	Ensign 33d	151 65	Do. do.
55	George Scammon	Lieutenant	35 61	Do. do.
56	Eleazer D. Wood	Colonel	80 00	Do. do.
58	Charles Duvant	Lieutenant 40th infantry	143 68	Do do.
58	Jacint Laval	Lieutenant colonel	108 41	Balance February 23, 1823.
59	Samuel T. Dyson	Captain	1,442 13	Balance July 10, 1820.
59	Robert H. Craig	Lieutenant 2d dragoons	2,386 29	Balance November 21, 1825.
60	Samuel G. Hopkins	Captain	6,813 13	Balance July 28, 1823.
62	David Vanderhaden	Lieutenant	2,182 00	Balance January 1, 1820.
62	Patrick Ford	do	131 10	Do. do.
63	Amasa J. Brown	Captain 30th	82 74	Balance February 26, 1828.
64	Simeon Hatheway	Ensign	395 52	Balance September 20, 1824.
66	Samuel Brady		12 00	Balance January 1, 1820.
67	Joseph C. Adams	Captain 34th	183 98	Balance August 11, 1823.
68	George Keese	Lieutenant 6th	565 07	Balance August 12, 1820.
70	George Armistead	Colonel	1,133 82	Balance November 4, 1831.
72	John Bliss	A. D. Q. M. G	50 00	Balance January 1, 1820.
74	William H. Newman	Lieutenant	687 24	Do. do.
75	Joseph Gleason	Captain	714 35	Balance April 6, 1822.
76	Buford Scruggs	Lieutenant 7th	287 24	Balance January 1, 1820.
76	David Riddle	Major	1,096 00	Balance June 14, 1826.
77	James H. Dearing	Lieutenant	294 77	Balance January 1, 1820.
78	William Alexander	Captain	845 72	Do. do.
79	John A. Graham	Lieutenant	300 00	Do. do.
80	John Simple	do	390 00	Balance December 21, 1820.
80	James McMahon	Captain	57 42	Balance January 1, 1820.
82	Wade Hampton	Major general	719 79	Balance December 4, 1820.
85	Charles B. Hopkins	Lieutenant	631 80	Balance July 30, 1861.
86	Thomas L. Butler	Captain	178 16	Balance December 1, 1820.
89	Benjamin Poland	Captain 34th	120 00	Balance January 1, 1820.
90	Rufus K. Lane	Lieutenant 33d	42 16	Balance June 19, 1824.
91	William Laprade	Lieutenant 8th	218 44	Balance January 1, 1820.
92	William C. Wayne	do	1,300 00	Balance March 10, 1821.
92	Samuel Coleman	Lieutenant 19th	304 30	Balance October 5, 1824.
93	John Armstrong	Late R. R.	1 84	Balance January 1, 1820.
93	Joseph Woodruff	Captain	250 26	Balance May 10, 1828.
95	John Kennedy	do	261 13	Balance January 1, 1820.

Statement of balances—Continued.

Pages.	Names.	Rank.	Amount.	Remarks.
				Arrearages:
95	Thomas Berry	Lieutenant	$362 94	Balance January 1, 1820.
95	Cornelius N. Lewis	do	1,427 25	Do. do.
96	James P. Hulse	Ensign	156 80	Do. do.
96	Robert Brackinridge	Captain	1,700 00	Do. do.
96	Benjamin Strother	Lieutenant	1,150 00	Do. do.
97	Benjamin Desher	Captain	135 98	Do. do.
98	William Scott	Lieutenant	186 25	Balance February 23, 1822.
99	William Chilton	do	126 00	Balance January 1, 1820.
101	Moses I. Chase	do	359 46	Do, do.
101	E. B. Morse	Captain	3,537 26	Balance January 1, 1820.
102	James S. Wade	Lieutenant	84 00	Balance May 6, 1823.
102	John Peebles	Lieutenant 18th	49 14	Balance January 1, 1820.
104	John Chapman	Lieutenant 6th	144 00	Do. do.
105	John Bayley	Lieutenant colonel	42 00	Do. do.
106	E. B. Billings	Lieutenant 44th infantry	575 77	Do. do.
106	Thomas Bomford	Lieutenant 7th	33 31	Do. do.
108	Lawrence Mawning	Major	573 10	Balance May 27, 1823.
109	George T. Ross	Colonel 44th	10,128 77	Balance January 1, 1820.
109	Samuel Brown	Major	9,889 76	Balance September 30, 1822.
112	Willis N. Boyan	Ensign	41 77	Balance May 19, 1820.
112	Daniel G. Brown	Ensign 28th	861 79	Balance May 21, 1822.
113	Patterson B. Clark	Ensign	698 00	Balance January 1, 1820.
114	Thomas Griffith	Lieutenant 28th	2,217 42	Do. do.
115	Edmund Hall	Ensign	260 00	Do. do.
115	J. E. London	Lieutenant 28th	1,300 00	Do. do.
115	Asa Morgan	Captain	234 65	Do. do.
116	Johnston McGowan	do	3,074 00	Balance April 7, 1825.
116	James Monday	Lieutenant	279 75	Balance January 1, 1820.
117	M. Sturges	Lieutenant 24th	1,583 63	Balance November 24, 1821.
118	B. W. Sanders	Captain 17th	1,724 28	Balance October 13, 1822.
118	John Wyatt	Lieutenant 28th	250 00	Balance January 1, 1820.
119	George Hamilton	Lieutenant 41st	36 00	Do. do.
120	John A. Watson	A. Q. M. General	301 94	Balance January 5, 1821.

120	T. V. Gray	D. Q. M. General	100	00	Balance December 15, 1821.
125	George W. Wight	Lieutenant	3,706	85	Balance January 1, 1820.
127	John Darrington	Colonel 4th infantry	132	82	Balance December 24, 1825.
127	P. Wheelock	Lieutenant 4th infantry	4	00	Balance January 1, 1820.
128	D. T. McRae	Ensign 3d infantry	888	00	Do. do
129	Mathew Chapman	Lieutenant	218	80	Do. do.
130	Luther Scott	do	926	76	Do. do.
131	William Smith	Lieutenant 18th	2,194	00	Do. do.
131	William Taylor	Captain	200	00	Do. do.
131	E. D. Dick	Lieutenant 18th	1,830	58	Do. do.
132	Samuel W. Smith	do	1,210	00	Do. do.
134	Samuel M. Dewey	Captain	463	72	Do. do.
134	Thomas B. Guy	Lieutenant	4	00	Do. do.
135	John Street	Lieutenant 18th	291	95	Balance January 6, 1820.
136	Timothy Dix	Major	2,036	33	Balance March 21, 1821.
136	John B. Sparks	Lieutenant 14th	375	59	Do. do.
136	Peter Rich	do	635	50	Balance January 1, 1820.
137	James W. Lent, jr	Lieutenant	121	96	Balance March 6, 1827.
138	Abraham Allison	do	95	00	Balance January 1, 1820.
141	George Reab	Lieutenant 13th	2	25	Do. do.
142	Lewis Dent	Paymaster	1,184	41	Balance February 28, 1821.
143	George Read	Lieutenant 16th	243	16	Balance January 1, 1820.
143	William Jones	Captain	475	32	Do. do.
147	Robert Y. Marye	Lieutenant	231	96	Do. do.
147	Joseph Oliver	Lieutenant 43d	392	91	Do. do.
147	William H. Fairchild	do	320	83	Balance February 3, 1820.
148	Robert B. Stark	Lieutenant	20	00	Balance January 1, 1820.
148	T. Reynolds	do	404	50	Balance June 8, 1820.
149	James Harris	Lieutenant 40th	10	60	Balance January 1, 1820.
151	Daniel Holden	Captain 45th	16	00	Do. do.
155	Thomas Post	Captain 12th	1,870	00	Balance November 3, 1820.
156	Philip White	Captain	427	10	Balance January 1, 1820.
157	Samuel Grantland	Lieutenant 12th	300	00	Do. do.
157	Enoch Manning	Lieutenant 40th	432	71	Do. do.
158	Joseph McComb	Lieutenant	52	50	Do. do.
158	E. T. Hall	Paymaster	1,006	67	Balance August 20, 1820.
159	James Wiley	Lieutenant 23d infantry	91	66	Balance January 1, 1820.
162	George Maxwell	Ensign 41st infantry	175	00	Do. do.
163	Abner H. Hicks	Lieutenant	220	00	Balance July 18, 1826.
164	William G. Green	Captain 4th	1,442	61	Balance November 25, 1822.
165	Joseph Irby	Lieutenant 43d	79	40	Balance June 8, 1820.

Statement of balances—Continued.

Pages.	Names.	Rank.	Amount.	Remarks.
				Arrearages:
165	John Mitchell	Lieutenant	$93 50	Balance August 19, 1822.
166	Oliver Vance	Lieutenant 27th	298 14	Balance January 1, 1820.
167	Royal D. Simons	Lieutenant 34th	709 00	Do. do.
169	Daniel Cushing	Captain	2,397 39	Balance July 20, 1835.
170	James F. McElroy	Captain 16th	304 52	Balance July 18, 1820.
174	George Keyser	Major	10,472 65	Balance January 1, 1820.
174	Fred. W. Hoffman	Lieutenant 28th	30 00	Do. do.
175	George W. Porter	Lieutenant 38th	53 18	Do. do.
175	William H. Addison	Ensign 38th	426 63	Do. do.
176	Isaac Aldridge	Captain 38th	3,122 42	Do. do.
177	William Welch	Lieutenant 43d	74 10	Do. do.
178	Duncan McArthur	Brigadier general	738 00	Balance November 23, 1822.
179	Reuben G. Beasley	Agent	3,428 86	Balance January 1, 1820.
181	Martin L. Seldon	Lieutenant 30th	344 41	Do. do.
181	Elisha Smith	do	96 13	Do. do.
181	Thomas F. Hargis	Lieutenant 32d	751 15	Do. do.
186	James Piatt	Lieutenant 15th	1,256 87	Balance June 18, 1821.
186	Robert C. Jennings	Deputy commissary	189,635 80	Balance February 9, 1821.
186	James Gibson	Captain 12th	152 06	Balance January 1, 1820.
187	Dominick Cornyn	Lieutenant 22d	2,730 00	Do. do.
187	Armstrong Irvine	Captain 42d	1,130 20	Balance October 15, 1825.
188	William Nicholas	Captain	3,155 38	Balance July 8, 1824.
188	Jacob Swoyer	Lieutenant 5th	454 20	Balance January 1, 1820.
189	James McKenney	Lieutenant 22d	57 50	Do. do.
189	Thomas Tindley	Lieutenant 16th	300 00	Do. do.
189	John Arrison	Captain 22d	571 75	Balance March 1, 1824.
190	Hector Burnes	Ensign	163 65	Balance January 1, 1820.
190	Benj. S. Ogden	Captain	4,716 00	Do. do.

194	Robert R. Hall	Lieutenant 22d	246 71	Do. do.
195	Benj. Branch	Captain	100 00	Do. do.
195	E. L. Whitlock	Major 15th	16 00	Do. do.
196	T. Horrell	Lieutenant 16th	893 79	Do. do.
196	John Rahm	...do	89 59	Do. do.
196	Elias Smurr	Lieutenant 4th R	231 51	Do. do.
197	Martin Fishback	Lieutenant 5th	2,014 00	Balance September 29, 1820.
197	Robert Mears	Ensign 5th	1,700 00	Balance January 1, 1820.
198	George Red	Lieutenant 5th	500 00	Do. do.
200	Francis Le Barron	Lieutenant, (apothecary general)	300 00	Balance November 25, 1825.
200	Elisha Hall	Captain 45th	183 86	Balance January 1, 1820.
201	Thomas I. Robeson	Major	6,564 50	Balance October 24, 1823.
202	John B. Troax	Ensign 33d	1,583 32	Balance January 1, 1820.
202	Fielder Ridgeway	Captain	2,416 80	Do. do.
203	David Scott	...do	345 73	Balance May 15, 1820.
203	Jacob Myers	Lieutenant 13th	1,002 00	Balance September 28, 1824.
204	Parker Greenough	Lieutenant 4th	126 06	Balance January 1, 1820.
205	Hugh W. Doneale	Captain 36th	683 50	Do. do.
206	Aaron McIntire	Ensign 23d	653 33	Balance December 14, 1821.
207	R. C. Smyth	Agent and lieutenant	2,562 30	Balance January 12, 1820.
209	M. Hughes	Lieutenant 12th	735 00	Balance March 23, 1820.
209	Angus McDonald	...do	1,923 38	Balance January 1, 1820.
210	James Charlton	Captain 12th	1,638 45	Balance April 15, 1822.
210	James Craig	Lieutenant 21st	209 66	Balance January 1, 1820.
211	Samuel Legate	Lieutenant	1,731 93	Balance June 28, 1821.
213	William C. Bird	Lieutenant	349 83	Balance January 1, 1820.
214	James H. Boyle	Captain artillery	100 00	Do. do.
215	Abraham Hawkins	Captain 4th infantry	63 95	Do. do.
215	Charles Smith	Lieutenant 44th	411 31	Do. do.
216	Frederick L. Amelung	Captain 1st	337 31	Balance June 21, 1826.
218	James Dorman	Major	90 74	Balance October 30, 1828.
218	James Wells	Lieutenant 11th	186 41	Balance January 1, 1820.
219	Henry J. Blake	...do	1,140 00	Do. do.
219	Josiah Shields	Ensign 11th	1,081 00	Do. do.
220	Joseph Bucklin	Captain 9th	1,167 00	Do. do.
220	William King	Lieutenant of artillery	41 04	Do. do.
221	James T. B. Romayne	Captain	523 00	Do. do.
222	S. L. Tracy	Lieutenant	36 00	Do. do.
223	Mathew D. Danvers	Captain 29th	5,437 03	Balance January 6, 1820.
224	Asa B. Sizer	Major 29th	123 14	Balance January 7, 1823
225	Isaac B. Barbour	Captain 9th	213 98	Balance January 1, 1820.

Statement of balances—Continued.

[P]ages.	Names.	Rank.	Amount.	Remarks.
				Arrearages:
226	F. Y. Waterman	Captain 29th	$51 59	Balance January 1, 1820.
226	A. P. Spencer	Captain 29th	5,768 80	Do. do.
229	Charles Page	Captain 12th	1,209 36	Do. do.
229	John Kenney	Lieutenant 12th	60 04	Do. do
230	Andrew L. Madison	Captain 12th	624 00	Balance April 11, 1821.
231	Nathaniel Stanley	Captain 45th	38 00	Balance January 1, 1820.
232	Nicholas Robinson	Lieutenant 14th	193 75	Do. do.
232	George McLaughlin	Lieutenant 20th	83 30	Balance November 5, 1822.
233	John Watkins	Lieutenant 18th	9 75	Balance January 1, 1820.
233	Daniel M. Darrow	Lieutenant 27th	142 00	Do. do.
234	James M. Stewart	Lieutenant 22d	159 50	Do. do.
235	Lewis G. A. Armistead	Captain R. R.	19 63	Do. do.
236	John Hatch	Lieutenant 31st	290 47	Do. do.
237	John J. Fontaine	Lieutenant 2d artillery	55 00	Do. do.
239	Francis Woodward	Lieutenant 24th	1,876 00	Balance December 4, 1821.
240	Alexander Hamilton	Ensign 24th	300 00	Balance March 31, 1821.
242	James W. Sproat	Ensign 16th	149 73	Balance January 1, 1820.
242	Thomas Mahon	do	950 16	Do. do.
246	Henry Garrett	Captain 43d	371 16	Do. do.
247	Francis Bealmear	Acting paymaster	11 48	Do. do.
248	John McCarty	Lieutenant 23d	343 89	Do. do.
248	Moses Clough	Lieutenant 34th	978 24	Do. do.
249	Supply B. Gookin	do	274 70	Do. do.
250	Nathaniel Webster	Ensign 33d	505 66	Do. do.
251	Isaac Carter	Captain 34th	1,193 24	Do. do.
251	William Stephens	Lieutenant 34th	369 00	Do. do.
252	George B. Shelden	Lieutenant 4th rifle	1,708 00	Do. do.
253	Abraham Schuyler	do	361 44	Do. do.
256	William L. Foster	Captain 9th	40 00	Do. do.
258	Robert Goode	Lieut. corps of artillery	1,206 50	Balance August 26, 1824.
259	Charles Fuller	Captain 4th	8 00	Balance January 1, 1820.
259	Robert Steuart	Late lieut. 2d artillery	49 92	Do. do.
261	White Youngs	Major 15th	245 03	Balance April 30, 1822.

262	Zebulon M. Pike	Brigadier general	1,491 34	Balance May 7, 1823.
263	Elijah Haynie	Lieutenant 24th	296 50	Balance January 1, 1820.
265	Samuel Vail	Captain 7th	1,368 00	Balance May 6, 1823.
268	John Archer	Lieutenant and paymaster	2,032 74	Balance April 27, 1820.
269	Washington Lee	Deputy paymaster	136 18	Balance October 25, 1823.
273	Nehemiah Gregory	Major 27th	427 32	Balance February 20, 1822.
274	John Pendleton	Lieutenant 3d rifles	15 85	Balance May 2, 1826.
277	Daniel George	Lieutenant 45th	39 04	Balance January 1, 1820.
281	Daniel C. Bryant	Captain 31st	334 26	Do. do.
282	Elihu Emmons	Lieutenant 31st	216 02	Do. do.
288	William G. Mills	Late lieutenant 14th	298 33	Do. do.
288	John Mather	Lieutenant 2d infantry	2,275 00	Balance May 9, 1822.
288	Marshall Baker	Lieutenant 45th infantry	4 00	Balance January 1, 1820.
294	Samuel B. Romayne	Late 41st infantry	32 00	Do. do.
295	John Machesney	Captain 16th	688 74	Balance May 17, 1820.
296	Stephen Bean	Captain 33d	297 16	Balance January 1, 1820.
297	Caleb H. Holders	Late lieutenant 17th	1,747 09	Balance October 1, 1821.
297	Florant Meline	Late lieutenant 15th	1,939 88	Balance January 18, 1821.
299	John Gates, Jr	Paymaster artillery	62 00	Balance January 1, 1820.
300	Jonathan Beall	Ass't deputy paymaster	5,875 43	Do. do.
301	Jesse Barlow		200 00	Do. do.
303	Samuel B. Hickcox	Lieutenant 29th	448 00	Do. do.
307	R. W. Scott	Lieutenant 7th, late 35th	805 00	Do. do.
309	Rodolphus R. Childs	Lieutenant 30th	41	Do. do.
312	Terah Jones	Lieutenant	407 92	Balance January 10, 1822.
313	J. Wilcocks	Major	2,245 20	Balance January 1, 1820.
313	Samuel Weston	Paymaster volunteers	2,580 20	Do. do.
314	Daniel Adams	do	2,312 19	Balance July 12, 1820.
314	Charles G. Boerstler	Lieutenant colonel 14th	98 18	Balance June 28, 1821.
314	J. L. Dubois	Ensign 6th	4,940 00	Balance January 1, 1820.
315	Benjamin Forsyth	Captain R. Reg.	301 62	Balance January 3, 1821.
315	David Fleming	Captain 3d artillery	2,250 00	Balance January 1, 1820.
316	Charles Steuart	Lieutenant 15th	1,858 00	Do. do.
316	Charles Smith	Capt. 2d light dragoons	3,992 70	Do. do.
318	Isaiah H. Marshall	Lieut. Pennsylvania volunteers	640 00	Do. do.
320	John R. Guy	Lieutenant	233 76	Balance October 29, 1828.
324	Joshua Wildey	Captain 23d	464 96	Balance January 1, 1820.
325	Samuel R. Hill	Ensign 23d	346 25	Do. do.
325	Richard Philips	do	160 00	Balance August 27, 1822.
326	John Jones	do	300 00	Balance September 6, 1823.
326	Ezra Post	Captain	90 75	Balance January 1, 1820.

Statement of balances—Continued.

Pages.	Names.	Rank.	Amount.	Remarks.
				Arrearages:
328	Caleb G. Forbes	Lieutenant 24th	$1,126 06	Balance January 1, 1820.
331	Cornelius R. French	Doctor	65 00	Do. do.
333	R. N. Yates	Lieutenant 4th rifle	122 28	Do. do.
338	John Hollingshead	Late Lt. dragoons	241 35	Do. do.
339	Peter Rivery		172 90	Do. do.
339	Henry Northup	Captain	647 61	Balance October 18, 1824.
342	Enoch Cooper	Lieutenant 11th reg	252 00	Balance January 1, 1820.
343	Smith Newcomb	Ensign 29th	769 93	Balance September 25, 1824.
343	Augustus F. Conant	Lieutenant	130 06	Balance June 8, 1820.
343	Henry Van Antwerp	do	829 78	Balance January 1, 1820.
344	John Wynkoop	Ensign 34th	76 00	Balance January 6, 1820.
344	Thomas Turner	do	124 00	Balance April 28, 1820.
345	N. H. Moore	Captain	30,098 00	Balance January 1, 1820.
345	Francis Smith	Ensign 2d rifle	268 00	Do. do.
355	Bailey Buckner	do	85 57	Balance April 12, 1834.
355	George Bryan	Lieutenant	2,500 00	Balance September 4, 1821.
355	J. M. Burnside	Lieutenant 16th infantry	1,400 00	Balance September 1, 1821.
356	Josiah S. Carty	Lieutenant 42d	300 00	Balance June 14, 1822.
356	Francis D. Cummings	Captain 16th	172 00	Balance March 24, 1820.
357	Jacob Fetter	Lieutenant 22d infantry	152 73	Balance December 20, 1824.
358	A. McIlhenny	Captain 5th	1,369 10	Balance April 20, 1822.
358	P. McDonag	Lieutenant artillery	504 00	Balance January 1, 1820.
358	Henry Meyer	Ensign	2,812 00	Balance August 23, 1821.
359	Edward Ross	Captain Lt. dragoons	1,100 00	Balance September 15, 1821.
359	John Sisk	Ensign 6th	2,910 00	Balance January 18, 1820.
360	Joseph Stahle	Ensign 22d	158 00	Balance February 16, 1820.
361	Larkin T. Baldwin	Ensign 43d	23 05	Balance January 1, 1820.
361	John Armstrong	Lieutenant 22d	20 00	Do. do.
362	Edward White	Lieutenant	747 00	Balance May 23, 1822.

369	Thomas H. Richardson	Lieutenant 7th	1,526 00	Balance January 1, 1820.
372	John G. Bull	Acting paymaster	21 94	Balance February 2, 1822.
373	Robert B. Colvin	Paymaster	12 00	Balance January 1, 1820.
376	Robert Gray	Major	1 00	Balance March 10, 1823.
377	James Smith	Lieutenant 30th	340 00	Balance January 1, 1820.
377	Henry Hendrix	Ensign 30th	426 94	Do. do.
378	William O. Allen	Captain 35th	246 91	Balance March 12, 1823.
378	J. E. A. Masters	Captain 6th	650 00	Balance November 26, 1821.
381	William F. Hobart	Lieutenant light artillery	5,001 00	Balance November 27, 1826.
385	Thomas Bodley	Quartermaster Gen. Ky. militia	22,247 59	Balance May 17, 1821.
385	Thomas S. Wingate	Quartermaster Ky. militia	135 75	Balance November 10, 1823.
386	Francis Thompson	Late paymaster 43d Md. militia	23 78	Balance January 1, 1820.
387	Benjamin Wright	Captain 39th	555 64	Do. do.
388	Elizha Fields	Captain 40th	539 85	Do. do.
389	Alexander F. F. Bill	Lieutenant 25th	3,328 24	Balance May 30, 1828.
389	John Jameson	Indian agent	100 00	Balance July 23, 1824.
390	Henry Philips	Late deputy paymaster	11,459 54	Balance December 27, 1822.
390	Henry Philips	Late lieutenant	389 65	Balance October 22, 1822.
391	Abel Farwell	Lieutenant 11th	255 91	Balance March 29, 1821.
391	Phineas Williams	Captain	1,245 00	Balance January 1, 1820.
392	Noadiah Kibb	Lieutenant 31st	491 94	Do. do.
397	Philip D. Spencer	Late ass't deputy paym'r gen'l	24,658 31	Do. do.
399	Josephus B. Stewart	Lieutenant and paymaster	17,813 52	Balance March 7, 1822.
399	Thomas M. Powers	Paymaster 16th infantry	2,984 59	Balance August 1, 1820.
400	Stephen F. Donaldson	Paymaster 14th infantry	16,442 87	Balance July 18, 1820.
403	Robert Purdy	Colonel 4th infantry	60 00	Balance January 1, 1820.
404	G. D. Young	Lieutenant colonel 29th	2,000 00	Balance December 19, 1821.
405	Robert S. Gardiner	Paymaster 13th	3,581 42	Balance April 27, 1820.
407	Farquhar McRea	Paymaster 10th infantry	542 11	Balance June 14, 1822.
408	John Maul	Lieutenant and quartermaster	87 42	Balance January 1, 1820.
411	John Farrant	Lieutenant	640 00	Balance May 6, 1823.
412	William McDonald	Major artillery	792 76	Balance February 7, 1823.
413	Robert Lamar	Lieutenant 8th	421 44	Balance January 1, 1820.
413	William McQueen	Captain 8th	239 88	Balance November 20, 1824.
414	Thomas C. Lovett	Ensign 8th	162 56	Balance March 10, 1821.
414	Samuel Haring	Captain 13th	6,521 29	Balance August 25, 1820.
415	Moses C. Cantine	Lieutenant 13th	1,846 00	Balance January 1, 1820.
415	John Murphy	Ensign 13th	821 00	Do. do.
415	William Burrill	Lieutenant 13th	814 59	Balance August 26, 1824.
416	Thomas W. Denton	do	100 00	Balance January 1, 1820.
422	A. L. Langham	Captain 19th infantry	2,775 35	Balance January 23, 1855.

				Arrearages:
424	William C. C. Clairborne	Governor	$5,000 00	Balance May 6, 1823.
427	Aaron Sutphur	Captain 15th	2,540 24	Balance November 26, 1821.
427	John Knapp	Lieutenant 15th	1,968 00	Balance November 12, 1821.
428	Francis Walters	do	500 00	Balance January 1, 1820.
428	Charles W. Lee	do	243 33	Do. do.
428	George Echfeldt	Lieutenant 16th	590 00	Balance May 30, 1822.
429	Charles Smith, jr	do	150 00	Balance January 1, 1820.
429	William Shannon	Lieutenant	1,093 00	Balance May 16, 1821.
430	Benjamin Brearly	Lieutenant 3d artillery	1,872 00	Balance July 16, 1824.
430	John Davis	Captain	208 50	Balance October 13, 1821.
430	James Lane	Lieutenant	150 00	Balance January 1, 1820.
431	John P. Bartlett	Lieutenant 3d artillery	1,121 92	Do. do.
431	John M. Connelly	Captain 3d artillery	514 55	Balance April 8, 1820.
431	William De Peyster	Lieutenant	249 52	Balance April 13, 1836.
432	Daniel Smalley	do	449 57	Balance May 19, 1820.
432	Benjamin S. Rue	Lieutenant 24th	58 92	Balance January 1, 1820.
434	John G. Bostick	Lieutenant 8th	362 21	Balance February 4, 1823.
434	M. A. Roberts	do	8 00	Balance April 16, 1821.
435	Beverly Martin	do	706 24	Balance January 1, 1820.
435	Thomas B. Randolph	Lieutenant light artillery	150 00	Do. do.
436	Thomas Sangster	Captain 4th infantry	4,916 60	Do. do.
438	Charles R. Rose	Lieutenant 35th	25 75	Do. do.
438	Theodorick B. Rice	Lieutenant 7th	90 75	Do. do.
439	Lewis M. Ayer	Lieutenant 24th	58 19	Do. do.
440	John Fendall	Late lieutenant 5th	218 24	Do. do.
442	Abraham C. Ashton	Paymaster 1st reg. N. Y. militia	158 51	Do. do.
443	Jonathan Carleton	Paymaster 1st reg. Ohio militia	51,127 88	Balance September 11, 1827.
443	Augustus Belknap	Paymaster New York militia	425 27	Balance January 1, 1820.
444	George C. Allen	Late lieutenant 7th infantry	186 95	Balance June 14, 1822.
444	Augustus Dousset	Ensign 8th	690 20	Balance March 10, 1821.
445	Joseph P. Prince	Captain artillery	7,526 33	Balance June 8, 1820.
446	William Christy	Assistant dep. quarterm'r gen	60 96	Balance January 1, 1820.

448	Joseph Duncan	Lieutenant 17th	239 09	Balance March 28, 1825.
449	Daniel Gregg	Late captain 45th	8 00	Balance January 1, 1820.
450	Robert Fenner	Captain	482 57	Do. do.
451	William Edmonston	Late lieutenant 43d	51 50	Balance February 21, 1824.
452	H. H. Hickman	Captain 17th	1,799 82	Balance January 1, 1820.
452	William H. Shang	Ensign 17th	1,870 00	Do. do.
453	William Featherston	do.	1,083 03	Do. do.
453	Jonathan Rees	Lieutenant 17th	1,880 00	Balance March 21, 1822.
454	Arthur Fox	Lieutenant 10th	233 84	Balance September 4, 1820.
454	John Swearingen	Lieutenant 2d rifles	318 00	Balance January 1, 1820.
454	Andrew Gilmore	Ensign rifle regiment	303 13	Do. do.
455	Allison C. Looker	do.	449 43	Do. do.
456	James Crutcher	Paymaster 3d reg. Ky. militia	5 00	Balance February 24, 1820.
459	Alex. Gray	Captain 24th infantry	1,923 50	Balance June 27, 1822.
459	William H. Puthuff	Captain	6,936 36	Balance January 4, 1822.
460	Frederick H. Lissenhoff	Paymaster Georgia militia	7,448 60	Balance July 18, 1826.
463	John Flanagan	Paymaster Pennsylvania vols.	88 42	Balance April 24, 1822.
464	Bartholomew Labuzan		5,257 14	Balance June 14, 1823.
464	Simon Brown	Lieutenant 37th	169 93	Balance January 1, 1820.
465	Joseph Atherton	Lieutenant 31st	201 40	Balance September 5, 1822.
465	Samuel E. Albro	Ensign 31st	530 00	Balance January 1, 1820.
465	A. W. Brown	Lieutenant 31st	84 65	Balance March 13, 1821.
466	Isaac Briggs	Ensign 31st	54 39	Balance January 1, 1820.
466	John Farwell	Lieutenant 31st	510 00	Balance September 7, 1821.
467	S. M. Perkins	Ensign 31st	580 00	Balance January 1, 1820.
468	Salmon Clark	Captain 30th	1,075 00	Balance September 20, 1821.
469	Asa Peabody		130 00	Balance January 1, 1820.
469	Phelps Smith	Lieutenant 30th	366 00	Do. do.
469	Levi Cox		341 25	Balance October 5, 1820.
470	Ebenezer W. Bohonon	Ensign 31st	400 00	Balance January 9, 1821.
471	William Baird	Captain 19th infantry	13 00	Balance May 17, 1820.
471	Robert Smith	Lieutenant 19th	500 00	Balance August 8, 1826.
472	C. A. Sparks	Lieutenant 3d rifles	40 00	Balance January 1, 1820.
472	William Keller	do.	30 00	Do. do.
472	Thomas Evans	Ensign 16th	64 05	Balance August 1, 1820.
473	Thomas M. Church	Late lieutenant 16th	139 41	Balance January 1, 1820.
473	Jacob Whistler	Ensign 16th	659 99	Balance January 7, 1823.
474	David T. Hopkins	Lieutenant 21st	300 00	Balance August 3, 1822.
474	Charles E. Toby	Captain 21st	450 00	Balance September 15, 1821.
475	Charles Proctor	do.	561 02	Balance June 17, 1824.
475	Charles Peters	Lieutenant 44th	818 50	Balance January 1, 1820.

				Arrearages:
477	Robert C. Respass	Paymaster 10th reg. dtd. Ky. ma.	$13,969 19	Balance May 18, 1820.
478	Alexander J. Williams	Captain	1,497 61	Balance April 5, 1824.
478	James Taylor	Captain 30th	64 18	Balance January 1, 1820.
478	Simeon Robinson	Lieutenant 30th	245 00	Do. do.
479	John L. Thompson	Late lieutenant 43d	184 55	Do. do.
480	Alexander Hamilton	Late captain 41st	44 00	Balance September 8, 1823.
480	Richard Doane	Late captain 45th	34 00	Balance January 1, 1820.
482	Joseph L. Barton	Captain 15th	1,926 00	Balance January 18, 1821.
482	Jacob Dickerson	Ensign 15th	578 05	Balance January 1, 1820.
483	John L. Hoppock	Captain	600 00	Balance August 3, 1822.
484	M. O. Bloomfield	Lieutenant	1,715 00	Balance May 28, 1822.
484	William Lancaster	Lieutenant 10th	700 85	Balance June 3, 1822.
485	William Ward	do	266 96	Balance January 1, 1820.
485	William F. Pendleton	Ensign 20th	470 19	Do. do.
486	M. M. Claiborne	Ensign 12th	178 00	Do. do.
488	William B. Jackson	Lieutenant 1st	102 00	Balance November 22, 1825.
489	Thomas W. Farrar	Captain 10th	140 71	Balance January 1, 1820.
492	Wilson P. Greenup	Late lieutenant 28th	872 00	Balance February 1, 1821.
493	German Senter	Surgeon's mate 3d artillery	345 22	Balance January 1, 1820.
494	D. Neilson	Apothecary general	560 00	Balance November 6, 1821.
494	A. McFarland	Lieutenant 2d dragoons	50 00	Balance January 1, 1820.
495	William Johnson	Cornet	126 64	Do. do.
495	Benjamin T. Robb	Lieutenant artillery	2,310 00	Do. do.
495	Charles Newkirk	do	50 00	Do. do.
497	George McChain	Lieutenant 25th	750 00	Do. do.
497	Lewis Norris	Ensign 9th	189 14	Do. do.
498	William Henry	Lieutenant 3d artillery	70 00	Balance April 30, 1822.
498	Lodowick Morgan	Captain rifles	5,438 34	Balance January 1, 1820.
499	Benjamin Price	Ensign	5 00	Do. do.
499	John Winters	Lieutenant	275 00	Do. do.
499	Gabriel H. Browne	Wagon master	420 00	Do. do.

501	John Lytle	do	1,408 94	Balance November 19, 1823.
501	George F. Dunkle		32 26	Balance March 21, 1821.
502	Thomas Hewson	Wagon master	300 00	Balance January 1, 1820.
502	Chester Lyman	Major	1,868 12	Balance November 24, 1821.
503	D. McFarland	Major 23d	947 00	Balance January 1, 1820.
503	Richard Smith	Captain	500 00	Balance December 13, 1821.
503	David Waters	Lieut. and Q. M. N. Y. militia	400 00	Balance September 21, 1821.
504	Thompson Maxwell	Captain	62 00	Balance January 1. 1820.
505	William Jenkins	Brigadier, Q. M. N. Y. militia	59 72	Do do.
507	Joshua Conkey	Captain N. Y. State volunteers	135 00	Do. do.
507	Frederick E. Hedges	Lieutenant 5th	187 25	Do. do.
508	James M. Porter	Captain, &c	64 91	Do. do.
509	Littleton Johnston	Ensign 24th	1,440 56	Do. do.
510	S. R. Proctor	Captain	812 19	Balance January 3, 1822.
511	Daniel Appling	do	796 95	Balance April 18, 1821.
511	William N. Earle	Lieutenant 36th	14 73	Balance January 1, 1820.
511	John R. Pettibone	Ensign 30th	49 40	Do. do.
513	Reuben Taylor	Lieutenant 17th	10 00	Balance July 13, 1822.
513	James Gibson	Colonel 4th rifles	4,485 96	Balance August 10, 1821.
516	David Herrin	Lieutenant 26th	13 39	Balance February 16, 1820.
516	Joseph Perkins	Lieutenant 24th	1,263 00	Balance November 4, 1830.
520	Robert Gray	Paymaster	309 98	Balance May 22, 1822.
521	Martin Strobel	do	329 96	Balance October 29, 1821.
522	William Coffee	Lieutenant 15th	676 00	Balance November 21, 1821.
523	Ebenezer Thompson	Late captain 9th	659 37	Balance January 1, 1820.
523	John Reed	Lieutenant 9th	50 00	Do. do.
525	Levi Hukill	Lieutenant 1st regiment	294 87	Balance September 19, 1822.
526	Joel Millikin	Captain 33d	273 03	Balance October 20, 1821.
528	Elijah Hall	Captain	55 93	Balance January 1, 1820.
529	Lewis Peckham	Lieutenant 4th	103 82	Do. do.
530	Levi Powers	Late captain 21st	176 17	Do. do.
530	Zacquille Morgan	Deceased; late captain 12th	459 00	Do. do.
531	Thomas Campbell	Captain, &c	5,683 50	Balance March 10, 1823.
532	James Powell	Lieutenant 33d	144 98	Balance January 1, 1820.
534	John Campbell	Late captain 13th	198 71	Do. do.
534	Amasa J. Bruce	Lieutenant 12th	1,787 26	Do. do.
535	George Pease		533 75	Do. do.
536	Archibald Neilson	Late lieutenant 7th	865 50	Do. do.
537	James Hackley	Lieutenant 17th	1,308 20	Balance July 13, 1827.
537	Philip S. Sharer	Ensign 17th	200 00	Balance January 1, 1820
537	Thomas J. Overton	Lieut. and quartermaster 17th	1,146 01	Do. do.

Statement of balances—Continued.

Pages.	Names.	Rank.	Amount.	Remarks.
				Arrearages:
538	Isaac Townsend	Lieutenant 34th	$178 00	Balance January 1, 1820.
540	Beverly Turpin	Lieutenant 2d dragoons	956 56	Balance January 3, 1822.
541	James Martin	Lieutenant dragoons	1,017 00	Balance November 24, 1821.
541	James Trippe	Lieutenant 2d dragoons	653 00	Balance January 1, 1820.
542	George G. Steele	Captain 16th	1,603 62	Balance January 10, 1822.
542	John N. McIntosh	Captain light artillery	265 10	Balance January 1, 1820.
543	Moses M. Russell	Lieutenant artillery	814 00	Do. do.
543	Charles Canty	Lieutenant 43d	244 00	Do. do.
545	Peter Simons	Ensign	198 98	Do. do.
546	Andrew P. Cochran	Captain 45th	16 00	Do. do.
547	William Mooney	Captain 22d	340 25	Do. do.
549	Christian Hartlett	Captain 27th	68 00	Do. do.
549	Smith W. Gordon	Lieutenant 44th	110 00	Do. do.
550	John Mason	Captain 28th	1,500 39	Do. do.
550	Marshall T. Alexander		34 82	Do. do.
551	Timothy Aldrick	Lieutenant 11th	374 30	Balance September 20, 1822.
551	George W. Jackson	Captain	15,629 75	Balance June 26, 1821.
554	Philip Smith	Lieutenant 26th	107 60	Balance January 1, 1820.
556	Francis Geslain	Hospital surgeon mate	30 00	Do. do.
556	John H. Ryan	Lieutenant R. R	200 00	Balance March 24, 1820.
557	John Atwood	Lieutenant 31st	157 85	Balance January 1, 1820.
558	Elisha M. Walker	Lieutenant 24th	548 00	Do. do.
558	Benjamin Davis	Lieutenant	15 00	Balance March 31, 1821.
559	John Campbell	Captain 26th	3,190 00	Balance October 26 1821.
559	Thomas J. Morgan	Ensign 17th	390 55	Balance January 1, 1820.
559	Robert Anderson	Lieutenant 26th	94 80	Do. do.
560	Nathaniel Pryor	Captain 44th	398 00	Do. do.
560	Edward W. Miller	Lieutenant 2d rifles	16 98	Do. do.
561	Alexander Pagan		283 50	Do. do.
562	James Perry	Captain 40th	721 56	Do. do.
562	Anthony Dearing	Ensign 39th	1,500 00	Do. do.

565	Augustus Sevake	Lieutenant 26th	25 00	Balance January 1, 1820.
578	Elias Stallings	Captain 1st rifles	470 34	Do. do.
579	John Warring	Lieutenant 14th	10 00	Do. do.
579	George Mytinger	Ensign 22d	272 85	Do. do.
580	Silas Remington	Surgeon	250 00	Balance November 9, 1821.
581	Elisha Kellog	Paymaster reg. N. Y. militia	32 31	Balance January 1, 1820.
582	Adrian Niel	Lieutenant 2d artillery	76 98	Do. do.
582	Thomas Shubrick	Lieutenant	100 00	Do. do.
583	Richard M. Bayley	....do	7 50	Balance April 24, 1820.
583	John C. Walker	Lieutenant 26th	1,459 36	Balance October 15, 1822.
584	Lewis Diffenbaick	Ensign 16th	70 50	Balance January 1, 1820.
585	Elisha Brimhall	Lieutenant 9th	92 00	Do. do.
585	Daniel G. Kelley	Lieutenant 45th	50 84	Do. do.
586	John B. Cooper	D. quartermaster	1,085 02	Balance November 18, 1822.
588	Moses Blackly	Captain 13th	244 00	Balance January 1, 1820.
589	Robert McClellan	Lieut. and paymaster 6th	8,990 57	Balance June 13, 1822.
589	Jacob Miller	Captain 7th	192 17	Balance January 1, 1820.
590	Elisha Jones	Captain 9th infantry	626 37	Do. do.
590	Charles Foster	Ensign 9th	621 00	Balance October 6, 1827.
591	Richard Mitchell	Ensign 17th	626 00	Balance January 1, 1820.
591	Jeremiah York	Lieutenant 31st	120 95	Do. do.
592	L. Egerton	Captain 31st	7 13	Balance May 19, 1820.
592	Joseph McClure	Lieutenant 34th	610 42	Balance January 1, 1820.
593	Nicholas C. Kinney	Lieutenant, &c	250 00	Do. do.
593	Isaac Jaquett	Lieutenant 4th rifles	225 29	Do. do.
594	James F. Moore	Lieutenant 28th	200 00	Do. do.
594	Samuel Rockwell	Lieutenant artillery	216 77	Do. do.
595	Byram Williams	Ensign 28th	266 00	Balance January 1, 1820.
596	Bracket Paine	Late lieutenant 21st	87 56	Do. do.
598	John Merrill	Lieutenant 31st	133 32	Balance December 27, 1820.
602	Thomas Butler		550 00	Balance May 25, 1825.
603	Abijah Johns	Ensign 19th	207 69	Balance January 1, 1820.
603	William M. Crawford	Lieutenant 24th	88 25	Do. do.
606	James W. Bryson	Late ass't deputy q. m. general	2,949 21	Balance August 29, 1829.
607	Caleb Benjamin	Captain, &c	2,148 54	Balance July 22, 1822.
607	Thomas Y. Sprogell	Lieutenant 22d	1,049 97	Balance February 2, 1824.
608	Joseph S. Simpson	Late ensign 14th	501 00	Balance January 1, 1820.
609	Oliver H. Nielson	Lieutenant 38th	27 25	Do. do.
609	Abiel Wilson	Ensign 4th infantry	190 75	Do. do.
609	Stephen Webb	Lieutenant 30th	38 10	Do. do.
610	Thomas Stephens	....do	65 98	Do. do.

				Arrearages:
612	William B. Ferris	Ensign 30th	$661 00	Balance January 1, 1820.
614	Felix B. Warley	Captain 8th	177 80	Balance April 16, 1821.
615	Samuel Coleman	Ensign 8th	200 00	Balance June 14, 1822.
617	Nicholas Edgecomb	Lieutenant 33d	42 00	Balance January 1, 1820.
618	Jonathan H. Falconer	Lieutenant 14th	230 45	Do. do.
619	Samuel Annin	Late paymaster Harper's Ferry	15,303 83	Balance October 12, 1820.
620	Cary Nicholas	Lieutenant, now captain 7th	817 92	Balance August 14, 1821.
622	Josiah Bacon	Lieutenant 4th	1,397 44	Balance October 10, 1822.
622	John Hazleton	Lieutenant 19th	239 49	Balance June 3, 1823.
623	John D. Rogers	Lieutenant dragoons	40 00	Balance January 1, 1820.
627	Otis Fisher	Assistant deputy q. m. general	242 97	Balance February 5, 1833.
629	Samuel Conrad	Paymaster Pennsylvania militia.	28 75	Balance January 13, 1823.
629	H. H. Davis	Captain 32d	239 00	Balance October 23, 1821.
630	Michael C. Hays	Captain R. R.	299 16	Balance January 1, 1820.
630	James Green	Lieutenant 3d rifles	490 49	Balance April 6, 1822.
631	John Williams	Ensign 3d rifles	349 63	Balance March 14, 1820.
632	Ethan A. Allen	Late ass't deputy q. m. general	425 19	Balance June 29, 1826.
632	Joseph Griswold	Captain	40 00	Balance January 1, 1820.
632	Moody Bedel	Lieutenant colonel	12,180 21	Balance December 23, 1826.
633	Joseph M. Wilcox	Lieutenant 3d infantry	301 43	Balance January 1, 1820.
634	John S. Langham	Acting paymaster	4,797 10	Do. do.
635	William Johnston	Lieutenant 24th	489 26	Do. do.
636	James Hedges	Captain 26th	1,366 32	Do. do.
636	Stephen Ford	Lieutenant 8th	47 00	Do. do.
636	Edward L. Pegram	Lieutenant 35th	763 00	Do. do.
637	William D. Hayden	Lieutenant and paymaster 28th.	24,972 82	Do. do.
639	Alton Nelson	Lieutenant 29th	119 22	Do. do.
639	Hollyman Battle	Lieutenant 43d	560 63	Do. do.
643	John Milligan	Lieutenant 19th	550 62	Do. do.
643	Wilson Elliott	Captain 19th	976 00	Balance May 23, 1822.
648	Thomas B. Young	Lieutenant 24th	124 00	Balance January 1, 1820.

650	Clarkson Price	Lieutenant 26th	296	00	Balance February 7, 1820.
653	Luther Bugbee	Lieutenant 31st	11	40	Balance January 1, 1820.
655	Robert L. Combs	Lieutenant 1st	550	00	Balance September 20, 1823.
656	Thomas Monroe	Lieutenant 20th infantry	52	98	Balance January 1, 1820.
656	Thompson Gaines	Late paymaster 7th Ky. militia	184	07	Balance November 9, 1820.
658	Jonathan Cox	Ensign 12th	25	91	Balance January 1, 1820.
658	Archibald C. Randolph	Captain	750	00	Do. do.
659	John C. Avery	Lieutenant 26th	163	95	Balance August 12, 1823.
660	Collin McLoud	do	73	00	Balance November 27, 1821.
662	William Morrow	Late paymaster 2d Ohio militia	746	55	Balance March 13, 1822.
667	Alexander D. Orr	Assistant deputy q. m. general	134	85	Balance March 6, 1823.
668	John C. Bartlett	Field commissary	32,754	82	Balance March 12, 1821.
668	James Meed	Deceased, late captain 17th	131	24	Balance January 1, 1820.
670	Benjamin T. Elmore	Captain	65	59	Balance April 26, 1823.
672	William B. Jones	Lieutenant 24th	16	00	Balance January 1, 1820.
672	Winfield Jones	Lieutenant 35th	529	20	Balance December 4, 1821.
673	Alexander R. McKnight	Lieutenant 29th	120	02	Balance January 1, 1820.
673	Thompson Douglass	Deputy paymaster	28,080	57	Do. do.
674	Jonas Gates	Lieutenant 31st	120	22	Do. do.
675	Edward Jones	Lieutenant 39th	133	62	Do. do.
676	Benjamin H. Scott	Lieutenant 9th	179	25	Do. do.
680	Israel Turner	Late captain 13th	176	07	Balance August 24, 1820.
681	Clement Sullivan	Captain 14th	44	38	Balance January 1, 1820.
681	William A. Covington	Lieutenant 39th	496	00	Do. do.
682	John Foster	Captain 22d	1,054	21	Do. do.
682	John S. Williamson	Lieutenant 24th	431	94	Do. do.
683	Wyley Martin	Captain	866	24	Do. do.
685	Thomas Duncan	Paymaster	80	27	Balance February 6, 1824.
689	James S. Wynkoop	Lieutenant 29th	106	08	Balance January 1, 1820.
690	Charles Hutchins	Late lieutenant 35th	98	30	Do. do.
690	Richard Edsall	Late lieutenant 15th	19	00	Do. do.
691	Jacob B. Ion	Captain artillery	18	62	Do. do.
691	Leonard J. M. Littlejohn	Late paymaster 3d Md. militia	224	38	Balance January 6, 1825.
691	William Rogers	Captain 15th	309	23	Balance February 26, 1824.
692	N. N. Hall	Lieutenant	250	00	Balance August 3, 1822.
692	Ira Drew	do	493	71	Balance November 2, 1821.
694	Ralp Martin	Major 22d	2,818	13	Balance December 21, 1820.
697	M. S. Massey	Lieutenant 2d artillery	404	94	Balance July 15, 1824.
698	Return J. Meigs	Indian agent	624	23	Balance June 20, 1824.
699	Heman A. Fay			17	Balance December 31, 1822.
702	George W. Melvin	Lieutenant artillery	3,740	62	Balance July 3, 1824.

				Arrearages:
705	Samuel Owings	Late paymaster 6th cavalry	$121 72	Balance January 1, 1820.
706	Robert Gibson	Lieutenant 34th	90 59	Do. do.
707	William Watkins	Paymaster New York militia	2,106 90	Do. do.
708	Daniel Forward	Lieutenant 25th	803 00	Balance September 7, 1821.
709	Jacob Lentner	Lieutenant 32d	57 08	Balance May 30, 1822.
711	William S. Heaton	Lieutenant 11th	18 24	Balance January 1, 1820.
711	Tunis Hanson	Lieutenant 29th	35 64	Do. do.
712	Loring Palmer	Late captain 9th	150 00	Do. do.
714	Anthony Palmer	Lieutenant 39th	606 00	Do. do.
714	Joel Denton	do	128 47	Balance September 16, 1829.
718	George Eckridge	Ensign 12th	100 02	Balance January 1, 1820.
718	Francis T. Wheeler	Lieutenant 13th	523 65	Do. do.
719	Jesse O. Tate	Lieutenant 39th	8 00	Do. do.
719	James Davis	Captain 39th	2,382 00	Balance December 9, 1828.
720	George Hallum	do	112 50	Balance January 1, 1820.
720	Guy Smith	Lieutenant 39th	360 07	Balance November 29, 1822.
722	Robert Wood	Late ensign 10th	451 00	Balance January 1, 1820.
722	Fifield Lyford	Lieutenant 31st	50 63	Balance December 19, 1821.
723	Josiah A. Smith	Late paymaster Maryland militia	123 90	Balance January 1, 1820.
723	Frederick J. Prevost	Lieutenant 6th	240 00	Do. do.
724	Lewis Dunham	Surgeon	4 92	Do. do.
725	David G. Cowan	Lieutenant 28th	105 24	Balance March 16, 1826.
734	Robert Brett	Lieutenant infantry	250 00	Balance December 8, 1821.
734	Henry Hart	Ensign	153 00	Balance August 24, 1820.
739	Jasper Y. Smith	Paymaster R. R	428 63	Balance January 1, 1820.
739	John Stannard	Lieutenant colonel	330 00	Balance September 6, 1820.
740	John W. Kincaid	Lieutenant	1,568 00	Balance November 17, 1821.
740	William Huston	Lieutenant 26th	238 00	Balance January 1, 1820.
741	Alexander Steuart	Major	251 83	Balance May 1, 1825.
742	William C. Hobbs	Lieutenant	100 00	Balance January 1, 1820.
742	Henry C. Neale	Captain 36th	328 67	Balance September 24, 1822.
743	James Neale	Lieutenant	600 00	Balance December 5, 1821.

744	Robert Call	Ensign 12th	40 46	Balance July 11, 1820.
744	John Robinson	do	1,524 50	Balance August 31, 1821.
744	Thomas P. Wagnon	Lieutenant 28th	158 00	Balance January 1, 1820.
745	Edward J. Roberts	Lieut. and paymaster 1st infantry	5,564 73	Do. do.
746	Asa Minor	Ensign 29th	72 20	Do. do.
746	John H. Bryson	Late captain 16th	912 45	Do. do.
747	Robert Young	Paymaster 19th	207 34	Balance July 14, 1823.
747	Andrew Noble	Paymaster, &c	9 74	Balance June 17, 1824.
748	John K. Stokes	Captain 2d dragoons	1,178 95	Balance August 13, 1822.
749	Chastien Scott	Lieutenant 17th	361 25	Balance March 29, 1820.
750	John G. Scholtz	Lieutenant 27th	5,592 96	Balance January 1, 1820.
750	Robert Peyton	Late captain	159 96	Do. do.
751	Sandford Bartlett	Ensign	380 00	Do. do.
753	Robert Edwards	Captain 17th	100 00	Do. do.
755	John Ruffin	Lieutenant artillery	632 00	Do. do.
756	Archibald Dobbin	Assistant deputy paymaster	6,782 13	Balance July 3, 1821.
756	William N. Irvine	Colonel	35,915 00	Balance October 30, 1821.
757	Christopher Kieser	Lieut. ord. and asst. D. Q. M. G.	363 75	Balance January 1, 1820.
758	Joseph Clark	Lieutenant 28th	500 00	Balance June 2, 1821.
759	Richard Perkins	Late paymaster 3d Va., militia.	421 00	Balance January 1, 1820.
760	Samuel H. Bryant	Lieutenant	190 00	Do. do.
761	Joseph Bryant	Late captain 10th	519 61	Do. do.
761	Benajah White	Lieutenant colonel 10th	4,055 50	Balance May 16, 1820.
762	John Henderson	Lieutenant	50 00	Balance January 1, 1820.
764	Benjamin Nicholson	Lieutenant 14th	457 67	Do. do.
766	Samuel A. Kippey	Late lieutenant 22d	60 00	Do. do.
767	Stephen Lee	Lieutenant 19th	276 57	Balance March 18, 1822.
767	James Duncan	Captain 17th	17 52	Balance November 1, 1821.
768	Joseph A. Martin	Ensign 24th	250 00	Balance June 14, 1822.
768	Lewis Saunders		20,000 00	Balance January 1, 1820.
769	Thomas Mountjoy	Ensign 17th	222 00	Do. do.
769	M. L. Hawkins	Lieutenant	75 00	Balance July 28, 1823.
769	Joseph Clay	Captain 10th	92 95	Balance June 4, 1840.
770	Neal McFadden	Lieutenant 19th	538 28	Balance January 1, 1820.
770	James Blair	do	71 20	Balance January 7, 1822.
771	Isaac McLain	Paymaster Virginia militia.	385 22	Balance January 1, 1820.
772	James Doherty	Major 26th	121 24	Do. do.
772	Wilson Creed	Ensign 7th	46 00	Balance May 6, 1820.
773	John Henderson	Paymaster 1st reg't Va. militia.	809 78	Balance January 1, 1820.
773	Jackson Durant	Lieutenant 4th	221 71	Do. do.
774	Burnell Goodwin	Late lieutenant 10th [illegible]	192 63	Do. do.

				Arrearages:
774	Spencer Hinton	Lieutenant 10th	$420 00	Balance August 3, 1822.
775	Solomon Sutherland	Captain 29th	144 34	Balance January 1, 1820.
775	Samuel Lane	Late maj. 14th, now lt. col. 32d.	912 52	Do. do.
780	Abil Gibbs	Lieutenant 30th	224 00	Do. do.
780	William R. Duncan	Captain artillery	98 00	Do. do.
781	Edward Upham	Ensign	1,010 00	Balance December 5, 1821.
781	A. Gates	do	1,000 00	Balance November 5, 1821.
782	Francis Carr	Ensign 21st	348 49	Balance January 1, 1820.
784	John V. H. Huych	Major	3,901 08	Balance April 30, 1822.
785	William S. Horner	Hospital surgeon's mate	20 00	Balance January 1, 1820.
786	Robert Morris	Late ensign 13th	234 16	Do. do.
787	Charles Livermore	Lieutenant 13th	106 30	Do. do.
787	James Brown, jr	Lieutenant 7th	96 00	Do. do.
788	William S. Wells	Lieutenant 24th, late 17th.	512 50	Do. do.
791	Gassaway Watkins	Lieutenant 38th	434 00	Balance September 13, 1825.
791	Addison Carrick	Late asst. deputy q. m. general.	4,429 64	Balance May 15, 1829.
792	Abraham Clark	Lieutenant 14th	159 41	Balance September 23, 1829.
794	Meredith W. Fisher	Lieutenant 17th	673 80	Balance January 1, 1820.
794	William Billings	Captain	101 80	Balance June 1, 1821.
795	John Sampson	Quartermaster New York militia.	155 68	Balance November 4, 1820.
796	William Bingham	Lieutenant 31st	52 25	Balance September 12, 1829.
796	Thomas Bangs	Ensign 9th	424 00	Balance November 16, 1826.
797	John Perley	Lieutenant 9th	451 69	Balance June 25, 1824.
798	Daniel C. Lane	Quartermaster brig. Ky. militia.	739 40	Balance August 24, 1830.
799	James Awl	Ensign 16th	263 20	Balance January 1, 1820.
802	John Lee	Lieutenant 34th	319 37	Do. do.
803	John H. Smith	Paymaster 1st Ohio militia	7,951 55	Do. do.
812	Thomas C. Wilbight	Act'g asst. subsistence Ft. Scott.	710 00	Do. do.
815	Robert Torrance		2,520 00	Balance July 24, 1822.
817	John Bayley	Paymaster 57th Va. militia	17 71	Balance September 25, 1820.
817	Samuel Scott	Paymaster 24th infantry	32,702 20	Balance January 17, 1821.

821	Reuben B. Patterson	Paymaster Virginia militia	388 58	Balance June 30, 1820.
822	Jonathan Pugh	...do	46 89	Balance October 9, 1821.
824	Ashton Garrett	Paymaster 17th	32,703 56	Balance October 21, 1834.
824	Joseph M. Hays	To pay Ohio militia	314 94	Balance January 1, 1820.
826	Frederick Leonard	To pay Delaware militia	342 92	Balance November 8, 1820.
826	John McDougal	Paymaster Ohio militia	16,811 01	Balance March 8, 1820.
827	Lewis M. Prevost	Paymaster Penn'a militia	1,608 32	Balance October 24, 1820.
828	Nathaniel Shewell	...do	302 82	Balance June 8, 1825.
830	W. H. Curtis	Lieutenant 12th	215 00	Balance September 28, 1829.
832	William Campbell	Captain light artillery	2,718 26	Balance May 25, 1825.
833	George Strother	Captain 10th	16 75	Balance January 1, 1820.
833	Clement White	Captain 20th	4 12	Do. do.
834	Thomas Ramsay	Captain 1st	334 60	Do. do.
834	Simon D. Wattles	Captain 23d	175 00	Balance August 27, 1822.
835	William Kenny	Lieutenant corps of artillery	24	Balance January 1, 1820.
835	Simon Larned	Colonel 9th	539 76	Do. do.
835	Miles Greenwood	Captain 16th	448 00	Balance July 17, 1822.
838	Thomas W. Blackledge	Lieutenant 3d	320 40	Balance October 3, 1823.
841	J. Leach	Lieutenant 7th	200 00	Balance January 1, 1820.
842	John Noble	...do	250 00	Do. do.
842	William Prince	Late paymaster 14th Ky. militia	12,813 59	Balance January 15, 1824.
843	N. G. Bean	Lieutenant 21st	12 79	Balance September 10, 1821.
844	Henry Draper	Ensign	80 00	Balance December 11, 1822.
845	John Ritchie	Captain artillery	1,453 40	Balance January 1, 1820.
846	John Nye	Captain 9th	142 39	Do. do.
847	Adam King	Acting paymaster, &c	223 85	Do. do.
847	David Perry	Captain 5th, late 9th, infantry	2,100 00	Balance November 5, 1821.
851	John Johnson	Lieutenant 12th	1,600 00	Balance January 1, 1820.
858	William Gutridge	Ensign 26th	112 00	Do. do.
858	Joseph Kerr		5,434 05	Do. do.
859	William Cocks	Late captain artillery	78 00	Do. do.
860	Philip T. Richardson	Ensign 26th	800 00	Do. do.
861	Frederick Brooks	Captain, &c	63 07	Do. do.
862	Edward Norton	Ensign	270 07	Do. do.
862	Charles Ketchline	Captain	280 00	Do. do.
864	Fayette Roane	Lieutenant dragoons	426 30	Balance February 21, 1825.
864	John G. Clark	Lieutenant 5th	76 00	Balance September 28, 1829.
864	Richard Arrell	Lieutenant 14th	210 00	Balance March 21, 1821.
865	Kennel Goodwin	...do	40 00	Balance November 2, 1821.
865	Lemuel Bradford	Captain 21st	1,083 01	Balance September 7, 1821.
866	Frederick Conkling	Lieutenant 4th	1,369 75	Balance January 1, 1820.

				Arrearages:
867	John D. Hart	Lieutenant dragoons	$675 57	Balance May 15, 1820.
869	N. R. Packard	Brigade quartermaster	391 82	Balance May 8, 1821.
870	Salomon Ellis	Late contractor	11,485 11	Balance June 30, 1822.
872	Ephraim L. Phelps		1,605 09	Balance May 16, 1828.
872	Lawrence Van Buren	Late quartermaster general	364 71	Balance October 16, 1821.
873	Jesse Robinson	Captain 2d artillery	119 14	Balance January 1, 1820.
873	Benjamin P. Head	Lieutenant 38th	606 00	Do. do.
875	Timothy Bacon	Lieutenant 34th	191 24	Do. do.
876	Simon Owens	Captain 1st	639 13	Do. do.
877	Festus Cone	Captain	122 00	Balance September 28, 1829.
880	Henry Wellington	Lieutenant 9th	171 44	Balance January 1, 1820.
880	Barrent Schuyler	Captain 29th	5,672 84	Balance November 30, 1821.
880	P. B. Van Beuren	do	1,450 34	Balance January 1, 1820.
880	Joel Peebles	Lieutenant 29th	1,000 00	Balance October 5, 1821.
881	Gad Dumbleton	do	1,588 52	Balance October 25, 1821.
881	S. D. Kellog	do	2,022 80	Balance July 6, 1821.
882	John King	Captain 23d	34 25	Balance January 1, 1820.
882	Benjamin Smead	Captain 11th	278 38	Do. do.
883	William Ray	Late quartermaster, &c	1,300 00	Do. do.
883	John H. Plummer	Late deputy commissary	13,775 57	Do. do.
884	Josiah Hill	Lieutenant rifles	30 00	Do. do.
885	Thomas M. Kead		743 86	Balance January 26, 1821.
886	John S. Brush	Late lieutenant artillery	800 44	Balance January 1, 1820.
888	Thomas A. Helms	Late captain dragoons	1,289 58	Balance February 16, 1820.
888	Aaron Bidgelow	Ensign 21st	675 24	Balance January 1, 1820.
888	John McCluney	Major 23d	2,530 50	Do. do.
889	Gabriel Barbour		1,770 00	Do. do.
889	John Burnett	Late lieut. and quarterm'r 3d	1,666 25	Do. do.
890	Thomas Bailey	Late lieutenant 34th	1,261 37	Do. do.
891	John M. Burgess	Late lieutenant 36th	700 00	Do. do.
891	Ralph B. Cuyler	Late lieutenant 6th	1,562 36	Do. do.
891	George Cloud	Late captain 10th	883 47	Balance January 6, 1820.

897	Willie J. Gordon	Late lieutenant 10th	2,222 00	Do. do.
898	Benjamin R. Bostwick	Late bar. mas	5,649 60	Do. do.
899	Thomas Vail	Late ensign 29th	1,755 00	Do. do.
899	Robert Steele	Captain	1,074 00	Do. do.
903	Wait Martin	Late lieutenant 23d	276 00	Do. do.
904	Isaac Myers	Ensign 16th	346 00	Balance February 14, 1828.
905	Charles Follett	Late captain 11th	3,248 00	Balance January 1, 1820.
907	Robert Beall	Late lieutenant 14th	2,706 62	Balance June 14, 1823.
907	William Morris, jr	Late lieutenant 33d	369 14	Balance January 1, 1820.
908	George W. Ten Broeck	Captain 6th	7,259 96	Do. do.
908	John Williby	Lieutenant 27th	75	Do. do.
908	Robert Stockton	Lieutenant 19th	470 00	Balance May 31, 1825.
909	Arthur Simkins	Captain 10th	724 21	Balance July 26, 1820.
909	Alexander Worster	Lieutenant 33d	15 51	Balance January 1, 1820.
909	Alexander McCalley	Late lieutenant 33d	140 34	Do. do.
910	Timothy Stuart	Late paymaster 2d N. Y. militia	1,166 82	Balance May 8, 1820.
910	William Young	Late lieutenant 7th	92 00	Balance January 1, 1820.
910	John Vail	Captain 18th	57 37	Do. do.
911	David Skinner	Paymaster New York militia	649 77	Balance August 22, 1826.
912	John McClelland	Late captain 3d infantry	831 77	Balance November 30, 1822.
912	Charles Quirey	Late captain 17th	3,050 00	Balance January 1, 1820.
912	Alexander Parris	Captain, &c	1,050 00	Do. do.
912	William Triplett	Late lieutenant 3d	1,027 00	Do. do.
913	John Miller	Captain, &c	19,359 09	Balance December 10, 1822.
913	Thomas Daggett	Lieutenant 2d regiment	600 00	Balance January 1, 1820.
913	George Templeman	Lieutenant and acting, &c	952 40	Do. do.
915	Robert Andrews	A. D. Q. M	425 32	Do. do.
916	Silas Amberson	Captain 22d	100 00	Balance July 6, 1822.
917	A. B. Armstead	Captain	1,333 06	Balance June 25, 1822.
917	Elbert Anderson	Cornet	257 79	Balance November 26, 1821.
918	James M. Anderson	Captain 8th	310 00	Balance October 7, 1820.
918	Nathaniel F. Adams	Paymaster 4th	9,709 73	Balance December 15, 1820.
918	Hanibal M. Allen	Captain	604 00	Balance January 1, 1820.
920	Marshall Ayers	Lieutenant 43d	570 00	Balance August 18, 1821.
920	William S. Allen		48	Balance January 1, 1820.
921	James G. Aiken	Ensign	425 56	Balance January 28, 1820.
921	Peter Albright	Ensign 1st rifles	12 07	Balance January 1, 1820.
921	P. Anspack	Cornet dragoons	166 00	Balance September 21, 1821.
922	Philo. Andrews	A. D. Q. M. general	603 16	Balance November 17, 1825.
922	William Aull	Lieutenant 4th rifles	231 26	Balance September 21, 1821.
923	Oliphant Martin		35 50	Balance January 1, 1820.

				Arrearages:
1240	Melancton Smith	Colonel	$20,998 89	Balance May 17, 1826.
1240	Aaron Walters	Lieutenant 29th	450 00	Balance January 6, 1820.
1240	Lemuel H. Mitchell	do	125 00	Do. do.
1241	George W. Barker	Captain 42d	200 00	Balance October 1, 1821.
1241	Richard Dennis	Colonel	24,640 18	Balance January 10, 1822.
1242	Joseph W. Edwards	Lieutenant 29th	150 00	Balance January 6, 1820.
1242	Jeremiah Emery	Captain 33d	199 65	Do. do.
1242	Thomas Lawrence	Lieutenant 22d	362 05	Balance January 11, 1820.
1243	Abraham Shane	Late lieutenant 27th	15 34	Balance August 21, 1824.
1243	Walter German	Captain 4th	31 40	Balance January 11, 1820.
1244	James B. Wilkinson	Captain 2d artillery	1,864 67	Balance July 18, 1823.
1244	William B. Staats	Ensign 6th	2,725 13	Balance September 7, 1820.
1244	Ebenezer Knox	Ensign 21st	483 77	Balance January 17, 1820.
1245	James Leith	Late lieutenant 39th	868 00	Balance January 1, 1820.
1245	Charles Lothorp	Late captain 33d	157 41	Balance January 18, 1820.
1246	Nathan C. Wade	Late ensign 10th	230 00	Balance January 1, 1820.
1246	Daniel Guin	Late lieutenant 24th	20 00	Do. do.
1247	Michael Walsh	Late captain artillery	692 00	Balance January 25, 1820.
1255	William Walker	Late captain 25th	565 30	Balance January 1, 1820.
1255	Moses Hammons	Ensign 33d	10 00	Do. do.
1256	Walter G. Hays	Late 20th infantry	2,354 55	Do. do.
1257	Abel Morse	Lieutenant 6th	2 50	Do. do.
1257	Peleg Barker	Late captain	130 40	Balance February 11, 1820.
1257	Owen Clinton	Captain 18th	878 98	Balance February 12, 1820.
1258	Daniel A. Blauvelt	Late paymaster 83d N. Y. militia	25 49	Balance January 22, 1824.
1258	Samuel Hairston	Lieutenant 20th	76 21	Balance February 11, 1820.
1259	William M. Dyer	Lieutenant 9th	78 20	Balance November 2, 1821.
1259	George Henry	Lieutenant 15th	50 00	Balance February 12, 1820.
1260	Jonathan B. Eastman	D. paymaster	16,984 83	Balance July 24, 1823.
1260	Leonard Cole	Late ensign 26th	66 80	Balance February 11, 1820.
1260	Samuel A. Taylor	Late lieutenant 43d	45 38	Balance February 16, 1820.
1261	Valentine P. Luckett	Late lieutenant dragoons	724 00	Do. do.

[illegible]	John Phagan	Late captain 39th	132 04	Balance March 15, 1821.
1262	Jesse Wormack	Late lieutenant 8th	126 00	Balance February 23, 1820.
1265	Henry W. Warner	Late paymaster 2d N. Y. militia	110 40	Balance March 7, 1820.
1265	Lemuel Morris	Captain, &c	2,282 79	Balance March 8, 1820.
1266	William Lavall	Late lieutenant 3d infantry	970 00	Balance March 14, 1820.
1266	Homer V. Milton	Colonel 3d infantry	1,997 62	Balance May 10, 1820.
1267	Waters Allen	Paymaster	8,653 24	Balance February 26, 1830.
1267	Robert W. Kent	Late captain 14th	23 72	Balance March 18, 1820.
1268	Melchor Keener	Lieutenant 36th	200 00	Balance January 1, 1820.
1269	Zachariah Schoonmaker	Late paymaster N. Y volunteers	5,106 15	Balance September 25, 1824.
1269	Henry A. Hobert	Lieutenant artillery	245 00	Balance March 23, 1820.
1270	William Townsley	Lieutenant 1st rifles	51 62	Balance March 24, 1820.
1270	Robert R. Conrad	Late lieutenant 35th	542 66	Balance June 19, 1822.
1271	Henry Grindage	Captain 14th	400 00	Balance June 7, 1825.
1271	Jacob Schenor	Captain 16th	347 43	Balance April 25, 1842.
1272	Harvey Weed	Late paymaster 2d N. Y. militia	1 86	Balance October 6, 1826.
1272	John Hamilton	Lieutenant 17th	102 66	Balance April 1, 1820.
1273	Londus L. Buck	Lieutenant 6th	1,122 00	Balance April 7, 1820.
1273	Edmund Badger	Lieutenant 9th	283 67	Balance August 21, 1821.
1274	William Rodes	Late paymaster 15th Ky. militia	156 80	Balance July 21, 1821.
1274	Melancton Woolsey	Assistant deputy q. m. general	13,142 26	Balance October 11, 1822.
1276	John Roberts	3d wagon-master	760 20	Balance November 6, 1822.
1276	Ferdinand Marsteller	Late paymaster, &c	62 45	Balance April 24, 1820.
1277	Jeremiah Chapman	Captain 21st	724 00	Balance January 25, 1822.
1278	Thomas Camp	Late as't deputy q. m. General	687 78	Balance October 11, 1823.
1280	Thomas French	Lieutenant 26th	846 00	Balance May 4, 1820.
1280	William Nelson	Late lieutenant 24th	1,104 00	Do. do.
1281	Jacob Tipton	Lieutenant 1st rifles	96 00	Balance May 9, 1820.
1282	John R. Spann	Captain light artillery	4 07	Balance May 10, 1820.
1283	Wilson Whatley	Late ensign 18th	1,126 60	Balance November 26, 1821.
1283	Thomas Hoxey	Paymaster Georgia militia	1,303 60	Balance May 3, 1824.
1284	Walter Smith	Late ensign 29th	10 00	Balance May 16, 1820.
1286	Thomas Steuart	Captain 39th	422 91	Balance February 13, 1833.
1286	Richard Doyle	Lieutenant 17th	128 13	Balance May 19, 1820.
1286	Michael J. Kenan	Late captain 18th	359 49	Balance May 16, 1820.
1288	Gerrit H. Van Schaick	Late paymast'r 156th N. J. militia	267 11	Balance May 19, 1820.
1289	George H. Green	Late paymas'r 118th N. Y. militia	19 60	Balance May 22, 1820.
1290	Frost Thorn	Late paymaster 2d N. Y. militia	66 67	Balance May 30, 1820.
1290	Samuel H. Eakin	Late deputy paymaster	9,067 43	Balance March 17, 1827.
1292	Joseph Jenkins	Lieutenant	1,550 00	Balance August 30, 1821.
1292	Thomas J. Martin	Lieutenant 16th	550 00	Balance June 22, 1827.

Pages.	Names.	Rank.	Amount.	Remarks.
				Arrearages:
1292	John Martin	Lieutenant 16th	$570 00	Balance June 22, 1827.
1293	Thomas A. Patterson	Captain R. R.	162 40	Balance June 8, 1820.
1296	William Griswold	Late paymaster N. Y. militia	99 11	Balance September 22, 1823.
1296	George R. Bridges	Late lieutenant 10th	928 84	Balance June 12, 1820.
1297	Hugh H. Carson	do	1,072 43	Balance January 1, 1820.
1297	John Collins	Ensign 15th	182 00	Balance September 29, 1829.
1298	Hugh Robinson	Late lieutenant 13th	78 26	Balance August 21, 1820.
1299	William A. Shelton	Late captain 20th	467 70	Balance June 27, 1820.
1299	Carter H. Bradley	Ensign 20th	501 00	Balance December 7, 1821.
1299	John Lynch	Late ensign 14th	102 91	Balance July 1, 1820.
1300	Aaron Kay	Wagon master	200 00	Balance January 1, 1820.
1300	Edward L. Lomax	Late ensign	100 00	Do. do.
1300	Robert H. Morris	Late captain 13th	585 70	Do. do.
1301	William Ross	Late ensign 21st	241 32	Balance May 13, 1820.
1301	John C. Radcliff	Paymaster, &c	67 44	Balance October 25, 1820.
1303	John Johnson, deceased	Major 21st	208 88	Balance January 1, 1820.
1303	Thomas Lyon	Captain 16th	228 00	Do. do.
1306	Elam Lynds	Captain 29th	61 33	Balance April 30, 1821.
1307	Ferdinand Fairfax	Citizen	70 00	Balance August 4, 1820.
1308	Sylvester Boothe	Late lieutenant 4th	4,053 00	Balance May 7, 1822.
1309	Freeman, Nickerson	Lieutenant 31st	320 00	Balance January 1, 1820.
1309	Thomas Winn	Lieutenant artillery	590 00	Do. do.
1330	Thomas Lyon	Late lieutenant 16th	248 00	Balance July 17, 1820.
1330	Joseph G. Wall	Lieutenant	544 00	Balance January 1, 1820.
1330	Silas Harmon	Paymaster New York militia	26 97	Balance August 19, 1820.
1331	John Chrystie	Lieutenant colonel	488 30	Balance May 11, 1821.
1334	John Duncan	Ensign 21st	77 34	Balance August 29, 1820.
1335	Thomas Yerby	Cornet 41st Virginia militia	34 00	Do. do.
1335	William Cogswell	Forage master	3,812 04	Balance April 20, 1822.
1335	James Green	Lieutenant colonel militia	1,250 00	Balance August 28, 1820.
1336	James Payne	Late acting paymaster	14 93	Balance August 30, 1820.
[illegible]	[illegible]	Captain, &c	11 30	Balance August 31, 1820.

1337	John Furman	Lieutenant	185 00	Balance January 1, 1820.
1337	Samuel Delong	Ensign	176 00	Do. do.
1338	Benjamin Mosby	Captain 28th	1,415 00	Do. do.
1339	Adam J. Roof	Late paymaster N. Y. militia	15 71	Balance October 13, 1821.
1340	Tilman Turner	Lieutenant 3d infantry	600 00	Balance January 1, 1820.
1340	Enos Walker	Late lieutenant 31st	135 00	Do. do.
1341	Henry Deyo	Late ensign 13th	73 58	Balance September 25, 1820.
1341	William Gale	Cornet	2,884 00	Balance September 27, 1820.
1342	John Wingate	Brigadier General Ohio militia	5 00	Balance February 2, 1824.
1242	James G. Chalmers	Paymaster	17,127 25	Balance October 1, 1821.
1342	Barnet Williams	Paymaster 1st reg. Ky. militia	754 79	Balance January 3, 1827.
1345	Cephas L. Rockwood	Captain 31st	50 00	Balance September 5 1822.
1346	James Meeker	Lieutenant militia cavalry	150 00	Balance January 1, 1820.
1347	John Butler	Late captain dragoons	4,800 00	Balance October 13, 1825.
1347	Charles Mitchell	Ensign 19th	1,395 00	Balance October 4, 1822.
1347	William Morrow	Lieutenant 22d	200 00	Balance January 1, 1820.
1348	Lemuel P. Montgomery	Major 39th	229 33	Do. do.
1348	Hugh McClelland	Late lieutenant 32d	384 54	Balance October 21, 1820.
1348	William H. Miles	Lieutenant 43d	21 55	Balance June 10, 1858.
1349	George Nelson	Captain	850 00	Balance January 1, 1820.
1349	Dabney Morris	Ensign	262 89	Do. do.
1349	John McClintic	Captain Pennsylvania vols.	794 00	Do. do.
1350	Robert B. Moore		447 33	Do. do.
1350	John B. McIntire	Ensign 34th	170 00	Do. do.
1350	Henry Carberry	Late colonel 36th	3,107 53	Balance April 22, 1824.
1351	Samuel Maclay	Lieutenant artillery	200 00	Balance January 1, 1820.
1351	Arthur Morgan	Captain	1,848 00	Balance May 6, 1823.
1352	Joseph Markle	do	20 00	Balance November 16, 1821.
1353	Benjamin W. Moss	Paymaster 1st reg. Va. militia	161 68	Balance March 23, 1824.
1354	J. P. Ragland	Paymaster 6th Virginia militia	48 20	Balance May 15, 1822.
1354	Daniel Sangford	Paymaster Virginia cavalry	405 33	Balance December 31, 1827.
1354	Edmund Tyler	Paymaster 5th Virginia militia	44 47	Balance June 26, 1822.
1356	Benedict Bacon	Quartermaster	75 00	Balance January 1, 1820.
1357	Henry Burbeck	Colonel	60 96	Do. do.
1357	R. B. Brown	Captain 24th	154 70	Balance February 24, 1841.
1358	Richard Bean	Lieutenant	44 70	Balance January 1, 1820.
1358	William Blanchard	Lieutenant 19th	600 00	Do. do.
1359	Josiah Brady	Lieutenant 26th	545 00	Balance March 30, 1822.
1359	Benjamin Bailey	Captain 34th	01	Balance January 1, 1820.
1360	Thomas Bruff	Late doctor and dentist	500 00	Do. do.
1360	David C. Butts	Captain 31st	34 09	Do. do.

				Arrearages:
1361	Bailey Bruce	Lieutenant 12th	$917 25	Balance January 1, 1820.
1361	Henry Brooks	Lieutenant	100 00	Do. do.
1362	N. Branton	Lieutenant 7th	50 00	Do. do.
1362	Moses Bixbee, jr		100 00	Do. do.
1363	Francis Blaise	Ensign 23d	578 00	Balance November 8, 1824.
1363	William R. Boote	Captain 2d infantry	1 50	Balance January 1, 1820.
1364	Samuel Borden	Lieutenant and quar'master 4th	975 50	Do. do.
1364	Jonathan Brooks	Captain 6th	863 50	Do. do.
1364	John Ballinger	Captain 24th	1,228 19	Balance December 28, 1824.
1365	Ross Bird	Captain 3d	200 00	Balance January 1, 1820.
1365	George M. Beall	Lieutenant 17th	770 00	Balance October 1, 1824.
1366	Henry Branch	Captain 20th	564 58	Balance October 19, 1824.
1366	P. Britton	Captain	40 01	Balance January 1, 1820.
1366	Henry Brown	Lieutenant	30 00	Balance January 1, 1820.
1367	Peter Bradley	Captain	1,918 00	Balance May 10, 1822.
1367	Rufus Bucklin	Lieutenant 11th	1 81	Balance January 1, 1820.
1368	Thomas S. Bailey	Lieutenant 8th	283 38	Do. do.
1368	Ebenezer Beebe	Captain	1,891 04	Do. do.
1368	Edward Barnaville	Lieutenant 34th	261 52	Balance September 15, 1829.
1369	Julius Bernard	Lieutenant dragoons	300 00	Balance January 11, 1821.
1369	Peter Bryan	Lieutenant 28th	668 85	Balance January 1, 1820.
1370	Henry Bender	Lieutenant 21st	50 00	Do. do
1370	Adolphus Bughardt	Ensign 9th	271 84	Balance September 7, 1829.
1372	Jeremiah Brown	Ensign	20 00	Balance January 1, 1820.
1372	Richard Bache	Captain volunteer artillery	100 00	Do. do.
1372	Joseph Barnett	Lieutenant 20th	434 00	Do. do.
1373	Walter Berryman	Lieutenant 2d artillery	64 05	Do. do.
1374	James Bailey	Lieutenant 6th	533 90	Balance August 13, 1828.
1374	Jonas G. Brooks	Ensign	28 00	Balance January 1, 1820.
1375	Joseph Berry	do	120 00	Balance September 10, 1829.
1375	W. Butler	Captain 3d infantry	2,178 00	Balance May 6, 1823.

1376	Joseph Bender	Lieutenant 32d	133 33	Balance January 1, 1820.
1377	Daniel A. A. Buck	Captain 31st	89 76	Do. do.
1377	Asa Baker	Lieutenant 31st	158 71	Do. do.
1378	Cyrus A. Baylor	Lieutenant 17th	1,250 00	Balance July 24, 1821.
1378	Samuel S. Berry	do	178 13	Balance January 1, 1820.
1379	Philip Berringer	Lieutenant	40 00	Do. do.
1379	Edward Baynton	Lieutenant 3d artillery	500 00	Balance January 11, 1821.
1380	Samuel G. Balch	Lieutenant 24th	300 00	Balance December 10, 1821.
1380	Narcissus Broutin	Lieutenant 7th	1,100 00	Balance October 1, 1824.
1381	Walter Bourke	Lieutenant 3d	1,034 00	Balance May 6, 1823.
1381	M. D. Burnett	Captain 46th	100 00	Balance September 9, 1829.
1383	John Beckett	Lieutenant	25 00	Balance January 1, 1820.
1383	Ebenezer Benedict	Lieutenant 27th	594 00	Do. do.
1383	Gideon Brownson	Lieutenant 30th	8 00	Do. do.
1384	William D. Beall	Colonel 36th	547 83	Balance February 1, 1821.
1384	Samuel Burr	Ensign 29th	500 00	Balance January 1, 1820.
1385	Abijah Bennett	Lieutenant 23d	249 25	Balance September 12, 1829.
1385	Thomas M. Buckley	Lieutenant 11th	82 34	Balance October 8, 1829.
1386	Walter B. Brown	Ensign 11th	109 82	Balance January 1, 1820.
1386	William P. Blair	Ensign 26th	1,300 00	Balance January 1, 1821.
1386	Reuben Crawford	Lieutenant 20th	622 53	Balance July 19, 1827.
1387	James Calhoun, jr., deceased		20 00	Balance May 26, 1821.
1387	Wm. W. Carr	Lieutenant 13th	739 11	Balance June 2, 1821.
1388	Jonathan Chase	Quartermaster Vermont militia	30 00	Balance April 17, 1822.
1388	Lemuel Childress	Ensign 39th	200 00	Balance May 25, 1825.
1388	Malachi Corning	Lieutenant 11th	805 87	Balance February 28, 1822.
1389	D. L. Carney	Lieutenant 19th	651 94	Balance September 6, 1821.
1389	Isaac Craton	Lieutenant 10th	25 00	Balance January 1, 1820.
1390	Samuel B. Canty	Lieutenant 18th	2 00	Do. do.
1390	Calvin Crooker	Lieutenant 34th	180 00	Balance May 18, 1822.
1390	Daniel Crossman	Captain 34th	233 08	Balance January 1, 1820.
1391	Thomas Clark	Lieutenant 34th	585 00	Balance September 6, 1821.
1391	Peter Chadwick	Captain 34th	2,150 48	Balance January 29, 1823.
1391	John Carney	Ensign 10th	24 00	Balance January 1, 1820.
1392	Wm. B. Carroll	Lieutenant 36th	448 00	Balance September 6, 1821.
1396	William Cock	Captain 6th	151 09	Balance January 1, 1820.
1395	John Campbell	Ensign 2d infantry	142 29	Do. do.
1395	John Cooper	Surgeon's mate	25 50	Do. do.
1396	Joseph Cross	Captain artillery	221 52	Do. do.
1396	Samuel Cherry	Lieutenant 6th	134 40	Do. do.
1397	Joseph Constant	Lieutenant colonel	54 00	Do. do.

				Arrearages:
1397	John Campbell	Lieutenant 1st	$40 00	Balance January 1, 1820.
1398	William Chisholm	Captain 8th	12 59	Balance November 8, 1824.
1398	Robert Clark	Lieutenant 4th	534 11	Balance June 7, 1824.
1399	James Chrystie	Lieutenant 14th	747 53	Balance November 11, 1824.
1399	Charles Crawford	Captain 8th infantry	178 48	Balance November 10, 1824.
1400	Charles Carson	Captain 15th	50 00	Balance January 1, 1820.
1401	Robert Clark	Lieutenant 28th	52 92	Balance May 28, 1832.
1402	Giles J. Chittenden	Contractor	44 82	Balance October 29, 1821.
1403	James Cummings	Ensign	50 00	Balance January 1, 1820.
1403	Charles Chase	Captain	50 00	Do. do.
1404	John J. Cromwell	Lieutenant 3d artillery	173 75	Balance April 15, 1822.
1404	Andrew Cowan	Ensign	124 32	Balance January 13, 1823.
1405	William Chappell	Captain 45th	632 00	Balance January 1, 1820.
1405	Samuel S. Connor	Lieutenant colonel 13th	7 51	Do. do.
1406	John B. Cole	Lieutenant 35th	54 50	Do. do.
1406	Robert A. Crowder	Lieutenant 37th	88 79	Balance January 25, 1821.
1406	Robert W. Carr	Ensign 35th	833 00	Balance January 1, 1820.
1407	Francis D. Charlton	Lieutenant 35th	70 55	Do. do.
1407	Joseph I. Clinch	Lieutenant 10th	174 00	Balance September 30, 1829.
1408	John Caldwell	Lieutenant	50 00	Balance January 1, 1820.
1409	F. L. Clairborn	Brigadier general volunteers	2,976 00	Balance July 16, 1821.
1409	John G. Crump	Lieutenant	100 00	Balance October 3, 1829.
1410	James Campbell	Lieutenant 17th	487 44	Balance November 10, 1824.
1410	Calvin Cummings	Ensign 21st	50 00	Balance January 1, 1820.
1410	John Carroll	Lieutenant 27th	400 00	Balance July 1, 1823.
1411	E. A. Clary	Lieutenant 40th	57 75	Balance January 1, 1820.
1411	Henry L. Duffell	Lieutenant 12th	19 59	Do. do.
1412	James Dunlap	Major	384 30	Balance September 30, 1822.
1412	Don C. Dixon	Lieutenant and paymaster 24th	230 46	Balance March 30, 1822.
1413	John E. Dorsey	Contractor	2,820 40	Balance January 1, 1820.
1413	A. M. Dixon	Ensign	50 00	Do. do.

[illegible]	John Dubois	Captain, &c.	37 10	Balance February 11, 1825.
1414	Thomas Dearborn	Lieutenant 33d	81 60	Balance January 1, 1820.
1415	Francis Drew	Captain 33d	6 00	Do. do.
1415	Isaac Davis	Surgeon 6th infantry	375 60	Balance October 14, 1829.
1416	Peter Donnelly	Lieutenant 13th	64 00	Balance January 1, 1820.
1416	Joseph H. Dwight	Ensign 13th	233 09	Balance October 17, 1829.
1417	Otis Dyer	Lieutenant 8th	364 79	Balance January 1, 1820.
1417	John Darnell	Lieutenant 2d infantry	64 80	Do. do.
1418	Richard C. Downes	Surgeon's mate 14th	5 00	Do. do.
1418	Thomas Davidge	Ensign 14th	150 00	Balance March 26, 1830.
1419	Silas Dickinson	Captain 31st	748 36	Balance January 1, 1820.
1419	Richard Dodge	Brigadier general militia	231 20	Do. do.
1420	Thomas Denny	Cadet	150 00	Balance March 20, 1820.
1420	Benjamin Darby	Lieutenant 30th	109 22	Balance January 1, 1820.
1420	John Doherty	Lieutenant militia cavalry	470 00	Balance October 13, 1821.
1421	Samuel Duncan	Assistant quartermaster general.	350 74	Do. do.
1422	Jeremiah Downes	Captain rifles, militia	10 27	Balance January 1, 1820.
1422	John F. Dixey	Lieutenant 40th	20 00	Do. do.
1422	Jeremiah Diman	Lieutenant	515 00	Balance November 6, 1822.
1423	Gaspard Dupey	Lieutenant 44th	372 00	Balance January 1, 1820.
1423	T. E. Danielson	Ensign 19th	89 00	Balance May 4, 1821.
1424	Jeremiah Edes	Lieutenant 34th	1,093 82	Balance January 25, 1821.
1424	Farley Eddy	Lieutenant	24	Balance January 1, 1820.
1425	Thomas Edmonson	Lieutenant 28th	58 00	Do. do.
1426	Nicholas Emigh	Captain militia	50 00	Do. do.
1426	Tisdale Eddy	Major	248 00	Balance October 16, 1821.
1426	Calvin Everist		150 00	Balance January 1, 1820.
1427	Jonathan Eddy	Lieutenant 31st	274 31	Do. do.
1427	Thomas Easton	Quartermaster militia	36 20	Do. do.
1427	William Eubank	Lieutenant 17th	390 00	Do. do.
1428	A. Evans	Ensign	190 00	Do. do.
1429	John Findley	Lieutenant	160 01	Do. do.
1429	John Fraser	Lieutenant 29th	113 51	Balance August 27, 1822.
1429	Amos Farnsworth	Surgeon's mate	50 00	Balance January 1, 1820.
1430	James Faulkner	Major artillery	70 00	Do. do.
1431	William Fowler	Quartermaster, N. Y. militia	118 24	Do. do.
1431	Thomas P. Finley	Lieutenant and paymaster	8,390 07	Balance January 30, 1821.
1432	Philip Fisher	Ensign 36th	46 00	Balance January 1, 1820.
1432	Bradbury Farnum	Lieutenant 21st	11 87	Do. do.
1433	G. Frisbee	Captain New York volunteers	150 00	Do. do.
1433	Henry F. Farley	Ensign	42 00	Do. do.

				Arrearages:
1433	Charles Farnham	Lieutenant 4th	$100 00	Balance January 1, 1820.
1434	James Fullington		25 00	Do. do.
1435	E. DeFlechier	Quartermaster 44th	400 00	Do. do.
1435	J. P. Favrot	Lieutenant 24th	976 00	Balance March 6, 1830.
1436	Amos Gustine	Lieutenant 4th	42 02	Balance January 1, 1820.
1436	Nathaniel Gookin	Lieutenant 34th	45 38	Balance December 8, 1824.
1437	James Green	Lieutenant 11th	1,063 00	Balance September 14, 1824.
1437	Valentine R. Goodrick	...do	55 00	Balance January 1, 1820.
1439	John Gibson	Acting Governor Indian Terr'y.	702 94	Balance June 1, 1826.
1439	Henry R. Graham	Lieutenant rifles	20 00	Balance January 1, 1820.
1440	Philip B. Greenwell	Lieutenant 5th	250 50	Balance December 31, 1824.
1441	Henry Glenn	Acting post quartermaster	115 65	Balance August 4, 1825.
1441	John Gilbreath	Lieutenant 24th	507 68	Balance January 1, 1820.
1441	John Gilbert	Ensign 30th	1,100 00	Balance July 5, 1821.
1442	John Goode	Lieutenant 26th	821 37	Balance October 17, 1829.
1442	John Gill	Captain, &c	19 81	Balance January 1, 1820.
1443	Asa Grimes	Lieutenant 31st	135 00	Balance May 18, 1822.
1444	Lemuel Grisham	Lieutenant	260 69	Balance April 2, 1823.
1445	William Gibson	Lieutenant 36th	64 94	Balance November 24, 1828.
1445	Robert Gilmore	Captain Ohio militia	93 00	Balance August 5, 1823.
1446	Orin Granger	Lieutenant 19th	1,250 00	Balance August 30, 1821.
1446	John S. Grantt	Lieutenant 11th	307 19	Balance January 1, 1820.
1446	Harry Gilman	Ensign 31st	287 35	Do. do.
1447	Jasper Scull	Paymaster 2d Pa. militia	100 22	Balance August 25, 1826.
1448	John Kercheval	Assistant quartermaster militia	12 00	Balance November 9, 1820.
1448	William Robinson	Under contract Nov. 18, 1812	76 26	Balance November 14, 1820.
1448	George P. Miller	Late paymaster 13th Ky. militia.	1,312 18	Balance January 24, 1824.
1449	Alexander Robertson	Lieutenant 17th	11 15	Balance April 20, 1826.
1449	Jacob D. Petrie	Paymaster New York militia	370 71	Balance November 17, 1820.
1450	Matthew Oliver	...do...do	31 97	Balance November 23, 1820.
1450	Daniel Libbey	Captain 21st	242 79	Do. do.

1452	Samuel Nye	Major artillery	83 69	Balance August 18, 1832.
1453	Peter C. Johnson	Lieutenant 12th	927 33	Balance January 1, 1820.
1453	David Johnson		1,000 00	Do. do.
1454	Matthew Jenkins	Lieutenant 3d artillery	1,080 00	Do. do.
1454	David Hunter	Lieutenant 12th	143 65	Do. do.
1455	William S. Henshaw	Lieutenant 5th	274 06	Do. do.
1455	W. W. Hazard	Hospital surgeon's mate	700 00	Do. do.
1456	R. G. Hite	Assistant adjutant general	270 00	Do. do.
1456	Abraham F. Hull	Captain 9th	859 81	Do. do.
1457	William Hazard	Lieutenant 2d	11 06	Do. do.
1457	James R. Hanham	Captain artillery	2,310 33	Balance December 31, 1821.
1458	Henry O. Hill	Lieutenant 5th	301 40	Balance January 1, 1820.
1458	Thomas Hawkins	Ensign 17th	100 00	Do. do.
1459	David Holt	Captain 17th	1,044 63	Balance May 21, 1830.
1459	Thomas Harris	Lieutenant 20th	440 32	Balance August 20, 1823.
1460	H. P. Helm	Lieutenant 7th	430 00	Do. do.
1461	Henry Huber	Lieutenant 38th	20 00	Balance January 1, 1820.
1461	Richard M. Harrison	Lieutenant 23d	112 76	Do. do.
1462	B. Hughes	A. D. quartermaster general	149 89	Do. do.
1463	John Hall	Captain 45th	1,616 00	Balance October 12, 1827.
1463	Abner Hines	Lieutenant 24th	1,000 00	Balance September 6, 1823.
1463	Bartlett Holmes	Master mason	50 00	Balance January 1, 1820.
1464	Nathaniel Hinkley	Ensign 21st	304 61	Do. do.
1464	Lewis Howard	Captain	100 00	Do. do.
1465	George K. Hall	Lieutenant 32d	133 33	Do. do.
1465	Joshua Hamilton	Captain rifles	115 77	Do. do.
1465	John Hogan	Captain 39th	70 00	Do. do.
1466	Perry Hawkins	Lieutenant	22 25	Do. do.
1466	Benjamin Harvey	Lieutenant 3d	850 00	Balance May 6, 1823.
1466	H. A. Hays	Lieutenant dragoons	1,281 92	Balance June 14, 1822.
1467	George H. Hunter	Major	370 00	Balance January 1, 1820.
1467	John Wood	Lieutenant	59 00	Do. do.
1467	Joseph Hutchinson	Lieutenant 25th	208 45	Do. do.
1468	F. T. Helmes	Lieutenant 13th	58 00	Do. do.
1468	Benjamin Hardaway	Ensign	700 23	Do. do.
1468	A. H. Holmes	Captain 8th	974 00	Balance May 6, 1823.
1469	L. Heath	Lieutenant	200 00	Balance January 1, 1820.
1469	John Hopewell	Lieutenant 12th	685 00	Do. do.
1470	Jacob Heet	Ensign 6th	60 00	Do. do.
1470	Edward Halloway	Lieutenant	98 63	Balance March 10, 1821.
1471	Mortimer D. Hall	Captain	837 32	Balance November 15, 1821.

				Arrearages:
1471	H. W. Huntington	Lieutenant 37th	$4 00	Balance January 1, 1820.
1471	T. S. Hopkins	Brigadier general militia	50 00	Do. do.
1472	William Hull	Captain	400 00	Do. do.
1472	Gideon Hawley	Lieutenant 30th	40 01	Do. do.
1472	Samuel Harper	Lieutenant	50 00	Do. do.
1473	Michael Hahn	Lieutenant 27th	200 00	Do. do.
1473	William Hughes	Lieutenant 17th	180 00	Do. do.
1473	John S. Hackett	Lieutenant 24th	170 00	Do. do.
1474	Carlisle Humphreys	Surgeon's mate	20 00	Do. do.
1474	Joseph K. Jacobs	Ensign 9th	50 00	Do. do.
1475	Lewis Johnson	Quartermaster 26th vol. rifles	487 00	Balance July 27, 1827.
1476	Thomas S. Johnson	Lieutenant 2d regiment	220 00	Balance January 1, 1820.
1476	James Johnston	Lieutenant 14th	175 50	Do. do.
1476	Jonas Jordan	Lieutenant 26th	100 00	Do. do.
1477	Charles G. Jones	Captain 29th	300 00	Do. do.
1477	Henry B. Jones	Lieutenant	113 00	Do. do.
1478	Benjamin Jackman	Lieutenant 21st	650 00	Do. do.
1478	Benjamin B. Jones	Captain 35th	602 03	Do. do.
1478	William Jordan	A. D. quartermaster general	1,000 00	Do. do.
1479	James Erwin	Captain of guides	50 00	Do. do.
1479	Isaac Keys	Lieutenant 12th	26 87	Do. do.
1480	John D. Kehr	Ensign	374 00	Do. do.
1480	Thomas D. Kelly		130 00	Do. do.
1480	Samuel Kercheval	Lieutenant 7th	500 00	Do. do.
1481	Jacob Koontz	Lieutenant 20th	529 67	Do. do.
1482	Archibald Kerr	Lieutenant	220 00	Balance April 11, 1821.
1482	Jesse Kean	Ensign 14th	264 48	Balance January 1, 1820.
1482	Charles Kean	Lieutenant 22d	1,409 52	Balance November 17, 1821.
1483	Francis B. King	Lieutenant 16th	400 00	Balance August 20, 1825.
1483	Lawson Kingsbury	Lieutenant 9th	75 00	Balance January 1, 1820.
1484	William King	Lieutenant 5th	200 00	Do. do.
1484	Abraham Kinney	Contractor	45 60	Do. do.

1485	Samuel Kirby	Lieutenant 35th	800 00	Balance January 1, 1820.
1486	Julius Keys	Brigade major	300 00	Do. do.
1487	Isaac Lee	Cornet of militia	40 00	Do. do.
1487	I. R. N. Luckett	Lieutenant 2d infantry	240 00	Do. do.
1487	John B. Long	Captain 39th	2,100 00	Do. do.
1488	William Leavitt	Lieutenant 19th	1,260 00	Do. do.
1488	Daniel Lane	Lieutenant 33d	50 00	Do. do.
1488	William Lithgow	Lieutenant	30 00	Do. do.
1489	Prentis Law	Captain 3d infantry	200 00	Balance May 20, 1821.
1489	Robert Lytle	Lieutenant	100 00	Balance January 1, 1820.
1490	S. C. Leakin	Captain 38th	50 00	Do. do.
1490	Joseph Loring	Colonel	28 00	Do. do.
1491	Charles Larned	Lieutenant 28th	100 00	Do. do.
1492	William Lewis	Lieutenant colonel	521 00	Balance August 15, 1823.
1492	John Lucas	Captain 26th	151 69	Balance November 20, 1821.
1492	Jacob C. Leslie	Lieutenant 26th	505 00	Balance February 7, 1823.
1493	William B. Ligon	Ensign 43d	55 51	Balance January 1, 1820.
1494	Granville N. Love	Ensign 17th	80 88	Balance January 12, 1832.
1494	John H. Lawson	Ensign 43d	350 00	Balance January 1, 1820.
1495	James A. Lewis	Ensign 20th	348 00	Do. do.
1495	John T. Lacy		500 00	Balance October 20, 1821.
1495	William M. Loftin	Lieutenant 3d rifles	2,228 78	Balance June 28, 1821.
1496	R. Lewis	Forage master	100 00	Balance January 1, 1820.
1496	M. M. Lane	Lieutenant 33d	78 75	Do. do.
1496	James Lawrence	Ensign 43d	54 00	Balance April 16, 1821.
1497	John M. Lawson	Ensign	44 00	Balance January 24, 1821.
1497	Lewis Morgan	Lieutenant 2d artillery	327 24	Balance April 18, 1823.
1497	Samuel McGuire	Captain 35th	1,674 00	Balance January 1, 1820.
1498	Horace Morris	Ensign 11th	48 00	Do. do.
1498	Samuel A. Morse	Quartermaster	71 14	Do. do.
1499	Stephen Morrill, jr	Ensign 34th	171 51	Do. do.
1499	Elias Morse	do	272 65	Balance May 4, 1822.
1500	John McIntire	Lieutenant 3d rifle	8 29	Balance January 1, 1820.
1501	Alexander A. Meeks	Lieutenant 17th	192 00	Do. do.
1501	Charles Mitchell	Lieutenant 15th	90 00	Do. do.
1501	George Murray	Lieutenant 5th	50 00	Do. do.
1502	Thomas Means	Captain 33d	23 60	Do. do.
1502	Joseph Marquand	Agent	500 00	Balance November 15, 1821.
1503	William McMillan	Lieutenant colonel 17th	637 37	Balance January 1, 1820.
1503	Charles C. McKenzie	Lieutenant 3d rifles	78 79	Do. do.
1503	Thomas G. Murray	Lieutenant artillery	1,244 00	Balance June 22, 1827.

Statement of balances—Continued.

Pages.	Names.	Rank.	Amount.	Remarks.
				Arrearages:
1504	Benjamin Mifflin	Late deputy commissary	$459 43	Balance January 1, 1820.
1504	James S. McKelvey	Captain	200 00	Balance June 28, 1827.
1505	John E. Morgan		150 00	Balance January 1, 1820.
1505	John McColl	Surgeon's mate	55 00	Do. do.
1506	James McGee	Lieutenant 22d	8 00	Do. do.
1507	Andrew McClary	Captain 11th	339 15	Balance October 17, 1825.
1507	John T. Mason	Lieutenant 36th	103 81	Balance January 1, 1820.
1507	D. McCrimmin	Adjutant 14th	250 00	Do. do.
1508	James McDonald	Lieutenant 39th	154 01	Do. do.
1508	D. D. McNair	Lieutenant 28th	1,150 00	Balance July 19, 1825.
1508	John McNair	Ensign 28th	100 00	Balance January 1, 1820.
1509	Jonas Munroe	Lieutenant	20 00	Do. do.
1509	David Morris	Lieutenant 19th	50 00	Do. do.
1510	Thomas Machin	Captain 29th	60 00	Do. do.
1511	S. Martindale	Lieutenant colonel militia	200 00	Do. do.
1511	William Martin	Ensign New York militia	60 0	Do. do.
1512	Aaron Matson, jr	Ensign 31st	360 00	Do. do.
1512	William Myrick	Lieutenant	115 51	Do. do.
1513	Samuel W. Magruder	Surgeon's mate	28 74	Do. do.
1513	James Minor	Lieutenant 35th	200 00	Do. do.
1514	William Macomb		250 00	Do. do.
1514	James A. Magruder	Late q. m. Columbia militia	700 00	Do. do.
1515	Philip Moses	Ensign 4th	450 00	Do. do.
1516	D. McClellan	Assistant deputy q. m. g	1 05	Do. do.
1516	John Morris		107 78	Do. do.
1517	John Mills	Ensign 37th	389 86	Do. do.
1517	Samuel McCormick	Captain	15 00	Do. do.
1518	George McClure	Brigadier general militia	502 14	Do. do.

1520	John Mershon	do	148 70	Balance April 22, 1824.
1520	De Town Madox	Lieutenant 24th	100 00	Balance January 1, 1820.
1521	Wm. A. Nash	Lieutenant 34th	68 00	Do. do.
1521	Wm. Nevers	do	32 31	Balance December 2, 1820.
1522	George Newbogin	Lieutenant 33d	12 80	Balance July 27, 1824.
1522	Presley J. Neville	Lieutenant artillery	372 94	Balance August 5, 1822.
1522	Joshua Norvell	Lieutenant	60 00	Balance January 1, 1820.
1523	Montgomery Newman	Lieutenant 2d artillery	100 00	Do. do.
1523	George Nicholas	Surgeon's mate	20 00	Do. do.
1524	Martin Nash	Major militia	20 00	Do. do.
1524	C. A. Norton	Lieutenant 26th	200 00	Do. do.
1524	Robert Nevill	do	560 00	Balance May 24, 1820.
1525	John Nicholson	Captain	240 00	Balance January 1, 1820.
1525	Christian Noyes	Lieutenant 15th	25 00	Do. do.
1525	Francis Neale	Quartermaster 36th	100 00	Do. do.
1526	Robert Neale	Lieutenant 40th	230 60	Do. do.
1526	Walter H. Overton	Captain	235 63	Balance March 25, 1824.
1527	Ferdinand A. Oneal	Lieutenant	10 00	Balance January 1, 1820.
1527	John O'Connor	Surgeon's mate	20 00	Do. do.
1528	Peter V. Ogden	Captain volunteers	350 00	Do. do.
1528	Richard Plummer	Lieutenant 10th	610 00	Do. do.
1529	Paul Peckham	Ensign 4th	1,128 00	Do. do.
1529	Peter Pifer		110 84	Do. do.
1530	George E. Pendergrast	Hospital surgeon	20 00	Do. do.
1530	Edward Pasteur	Colonel	50 50	Do. do.
1530	William Pennell	Captain 6th	10 00	Do. do.
1531	John J. Plume	Lieutenant and q. m. 6th	280 00	Do. do.
1531	James R. Peyton	Lieutenant	200 00	Do. do.
1531	Thomas Parker	Captain	184 00	Do. do.
1532	William Parker	Lieutenant 3d rifles	3:8 02	Do. do.
1532	Daniel Patch	Lieutenant	500 00	Do. do.
1532	Wm. K. Paulding	Ensign 24th	524 96	Do. do.
1533	Thomas Pitts		32 00	Do. do.
1533	Aaron Palmer	Captain	100 00	Do. do.
1533	Daniel Paige	Lieutenant	508 00	Do. do.
1534	John Putnam	Lieutenant 31st	77 82	Balance November 6, 1822.
1534	William Prosser	Lieutenant 7th	1,516 00	Balance May 6, 1823.
1534	Samuel Price	Captain artillery	587 83	Balance January 1, 1820.
1535	James Pike	Lieutenant 4th infantry	200 00	Do. do.
1536	Chauncey Pettibone	Lieutenant 6th	70 00	Do. do.
1536	Abner P. Pinney	Captain 27th	500 00	Balance July 19, 1825.

Statement of balances—Continued.

Pages.	Names.	Rank.	Amount.	Remarks.
				Arrearages:
1537	Wm. Pricbard	Captain 2d rifles	$869 31	Balance January 1, 1820.
1538	John Rutland	Captain	160 00	Do. do.
1538	Phineas Read	Brigade quartermaster	340 00	Do. do.
1540	James Read	Captain artillery	408 24	Do. do.
1540	Richard H. Root	Lieutenant 13th	143 70	Balance December 15, 1820.
1540	John Riddle	Lieutenant	40 00	Balance January 1, 1820.
1541	Wm. B. Read	Lieutenant 3d artillery	86 50	Do. do.
1541	Thomas Richie	Lieutenant 36th	100 00	Do. do.
1541	Jonas Rhodes	Ensign 28th	750 00	Do. do.
1542	Benjamin Ricketts	Ensign 14th	450 00	Balance March 21, 1821.
1542	Thomas Ripetto	Lieutenant 20th	2,557 36	Balance January 1, 1820.
1543	Samuel Robinson	Ensign	10 00	Do. do.
1544	G. H. Rogers	do	336 24	Do. do.
1544	Thomas Ragland	Ensign 3d rifles	50 00	Do. do.
1544	John T. Riding	Lieutenant	50 00	Do. do.
1545	L. Robinson	Lieutenant 26th	467 00	Do. do.
1545	Neil B. Rose	Brigade Q. M. Tenn. militia	192 11	Do. do.
1546	Robert P. Ross	Lieutenant 27th	720 00	Do. do.
1547	Alexander E. Rose	Captain 6th	120 00	Do. do.
1547	Henry Renschner	Lieutenant 10th	508 00	Do. do.
1548	Mason Ronalds	Lieutenant 13th	408 00	Do. do.
1548	Isaac Ruland	Ensign militia	60 00	Do. do.
1549	James W. Riddle	Ensign 14th	203 59	Do. do.
1549	Jonathan Stark	Captain 11th	600 73	Balance March 30, 1823.
1550	Wm. G. Scott	Lieutenant	35 63	Balance March 3, 1824.
1550	Mason Seward	Lieutenant 19th	92 00	Balance January 1, 1820.
1550	George W. Stall	do	671 77	Balance October 4, 1822.
1551	John Simmons	Ensign 19th	648 08	Balance June 18, 1824.

1553	Asa W. Simons	Ensign 11th	1,000 00	Do. do.
1554	Robert Simpson	Doc. St. Louis	77 03	Do. do.
1554	John Smith	Lieutenant colonel 3d infantry	400 00	Do. do.
1554	Thomas Spencer	Lieutenant	60 43	Do. do.
1555	Robert G. Seeley	Lieutenant 2d infantry	48 39	Do. do.
1555	Nathaniel Sherman	Lieutenant 6th	450 00	Do. do.
1556	Francis W. Small		411 17	Do. do.
1556	Neal Shaw	Lieutenant 6th	28 75	Do. do.
1556	Charles Scott		2,500 00	Do. do.
1557	Sufferers of the Connecticut Land Company		706 26	Do. do.
1557	John W. Smoot	Lieutenant 5th	72 69	Do. do.
1557	Daniel Saint	Lieutenant 42d	669 75	Do. do.
1558	Willis R. Smith	Lieutenant 17th	300 00	Do. do.
1559	Thomas W. Shanks	Ensign 26th	100 00	Do. do.
1559	Wm. Sturgiss	Lieutenant 22d	1,195 81	Do. do.
1559	Robert Sterry	Major and inspector general	193 69	Do. do.
1560	Joseph Sumner	Lieutenant 34th	300 00	Do. do.
1560	James P. Sanderson		200 00	Do. do.
1561	Benjamin Smith	Lieutenant 2d dragoons	230 00	Do. do.
1561	Thomas S. Seymour	Ensign 25th	918 00	Balance May 24, 1823.
1562	C. Sackrider	Major	300 00	Balance January 1, 1820.
1562	Wm. Shotwell	Captain 42d	3,088 00	Do. do.
1562	Nathaniel Smith	Lieutenant	695 51	Balance August 26, 1824.
1563	Anderson Spencer	Lieutenant 26th	284 00	Balance December 27, 1822.
1563	John Stewart	Ensign 32d	326 91	Balance January 1, 1820.
1564	Nathaniel Spalding	Lieutenant 30th	378 26	Do. do.
1564	Wm. W. Smith	Lieutenant artillery	100 00	Do. do.
1565	John W. Stith	Captain 35th	300 00	Do. do.
1565	Joseph Schofield	Lieutenant 15th	100 00	Do. do.
1566	Benjamin Smith	Lieutenant 46th	350 00	Do. do.
1566	Asahel Schovel	Captain	75 00	Balance March 19, 1822.
1567	Robert Scott	Captain 4th rifles	40 13	Balance January 1, 1820
1567	Israel Stoor	Lieutenant 37th	30 00	Do. do.
1568	Matthew S. Steel	Ensign	10 00	Do. do.
1569	Daniel Smith	Lieutenant 29th	361 09	Do. do.
1569	Reuben Sallisbury	Lieutenant 30th	118 00	Do. do.
1570	David Smith	Lieutenant	50 00	Do. do.
1570	Drury Stith	Ensign	891 00	Do. do.
1571	George W. Thomas	Ensign 34th	60 00	Do. do.
1571	Richard Taylor	Deputy q. m. general	1,039 00	Balance February 21, 1833.
1572	Joseph Thompson	Captain 26th	231 15	Balance January 1, 1820.

				Arrearages:
1572	Solomon D. Townson		$33 00	Balance January 1, 1820.
1572	Adamson Tannehill	Brigadier general militia	500 00	Do. do.
1573	J. C. Taite	Lieutenant 39th	50 00	Do. do.
1573	John Trimbo	Lieutenant 28th	150 00	Do. do.
1573	Noah Terry	Captain, &c	200 00	Do. do.
1574	S. Turner	Lieutenant	460 00	Do. do.
1574	Ebenezer Taylor	Captain	200 00	Do. do.
1574	M. Talliaferro	Captain 35th	20 00	Do. do.
1575	R. C. Talbott	Captain 26th	280 02	Balance February 7, 1823.
1576	David Tracey	Lieutenant 37th	104 00	Balance January 1, 1820.
1576	Nathaniel Taylor	Brigadier general	500 00	Do. do.
1577	William Tatham		100 00	Do. do.
1577	John Valleau	Lieutenant 13th	125 25	Do. do.
1577	Peter J. Vosbury	Lieutenant colonel 9th	650 00	Do. do.
1578	N. J. Vischer	Captain rifles	161 51	Do. do.
1578	Storm T. Vanderzee	Wagon master	135 14	Do. do.
1579	Joseph Warner	Quartermaster Ohio militia	26 32	Balance November 19, 1823.
1580	Nathaniel Wilson	Surgeon	100 00	Balance January 1, 1820.
1580	Daniel B. Wilcox	Lieutenant 13th	743 67	Do. do.
1580	J. West	Assistant adjutant general	300 00	Balance July 23, 1823.
1581	Ebenezer White	Captain 21st	370 00	Balance January 1, 1820.
1581	George Wyche	Lieutenant	121 60	Balance June 26, 1821.
1581	Benjamin Woodman	Lieutenant 34th	130 37	Balance March 18, 1823.
1582	Wm. L. Wilkinson	Lieutenant	131 78	Balance April 9, 1823.
1582	Benedict White	Lieutenant 36th	110 50	Balance January 1, 1820
1582	James Ward	Lieutenant 38th	30 00	Do. do.
1584	Alexander Wentzel		40 00	Do. do.
1584	Jonathan Williams	Colonel United States army	650 00	Do. do.
1585	Hays G. White	Brigade quartermaster	223 55	Do. do.
1585	John C. Wallace	Militia	80 00	Do. do.

1587	[illegible]atson	Lieutenant 25th	220 00	Do. do.
1588	Jon'n Williams	Lieutenant colonel Vt. militia	200 00	Do. do.
1588	John S. Willard	Lieutenant 31st	250 00	Do. do.
1588	Uriah Ward	Captain 31st	5 06	Do. do.
1589	John Wilson	Lieutenant	11 28	Do. do.
1589	Ira Westover	Ensign 4th	50 00	Do. do.
1590	John Williams	Lieutenant New York militia	40 00	Do. do.
1590	Linneus T. Wheelock	Ensign 31st	1,070 00	Do. do.
1590	John Watson	Captain militia cavalry	30 00	Do. do.
1591	George Watts	Lieutenant dragoons	30 00	Do. do.
1591	George Will	Ensign 26th	167 06	Do. do.
1592	Heman Wadham	Lieutenant 30th	695 00	Balance February 19, 1821.
1593	Sheorick Weeks		236 00	Balance January 1, 1820.
1593	John C. Wooding	Ensign 1st infantry	300 00	Do. do.
1594	William Walker	Sub-agent	608 24	Do. do.
1594	Robert Young	Ensign 26th	71 84	Balance June 30, 1823.
1595	James M. Young	Lieutenant 30th	299 00	Balance January 1, 1820.
1595	Philip Yost	Lieutenant 1st infantry	171 64	Balance November 26, 1825.
1595	William C. Yeates	Ensign 5th	33 40	Balance January 1, 1820.
1596	Jonathan W. Young	Lieutenant 30th	191 32	Do. do.
1605	R. D. Richardson	Captain of ordnance	4 00	Balance December 1, 1820.
1606	Barzillia Worth	Late paymaster, &c	380 73	Balance April 5, 1821.
1607	Richard Rudd	Late paymaster 2d Ky. m'ted vols	575 34	Balance December 19, 1820.
1608	Samuel Edmonds	Paymaster general N. Y. militia	10,498 08	Balance September 12, 1823.
1608	Samuel Edmonds	Late do	4,152 09	Balance January 28, 1825.
1610	James Nash	Paymaster, &c	938 98	Balance January 17, 1821.
1611	Thomas H. Ferguson	Ensign	550 00	Balance February 23, 1821.
1613	Wm. P. Anderson	Late colonel 24th	11,811 33	Balance November 9, 1835.
1614	Avery Clark	Late lieutenant 24th	154 00	Balance October 3, 1829.
1614	Tilden Taylor	do	50 00	Balance March 31, 1821.
1614	Kenneth McKenzie	Captain 14th	100 00	Balance March 21, 1821.
1616	John S. Peyton	Captain artillery	96 00	Balance April 11, 1821.
1616	John A. Beaulard	Lieutenant 8th infantry	50 00	Balance April 16, 1821.
1618	Hamlin Cook	Deputy paymaster	37,467 72	Balance July 2, 1823.
1618	Irvine Keith	Captain 8th	15 00	Balance April 18, 1821.
1620	Martin H. Wickliff	Late paymaster 5th Ky. militia	9 15	Balance April 23, 1821.
1620	Peter G. Voorhies	Deputy paymaster	27,614 13	Balance January 1, 1824.
1620	William Whitsett	Late paymaster, &c	1,080 40	Balance May 8, 1822.
1621	James T. Pendleton	Paymaster	563 37	Balance July 2, 1821.
1621	Wm. C. Vaught	Paymaster Ky. militia	2,410 37	Balance December 10, 1823.
1621	Wm. Whitsett	Paymaster, &c	3,413 51	Balance May 8, 1822.

Pages.	Names.	Rank.	Amount.	Remarks.
				Arrearages:
1622	James S. Swearengen	Late captain	$4 00	Balance May 3, 1821.
1623	George Todd	Late colonel 17th	3,869 22	Balance March 21, 1822.
1623	John K. Paige	Late captain 13th	554 16	Balance May 8, 1821.
1624	Lewis Yancey	Late lieutenant 10th	2,530 04	Balance May 25, 1821.
1624	John H. Simons		207 94	Balance January 1, 1820.
1625	Philip C. Whitehead	Late lieutenant 15th	25 00	Balance June 18, 1821.
1626	P. F. Hunn	Late paymaster N. Y. militia	53 77	Balance January 19, 1822.
1526	Ebenezer Way	Late captain 4th infantry	279 56	Balance June 26, 1821.
1628	Abraham Reynolds	Captain 15th	49 00	Balance August 31, 1821.
1628	Joseph Provaux	Lieutenant 1st regiment artillery	250 00	Balance August 13, 1821.
1630	Alpheous Rouse	Late quartermaster N. Y. militia	300 00	Balance October 16, 1821.
1630	John Vernor, jr	Forage master, &c	130 00	Do. do.
1630	Andrew Backus	Late forage master N. Y. militia	100 00	Do. do.
1631	Richard Caldwell	Captain 25th	178 77	Balance February 2, 1822.
1631	John Garrett	Ensign 10th infantry	30 00	Balance November 6, 1821.
1631	James Wilkinson	Late major general	3,879 71	Balance November 12, 1842.
1640	John Levake	Late captain 26th	832 35	Balance November 22, 1822.
1640	William Barney	Lieutenant 30th	50 00	Balance November 30, 1821.
1640	Henry Whiting	Lieutenant 1st dragoons	20 00	Do. do.
1641	Charles Lawton	Captain volunteers	60 00	Balance December 28, 1826.
1642	James Smith	Paymaster 1st O. militia	2,232 71	Balance October 16, 1825.
1643	William Scott	Lieutenant 24th	17 85	Balance October 1, 1834.
1644	Nathaniel Hamlin	Quartermaster militia	348 50	Balance March 19, 1822.
1645	Luke Parsons	Captain militia	45 00	Do. do.
1645	Rufus How, cornet, and Isaac Eames, lieutenant militia		20 00	Do. do.
1646	Caleb B. Campbell	Ensign 19th	100 00	Balance March 21, 1822.
1647	John Eagan	Late lieutenant 27th infantry	116 10	Balance March 30, 1822.
1647	Philip Houts	do	274 50	Do. do.
1648	Beverly Roy	Lieutenant 24th	60 00	Balance July 6, 1822.
1650	Wilson P. Greenup	Late p. m., 1st reg. Ky. lt. d'gs.	17,800 00	Balance February 1, 1821.
1650	Wilson P. Greenup	do	2,259 73	Balance May 16, 1822.
1650	James Clark	Captain 32d infantry	300 00	Balance October 19, 1822.
1651	[illegible]nt E. Loockerman	do	100 00	Balance May 30, 1822.

[illegible]	Samuel P. Davis	Lieutenant 32d	100 00	Do. do.
1655	Thomas B. Van Horne	Lieutenant colonel 19th, &c	9 10	Balance August 9, 1832.
1655	John Martin	Late lieutenant 44th	343 00	Balance June 22, 1822.
1655	Daniel Hoffman		88 00	Balance June 17, 1822.
1656	Paul D. Butler	Major commanding Sandusky	500 00	Do. do.
1656	William McClellan	Late captain 7th	600 00	Balance June 14, 1822.
1658	Thomas F. Wells	Lieutenant 8th infantry	101 60	Balance August 17, 1822.
1659	D. E. Jackson	Ensign	200 00	Balance October 4, 1822.
1670	Wadsworth Bull		500 00	Balance October 11, 1822.
1670	James Ligget	Ensign	25 50	Balance October 15, 1822.
1671	William Watson	Ensign 26th	155 00	Balance November 23, 1822.
1672	Robert Gray	Paymaster colonel militia	95 89	Balance November 6, 1822.
1672	John Miller	Late colonel 19th	375 00	Balance July 13, 1827.
1674	John T. Pemberton	Late deputy paymaster	11,568 23	Balance January 18, 1823.
1674	Seth Bannister	Captain 9th	471 87	Balance May 16, 1823.
1676	John MacQueen	Late lieutenant 10th	120 00	Balance February 12, 1823.
1677	John P. Houston	Brigade inspector Tenn. militia	500 00	Balance March 18, 1823.
1678	Thomas P. Moore	Late Captain 12th, &c	212 95	Balance April 14, 1823.
1678	John Kirby	Late lieutenant	150 00	Balance April 29, 1823.
1678	Jonathan Grant	Ensign	200 00	Balance May 6, 1823.
1679	Michael McClelland	Captain 7th	214 09	Balance January 7, 1825.
1679	Francis Newman	Captain artillery	200 00	Balance May 6, 1823.
1680	Edward King	Captain 18th	203 62	Balance May 31, 1823.
1681	Samuel Turner	Late deputy paymaster	46,749 77	Balance January 24, 1825.
1681	Daniel Dana	Late colonel 31st	2,972 75	Balance June 24, 1823.
1682	James H. Watts	Lieutenant 23d infantry	266 37	Balance July 17, 1823.
1682	Jared Ingersoll	Late captain	475 00	Balance August 4, 1823.
1682	Batteal Harrison	Captain 2d rifles	23 91	Balance December 12, 1823.
1683	Joshua Clark	Late paymaster Georgia militia	27 39	Balance February 13, 1824.
1686	John S. Gans	Late major general O. militia	436 16	Balance December 18, 1823.
1688	John Merrill	Late paymaster 34th	519 71	Balance January 21, 1824.
1691	Philip Grymes	Dist. attorney at New Orleans	7,333 90	Balance March 24, 1824.
1696	William Smyth	Captain 1st rifles	4,279 16	Balance April 22, 1824.
1697	Skelton Felton	Late lieutenant 9th infantry	71 95	Balance May 18, 1824.
1698	Nathan McLaughlin, deceased	late 16th infantry	266 32	Balance August 23, 1824.
1699	Joseph H. Windle	Late assistant deputy paymaster	18,060 61	Balance March 12, 1825.
1699	William Gill	Captain 19th	19 93	Balance October 18, 1824.
1700	Benjamin Hodges	Late paymaster Md. militia	46 35	Balance December 11, 1824.
1700	Robert R. Ruffin	Late paymaster 2d regiment art	1,511 11	Balance September 23, 1826.
1701	Daniel D. Tompkins	Late governor New York	304 00	Balance January 28, 1825.
1710	James Howerton	Late lieutenant 28th infantry	100 00	Balance April 7, 1825.

Statement of balances—Continued.

Pages.	Names.	Rank.	Amount.	Remarks.
				Arrearages:
1711	Robert Stockton	Lieutenant 28th infantry	$130 00	Balance May 31, 1825.
1711	Joseph Coleman	Late deputy paymaster	79,907 09	Balance March 18, 1826.
1712	William Bowman	Lieutenant 21st infantry	50 00	Balance June 24, 1825.
1713	Benjamin Ropes	Captain 21st infantry	1,191 96	Balance February 6, 1826.
1714	Peter L. Hogeboom	Late paymaster 23d infantry	5,761 83	Balance May 24, 1826.
1714	Joseph Wescott	Late captain volunteers	1,247 61	Balance September 13, 1825.
1715	Seth Phelps	Late captain 11th infantry	67 48	Balance October 17, 1825.
1716	John Weakley	Captain Tennessee militia	20 00	Balance November 25, 1825.
1716	P. Grayson	Adjutant general	50 00	Do. do.
1717	J. W. Harris	Lieutenant Tennessee militia	15 00	Do. do.
1717	David Abbott	do	50 00	Do. do.
1717	James Gray	Captain Tennessee militia	5 00	Do. do.
1718	D. M. Bradford	do	5 00	Do. do.
1718	James Barnes	Lieutenant	75 00	Do. do.
1721	Samuel Champlain	Late deputy paymaster	56,127 20	Balance March 15, 1827.
1721	Samuel Champlain	Late deputy q. m. general	52,986 97	Balance July 18, 1826.
1730	William McCarr	Hospital surgeon	200 00	Do. do.
1730	Joseph H. Rees	Late asst. dep. paymaster gen	2,254 94	Balance November 19, 1828.
1730	Alexander A. Meek	Late district attorney	1,279 04	Balance March 7, 1828.
1732	Samuel Kratzer	Late paymaster, &c	159 84	Balance February 27, 1827.
1732	Samuel Kratzer	Late acting paymaster, &c	57 30	Balance June 16, 1828.
1733	Thomas P. Baldwin	Late asst. dep. q. m	5,770 00	Balance March 17, 1827.
1734	Thomas Doyle	Lieutenant volunteers	40 00	Balance March 28, 1827.
1734	Storm A. Vanderzee	do	10 00	Do. do.
1735	Hamlin Cook	Late paymaster 8th infantry	3,810 96	Balance December 10, 1831.
1736	Robert Crockett	Marshal for the Kentucky dist	246 29	Balance January 25, 1828.
1738	Alexander Dunlap	Captain volunteers	100 00	Balance August 4, 1828.
1738	Isaac Pangle	Lieutenant 39th	177 00	Balance December 9, 1828.
1739	Richard H. Lee	Lieutenant rifles	578 09	Balance December 21, 1828.
1742	Joseph E. Merritt	Late assisant deputy paymaster	12,781 43	Balance December 16, 1829.
1743	Walter Wilkinson	Captain 24th infantry	938 68	Balance November 4, 1830.

1746	Joseph Owens	Late paymaster 5th infantry	907 32	Balance February 26, 1834.
1747	Thomas D. Owens	Late colonel 28th infantry	11,502 90	Balance March 16, 1831.
1752	Silas Parlin, jr	Captain volunteers	2 41	Balance June 2, 1831.
1753	John Lucas and John Abercrombie	Sureties of Hamlin Cook	1,268 98	Balance August 23, 1832.
1756	Adam Peck	Lieutenant 24th infantry	32 00	Balance March 2, 1832
1758	Benjamin Wallace	Major	3,010 21	Balance May 28, 1833.
1759	Archibald H. Sneed	Late battalion paymaster	18,436 07	Balance June 3, 1849.
1765	R. Skinner	Late United States artillery	157 69	Balance April 18, 1834.
1769	James Collingsworth	United States artillery	7,404 67	Balance August 29, 1836.
1769	Nicholas L. Dawson	Late paymaster Md. militia	1,419 22	Balance April 11, 1836.
1771	Henry S. Geyer	Late paymaster 38th infantry	14,097 01	Balance May 27, 1856.
1773	Alpha Kingsley	Late deputy paymaster	26,582 82	Balance June 9, 1837.
1774	Thomas Barker	Late lieutenant 10th infantry	176 00	Balance July 28, 1840.
1778	Matthew Ernest	Agent of Q. M. Gen. Wilkins	3,169 88	Balance November 12, 1842.
1778	Samuel Hodgdon	do	3,376 58	Do. do.
1772	William H. Winder	Late major general	1,958 75	Balance September 10, 1836.

Balances outstanding from May, 1792, to July 1, 1815, under the head of arrearages, $2,831,889 86.

REPORT OF THE FOURTH AUDITOR.

TREASURY DEPARTMENT,
FOURTH AUDITOR'S OFFICE,
October 28, 1868.

SIR: I have the honor again to submit for your consideration a summary statement of the business of this office during the fiscal year ending with June 30, 1868. The details into which I have heretofore entered render it unnecessary to recapitulate the explanations then submitted, or to do much more at the present time than to present tabular statements of the operations of the various divisions of the office. These I shall consecutively offer for your consideration.

I.—RECORD DIVISION.

Statement of the correspondence of the Fourth Auditor's office for the fiscal year ending June 30, 1868, *and the work of the record division.*

Date.	Letters received.	Letters written.	Letters recorded.	Letters indexed and double indexed.	Letters filed.	No. of accounts reported and recorded.	Licenses recorded and registered.	Letters referred to other bureaus.	Dead letters registered.	Letters written by record division.
1867.										
July	2,277	2,751	3,248	16,288	1,727	190	32	31	42	85
August	2,078	2,779	2,183	11,548	1,477	20	50	44	59	57
September	1,965	2,219	3,382	28,421	258	21	6	30	51	56
October	2,212	2,702	2,287	24,478	352	....	15	51	45	71
November	1,951	2,461	3,128	16,333	2,270	77	6	20	35	49
December	1,866	2,268	1,742	3,763	395	28	8	13	35	55
1868.										
January	2,233	3,305	4,025	7,550	1,366	49	4	39	44	69
February	1,994	2,576	3,649	7,824	1,060	....	4	4	52	56
March	2,020	2,834	2,902	9,468	1,732	67	1	25	5	53
April	1,850	3,235	2,965	10,218	1,111	40	146	28	35	706
May	1,707	3,246	3,197	8,958	963	93	196	14	64	207
June	1,506	2,377	3,192	12,799	882	53	52	21	63	76
Total	23,659	32,753	35,900	157,648	13,593	638	520	320	530	1,540

Besides the above, about 314,000 names have been indexed, of which no separate record was kept. The average number of clerks employed in the "record division," during the year, was 15. The chief of this division is Charles Cook.

II.—BOOKKEEPERS' DIVISION.

Statement exhibiting the number and amounts of requisitions entered upon the books of this office during the fiscal year ending June 30, 1868, and also the amount of internal revenue and hospital fund credited to those funds respectively.

	No.	Amount.
Cash requisitions	1266	$30,512,704 97
Cash refunding requisitions	293	4,620,033 32
Internal revenue		370,878 91
Hospital fund		95,047 51
Total		35,598,664 71

The average number of clerks employed in this division during the year was two.

The chief of this division is Paris H. Folsom.

III.—PRIZE MONEY DIVISION.

Statement of prize money disbursed by the Fourth Auditor during the fiscal year ending June 30, 1868.

Date.	Claims received.	Claims settled.	Amount.
1867:			
July	310	268	$158,775 29
August	562	538	124,360 83
September	261	257	11,307 67
October	156	137	15,222 12
November	278	267	16,081 70
December	1,039	1,060	24,265 14
1868:			
January	652	674	27,278 13
February	150	126	11,808 46
March	1,301	1,301	12,109 34
April	1 746	1,700	16,164 60
May	321	276	7,818 10
June	235	275	13,333 67
Total	7,011	6,879	438,525 05

The average number of clerks employed is seven.

The chief of this division is Silas M. B. Servoss.

IV.—DIVISION OF NAVY PENSIONS, MARINE CORPS, ETC.

Statement of the business transacted in the pension and marine division of the Fourth Auditor's Office during the fiscal year ending on the 30th of June, 1868.

The total number of accounts settled is 345, involving disbursements to the amount of $1,772,986 08, viz:

235 accounts of pension agents	$329,709 61
44 individual accounts of pensioners	3,241 76
14 accounts of disbursing officers of the marine corps	1,330,963 12
45 individual accounts of officers and privates of the marine corps	4,939 23
7 accounts of naval storekeepers	104,132 36

The number of letters written during the said fiscal year is 1,263.

The number of requisitions issued is 109, viz.: 53 requisitions drawn by the Secretary of the Department of the Interior for advances to pension agents; 48 requisitions for payment of arrearages due to pensioners; 8 refunding requisitions.

The number of pensioners whose names have been added to the pension list during the year is 456.

The accounts of officers of the marine corps in charge of clothing, &c., have been examined and entered on the books as far as returns have been received.

The number of clerks employed in this division is three, and the chief is Geo. M. Head.

V.—ALLOTMENT DIVISION.

Statement of work performed in allotment division for the fiscal year ending June 30, 1868.

Date.	Letters received.	Letters written.	Allotments examined and adjusted.	Allotments registered.	Allotments discontinued.
1867.					
July	138	165	189	14	189
August	109	141	112	221	112
September	139	190	61	61	199
October	125	160	64	64	219
November	99	135	45	45	124
December	109	129	94	94	121
1868.					
January	131	167	157	157	58
February	112	154	92	92	153
March	99	111	51	51	87
April	85	97	35	35	113
May	76	102	69	69	67
June	63	87	31	31	59
Total	1,285	1,638	1,000	934	1,501

The number of clerks employed is two.

The chief of this division is William L. Waller.

VI.—PAYMASTERS' DIVISION.

Statement of accounts received and settled in the paymasters' division from July 1, 1867, to June 30, 1868, with the amount of cash disbursed in those settled, and the number of letters written in relation to the same.

Date.	Accounts received.	Accounts settled.	Letters written.	Cash disbursements.
1867.				
July	19	33	179	$1,258,908 94
August	37	31	150	610,438 89
September	18	28	135	2,212,499 85
October	19	32	164	2,224,480 16
November	18	14	172	588,570 65
December	25	36	151	2,080,642 71
1868.				
January	22	23	243	734,145 60
February	16	17	176	533,066 25
March	30	27	233	1,529,335 40
April	20	19	209	970,163 44
May	26	20	188	656,490 27
June	23	41	140	2,651,632 91
Total	273	321	2,140	16,050,375 07

Average number of clerks employed, 20¾.
The chief of this division is William Conard.

VII.—NAVY AGENTS' DIVISION.

Annual report of the navy agents' division for the fiscal year ending June 30, 1868.

Date.	Accounts received.	Accounts settled	Cash disbursements.	Letters written.	Letters received.
1867.					
July	3	2	$1,316,205 37	24	19
August	3	2	3,627,170 91	30	23
September	3	1	544,582 54	8	14
October	2	2	2,548,503 40	40	23
November	4	4	4,088,557 65	29	27
December	2	4	2,197,922 93	20	19
1868.					
January	8	12	2,507,791 41	45	28
February	3	10	1,208,483 00	37	26
March	7	6	1,834,891 76	30	16
April	8	8	2,167,323 33	26	26
May	5	6	1,884,321 16	35	21
June	2	5	2,554,553 76	29	21
Total	50	62	26,480,323 22	353	263

Statement of amount paid by navy agents for allotments during the year 1867.

Station.	Amount.
New York	$173,233 00
Boston	112,425 00
Philadelphia	101,796 50
Washington	34,240 00
Baltimore	33,575 00
Portsmouth	14,851 50
San Francisco	90 00
Total	470,211 00

Accounts remaining on hand June 30, 1868, five; average number of clerks employed, seven; number of vouchers examined, 90,000.

The chief of this division is William F. Stidham.

VIII.—GENERAL CLAIM DIVISION.

Annual report of the general claim division for the fiscal year ending June 30, 1868.

Claims received.	Number.	Claims adjusted.	Number.	Amount.
On hand July 1, 1867	314			
Received in July, 1867	360	Adjusted in July, 1867	360	$21,052 83
Received in August, 1867	314	Adjusted in August, 1867	261	16,603 37
Received in September, 1867	373	Adjusted in September, 1867	223	11,620 18
Received in October, 1867	367	Adjusted in October, 1867	170	14,641 99
Received in November, 1867	470	Adjusted in November, 1867	406	16,836 46
Received in December, 1867	390	Adjusted in December, 1867	369	18,341 51
Received in January, 1868	407	Adjusted in January, 1868	450	25,093 37
Received in February, 1868	319	Adjusted in February, 1868	322	20,150 84
Received in March, 1868	393	Adjusted in March, 1868	553	19,943 07
Received in April, 1868	258	Adjusted in April, 1868	322	17,266 91
Received in May, 1868	256	Adjusted in May, 1868	289	23,626 55
Received in June, 1868	202	Adjusted in June, 1868	278	14,128 68
Total	4,428		4,003	219,305 76

Number of letters written, 12,390; number of reports on applications for pensions, 119; number of reports on applications for bounty land, 35; number of reports on applications for admission to naval asylum, 19.

The chief of this division is Alan C. Adamson.

IX.

Virtually, though perhaps not technically, there is still another division in the office, whose duties, however, are performed by one person, B. P. Davis. He acts as disbursing clerk, as assistant and deputy for the chief clerk, and attends to a number of important and miscellaneous duties which could not be enumerated without considerable detail.

The practice alluded to in my last annual report as having been introduced concerning allotments, requiring "monthly statements" of the several navy paymasters of amounts paid by them on all expired and discontinued allotments, continues to be regularly made, and is found to facilitate the settlement of accounts in which allotments are involved.

A number of the accounts settled in the different divisions during the fiscal year ending with June 30, 1868, were supplemental settlements, and contained no vouchers and embraced no cash disbursements; but containing, as they did, suspensions for irregular and informal payments running through several years, required careful investigation and consumed more time in their settlement than the regular quarterly accounts; while the labor involved and time consumed is not made apparent in the column of "cash disbursements," or in the number of vouchers examined.

In order to illustrate this, I will take the case of the navy agent at New York. A supplemental settlement of that account has been in progress, at the present writing, about nine months, employing two clerks constantly in investigating the suspensions and passing upon the validity of corrected vouchers now furnished by the agent to reduce the large balance shown against him by the settlement of his final account, viz., more than $700,000. And yet the labor involved in this settlement is only shown in the tabular report as *one* account settled, and the vouchers and expenditures having been included in the previous accounts, (and having been there suspended,) are not reported in the present table.

This explanation is necessary in order to understand that neither the column of "cash disbursements" nor "accounts settled" can be taken as the only guides in estimating the actual labor involved in the settlement of the accounts in this office.

Tabular statements are valuable because they give, oftentimes, a close approximation to the amount of work performed. It is, however, a great error to suppose that the sum involved in an account is an index to the labor required for its settlement, as I have just partially illustrated. In fact, in cases where the number of clerks employed, the amount of time consumed, and the sum total of dollars and cents involved, are all duly given, there would still be a probability of error in the judgment of an examiner who was personally unacquainted with the details, because in an account of $5,000 there is frequently vastly more work than in another of several millions, owing to the blunders and incapacity of those who kept them, or arising from inevitable complications, destruction of papers by fire and water, and various and numerous circumstances. In this connection let me refer to the paymasters' division in this office.

To account for the falling off in the number of accounts settled in the paymasters' division, and the amount of cash disbursements shown therein, since the report of 1865–'66, I beg leave to repeat that it is impossible to form more than an approximate estimate of the amount of labor performed by reference to the figures shown in the yearly report. Among the vast number of volunteer paymasters appointed during the late rebellion were many who were entirely unacquainted with the rules and regulations of the service, and many inaccuracies arose thereby which affected not only their accounts, but also the accounts of nearly all with whom they had transactions.

These imperfect accounts, having to await their regular turn, were not taken up for settlement until recently, and, although showing a comparatively small amount of cash disbursements, they required an unusual amount of care and labor in their settlement.

Many supplementary settlements have also been made of the accounts of receiving ships whereon the largest disbursements were made, the re-examination of which has required at least three times the amount of labor more than the original settlements, and yet which show no disbursements at all, the whole amount having been stated in the report of the

as an illustration. The clerk must, in the first place, address a letter to the Bureau of Equipment and Recruiting, in order that he may learn whether or not the applicant enlisted as a volunteer, and when this information is before him the rolls of every vessel upon which the man served while in the navy must be carefully examined for fear he may have been credited with one or more instalments during the time he was in the service, and if all the rolls should not be on file it would be necessary to write another letter to the paymaster to know what amount, if any, was paid by him. If the man should prove to be a substitute, an additional letter must be written to the Adjutant General for information in regard to his principal. Such a claim will at most amount to not more than $300, and in the settlement from one to four letters must be written, and the rolls of from one to a dozen vessels carefully examined, involving an extent of time and labor which a tabular statement does not exhibit.

In the settlement of an ordinary claim for arrears of pay it frequently happens that the clerk is compelled to make more search and consume more time in the settlement, where the amount claimed is for a small sum, than when it is for a large amount. This commonly occurs in cases where the party had an allotment running, (which will sometimes give rise to considerable correspondence,) or an error has been made in his transfer from one vessel to another. The clerk would, after all, receive credit for one or two letters, and the settlement of one claim for a few dollars, which, perhaps, cost him several days' labor.

All applications for admission to the United States Naval Asylum are referred to this office by the Bureau of Yards and Docks, for the purpose of verifying the applicant's statement of his service, which must not be less than 20 years in order to secure admission. It will be readily seen that a man cannot be traced over a period of 20 years from one vessel to another, under the most favorable circumstances, in less than two days; but in some instances it cannot be done in less than a week. The clerk in either case would only receive tabular credit for writing a letter of about 10 lines.

To give one instance more in relation to this division. A large number of applications for pension under the act of March 2, 1867, are referred to this division from the Bureau of Equipment and Recruiting for verification of service. Pensions are granted under this law to persons who served 20 years, and also to those who served 10 years, but for a less sum, provided they were not discharged for misconduct. The same investigation must be made in these cases as that required for the Naval Asylum; and in addition, great care must be taken to observe that the claimant was not at any time dishonorably discharged, or marked as a deserter, either of which would deprive him of the benefit of the law. But after all this labor, the clerk who investigated such a case would only receive credit for one letter of about 10 lines.

I might add similar illustrations in regard to the other divisions, but believe I have said enough to show that the amount involved in a settlement, and the number of accounts adjusted in a given time, are not correct criterions of the labor expended in these cases. It has been my endeavor, during the past year, to employ the force of this office constantly, and to employ it, likewise, usefully for the government. The amount of work will ultimately be less, when the accumulation of business occasioned by the war is cleared off and the necessary records now in progress are completed. When this exigency arises it will, of course, be my duty to recommend the dismission of such clerks as are no longer needed. During the past year the number of male clerks on the roll has been 10 less than the number allowed by the statute regulating the office, and the number of females employed is four less than hitherto. There has been a large percentage of sickness in the office during the past year, and in several instances cases of disease have occurred which endured not only for weeks, but for months. As monthly reports of these facts, however, have been regularly made, I have not felt at liberty to recommend dismissions on account of such visitations, although the working force of the office has been diminished thereby to the amount of not less than five clerks. I am pleased that I can reiterate the praise which I have hitherto bestowed upon the clerks of this office, as persons who are both faithful and capable, notwithstanding some occasional instances of a want of that prompt and continued attention to duty which completes and rounds the character of invariable good conduct.

The chiefs of the various divisions, who are now in charge, have uniformly discharged their functions with gratifying and laudable ability. To my chief clerk, Mr. William B. Moore, I would again award the high commendation he so justly deserves for the unfailing and valuable assistance he has so constantly given me in the management and conduct of the office. I am greatly indebted to him for its order and efficiency, and during the past year many improvements in the modes of transacting and despatching business have been introduced. The files of the office are very voluminous, but they are now in more complete order than they have ever heretofore been. In finally casting a glance over the office, I am pleased with its condition, and trust it will be found that all its business has been transacted with courtesy, promptitude, and correctness. With thanks for your personal kindness, and for the regard you have ever manifested towards those who compose your department, I am, sir, very respectfully, your obedient servant,

STEPHEN J. W. TABOR,
Auditor.

Hon. HUGH MCCULLOCH,
Secretary of the Treasury.

REPORT OF THE FIFTH AUDITOR.

TREASURY DEPARTMENT,
FIFTH AUDITOR'S OFFICE,
November 1, 1868.

SIR: I have the honor to submit herewith the usual annual exhibit of the business operations of this office. During the fiscal year ended June 30, 1868, the number of accounts entered for settlement in the office was 14,575, and the number of letters written 5,354. A large amount of incidental labor, such as examining vouchers, copying and comparing accounts, &c., has been performed. For more particular information you are respectfully referred to the schedules herewith, marked A to N, inclusive.

A comparison of the annual salaries paid to and fees received from the consular officers of the government during the past 10 years shows the following:

Year.	Salaries paid to all consular officers.	Total fees received.		
1858	$251,544 94	$110,802 89	Deficit, paid out of treasury	$140,742 05
1859	255,540 85	98,383 41	....do......do......do......	157 157 44
1860	263,206 98	110,896 78	....do......do......do......	152,310 20
1861	250,714 19			
Loss in exchange.	8,809 08			
	259,523 27	99,113 23	....do......do......do......	160,410 04
1862	271,655 74			
Loss in exchange	12,899 80			
	284,555 54	95,562 86	....do......do......do......	188,992 68
1863	351,032 29			
Loss in exchange	54,368 08			
	405,400 37	152,982 94	....do......do......do......	252,417 43
1864	334,920 47			
Loss in exchange.	28,859 52			
	363,779 99	254,218 34	....do......do......do......	109,561 65
1865	345,053 48			
Loss in exchange	13,708 16			
	358,761 64	287,108 00	....do......do......do......	71,653 64
1866	340,899 34			
Loss in exchange.	9,671 60			
	350,570 94	442,477 56	Excess of fees	91,906 62
1867	371,292 63			
Loss in exchange.	10,717 77			
	382,010 42	424,099 17	...do....do..............	42,089 77
1868	363,556 35			
Loss in exchange.	10,194 54			
	373,750 89	435,179 73	...do....do..............	61,428 84

It is believed that the annual revenue from consular fees should be much greater even than it has been during the last three years, but it is exceedingly difficult to obtain full and honest returns from all the consulates. Constant vigilance is, however, exercised in this behalf, and all omissions and delinquencies are promptly dealt with so far as practicable.

Schedule H, showing the expenses of assessing the internal revenue for the fiscal year, makes the gross amount $6,142,931 77. In my last report the gross expenses for assessing during the year ending June 30, 1867, appear at $3,921,598 49, (including tax on compensation of assessors and assistants.) The apparent excess of expense in assessing of 1868 over 1867 is mainly accounted for by the fact that at the time the report for 1867 was made a large number of disbursing agents' accounts for that year had not been adjusted. These accounts have since been received and settled, and as a consequence the following expenses belonging to the year 1867 are included in the exhibit for 1868, now submitted, viz:

Compensation of assistant assessors	$816, 801 71
Salaries of assessors	77, 727 89
Clerk hire allowed to assessors	67, 222 20
Total	961, 751 80

This amount should therefore be deducted from the aggregate expense of assessing for the year 1868 and added to that for the year 1867. Thus, according to the accounts as adjusted and finally certified, the cost of assessing in 1867 was $4,883,350 29, and in 1868 $5,181,179 97. The difference still remaining between the two years is mainly caused by the increase in the *per diem* allowance of assistant assessors from $4 to $5 per day.

The proper transaction of the public business in any office depends in a great degree on the character of its subordinates, the value of whose services should ever be borne in mind. It is with pleasure, therefore, that I assure you that the clerks connected with this office continue to discharge their varied duties with a fidelity and ability deserving of public commendation.

Very respectfully,

C. M. WALKER, *Auditor*.

Hon. H. McCULLOCH,
Secretary of the Treasury.

A.—*Statement of the expenses of all missions abroad for salaries, contingencies, and loss by exchange from the* 1st *July*, 1867, *to the* 30*th June*, 1868, *as shown by accounts adjusted in this office.*

Mission.	Salary.	Contingencies.	Loss by exchange.	Total.
GREAT BRITAIN.				
Charles F. Adams, minister, from July 1, 1867, to May 13, 1868	$15, 192 31	$1, 541 68		
Benj. Moran, secretary of legation, from July 1, 1867, to May 13, 1868	2, 169 57			
Benj. Moran, chargé d'affaires, from May 13 to June 30, 1868	1, 130 30	305 28		
D. R. Alward, assistant secretary of legation, from July 1, 1867, to June 30, 1868	1, 475 00			

Statement A—Continued.

Mission.	Salary.	Contingencies.	Loss by exchange.	Total.
FRANCE.				
John A. Dix, minister, from July 1, 1867, to June 30, 1868	$16,675 00	$3,602 27	$132 83	
W. Hoffman, secretary of legation, from July 1, 1867, to June 30, 1868	2,543 76	....	23 57	
John W. Dix, assistant secretary of legation, from July 1, 1867, to June 30, 1868.	1,475 00	....	9 93	
	20,693 76	3,602 27	166 33	$24,462 36
RUSSIA.				
C. M. Clay, minister, from July 1, 1867, to June 30, 1868	11,450 00	1,200 00		
J. Curtin, secretary of legation, from July 1, 1867, to June 30, 1868	1,760 00			
	13,210 00	1,200 00	....	14,410 00
PRUSSIA.				
George Bancroft, minister, from July 1, 1867, to June 30, 1868	11,450 00	921 94		
Alex. Bliss, secretary of legation, from July 1, 1867, to June 30, 1868	1,760 00			
	13,210 00	921 94	....	14,131 94
AUSTRIA.				
John Hay, chargé d'affaires, from July 1, 1867, to June 30, 1868	5,750 00	953 44	....	6,703 44
MEXICO.				
E. L. Plumb, chargé d'affaires, from October 8, 1867, to June 30, 1868	4,189 54	1,346 01		
E. L. Plumb, secretary of legation, from July 1, 1867, to October 7, 1867	473 48			
	4,663 02	1,346 01	....	6,009 03
SPAIN.				
J. P. Hale, minister, from July 1, 1867, to June 30, 1868	11,450 00	2,559 93	171 27	
H. J. Perry, secretary of legation, from July 1, 1866, to June 30, 1868	1,760 00			
	13,210 00	2,559 93	171 27	15,769 93
BRAZIL.				
J. W. Webb, minister, from July 1, 1867, to June 30, 1868	11,450 00	1,000 00	....	12,450 00
BELGIUM.				
H. S. Sanford, minister, from July 1, 1867, to June 30, 1868	6,175 00	807 49	62 41	
Aaron Goodrich, secretary of legation, from July 1, 1867, to June 30, 1868	1,475 00			

Statement A—Continued.

Mission.	Salary.	Contingencies.	Loss by exchange.	Total.
PERU.				
A. P. Hovey, minister, from July 1, 1867, to June 30, 1868	$9,550 00	$512 13		
H. M. Brent, secretary of legation, from July 1, 1867, to June 30, 1868	1,475 00			
	11,025 00	512 13	....	$11,537 13
CHINA.				
A. Burlingame, late minister, from July 1, 1867, to November 21, 1867	4,475 43	325 00	$175 00	
S. W. Williams, secretary of legation and interpreter, from July 1, 1867, to November 21, 1867	1,850 00			
S. W. Williams, chargé d'affaires, from November 22, 1867, to June 30, 1868	3,503 17	713 00		
	9,828 60	1,038 00	175 00	11,041 60
TURKEY.				
E. Joy Morris, minister, from July 1, 1867, to June 30, 1868	7,175 00	2,793 73	257 31	10,226 04
ITALY.				
George P. Marsh, minister, from July 1, 1867, to June 30, 1868	11,450 00	491 00	35 00	
Green Clay, secretary of legation, from July 1, 1867, to June 30, 1868	1,760 00			
	13,210 00	491 00	35 00	13,736 00
SWEDEN.				
J. J. Bartlett, minister, from July 1, 1867, to June 30, 1868	7,175 00	455 61	6 97	7,637 58
DENMARK.				
G. H. Yeaman, minister, from July 1, 1867, to June 30, 1868	7,175 00	732 25	....	7,907 25
GUATEMALA.				
Fitz H. Warren, minister, from July 1, 1867, to June 30, 1868	7,175 00	608 88	361 00	8,144 88
NEW GRENADA.				
P. J. Sullivan, minister, from July 1, 1867, to June 30, 1868	7,175 00	881 09	....	8,056 09
SWITZERLAND.				
G. Harrington, minister, from July 1, 1867, to June 30, 1868	7,175 00	412 98	....	7,587 98
NETHERLANDS.				
Hugh Ewing, minister, from July 1, 1867, to June 30, 1868	7,175 00	441 67	....	7,616 67

Statement A—Continued.

Mission.	Salary.	Contingencies.	Loss by exchange.	Total.
HONDURAS.				
R. H. Rousseau, minister, from July 1, 1867, to June 30, 1868	$7,175 00	$400 00	....	$7,575 0
HAWAIIAN ISLANDS.				
E. M. McCook, minister, from July 1, 1867, to June 30, 1868	7,175 00	98 88	$18 56	7,292 4
ARGENTINE CONFEDERATION.				
A. Asboth, late minister, from July 1, 1867, to January 21, 1868	3,922 50	279 21		
H. G. Worthington, minister, from January 22, 1868, to June 30, 1868	3,252 50	237 36		
	7,174 00	516 57	....	7,690 5
COSTA RICA.				
A. G. Lawrence, minister, from July 1, 1867, to June 30, 1868	7,175 00	26 80	368 26	7,570 0
NICARAGUA.				
A. B. Dickinson, minister, from July 1, 1867, to June 30, 1868	7,175 00	680 25	....	7,855 2
CHILI.				
J. Kilpatrick, minister, from July 1, 1867, to June 30, 1868	9,550 00	800 00	161 09	
S. M. Carpenter, secretary of legation, from August 7, 1867, to June 30, 1868	1,241 59	....	42 64	
	10,791 59	800 00	203 73	11,795 3
PARAGUAY.				
C. A. Washburn, minister, from July 1, 1867, to June 30, 1868	7,175 00	473 44	460 00	8,128 4
ECUADOR.				
W. T. Coggeshall, late minister, from July 1, 1867, to August 2, 1867	643 41	....	....	643 4
VENEZUELA.				
J. Wilson, minister, from July 1, 1867, to August 8, 1867	760 40			
T. N. Stillwell, minister, from October 4, 1867, to June 30, 1868	5,322 76	208 21	16 87	
	6,083 16	208 21	16 87	6,308 2
HAYTI.				
G. H. Hollister, minister, from February 5, 1868, to June 30, 1868	2,897 59	75 00	....	2,972 5

Statement A—Continued.

Mission.	Salary.	Contingencies.	Loss by exchange.	Total.
SALVADOR.				
A. S. Williams, minister, from July 1, 1867, to June 30, 1868	$7,175 00	$198 39	$57 00	$7,430 39
LIBERIA.				
John Seys, minister, from July 1, 1867, to June 30, 1868	3,850 00	125 00	....	3,975 00
JAPAN.				
R. B. Van Valkenburgh, minister, from July 1, 1867, to June 30, 1868	7,175 00	725 00	650 00	
A. L. C. Portman, secretary of legation, from July 1, 1867, to June 30, 1868	2,425 00	....	322 00	
	9,600 00	725 00	972 00	11,297 00
PORTUGAL.				
C. A. Munro, chargé d'affaires, from July 18, 1867, to June 30, 1868	1,406 85	194 71	84 25	1,685 81
PONTIFICAL STATES.				
Rufus King, minister, from July 1, 1867, to July 30, 1867	933 42	....	....	933 42
BARING BROS. & CO., BANKERS, LONDON.				
Loss by exchange during year	....	....	1,257 85	1,257 85
JUDGES AND ARBITRATORS.				
Under the provisions of treaty with Great Britain of April 7, 1862.				
Truman Smith, judge at New York, from July 1, 1867, to June 30, 1868	2,425 00	100 00		
Benj. Pringle, judge at Capetown, from July 1, 1867, to June 30, 1868	2,425 00	169 40	130 40	
G. W. Palmer, judge at Sierra Leone, from July 1, 1867, to June 30, 1868	2,425 00	....	116 89	
W. L. Avery, arbitrator, Capetown, from July 1, 1867, to June 30, 1868	1,950 00	....	53 60	
T. A. Whittlesey, arbitrator, Sierra Leone, from July 1, 1867, to June 30, 1868	1,950 00	....	30 00	
Cephas Brainard, arbitrator, New York, from July 1, 1867, to June 30, 1868	1,000 00	....	....	
	12,175 00	269 40	330 89	12,775 29
Total	....	....	....	325,948 04

B.—*Statement of consular returns of salaries, fees, and loss in exchange for the fiscal year ending June 30, 1868.*

No.	Consulates.	Salaries.	Fees.	Loss in exchange.
	A.			
1	Amoor River	$1,000 00	$103 46	....
2	Algiers	1,500 00	14 50	$76 23
3	Antwerp	2,625 00	3,015 00	....
4	Amsterdam	1,000 00	830 53	16 62
5	Aix-la-Chapelle	2,500 00	2,016 75	....
6	Alexandria	3,500 00	150 00	....
7	Amoy	4,037 46	686 43	626 35
8	Apia	750 00	73 73	1,737 30
9	Aux Cayes	500 00	408 80	....
10	Acapulco	1,918 00	1,000 35	....
11	Aspinwall	2,500 00	4,147 07	....
	B.			
12	Bristol*	....	....	....
13	Belfast	2,315 31	8,282 58	....
14	Bay of Islands	....	....	....
15	Bordeaux	2,277 17	6,293 00	....
16	Barcelona	1,500 00	1,054 37	24 35
17	Batavia	1,000 00	354 80	56 83
18	Bremen	3,000 00	2,778 25	....
19	Basle	2,000 00	1,804 86	39 27
20	Beirut	2,250 00	210 84	....
21	Bahia	1,250 00	1,237 26	....
22	Buenos Ayres	3,052 89	6,992 48	....
23	Bangkok	1,000 00	165 52	19 25
24	Brindisi	1,500 00	....	53 19
25	Boulogne	1,500 00	119 00	49 53
26	Bradford	....	4,525 04	....
27	Berlin	....	3,419 43	....
	C.			
28	Cork	2,000 00	285 90	36 65
29	Calcutta	5,000 00	3,972 12	....
30	Cape Town	1,000 00	294 29	53 90
31	Cadiz	1,500 00	840 28	54 88
32	Constantinople	3,000 00	530 37	180 76
33	Canea	1,000 00	2 00	....
34	Cyprus	1,000 00	....	68 76
35	Canton	8,066 82	2,192 09	731 34
36	Cape Haytien	1,000 00	565 93	....
37	Carthagena	500 00	591 12	7 17
38	Callao	4,500 00	2,884 10	....
39	Cobija	....	....	....
40	Coaticook	1,500 00	5,840 00	13 84
41	Chin Kiang	4,385 87	465 85	303 62
42	Clifton	1,500 00	1,447 00	5 54
43	Ceylon	1,500 00	262 70	302 84
44	Chemnitz	2,000 00	7,124 75	....
	D.			
45	Dundee	2,000 00	4,830 44	3 26
46	Demerara	2,000 00	1,791 32	....
	E.			
47	Elsinore	1,500 00	32 50	60 99

* Fees.

B.—*Statement of consular returns of salaries, fees, &c.*—Continued.

No.	Consulates.	Salaries.	Fees.	Loss in exchange.
	F.			
48	Fort Erie	$1,500 00	$3,887 75	....
49	Funchal	1,500 00	127 60	$33 67
50	Fayal	750 00	504 18	....
51	Frankfort-on-the-Main	5,113 74	1,641 00	72 81
52	Foo-Choo	875 00	232 37	....
	G.			
53	Genoa	1,500 00	1,376 68	16 57
54	Glasgow	3,000 00	8,663 82	....
55	Geneva	1,500 00	949 00	42 64
56	Gaspé Basin	....	....	....
57	Guayaquil	731 09	194 70	....
58	Gaboon	1,000 00	26 97	....
59	Guayamas	1,192 00	714 25	....
60	Gibraltar	1,500 00	536 84	....
61	Goderich	1,500 00	1,681 78	....
	H.			
62	Hong Kong	4,375 00	7,395 54	....
63	Halifax	2,000 00	3,761 26	....
64	Havre	6,000 00	5,803 12	1 87
65	Havana	15,529 04	36,723 93	....
66	Hamburg	2,000 00	7,066 27	126 26
67	Honolulu	6,428 10	7,459 14	....
68	Hankow, China	3,750 00	471 03	369 84
69	Hamilton	....	1,273 36	....
	J.			
70	Jerusalem	1,663 46	....	152 65
	K.			
71	Kingston, Jamaica	2,000 00	1,668 30	10 78
72	Kanagawa	3,000 00	3,233 58	296 76
73	Kingston, C. W	1,500 00	1,716 70	....
	L.			
74	London	5,625 00	27,558 44	....
75	Liverpool	7,500 00	34,012 22	....
76	Leeds	2,000 00	1,167 75	....
77	Lisbon	1,500 00	587 12	46 71
78	Lyons	2,750 00	5,386 00	16 22
79	La Rochelle	1,500 00	326 00	64 35
80	Leipsic	1,500 00	5,303 75	12 50
81	Leghorn	1,500 00	1,651 29	18 15
82	Lanthala	945 14	7 50	234 66
83	Laguayra	1,500 00	528 70	....
84	Lahaina	3,000 00	180 47	39 60
85	Leith	....	768 99	....
	M.			
86	Manchester	3,000 00	17,956 00	....
87	Melbourne	6,642 27	4,564 21	14 65
88	Malta	1,500 00	268 72	61 79
89	Montreal	4,461 96	5,619 31	....

B.—*Statement of consular returns of salaries, fees, &c.*—Continued.

No.	Consulates.	Salaries.	Fees.	Loss in exchange.
90	Moscow	$2,586 73	$16 00	$271 64
91	Marseilles	2,500 00	3,804 87	
92	Malaga	1,500 00	1,471 71	
93	Matanzas	2,500 00	5,203 20	
94	Munich	1,500 00	862 25	44 79
95	Messina	1,500 00	1,623 86	
96	Mexico	692 94	378 00	
97	Matamoras	1,013 57	1,876 02	
98	Montevideo	1,250 00	2,842 92	
99	Maranham	1,000 00	496 18	
100	Mauritius	2,500 00	203 66	37 95
	N.			
101	Naples	1,190 22	665 19	34 53
102	Nassau	8,880 42	11,701 32	
103	Newcastle	1,500 00	1,005 00	7 08
104	Nantes	1,500 00	236 56	83 87
105	Nice	1,471 66	324 50	40 75
106	Nagasaki	3,181 32	817 59	645 14
107	Nuremberg		3,282 84	
	O.			
108	Odessa	2,000 00	113 50	274 42
109	Oporto	1,500 00	314 67	88 81
110	Omoa and Truxillo	1,000 00	51 75	
	P.			
111	Paris	7,250 00	42,380 75	72 03
112	Prince Edward's island	3,370 46	1,662 88	19,92
113	Port Mahon	1,500 00	251 34	61 34
114	Port Stanley			
115	Paso del Norte	500 00	44 00	
116	Panama	2,349 18	1,197 29	
117	Pernambuco	2,000 00	1,218 26	87 23
118	Para	1,000 00	2,224 81	
119	Payta	500 00	191 48	
120	Pictou	1,500 00	357 42	
121	Palermo	1,500 00	1,519 31	
122	Piræus	396 60		47 14
123	Prescott	1,500 00	1,935 88	
	Q.			
124	Quebec	1,548 33	782 08	4 84
	R.			
125	Rio de Janeiro	6,000 00	6,656 48	
126	Revel	2,000 00		315 82
127	Rotterdam	2,000 00	2,223 02	25 93
128	Rio Grande, Brazil	1,000 00	530 32	11 35
129	Rome	1,500 00	934 50	14 42
	S.			
130	St. Petersburg	2,000 00	1,241 61	115 60
131	St. Paul de Loanda	1,250 00	126 47	
132	St. Thomas	4,260 87	2,526 57	
133	St. Domingo	1,500 00	147 15	
134	St. Catharine's	1,500 00	661 62	

B.—*Statement of consular returns of salaries, fees, &c.*—Continued.

No.	Consulates.	Salaries.	Fees.	Loss in exchange.
135	Singapore	$2,500 00	$605 22	$112 84
136	Santiago de Cuba	2,500 00	475 22	....
137	San Juan	2,500 00	1,306 25	....
138	Santiago, Cape Verde	1,130 80	158 55	84 15
139	Santa Cruz	1,500 00	310 83	....
140	Stuttgart	1,000 00	2,972 75	12 07
141	Spezzia	1,500 00	6 00	61 36
142	Smyrna	2,000 00	1,349 53	89 72
143	Shanghai	6,096 14	3,814 61	299 45
144	Swatow	3,500 00	216 52	184 61
145	San Juan del Norte	2,000 00	471 09	....
146	San Juan del Sur	2,413 98	363 87	....
147	Sabanilla	375 00	451 40	....
148	Santos	....	....	....
149	Stettin	1,000 00	147 60	12 47
150	Southampton	2,000 00	259 94	....
151	St. Helena	1,125 00	256 05	....
152	St. John, Canada East	1,500 00	3,280 66	....
153	Sarnia	1,500 00	1,014 50	....
154	Sheffield	....	1,872 28	....
	T.			
155	Tangiers	3,000 00	....	171 69
156	Trieste	2,000 00	1,255 30	....
157	Tampico	1,500 00	1,045 78	....
158	Trinidad de Cuba	2,500 00	1,251 58	....
159	Tripoli	3,000 00	....	208 55
160	Tunis	2,559 78	3 93	41 36
161	Turk's island	1,500 00	334 77	....
162	Tumbez	....	....	....
163	Tahiti	1,000 00	326 94	71 86
164	Talcahuano	1,000 00	864 13	....
165	Toronto	1,500 00	4,983 41	10 00
166	Tamatave	2,000 00	36 18	244 56
	V.			
167	Valparaiso	3,000 00	3,709 70	....
168	Vienna	1,500 00	4,560 50	....
169	Venice	750 00	512 50	24 79
170	Vera Cruz	3,500 00	1,582 09	....
	W.			
171	Windsor	1,500 00	1,245 19	....
	Z.			
172	Zurich	750 00	1,166 00	....
173	Zanzibar	912 03	331 48	105 51
	Total	363,556 35	435,179 73	10,194 54

Total amount of fees		$435,179 73
Total amount paid salaries	$363,556 35	
Loss in exchange	10,194 54	
		373,750 89
Excess of fees over expenditures		61,428 84

REMARKS.

No.

1. Second quarter 1868 not received.
3. Including salary of B. M. Wilson, consular clerk, from July 1, 1867, to March 31, 1868, second quarter 1868 not received.
7. Including salary of W. P. Jones, from November 1, 1865, to November 11, 1865, and while making transit from post of duty from February 1, 1868, to May 25, 1868.
8. Including salary for second quarter 1867, first and second quarters 1868 not received.
12. Returns incomplete.
13. Including salary of G. H. Heap, from June 13, 1867, to June 29, 1867, while making transit to post of duty, and from July 1, 1867, to August 8, 1867, while making transit from post of duty.
14. No returns.
15. Including salary from July 1, 1866, to August 20, 1866.
20. Including salary of L. M. Johnson, consular clerk, from January 1, 1868, to March 31, 1868.
21. Including second quarter 1867.
22. Including salary of H. R. Helper, from July 1, 1866, to October 30, 1866, and while making transit from post of duty, from November 25, 1866, to February 2, 1867.
23. First and second quarters 1868 not received.
26. Settled up to August 22, 1868.
35. Including salary of O. H. Perry, from October 1, 1866, to March 31, 1867, and while receiving instructions from April 27, 1855, to May 15, 1855, and while making transit to post from May 18, 1855, to August 3, 1855, and while making transit home from September 11, 1867, to February 2, 1868.
38. Including salary of A. C. Hyer, jr., consular clerk, from July 1, 1868, to June 30, 1868.
39. No returns.
41. Including salary of J. L. Kiernan, from January 1, 1867, to March 31, 1867, and for transit heretofore disallowed from October 4, 1865, to December 20, 1865.
51. Including salary of Franklin Olcott, consular clerk, from October 1, 1867, to March 31, 1868. Salary of Hobert Miller, consular clerk, from April 1, 1867, to September 8, 1867, Salary of Samuel Ricker, late consul general from October 1, 1861, to November 25, 1861, and while making transit from post, from November 11, 1865, to December 11, 1865. Also salary of Augustus Gleaser, consular clerk, from January 14, 1868, to June 30, 1868.
52. Fourth quarter 1867. First and second quarters 1868 not received.
56. No returns.
62. Including salary from April 1, 1867, to June 30, 1867.
65. Including salary of R. W. Shoffeld, from April 4, 1863, to April 9, 1863.
67. Including salary of Thomas F. Wilson, consular clerk, from February 15, 1867, to October 14, 1867. Salary of Alfred Caldwell, from October 1, 1866, to January 7, 1867, and while making transit home from March 11, 1867, to May 13, 1867.
70. Including salary of L. M. Johnson, consular clerk, from April 1, 1868, to May 30, 1868.
74. Second quarter 1868 not received
78. Including salary of Albert J. Dezeyk, consular clerk, from July 1, 1867, to March 31, 1868.
82. Including salary of Kintzing Pritchette, from April 18, 1867, to November 27, 1867, while making transit to post of duty.
85. Account settled only to November 6, 1867.
86. Including salary from January 1, 1867, to June 30, 1867. First and second quarters 1868 not received.
87. Including salary of William Blanchard from October 1, 1866, to October 31, 1866, and while making transit from post of duty, from December 12, 1866, to April 8, 1867. Also salary of H. J. Hart, from April 1, 1867, to June 30, 1867.
89. Including salary of Franklin Olcott, consular clerk, from July 1, 1867, to September 30, 1867. Salary of Thomas F. Wilson, consular clerk, from October 15, 1867, to December 31, 1867.
90. Including salary of Eugene Schuyler, from August 24, 1867, to October 24, 1867, while making transit to post of duty, and from October 25, 1867, to November 9, 1867, while awaiting his exequatur.
96. Second quarter 1868 not received.
97. Including salary of T. W. Scott, from September 14, 1867, to October 2, 1867, while receiving instructions, and from October 16, 1867, to October 26, 1867, while making transit to post of duty.
98. Including salary from April 1, 1867, to June 30, 1867.
102. Including salary from January 1, 1865.
105. Second quarter 1868 not received.
106. Including salary for first quarter 1867.
107. Excess of fees received from July 26, 1866, to August 17, 1867.
111. Including salary of James Hand, consular clerk, and William Heine, consular clerk, from July 1, 1867. Salary of Franklin Olcott, consular clerk, for second quarter 1868.

112. Including salary of Jay. H. Sherman, from April 1, 1866, to June 20, 1866. Salary of E. Parker Scammon, from July 1, 1866, to December 31, 1867, and salary of Joseph Covell, from January 1, 1865, to March 6, 1866.
114. Returns incomplete.
116. Second quarter 1868 not received.
124. Including salary of Charles Robinson, from April 6, 1868, to April 25, 1868, while receiving instructions, from April 26, 1868, to April 30, 1868, while making transit to post of duty, and from May 1, 1868, to May 11, 1868, while awaiting his exequator.
131. Including salary from April 1, 1867, to June 30, 1867.
132. Including salary of Joseph H. Thompson, from October 28, 1867, to November 20, 1867, while receiving instructions.
138. Including salary of Benjamin Tripp, jr., from September 25, 1867, to October 25, 1867, while receiving instructions, and from October 26, 1867, to December 4, 1867, while making transit to post of duty.
140. Including salary for second quarter of 1867.
143. Including salary of B. R. Lewis, consular clerk, from July 1, 1867, to June 30, 1868. Salary of O. B. Bradford, consular clerk, from May 27, 1867, to June 30 1868
146. Including salary of Rufus Mead, from October 20, 1867, to November 20, 1867, while receiving instructions, and from December 2, 1867, to January 16, 1868, while making transit to post of duty.
147. Second quarter 1868 not received.
148. No returns.
151. Second quarter 1868 not received.
154. Adjusted up to December 31, 1867.
160. Including 10 mouths and three days' salary, while in transit to post of duty.
161. Second quarter 1868 not received.
162. Returns incomplete.
172. First and second quarters 1868 not received.
173. Second quarter 1868 not received.

C.—*Statement showing the amount expended by the consular officers of the United States for the relief of American seamen at the consulates, the amount received by them as extra wages of discharged seamen, and the amount of loss in exchange incurred by them in drawing for balances due them, as appears from the settlement, in the Fifth Auditor's office, of the consular accounts for the fiscal year ending June* 30, 1868.

Consulate.	Disbursements.*	Loss in exchange.	Receipts.
Acapulco	$531 63		$153 10
Alexandria	130 41		
Amoy	317 27		446 13
Antwerp	210 51		234 60
Aspinwall	438 88		104 00
Aux Cayes	394 57		
Bahia	68 20		
Barbadoes	295 64		360 00
Barcelona	48 03		251 56
Batavia	1,042 87	$30 25	917 00
Bathurst	187 65		
Beirut	15 00		
Belfast	97		
Bermuda	231 59		231 00
Bombay	1,065 61		357 00
Bordeaux	87 10		338 18
Boulogne	72 27	1 44	
Bremen			17 50
Buenos Ayres	10,519 48		13,834 69
Cadiz	260 17	20 85	22 04
Calcutta	634 05		1,150 30
Callao	1,992 90		791 18
Cape Haytien	132 00		

Statement—Continued.

Consulate.	Disbursements.	Loss in exchange.	Receipts.
Cape Town	$200 09		$208 47
Ceylon	6 78		
Clifton	12 00	$0 18	
Constantinople	172 86	13 66	87 51
Curaçoa	142 75		
Demerara	82 34		71 45
Dundee	388 43		428 58
Fayal	11,427 67		4,739 44
Genoa	42 61		43 00
Gibraltar	92 18		
Glasgow	31 70		50 86
Goderich	24 00		
Guayaquil	32 60		
Halifax	59 82		
Havana	1,390 65		1,185 01
Havre	482 07	10 24	311 02
Hilo	770 63		948 00
Hong Kong	1,251 21		1,097 15
Honolulu	10,476 86		8,617 21
Kanagawa	3,939 59	116 25	5,737 52
Kingston, Jamaica	390 70	13 06	
Laguayra	31 72		
Lahaina	290 60		372 00
Lambayeque	33 50		
La Paz	586 04		
Leeds	21 94		
Leghorn	46 95		30 00
Leipsic	4 14		
Liverpool	2,696 38		14,917 35
London	102 01		30 50
Malaga	3,632 35	307 74	125 20
Manila	135 00	48 28	112 53
Marseilles	591 45	13 24	211 73
Matanzas	213 31		126 00
Mauritius	90 75	5 76	
Mazatlan	221 00		663
Melbourne	252 65	1 10	199 74
Minatitlan	126 75	5 20	
Montevideo	847 96		1,256 44
Montreal	15 75		75 00
Nagasaki	724 02		1,097 69
Nantes	318 37		463 47
Nassau, West Indies	921 03		
New Castle upon Tyne	118 32		
Odessa	36 81	5 50	
Oporto	503 10	38 63	
Panama	890 60		252 00
Para	67 23		
Paris	67 74		
Payta	4,262 25		540 00
Pernambuco	929 98	62 14	387 99
Port Mahon	243 45		323 45
Quebec	10 00		
Rio de Janeiro	1,246 22		1,547 70
Rio Grande do Sul	455 47		
Rotterdam			37 22
Santa Cruz			21 43
Santiago, Verde islands	524 23	24 06	72 00
Shanghai	1,245 47		2,519 02
Sheffield	14 51		
Singapore	989 07	14 80	1,291 55
Sisal	96 50		

Statement—Continued.

Consulate.	Disbursements.	Loss in exchange.	Receipts.
Smyrna	$15 00	$1 05	
St. Catherine, Brazil	312 00		$420 00
St. Helena	1,189 87		1 047 00
St. John, New Brunswick	79 80		
St. Martin, West Indies	47 42		
St. Pierre, Miquelon	68 73		
St. Petersburg	61 64		
St. Thomas, West Indies	585 15		203 82
Stockholm	91 00		
Sydney, New South Wales	512 22	52 36	288 20
Tahiti	5,214 95	565 33	720 00
Talcahuano	3,818 00		1,094 00
Teneriffe	45 45		77 85
Trinidad (island)	3 50		
Tumbez	1,700 37	80 03	192 00
Turk's Island	263 14		283 71
Valencia	20 20		13 35
Valparaiso	3,965 64		2,890 70
Vera Cruz	369 75		
Victoria, V. I.	1,244 00		
Zanzibar	570 72	89 20	189 42
Total	93,877 51	1,520 35	76,170 19

RECAPITULATION.

Total amount of expenditures and loss in exchange	$95,397 86
Amount of receipts	76,170 19
Excess of disbursements over receipts	19,227 67

D.—*Statement showing the amount refunded citizens, seamen, or their representatives directly from the United States treasury during the fiscal year ending June* 30, 1868, *the several sums having been previously received at the consulates.*

Edward Rock, citizen, estate of	$276 09
Charles J. Lewis..do......do	329 14
John A. Campbell.do......do	238 06
J. D. Athey......do......do	56 33
A. M. Hart.......do......do	497 32
C. P. Casseles....do......do	37 64
James H. Wiley..do......do	417 25
E. J. Moore.......do......do	1,297 03
L. Hoadley, seaman.......do	69 20
Robert Easby..do.......do	137 15
P. McGinley...do....wages refunded	90 00
W. J. Scott....do.........do	80 00
John Brown...do.........do	35 33
Geo. Jackson...do.........do	60 00
Theie, Seilter & Co., consiguees. } money erroneously collected	25 50
E. Maxfield, owner } money erroneously collected	72 50
Total	3,718 54

E.—*Statement showing the amount expended by the United States consulate for expenses incurred on account of criminal seamen for the fiscal year ending June* 30, 1868.

Acapulco	$121 50
Funchal	126 55
Havana	330 74
Havre	149 83
Honolulu	85 25
Monrovia	672 18
Turk's Island	15 00
Total	1,501 05

F.—*Statement of the number of destitute American seamen sent to the United States, and the amount paid for their passage, from the following consulates, during the fiscal year ending June* 30, 1868.

Consulates.	No of seamen.	Amount.
Acapulco	25	$250 00
Aux Cayes	3	90 00
Amoy	2	20 00
Aspinwall	38	380 00
Bahia	7	70 00
Barbadoes	22	220 00
Batavia	1	10 00
Bahamas	43	515 00
Beirut	2	60 00
Bermuda	5	65 00
Buenos Ayres	1	10 00
Bombay	1	10 00
Cadiz	3	30 00
Callao	3	30 00
Cape town	12	170 00
Cape Haytien	7	70 00
Cienfuegos	1	10 00
Cow Bay	1	10 00
Curaçoa	8	125 00
Fayal	45	995 00
Gibraltar	5	50 00
Glasgow	1	10 00
Halifax	3	30 00
Havre	4	40 00
Havana	34	340 00
Honolulu	136	1,675 00
Hong Kong	1	10 00
Jacmel	1	10 00
Kanagawa	18	180 00
Kingston, Jamaica	5	50 00
La Paz	17	170 00
Liverpool	12	120 00
London	12	120 00
Malaga	1	10 00
Manila	1	10 00
Matanzas	8	80 00
Mazatlan	10	100 00
Mayaguez	1	10 00
Messina	2	20 00
Minatitlan	7	70 00
Montreal	3	34 50
Neuvitas	2	20 00
Panama	9	90 00
Para	8	80 00
Pernambuco	11	$125 00
Plaister Cove, N. S	3	30 00
Rio Janeiro	55	550 00
Rio Grande do Sul	3	30 00
Rotterdam	1	10 00
Sagua la Grande	1	10 00
Santiago de Cuba	1	10 00
Shanghai	7	70 00
St. Cruz	3	30 00
St. Helena	31	360 00
St. John, N. B	39	310 00
Santiago, Cape de Verde	11	185 00
St. Martin	15	175 00
St. Thomas, W. I	26	260 00
Sidney, N. S. W	4	40 00
Sisal	4	40 00
Tahiti	2	20 00
Talcahuano	3	30 00
Trinidad Island	3	30 00
Valparaiso	3	30 00
Vera Cruz	48	624 00
Victoria, V. I	28	280 00
Zanzibar	4	40 00
Amount paid for transportation of shipwrecked American seamen from Howland's island, Pacific ocean, to Honolulu	20	600 00
Amount paid for transportation of shipwrecked American seamen from Baker and McKean's island, Pacific ocean, to Honolulu	52	1,560 00
Picked up at sea and carried to Baltimore.	7	90 00
From Chiltepec bar (Mexico) to Boston	8	130 00
Total	924	12,138 50

G.—*Department accounts, &c., received and allowed during the fiscal year ending June 30, 1868.*

Description.	Accounts.	Amounts.
STATE DEPARTMENT.		
Proof-reading, packing, &c	4	$4,481 98
Miscellaneous items	4	2,902 83
Office rent of consuls	4	18,675 38
Extra clerk hire	4	23,731 04
Contingent expenses, foreign intercourse	4	56,016 85
Rescue of American citizens from shipwreck	3	4,950 00
Copper-plate printing, books, maps, &c	4	3,783 26
Contingent expenses of all the missions abroad	4	20,773 78
Stationery, blank books, &c	3	8,453 37
Blank books, &c., for consuls	4	45,803 33
To encourage immigration	4	15,064 08
Expenses Universal Exposition at Paris	4	13,723 98
Expenses under the neutrality act	4	17,631 54
Bringing home from foreign countries persons charged with crime	2	30,614 52
Publishing laws in pamphlet form	4	65,057 95
Total	56	331,063 89
Archibald Campbell, commissioner northwest boundary survey, for running northwest boundary line	4	$15,773 21
N. M. Beckwith, United States commissioner general to the Universal Exhibition of 1867, expenses during the fiscal year ending June 30, 1868	4	$159,929 73
INTERIOR DEPARTMENT.		
Expenses of taking the eighth census	4	$22,736 83
Suppression of the slave trade	1	520 12
Packing and distributing documents	4	7,252 40
Preservation of collections of exploring expeditions	2	3,116 31
Census of Arizona Territory	1	287 00
United States Statutes at Large	1	945 00
Total	13	34,857 66
PATENT OFFICE.		
Contingent expenses	5	$358,527 06
Illustrations for reports	5	22,922 60
Fitting up cases of copyrights	4	1,605 90
Repairing saloon in north wing	5	19,311 41
Total	19	402,366 97
POST OFFICE.		
Blank books, &c	3	$80,821 17
Extension	1	39,999 96
Repairing and republishing post route maps	1	9,969 19
Total	5	130,790 32

H.—*Statement showing the expense of assessing the internal revenue taxes in the several collection districts, including the salaries, commissions, and extra allowances of the assessors, their contingent expenses, and the compensation of assistant assessors, from July 1, 1867, to June 30, 1868.*

District.	Gross compensation.	Tax.	Net compensation.	Clerk hire.	Stationery.	Printing and advertising.	Postage and express.	Rent of assessor.	Compensation of assistant assessors.	Tax.	Net compensation of assistant assessors.	Rent of assistant assessors.	Total.
MAINE.													
1st district	$3,971 89	$136,07	$3,835 82	$1,625 00	$46 92	$25 75	$50 43	$300 00	$11,648 66	$222 57	$11,426 09	....	17,310 01
2d district	3,266 66	96 52	3,170 14	666 56	184 52	21 00	119 15	100 00	11,910 63	223 23	11,687 40	....	15,948 77
3d district	1,247 29	39 26	1,208 03	650 00	115 96	....	74 79	110 00	8,390 08	155 68	8,234 40	....	10,393 18
4th district	1,588 60	29 42	1,559 18	799 99	162 27	13 75	87 55	100 00	9,260 19	170 81	9,089 38	....	11,812 12
5th district	2,171 13	40 02	2,131 11	708 39	134 02	6 00	21 09	75 00	11,667 89	236 74	11,431 15	....	14,506 76
Total	12,245 57	341 29	11,904 28	4,449 94	643 69	66 50	353 01	685 00	52,877 45	1,009 03	51,868 42	....	69,970 84
NEW HAMPSHIRE.													
1st district	3,327 50	122,06	3,205 44	750 00	222 98	22 50	34 84	93 75	9,512 15	177 72	9,334 43	....	13,663 94
2d district	3,835 79	141 76	3,694 03	867 32	174 71	16 00	115 44	200 00	8,609 71	162 64	8,447 07	$6 67	13,521 24
3d district	2,401 12	57 54	2,343 58	938 46	105 32	25 58	127 42	75 00	12,646 02	236 30	12,409 72	5 00	16,030 08
Total	9,564 41	321 36	9,243 05	2,555 78	503 01	64 08	277 70	368 75	30,767 88	576 66	30,191 22	11 67	43,215 26
VERMONT.													
1st district	2,533 53	64 16	2,469 37	369 50	31 32	14,75	35 38	61 25	10,766 54	203 62	10,562 92	35 88	13,580 37
2d district	2,699 74	72 47	2,627 27	138 00	33 60	12 25	141 61	75 00	9,126 40	173 32	8,953 08	....	11,980 81
3d district	2,026 09	34 52	1,991 57	666 65	210 56	34 11	73 99	200 00	14,211 28	263 30	13,947 98	....	17,124 86
Total	7,259 36	171 15	7,088 21	1,174 15	275 48	61 11	250 98	336 25	34,104 22	640 24	33,463 98	35 88	42,686 04
MASSACHUSETTS.													
1st district	3,865 33	125 84	3,739 49	1,741 61	101 74	5 00	133 78	187 50	24,454 34	477 28	23,977 06	....	29,886 18
2d district	3,839 40	141 96	3,697 44	1,800 00	223 87	8 00	56 08	200 00	18,802 25	353 05	18,449 20	5 00	24,439 59
3d district	4,375 00	156 25	4,218 75	3,675 00	685 08	15 00	320 17	1,050 00	37,013 47	730 81	36,282 66	....	40,246 66
4th district	4,504 16	160 12	4,344 04	3,018 15	266 45	26 75	146 43	525 00	21,940 06	435 23	21,504 83	....	29,831 65
5th district	3,852 51	142 61	3,709 90	2,237 02	303 06	51 00	19 73	181 00	19,907 82	374 35	19,533 47	....	26,035 18
6th district	4,375 00	156 25	4,218 75	2,584 00	336 44	12 95	203 54	400 00	21,497 78	410 96	21,086 82	....	28,842 50
7th district	4,375 00	156 25	4,218 75	2,823 29	227 77	12 00	99 13	150 00	23,185 53	440 79	22,744 74	3 33	30,279 01

9th district	3,838 53	141 91	3,696 62	1,554 00	229 88	46 25	100 29	200 00	19,996 23	369 67	19,626 56	....	25,453 60
10th district	4,306 18	152 79	4,153 39	2,499 96	408 27	29 62	198 20	175 00	30,820 03	571 46	30,248 57	....	37,704 01
Total	41,331 10	1,483 98	39,847 12	23,833 70	3,083 44	232 32	1,391 79	3,468 50	235,997 11	4,508 23	231,488 88	8 33	303,354 08
RHODE ISLAND.													
1st district	4,000 00	150 00	3,850 00	2,499 96	78 91	....	8 00	....	22,889 14	436 32	22,452 82	....	28,889 69
2d district	3,473 19	123 65	3,349 54	799 99	23 07	18 37	27 23	200 00	7,780 80	143 81	7,636 99	....	12,055 19
Total	7,473 19	273 65	7,199 54	3,299 95	101 98	18 37	35 23	200 00	30,669 94	580 13	30,089 81	....	40,944 88
CONNECTICUT.													
1st district	4,249 69	154 19	4,095 50	1,312 48	133 16	35 82	106 64	280 00	21,508 79	407 69	21,101 10	....	27,064 70
2d district	3,952 59	147 63	3,804 96	1,200 00	464 89	9 90	214 42	100 00	14,929 99	280 10	14,649 89	....	20,444 06
3d district	4,084 04	141 69	3,942 35	1,249 95	159 73	12 75	115 57	250 00	15,101 28	284 99	14,816 29	22 50	20,569 14
4th district	3,693 07	134 64	3,558 43	999 98	32 80	19 00	64 77	75 00	13,505 69	252 42	13,253 27	....	18,003 25
Total	15,979 39	578 15	15,401 24	4,762 41	790 53	77 47	501 40	705 00	65,045 75	1,225 20	63,820 55	22 50	86,081 15
NEW YORK.													
1st district	....	....	....	3,000 00	522 38	19 25	45 61	731 81	24,680 02	453 49	24,226 53	....	28,545 58
2d district	3,999 98	150 00	3,849 98	4,999 93	236 26	69 48	79 00	800 00	25,547 35	474 50	25,072 85	....	35,107 50
3d district	4,344 50	170 83	4,173 67	6,344 15	870 66	97 64	20 55	1,250 00	36,931 39	701 06	36,230 33	....	48,987 00
4th district	3,999 99	150 00	3,849 99	5,000 00	560 90	31 20	13 00	1,208 34	42,219 94	794 16	41,425 78	16 00	52,105 21
5th district	3,742 55	137 73	3,604 82	4,000 03	556 35	47 00	....	650 00	21,243 99	398 45	20,845 54	....	29,703 74
6th district	3,847 72	142 38	3,705 34	5,000 00	133 89	39 00	10 00	625 00	24,519 12	462 93	24,056 19	....	33,569 42
7th district	3,898 95	144 94	3,754 01	4,000 00	213 51	36 00	....	2,500 00	23,810 25	449 21	23,361 04	....	33,864 56
8th district	4,482 44	158 40	4,324 04	5,599 84	496 76	75 25	19 00	1,033 33	54,042 66	1,006 80	53,035 86	....	64,584 08
9th district	3,894 07	144 69	3,749 38	3,979 92	155 43	16 20	42 00	840 00	40,279 89	737 61	39,542 28	....	48,325 21
10th district	3,726 56	136 31	3,590 25	1,999 92	261 47	10 25	39 79	400 00	24,356 92	448 91	23,908 01	....	30,209 69
11th district	2,806 68	90 23	2,716 45	999 97	101 10	13 10	79 67	60 00	13,359 24	233 32	13,125 92	....	17,096 21
12th district	3,216 26	110 79	3,105 47	1,800 00	128 94	8 40	21 65	110 00	18,092 00	334 03	17,757 97	....	22,932 43
13th district	3,184 33	72 49	3,111 84	2,600 00	64 07	16 50	38 62	75 00	20,845 87	439 68	20,406 19	....	26,312 22
14th district	4,000 00	150 00	3,850 00	3,200 00	451 96	35 00	250 84	500 00	22,834 89	435 29	22,399 60	7 50	30,694 90
15th district	3,558 91	127 93	3,430 98	2,113 50	163 07	54 65	163 23	500 00	17,075 37	319 58	16,755 79	....	23,181 22
16th district	2,570 67	76 08	2,494 59	483 01	206 77	6 50	131 62	7 91	7,040 51	131 09	6,909 42	....	10,239 83
17th district	1,621 10	42 87	1,578 23	90 00	101 40	....	28 69	50 83	8,645 16	159 94	8,485 22	....	10,334 37
18th district	2,409 65	70 47	2,339 18	1,725 00	148 20	45 35	17 26	200 00	14,192 51	272 69	13,919 82	....	18,394 81
19th district	2,106 67	51 43	2,055 24	650 00	289 69	30 07	45 07	168 75	12,117 00	225 32	11,891 68	10 00	15,140 50
20th district	2,517 46	75 87	2,441 59	682 61	251 72	40 00	6 57	120 00	9,605 11	179 24	9,425 87	....	12,968 36
21st district	3,570 17	120 12	3,450 05	1,977 36	237 03	....	234 08	300 00	20,750 80	384 28	20,366 52	....	26,565 04
22d district	2,227 79	61 37	2,166 42	1,200 00	215 68	7 40	207 93	100 00	14,362 30	265 15	14,097 15	....	17,994 58
23d district	2,321 12	70 16	2,250 96	2,016 63	144 31	10 50	58 71	250 00	14,400 42	270 15	14,130 27	....	18,861 38
24th district	3,688 78	134 42	3,554 36	856 26	213 86	31 85	233 41	61 56	17,781 55	330 73	17,450 82	....	22,402 12
25th district	2,250 00	40 78	2,209 22	1,349 10	338 90	18 40	77 09	65 00	12,523 60	249 18	12,274 62	11 00	16,343 33
26th district	2,618 50	80 91	2,537 59	999 96	171 42	5 10	73 30	157 53	10,690 00	201 66	10,488 34	....	14,433 24
27th district	2,765 77	75 77	2,690 00	1,249 95	266 85	10 84	51 63	237 50	14,761 72	278 15	14,483 57	....	18,990 34
28th district	3,356 88	117 83	3,239 05	1,800 00	120 74	39 00	64 93	350 00	16,623 05	311 89	16,311 16	....	21,924 88
29th district	3,716 90	105 93	3,610 97	1,249 96	77 92	7 30	74 65	150 00	28,352 46	528 62	27,823 84	....	32,994 64

Statement showing the expense of assessing the internal revenue taxes, &c.—Continued.

District.	Gross compensation.	Tax.	Net compensation.	Clerk hire.	Stationery.	Printing and advertising.	Postage and express.	Rent of assessor.	Compensation of assistant assessors.	Tax.	Net compensation of assistant assessors.	Rent of assistant assessors.	Total.
NEW YORK.													
30th district	$4,308 55	$150 21	$4,158 34	$5,143 00	$458 00	....	$75 99	$400 00	$36,241 75	$710 64	$35,531 11	$78 75	$45,847 19
31st district	2,508 55	62 92	2,445 63	782 50	204 19	$12 20	138 16	112 50	11,870 92	222 15	11,648 77	30 33	15,374 28
32d district	3,873 64	147 89	3,725 75	5,000 01	640 61	....	....	875 00	56,945 00	1,068 30	55,876 70	....	66,118 07
Total	101,135 14	3,371 75	97,763 39	81,894 61	9,004 04	833 43	2,342 05	14,890 06	716,742 96	13,478 20	703,264 76	153 58	910,145 92
NEW JERSEY.													
1st district	6,133 11	241 64	5,891 47	1,200 01	89 30	....	85 78	150 00	13,764 58	255 75	13,508 83	....	20,925 39
2d district	2,929 59	96 45	2,833 14	1,299 99	152 74	16 56	82 88	137 50	15,511 21	288 48	15,222 73	....	19,745 54
3d district	3,639 95	131 98	3,507 97	2,009 03	204 97	32 10	104 16	200 00	20,634 28	385 08	20,249 20	5 00	26,303 43
4th district	3,980 78	134 75	3,846 03	2,133 28	145 96	47 45	131 93	200 00	28,407 69	529 53	27,878 16	7 50	34,390 31
5th district	3,999 99	150 00	3,849 99	4,216 65	222 80	37 70	4 99	812 50	31,454 84	597 33	30,857 51	....	40,002 14
Total	20,683 42	754 82	19,928 60	10,849 96	815 77	133 81	409 74	1,500 00	109,772 60	2,056 17	107,716 43	12 50	141,366 81
PENNSYLVANIA.													
1st district	4,648 02	165 00	4,483 02	6,637 63	812 31	....	32 60	927 49	55,932 27	1,056 13	54,876 14	....	67,769 19
2d district	4,647 51	182 37	4,465 14	3,999 99	476 56	25 20	....	850 00	32,475 68	645 19	31,830 49	20 00	41,667 38
3d district	5,027 30	186 23	4,841 07	5,383 33	399 62	216 60	76 95	825 00	40,765 06	761 61	40,003 45	69 96	51,815 98
4th district	4,610 65	183 99	4,426 66	3,916 61	946 01	64 47	5 24	625 00	28,258 86	593 27	27,665 59	161 32	38,210 90
5th district	2,774 86	88 72	2,686 14	3,479 99	359 90	17 45	87 85	500 00	21,631 17	399 27	21,231 90	....	28,363 23
6th district	3,175 53	109 27	3,066 26	800 00	98 02	4 00	....	175 00	15,411 10	286 44	15,124 66	....	19,267 94
7th district	2,828 21	91 40	2,736 81	1,800 00	192 94	....	57 25	312 50	19,305 15	355 23	18,949 92	30 83	24,080 25
8th district	3,004 99	87 75	2,917 24	1,466 64	60 75	....	35 02	200 00	19,623 29	372 59	19,250 70	....	23,930 35
9th district	4,859 41	170 73	4,688 68	1,699 00	280 96	12 00	92 33	187 50	23,372 20	448 63	22,923 57	....	29,884 04
10th district	12 50	21	12 29	1,200 00	129 25	9 75	22 00	300 00	13,877 33	263 37	13,613 96	....	15,287 25
11th district	3,166 48	95 39	3,071 09	1,461 62	25 31	38 50	83 11	213 71	15,185 63	288 29	14,897 34	5 00	19,795 68
12th district	1,262 33	42 36	1,219 97	883 61	220 79	30 75	330 15	142 83	17,476 78	322 63	17,153 95	55 76	20,036 81
13th district	1,755 51	41 89	1,713 62	799 99	82 65	64 40	55 02	145 31	13,517 22	248 08	13,269 14	76 66	16,206 79
14th district	2,524 34	84 78	2,439 56	1,199 95	284 26	11 00	135 94	300 00	21,626 90	396 20	21,230 70	35 41	25,636 82
15th district	2,841 12	88 65	2,752 47	1,500 00	166 72	45 50	60 32	165 54	20,306 13	372 17	19,933 96	14 74	24,639 25
16th district	2,296 98	54 12	2,242 86	1,066 68	117 20	30 00	29 28	79 40	21,487 45	405 42	21,082 03	43 50	24,690 95
17th district	1,927 34	44 04	1,883 30	337 00	72 69	18 00	38 03	100 00	9,992 06	184 78	9,807 28	....	12,256 30
18th district	2,237 04	61 83	2,175 21	800 00	129 28	28 25	118 45	100 00	17,780 80	326 03	17,454 77	....	20,805 96

20th district	3,194 15	109 70	3,084 45	1,400 00	285 20	39 00	161 54	187 50	18,338 05	339 59	17,998 46	....	23,156 15
21st district	2,532 09	100 09	2,432 00	999 95	222 50	15 50	22 34	93 00	20,710 10	380 67	20,329 43	....	24,114 72
22d district	4,000 00	149 99	3,850 01	3,399 92	420 90	2 25	29 50	625 00	18,429 39	356 47	18,072 92	....	26,493 83
23d district	3,395 40	119 76	3,275 64	1,530 00	200 12	18 50	24 82	300 00	14,336 41	274 39	14,062 02	93 33	19,381 10
24th district	1,547 91	39 88	1,508 03	600 00	193 08	14 07	137 64	133 00	18,098 04	330 86	17,767 18	14 59	20,367 59
Total	71,449 04	2,407 10	69,041 94	47,266 91	6,321 86	756 94	1,660 89	7,527 78	510,129 79	9,634 25	500,495 54	1,037 77	634,109 63
DELAWARE	3,399 74	119 96	3,279 78	1,800 00	191 28	14 90	66 04	75 00	22,846 48	439 36	22,407 12	....	27,834 12
MARYLAND.													
1st district	1,673 53	33 67	1,639 86	600 00	126 00	40 23	61 31	102 00	15,258 56	278 77	14,979 79	....	17,549 19
2d district	4,136 77	146 50	3,990 27	1,403 67	75 44	....	5 90	500 00	12,141 41	228 15	11,913 26	....	17,888 54
3d district	4,608 94	161 84	4,447 10	4,399 88	265 07	32 25	24 48	....	44,651 47	853 28	43,798 19	....	52,966 97
4th district	3,698 02	126 10	3,571 92	778 45	118 52	51 50	12 85	90 00	16,234 56	30 64	15,927 92	....	20,551 16
5th district	3,206 77	93 52	3,113 25	566 62	97 28	28 50	11 89	37 50	25,657 56	468 04	25,189 52	....	29,044 56
Total	17,324 03	561 63	16,762 40	7,748 62	682 31	152 48	116 43	729 50	113,943 56	2,134 88	111,808 68	....	138,000 42
DIST. COLUMBIA	3,668 42	120 91	3,547 51	2,356 99	140 12	30 00	....	420 00	18,593 06	355 96	18,237 10	....	24,731 72
OHIO.													
1st district	1,658 10	56 92	1,601 18	3,499 99	370 23	47 00	13 25	1,200 00	27,188 26	513 02	26,675 24	....	33,406 89
2d district	4,324 35	153 89	4,170 46	2,075 00	108 32	27 00	20 00	771 67	25,450 13	482 41	24,967 72	....	32,140 17
3d district	3,526 00	126 30	3,399 70	1,800 00	312 33	23 85	112 62	416 67	25,323 27	470 26	24,853 01	....	30,918 18
4th district	1,684 09	58 95	1,625 14	1,216 66	350 24	20 50	38 08	135 00	9,188 58	172 37	9,016 21	....	12,401 83
5th district	1,529 10	26 45	1,502 65	350 00	171 31	45 00	24 60	60 00	7,186 93	134 66	7,052 27	....	9,205 83
6th district	2,053 41	56 79	1,996 62	906 51	522 09	17 00	87 79	106 25	12,108 58	225 11	11,883 47	....	15,519 73
7th district	3,234 76	111 73	3,123 03	1,479 00	271 27	58 37	158 23	112 50	16,983 81	320 13	16,663 68	....	21,866 08
8th district	2,082 68	39 78	2,042 90	712 50	291 97	16 50	21 73	100 00	11,128 44	208 88	10,919 56	....	14,107 16
9th district	2,991 84	83 22	2,908 62	1,084 50	269 88	56 80	55 75	100 00	19,361 87	362 88	19,018 99	....	23,494 54
10th district	3,673 65	133 68	3,539 97	70 00	63 68	33 30	41 38	....	7,798 47	145 04	7,653 43	....	11,401 76
11th district	3,002 19	85 93	2,916 26	....	83 51	30 75	20 00	131 25	10,298 67	192 89	10,105 78	....	13,287 55
12th district	3,140 18	106 98	3,033 20	1,000 00	74 47	29 00	62 37	150 00	12,931 34	239 99	12,691 35	....	17,040 39
13th district	3,426 60	113 81	3,312 79	800 00	156 65	13 75	116 16	120 00	10,474 90	195 22	10,279 68	21 67	14,820 70
14th district	2,334 72	48 20	2,286 52	583 81	52 88	20 75	28 60	100 00	14,916 78	286 31	14,630 47	....	17,703 03
15th district	2,667 21	83 26	2,583 95	600 00	136 32	34 50	121 91	100 00	6,667 92	124 73	6,543 19	17 50	10,137 37
16th district	1,646 83	32 58	1,614 25	501 96	123 47	38 25	28 86	47 50	7,525 10	140 94	7,384 16	24 17	9,762 62
17th district	3,284 00	92 55	3,191 45	1,800 00	99 17	24 50	89 46	150 00	14,766 70	291 70	14,475 00	....	19,829 58
18th district	3,876 35	147 94	3,728 41	2,000 00	325 42	14 25	46 00	500 00	21,368 44	395 42	20,973 02	....	27,587 10
19th district	1,902 25	49 22	1,853 03	526 00	126 51	12 50	38 26	107 50	9,508 97	179 81	9,329 16	....	11,992 96
Total	52,038 31	1,608 18	50,430 13	21,005 93	3,909 72	565 57	1,125 05	4,408 34	270,197 16	5,081 77	265,115 39	63 34	346,623 47

Statement showing the expense of assessing the internal revenue taxes, &c.—Continued.

District.	Gross compensation.	Tax.	Net compensation.	Clerk hire.	Stationery.	Printing and advertising.	Postage and express.	Rent of assessor.	Compensation of assistant assessors.	Tax.	Net compensation of assistant assessors.	Rent of assistant assessors.	Total.
INDIANA.													
1st district	$3,015 91	$100 79	$2,915 12	$964 63	$245 58	$17 50	$1 10	$105 00	$11,659 10	$217 48	$11,441 62		$15,690 55
2d district				999 96	117 08	86 50	48 98	480 00	7,291 65	136 29	7,155 36	$4 00	8,891 88
3d district	1,688 32	34 40	1,653 92	800 00	134 63	34 00	30 29	200 00	9,313 73	173 12	9,140 61		11,993 45
4th district	2,329 07	64 13	2,264 94	946 25	62 64	27 00	32 82	96 00	9,899 95	189 10	9,710 85	10 00	13,150 50
5th district	2,195 66	45 60	2,150 06	1,000 03	141 55		73 53	96 00	12,232 13	231 48	12,000 65	15 00	15,476 82
6th district	3,002 44	100 11	2,902 33	1,083 00	282 42	15 00	41 94		11,378 25	215 62	11,162 63		15,487 32
7th district	2,052 56	52 75	1,999 81	623 08	56 45	113 75	10 10	93 75	7,121 42	134 08	6,987 34		9,884 28
8th district	1,751 33	41 68	1,709 65	825 00	42 27	4 00		150 00	9,266 75	172 85	9,093 90	41 66	11,866 48
9th district	2,040 05	52 00	1,988 05	273 00	95 19	54 75	68 94	50 00	10,199 76	191 66	10,008 08	13 00	12,551 01
10th district	1,770 52	38 50	1,732 02	584 00	88 88	16 50	46 70	100 00	6,080 23	115 33	5,964 90		8,533 00
11th district	2,004 17	33 41	1,970 76	798 00	101 63		7 15	225 00	16,884 56	311 98	16,572 58	139 00	19,814 12
Total	21,850 03	563 37	21,286 66	8,896 95	1,368 32	369 00	361 55	1,595 75	111.327 53	2,089 01	109,238 52	222 66	143,339 41
ILLINOIS.													
1st district	4,374 91	156 25	4,218 66	4,871 77	310 88	61 60	116 04	1,000 00	40,381 43	785 93	39,595 50		50,174 45
2d district	2,481 09	57 25	2,423 84	1,200 03	415 30	24 30	100 19	127 50	16,554 14	312 53	16,241 61		20,532 74
3d district	3,266 59	81 49	3,185 10	1,583 27	71 61	33 40	85 64	180 00	30,241 30	630 97	29,610 33		34,749 35
4th district	3.436 64	109 32	3,327 32	1,500 00	267 81	35 00	208 07	300 00	19,805 17	368 63	19,436 54		25,074 74
5th district	4,251 14	142 53	4,108 61	1,854 00	472 17	35 65	176 78	300 00	25,647 21	481 57	25,165 64	45 67	32,158 52
6th district	2,166 85	45 96	2,120 89	888 00	73 30	13 10	40 67	250 00	19,998 88	373 27	19,625 61		23,011 57
7th district	2,622 24	68 60	2,553 64	1,125 00	122 95		49 62	181 25	21,879 05	403 60	21,475 45	25 32	25,533 23
8th district	3,797 38	127 43	3,669 95	1,500 00	779 95	29 50	187 62	350 00	20,349 13	383 83	19,965 30		26,482 32
9th district	1,613 44	31 97	1,581 47	1,282 50	96 96	7 00	60 19	100 00	10,711 26	202 13	10,509 13		13,637 25
10th district	2,170 62	56 04	2,114 58	641 00	225 57	46 70	74 30	150 00	16,030 27	298 36	15,731 91		18,984 06
11th district	1,613 30	30 65	1,582 65	800 03	63 28	13 00	31 49	77 38	13,996 23	257 22	13,739 01		16,306 84
12th district	3,463 87	108 74	3,355 13	746 33	144 02	36 67	78 48	168 00	17,740 48	332 07	17,408 41		21,937 04
13th district	1,628 82	31 02	1,597 80	246 00	95 89	5 00	3 00	60 00	8,371 61	155 23	8,216 38		10,224 07
Total	36,886 89	1,047 25	35,839 64	18,227 90	3,139 69	340 92	1,212 09	3,244 13	261,706 16	4,985 34	256,720 82	70 99	318,806 18
MICHIGAN.													

4th district	2,822 78	71 64	2,751 14	1,219 74	191 18	20 60	23 23	206 25	11,005 04	219 46	10,785 58	87 89	15,285 61
5th district	2,133 25	42 95	2,090 30	999 97	43 18	24 20	215 24	183 38	12,899 58	242 52	12,657 06	....	16,213 33
6th district	2,207 23	53 80	2,153 43	1,346 68	45 17	54 15	130 63	175 00	20,427 09	384 24	20,042 85	....	23,947 91
Total	17,479 10	505 08	16,974 02	7,986 88	797 84	293 35	699 98	1,322 96	101,804 98	1,949 44	99,855 54	138 72	128,069 29
WISCONSIN.													
1st district	3,762 49	138 11	3,624 38	2,583 46	79 92	12 00	78 49	400 00	18,294 46	343 52	17,950 94	....	24,729 19
2d district	2,199 07	59 94	2,139 13	1,266 30	215 29	25 70	156 97	150 00	13,300 62	251 39	13,049 23	....	17,002 62
3d district	1,614 19	30 70	1,583 49	531 97	117 49	20 30	123 31	120 00	9,405 97	172 85	9,233 12	8 33	11,738 01
4th district	....	....	....	799 92	185 38	39 90	135 03	150 00	9,891 00	183 26	9,707 74	....	11,017 97
5th district	2,195 39	55 70	2,139 69	865 38	234 68	7 70	48 78	75 00	19,293 48	374 61	18,918 87	....	22,290 10
6th district	1,587 77	29 38	1,558 39	300 00	86 93	24 50	119 44	87 00	9,685 43	179 33	9,506 10	....	11,682 36
Total	11,358 91	313 83	11,045 08	6,347 03	919 69	130 10	662 02	982 00	79,870 96	1,504 96	78,366 00	8 33	98,460 25
IOWA.													
1st district	3,831 08	127 66	3,703 42	860 28	70 16	77 00	73 90	167 50	23,390 17	478 92	22,911 25	33 00	27,896 51
2d district	2,258 84	50 43	2,208 41	750 00	102 31	34 40	65 09	65 00	14,497 49	276 94	14,220 55	16 25	17,462 01
3d district	2,798 55	77 41	2,721 14	867 35	167 62	23 50	34 67	....	14,530 91	272 46	14,258 45	....	18,072 73
4th district	1,625 13	31 25	1,593 88	699 96	174 74	63 40	63 66	120 16	10,461 39	203 14	10,258 25	....	12,974 05
5th district	1,623 01	28 83	1,594 18	379 21	113 07	78 25	....	48 00	6,554 18	136 98	6,417 20	23 33	8,653 24
6th district	2,999 68	63 28	2,936 40	798 40	54 40	195 50	17 84	144 00	10,825 74	216 97	10,608 77	30 00	14,785 31
Total	15,136 29	378 86	14,757 43	4,355 20	682 30	472 05	253 16	544 66	80,259 88	1,585 41	78,674 47	102 58	99,843 85
MINNESOTA.													
1st district	2,847 30	62 34	2,784 96	731 80	89 28	....	15 01	100 00	14,378 72	294 05	14,084 67	....	17,805 72
2d district	2,247 75	62 37	2,185 38	654 10	177 57	27 62	48 07	300 00	10,303 83	192 07	10,111 76	73 53	13,578 03
Total	5,095 05	124 71	4,970 34	1,385 90	266 85	27 62	63 08	400 00	24,682 55	486 12	24,196 43	73 53	31,383 75
KANSAS	3,171 32	94 36	3,076 96	1,875 00	403 23	120 75	355 45	450 00	20,010 02	388 22	19,621 80	24 67	25,927 86
CALIFORNIA.													
1st district	5,750 00	225 50	5,524 50	8,327 50	294 43	30 00	13 55	....	44,982 98	1,379 67	43,603 31	....	57,793 29
2d district	4,427 03	171 42	4,255 61	1,644 00	204 46	58 75	90 92	300 00	21,176 39	643 47	20,532 92	58 34	27,145 00
3d district	3,688 90	125 70	3,563 20	1,350 00	197 11	38 00	130 60	360 00	16,236 30	489 14	15,747 16	....	21,386 07
4th district	6,399 30	243 32	6,155 98	5,322 00	395 69	309 83	231 80	652 30	68,440 38	2,265 65	66,174 73	202 50	79,444 83
5th district	4,207 57	147 89	4,059 68	1,875 00	168 20	66 70	61 56	300 00	22,657 40	689 00	21,968 40	....	28,499 54
Total	24,472 80	913 83	23,558 97	18,518 50	1,259 89	503 28	528 43	1,612 30	173,493 45	5,466 93	168,026 52	260 84	214,268 73
OREGON	5,283 71	201 64	5,082 07	2,545 00	189 44	80 50	60 08	420 00	21,862 51	660 48	21,202 03	83 33	29,662 45

Net compensation of assistant assessors.	Rent of assistant assessors.	Total.
$9, 363 61	$79 83	$12, 935 35
16, 189 38	....	22, 796 62
21, 517 24	87 50	26, 932 75
14, 478 12	....	20, 274 79
9, 966 01	....	15, 100 91
9, 079 34	....	13, 266 25
1, 322 21	....	2, 237 87
2, 301 26	....	6, 784 38
12, 450 30	....	17, 708 35
11, 914 32	....	17, 962 43

VIRGINIA.													
1st district	1,373 64	22 90	1,350 74	200 00	46 76	....	....	22 50	13,271 48	241 54	13,029 94	....	14,649 94
2d district	3,530 66	126 60	3,404 06	2,000 02	235 35	7 70	....	....	17,369 29	322 90	17,046 39	....	22,693 52
3d district	3,762 25	142 36	3,619 89	1,919 41	97 15	30 00	51 03	....	14,845 58	273 37	14,572 21	....	20,289 69
4th district	875 05	22 96	852 09	750 00	128 13	26 50	13 53	252 52	13,381 15	242 03	13,139 12	81 66	15,243 55
5th district	5,317 98	177 21	5,140 77	2,300 00	142 23	....	22 15	375 00	17,296 65	364 41	16,932 24	....	24,912 39
6th district	1,515 68	38 27	1,477 41	900 00	155 18	....	103 95	200 00	13,209 91	241 91	12,968 00	....	15,804 54
7th district	1,589 77	29 49	1,560 28	600 00	69 80	10 25	16 68	180 00	15,300 77	281 76	15,019 01	....	17,456 02
8th district	1,874 99	31 25	1,843 74	1,416 62	22 41	....	26 79	250 00	8,899 67	167 67	8,732 00	....	12,291 56
Total	19,840 02	591 04	19,248 98	10,086 05	897 01	74 45	234 13	1,280 02	113,574 50	2,135 59	111,438 91	81 66	143,341 21
KENTUCKY.													
1st district	2,077 25	40 19	2,037 06	1,912 10	89 99	20 00	10 50	275 00	14,626 70	273 39	14,413 31	....	18,756 96
2d district	1,823 29	32 79	1,790 50	1,500 00	66 57	....	13 89	264 00	13,696 94	253 18	13,443 76	....	17,078 72
3d district	1,968 99	35 95	1,933 04	1,875 00	96 10	....	22 02	162 50	20,015 68	368 05	19,647 63	....	23,736 29
4th district	2,267 52	50 85	2,216 67	2,250 00	340 02	11 50	10 57	360 00	20,808 87	384 67	20,424 20	....	25,612 96
5th district	5,652 07	220 10	5,431 97	3,124 95	174 73	43 50	44 00	....	24,868 23	471 06	24,397 17	....	33,216 32
6th district	4,086 90	141 83	3,945 07	2,235 00	310 73	10 50	24 20	250 00	37,498 42	725 87	36,772 55	....	43,548 05
7th district	4,222 06	144 26	4,077 80	1,300 00	277 73	28 00	22 10	240 00	37,768 49	771 88	36,996 61	....	42,942 24
8th district	2,004 16	33 40	1,970 76	1,066 72	59 62	4 50	1 75	150 00	19,281 01	387 03	18,893 98	....	22,147 33
9th district	2,437 07	59 17	2,377 90	316 25	201 74	4 75	70 79	275 00	15,591 24	287 26	15,303 98	....	18,550 41
Total	26,539 31	758 54	25,780 77	15,580 02	1,616 23	122 75	219 82	1,976 50	204,215 58	3,922 39	200,293 19	....	245,589 28
MISSOURI.													
1st district	5,116 65	191 01	4,925 64	5,171 33	345 02	32 90	56 07	1,000 00	33,211 46	639 74	32,571 72	....	44,102 68
2d district	2,571 80	58 52	2,513 28	1,189 76	159 68	8 50	183 97	150 00	13,973 37	285 30	13,688 07	....	17,878 26
3d district	3,473 15	102 17	3,370 98	2,400 00	102 22	44 00	111 08	200 00	14,007 37	285 94	13,721 43	....	19,949 71
4th district	3,250 94	98 23	3,152 71	874 95	35 65	50 25	59 30	100 00	9,725 30	181 48	9,543 82	....	13,816 68
5th district	1,513 93	42 43	1,471 50	800 02	154 10	41 75	99 84	216 00	9,775 17	182 09	9,593 08	14,50	12,390 79
6th district	3,559 06	110 49	3,448 57	2,681 00	262 14	51 85	144 72	420 00	31,812 14	543 76	31,268 38	....	38,276 66
Total	19,485 53	602 85	18,882 68	13,117 06	1,058 81	229 25	639 98	2,086 00	112,504 81	2,118 31	110,386 50	14,50	146,414 78
TENNESSEE.													
1st district	6,509 75	202 57	6,307 18	1,455 67	45 00	....	....	163 68	31,254 82	808 53	30,446 29	....	38,417 82
2d district	3,917 12	114 10	3,803 02	2,736 62	81 81	21 50	9 90	400 00	20,708 46	485 87	20,222 59	....	27,275 44
3d district	2,807 11	67 53	2,739 58	3,166 00	428 20	16 00	92 00	300 00	20,605 97	440 13	20,165 84	....	26,907 62
4th district	4,915 23	178 02	4,737 21	1,136 40	108 90	....	19 25	72 00	15,953 32	347 79	15,605 53	....	21,679 29
5th district	4,989 19	168 18	4,821 01	3,150 00	3 51	....	10 00	390 00	30,291 02	706 44	29,584 58	10 00	37,969 10
6th district	4,225 77	156 71	4,069 06	1,766 66	141 72	....	34 15	158 00	27,535 90	595 23	26,944 67	39 99	33,154 25
7th district	3,273 93	86 99	3,186 94	2,255 12	308 64	33 50	22 50	100 00	19,166 91	414 03	18,752 88	....	24,659 58
8th district	4,412 19	155 65	4,256 54	2,450 00	204 82	43 50	....	800 00	26,276 14	578 20	25,697 94	....	33,452 80
Total	35,050 29	1,129 75	33,920 54	18,106 47	1,322 60	114 50	197 80	2,383 68	191,796 54	4,376 22	187,420 32	49 99	243,515 90

Statement showing the expenses of assessing the internal revenue taxes, &c.—Continued

District.	Gross compensation.	Tax.	Net compensation.	Clerk hire.	Stationery.	Printing and advertising.	Postage and express.	Rent of assessor.	Compensation of assistant assessors.	Tax.	Net compensation of assistant assessors.	Rent of assistant assessors.	Total.
LOUISIANA.													
1st district	$5,386 33	$201 34	$5,184 99	$7,111 91	$1,008 02	$562 50	$28 70	....	$87,457 59	$2,329 49	$85,128 10	$30 00	$99,054 22
2d district	4,395 22	169 75	4,225 47	3,150 98	357 59	....	25 41	$420 00	34,900 37	922 39	33,977 98	102 50	42,259 93
3d district	2,404 66	101 19	2,303 47	903 32	250 34	154 25	40 50	555 00	25,573 02	685 73	24,887 29	37 50	29,131 67
Total	12,186 21	472 28	11,713 93	11,166 21	1,615 95	716 75	94 61	975 00	147,930 98	3,237 61	143,993 37	170 00	170,445 82
NORTH CAROLINA.													
1st district	2,008 03	54 47	1,953 56	1,116 65	39 29	....	28 35	120 00	16,374 70	373 32	16,001 38	....	19,259 23
2d district	4,638 50	146 99	4,491 51	1,666 65	206 09	19 00	59 65	300 00	20,692 94	440 82	20,252 12	54 50	27,049 52
3d district	3,663 44	133 16	3,530 28	687 50	34 98	4 25	19 90	150 00	11,732 81	258 67	11,494 14	....	15,921 05
4th district	3,460 64	110 53	3,350 11	1,875 00	133 94	36 00	43 89	300 00	23,063 37	491 44	22,571 93	10 00	28,320 87
5th district	2,907 08	103 69	2,803 39	875 00	35 40	10 00	28 29	200 00	13,636 15	294 24	13,341 91	....	17,293 99
6th district	3,168 67	96 09	3,072 58	1,875 00	40 40	16 00	41 50	300 00	9,589 75	206 75	9,383 00	....	14,728 48
7th district	2,839 41	72 35	2,767 06	1,850 00	151 72	....	70	187 50	18,188 52	404 58	17,783 94	35 00	22,775 92
Total	22,685 77	717 28	21,968 49	9,945 80	641 82	85 25	222 28	1,557 50	113,298 24	2,469 82	110,828 42	99 50	145,349 06
SOUTH CAROLINA.													
1st district	5,997 28	231 11	5,766 17	1,970 88	175 41	41 75	93 85	68 75	24,467 51	631 76	23,835 75	13 61	31,966 17
2d district	4,624 99	168 73	4,456 26	2,369 44	115 40	38 75	59 66	225 00	25,488 55	660 04	24,828 51	....	32,003 02
3d district	4,944 54	179 96	4,764 58	2,230 00	27 55	47 95	49 74	182 50	51,787 71	1,409 09	50,378 62	133 17	57,814 11
Total	15,566 81	579 80	14,987 01	6,570 32	318 36	128 45	203 25	476 25	101,743 77	2,700 89	99,042 88	146 78	121,873 30
GEORGIA.													
1st district	4,600 27	167 51	4,432 76	2,625 00	120 99	11 25	31 50	475 00	22,672 36	582 31	22,090 05	....	20,786 55
2d district	3,999 99	150 00	3,849 99	2,973 99	210 87	56 50	61 49	500 00	33,225 60	849 31	32,376 29	....	40,029 13
3d district	5,161 17	184 85	4,976 32	4,249 99	538 21	18 00	103 57	500 00	49,119 04	1,273 38	47,845 66	....	58,231 75
4th district	4,630 34	169 99	4,460 35	2,548 18	132 04	116 12	183 91	450 00	33,690 77	872 94	32,817 83	....	40,708 43
Total	18,391 77	672 35	17,719 42	12,397 16	1,002 11	201 87	380 47	1,925 00	138,607 77	3,577 94	135,129 83	....	168,755 86

ALABAMA.													
1st district	5,393 70	190 66	5,203 04	5,066 64	152 14	272 00	165 35	....	56,010 25	1,462 13	54,548 12	....	65,407 29
2d district	5,043 65	184 60	4,859 35	4,974 96	242 41	93 50	166 35	550 00	45,906 40	1,229 60	44,736 80	87 50	55,710 87
3d district	4,624 91	172 03	4,452 88	2,411 00	128 17	36 50	68 85	75 00	31,175 14	872 33	30,301 81	....	37,475 21
Total	15,062 56	547 29	14,515 27	12,452 60	522 72	402 00	400 55	625 00	133,151 79	3,564 06	129,587 73	87 50	158,593 37
MISSISSIPPI.													
1st district	5,233 84	211 69	5,022 15	1,500 00	82 88	35 50	130 51	214 00	16,679 83	436 60	16,243 23	58 33	23,286 60
2d district	2,953 88	118 89	2,834 99	875 00	248 17	....	46 55	450 00	23,812 06	625 64	23,186 42	....	27,641 13
3d district	3,835 60	142 53	3,693 07	1,600 00	139 85	66 00	19 23	500 00	20,746 12	579 59	20,166 53	99 44	26,284 12
Total	12,023 32	473 11	11,550 21	3,975 00	470 90	101 50	196 29	1,164 00	61,238 01	1,641 83	59,596 18	157 77	77,211 85
TEXAS.													
1st district	5,224 81	200 06	5,024 75	2,655 58	200 70	49 95	65 70	305 00	21,125 69	581 12	20,544 57	116 66	28,962 91
2d district	4,152 82	155 23	3,997 59	2,395 05	270 40	40 75	246 46	500 00	40,641 38	1,191 31	39,450 07	343 33	47,243 65
3d district	4,989 44	185 20	4,804 24	3,184 15	80 82	36 79	276 23	400 00	25,676 99	671 37	25,005 62	41 67	33,829 52
4th district	4,826 48	183 10	4,643 38	1,916 63	246 41	40 25	42 00	480 00	20,573 23	575 78	19,997 45	87 50	27,453 62
Total	19,193 55	723 59	18,469 96	10,151 41	798 33	167 74	630 39	1,685 00	108,017 29	3,019 58	104,997 71	589 16	137,489 70
ARKANSAS.													
1st district	8,099 08	299 14	7,799 94	2,341 64	503 82	274 50	111 95	541 66	39,765 97	1,097 34	38,668 63	130 83	50,372 97
2d district	5,034 89	191 42	4,843 47	3,805 33	163 81	110 25	39 09	750 00	32,114 71	857 78	31,256 93	116 65	41,085 53
3d district	3,033 62	90 23	2,943 39	2,698 33	237 63	42 75	63 47	270 00	16,653 26	435 51	16,217 75	....	22,473 32
Total	16,167 59	580 79	15,586 80	8,845 30	905 26	427 50	214 51	1,561 66	88,533 94	2,390 63	86,143 31	247 48	113,931 82

RECAPITULATION.

District.	Gross compensation.	Tax.	Net compensation.	Clerk hire.	Stationery.	Printing and advertising.	Postage and express.	Rent of assessor.	Compensation of assistant assessors.	Tax.	Net compensation of assistant assessors.	Rent of assistant assessors.	Total.
Maine	$12,245 57	$341 29	$11,904 28	$4,449 94	$643 69	$66 50	$353 01	$685 00	$52,877 45	$1,009 03	$51,868 42	....	$69,970 84
New Hampshire	9,564 41	321 36	9,243 05	2,555 78	503 01	64 08	277 70	368 75	30,767 88	576 66	30,191 22	$11 67	43,215 26
Vermont	7,259 36	171 15	7,088 21	1,174 15	275 48	61 11	250 98	336 25	34,104 22	640 24	33,463 98	35 88	42,686 04
Massachusetts	41,331 10	1,483 98	39,847 12	23,833 70	3,083 44	232 32	1,391 79	3,468 50	235,997 11	4,508 23	231,488 88	8 33	303,354 08
Rhode Island	7,473 19	273 65	7,199 54	3,299 95	101 98	18 37	35 23	200 00	30,669 94	580 13	30,089 81	....	40,944 88
Connecticut	15,979 39	578 15	15,401 24	4,762 41	790 58	77 47	501 40	705 00	65,045 75	1,225 20	63,820 55	22 50	86,081 15
New York	101,135 14	3,371 75	97,763 39	81,894 61	9,004 04	833 43	2,342 05	14,890 06	716,742 96	13,478 20	703,264 76	153 58	910,145 92
New Jersey	20,683 42	754 82	19,928 60	10,849 96	815 77	133 81	409 74	1,500 00	109,772 60	2,056 17	107,716 43	12 50	141,366 81
Pennsylvania	71,449 04	2,407 10	69,041 94	47,266 91	6,321 86	756 94	1,660 89	7,527 78	510,129 79	9,634 25	500,495 54	1,037 77	634,109 63
Delaware	3,399 74	119 96	3,279 78	1,800 00	191 28	14 90	66 04	75 00	22,846 48	439 36	22,407 12	....	27,834 12
Maryland	17,324 03	561 63	16,762 40	7,748 62	682 31	152 48	116 43	729 50	113,943 56	2,134 88	111,808 68	....	138,000 42
Dist. of Columbia	3,668 42	120 91	3,547 51	2,356 99	140 12	30 00	....	420 00	18,593 06	355 96	18,237 10	....	24,731 72
Ohio	52,038 31	1,608 18	50,430 13	21,005 93	3,909 72	565 57	1,125 05	4,408 34	270,197 16	5,081 77	265,115 39	63 34	346,623 47
Indiana	21,850 03	563 37	21,286 66	8,896 95	1,368 32	369 00	561 55	1,595 75	111,327 53	2,089 01	109,238 52	222 66	143,339 41
Illinois	36,886 89	1,047 25	35,839 64	18,237 90	3,139 69	340 92	1,212 09	3,244 13	261,706 16	4,985 34	256,720 82	70 99	318,806 18
Michigan	17,479 10	505 08	16,974 02	7,986 88	797 84	293 35	699 98	1,322 96	101,804 98	1,949 44	99,855 54	138 72	128,069 29
Wisconsin	11,358 91	313 83	11,045 08	6,347 03	919 69	130 10	662 02	982 00	79,870 96	1,504 96	78,366 00	8 33	98,460 25
Iowa	15,136 29	378 86	14,757 43	4,355 20	682 30	472 05	255 16	544 66	80,259 88	1,585 41	78,674 47	102 58	99,843 85
Minnesota	5,095 05	124 71	4,970 34	1,385 90	266 85	27 62	63 68	400 00	24,682 55	486 12	24,196 43	73 53	31,383 75
Kansas	3,171 32	94 36	3,076 96	1,875 00	403 23	120 75	355 45	450 00	20,010 02	388 22	19,621 80	24 67	25,927 86
California	24,472 80	913 83	23,558 97	18,518 50	1,259 89	503 28	528 43	1,612 30	173,493 45	5,466 93	168,026 52	260 84	214,268 73
Oregon	5,283 71	201 64	5,082 07	2,545 00	189 44	80 50	60 08	420 00	21,862 51	660 48	21,202 03	83 33	29,662 45
Nebraska	1,784 30	34 69	1,749 61	1,125 00	238 44	71 55	57 31	250 00	9,544 57	180 96	9,363 61	79 83	12,935 35
Nevada	4,779 36	176 87	4,602 49	1,242 40	104 69	150 00	27 66	480 00	16,698 05	508 67	16,189 38	....	22,796 62
New Mexico	3,152 63	94 58	3,058 05	1,260 70	617 42	30 00	61 84	300 00	22,192 35	675 11	21,517 24	87 50	26,932 75
Utah	3,738 21	117 27	3,620 94	1,357 64	156 10	20 00	41 99	600 00	14,981 49	503 37	14,478 12	....	20,274 79
Colorado	3,124 99	93 75	3,031 24	1,541 65	95 01	54 00	48 00	365 00	10,276 68	310 67	9,966 01	....	15,100 91
Washington	3,250 00	108 50	3,141 50	650 00	73 28	60 00	42 13	240 00	9,331 03	251 69	9,079 34	....	13,286 25
Dakota	802 35	13 38	788 97	....	33 00	18 00	4 49	71 20	1,365 79	43 58	1,322 21	....	2,237 87
Arizona	4,164 15	136 53	4,027 62	....	131 48	20 00	4 02	300 00	2,373 07	71 81	2,301 26	....	6,784 38
Idaho	4,594 13	147 89	4,446 24	48 00	78 91	36 33	48 57	600 00	12,871 12	420 82	12,450 30	....	17,708 35
Montana	4,960 50	173 77	4,786 73	661 00	60 38	....	....	540 00	12,296 78	382 46	11,914 32	....	17,962 43
West Virginia	7,730 22	223 36	7,506 86	2,433 18	254 95	117 86	19 87	333 46	40,704 53	767 62	39,936 91	62 42	50,665 51
Virginia	19,840 02	591 04	19,248 98	10,086 05	897 01	74 45	234 13	1,280 02	113,574 50	2,135 59	111,438 91	81 66	143,341 21
Kentucky	26,539 31	758 54	25,780 77	15,580 02	1,616 23	122 75	219 82	1,976 50	204,215 58	3,922 39	200,293 19	....	245,589 28
Missouri	19,485 53	602 85	18,882 68	13,117 06	1,058 81	229 25	639 98	2,086 00	112,504 81	2,118 31	110,386 50	14 50	146,414 78
Tennessee	35,050 29	1,129 75	33,920 54	18,106 47	1,322 60	114 50	197 80	2,383 68	191,796 54	4,376 22	187,420 32	49 99	243,515 90

South Carolina	15,566 81	579 80	14,987 01	6,570 32	318 36	128 45	203 25	476 25	101,743 77	2,790 89	99,042 88	146 78	121,873 30
Georgia	18,391 77	672 35	17,719 42	12,397 16	1,002 11	201 87	380 47	1,925 00	138,707 77	3,577 94	135,129 83	....	168,755 86
Florida	7,793 95	307 08	7,486 87	2,875 00	147 04	49 50	65 77	513 33	27,039 83	764 66	26,275 17	190 34	37,603 02
Alabama	15,062 56	547 29	14,515 27	12,452 60	522 72	402 00	400 55	625 00	133,151 79	3,564 06	129,587 73	87 50	138,593 37
Mississippi	12,023 32	473 11	11,550 21	3,975 00	470 90	101 50	196 29	1,164 00	61,238 01	1,641 83	59,596 18	157 77	77,211 85
Texas	19,193 55	723 59	18,469 96	10,151 41	798 33	167 74	630 39	1,685 00	108,017 29	3,019 58	104,997 71	589 16	137,489 70
Arkansas	16,167 59	580 79	15,586 80	8,845 30	905 26	427 50	214 51	1,561 66	88,533 94	2,390 63	86,143 31	247 48	113,931 82
Total	786,352 74	25,733 20	760,619 54	428,735 28	48,651 33	8,743 80	16,783 88	68,174 58	4,781,094 51	101,572 28	4,679,522 23	4,395 65	6,015,626 29
Add tax on compensation of assessors and assistant assessors													127,305 48
Total cost of assessing													6,142,931 77

I.—*Statement showing the expenses of collecting the internal revenue taxes in the several collection districts, including the commissions, salaries, and extra allowances of the collector; the office expenses which are paid out of the commissions and extra allowances, and the assessments and collections from July* 1, 1866, *to June* 30, 1867.

Districts.	Gross compensation.	Tax.	Net compensation.	Stationery and blank books.	Postage.	Express and dep. money.	Advertising.	Total expense of collecting.	Expenses of administering office.	Assessments.	Collections.
MAINE.											
1st district	$21,286 56	$572 49	$20,714 07	$394 56	$653 64	$96 56	$76 76	$22,508 08	$8,997 26	$2,325,630 32	$2,233,291 90
2d district	7,706 17	317 91	7,388 26	169 02	265 79	5 25	38 18	8,204 41	1,516 03	638,785 83	551,526 83
3d district	6,926 92	204 71	6,722 21	52 46	393 23	....	27 25	7,399 86	2,098 25	343,592 47	342,692 06
4th district	6,633 03	216 49	6,416 54	98 10	207 99	....	146 75	7,085 87	1,635 24	236,702 08	227,314 27
5th district	6,160 11	106 51	6,033 60	120 02	59 82	157 32	52 04	6,549 31	3,403 32	169,622 82	150,730 68
Total	48,712 79	1,418 11	47,294 68	854 16	1,580 47	259 13	340 98	51,747 53	17,650 10	3,714,333 52	3,505,555 74
NEW HAMPSHIRE.											
1st district	10,149 63	356 64	9,792 99	250 22	290 49	256 00	90 99	11,037 33	3,338 68	957,500 09	929,926 74
2d district	11,155 15	367 96	10,787 19	190 05	156 18	47 78	25 50	11,574 66	4,245 45	1,524,905 67	1,524,124 28
3d district	7,146 06	159 07	6,986 99	234 62	206 64	28 40	104 00	7,719 72	3,237 83	415,899 89	396,812 67
Total	28,450 84	883 67	27,567 17	674 89	653 31	332 18	220 49	30,331 71	10,821 96	2,898,305 85	2,850,863 69
VERMONT.											
1st district	6,955 36	167 00	6,788 36	95 26	200 00	85 40	128 15	7,464 17	2,880 93	372,095 58	345,536 40
2d district	7,315 37	202 36	7,113 01	96 05	187 29	101 45	114 80	7,814 96	2,493 75	408,180 13	381,537 03
3d district	5,928 33	180 68	5,747 65	123 33	129 64	10 75	43 58	6,235 63	1,580 44	289,230 64	242,733 19
Total	20,199 06	550 04	19,649 02	314 64	516 93	197 60	286 53	21,514 76	6,955 12	1,069,506 35	969,806 62

I.—*Statement showing the expenses of collecting the internal revenue taxes, &c.*—Continued.

District.	Gross compensation.	Tax.	Net compensation.	Stationery and blank books.	Postage.	Express and dep. money.	Advertising.	Total expense of collecting.	Expenses of administering office.	Assessments.	Collections.
MASSACHUSETTS.											
1st district	$10,534 43	$256 36	$10,278 07	$683 39	$411 56	$70 24	$18 75	$11,718 37	$5,209 90	$1,412,964 90	$1,431,042 66
2d district	11,995 81	283 02	11,712 79	138 52	....	14 00	13 75	12,162 08	6,114 53	1,572,044 00	2,197,256 84
3d district	16,474 87	493 57	15,981 30	858 19	1,096 00	....	14 00	18,443 06	7,834 31	6,038,199 07	5,937,559 98
4th district	13,782 68	275 98	13,506 70	388 54	571 70	....	37 87	14,780 79	7,990 65	3,916,631 53	3,703,579 92
5th district	11,824 11	308 10	11,516 01	98 52	252 46	246 32	73 29	12,494 70	5,626 33	2,131,611 18	2,059,295 70
6th district	13,113 92	281 75	12,832 17	279 29	457 80	3 40	78 50	13,932 91	7,054 64	2,646,721 43	3,081,856 92
7th district	12,556 77	360 23	12,196 54	155 02	710 56	9 00	94 00	13,525 35	5,863 79	2,644,807 23	2,646,662 33
8th district	12,976 63	333 57	12,643 06	199 50	142 23	....	121 50	13,439 86	6,296 29	2,945,016 20	2,987,932 28
9th district	11,281 22	274 38	11,006 84	143 31	356 94	6 20	98 00	11,885 67	5,509 39	1,402,082 50	1,624,978 84
10th district	12,032 36	180 35	11,852 01	281 47	106 00	179 55	77 97	12,677 35	7,690 98	2,326,693 00	2,225,891 63
Total	126,572 80	3,047 31	123,525 49	3,225 75	4,105 25	528 71	627 63	135,060 14	65,190 81	27,636,771 04	27,899,057 10
RHODE ISLAND.											
1st district	14,016 70	426 19	13,590 51	230 92	300 97	....	158 49	14,707 08	6,248 36	3,947,057 10	3,816,886 31
2d district	10,759 17	296 32	10,462 85	199 11	50 00	....	55 49	11,063 77	4,631 35	1,215,341 76	1,207,336 14
Total	24,775 87	722 51	24,053 36	430 93	350 97	....	213 98	25,770 85	10,879 71	5,162,398 86	5,024,222 45
CONNECTICUT.											
1st district	12,166 31	301 84	11,864 47	249 56	370 60	11 20	60 76	12,858 43	6,105 82	2,224,023 11	2,439,436 26
2d district	12,066 90	334 99	11,731 91	371 53	423 90	....	61 00	12,923 33	5,529 44	2,003,565 99	2,253,520 81
3d district	10,965 92	276 97	10,688 95	159 08	239 90	5 85	155 62	11,526 37	5,161 34	1,389,897 70	1,372,755 23
4th district	11,225 96	282 38	10,943 58	400 93	534 58	150 96	38 26	12,350 69	5,333 66	1,349,158 45	1,580,765 87
Total	46,425 09	1,196 18	45,228 91	1,181 10	1,568 98	168 01	315 64	49,658 82	22,149 66	6,966,645 25	7,646,478 17
NEW YORK.											
1st district	10,880 23	38 28	10,841 95	1,013 47	96 01	9 95	14 83	12,014 49	13,504 15	1,379,000 54	1,305,323 45
2d district	12,607 85	179 67	12,428 18	430 10	199 01	....	51 00	13,287 96	8,435 55	2,859,396 67	2,657,072 37
3d district	12,915 05	177 90	12,737 15	476 74	237 17	....	212 32	13,841 28	8,995 91	3,447,159 99	3,257,429 60
4th district	16,442 35	38 28	16,404 07	756 68	937 80	....	111 75	18,248 58	18,847 26	6,650,951 07	5,763,282 46
5th district	11,299 02	178 98	11,120 04	266 14	225 03	....	78 00	11,868 16	6,985 00	1,877,846 02	1,642,997 44

11th district	9,703 17	244 19	9,458 98	213 08	160 99	45 55	140 00	10,262 79	4,244 30	846,364 78	803,509 11
12th district	10,414 99	131 50	10,283 49	194 32	234 31	29 12	160 47	11,033 21	7,050 64	1,106,058 73	978,181 16
13th district	7,281 23	92 77	7,168 46	147 75	21 71	....	24 00	7,474 69	4,691 43	548,575 84	420,556 70
14th district	12,896 50	365 99	12,530 51	437 24	232 69	....	277 45	13,813 88	5,967 51	2,350,515 57	2,9.8,148 78
15th district	10,901 13	331 84	10,569 29	699 21	703 82	14 40	98 20	12,416 76	4,403 59	1,356,522 09	1,322,524 39
16th district†	6,125 59	185 74	5,939 85	177 08	176 38	75	71 57	6,551 37	1,723 79	310,346 19	292,194 12
17th district	5,676 65	95 53	5,581 12	127 95	182 70	17 00	84 29	6,088 58	2,731 75	217,338 95	187,604 54
18th district	9,116 05	129 68	8,986 37	184 35	338 31	6 20	33 90	9,678 81	5,798 00	693,623 70	543,209 63
19th district	6,272 27	97 77	6,174 50	133 43	197 33	5 55	41 50	6,650 08	3,582 42	334,409 02	278,205 03
20th district	8,145 74	130 85	8,014 89	168 54	242 30	1 75	52 00	8,610 33	4,794 36	560,904 30	529,520 44
21st district†	9,109 85	330 81	8,779 04	373 23	42 49	80	29 00	9,555 37	3,159 13	1,133,690 90	1,110,469 39
22d district	7,971 23	147 09	7,824 14	293 58	268 80	54 01	108 49	8,696 11	4,295 05	481,248 17	494,610 50
23d district†	9,957 23	266 23	9,691 00	194 38	233 00	70 80	24 60	10,480 01	3,909 29	1,236,407 59	*1,093,123 33
24th district	9,152 55	193 22	8,959 33	291 86	216 70	56 99	46 90	9,765 00	4,553 81	796,594 70	719,504 49
25th district†	6,829 33	127 73	6,701 60	180 42	246 48	9 95	34 82	7,301 00	3,548 62	384,774 49	308,691 02
26th district	7,958 47	167 73	7,790 74	135 44	123 57	4 00	35 55	8,257 03	3,869 49	515,971 35	491,850 07
27th district	7,672 95	149 46	7,523 49	136 74	418 00	3 65	42 95	8,274 29	3,949 32	524,619 85	434,590 03
28th district	10,608 94	355 29	10,253 65	169 97	222 32	....	50 00	11,051 23	3,815 05	1,286,165 47	1,088,977 19
29th district	8,125 63	142 67	7,982 96	251 22	135 03	8 40	97 00	8,617 28	4,537 01	601,034 04	525,126 80
30th district	11,096 77	227 99	10,868 78	416 49	210 00	121 47	....	11,844 73	6,360 52	2,020,579 37	2,036,413 90
31st district†	4,669 08	62 13	4,606 95	263 91	60 82	3 70	13 90	5,011 41	2,834 16	288,246 52	263,415 35
32d district	30,700 75	213 28	30,487 47	2,493 31	1,103 80	1 56	277 70	34,577 12	25,700 75	10,263,207 90	9,693,537 84
Total	337,643 98	6,534 14	331,109 84	13,315 48	8,915 81	465 60	3,385 56	363,726 43	205,677 33	60,007,502 77	55,394,761 22
NEW JERSEY.											
1st district	8,714 18	248 27	8,465 91	127 39	402 58	435 00	....	9,680 15	3,272 25	665,053 22	642,836 77
2d district	9,401 09	173 33	9,227 76	220 20	566 00	....	83 80	10,271 09	5,075 09	791,740 54	780,907 22
3d district	10,904 73	217 60	10,687 13	328 22	825 42	110 65	52 95	12,221 97	5,771 24	1,306,048 07	1,325,157 22
4th district	20,540 06	802 53	19,737 53	797 42	169 44	1 20	60 75	21,568 87	3,975 89	1,020,394 89	961,789 13
5th district	13,762 84	244 84	13,518 00	1,269 12	497 99	78 80	....	15,608 75	8,471 36	4,011,352 53	4,366,804 30
Total	63,322 90	1,686 57	16,636 33	2,742 35	2,461 43	626 65	197 50	69,350 83	26,565 83	7,794,589 25	8,077,494 64
PENNSYLVANIA.											
1st district	13,485 00	291 99	13,193 01	792 02	12 50	....	66 16	14,355 68	8,150 37	4,288,751 24	4,893,873 94
2d district	13,287 54	197 48	13,090 06	521 06	319 12	....	31 50	14,159 22	6,451 41	3,514,650 60	3,410,765 36
3d district	11,780 47	235 48	11,544 99	631 70	....	....	123 85	12,536 02	6,500 00	2,169,602 22	2,029,946 09
4th district	10,969 23	565 87	10,403 36	465 36	168 00	....	149 08	11,691 67	2,218 72	2,468,491 07	2,067,402 57
5th district†	1,952 53	35 27	1,917 26	172 57	45 82	7 70	....	2,178 62	1,046 46	590,299 02	396,629 93
6th district	10,270 13	362 51	9,907 62	196 86	256 01	4 00	44 05	10,771 05	3,390 80	1,033,781 75	954,025 27
7th district	8,651 71	267 71	8,384 00	406 63	233 76	....	44 34	9,336 64	3,115 79	684,658 16	718,523 73
8th district	8,852 78	284 95	8,567 83	43 68	63 69	....	40 50	9,000 65	2,947 41	699,731 45	670,556 02
9th district	6,049 50	204 32	5,845 18	360 97	191 40	....	61 66	6,663 53	2,039 68	448,248 75	443,778 15
10th district	8,753 81	273 74	8,480 07	127 71	125 00	....	19 50	9,026 02	2,993 04	608,120 10	653,762 67
11th district	8,827 12	113 45	8,713 67	352 57	255 32	....	103 00	9,538 01	5,823 67	646,639 38	666,358 91
12th district	7,331 54	174 62	7,156 92	158 47	428 94	17 70	90 30	8,626 95	3,251 26	586,149 92	520,641 86
13th district	5,950 09	176 01	5,774 08	187 58	221 29	....	12 50	6,371 46	1,658 48	234,183 86	245,038 87
14th district	7,796 77	245 03	7,551 74	310 07	291 84	1 95	152 25	8,552 88	2,395 69	538,032 71	459,555 84
15th district	16,081 64	679 34	15,402 30	412 30	406 71	55	41 09	16,942 20	1,911 22	1,280,379 27	1,197,862 69

I.—*Statement showing the expenses of collecting the internal revenue taxes, &c.*—Continued.

District.	Gross compensation.	Tax.	Net compensation.	Stationery and blank books.	Postage.	Express and dep. money.	Advertising.	Total expense of collecting.	Expenses of administering office.	Assessments.	Collections.
16th district †	$5,037 26	$91 54	$4,945 72	$231 86	$213 95	$99 57	$50 25	$5,632 89	$2,685 11	$199,894 21	$190,163 46
17th district	6,065 36	137 50	5,927 86	69 63	271 28	....	25 00	6,431 27	2,749 41	307,426 20	296,462 55
18th district †	5,161 58	40 79	5,120 79	269 88	164 75	....	57 50	5,653 71	3,986 44	312,147 33	222,225 76
19th district	8,116 22	143 57	7,972 65	191 99	400 30	18 00	....	8,716 51	4,510 33	511,117 59	523,256 55
20th district	12,093 95	152 43	11,941 52	299 80	438 76	....	37 00	12,869 51	8,311 09	1,109,798 07	951,246 74
21st district	8,141 71	154 20	7,987 51	411 02	169 37	15 05	30 75	8,767 90	4,322 22	336,546 63	324,351 04
22d district	28,682 52	746 90	27,935 62	1,047 25	703 48	1 00	115 60	30,549 85	13,514 19	7,636,901 97	8,157,049 67
23d district	9,118 75	236 17	8,882 58	231 55	190 99	....	52 25	9,593 54	4,393 52	1,041,184 14	1,044,772 51
24th district	6,516 17	100 24	6,415 93	197 86	318 49	9 80	74 80	7,117 12	3,833 29	416,747 55	373,141 98
Total	228,973 38	5,911 11	223,062 27	8,080 59	5,830 77	175 32	1,422 84	244,482 90	102,226 51	31,663,483 00	31,348,376 06
DELAWARE	9,385 29	207 00	9,178 29	342 67	356 05	....	39 40	10,123 41	4,510 94	770,071 71	777,057 23
MARYLAND.											
1st district †	3,761 97	123 33	3,638 64	120 99	108 56	....	71 25	4,062 77	721 10	253,650 69	111,781 68
2d district	10,687 75	280 31	10,407 44	241 11	85 00	2 35	100 12	11,116 33	4,841 00	1,257,910 16	1,165,701 60
3d district	19,828 38	625 61	19,202 77	547 52	298 00	....	87 13	20,761 03	8,028 97	6,598,304 29	6,280,841 02
4th district †	5,652 81	159 73	5,493 08	162 54	90 57	80	40 00	5,946 72	2,070 21	305,618 37	299,294 03
5th district †	5,746 84	151 69	5,595 15	241 14	130 80	60 50	97 48	6,276 76	2,677 58	275,366 76	330,428 73
Total	45,677 75	1,340 67	44,337 08	1,313 30	712 93	63 65	395 98	48,163 61	18,338 86	8,690,850 27	8,188,047 06
DISTRICT OF COLUMBIA	8,958 89	225 47	8,733 42	152 20	85 00	....	141 83	9,337 92	3,678 58	868,004 93	692,584 22
OHIO.											
1st district †	17,693 13	517 91	17,175 22	867 93	90 00	....	59 63	18,701 69	9,063 31	7,519,746 51	7,023,357 15
2d district	12,694 57	265 93	12,428 64	403 14	93 25	....	83 25	13,274 21	6,441 74	2,389,867 02	2,366,737 77
3d district	10,898 24	184 95	10,713 29	684 62	483 03	60 45	58 90	12,185 24	6,464 77	1,305,428 07	1,213,669 16
4th district †	5,311 69	275 82	5,035 87	276 51	192 72	....	91 00	5,871 92	740 00	864,351 37	793,084 40

12th district	6,736 70	115 48	6,621 22	433 97	121 25	5 55	17 00	7,314 47	3,292 60	517,285 91	315,626 73
13th district	7,627 13	169 02	7,458 11	119 02	223 40	30 75	52 15	8,052 45	3,512 24	465,602 02	422,079 15
14th district	6,821 61	151 43	6,670 18	202 06	229 39	30 90	38 50	7,322 46	2,742 67	188,526 01	200,261 77
15th district†	6,068 42	95 13	5,973 29	135 69	75 39	....	28 00	6,307 50	3,455 62	401,221 16	320,963 56
16th district	5,043 01	98 85	4,944 16	117 79	154 02	21 04	43 25	5,379 11	2,331 56	198,078 47	154,311 25
17th district	7,914 71	155 59	7,759 12	331 71	268 49	1 75	68 12	8,584 78	4,003 00	497,789 00	464,843 62
18th district†	12,298 93	277 49	12,021 44	1,111 49	364 67	....	54 70	13,829 79	7,030 87	3,476,251 44	2,877,635 41
19th district	7,398 84	146 21	7,252 63	307 88	414 50	32 77	59 85	8,213 84	3,740 29	446,400 30	390,986 48
Total	159,095 16	3,491 71	155,603 45	7,614 23	3,804 35	271 51	1,155 75	171,941 00	80,513 76	21,930,227 24	19,910,413 53
INDIANA.											
1st district	9,191 08	157 63	9,033 45	164 16	74 11	25 90	54 50	9,509 75	5,305 03	720,095 17	730,732 18
2d district	15,784 91	339 34	15,445 57	309 54	165 80	....	132 80	16,393 05	7,663 44	1,029,038 11	958,004 56
3d district†	7,744 33	236 20	7,508 13	506 49	222 15	111 25	57 25	8,641 47	2,643 77	698,207 72	653,465 69
4th district†	6,865 69	183 61	6,682 08	317 19	348 99	....	80 50	7,612 37	2,963 31	390,646 70	293,078 07
5th district	5,968 54	142 41	5,726 13	164 65	232 16	....	69 25	6,334 60	2,261 83	269,985 68	214,995 21
6th district	7,778 05	170 38	7,607 67	135 80	142 59	....	56 25	8,112 69	3,836 50	582,318 34	503,960 70
7th district	5,724 31	107 59	5,616 72	81 98	49 38	....	52 00	5,907 67	2,838 11	275,185 81	225,838 14
8th district	7,117 30	192 44	6,924 86	378 43	126 00	1 50	67 15	7,690 38	8,831 48	396,992 74	379,729 34
9th district	5,555 19	124 81	5,430 38	60 67	45 67	83 17	103 50	5,848 20	2,438 41	282,581 59	256,218 05
10th district	5,631 96	103 65	5,528 31	102 06	64 08	31 25	164 00	5,993 35	2,724 65	249,726 78	203,195 96
11th district†	3,482 47	69 17	3,413 30	218 43	116 88	30 60	120 75	3,969 13	1,665 93	115,647 09	87,910 02
Total	80,743 83	1,827 23	78,916 60	2,439 40	1,587 81	283 67	957 95	86,012 66	43,172 46	5,010,425 73	4,507,127 92
ILLINOIS.											
1st district	16,024 98	250 61	15,774 37	740 18	622 48	....	69 20	17,456 84	10,729 66	4,832,088 74	5,404,660 22
2d district†	8,245 62	261 86	7,983 76	249 54	270 22	59 03	86 35	8,910 76	2,364 46	493,447 59	411,870 44
3d district†	7,297 26	211 68	7,085 58	197 28	114 19	....	64 50	7,673 23	1,549 83	521,784 02	414,278 63
4th district	11,407 25	200 69	11,206 56	595 55	167 05	....	79 00	12,248 85	6,534 00	1,654,086 66	1,627,087 95
5th district	10,508 64	341 39	10,167 25	640 81	380 00	6 25	119 15	11,654 85	3,862 28	710,307 40	588,418 79
6th district	11,249 78	156 62	11,093 16	497 03	539 92	146 70	47 90	12,481 33	8,202 83	443,203 55	377,673 11
7th district	10,552 76	173 66	10,379 10	306 16	261 45	139 80	87 00	11,347 17	6,210 21	1,186,628 91	1,041,540 47
8th district†	10,765 86	244 22	10,521 64	250 12	246 86	423 67	194 18	11,880 69	5,530 80	988,159 45	920,594 07
9th district	5,163 10	81 28	5,081 82	332 90	175 59	10 36	91 50	5,773 45	3,092 77	231,965 32	197,716 90
10th district	5,746 42	48 80	5,697 62	173 93	227 19	58 50	105 45	6,311 49	4,715 26	347,317 04	266,841 89
11th district	7,508 44	102 89	7,405 55	150 28	237 91	3 60	136 63	8,036 86	4,283 81	140,932 89	91,690 51
12th district	7,658 87	72 71	7,586 16	422 66	909 54	9 20	313 00	9,313 27	5,686 32	562,399 40	426,648 82
13th district	5,375 91	59 42	5,316 49	38 81	73 00	....	57 50	5,545 22	3,795 07	203,838 07	185,790 52
Total	117,504 89	2,205 83	115,299 06	4,595 25	4,225 40	857 11	1,451 36	128,634 01	66,557 30	12,316,159 04	11,954,812 32
MICHIGAN.											
1st district	11,577 21	242 03	11,335 18	524 39	523 74	2 90	43 40	12,671 64	6,214 05	2,199,013 60	1,878,137 6
2d district	9,980 60	89 43	9,891 17	79 28	260 58	98 29	43 90	10,462 65	6,625 52	338,967 53	246,286 6

I.—*Statement showing the expenses of collecting the internal revenue taxes, &c.*—Continued.

District.	Gross compensation.	Tax.	Net compensation.	Stationery and blank books.	Postage.	Express and dep. money.	Advertising.	Total expense of collecting.	Expenses of administering office.	Assessments.	Collections.
3d district†	$5,291 15	$87 53	$5, 20362	$219 57	$165 03	$41 85	$58 60	$5,776 20	$4,313 21	$352,179 84	$294,761 40
4th district†	4,922 31	67 07	4,855 24	181 37	113 02	....	19 80	5,236 50	2,924 22	272,161 47	184,911 55
5th district†	7,082 68	201 47	6,881 21	451 81	309 41	77 12	21 95	7,942 97	2,387 32	339,933 75	266,206 77
6th district†	3,574 14	26 92	3,547 22	334 15	95 73	9 20	9 50	4,022 72	3,116 08	234,054 73	113,138 50
Total	42,428 09	714 45	41,713 64	1,790 57	1,467 51	229 36	197 15	46,112 68	25,580 40	3,736,300 92	2,983,442 53
WISCONSIN.											
1st district†	10,153 08	298 62	9,854 46	310 03	468 52	17 80	144 95	11,094 38	4,173 94	1,671,643 48	1,689,835 32
2d district	6,142 30	144 01	5,998 29	215 30	336 94	3 90	34 75	6,733 19	2,604 37	290,000 44	288,482 20
3d district	5,091 50	61 63	5,029 87	112 72	134 80	41 25	50 75	5,431 02	3,160 21	153,151 32	116,888 70
4th district†	5,167 19	107 25	5,059 94	340 94	303 55	64 60	39 00	5,915 28	2,351 65	244,052 28	189,095 73
5th district†	8,521 44	40 95	8,480 49	867 57	103 14	70 72	31 15	9,594 02	4,536 89	218,521 46	150,995 35
6th district	5,662 88	53 28	5,609 60	170 56	87 01	23 83	41 40	5,985 68	4,378 94	156,279 78	135,766 32
Total	40,738 39	705 74	40,032 65	2,017 12	1,433 96	222 10	342 00	44,753 57	21,206 00	2,733,648 76	2,571,063 62
IOWA.											
1st district	9,012 12	295 54	8,716 58	409 44	182 02	54 40	115 00	9,772 98	3,053 41	765,192 18	738,308 22
2d district†	6,311 03	128 96	6,182 07	446 53	114 35	6 60	82 50	6,961 01	3,833 85	377,950 24	272,420 98
3d district	8,637 40	164 19	8,473 21	651 14	329 00	8 00	95 00	9,720 51	8,454 48	690,862 80	627,480 56
4th district†	5,024 96	132 81	4,892 15	369 19	116 08	117 67	57 50	5,685 40	1,712 29	209,303 02	185,969 15
5th district†	4,027 10	36 58	3,990 52	180 75	118 86	10 52	99 70	4,436 93	3,142 57	152,070 89	120,126 22
6th district†	2,101 52	21 39	2,080 13	109 51	76 10	18 90	51 70	2,357 73	1,967 52	96,295 45	61,076 19
Total	35,114 13	779 47	34,334 66	2,166 56	936 41	216 09	501 40	38,934 59	22,164 13	2,291,674 58	2,005,381 32
MINNESOTA.											
1st district†	4,227 75	50 93	4,176 82	1 85	275 04	101 79	97 17	4,703 60	3,427 40	182,003 28	107,548 83
2d district†	5,763 56	35 55	5,728 01	453 48	142 97	105 33	71 72	6,537 06	6,803 90	375,937 53	274,285 60
Total	9,991 31	86 48	9,904 83	455 33	418 01	207 12	168 89	11,240 66	10,231 30	557,940 81	381,834 43

3d district	12,336 90	138 17	12,198 73	258 00	76 40	1,065 33	277 00	14,013 63	1,723 93	235,126 74	182,319 35
4th district	21,769 21	7 06	21,762 15	491 10	278 00	1,731 81	404 46	24,674 58	17,769 21	748,534 36	707,848 47
5th district	15,493 85	138 28	15,355 57	452 34	130 51	1,852 39	260 35	18,189 44	8,416 29	206,543 03	118,203 62
Total	85,523 06	816 32	84,706 74	2,027 82	894 01	5,816 76	1,061 56	95,313 21	60,691 24	6,781,459 75	6,630,589 25
OREGON	14,541 65	152 03	14,389 62	282 38	85 92	104 00	50 00	15,063 95	11,900 54	317,053 56	338,093 11
NEBRASKA	6,733 46	77 59	6,655 87	160 60	58 51	9 35	63 50	7,025 42	4,447 29	109,587 41	111,919 05
NEVADA	6,161 43	38 16	6,123 27	204 31	70 67	5,342 43	116 00	11,894 84	13,198 15	317,812 15	267,092 96
NEW MEXICO	6,000 00	95 76	5,904 24	119 76	34 85	....	31 50	6,166 11	5,515 92	88,284 70	49,591 90
UTAH	15,216 64	138 28	15,078 36	348 70	33 73	26 25	13 00	15,638 32	8,007 80	83,412 24	63,547 86
COLORADO	12,600 00	112 45	12,487 55	327 48	126 66	35 70	87 00	13,176 84	9,616 55	166,103 31	150,870 95
WASHINGTON	12,880 00	165 78	12,694 22	424 26	107 75	33 43	90 00	13,535 44	8,762 88	118,773 09	124,222 29
DAKOTA	1,557 36	38 28	1,519 08	130 27	....	....	8 00	1,695 63	....	1,328 58	1,912 00
ARIZONA	1,479 62	37 67	1,441 95	....	....	153 53	....	1,633 15	....	2,747 09	....
IDAHO	2,953 73	74 53	2,879 20	182 50	19 71	13 57	26 00	3,195 51	3,847 96	81,922 58	74,015 93
MONTANA	17,325 00	163 28	17,161 72	....	20 00	600 00	....	17,945 00	9,975 00	76,454 67	93,807 41
WEST VIRGINIA.											
1st district	8,892 57	177 11	8,715 46	197 83	106 95	7 30	102 00	9,306 65	4,637 39	770,599 51	727,764 24
2d district	3,231 25	54 37	3,176 88	519 09	55 80	81 99	88 00	3,976 04	2,194 49	106,107 26	70,469 42
3d district	4,795 40	114 43	4,680 97	54 52	45 48	11 60	....	4,907 00	1,733 00	85,485 59	119,650 38
Total	16,919 22	345 91	16,573 31	771 35	208 23	100 89	190 00	18,189 69	8,564 88	962,192 36	917,914 04
VIRGINIA.											
1st district	2,926 41	46 90	2,879 51	184 72	30 95	....	3 25	3,145 33	1,333 33	45,630 73	43,426 06
2d district	8,864 17	243 95	8,620 22	17 46	....	....	....	8,881 63	3,400 00	920,590 03	654,547 87
3d district	10,298 04	367 71	9,930 33	334 41	141 58	....	155 75	10,929 78	3,347 34	713,191 61	656,899 54

I.—*Statement showing the expenses of collecting the internal revenue taxes, &c.*—Continued.

District.	Gross compensation.	Tax.	Net compensation.	Stationery and blank books.	Postage.	Express and dep. money.	Advertising.	Total expense of collecting.	Expenses of administering office.	Assessments.	Collections.
4th district	$4,917 36	$155 38	$4,761 98	$338 11	$118 55	....	$69 00	$5,443 03	$1,026 00	$139,681 62	$114,093 27
5th district	5,643 83	101 26	5,542 57	244 63	....	....	....	5,888 46	2,884 20	279,194 98	175,654 06
6th district	5,117 47	51 15	5,066 32	320 71	148 00	$3 50	18 50	5,608 18	3,360 00	171,161 56	158,074 79
7th district	4,733 47	62 55	4,670 92	451 40	233 23	26 93	80 60	5,625 63	3,269 72	170,939 69	120,010 48
8th district	3,995 48	78 35	3,917 13	306 85	70 56	55 32	82 75	4,510 96	1,646 39	104,891 01	79,199 25
Total	46,496 23	1,107 25	45,388 98	2,298 29	742 87	85 75	409 85	50,032 99	20,266 98	2,545,281 23	2,001,905 32
KENTUCKY.											
1st district	8,564 81	154 57	8,410 24	312 77	23 37	76 93	76 50	9,054 38	4,545 80	492,171 44	393,742 83
2d district	11,629 18	281 08	11,348 10	232 90	106 91	1 65	25 50	11,996 14	3,892 03	370,659 14	560,518 86
3d district	5,792 23	66 77	5,725 46	386 57	96 25	30 55	62 50	6,268 10	3,722 54	271,486 80	229,722 62
4th district	5,768 52	45 44	5,723 08	374 28	243 27	151 30	253 50	6,790 87	4,261 48	159,048 89	241,609 56
5th district	12,548 88	288 33	12,260 55	278 24	120 00	....	95 75	13,042 87	6,600 92	2,844,819 42	2,671,953 15
6th district	16,941 52	558 71	16,382 81	413 26	299 90	67 02	43 00	17,764 70	7,788 00	1,167,315 62	1,064,153 86
7th district	9,479 50	164 71	9,314 79	496 21	....	2 75	109 60	10,088 06	6,843 26	612,747 46	520,502 62
8th district†	4,058 84	61 74	3,997 10	451 52	83 75	50	47 00	4,641 61	1,675 55	113,807 09	97,560 80
9th district†	3,767 11	147 95	3,619 16	....	24 50	....	....	3,791 61	529 15	142,701 57	142,701 18
Total	78,550 59	1,769 30	76,781 29	2,845 75	997 95	330 70	713 35	83,438 34	39,858 73	6,174,757 43	5,922,465 48
MISSOURI.											
1st district	17,592 84	178 01	17,414 83	1,123 58	646 80	....	38 46	19,401 68	14,154 57	5,486,424 02	4,842,793 84
2d district†	3,308 88	35 86	3,273 02	114 05	169 84	75 13	2 50	3,670 40	4,081 42	187,340 25	198,096 36
3d district†	6,239 33	269 83	5,969 50	300 85	122 00	12 25	97 00	6,771 43	1,388 43	553,663 94	485,157 74
4th district	7,720 35	315 10	7,405 25	134 39	185 00	364 80	41 25	8,445 79	1,454 50	443,836 63	444,070 76
5th district†	2,267 31	62 95	2,204 36	107 44	111 50	....	59 50	2,545 75	1,348 62	163,613 49	78,445 95
6th district†	9,263 53	177 05	9,086 48	376 33	378 85	687 03	217 50	10,923 24	6,972 98	593,282 47	596,391 50
Total	46,392 24	1,038 80	45,353 44	2,156 64	1,613 95	1,139 21	456 21	51,752 29	29,400 52	7,428,160 80	6,644,956 15
TENNESSEE.											
1st district†	16,804 89	555 26	16,249 63	....	....	....	....	16,804 89	4,463 09	788,249 24	549,606 74
2d district†	6,858 16	204 84	6,653 32	552 48	54 00	33 00	38 00	7,535 64	3,687 74	691,556 74	502,387 17
3d district	228 01	2 06	225 95	....	10 00	....	16 00	254 01	160 00	28,191 71	3,479 37

8th district	7,679 90	83 97	7,595 93	219 57	61 60	14 00	12 50	7,987 57	5,466 66	1,211,663 70	1,255,411 41
Total	43,627 19	921 24	42,705 95	1,278 76	161 20	64 00	220 00	45,351 15	24,378 72	3,667,846 35	3,198,585 91
LOUISIANA.											
1st district	25,257 84	602 57	24,655 27	1,240 34	14 39	....	564 10	27,076 67	29,810 38	6,320,680 79	4,980,996 52
2d district	18,708 00	153 76	18,554 24	523 97	85 74	120 40	36 25	19,474 36	13,827 65	1,426,965 28	1,317,863 59
3d district	8,176 00	38 28	8,137 72	555 80	80 25	....	187 50	8,999 55	15,260 72	1,141,941 57	645,088 62
Total	52,141 84	794 61	51,347 23	2,320 11	180 38	120 40	787 85	55,550 58	58,898 75	8,889,587 64	6,943,948 73
NORTH CAROLINA.											
1st district	3,623 94	54 56	3,569 38	224 40	60 46	19 74	....	3,928 54	2,054 85	187,048 56	80,505 34
2d district	10,421 00	138 33	10,282 67	449 47	121 13	59 05	272 29	11,322 94	6,921 60	817,779 68	721,022 48
3d district	6,350 53	44 94	6,305 59	9 50	23 00	184 15	22 00	6,589 18	5,929 48	297,113 64	284,386 85
4th district	5,269 13	84 90	5,184 23	412 69	19 06	26 55	35 00	5,762 43	2,906 78	260,568 05	210,691 29
5th district	4,975 48	167 16	4,808 32	71 98	9 40	13 00	24 00	5,093 86	697 68	282,344 06	139,240 60
6th district	5,587 10	43 76	5,543 14	107 92	24 82	32 96	90 50	5,843 30	4,145 50	175,966 98	208,142 07
7th district	2,595 89	45 79	2,550 10	568 30	33 60	312 65	12 00	3,522 44	871 48	45,603 05	28,974 46
Total	38,823 07	579 64	38,243 43	1,844 26	291 47	648 10	455 79	42,062 69	23,726 77	2,066,424 02	1,672,963 09
SOUTH CAROLINA.											
1st district	6,670 64	329 01	6,341 63	249 23	30 00	75	12 00	6,962 62	747 00	434,073 61	437,399 78
2d district	8,350 19	65 54	8,284 65	295 27	129 66	....	82 70	8,857 82	6,847 87	667,491 52	567,898 98
3d district	10,737 83	123 37	10,614 46	725 59	11 00	47 74	24 90	11,547 06	7,713 83	676,892 15	984,533 78
Total	25,758 66	517 92	25,240 74	1,270 09	170 66	48 49	119 60	27,367 50	15,308 70	1,778,457 28	1,989,828 54
GEORGIA.											
1st district	8,023 20	87 73	7,935 47	128 02	12 00	....	28 50	8,191 72	5,602 33	516,844 07	505,949 11
2d district	11,953 48	38 28	11,915 20	1,202 88	83 50	152 04	189 00	13,580 90	16,890 29	2,233,198 00	2,166,025 94
3d district	18,741 13	428 83	18,312 30	464 06	94 75	99 90	56 10	19,455 94	9,780 27	2,384,389 88	2,279,219 57
4th district	20,081 83	243 71	19,838 12	507 56	44 74	....	44 75	20,678 88	13,948 01	627,357 20	594,763 89
Total	58,799 64	798 55	58,001 09	2,302 52	234 99	251 94	318 35	61,907 44	46,220 95	5,761,789 15	5,545,958 51
FLORIDA	18,390 09	631 25	17,758 84	754 47	98 06	735 31	6 00	19,983 93	16,933 52	668,383 88	646,966 48
ALABAMA.											
1st district	11,485 11	38 28	11,446 83	....	....	6 25	117 00	11,608 36	11,892 50	2,530,320 05	1,840,961 22
2d district	23,042 00	163 28	22,878 72	657 35	196 00	288 23	231 43	24,415 01	29,392 00	1,997,982 53	1,915,784 23
3d district	10,324 01	138 00	10,186 01	315 78	47 43	14 55	49 00	10,750 77	11,048 30	493,373 29	304,270 97
Total	44,851 12	339 56	44,511 56	973 13	243 43	309 03	397 43	46,774 14	52,332 80	5,021,675 87	4,061,016 42

I.—*Statement showing the expenses of collecting the internal revenue taxes, &c.*—Continued.

District.	Gross compensation.	Tax.	Net compensation.	Stationery and blank books.	Postage.	Express and dep. money.	Advertising.	Total expense of collecting.	Expenses of administering office.	Assessments.	Collections.
MISSISSIPPI.											
1st district	$16,664 30	$268 30	$16,396 00	$392 24	....	$70 58	$228 15	$17,355 27	$10,315 68	$1,173,271 70	$1,022,205 92
2d district	11,446 40	459 97	10,995 42	118 75	$86 74	123 45	6 00	11,781 34	18,538 00	2,541,828 37	2,216,121 25
3d district	14,588 40	360 24	14,228 16	2 00	....	115 96	....	14,706 36	6,938 70	1,819,521 58	1,811,078 77
Total	42,699 10	1,079 51	41,619 59	512 99	86 74	309 99	234 15	43,842 97	35,792 38	5,534,621 65	5,049,465 94
TEXAS.											
1st district	10,687 03	151 17	10,535 86	509 84	16 30	35 67	106 75	11,355 59	6,929 17	1,142,994 62	1,172,243 82
2d district	12,691 37	141 11	12,550 26	168 56	66 14	759 15	83 00	13,788 22	9,391 12	889,907 35	776,775 88
3d district	7,780 41	113 96	7,666 45	125 23	106 07	600 00	53 25	8,664 96	10,707 76	535,058 26	509,126 74
4th district	4,025 57	150 06	3,875 51	1,205 68	54 41	10 02	42 00	5,337 68	3,606 00	1,199,203 25	660,701 47
Total	35,184 38	556 30	34,628 08	2,029 31	242 92	1,404 84	285 00	39,146 45	30,234 05	3,767,163 48	3,118,847 91
ARKANSAS.											
1st district	12,132 45	517 23	11,615 22	1,044 76	47 15	36 00	13 00	13,273 36	2,553 69	922,908 19	835,307 50
2d district	6,814 86	21 40	6,793 46	730 67	21 79	773 75	17 50	8,356 57	10,147 93	893,696 28	821,719 68
3d district	2,999 19	30 56	2,968 63	....	8 00	18 00	....	3,025 19	1,942 00	176,897 32	76,969 88
Total	21,946 50	569 19	21,377 31	1,775 43	76 94	827 75	30 50	24,657 12	14,643 92	1,993,501 79	1,733,997 06

RECAPITULATION.

District.	Gross compensation.	Tax.	Net compensation.	Stationery and blank books.	Postage.	Express and dep. money.	Advertising.	Total expense of collecting.	Expenses of administering office.	Assessments.	Collections.
Maine	$48,712 79	$1,418 11	$47,294 68	$854 16	$1,580 47	$259 13	$340 98	$51,747 53	$17,650 10	$3,714,333 52	$3,505,555 74
New Hampshire	28,450 84	883 67	27,567 17	674 89	653 31	332 18	240 49	30,331 71	10,821 96	2,898,305 85	2,851,863 69
Vermont	20,199 06	550 04	19,649 02	314 64	516 93	197 60	286 53	21,514 76	6,955 12	1,069,506 35	969,806 62
Massachusetts	126,572 80	3,047 31	123,525 49	3,225 75	4,105 25	528 71	627 63	135,060 14	65,190 81	27,036,771 04	27,809,157 10

New Jersey	63,322 95	1,686 57	61,636 33	2,742 35	2,461 43	626 65	197 50	69,350 83	26,565 83	7,794,589 25	8,077,494 64
Pennsylvania	228,973 38	5,911 11	223,062 27	8,080 59	5,830 77	175 32	1,422 84	244,482 90	102,226 51	31,663,483 00	31,348,376 06
Delaware	9,385 29	207 00	9,178 29	342 67	356 05		39 40	10,123 41	4,510 94	770,671 71	777,057 23
Maryland	45,677 75	1,340 67	44,337 08	1,313 30	712 93	63 65	395 98	48,161 61	18,338 86	3,690,850 27	8,188,047 06
District of Columbia	8,958 89	225 47	8,733 42	152 20	85 00		141 83	9,337 92	3,678 58	868,004 93	692,524 22
Ohio	159,195 16	3,491 71	155,603 45	7,614 23	3,804 35	271 51	1,155 75	171,941 00	80,513 76	21,930,227 24	19,910,413 53
Indiana	80,743 83	1,827 23	78,916 60	2,439 40	1,587 81	283 67	957 95	86,012 66	43,172 46	5,010,425 73	4,507,127 92
Illinois	117,504 89	2,205 83	115,299 06	4,595 25	4,223 40	857 11	1,451 36	128,634 01	66,557 30	12,316,159 04	11,954,812 32
Michigan	42,428 69	714 45	41,713 64	1,790 57	1,467 51	229 36	197 15	46,112 68	25,580 40	3,736,300 92	2,980,442 53
Wisconsin	40,738 39	705 74	40,032 65	2,017 12	1,433 96	222 10	342 00	44,753 57	21,206 00	2,733,648 76	2,571,063 62
Iowa	35,114 13	779 47	34,334 66	2,166 56	936 41	216 09	501 40	38,934 59	22,164 12	2,291,674 58	2,005,381 32
Minnesota	9,991 31	86 48	9,904 83	455 33	418 01	207 12	168 89	11,240 66	10,231 30	557,040 81	381,834 43
Kansas	6,643 53	68 24	6,575 29	233 46	277 03	5 00	46 00	7,205 02	4,749 56	466,269 64	366,812 65
California	85,523 06	816 32	84,706 74	2,027 83	884 01	5,816 76	1,061 56	95,313 21	60,691 24	6,781,459 75	6,630,589 25
Oregon	14,541 65	152 03	14,389 62	262 38	85 92	104 00	50 00	15,063 95	11,900 54	317,053 56	338,093 11
Nebraska	6,733 46	77 59	6,655 87	160 60	58 51	9 35	63 50	7,025 42	4,447 29	109,587 41	111,919 05
Nevada	6,161 43	38 16	6,123 27	204 31	70 67	5,342 43	116 00	11,894 84	13,198 15	317,812 15	267,092 96
New Mexico	6,000 00	95 76	5,904 24	119 76	34 85		31 50	6,186 11	5,515 92	88,284 70	49,591 90
Utah	15,216 64	138 28	15,078 36	348 70	33 73	26 25	13 00	15,638 32	8,007 80	83,412 24	63,547 86
Colorado	12,600 00	112 45	12,487 55	327 48	126 66	35 70	87 00	13,176 84	9,616 55	166,103 31	150,870 95
Washington	12,880 00	185 78	12,694 22	424 26	107 75	33 43	90 00	13,535 44	8,762 88	118,773 09	124,222 29
Dakota	1,557 36	38 28	1,519 08	130 27			8 00	1,695 63		1,328 58	1,912 00
Arizona	1,479 62	37 67	1,441 95			153 53		1,633 15		2,747 09	
Idaho	2,953 73	74 53	2,879 20	182 50	19 71	13 57	26 00	3,195 51	3,847 96	81,922 58	74,015 93
Montana	17,325 00	163 28	17,161 72		20 00	600 00		17,945 00	9,975 00	76,454 67	93,867 41
West Virginia	16,919 22	345 91	16,573 31	771 35	208 23	100 89	190 00	18,189 69	8,564 88	962,192 36	917,914 04
Virginia	46,496 23	1,107 25	45,388 98	2,298 29	742 87	85 75	409 85	50,032 99	20,266 98	2,545,281 23	2,001,905 32
Kentucky	78,550 59	1,769 30	76,781 29	2,845 75	997 95	330 70	713 35	83,438 34	39,858 73	6,174,757 42	5,922,465 48
Missouri	46,392 24	1,038 80	45,353 44	2,156 64	1,613 99	1,139 21	456 21	51,758 29	29,400 52	7,428,169 90	6,644,956 15
Tennessee	43,627 19	921 34	42,705 95	1,278 76	161 20	64 00	220 00	45,351 15	24,378 72	3,667,846 35	3,198,585 91
Louisiana	52,141 84	794 61	51,347 23	2,320 11	180 38	120 40	787 85	55,550 58	58,898 75	8,889,587 64	6,943,948 73
North Carolina	38,823 07	579 64	38,243 43	1,844 26	291 47	648 10	455 79	42,062 69	23,726 77	2,066,424 02	1,672,963 09
South Carolina	25,758 66	517 92	25,240 74	1,270 09	170 66	48 49	119 60	27,367 50	15,308 70	1,778,457 28	1,989,628 54
Georgia	58,799 64	798 55	58,001 09	2,302 52	234 99	251 94	318 35	61,907 44	46,220 95	5,761,789 15	5,545,958 51
Florida	18,390 09	631 25	17,758 84	754 47	98 06	735 31	6 00	19,983 93	16,933 52	668,383 88	646,966 48
Alabama	44,851 12	339 56	44,511 56	973 13	243 43	309 03	397 43	46,774 14	52,332 80	5,021,675 87	4,061,016 42
Mississippi	42,699 10	1,079 51	41,619 59	512 99	86 74	309 99	234 15	43,842 97	35,792 38	5,534,621 65	5,049,405 94
Texas	35,184 38	556 30	34,628 08	2,029 31	242 92	1,404 84	285 00	39,146 45	30,234 05	3,767,163 48	3,118,847 91
Arkansas	21,946 50	569 19	21,377 31	1,775 43	76 94	827 75	30 50	24,657 12	14,643 92	1,993,501 79	1,733,997 06
Grand total	2,234,909 79	46,581 09	2,188,328 70	81,280 26	48,080 02	23,620 23	18,579 50	2,406,469 89	1,321,345 41	270,089,891 58	254,409,614 81

* This includes the reports for the previous year.

† Returns for the year not complete.

K.—*Statement of disbursements for salaries and contingent expenses in collecting taxes, &c., in insurrectionary districts during the fiscal year ending June* 30, 1868.

State.	Salary.	Tax.	Net salary.	Miscellaneous.	Total.
South Carolina	$6,000 00	$200 00	$5,800 00	....	$5,800 00
Florida	1,768 25	51 96	1,716 29	....	1,716 29
Mississippi	....	....	....	$32 05	32 05
Total	7,768 25	251 96	7,516 29	32 05	7,548 34

L.—*Statement showing the amounts paid to revenue and special agents of internal revenue for salary and expenses; also, the contingent expenses of the office of internal revenue, including salaries of Commissioner and deputy commissioners, clerks, &c., printing, &c., stationery, expressage, counsel fees, moieties and rewards, and taxes erroneously assessed and collected, refunded from July* 1, 1867, *to June* 30, 1868.

Revenue and special agents:			
Salary	$95,360 04		
Tax	2,447 67		
Net salary		$92,912 37	
Expenses		60,501 27	
			$153,413 64
Contingent expenses, salary, &c., of Commissioner, deputies, &c.:			
Salary	$366,461 58		
Tax	4,871 93		
Net salary		331,589 65	
Travelling expenses	14,080 79		
Tax	23 64		
Net travelling expenses		14,057 15	
Printing, &c		252,810 52	
Stationery		13,492 78	
Expressage		19,495 20	
			631,445 30
Counsel fees, moieties and rewards:			
Fees		32,639 53	
Moieties		868 77	
Rewards		15,300 00	
			48,808 30
Taxes erroneously assessed and collected, refunded			1,016,515 79
Total			1,850,183 03

M.—*Statement of the amounts paid to internal revenue inspectors in the several States for salary and travelling expenses for the fiscal year ending June 30, 1868.*

States.	Salary.	Tax.	Net salary.	Expenses.	Total.
Maine	$2,332 00	$23 32	$2,308 68	$526 05	$2,834 73
New Hampshire	1,056 00	10 56	1,045 44	621 14	1,666 58
Vermont	1,108 00	11 08	1,096 92	930 36	2,027 28
Massachusetts	13,904 00	145 72	13,758 28	3,081 20	16,839 48
Rhode Island	1,072 00	10 72	1,061 28	111 35	1,172 63
Connecticut	3,286 00	32 86	3,253 14	1,253 89	4,507 03
New York	104,929 00	1,051 40	103,877 60	15,384 04	119,261 64
New Jersey	7,442 00	68 24	7,373 76	1,304 68	8,678 44
Pennsylvania	45,410 50	455 86	44,954 64	7,939 08	52,893 72
Maryland	5,872 00	61 77	5,810 23	589 37	6,399 60
District of Columbia	1,856 00	18 56	1,837 44	1,454 14	3,291 58
Ohio	21,131 00	208 28	20,922 72	7,964 49	28,887 21
Indiana	6,822 00	68 41	6,753 59	1,937 00	8,690 59
Illinois	13,730 00	137 30	13,592 70	7,070 44	20,663 14
Michigan	1,808 00	18 08	1,789 92	1,076 72	2,866 64
Wisconsin	2,280 00	22 80	2,257 20	1,397 72	3,654 92
Iowa	3,708 00	37 08	3,670 92	2,747 55	6,418 47
Minnesota	12 00	12	11 88	17 50	29 38
Kansas	2,244 00	22 44	2,221 56	1,485 52	3,707 08
California	7,688 00	205 26	7,482 74	2,573 26	10,056 00
West Virginia	2,316 00	23 16	2,292 84	2,149 99	4,442 83
Virginia	7,936 00	79 36	7,856 64	3,913 01	11,769 65
Kentucky	11,752 00	117 52	11,634 48	6,836 29	17,470 77
Missouri	2,428 00	24 28	2,403 72	1,098 30	3,502 02
Tennessee	5,658 00	81 30	5,576 70	4,067 93	9,644 63
Louisiana	3,572 00	81 64	3,490 36	322 10	3,812 46
North Carolina	214 00	2 14	211 86	196 40	408 26
South Carolina	1,280 00	23 01	1,256 99	1,642 16	2,899 15
Georgia	3,389 00	41 29	3,347 71	1,567 65	4,915 36
Florida	1,068 00	10 68	1,057 32	902 50	1,959 82
Alabama	928 00	9 28	918 72	600 65	1,519 37
Mississippi	444 00	4 44	439 56	455 40	894 96
Texas	2,584 00	58 00	2,526 00	691 69	3,217 69
Arkansas	348 00	3 48	344 52	1 66	346 18
Total	291,607 50	3,169 44	288,438 06	82,911 23	371,349 29

N.—*Statement of certificates issued and allowed for drawbacks on merchandise exported, as provided for under section* 171 *of the act of June* 30, 1864, *for the fiscal year ending June* 30, 1868.

Number of certificates received and allowed, 3,831 ; amount involved....... $1,399,753 06

REPORT OF THE SIXTH AUDITOR.

OFFICE OF THE AUDITOR OF THE TREASURY
FOR THE POST OFFICE DEPARTMENT,
October 24, 1868.

SIR: In accordance with the uniform custom of this office, I respectfully submit the subjoined statement of the clerical labors performed in this bureau during the past fiscal year.

The forthcoming annual report of this office to the Postmaster General will exhibit in detail all that pertains to the financial transactions of the Post Office Department.

SUMMARY OF PRINCIPAL LABORS.

The postal accounts between the United States and foreign governments have been promptly and satisfactorily adjusted to the latest period.

24,190 corrected quarterly accounts of postmasters have been examined, copied, re-settled, and mailed.

145,396 letters were received, endorsed, and properly disposed of.
109,055 letters were answered, recorded, and mailed.
14,506 drafts were issued to mail contractors.
4,932 warrants were issued to mail contractors.

The number of folio-post pages of correspondence recorded, viz:
4,465 pages in collection book.
190 pages in report book.
905 pages in suit book.
645 pages in miscellaneous book.
404 miscellaneous accounts were audited and reported for payment.
446 special agents' accounts were audited and paid.
4,400 letter-carriers' accounts were settled.
$996,370 77 was paid to letter-carriers.

MONEY-ORDER DIVISION.

1,295 letters relating to money-order affairs were written and mailed, all of which were copied.

The transactions of this branch of the public business involved the amount of $29,160,534 20.

PAY DIVISION.

24,646 mail contractors' accounts were adjusted, and reported for payment.

75,546 collection-orders were transmitted to mail contractors.

97,169 postmasters' accounts were examined, adjusted, and registered.

$337,184 82 was collected from special and mail messenger offices.

$2,336,796 86, aggregate amount of drafts issued to pay mail contractors.

$7,039,861 96, aggregate amount of warrants issued to pay mail contractors.

$2,084,691 05 was received of postmasters, by mail contractors, on collection orders.

$36,908 01 was paid for advertising.

$32,148 48 was collected by suit from late postmasters.

309 suits were instituted for the recovery of balances due the United States, amounting to $104,150 95.

278 judgments were obtained in favor of the United States.

34 accounts of attorneys, marshals, and clerks of the United States courts were reported for payment.

16,756 accounts of special contractors and mail messengers were adjusted and reported for payment.

9,687 accounts of postal clerks, route agents, &c., were audited and reported for payment.

COLLECTION DIVISION.

The collection division has had charge of the following numbers of accounts, viz:

26,481 accounts of present postmasters.

7,591 accounts of postmasters who became late.

$19,283 09 was collected from mail contractors by collection drafts, for over collections made by them from postmasters.

$66,002 53, amount of internal revenue tax received by postmasters, and amounts withheld from other persons, paid to the Commissioner of Internal Revenue.

In addition, many duties of an important character have been discharged, requiring much time and labor which it would not be practicable to particularize in this report.

I have the honor to be, sir, very respectfully,

H. J. ANDERSON, *Auditor.*

Hon. HUGH McCULLOCH,
Secretary of the Treasury.

REPORT OF THE SUPERVISING ARCHITECT OF THE TREASURY DEPARTMENT.

TREASURY DEPARTMENT,
OFFICE OF SUPERVISING ARCHITECT,
October 31, 1868.

SIR: I have the honor to submit the following report on the condition of the public property under the supervision of this office, and upon the work performed and expenditures made under its direction during the year ending September 30, 1868; and in so doing have to say that the business of the office has steadily increased, and is now greater than at any time since its organization.

The commencement of new buildings, the preparation of plans for others, the progress of the work on those now in course of erection, the repairing of those already completed, and the supervision of the large amount of real estate owned by the department, have involved a constant amount of care, attention, and anxiety. No pains have been spared to hasten the completion of the various works now in progress, though I regret to state that the results have not been in all cases satisfactory, owing to causes beyond the control of this office, which will be explained in detail. Prominent among these has been the impossibility of compelling contractors for the supply of material and manufactured work, who have taken contracts at rates that they deem unremunerative, to comply with their obligations; the principal difficulty having been with contractors for cut stone, they having, in many cases, owned or controlled the only quarries from which a supply could be obtained, thus placing the department entirely at their mercy. The contracts have been prepared under the advice and with the approval of the Solicitor of the Treasury, and are, it is believed, as stringent and thoroughly binding as any that could be made. It is true the penalty they prescribe for delay remains charged against the contractors, and will be enforced by the department; but an impression appears to prevail that it is only necessary to prove that the price paid them was inadequate in order to obtain relief from Congress. I trust that they may be mistaken, and that they will be held to the strict letter of their obligations.

Another serious cause of embarrassment has been the adoption of the eight-hour system on government works, which has greatly increased the cost and retarded the progress of the buildings under charge of this office. The idea that as much labor can be performed in eight as in ten hours has proved to be utterly fallacious; indeed, the experience of this office justifies the assertion that less labor per hour has, in most cases, been obtained under the eight than under the ten-hour system. It appears to me that the law in force up to the passage of the act in question, which authorized government officers to conform to the rules and prices established by custom in the different localities, was not only eminently just, but liberal; the uniform practice on all works under charge of this department having been to pay full market rates for labor, and to give the mechanics and laborers employed the full advantage of the interpretation of the local customs on all points, and to avoid interfering in any manner with these questions. It is also, in discussing this subject, worthy of remark, that a workman can earn a larger sum per annum when employed on public than on private buildings at the same per diem pay, there being a much smaller percentage of lost time, and employment being more permanent.

It is a matter of no personal importance to me whether mechanics and laborers work eight or ten hours; but it appears manifest that the system of paying the mechanic who is employed on government work the same price for eight hours that the one employed by private parties receives for ten hours' work is unjust. It has, at any rate, increased the cost of public buildings from twenty to twenty-five per cent. beyond the amount for which I can consent to be held responsible. I can see no reason why the price of labor should be regulated by law any more than that of provisions or other merchandise; or why the mechanic should receive more protection than agricultural laborers, whose pay is less and who work more hours.

The great pressure of important legislation upon the late Congress, and the consequent delay in the passage of the appropriation bills, compelled the suspension of work in some cases, and caused serious delay in others. In my last report I called the attention of the department to the difficulty of obtaining the services of competent and energetic superintendents, and the impossibility of controlling the cost or the quality of the work, or of enforcing a due observance of contracts without such superintendence; and as the Supervising Architect is held responsible for the cost and management of the work, and its success or failure, I would respectfully suggest that he should be authorized to nominate if not to appoint them. I also deem it my duty to say that the duties of a superintendent are sufficiently onerous and exacting to require the entire time and the exclusive attention of a thoroughly competent man; and I can see no reason why a superintendent, paid by the day, should be allowed to attend, during working hours, to private business, any more than a mechanic or laborer under his charge. It is true that the appointment of gentlemen of high social standing, who have a large and lucrative private business, may nominally secure the services of trustworthy and talented persons; but as the duties of a superintendent require, as I before stated, the entire time of just such talent as is necessary to oversee and supervise the execution of the plans of an architect, it is but proper that gentlemen accepting the superintendence of public buildings should understand that their entire time will be demanded by the work under their charge. The experience of the past year fully justifies these remarks, which, it is scarcely necessary for me to say, do not apply, neither are they intended to do so, in the cases of architects who have been employed under a percentage. I deem it my duty to add that the work executed under the supervision of this office has been, with scarcely an exception, carried out in a thoroughly honest and straightforward manner, and with the best intentions; but must say that the most favorable results have been attained at places where superintendents have devoted their entire time and attention to the work.

In my previous reports I have called attention to the fact that the great extent of country over which the supervision of this office extends, and the impossibility of inspecting the works in progress as frequently as the interests of the department demand, renders it important that its duties should be made in fact, as in name, of a more supervisory nature than at present, and that in the erection of the more important public buildings, which are invariably situated in large cities, authority should be given for the employment of resident architects who would act as the representatives of this office and operate as a direct check on the superintendents. This arrangement would also enable the department to avail itself of their knowledge of local peculiarities and prices and relieve this office of a vast amount of detail.

The experience of this office has justified the determination of the department to make no contract for the erection of buildings save in exceptional cases. The supplies of material and manufactured work have, however, been obtained after due advertisement therefor, and in no case has the contract been awarded to any save the lowest bidder. Could any system be devised that would restrict competition for the erection of public buildings to those only who are competent to estimate correctly the value of the works required and sufficiently responsible to meet their obligation, it would undoubtedly be the most desirable plan for performing the work. This principle can be, and is, carried out by private individuals, who have the right to select their own bidders; but I can see no means by which this system can be applied to public works until it is deemed proper to intrust government officers with the same discretion that is exercised by private persons. Until that can be done or some other remedy devised, I see no alternative except to continue the present system of executing the work under the immediate supervision of a superintendent. With the indiscriminate bidding necessarily allowed for public works, the contract must be allowed to the lowest bidder, although it may be evident that he cannot perform the work for the amount of his bid, or a discretion exercised that practically places the disposition of the contract in the hands of the officer making the award. The result is almost invariably that ignorant and incompetent bidders find the contract a source of loss instead of profit—delay and embarrass the work, and ultimately abandon it or involve the department in vexatious and often fruitless litigation. For these reasons the system of doing the work explained in my last report has been adhered to.

The repairing and remodelling of the old buildings has been proceeded with as rapidly as the means at the disposal of this office would permit, the most important work of this nature having been performed under the immediate charge of superintendents of repairs specially appointed for this purpose with gratifying results. The experience of the past year has been taken advantage of to inaugurate a system of monthly and quarterly reports from the superintendents that show in detail the quantities and cost of each item of work performed under their charge, the old forms having failed to furnish the information necessary to exercise a proper suspension over the progress of the work. It is proposed during the coming season to perfect this plan by the adoption of a uniform system of measurement, the discrepancies in the various localities having prevented as careful a comparison of the cost of work as was desired. I had intended furnishing herewith a schedule of the cost of work on each building, but find it impossible to do so without injustice to some superintendents, the rules of measurement differing materially. I propose in my next report to submit a table, showing the cost of work in each locality, which will be interesting and valuable for reference.

In the preparation of designs (as stated in my last report) I have not considered myself limited by the amount of the appropriation made, except in cases where the cost was specially restricted to the amount, but have prepared designs for buildings large enough to accommodate the offices for whose use the building was intended, and not more costly than the importance of the locality and the dignity of the government demanded. I believe that this system will be found in the end not only the most satisfactory but economical. The greatest portion of the appropriations which are annually expended for the repairs and preservation of buildings could have been saved had suitable structures been erected originally, while the results are at best unsatisfactory and the accommodations unsuitable. In accordance, however, with your instructions, detailed estimates of the cost of the buildings to be commenced have been prepared from the working plans and specifications, the prices being calculated from the rates paid on the Treasury extension, and are as accurate and complete as they can be made. These prices will of course be somewhat differed from owing to local causes and the efficiency or otherwise of the superintendent, but I can devise no better system. All efforts to obtain data from which to determine the value of work in the different localities have thus far proved unsuccessful, partly on account of the desire of the residents that work should be commenced and their consequent disposition to underrate difficulties and prices, and partly from the want of information as to the cost of the kind of work proposed.

The recent severe earthquakes on the Pacific coast have demonstrated the correctness of the opinions previously expressed by me as to the total unfitness of the custom-house lot at San Francisco as a site for the erection of permanent structures of the kind needed by the government, the property being land reclaimed from the bay and resting on a substrata of quicksand. The custom-house is badly shattered, and though repairs have been authorized, they are mere temporary expedients, the thorough and permanent protection of the building being impracticable. I would earnestly recommend that steps be taken to erect a suitable building in some locality where a good foundation can be obtained, and would suggest that the marine hospital property on Rincon Point, now owned by the government, is the most eligible spot in San Francisco for the purpose. I have also to report that the marine hospital at San Francisco has been abandoned as no longer tenantable. The building is an immense and wretchedly built, though very costly, structure, and has been a constant source of expense to the government from the original defects in its construction. The site, however, is a valuable and commanding one, and though, from the progress of the city in that direction, no longer desirable for hospital purposes, I consider it the most valuable property owned by the United States in that city. I would recommend that steps be taken to secure a suitable location for a new marine hospital building, and would suggest that a portion of some of the government reservations in the vicinity of the city might be found adapted to the purpose.

Through the earnest efforts of the commission appointed by joint resolution of Congress approved March 2, 1867, and the cordial co-operation and liberal action of the city of Boston, a cheap and admirable site

indispensable. No suitable accommodations could, however, be obtained until a most advantageous lease was effected, as stated in my last report, with the Merchants' Exchange Company for a portion of their building, including their spacious reading room, which has been converted into a business office that is believed to be equal, if not superior in convenience and comfort, to any in the country. The arrangement of the custom-house to utilize the space thus attained is nearly completed.

In my last report I urged the erection in the city of New York of suitable fire-proof warehouses for the examination and appraisal of merchandise entered at that port, and called particular attention to the unsuitable and unsatisfactory accommodations that were at present obtained, at an expense sufficient in a few years to pay the entire cost of erecting suitable buildings. I desire to renew the recommendation, and to urge the propriety of securing, if possible, the entire battery as a site for the revenue buildings needed in that city; and in this connection I have to state that, at the present rate of increase, the custom-house will, in a very short time, be found as inadequate for the transaction of the business of the port of New York as were the buildings formerly occupied at the date of removal from them, the entire building, including the upper and attic stories, which were occupied by the American Bank Note Company until May 1, 1866, now being crowded to its utmost capacity. The purchase of a portion of the Battery as a site for the proposed barge office, and the contemplated and necessary removal thereto of the entire surveyor's department, renders it highly important that steps should be taken to secure this valuable property from the city of New York, who are the owners, and from the liberality with which the city authorities have heretofore treated the government in similar cases, I believe that it can be obtained at a low rate, and that the present custom-house property can be sold for a sum that would enable the department to erect a building ample for the wants of the public business, creditable to the government, and an ornament to the city of New York.

I would respectfully recommend that authority be obtained for the sale or lease of the unoccupied portion of the custom-house lot at San Francisco, California, receiving therefrom, if leased, considerable revenue, the property, although valuable for mercantile purpose, being now of no use to the department; also, for the sale of the old custom-house and lot at Plymouth, North Carolina, which has not been in use for many years, the building being no longer tenantable; and for the sale of the old custom-house lot at Astoria, Oregon, which is at a considerable distance from the present site of the town, and of no value to the department. I would also recommend the sale of the old custom-house and lot at Charleston, South Carolina. It is untenantable and of no value for government purposes, and has not been occupied for any purpose since the recapture of the city.

The property at Waterford, Pennsylvania, the sale of which was authorized by the act approved March 4, 1868, has been disposed of at public auction for a small amount, it being of very little value. The old marine hospital property at Chelsea, Massachusetts, has been sold, except one lot which is considered very valuable, and for which no satisfactory offer could be obtained.

Sites have been purchased for the custom-houses at Astoria, Oregon, Wiscasset and Machias, Maine; the title to the latter has not yet, however, been perfected. A site has also been acquired for the United States branch mint at Dalles City, Oregon, the owner releasing to the government his interest in the property without consideration.

Work has been commenced on the extension of the custom-house at

Bangor, Maine, and on the custom-house at Wiscasset, Maine. Plans and specifiations for the custom-house at Astoria and for the branch mint at Dallas City, Oregon, have been forwarded to the superintendents and all arrangements made for the commencement of operations on the cession of jurisdiction over the property by the legislature of the State, as required by law; until then nothing more can be done. Plans for the branch mint at San Francisco have also been prepared and forwarded with instructions for the commencement of operations, which it is proposed to confine principally to quarrying stone and other preliminary steps until further appropriations are obtained.

Repairs and alterations have been made to the following buildings since the date of my last report, viz.: Custom-houses at Alexandria, Virginia; Bath, Maine; Bangor, Maine; Belfast, Maine; Boston, Massachusetts; Baltimore, Maryland; Buffalo, New York; Cleveland, Ohio; Charleston, South Carolina; Chicago, Illinois; Cincinnati, Ohio; Dubuque, Iowa; Detroit, Michigan; Eastport, Maine; Ellsworth, Maine; Erie, Pennsylvania; Galena, Illinois; Gloucester, Massachusetts; Kennebunk, Maine; Louisville, Kentucky; Milwaukee, Wisconsin; Mobile, Alabama; Middletown, Connecticut; Norfolk, Virginia; New Orleans, Louisiana; Newark, New Jersey; New Bedford, Massachusetts; New Haven, Connecticut; New London, Connecticut; Newport, Rhode Island; New York, New York; Oswego, New York; Petersburg, Virginia; Pittsburg, Pennsylvania; Plattsburg, New York; Providence, Rhode Island; Richmond, Virginia; Suspension Bridge, New York; San Francisco, California; Sandusky, Ohio; Savannah, Georgia; St. Louis, Missouri; Toledo, Ohio; Wilmington, North Carolina; Wheeling, West Virginia. Marine Hospitals at Chelsea, Massachusetts; Cleveland, Ohio; Detroit, Michigan; Louisville, Kentucky; Portland, Maine; San Francisco, California; St. Louis, Missouri. Court-houses at Baltimore, Maryland; Boston, Massachusetts; Indianapolis, Indiana; Philadelphia, Pennsylvania; St. Augustine, Florida; Windsor, Vermont.

The site of the marine hospital at Napoleon, Arkansas, which was selected with admirable sagacity, has been swept away by the river, which was perhaps the most favorable disposition of it that could have been suggested, the building having never been needed or used for hospital purposes since its erection, and all attempts to sell it having proved abortive. After all efforts to dispose of it had failed, the officer in charge was authorized, at his suggestion, to wreck the building and sell the material, which appears from his returns to have realized the net sum of thirty dollars, ($30.) The original cost of the building was $62,431 02.

I would suggest that some decision be made in regard to the immense and unsightly mass of granite, popularly known as the New Orleans custom-house. The temporary roof that was placed over it some years since will probably need extensive repairs before long. I called attention in my report of 1866 to this building and stated that it had then sunk upwards of two feet. An application having been recently received at this department for the position of gauger and recorder of the monthly settlement, from the gentleman who held that position before the war, it is presumed that the building is still going down. It is worthy of consideration whether an attempt should be made to remodel and complete the building at the least possible expense, or use the valuable material in the erection of a suitable and creditable structure that should not violate the true principles of architectural taste, as is the case with the present one. I am of the opinion that the latter plan would be the cheaper and more desirable one.

ELEVATION OF WEST FRONT TREASURY BUILDING

Showing the proposed Grade

Scale 80 feet to 1 inch

0 5 10 20 30 40 50 100 150 200 feet

A large portion of our public buildings and the approaches to them are blockaded and disfigured by stands for the sale of fruit, periodicals, and other articles of like nature. I can see no reason why one person should be permitted to occupy any portion of government property more than another; and as the whole system is an unmitigated nuisance, I recommend that it be prohibited by law.

TREASURY EXTENSION.

The completion of the north wing of the Treasury extension and approaches has been urged forward as rapidly as the means at the disposal of this office and the nature of the work would permit, and it is believed that the progress has been equal to that attained last year, though the work was not of a nature to attract as much attention. The three upper stories will be completed and can be occupied by the 1st of December next, and the remainder of the building, should no unforeseen difficulty occur, by the 1st of January following, or less than two years from the time the removal of the old State Department was completed, and twenty-one months from the date the first stone was laid in the foundation. The south wing was commenced on the 7th of September, 1855, and was completed for occupancy about the same time in 1861; the approaches were not, however, completed until some time subsequently.

In the completion of the north wing of the building I have endeavored to make it the best finished and most durable portion, and, as far as the original design would permit, the best and most artistic work that the skill of American mechanics could produce, and have especially avoided all shams and imitations. I could, it is true, have shown a large apparent saving and reduced the expenditures considerably by following the example of my predecessor, as explained in his report of September 30, 1863; or, in other words, by the omission of important and necessary portions of the interior finish and by lowering the standard of workmanship to that executed on ordinary buildings. I have, however, used every exertion to procure and produce the work at the lowest possible cost, and have the satisfaction of knowing that all contracts made by me have been at less than market rates.

I stated in my last report that arrangements had been made to provide a suitable business room for the cashier's department of the Treasurer's bureau, the one now occupied being a mere temporary expedient as before described. The proper method of arranging and completing this room (which is in fact the only strictly public one in the Treasury building) was carefully considered, and a thorough examination of the comparative cost of scagliola, frescoing, painting, and other modes of interior decoration made before the production of the present design, which was referred by the department to the Hon. William E. Chandler, assistant secretary, and the Treasurer of the United States, Hon. F. E. Spinner, and after careful consideration and investigation was approved by them. It was considered that this room should in the purity of its design, and by the avoidance of all shams and imitations of material, be emblematic of the dignity of the nation and the stability of its credit. The high character of these gentlemen will, it is believed, satisfy the most rigid economist that the design is not more costly than was demanded by the use for which it was intended. The work has been executed at so low a rate that it would be impossible to duplicate it unless at a greatly advanced cost, the contractors declining to furnish any more material at the rates paid. In this connection it is but just to express my obligations to Henry Parry, esq., of New York, who, though originally the contractor for but a comparatively small portion of the marble work, has supplied, at the original contract prices and at considerable inconvenience to himself, the deficiencies caused by the failure of other contractors to furnish the materials contracted for by them.

In my last report I called attention to the excessive height of the sub-base of the exterior balustrade, which, by destroying the proportion on which all the beauty of classic architecture depends, diminished the apparent height of the building and destroyed the harmony between it and the balustrade. In completing the north front the sub-base was lowered in accordance with those views. The result has fully justified my expectation and given general satisfaction. The completion of the building rendered it necessary to adopt the remarkable galvanized iron "acroterial ornaments" designed by my predecessor, and remove the stone balustrade, or remove the galvanized iron and restore the balustrade. It is scarcely necessary to say the balustrade was adopted, and the paltry galvanized iron work that has so long disfigured and disgraced the grand western front of the building has been removed. The leakage of the gutters on the south front rendered their reconstruction necessary. The balustrade on that front was therefore reduced to the same height, and the gutters repaired in such a manner as will, it is believed, protect the building from leakage, which has heretofore invariably followed each severe snow storm.

I desire to call attention to the unsightly protuberance over the west front, generally supposed to be a shot-proof turret on the "monitor" principle erected for the defence of the building, but which was supposed by its designer to be a sky-light. Efforts have been made to use it for that purpose since its completion, though without much success. I recommend its removal and the erection of a sky-light to the main stairway, that will give some light and ventilation to the building without disfiguring the exterior. I would also recommend that the inclined driveway and enormous area that now destroys the proportions of the western front be dispensed with, and the area reduced to such a width as will give sufficient light and ventilation to the cellar without affecting the architectural symmetry and proportion of the building. It was constructed in the belief that fuel could not otherwise be supplied to the building, which I have shown in the arrangements for the supply for the north wing to be an error. I would also call attention to the ingenious effort to destroy the architectural effect of the beautiful south portico by illuminating its background with a sky-light, and strongly recommend that the original design be restored, which can be done at a reasonable expense.

The design for the approaches to the north wing was adopted after much study and consideration, and is believed to be as satisfactory a solution of the problem as the location of the building would permit, and no more costly than the difficulties to be overcome and the character of the building required. In this connection I desire to recommend the removal of the driveway under the south portico, which is entirely unnecessary, and detracts so much from its architectural effect. The fence on each side of the same can then be dispensed with, and the gardens carried to the line of the area. I would also urge that the present fences and gates enclosing the south front be removed and the approaches completed in harmony with those of the remainder of the building. The cost would not be great, and when compared with the improvement this change would make in the appearance of that front, and particularly in the portico, would be trifling.

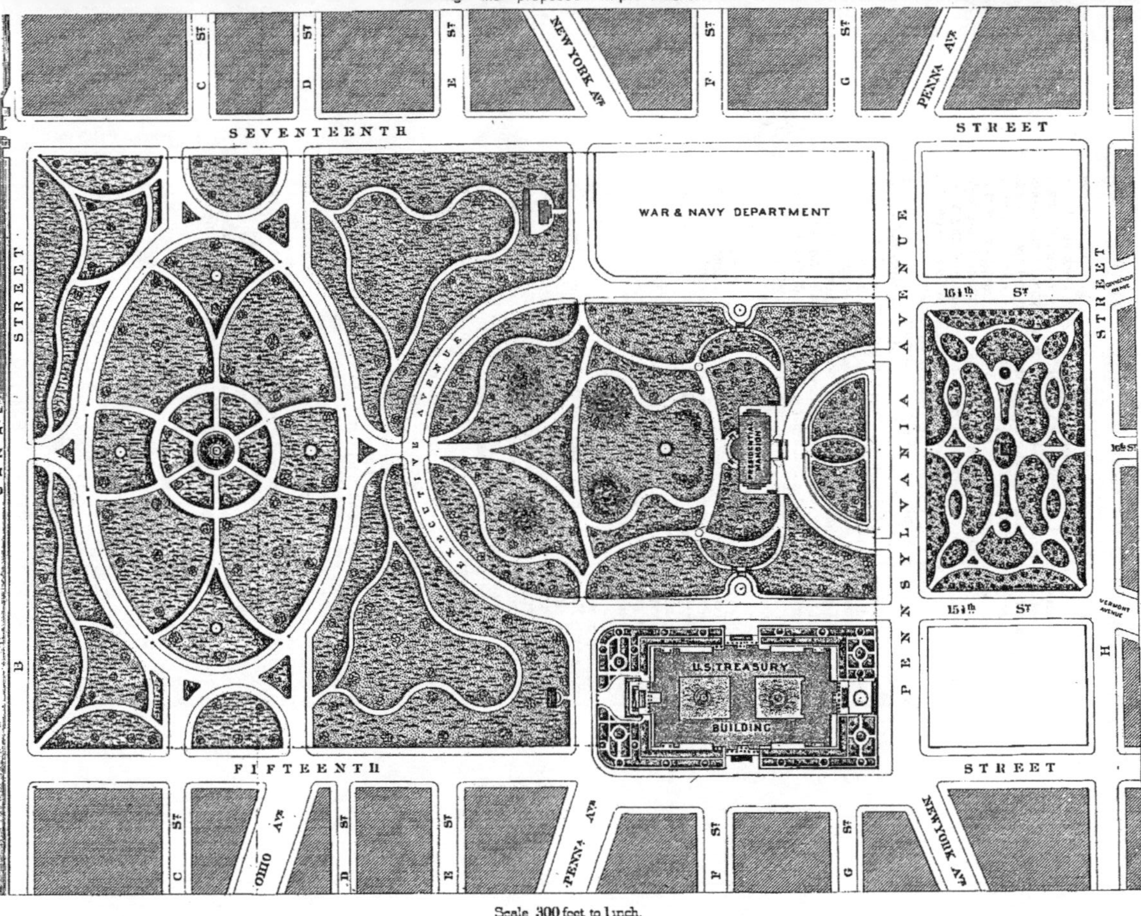

Scale 300 feet to 1 inch.

In my last report I urged the condemnation of a strip of land 61 feet wide on the east side of Fifteenth street, between New York and Pennsylvania avenues, and the removal of the street a corresponding distance from the Treasury building. I desire to renew my recommendations, and say that I believe that the adoption of this plan is indispensable to the proper completion of the building, and as each year adds to the value of the property and improvements thereon, I would strongly urge that immediate steps be taken to secure it. In this connection I desire to remark that in my opinion the extension of the Treasury building at its present level was an error, though I cannot too highly praise the design, for which the country is indebted to Thomas U. Walter, esq., whose knowledge of classic architecture is probably unsurpassed by any living architect. Unfortunately, other parties were intrusted with the execution of his design. The old building should have been raised to a proper grade, (which was entirely practicable at that time,) or a building according to Mr. Walter's design commenced nearer the Executive Mansion, which would probably have been the cheapest and most satisfactory arrangement, and would have avoided the present necessity for changing the line of Fifteenth street, and lowering its grade and that of Pennsylvania avenue on the north, from Seventeenth to Fifteenth streets, which in connection with the condemnation of this strip of land I desire to recommend. A careful survey has been made, and no practical or serious difficulty exists to prevent the adoption of this plan, which would relieve the Treasury building from the difficulty of its present location, and render it the grandest departmental building in the world. I inclose a plan showing the Treasury building and grounds, and an elevation of the west front of the building according to this plan. I also enclose plat of reservation No. 1, including the grounds of the Executive Mansion, and of the Treasury and War and Navy Departments, which has been prepared with a view to harmonize the recent improvement of the Treasury building and grounds and the proposed improvements of the War Department with the original design of the lamented Downing—to connect the Executive Mansion and the departments with the Capitol grounds by continuous drives through the mall and the reservations—a project which I strongly recommend be carried out at the earliest moment. No serious difficulty exists, and it can be accomplished at a small expense, giving Washington in her midst an ample park for the recreation and amusement of her citizens, and one that from its location is available to the poorest as well as the richest. The prominent feature of the plat I submit herewith is the extension of the avenue recently formed between the Executive Mansion and the Treasury on the arc of a circle towards Seventeenth street, and its ultimate extension between the Executive Mansion and the War and Navy Departments. I have been permitted by the courtesy of Brigadier General N. Michler, Commissioner of Public Buildings and Grounds, to complete the grading of this avenue to 17th street, without expense to the government, by depositing thereon the earth removed thereto from the Treasury extension. I would strongly recommend that authority be given to the Commissioner to open the avenue between the Executive Mansion and the War and Navy Departments, and to grade Pennsylvania avenue and Fifteenth street, as suggested, to such depth as may be found necessary.

A careful examination of the east front has shown the stone to be rapidly disintegrating, and extensive and costly repairs necessary. It has therefore been deemed desirable to take no action in the case until a decision has been made by Congress as to the propriety of rebuilding it in granite in a manner corresponding with the rest of the building, and changing the line of Fifteenth street in accordance with the plan herewith submitted.

CUSTOM-HOUSE, ASTORIA, OREGON.

An entire block, represented to be one of the best in the city, has been purchased as a site, for the sum of eight thousand (8,000) dollars. Plans and specifications, with full instructions, have been forwarded to the superintendent, and all necessary steps taken to commence work immediately on the cession of jurisdiction over the property by the State of Oregon, as required by the act approved September 11, 1841. Until this is done no further steps can be taken.

The building will be 60 by 45 feet, two stories in height, and will be practically fire-proof, the joists being deadened and isolated from the flooring and finish by a layer of cement. The exterior will be of rubble stone, with dressings of hammered work. Its estimated cost, at Washington prices, is $52,672 50, exclusive of fencing, grading, sewerage, and the supply of water and gas. The cost at Astoria will be considerably greater, but how much I have not the means of deciding.

CUSTOM-HOUSE, BURLINGTON, VERMONT.

In my last report I stated that this building had been remodelled and repaired. This was an error arising from the fact that the expenditure had been authorized but not made by the collector, no satisfactory proposals for the work having been obtained. The pressure of business has prevented the execution of the work during the present season, more urgent demands having also been made on the appropriation elsewhere. Such repairs as were indispensable have been executed under the immediate supervision of the collector, and arrangements made for the completion of the work during the coming season. New furnaces of improved design and sufficient capacity to heat the building have also been provided.

CUSTOM-HOUSE, BANGOR, MAINE.

The extension of this building, so much needed and so long contemplated, was commenced on the 18th of May last, and is progressing rapidly and favorably, under the judicious and able management of the superintendent. Great difficulties have, in consequence of the peculiar location of the building in the middle of the Kenduskeag river, been experienced in obtaining suitable foundations, and it has been found necessary to carry them to a considerably greater depth than was anticipated. The work was also delayed much in its early stages from the impracticability of working except at low tide. A fine foundation has, however, been obtained, and all difficulties successfully overcome. The superintendent reports that he will, should the weather prove favorable, complete the roof the present season; should he succeed, it will be, considering the nature of the work, one of the most rapid instances of construction within the knowledge of this office. The work has also been

Proposed Plan

for completing Treasury Building and grounds

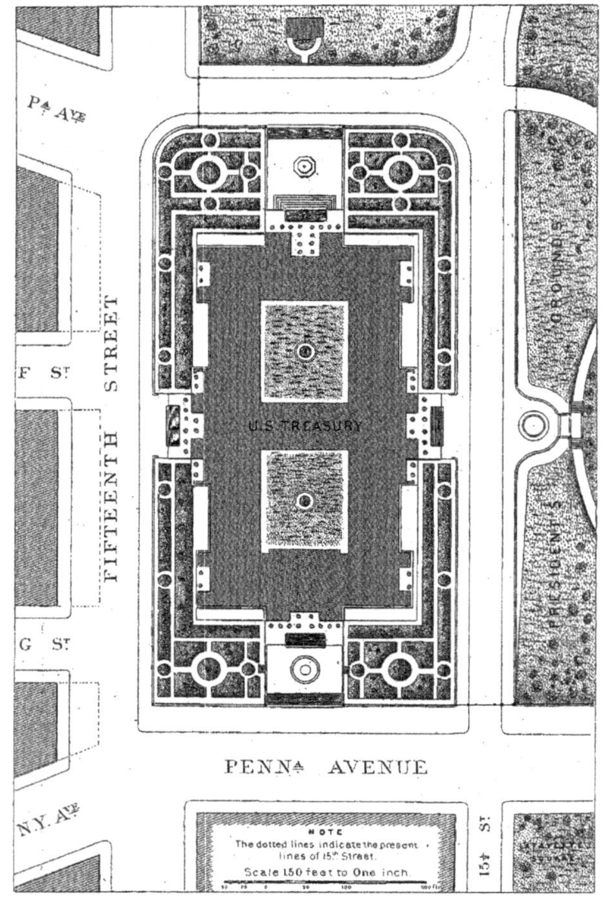

each working day. He has, however, neither claimed nor received any extra compensation, though he has performed twice the labor each day of any employé under his charge. No doubt exists as to the entire completion of the work during the coming season.

CUSTOM-HOUSE, BOSTON, MASSACHUSETTS.

The removal of the sub-treasury from this building having, as I before explained, been effected in a satisfactory manner, the department has been enabled to afford some relief to the overcrowded condition of the custom-house. The alterations necessary to utilize the space thus gained are in progress and will soon be completed, when the building will be not only in excellent repair, but it is believed as conveniently arranged as possible.

CUSTOM-HOUSE, BUFFALO, NEW YORK.

The lower story of this building, which is occupied by the Post Office department, has been remodelled and repainted, and is now well and conveniently arranged for post office purposes. A new roof is much needed, which will be constructed during the coming season, if practicable. The building is otherwise in good condition.

CUSTOM-HOUSE, CHICAGO, ILLINOIS.

This building has been thoroughly repaired and remodelled during the past season, at the cost of $23,320 36. The galvanized iron roof has been replaced by an excellent one of slate; the bonded warehouse removed from its basement, and the additional room thus obtained devoted to the post office department, which has been rearranged, provided with new and improved distributing tables, lock-boxes, &c., and is now one of the best and most convenient in the country.

Additional room has been obtained for the use of the officers of the judiciary by the rearrangement of the upper story. The building, though large, is inadequate for the proper transaction of the public business in that city, and with its rapid growth, I am of opinion that the day is not far distant when the interests of the public service and the convenience of the citizens of Chicago will demand the erection of a new and commodious structure for the accommodation of the revenue officers of the government, and the present building devoted exclusively as a post office and court-house.

CUSTOM-HOUSE, CAIRO, ILLINOIS.

Work was suspended on this building until the latter part of August of the present year, the former appropriation having been exhausted, and the new one not becoming available until about that time. Since its resumption it has been pressed rapidly forward, and it is hoped to have the entire building completed before the close of the coming season. Much difficulty has been experienced in consequence of the changes that have been made in the design during the progress of the work, the building having been originally designed as a two story structure, 73 feet 8 inches long by 59 feet wide, which was believed by the department ample for the wants of the city, and work was commenced on that basis. The length of the building was afterwards extended to 100 feet, at the request of the senators and a large majority of the representatives from Illinois. The act approved July 25, 1868, making it also a court-house, has necessitated a third change, which, it is trusted, will be the last, and that nothing will prevent its speedy completion.

CUSTOM-HOUSE, CINCINNATI, OHIO.

After long and urgent solicitations on the part of the officers in charge of the customs and post office departments of this building, authority was granted for certain changes in the portions of the building occupied by them. The interior of the building has also been thoroughly renovated and painted. These expenditures could have been avoided had the remodelling of the building on which so much time and so large a sum were expended in 1864, 1865, 1866, been properly performed. Other changes are much desired, but the means at the disposal of this office did not permit further expenditures. In this connection I desire to call attention to the inadequate size of the building and the urgent necessity of erecting one large enough to accommodate the wants of the public business in that city.

CUSTOM-HOUSE, DETROIT, MICHIGAN.

Steps have been taken to place this building in thorough repair, which is much needed. The roof and gutters are in bad condition and must be replaced. The interior requires thorough renovation and repair, and is at present in anything but a creditable condition. The improvement of this building has long been contemplated, but owing to the limited amount of funds at the disposal of this office, action could not be taken at an earlier date.

CUSTOM-HOUSE, EASTPORT, MAINE.

This building has been thoroughly repaired, the roof made tight, the interior, the wood and iron work of the exterior repainted, the brick-work repointed, sewer and pavement relaid, and the entire structure placed in as good condition as its bad design and worse construction would permit.

CUSTOM-HOUSE, GLOUCESTER, MASSACHUSETTS.

Repairs costing $1,060 have been made on this building during the past year, which included only such items as were absolutely necessary for its preservation and the comfort of the officers occupying it, as the repairs of the roof and gutters, removal of the old balustrade, (which in a building professedly fire-proof was of wood,) renovating the interior, &c. The present roof is of galvanized iron, and must be replaced at an early day, though the repairs lately made upon it will preserve it until another season. New furnaces are also required, the present ones being worthless.

CUSTOM-HOUSE, KENNEBUNK, MAINE.

This building was purchased in 1832, and is not of fire-proof construction or of much value. It has been thoroughly and judiciously repaired at a very small expense under the direction of the superintendent at Portland, and is now in good condition.

CUSTOM-HOUSE, LOUISVILLE, KENTUCKY.

In my report for the year ending September 30, 1866, I stated that the upper stories of this building had been remodelled and repaired, and that, with the exception of the lower or post office story, it was in good condition. Repeated complaints of the condition of the post office department had been received, but from the limited means at the disposal of this office, no relief could be afforded until the present season, when that portion of the building was remodelled under the personal supervision of Judson York, esq., superintendent of repairs. The entire building is now in good condition, and, it is believed, is as conveniently arranged as its structural defects will admit.

CUSTOM-HOUSE, MILWAUKEE, WISCONSIN.

The repairs and alterations of this building have been completed, and it is now in good condition. The steam heating apparatus, however, put in last season, was not completed in a satisfactory manner and will require some alterations to make it creditable to the contractors or to the department. No provision was made to aid the ventilation of the building, and even the imperfect arrangements previously provided were ignored. Arrangements have been made to remedy the defects and place it in proper condition.

CUSTOM-HOUSE, NEW BEDFORD, MASSACHUSETTS.

This building, which is old-fashioned but solidly constructed of undressed granite, with dressings of hammered work, has been renovated and the large business room made available for the business of the port. New sash have been provided for the windows and general repairs made. More are required, but those executed were the most pressing, and were all the means at the disposal of this office would permit.

CUSTOM-HOUSE, NEW YORK, N. Y.

The alterations and repairs of this building have been completed, including ventilation of the rotundo, the repairs and improvements in heating apparatus, and give general satisfaction. File-rooms have been provided in the attic story, and the customs records heretofore stored in the sub-treasury removed thereto. Many of the offices have been refurnished, the old furniture having been in constant use for many years, and the entire building is in very fine condition, though overcrowded and too small for the rapidly increasing business of the customs department in that city.

In this connection I desire to call attention to the recommendation contained in another portion of this report, in regard to the desirability of obtaining sufficient space on the Battery for the erection of suitable buildings for the revenue department at that port.

CUSTOM-HOUSE, NASHVILLE, TENNESSEE.

No steps have yet been taken towards the erection of this building, the site purchased some years since being entirely too small to permit the erection of a suitable structure. Efforts have been made to purchase sufficient additional property to make the lot adequate to the necessities of the proposed building, but the prices demanded have been, in the opinion ot the department, excessive. A lot of ample size, said to be in a good location, has been offered in exchange for the custom-house lot, and I would recommend that the department be authorized to exchange or sell the present lot and purchase a more suitable one with the proceeds.

CUSTOM-HOUSE, OGDENSBURG, NEW YORK.

This building is radidly approaching completion, the exterior walls being finished, and the roof so far advanced that no doubt of its completion during the coming season exists. At the urgent request of prominent citizens of Ogdensburg, and upon the recommendation of Hon. C. T. Hulburd, representative from the district, estimates were submitted for a dome not contemplated by the original desigu, which were approved by Congress. This addition not only greatly improves the appearance of the building, but affords a lookout from which au uninterrupted view of the river can be obtained for upwards of ten miles by the customs officers.

The building is constructed of Cleveland, Ohio, stone, with slate roof, the dome of iron and slate. The quality of the work is of the best, and the management of the superintendent is believed to be highly creditable to him. The whole of the stone for the basement was quarried under his immediate supervision, and the stone for the superstructure cut in the same manner by days' work. A contract has been made with James P. Wood & Co., of Philadelphia, for the heating of the building, and arrangements made for its completion during the coming season.

CUSTOM-HOUSE, PORTLAND, MAINE.

Work on this building has been pressed as rapidly as possible, though, I regret to say, with the most unsatisfactory results. No doubt was felt at the date of my last report as to the completion of the exterior, including the roof, during the present season, and had the contractor for the supply of granite-work fulfilled his obligations, no difficulty would have been experienced in accomplishing that result. Every effort has been made by the superintendent and the department to compel an observance of the terms of the contract as regards time of delivery, but as before stated, without success. The contractor having practically the control of the quarry, the department has been powerless in the matter. The workmanship is, however, unexcelled by that of any building in the country save the Treasury extension. In this connection I may say that the granite for the principal part of the basement story (which was not included in the contract) was purchased for the department and cut under the immediate supervision of the superintendent, with the most gratifying results. Had this plan been adopted with regard to the remainder of the building, no difficulty would have been experienced; and though the first cost would have been somewhat greater, (the contract having been taken at extremely low rates,) it is believed that the ultimate cost of the building would have been less, as the expenses rendered necessary by delay in the delivery of material would have been avoided. Arrangements have, however, been made that will prevent any delay during the coming season.

CUSTOM-HOUSE, PORTLAND, OREGON.

Designs for this building are in progress, but it is feared, from information recently received at this office of the prices of work and material on the Pacific coast, and of the size of the building required, that the amount to which the department is limited by the act approved July 20, 1868, will prove insufficient for its completion. I would, therefore, recommend that authority be obtained for the expenditure of a sum that will make the building a satisfactory and creditable one—one that will not, as has been too often the case, require rebuilding in a few years to meet the increased demands of the public business. Portland being the second commercial port on the Pacific coast, it appears to me desirable that ample and sufficient accommodations should be provided, and that the building, when erected, should be creditable to the government.

CUSTOM-HOUSE, PITTSBURG, PENNSYLVANIA.

This is perhaps the worst and most unsightly building of any importance under charge of this office, and is utterly unfit for government use. The post office is wretched in the extreme, without light, ventilation, or ordinary conveniences. The other portions of the building are little better, and the entire structure is a disgrace to the government. The building was, I have been informed, originally designed for a warehouse; and though rather a costly structure for such a purpose, is certainly better fitted for that than its present use.

CUSTOM-HOUSE, PHILADELPHIA, PENNSYLVANIA.

The general business room of this building has been rearranged, refitted, and painted, and the old and much worn wooden floor replaced by marble tile. It is now convenient and well arranged for the transaction of business, and entirely satisfactory to the officers of customs, though from the excessive height of the counter screen not as elegant as was designed. Other repairs have been made and the building is in creditable condition.

CUSTOM-HOUSE, SAVANNAH, GEORGIA.

The lower story of this building, now partially occupied by the post office, was originally designed as a warehouse, and though suitable for such purposes is entirely unfit for its present use, being damp and illy ventilated and lighted. Efforts have been made to afford some relief, and a rearrangement of the post office portion of the building authorized that will greatly improve it, though not remove the principal causes of complaint. This building is much in need of thorough repairs, which it is proposed to make during the coming season.

CUSTOM-HOUSE, ST. LOUIS, MISSOURI.

I have before called attention to the unsuitable character of this building, and the utter impossibility of making it convenient and suitable for the transaction of the business for which it is used. The increase of the post office business at this point, caused principally by the rapid construction of the Pacific railroad, has rendered some changes necessary which are now in progress and will greatly improve the condition and increase the amount of accommodation in this department.

CUSTOM-HOUSE, SUSPENSION BRIDGE, NEW YORK.

This building, purchased in 1867 for the sum of six thousand dollars, ($6,000,) is now being remodelled and adapted to the wants of this department. Upon a careful examination more extensive repairs than were anticipated have been found necessary. A new slate roof has been constructed, and the interior arranged to accommodate the post office as well as the customs department, ample accommodations being obtained for each. The work is progressing favorably and will be completed at an early day. Furnaces of sufficient capacity to heat the building will be provided, and the entire structure placed in the best possible condition.

CUSTOM-HOUSE, ST. PAUL, MINNESOTA.

The progress of the work on this building has been less satisfactory than any under the supervision of this department, the walls being levelled up to the first floor only. The building will be of Norman architecture and constructed of rubble-stone, with dressings from a granite quarry recently discovered near the falls of St. Cloud, and opened to supply the stone for this building. It is of an excellent quality and will undoubtedly be a great acquisition to the resources of the west, and is peculiarly valuable and interesting as being the only known deposit of that valuable material in the Mississippi valley. Favorable contracts for the supply and cutting of the granite have been made, and it is hoped that the difficulties have been so far overcome as to enable good progress to be made during the coming season.

CUSTOM-HOUSE, TOLEDO, OHIO.

I desire to call attention to the disgraceful condition of this building, and recommend that an appropriation be obtained for remodelling and completing it, for fencing and grading the lot, and for paving the surrounding streets, or that the building be removed and a suitable and creditable one erected, the latter being in my opinion the more preferable.

CUSTOM-HOUSE, WISCASSET, MAINE.

The act making an appropriation for rebuilding the custom-house at this place authorized the Secretary of the Treasury to purchase a new site if deemed desirable, the old lot being found unsuitable and inadequate. A site, centrally and admirably located, has been purchased for the low sum of eighteen hundred dollars, ($1,800,) and the building not being of sufficient importance to warrant the employment of a resident superintendent, a contract for its erection has been made with William Hogan, esq., of Bath, Maine, for the moderate sum of seventeen thousand dollars, ($17,000,) he being the lowest bidder; the work to be done under the supervision of the superintendent of the extension of Bangor custom-house, who is authorized to visit and inspect it as often as may be necessary. The building will be two stories in height, 40 by 52 feet, and of the best hard-burned brick, with granite dressings. It will accommodate the post office, custom-house, and officers of internal revenue, and by the terms of the contract is to be completed on the 1st day of June, 1869.

MARINE HOSPITAL, CHELSEA, MASSACHUSETTS.

The indebtedness on this building has been discharged, leaving a balance of $1,851 14, which it is proposed to expend on the most important portions of the work that yet remain to be done, the cost of which is estimated at $3,570. The work performed on this building was in many respects equivalent to its reconstruction, and it is no exaggeration to say that nine-tenths of the expenditure could have been avoided had the work been properly designed and faithfully executed; in addition, many defects exist for which there is no practicable remedy. The building is however in creditable condition, admirably located, spacious, and, though defective in means of ventilation, one of the best marine hospitals in the country.

MARINE HOSPITAL, CHICAGO, ILLINOIS.

Great difficulty has been experienced in obtaining material for the exterior walls, and the progress of work has been much retarded thereby. I had expected the building would have been ready for the roof this season, and regret that its progress has not equalled my expectations; the work has, however, been done in the most substantial and workmanlike manner, and, considering the quality, at fair prices.

The work has been done in a much superior manner to the requirements of the specifications and the instructions of the department, though not, perhaps, better than the importance and nature of the building demand. The building, it is confidently expected, will be completed ready for occupancy during the coming season, and will, it is believed, be one of the most convenient and comfortable buildings of its kind in the country, and the best ventilated hospital in the world.

MARINE HOSPITAL, LOUISVILLE, KENTUCKY.

The repairs and remodelling of this building, which is one of the most admirably located in the country, was commenced in Septenber, 1867. The estimate of the cost of the work made by the superintendent amounted to $12,242 17, which was approved by this office. An allowance of $2,224 03 for extra work, reported by the superintendent to be found necessary during the progress of the repairs, was also made, which it was supposed and understood would complete the work. Greatly to the surprise of the department, a further estimate was subsequently forwarded by the superintendent for the sum of $4,474 02, which, after consideration, he was authorized to expend, provided he could complete all the work and place the entire building and premises in the best condition, but not otherwise. This sum he also expended and forwarded a further estimate for $5,862 12, upon receipt of which work was at once suspended and an investigation ordered. As to the results of which, as they are at present the subject of legal proceedings, it would perhaps be improper for me to do more than express my entire conviction that the work has cost enormously and been disgracefully done. The repairs have been completed by Judson York, esq., in connection with his investigation of the management of the previous superintendent, whose conduct, under any circumstances, is deserving of the highest censure.

MARINE HOSPITAL, NAPOLEON, ARKANSAS.

During the past season the last of this building, with its foundations, as previously remarked, was washed into the Arkansas river. It has been occupied for the last two years by an officer of the Freedmen's bureau, who also acted as custodian for this department. After ineffectual efforts to dispose of the property, and when it became evident that the building could stand but a short time longer, orders were given him to remove all the material possible and to dispose of the same on the best terms, but it appears from the report of the custodian that, after deducting the cost of removal and the expenses of sale, the material only realized the small net sum of thirty dollars, ($30.)

MARINE HOSPITAL, PORTLAND, MAINE.

Further complaints having been made of the defects in this building, a thorough examination was ordered and disclosed defects in the construction discreditable to the contractors and the superintendent under whose supervision it was erected, and which furnished conclusive evidence that the complaints of the physician in charge were not ill-founded. Extensive repairs have accordingly been made and the most serious defects partially remedied, but the quality of workmanship is so inferior the building will probably demand, as heretofore, a large annual outlay for repairs. The site is an admirable one, but the building is neither convenient or attractive.

MARINE HOSPITAL, SAN FRANCISCO, CALIFORNIA.

This costly but poorly constructed building has been abandoned for hospital purposes, the city having graded the streets adjoining the hospital lot to a depth of over forty (40) feet below its level, and the banks having receded so far as to affect the foundations on one side, it is reported to be in imminent danger. The title to the property being yet in litigation, the department has not felt authorized in expending any large amount thereon, more especially as the cost of retaining walls would have been greater than the value of the building. Steps have been taken to secure an early decision as to the title, and it is not doubted that it will be a favorable one. I consider the property the most valuable for government purposes in the city of San Francisco.

MARINE HOSPITAL, ST. LOUIS, MISSOURI.

This building is much in need of remodelling and rearranging, there being no means of heating or ventilation. The fumes of the laundry penetrate the entire building and are most offensive. The patients occupy during the summer a temporary but comfortable ward erected during the war while in charge of the War Department. Some changes and repairs were found necessary before they could be removed to the main building for the winter. These have been made, water and gas introduced into the building, and arrangements made for remodelling it during the coming season.

COURT-HOUSE, BOSTON, MASSACHUSETTS.

The repairs and remodelling of this building have been nearly completed. New windows have been cut, new sash provided for the old ones, the interior repainted and repaired, and the building placed in as good condition as practicable. It is not, however, suitable for the purpose, not being fire-proof, but of ordinary construction.

COURT-HOUSE, DES MOINES, IOWA.

A contract fort urnishing all the cut stone for the building, above the level of the water-table, was made on the 10th of February, 1868, with N. Osborn, esq., of Rochester, New York, for the sum of $47,735, he being the lowest bidder; the delivery of the material to be completed by the 1st of November, following. Every effort has been made to compel the fulfilment of the contract, without success, and it is believed the contractor is not entirely responsible for the delay—a strike at the quarries from which the stone was procured having rendered it impossible for him to obtain material at a time when most needed. The failure is to be the more regretted as the building could have been roofed during the present season, had the contractor complied with his obligations. The building will be 116 by 64 feet, two stories in height, with basement and attic, and is constructed of Joliet limestone, with ashlar from the Athens quarries.

COURT-HOUSE, MADISON, WISCONSIN.

Work on this building is progressing as rapidly as the difficulty of procuring labor and material will permit, and the quality is unsurpassed by any similar structure in the United States. The exterior is of cut stone; the ashlar from the quarry of cream-colored magnesian limestone, purchased by the department in the vicinity of Madison, and the dressings of the well-known Joliet limestone—the former quarry having failed to furnish stones of sufficient size for them. The work is finished more elaborately than was required by the specifications, or contemplated by the department, but it is believed that the superintendent has used every effort to reduce the cost, without depreciating the quality of the workmanship, and has made every endeavor to hasten its completion.

The principal expenditures having been for labor, (the stone being cut by days' work,) the eight-hour system has increased its cost and delayed its progress more than in some other cases. The building, when completed, will be inferior to none in the west.

COURT-HOUSE, PORTLAND, MAINE.

The remarks in regard to the custom-house at this place apply with even greater force to this building. No efforts have been spared, either by the department or superintendent, to procure material from the contractors, but with the most discouraging results. The material furnished has, however, proved entirely satisfactory in quality, and had the contractors fulfiled their obligations as well in the time of delivery as in other respects, no cause of complaint would have existed. It is proper and just to say that the superintendent is of opinion that they have exerted themselves to the utmost to meet their engagements, and that the means at their disposal were inadequate, and the supply of marble limited, the quarry having been recently opened.

COURT-HOUSE, SPRINGFIELD, ILLINOIS.

The exterior of the building, including the roof, has been completed, the windows glazed, and the outer doors hung. The amount of work performed by the superintendent does not equal the expectations of this office, but he reports unusual difficulties in obtaining labor, while the operation of the eight-hour system has been most unfavorable, the progress of the work being retarded and its cost greatly increased thereby. The detailed reports of the superintendent have not as yet been received, and I cannot therefore speak with the confidence I desire, but it is believed that the work has cost considerably more than at other places. Work is now suspended, and a full and searching investigation will be made before the resumption of operations.

The building is 60 by 120 feet, three stories in height, and is constructed of stone from the Nauvoo quarries. The design is extremely simple, and depends for its architectural effect entirely upon its proportion and the beauty of the material. A contract for heating it by low-pressure steam, on the principle of Gould's patent, has been made with Messrs. James P. Wood & Co., of Philadelphia.

POST OFFICE AND SUB-TREASURY, BOSTON, MASSACHUSETTS.

As previously stated in my report, an admirable site has been secured for this building, and all preliminary questions in regard to grades of the adjoining streets, &c., satisfactorily arranged. Plans for the building are in course of preparation, but are not yet sufficiently advanced to enable me to make an accurate estimate of its cost. It is expected, however, that it will be in the neighborhood of $800,000, though this sum may be reduced considerably.

BRANCH MINT, SAN FRANCISCO, CALIFORNIA.

Plans for the new mint have been prepared and forwarded, with instructions to commence quarrying stone for the building, which will be obtained from the government quarries on Angel island, permission having been obtained from the War Department, the entire island being under its jurisdiction.

The building will be two stories and a basement in height, and is a simple but imposing specimen of the Roman Doric. No ornamentation has been attempted, but dependence placed on the magnitude and proportion of the building for its architectural effect. No pains have been spared to make it, when complete, not only the finest and best constructed building on the Pacific coast, but the best arranged mint in the world.

The destruction of the custom-house and other buildings, public and private, in San Francisco by earthquakes has rendered it necessary to take every precaution to prevent a similar catastrophe to the proposed building, and I am willing to risk my professional reputation upon its stability if properly carried out according to my plans.

In determining the size of the building, and its internal arrangement, I have been governed by the opinions of the superintendent and officers of the present branch mint at San Francisco and of the present and late director of the mint, to whose inspection the plans have been submitted, and by whom they have been approved. A careful and detailed estimate of the cost of the building has been made, which amounts, at the cost of work on the north wing of the Treasury extension, to $939,289 90, exclusive of fencing and grading.

BRANCH MINT, CARSON CITY, NEVADA.

In my last report I stated that an examination of the expenditures on this building and the management of the superintendent had been ordered, the cost of work and material having greatly exceeded the expectations of the department. This has been made by J. F. Morse, esq., of this office, one of its oldest and most valued officers. He reports that a careful and searching investigation has failed to disclose the slightest suspicion of dishonesty or incompetency on the part of the superintendent, and that the work is of the most durable and substantial character The high reputation of the superintendent and of his endorsers, as well as of the disbursing agent, sustain the position of Mr. Morse. I am, therefore, of the opinion that the superintendent has acted with strict integrity as regards his expenditures, though, from the anxiety he shared in common with the citizens of Nevada to secure the erection of the building, he led the department to believe that it could be erected for a much less sum than has been found necessary, work having been once suspended, and only resumed on his promise to complete the building within the amount of the original estimate. The building has been constructed of rubble-stone, with hammered dressings, and is a handsome and convenient structure; it is now ready for the reception of the machinery, and will be, excepting the one at New Orleans, the most convenient branch mint in the country.

The cost of the building has been $180,154 35; of sewerage and water supply (the latter having been brought some distance from a valuable and unfailing spring) $16,033 26, making a total of $196,187 61.

BRANCH MINT, DALLES CITY, OREGON.

A suitable and well-located site has been obtained for this building without cost to the government. Plans and specifications, with full instructions, have been forwarded to the superintendent, and all necessary steps taken to commence work, as at Astoria, immediately on the cession of jurisdiction over the property by the legislature of Oregon, as required by law.

The building will be well and conveniently arranged for its intended use, and practically fire-proof. It is to be 90 by 63 feet, two stories in height, with a one-story engine house, 30 by 16 feet, and will cost, at Washington prices, the sum of $98,616 79, exclusive of fencing, grading, &c. The prices in Oregon being much greater than here, these figures will doubtless be considerably increased.

APPRAISERS' STORES, PHILADELPHIA, PENNSYLVANIA.

The old Pennsylvania bank building (on the site of which this building is being erected) has been removed, the walls of the basement and first and second stories completed, and the work suspended. The appropriations, which were reduced $25,000 below the estimates, and still further diminished by the eight-hour law, have been exhausted. The building will be of pressed brick, four stories in height, with basement and attic, and 248 by 77 feet. It will be, when completed, the only absolutely fire-proof warehouse of which I have any knowledge in the United States. It is believed that the revenue that may be derived from the lease of the upper stories of the building for storage will pay the interest on the whole investment, while the lower stories will give admirable accommodations for the entire appraisers' department, and also of the weighers, gaugers, &c. I cannot too strongly urge the completion of this important and much-needed structure.

BARGE OFFICE, NEW YORK, N. Y.

A contract has been made with C. P. Dixon, esq., of New York, for the erection of the sea-wall of the proposed revenue dock and pier on the battery extension, and work will be commenced without delay. The wall will be of solid granite masonry, and it is believed superior to anything in the country, and as durable as the material of which it is to be composed. No pains will be spared to make it one of the finest structures of the kind in the world. It is proposed, should a sufficient appropriation be obtained, to lay the foundation of the barge office during the coming season, and to make such arrangements as may be necessary for

CONCLUSION.

In submitting this report I desire to urge the importance of a reorganization of this office on a basis that will make it the interest of competent and valuable men to remain in its employ, instead of using it, as is too often the case at present, as a mere temporary expedient and a stepping-stone to business elsewhere. The peculiar character of government buildings, and other work under the supervision of this office, require a much higher order of talent than mere draughtsmen, and it is of the utmost importance that provision should be made for the retention of a class of men who have little inducement to remain under the present system.

In making these remarks I do not reflect upon the manner in which the gentlemen attached to this office have performed their duties; on the contrary, I have to express my satisfaction and to return my thanks for the cordial and earnest support I have received from them.

Very respectfully, your obedient servant,

A. B. MULLETT,
Supervising Architect.

Hon. HUGH McCULLOCH,
Secretary of the Treasury.

Tabular statement of custom-houses, court-houses, post offices, branch mints, &c., under charge of this office, exhibiting the cost of site, date of purchase, contract price of construction, actual cost of construction, and the total cost of the work, including site, alterations, and repairs, to September 30, 1868.

Nature and location of work.	Date of purchase.	Cost of site.	Contract price of construction.	Actual cost of construction.	Total cost to Sept. 30, 1868.	Remarks.
CUSTOM-HOUSES.						
Alexandria, Va., (old)	Nov. 25, 1820	*$6,000 00		$8,246 46	$14,396 46	
Alexandria, Va.	May 3, 1856	16,000 00	$37,149 37	57,913 64	78,861 89	
Astoria, Oregon, (old)	Mar. 27, 1856	900 00				
Astoria, Oregon	May 7, 1868	8,000 00				Not commenced.
Bath, Maine	Feb. 7, 1852	15,000 00	47,594 36	99,182 65	105,182 81	
Bangor, Maine	June 5, 1851	15,000 00	45,584 39	103,698 13	136,235 37	
Belfast, Maine	Oct. 4, 1856	5,600 00	17,500 00	34,340 25	38,534 82	
Burlington, Vt	Mar. 30, 1855	7,750 00	28,233 40	40,036 96	53,858 94	
Boston, Mass	Aug. 29, 1837	180,000 00		886,658 00	1,101,733 12	
Barnstable, Mass	April 24, 1855	1,500 00	17,250 00	34,433 71	36,658 71	
Baltimore, Md	July 16, 1817	*70,000 00				
	Feb. 10, 1853	*110,000 00		451,672 61	892,209 56	Including post office.
	May 28, 1857	*207,000 00				
Buffalo, N. Y	Jan. 22, 1855	45,000 00	117,769 05	191,764 34	282,029 25	
Bristol, R. I	Mar. 12, 1856	4,400 00	17,522 00	23,952 68	28,297 00	
Cleveland, Ohio	April 9, 1856	30,000 00	83,500 00	138,236 30	188,596 40	
Charleston, S. C., (old)	Feb. 14, 1818	*60,000 00			70,000 00	
Charleston, S. C	July 10, 1849	130,000 00		1,939,948 46	2,107,159 37	
Castine, Maine	April 6, 1833	1,200 00			1,458 53	
Chicago, Ill	Jan. 10, 1855	26,600 00				
	July 31, 1857	34,200 00	276,750 56	365,694 18	464,508 58	
	Jan. 26, 1865	8,400 00				
Cairo, Ill	April 28, 1866				81,790 28	Site donated.
Cincinnati, Ohio	Sept. 1, 1851	50,000 00		242,197 23	354,347 57	
Dubuque, Iowa	Feb. 17, 1857	20,000 00	87,334 50	173,607 53	194,070 27	
Detroit, Mich	Nov. 13, 1855	24,000 00	103,160 68	214,020 61	217,401 98	
Eastport, Maine, (old)	—— —, 1830					Acquired for debt.
Eastport, Maine	July 3, 1847	2,780 00	30,500 00	32,509 60	41,789 10	
Ellsworth, Maine	April 11, 1855	3,000 00	9,200 00	21,629 84	26,646 42	
Erie, Pa	July 2, 1849	*29,000 00			31,985 14	
Galena, Ill	Mar. 24, 1857	16,500 00	43,629 00	61,372 44	78,434 04	
Galveston, Texas	Sept. 1, 1855	6,000 00	94,470 74	108,359 82	129,266 91	
Georgetown, D. C	Oct. 23, 1856	5,000 00	41,582 00	53,736 11	64,778 87	
Gloucester, Mass	June 6, 1855	9,000 00	26,596 78	40,765 11	49,785 11	
Key West, Fla	July 26, 1833	*4,000 00			8,699 66	
Kennebunk, Maine	Nov. 19, 1832	*1,575 00			2,348 42	
Louisville, Ky	Oct. 7, 1851	16,000 00	148,158 00	246,640 75	300,370 04	
Milwaukee, Wis	Feb. 16, 1855	12,200 00	130,064 03	159,700 00	189,889 02	
Mobile, Ala	—— —, 1830	*16,300 00				Old building sold and removed, and present building erected on site.
	Oct. 13, 1851	12,500 00		382,159 93	400,484 05	

* Building and site.

Nature and location of work.	Date of purchase.	Cost of site.	Contract price of construction.	Actual cost of construction.	Total cost to Sept. 30, 1868.	Remarks.
CUSTOM-HOUSES—Continued.						
Middletown, Conn	Feb. 8, 1833	$3,500 00		$12,176 64	$27,764 47	
Norfolk, Va., (old)	Dec. 6, 1817	9,000 00			47,002 33	
Norfolk, Va	Feb. 28, 1852	13,500 00		273,893 75	295,341 16	
New Orleans, La	Jan. 27, 1848			2,929,264 50	2,975,705 60	Site donated.
Newark, N. J	May 30, 1855	50,000 00	$81,252 90	108,519 00	162,645 28	
New London, Conn	May 18, 1833	3,400 00		14,600 00	20,719 17	
New Haven, Conn	June 1, 1855	25,500 00	88,000 00	158,614 50	190,678 17	
Newport, R. I	Sept. 16, 1829	1,400 00		8,600 00	12,464 23	
Newburyport, Mass	Aug. 9, 1833	3,000 00		23,188 50	26,960 80	
New Bedford, Mass	April 13, 1833	4,900 00		24,500 00	33,071 54	
Nashville, Tenn	Feb. 17, 1857	20,000 00				
New York, N. Y., (old)	Dec. 16, 1816	*70,000 00				
	Jan. 9, 1833	200,000 00		858,846 76	1,314,435 41	Now sub-treasury.
New York, N. Y	April 29, 1865	1,000,000 00			1,227,126 66	
Oswego, N. Y	Dec. 15, 1854	12,000 00	77,255 00	121,092 89	133,708 18	
Ogdensburg, N. Y	Feb. 4, 1857	8,000 00			123,855 63	
Portsmouth, N. H	June 22, 1857	19,500 00	82,728 96	145,046 91	165,725 96	
Portland, Maine, (old)	Oct. 4, 1828	5,500 00				New custom-house being built on these sites.
	Dec. 31, 1866	35,000 00			206,730 92	
Portland, Maine, (new)	July 5, 1849	149,000 00				Building destroyed by fire January 8, 1854. Court-house in erection on site.
Petersburg, Va	Feb. 5, 1856	15,000 00	67,619 88	78,754 89	104,543 38	
Pensacola, Fla	——— —, ———		27,115 00	48,004 27	51,439 93	Built on government reservation.
Philadelphia, Pa	Aug. 27, 1844	*257,000 00			313,431 50	
Pittsburg, Pa	May 8, 1851	41,000 00	39,866 00	99,747 00	151,280 65	
Plattsburg, N. Y	June 10, 1856	5,000 00	51,224 94	71,450 17	72,890 90	
Providence, R. I., (old)	Nov. 26, 1817	3,000 00		10,504 00	16,492 26	
Providence, R. I	Oct. 9, 1854	40,000 00	151,000 00	202,334 33	258,078 25	
Plymouth, N. C	May 17, 1834	*2,506 00			2,932 70	
Perth Amboy, N. J	July 30, 1857	2,000 00			3,374 66	
Richmond, Va	June 22, 1853	61,000 00	110,000 00	194,404 47	260,424 41	
San Francisco, Cal	Sept. 5, 1854	150,000 00	400,000 00	628,581 49	790,368 31	
Sandusky, Ohio	Dec. 28, 1854	11,000 00	47,560 27	64,522 16	75,523 05	
Savannah, Ga	Dec. 16, 1945	20,725 00		156,434 35	172,771 31	
Salem, Mass	June 23, 1818	5,000 00		14,271 77	35,929 44	
St. Louis, Mo	Oct. 31, 1851	37,000 00	336,309 07	321,987 08	372,495 47	
Suspension Bridge, N. Y	May 25, 1867	*6,000 00			6,060 00	
St. Paul, Minn	April 10, 1867	16,000 00			72,173 02	
Toledo, Ohio	Feb. 20, 1855	12,000 00	45,530 11	64,522 16	77,246 00	
Wilmington, N. C	Mar. 19, 1819	*14,000 00				Old building destroyed by fire January 17, 1840. Present building erected on site.

Wilmington, Del	May 27, 1853	3, 500 00	29, 234 00	40, 146 34	45, 378 49	
Wiscasset, Maine, (old)	Nov. 23, 1848	*2, 000 00				Building destroyed by fire October 9, 1866.
Wiscasset, Maine	June 20, 1868	1, 800 00			9, 243 00	
Wheeling, W. Va	Sept. 7, 1855	20, 500 00	85, 070 82	96, 648 64	125, 165 56	
Waldoboro', Maine	Nov. 29, 1852	2, 000 00	15, 800 00	22, 624 68	25, 132 93	
MARINE HOSPITALS, ETC.						
Chelsea, Mass	June 12, 1858	50, 000 00	122, 185 39	233, 015 31	373, 345 61	
Chicago, Ill	Jan. 22, 1867	10, 000 00			105, 551 57	In course of erection.
Cleveland, Ohio	Oct. 11, 1837	12, 000 00	20, 000 00	79, 972 05	101, 582 88	
Detroit, Mich	Mar. 19, 1855	23, 000 00	54, 637 12	78, 215 14	106, 201 22	
Galena, Ill	Mar. 14, 1857	5, 052 00	29, 862 00	48, 2[illegible]2 93	53, 849 58	
Key West, Fla	Nov. 30, 1844	500 00		25, 600 00	31, 281 31	
Louisville, Ky	Nov. 3, 1842	6, 000 00		53, 591 26	82, 819 63	
Natchez, Miss	Aug. 9, 1837	7, 000 00		59, 785 37	66, 785 37	
Napoleon, Ark	Sept. 15, 1837	1, 000 00		58, 220 80	62, 431 02	Building sold September, 1868.
Norfolk, Va	Dec. 16, 1800	*6, 185 34			15, 695 35	
New Orleans, La	Aug. 7, 1855	12, 000 00	429, 395 79	496, 162 05	527, 934 34	
Ocracoke, N. C	May 15, 1843	1, 100 00			10, 327 07	
Pittsburg, Pa	Nov. 7, 1842	10, 253 60		50, 420 32	66, 976 05	
Portland, Me	Nov. 22, 1852	11, 000 00	66, 200 00	84, 758 73	104, 939 40	
San Francisco, Cal	Nov. 13, 1852	600 00		224, 000 00	230, 775 41	
St. Louis, Mo	Mar. 7, 1850			85, 712 63	93, 943 47	Ceded by War Department.
Vicksburg, Miss	June 25, 1853	4, 500 00				
	Feb. 28, 1856	4, 700 00	57, 021 02	67, 525 16	76, 975 16	Used by War Department.
Wilmington, N. C	Mar. 17, 1857	6, 500 00	28, 968 25	37, 346 04	43, 897 44	
Mobile, Ala	June 20, 1838	4, 000 00				
	Aug. 25, 1856	6, 000 00		51, 400 00	64, 540 00	
COURT-HOUSES AND POST OFFICES.						
Boston, Mass		*105, 000 00			116, 531 48	
Baltimore, Md	June 6, 1859	50, 000 00	112, 808 04	205, 176 97	255, 567 79	
Boston, Mass	Mar. 25, 1868	458, 415 00				
Des Moines, Iowa					67, 562 48	In course of erection.
Indianapolis, Ind	Nov. 5, 1856	17, 160 00	98, 983 79	148, 032 07	189, 212 00	
Memphis, Tenn	June 6, 1860	15, 000 00				
Madison, Wis	Mar. 25, 1867				113, 292 12	Site donated; building now in course of erection.
Portland, Me					100, 329 98	Building in course of erection on site of old custom-house.
Philadelphia, Pa	Oct. 6, 1860	*161, 000 00		73, 473 40	244, 742 33	
Rutland, Vt	July 4, 1857	1, 400 00				
	May 17, 1859	500 00	55, 701 75	62, 297 56	73, 663 48	
Raleigh, N. C	Aug. 7, 1860	7, 700 00				
Springfield, Ill	Mar. 2, 1857	6, 000 00			212, 666 58	Nearly finished.
Key West, Fla	Apr. 28, 1858	3, 000 00				
St. Augustine, Fla						Acquired from Spain.
Windsor, Vt	Mar. 4, 1857	4, 700 00	53, 258 84	68, 262 48	85, 401 13	

* Building and site.

Tabular statement of custom-houses, court-houses, post offices, branch mints, &c.—Continued.

Nature and location of work.	Date of purchase.	Cost of site.	Contract price of construction.	Actual cost of construction.	Total cost to Sept. 30, 1868.	Remarks.
UNITED STATES MINTS, ETC.						
Philadelphia, Pa.	July 18, 1792	*$5,466 66				
	Apr. 30, 1829	*31,666 67		$207,101 25	$230,508 03	
San Francisco, Cal., (old)	May 2, 1854	*283,929 10			300,000 00	
San Francisco, Cal.	Jan. 1, 1867	100,000 00			101,575 84	Not commenced.
New Orleans, La	June 19, 1835				614,825 88	Use of lot granted by city.
Charlotte, N. C	Nov. 2, 1835	1,500 00		66,849 82	101,699 02	
Dahlonega, Ga	Aug. 3, 1835	1,050 00		69,588 33	69,588 33	Used by War Department.
Carson City, Nev	May 3, 1865				170,107 46	Building nearly completed; site donated.
Denver City, Col	Nov. 25, 1862	*25,000 00			93,377 69	
Dallas City, Oregon						Not commenced.
Assay Office, N. Y.	Aug. 21, 1854	*530,000 00			713,358 75	
MISCELLANEOUS.						
United States Treasury extension					6,127,026 08	Includes cost of old building.
Penitentiary, Utah					53,361 90	
Capitol, N. M					57,851 20	
Penitentiary, N. M.					20,000 00	
Quarantine warehouse at New Orleans, La.	Sept. 23, 1858		$31,984 00		39,865 12	Site donated.
Boarding station, Southwest Pass	May 9, 1857	*3,500 00			7,335 70	
Boarding station, Pass à l'Outre	Feb. 1, 1856		10,900 00		12,000 00	Use of site granted.
Appraisers' stores, San Francisco			53,500 00		99,966 19	Built on custom-house lot.
Appraisers' stores, Philadelphia	Mar. 2, 1857	*250,000 00			393,770 55	Now being built on site of Pennsylvania Bank building.
Public store, Baltimore	June 10, 1833	*30,000 00			30,099 70	
No. 23 Pine street, New York		*11,137 60			11,206 57	
Barge office, New York	Mar. 30, 1867	10,000 00			13,702 24	

* Building and site.

Tabular statement of appropriations for the erection or repair of public buildings under control of this office, showing available balance September 30, 1868.

Nature and location of work.	Available Sept. 30, 1867.	Appropriated 1867-'68.	Authorized and expended in 1867-'68.	Available Sept. 30, 1868.	Remarks.
CUSTOM-HOUSES.					
Astoria, Oregon	$25,000 00		$325 00	$24,475 00	
Bangor, Me	35,919 60	$20,000 00	22,672 90	25,936 70	
Charleston, S. C	15,645 00		15,645 00		
Cairo, Ill	4,060 39	59,000 00	41,991 82	25,367 11	$4,298 54 from Staten Island wharves.
Chicago, Ill		20,000 00	20,000 00		
Dubuque, Iowa	756 72	1,005 05	865 73	896 04	
Island Pond, Vt	10,000 00				Transf'd to surplus fund.
Knoxville, Tenn	95,568 19				Transf'd to surplus fund.
Machias, Me	20,000 00		260 00	19,740 00	
Newport, Vt	10,000 00			10,000 00	
New York, N. Y		45,000 00	45,000 00		
Nashville, Tenn	104,215 69			104,215 69	
Ogdensburg, N. Y	56,786 36	40,000 00	71,786 36	25,000 00	
Portland, Me	50,017 99	150,000 00	123,721 78	76,296 21	
Philadelphia, Pa	21,436 58		16,400 00	5,036 58	
Perth Amboy, N. J	20,625 34			20,625 34	
Portland, Oregon		50,000 00		50,000 00	
St. Albans, Vt	10,000 00				Transf'd to surplus fund.
St. Paul, Minn	33,884 30	50,000 00	56,270 95	27,613 35	
Toledo, Ohio	13,409 33			13,409 33	
Wiscasset, Me	25,000 00		7,191 50	17,808 50	
MARINE HOSPITALS.					
Chelsea, Mass		45,000 00	43,148 86	1,851 14	
Chicago, Ill	119,928 99		89,650 92	30,278 07	
Louisville, Ky	10,000 00		10,000 00		
Pensacola, Fla	20,947 04				Transf'd to surplus fund.
Portland Bridge, Me	3,000 00			3,000 00	
COURT-HOUSES, ETC.					
Des Moines, Iowa	71,035 80	89,008 00	66,473 38	93,570 42	
Key West, Fla	40,908 26			40,908 26	
Memphis, Tenn	34,856 10			34,856 10	
Madison, Wis	38,284 15	100,000 00	101,705 62	36,578 53	
Portland, Me	116,153 40	100,000 00	72,441 36	143,712 04	
Springfield, Ill	53,841 03	55,000 00	103,301 53	5,539 50	
UNITED STATES MINTS.					
San Francisco (old)	45,000 00		11,300 00	33,700 00	
San Francisco (new)	199,340 20		566 00	198,418 16	
Carson City, Nevada		150,000 00	12,376 82	137,623 18	
Dallas City, Oregon	99,621 05		395 00	98,966 05	
MISCELLANEOUS.					
Appraisers' stores, Philadelphia	47,120 89	75,000 00	120,891 44	1,229 45	
Barge office, New York	37,197 96	50,000 00	900 20	86,297 76	
Warehouses, Staten isl'd, N. Y	4,298 54				Carried to Cairo, Illinois, court-house.
Treasury extension	262,500 44	301,882 40	537,351 12	27,031 72	
Repairs and preservation of public buildings	91,096 91	50,000 00	103,678 34	37,418 57	
Furniture and repairs of furniture for public buildings	45,718 54	20,000 00	41,195 54	24,523 00	
Heating apparatus for public buildings		35,000 00	20,165 77	14,834 23	
To replace corrugated galvanized iron roofs with copper or slate		30,000 00		30,000 00	
Vaults, safes, &c	20,778 58	25,000 00	21,523 85	24,254 73	

Tabular statement of buildings under control of this office in process of erection, showing available balance September 30, 1867, amount expended 1867–'68, and balance available September 30, 1868.

Nature and location of work.	Available Sept. 30, 1867.	Am't expended 1867–'68.	Available Sept. 30, 1868.	Remarks.
CUSTOM-HOUSES.				
Astoria, Oregon	$25,000 00	$525 00	$24,475 00	Plans forwarded.
Bangor, Me.	35,919 60	22,672 90	25,936 70	Enlarging.
Cairo, Ill	4,060 39	41,991 82	25,367 11	
Machias, Me	20,000 00	260 00	19,740 00	Plans in preparation.
Ogdensburg, N. Y	56,786 36	71,786 36	25,000 00	
Portland, Me	50,017 99	123,721 78	76,296 21	
St. Paul, Minn	33,884 30	56,270 95	27,613 35	
Wiscasset, Me	25,000 00	7,191 50	17,808 50	
MARINE HOSPITAL.				
Chicago, Ill	119,928 99	89,650 92	30,278 07	
COURT-HOUSES AND POST OFFICES.				
Des Moines, Iowa	71,035 80	66,473 38	93,570 42	
Madison, Wis	38,284 15	101,705 62	36,578 53	
Portland, Me	116,153 40	72,441 36	143,712 04	
Springfield, Ill	53,841 03	103,301 53	5,539 50	Nearly completed.
UNITED STATES MINTS.				
San Francisco, Cal	199,340 20	566 00	198,418 16	
Carson City, Nevada	....	12,376 82	137,623 18	
Dallas City, Oregon	99,621 05	395 00	98,966 05	Plans forwarded.
MISCELLANEOUS.				
Appraisers' stores, Philadelphia	47,120 89	120,891 44	1,229 45	
Barge office, New York	37,197 96	900 20	86,297 76	Plans in preparation.

Tabular statement exhibiting the amount of expenditures authorized and made from the appropriation for repairs and preservation of public buildings, and for heating apparatus and repairs of same, during the year ending September 30, 1868.

Nature and location of work.	Amount authorized and expended.	Nature and location of work.	Amount authorized and expended.
CUSTOM-HOUSES.		CUSTOM-HOUSES.	
Alexandria, Va	$1,160 95	Mobile, Ala	$516 47
Bath, Me	439 75	Middletown, Conn	100 00
Bangor, Me	325 31	Norfolk, Va	316 50
Belfast, Me	350 00	New Orleans, La	3,885 83
Boston, Mass	1,490 17	Newark, N. J	200 00
Baltimore, Md	2,970 81	New Bedford, Mass	1,912 00
Buffalo, N. Y	3,627 18	New Haven, Conn	240 76
Cleveland, Ohio	281 69	New London, Conn	756 55
Charleston, S. C	1,920 91	Newport, R. I	75 00
Chicago, Ill	3,320 36	New York, N. Y	†22,356 52
Cincinnati, Ohio	1,845 86	Oswego, N. Y	687 10
Dubuque, Iowa	180 82	Petersburg, Va	532 70
Detroit, Michigan	1,087 45	Pittsburg, Pa	220 13
Eastport, Maine	1,477 46	Plattsburg, N. Y	26 88
Ellsworth, Maine	300 00	Providence, R. I	995 86
Erie, Pa	7 75	Richmond, Va	463 25
Galena, Ill	308 50	Suspension Bridge, N. Y	30 00
Gloucester, Mass	1,060 00	San Francisco, Cal	1,004 00
Kennebunk, Maine	207 72	Sandusky, Ohio	147 00
Louisville, Ky	5,258 86	Savannah, Ga	1,960 00
Milwaukee, Wis	*12,515 86	St. Louis, Mo	1,054 59

Tabular statement exhibiting the amount of expenditures, &c.—Continued.

Nature and location of work.	Amount authorized and expended.	Nature and location of work.	Amount authorized and expended.
CUSTOM-HOUSES—Cont'd.		COURT-HOUSES, ETC.	
Toledo, Ohio	$669 50	Baltimore, Md	$390 82
Wilmington, N. C	43 00	Boston, Mass	3,625 00
Wheeling, West Va	94 20	Indianapolis, Ind	410 20
		Philadelphia, Pa	2,517 71
MARINE HOSPITALS.		St. Augustine, Fla	2,000 00
		Windsor, Vt	100 00
Chelsea, Mass	248 76		
Cleveland, Ohio	1,027 84	MISCELLANEOUS.	
Detroit, Mich	1,149 76		
Louisville, Ky	12,806 39	Sub-treasury, N. Y	5,829 38
Portland, Maine	4,255 00	Pine St. building, No. 23, N. Y.	153 97
San Francisco, Cal	610 00	Santa Fé, N. M	5,000 00
St. Louis, Mo	676 02		

Tabular statement of expenditures made and authorized from the appropriation for furniture and repairs of furniture for public buildings during the year ending September 30, 1868.

Nature and location of work.	Amount authorized and expended.	Nature and location of work.	Amount authorized and expended.
CUSTOM-HOUSES.		CUSTOM-HOUSES.	
Alexandria, Va	$313 25	New Bedford, Mass	$763 00
Bath, Maine	218 60	New York, N. Y	12,221 60
Bangor, Maine	597 42	Oswego, N. Y	286 74
Belfast, Maine	336 50	Portsmouth, N. H	215 00
Boston, Mass	25 00	Petersburg, Va	45 00
Baltimore, Md	578 45	Philadelphia, Pa	628 50
Buffalo, N. Y	401 29	Pittsburg, Pa	993 35
Cleveland, Ohio	638 12	Richmond, Va	2,013 50
Charleston, S. C	2,632 00	San Francisco, Cal	233 00
Chicago, Ill	6,493 11	Savannah, Ga	405 00
Cincinnati, Ohio	2,727 20	St. Louis, Mo	374 83
Dubuque, Iowa	635 99	St. Albans, Vt	25 00
Detroit, Mich	817 75	Wheeling, West Va	25 00
Galena, Ill	327 18		
Galveston, Texas	1,520 00	MARINE HOSPITALS.	
Kennebunk, Maine	10 00		
Louisville, Ky	2,751 60	Portland, Maine	175 00
Milwaukee, Wis	3,225 25	San Francisco, Cal	51 00
Mobile, Ala	22 50	St. Louis, Mo	250 00
Norfolk, Va	1,058 60	COURT-HOUSES, ETC.	
New Orleans, La	4,459 24		
New London, Conn	58 00	Indianapolis, Ind	35 00
New Haven, Conn	143 20	Philadelphia, Pa	1,613 24

REPORT OF THE TREASURER.

TREASURY OF THE UNITED STATES,
Washington, October 27, 1868.

SIR: In pursuance of provisions of statutory law, the following statements of the receipts and expenditures of the treasury of the United States are most respectfully submitted. They exhibit the business transactions of the office located at the seat of government, and including as well all the offices belonging thereto, by or through which money has been received or disbursed, all under their appropriate heads; and also showing the money movement of the office in the past as compared with the present, accompanied with suggestions for the future, for the fiscal year ending with the 30th day of June, 1868.

The books of the office were closed at the date specified, after the entry therein of all moneys received and disbursed, on authorized warrants, within said fiscal year, as follows, to wit:

Cash Dr.

Balance from last year		$170, 868, 814 40
Received from loans	$625, 111, 433 20	
Received from internal revenue	191, 087, 589 41	
Received from miscellaneous sources	46, 949, 033 09	
Received from direct tax	1, 788, 145 85	
Received from lands	1, 348, 715 41	
Received from War	24, 268, 876 34	
Received from Navy	9, 208, 110 99	
Received from Treasury	9, 314, 036 64	
Received from Interior	1, 783, 506 40	
		910, 859, 447 33
Received from customs (in gold)		164, 464, 599 56
Total		1, 246, 192, 861 29

Cash Cr.

Paid on account of public debt	$848, 445, 848 57	
Paid on account of internal revenue	11, 512, 376 12	
Paid on account of customs	15, 025, 787 95	
Paid on account of War	147, 515, 524 96	
Paid on account of Navy	34, 983, 613 71	
Paid on account of Interior	29, 628, 802 22	
Paid on account of diplomatic	1, 352, 557 82	
Paid on account of Treasury proper	19, 022, 744 40	
Paid on account of Treasury interior	4, 986, 205 41	
Paid on account of quarterly salaries	473, 833 72	
Paid on account of War (civil branch)	1, 479, 432 95	
Paid on account of Chickasaw trust fund	37, 773 28	
		1, 114, 464, 501 11
Unavailable transferred to Register, December 20, 1867	721, 827 93	
Unavailable transferred to Register, April 4, 1868	172, 094 29	
		893, 922 22
Balance—cash in treasury		130, 834, 437 96
Total		1, 246, 192, 861 29

The receipts were carried into the treasury by 10,098 covering warrants, which is an increase of 268 over last year. The payments were made on 30,222 authorized warrants, for the payment of which warrants there were issued 36,566 drafts, which is an increase of 2,544 over the number issued last year.

The two preceding tables show, the one, the cash on hand at the commencement of the fiscal year, and the amounts that were actually covered into the treasury by warrants, and they include repayments; and in the other there appear only such amounts, including a like amount of payments that were afterwards repaid, as were paid out on warrants, and the balance of cash remaining on hand at the close of the fiscal year; these statements, because they contain payments and repayments of the same amounts of money; and for the further reason that some of the warrants belonged to the preceding and some to the succeeding fiscal year, do not show the precise actual amount received within the year commencing with July 1, 1867, and ending with June 30, 1868.

Among the items of receipts, and also in those of expenditures, in the foregoing statements, appear payments and repayments of sums that had been paid out, and not being used were returned into the treasury, and should, therefore, to a correct understanding of the actual receipts and expenditures, be left out of the statement of receipts, and like amounts should be deducted from the corresponding items of payments. These are as follows, to wit:

On account of War	$18,609,173 53
On account of Navy	4,753,351 21
On account of Treasury	1,147,505 92
On account of Interior	930,959 22
Total of payments and repayments	25,440,989 88

With these corrections, of deducting all expenditures that were returned into the treasury, as above, from both sides of the book account, the actual receipts and payments would be, as then represented by the warrant ledger, as follows:

ACTUAL RECEIPTS.

(Per warrants, less counter warrants.)

On account of loans	$625,111,433 20
On account of internal revenue	191,087,589 41
On account of miscellaneous receipts	46,949,033 09
On account of direct tax	1,788,145 85
On account of lands	1,348,715 41
On account of War	5,659,702 81
On account of Navy	4,454,759 78
On account of Treasury	8,166,530 72
On account of Interior	852,547 18
Total of lawful money	885,418,457 45
Total of customs in gold	164,464,599 56
Total of all receipts	1,049,883,057 01
Balance from last year	170,868,814 40
Payments and repayments as stated	25,440,989 88
Footing as per books	1,246,192,861 29

ACTUAL EXPENDITURES.

(Per warrants, less counter warrants.)

On account of public debt	$848,445,848 57
On account of internal revenue	11,512,376 12
On account of War (military branch)	128,906,351 43
On account of War (civil branch)	1,479,432 95
On account of Navy	30,230,262 50
On account of Treasury	17,875,238 48
On account of Treasury Interior	4,986,205 41
On account of Interior proper	28,697,843 00
On account of diplomatic	1,352,557 82
On account of quarterly salaries	473,833 72
On account of Chickasaw trust fund	37,773 28
On account of customs	15,025,787 95
Actual payments	1,089,023,511 23
Payments and repayments as stated	25,440,989 88
Unavailable transferred to Register	893,922 22
Cash—balance in treasury	130,834,437 96
Footing as per books	1,246,192,861 29

The manner of keeping the books and the arrangement of the accounts has, to some extent, been changed within the year, so that the statements made from them may exhibit the real and actual, instead of merely apparent results, so that they may be more easily and correctly understood.

Now as the business of this office is not an exception to the general rule that everything in this world is comparative, it is believed that the money movement of the office, the amount of business transacted, and the increase or decrease of such business, or any part thereof, can be more easily comprehended and better understood by comparisons of items in any one given year with the like items in any other year or years. The statements heretofore published, commencing with 1861, have been changed so as to conform to the new mode of stating the accounts, and are thus continued, by adding the results of this year on the corrected basis of other years, but containing the same items, and none others, in each year, through the whole series of eight years.

The amount of payments and repayments, had they been stated as they were stated in former years, would have been	$44,574,530 37
The statement for these items is, however, now only	25,440,989 88
Difference, for received on sales of government property	19,133,540 49

To the extent of the last-named amount the comparative statements and tables that follow will disagree with the actual receipts and expenditures as they appear in the foregoing statements and tables.

Thus:

Net amount of receipts	$1,030,749,516 52

Expenditures, including amounts transferred	$1,070,783,892 96
Decrease of balance in treasury	40,034,376 44
	1,030,749,516 52

Or,

Net amount of expenditures	$1,069,889,970 74
Amounts transferred to Register	893,922 22
	1,070,783,892 96

Net amount of receipts	$1,030,749,516 52
Decrease of balance in treasury	40,034,376 44
	1,070,783,892 96

The following tables are corrected so as to exhibit the true receipts and expenditures by authorized warrants, excluding all such as were issued for payments and repayments, and all other counter-warrants, and all trust funds for the last eight years ending each with the 30th of June. They show a constant increase during the rebellion and a decrease in each year since.

The receipts were in the years—

1861	$83,206,693 56
1862	581,628,181 26
1863	888,082,128 05
1864	1,389,466,963 41
1865	1,801,792,627 51
1866	1,270,884,173 11
1867	1,131,060,920 56
1868	1,030,749,516 52
Total	8,176,871,203 98

The expenditures were in the years—

1861	$84,578,834 47
1862	570,841,700 25
1863	895,796,630 65
1864	1,298,056,101 89
1865	1,897,674,224 09
1866	1,141,072,666 09
1867	1,093,079,655 27
1868	1,069,889,970 74
Total	8,050,989,783 45

This again shows a decrease in the amount of expenditures in this as compared with the last fiscal year, of $23,189,684 53. But this is only apparent and not real. The aggregate of receipts and also of expenditures is largely augmented by the fact that the amounts of the redemption of the old and worn out legal tender notes and fractional currency, and the issue of new in their stead, enter into these two statements in all the tables. And from the further fact that the short securities maturing and matured, are under existing laws converted into the permanent stocks of the United States, and as this operation involves the redemption of the former and the issue of the latter named securities, these amounts are also necessarily constructively paid out and received again, and thus they enter into all the statements of receipts and into those of expenditures as well. This process of conversion is now nearly ended and will, in the statements for the next year, be comparatively small, and in succeeding years will disappear from them entirely.

These transactions for the last two years, compared, stand as follows:

Year.	Loans contracted.	Public debt paid.
1867	$640,426,910 29	$898,139,355 78
1868	625,111,433 20	848,445,848 57
Decrease	15,315,477 09	49,693,507 21

Cash ledger balances struck after all the cash accounts from all the offices constituting the treasury of the United States had been received and entered in the books of the treasury:

Cash Dr.

Ledger balance, June 30, 1867	$181, 704, 664 53
Actual receipts in the year	1, 044, 519, 537 08
Total	1, 226, 224, 201 61

Cash Cr.

Amount paid out on drafts	$1, 089, 023, 511 23
Transferred to Register's books	893, 922 22
Counter entry belonging to 1867	7, 337 84
Cash balance in treasury	136, 299, 430 32
Total	1, 226, 224, 201 61

How these results were arrived at appears in the following statement. The balance from last year and the actual receipts in money as per cash ledger were from the sources and for amounts as follows, viz:

Cash ledger balance, June 30, 1867		$181, 704, 664 53
Customs in gold		164, 428, 842 31
Six per cent. five-twenty bonds	$436, 547, 400	
Six per cent. twenty year bonds	113, 850	
Five per cent. ten-forty bonds	23, 157, 050	
Temporary loans	50, 035, 000	
Gold certificates	77, 939, 900	
Legal tender notes	10, 071, 560	
Fractional currency	25, 022, 624	
Loans		622, 887, 384 00
Internal revenue		191, 155, 777 34
Premium on coin, bonds, &c		29, 108, 052 27

Public lands	$1,534,661 94
Captured and abandoned property	1,518,498 04
Conscience money	49,114 11
Fines, penalties, and forfeitures	714,896 59
Interior Department	805,888 01
Indian and other trust funds	550,033 19
Prize captures	270,678 79
Real estate tax	49,308 40
Patent fees	695,404 26
Repayments	2,621,693 19
Total	1,226,224,201 61

The actual amounts of disbursements, as per cash ledger, were made on account of the—

Public debt	$848,434,025 93
Internal revenue	11,322,243 26
Customs	14,732,582 15
War—military branch	128,906,351 43
War—civil branch	1,478,367 42
Navy	30,230,262 50
Diplomatic	992,677 63
Treasury proper	18,753,092 49
Treasury Interior	4,965,573 20
Interior	28,697,843 00
Chickasaw fund	37,371 96
Quarterly salaries	473,120 26
Transferred to Register's books	893,922 22
Counter entry belonging to 1867	7,337 84
Balance cash in treasury	136,299,430 32
Total	1,226,224,201 61

In the preceding year these balances and the uncovered difference between the cash ledger and the warrant ledger stood as follows:

Cash ledger balance	$180,399,201 79	
Warrant ledger balance	170,868,814 40	
Amount uncovered, July 1, 1867		$9,530,387 39
Amount not covered, July 1, 1868		3,447,442 81
Difference in favor of this year		6,082,944 58

The aggregate business transactions, including all necessary entries in the cash accounts on the books in the office in the city of Washington for the last eight years, exhibited the following results by years, viz:

For the year 1861	$41,325,339 20
For the year 1862	929,630,814 38
For the year 1863	2,696,059,087 86
For the year 1864	3,889,171,151 00
For the year 1865	4,366,551,844 73
For the year 1866	2,889,157,017 49
For the year 1867	3,188,754,053 91
For the year 1868	3,004,098,870 97
Total for the eight years	21,004,748,179 54

The aggregate of receipts and disbursements for the year at the various offices which together constitute the treasury of the United States, exclusive of all agencies and agency accounts, but strictly on account of the treasury proper, and which enter into the accounts of this office, were, as per the books of this office	$2,190,682,470 22
For transfers from one office to another office	327,579,818 86
The business of this office, exclusive of the above	3,004,098,870 97
Grand total	5,522,361,160 05

In the preceding fiscal year these items stood as follows:

Receipts and disbursements by the treasury	$2,315,570,899 85
For transfer from one office to another office	426,142,988 14
The business of this office, exclusive of the above	3,188,754,053 91
Grand total	5,930,467,941 90

This shows a falling off in each one of the three items, which in the aggregate amounts to	$408,106,781 85

Now that the short securities have been converted into long loans, it is hoped these tables will in future be much diminished.

The following is a comparative statement of the business of the treasury, including all that was done at the office in Washington and so much of that transacted at other offices as necessarily enters into the accounts kept in the treasury at Washington, for the eight years commencing with July 1, 1860, and ending with June 30, 1868:

In the year 1861	$231,458,546 07
In the year 1862	2,294,674,642 09
In the year 1863	4,945,434,289 56
In the year 1864	7,332,385,024 16
In the year 1865	9,117,855,012 58
In the year 1866	6,403,203,990 72
In the year 1867	5,930,467,941 90
In the year 1868	5,522,361,160 05
Total book transactions for the eight years	41,777,840,607 13

Comparative statements of receipts and expenditures on authorized warrants for the fiscal years ending June 30, 1867 *and* 1868.

RECEIPTS.

On account of—	1867.	1868.
Balance brought forward	$132, 887, 549 11	$170, 868, 814 40
Loans	640, 426, 910 29	625, 111, 433 20
Internal revenue	266, 027, 537 43	191, 087, 589 41
Customs	176, 417, 810 88	164, 464, 599 56
Miscellaneous	56, 020, 318 44	58, 051, 215 58
War Department	22, 476, 564 53	24, 268, 876 34
Navy Department	12, 277, 201 56	9, 208, 110 99
Interior Department	1, 966, 163 68	1, 783, 506 40
Public lands	1, 163, 575 76	1, 348, 715 41
Totals	1, 309, 663, 631 68	1, 246, 192, 861 29

DISBURSEMENTS.

	1867.	1868.
Public debt	898, 139, 355 78	848, 445, 848 57
War Department	117, 700, 980 16	147, 515, 524 96
Navy Department	43, 311, 212 60	34, 983, 613 71
Interior Department	27, 545, 247 16	29, 628, 802 22
Civil and diplomatic	52, 098, 021 58	54, 784, 633 87
Balance in treasury	170, 868, 814 40	130, 834, 437 96
Totals	1, 309, 663, 631 68	1, 246, 192, 861 29

It appears from the foregoing statement that there has been a falling off in the receipts for this fiscal year, as compared with the year before, as follows, to wit: On—

Balance brought forward	$40, 034, 376 44
Loans	15, 315, 477 09
Internal revenue	74, 939, 948 02
Customs, (gold)	11, 953, 211 32

The expenditures have also fallen off as follows, to wit: On the—

Payment of the public debt	$49, 693, 507 21
Expenditures for the navy	8, 327, 598 89

The expenditures have increased as follows, to wit: For the—

Interior Department	$2, 083, 555 06
Civil, diplomatic	2, 686, 612 29
War Department	29, 814, 544 80

As there was paid for army bounties about $38, 000, 000, the expenditures for the War Department would be $8, 000, 000 less than the year before, but for these bounties paid.

Interest on the public debt has been paid within the year as follows, to wit:

In coin	$103, 469, 558 85
In currency	35, 425, 351 83
Total paid and advanced for the payment of interest	138, 894, 910 68

GOLD CERTIFICATES ISSUED.

From November 13, 1865, to June 30, 1866, inclusive		$98,493,660
From July 1, 1866, to June 30, 1867, inclusive		109,121,620
From July 1, 1867, to June 30, 1868, inclusive		77,960,400
Total issues		285,575,680
With Treasurer at Washington	$3,200,000	
Remaining in vault	3,163,200	
		$36,800
Forwarded to assistant treasurer New York	300,640,000	
Remaining in his vault	15,101,120	
		285,538,880
Issued up to June 30, 1868, as above stated		285,575,680
Total issued as above		$285,575,680
Redeemed as per following statements		267,897,040
Outstanding		17,678,640

GOLD CERTIFICATES REDEEMED.

From November 13, 1865, to June 30, 1866, inclusive	$87,545,800
From July 1, 1866, to June 30, 1867, inclusive	101,295,900
From July 1, 1867, to June 30, 1868, inclusive	79,055,340
Redemption to June 30, 1868	267,897,040
Outstanding as above	17,678,640
Total issues as above	285,575,680

The foregoing redemptions of gold certificates were made at the various places and for the amounts as stated below, viz:

Treasurer of the United States, Washington, D. C	$321,360
Assistant treasurer of the United States, Boston, Massachusetts	9,265,520
Assistant treasurer of the United States, New York, New York	250,903,000
Assistant treasurer of the United States, Philadelphia, Pennsylvania	539,320
Assistant treasurer of the United States, Charleston, South Carolina	190,200
Assistant treasurer of the United States, New Orleans, Louisiana	219,100
Assistant treasurer of the United States, St. Louis, Missouri	247,660
Assistant treasurer of the United States, San Francisco, California	1,040
Depositary of the United States, Baltimore, Maryland	5,557,120
Depositary of the United States, Buffalo, New York	58,040
Depositary of the United States, Chicago, Illinois	183,920

Depositary of the United States, Cincinnati, Ohio	$306,380
Depositary of the United States, St. Paul, Minnesota	9,000
Depositary of the United States, Louisville, Kentucky	13,620
Depositary of the United States, Mobile, Alabama	81,760
Total redemptions to June 30, 1868, as above	267,897,040

The gold certificates were redeemed by denominations, as follows:

21,932 in sums of $20 is	$438,640	
64,730 in sums of $100 is	6,473,000	
5,264 in sums of $500 is	2,632,000	
35,170 in sums of $1,000 is	35,170,000	
42,404 in sums of $5,000 is	212,020,000	
500 in sums of $10,000 is	5,000,000	
Total redemptions and destructions		$261,733,640
Redeemed and on hand		6,163,400
Outstanding June 30, 1868		17,678,640
Total issues as before stated		285,575,680

From the foregoing statements it will be seen that $34,635,880 in amount was redeemed at fourteen places other than the two from whence issued. Of the amount redeemed at this office, the most was received from the collectors of customs from all parts of the country. These facts go to show that these gold certificates serve a purpose in addition to the one for which they were authorized. They make a very convenient medium of exchange, without cost or change of any kind between the various places and sections of our wide spread country.

Detailed statements of unavailable funds transferred from the books of the Treasurer to those of the Register, as stated in the table of "Cash Cr." as of December 20, 1867, and April 4, 1868:

Hamilton Stuart, late designated depositary at Galveston, Texas, as per his return of March 21, 1861	$2,033 32
Jesse Thomas, late designated depositary at Nashville, Tennessee, as per his return of April 28, 1861	4,880 88
James T. Miller, late designated depositary at Wilmington, North Carolina, as per his return of April 1, 1861	6,088 80
T. Sanford, late designated depositary at Mobile, Alabama, as per his return of March 14, 1861	18,225 35
John Boston, late designated depositary at Savannah, Georgia, as per his return of February 1, 1861	4,874 11
Anthony J. Guirot, late treasurer of branch mint at New Orleans for bullion deposits with him	389,267 46
S. Garfield, late designated depositary at Olympia, Washington Territory, as per his return of July 31, 1860	516 79
P. T. Crutchfield, late designated depositary at Little Rock, Arkansas, as per his return of December 29, 1860	68,060 28
W. N. Haldeman, late designated depositary at Louisville, Kentucky, as per his return of June 15, 1861	2,410 91
T. J. Sherlock, late designated depositary at Cincinnati, Ohio, as per his return of May 15, 1861	1,118 61

A. L. Woodward, late designated depositary at Tallahassee, Florida, as per his return of March 15, 1861	$679 66
G. N. Carleton, late designated depositary at Memphis, Tennessee, as per report No. 159,036	223,671 76
Total transfer made December 20, 1867	721,827 93

Anthony J. Guirot, late assistant treasurer at New Orleans, Louisiana, as per report No. 155,441	$146,226 74
William M. Harrison, late designated depositary at Richmond, Virginia, as per his return of April 13, 1861	14,071 97
J. J. Simkins, late designated depositary at Norfolk, Virginia, as per his return of April 20, 1861	11,795 58
Total of transfers of April 4, 1868	172,094 29

Total of December 20, 1867	$721,827 93	
Total of April 4, 1868	172,094 29	
		$893,922 22

It will be observed that about three-fourths of this amount has stood as unavailable since the commencement of the rebellion.

The following is a correct statement of the balances standing to the credit of the Treasurer of the United States, and the overdrafts in the others of the various offices constituting the treasury, as per ledger, June 30, 1868:

Treasurer's office,	Washington	$11,054,952 81	
Ass't treasurer's office,	New York	73,801,569 99	
Do do	Philadelphia	6,453,549 47	
Do do	Boston	6,021,150 51	
Do do	St. Louis	428,913 47	
Do do	Charleston	178,444 91	
Do do	Denver	3,526 24	
Depositary's office,	Baltimore	1,718,219 82	
Do do	Cincinnati	2,682,650 18	
Do do	Chicago	922,921 48	
Do do	Louisville	233,289 23	
Do do	Buffalo	158,665 44	
Do do	Pittsburg	739,005 76	
Do do	Omaha	18 99	
Do do	Mobile	189,740 50	
Do do	Little Rock	590 00	
Do do	Santa Fé	106,507 51	
In 373 national bank depositaries		23,057,167 07	
Suspense account		1,002,814 28	
Assay office at New York		3,452,513 00	
Treasurer of the mint at	Philadelphia	994,654 16	
Do do	San Francisco	1,735,000 00	
Do do	Denver	3,100 00	
Unavailable in late insurrectionary States		59,950 03	
			$134,998,914 85

Deduct for overdrafts with offices as follows:

Assistant treasurer at San Francisco	$162, 718 91	
Do............. New Orleans..	489, 517 91	
Designated depositary at Olympia...	2, 266 28	
Do.....do...... Oregon City	6, 225 89	
Do......do...... St. Paul....	56, 305 09	
		$717, 034 08
Total cash ledger balance....................		134, 281, 880 77
This balance consists of gold and silver	99, 984, 561 28	
Lawful money......................	34, 297, 319 49	
		$134, 281, 880 77
Deduct for uncovered cash........................		3, 447, 442 81
Balance as per warrant ledger (see Cash Cr.)...		130, 834, 437 96

Amounts to the credit of United States disbursing officers with the several depositaries, June 30, 1868:

With Treasurer of the United States, Washington, D. C.	$2, 403, 160 51
Assistant treasurer United States, New York, N. Y.	9, 143, 248 54
Do..............do........ Boston, Mass.....	788, 211 94
Do..............do........ Philadelphia, Pa.	773, 000 00
Do..............do........ St. Louis, Mo.....	1, 259, 596 84
Do..............do........ Charleston, S. C.	386, 237 58
Do..............do........ New Orleans, La.	2, 284, 171 67
Do..............do........ San Francisco, Cal	3, 063, 711 84
Designated depository of the U. States, Baltimore, Md.	251, 155, 53
Do..........do........do.... Buffalo, N. Y.	6, 539 35
Do..........do........do.... Chicago, Ill...	678, 691 21
Do..........do........do.... Cincinnati, O.	702, 510 89
Do..........do........do.... Louisville, Ky.	454, 679 06
Do..........do........do.... Pittsburg, Pa..	128, 784 14
Do..........do........do.... St. Paul, Minn.	372, 440 25
Do..........do........do.... Oregon City, Or.	2, 768 49
Do..........do........do.... Santa Fé, N. M.	355, 152 10
Do..........do........do.... Mobile, Ala...	75, 792 58
Seventy-one national banks designated for that purpose	3, 460, 416 34
Total...	26, 590, 268 86

There were drawn during the year transfer checks on the offices of the assistant treasurers, of the kinds and numbers, and for the amounts as follows, viz.:

CURRENCY CHECKS.

53, 718 on New York for............	$44, 360, 515 06	
5, 855 on Boston for..............	1, 712, 107 37	
4, 413 on Philadelphia for..........	2, 409, 408 56	
339 on New Orleans for..........	657, 241 07	
86 on San Francisco for........	138, 604 58	
64, 411 total currency checks........................		$49, 277, 876 64

COIN CHECKS.

1, 432 on New York for	$2, 809, 538 50	
26 on Boston for	73, 912 39	
43 on Philadelphia for	75, 561 06	
2 on New Orleans for	550 00	
3 on San Francisco for	1, 735 50	
1, 506 total coin checks		$2, 961, 297 45
65, 917 checks.—Total of currency and coin		52, 239, 174 09

TRANSFER OF FUNDS.

To facilitate payments at points where the moneys were needed for disbursements, transfer letters, orders and bills of exchange were issued during the year, in number, in kind and for amounts, as follows:

4, 712 letters on national bank depositaries	$157, 640, 000 00
1, 189 transfer orders on national bank depositaries	18, 020, 000 00
67 exchanges drawn on national bank depositaries	1, 792, 942 28
24 bills of exchange on collectors of customs	43, 200 00
905 transfer orders on assistant treasurers and designated depositaries	150, 083, 676 58
Total transfers of funds	327, 579, 818 86

Of which amount there was in coin	$23, 963, 584 75	
And in currency	303, 616, 234 11	
		$327, 579, 818 86

OPEN ACCOUNTS.

There were at the close of the fiscal year open accounts as follows:

With assistant treasurers	9
With designated depositaries	12
With national banks designated as depositaries	373
With disbursing officers	109
Impersonal accounts	41
Total number of open accounts	544

NATIONAL BANKS.

The whole number of banks that had deposited United States securities preliminary to their organization to date of the last annual report, was	1, 672
The number of new banks that have since so deposited, is	10
Total of banks organized, to June 30, 1868	1, 682

The whole number of banks that had their securities still on deposit, and paid duties to the government, on the 30th day of June, 1868, was	1,655
Failed, money realized from sale of stocks prior to June 30, 1867	1
Failed, securities still held, before June 30, 1867	7
Withdrawn and deposited money before June 30, 1867	2
Withdrawn, having no circulation, before June 30, 1867	10
Failed, securities still held, in fiscal year	6
Withdrawn and deposited money in fiscal year	1
Total of banks organized up to and including June 30, 1868	1,682

The following ten new national banks made their first deposits during the fiscal year in the order in which they stand:

The National Bank of Royalton, Vermont; the National Security Bank of Boston, Massachusetts; Kearsarge National Bank of Warner, New Hampshire; the First National Bank of Honeybrook, Waynesburg, Pennsylvania; Greene County National Bank of Springfield, Missouri; the Union Stockyard National Bank of Chicago, Illinois; Central National Bank of Omaha, Nebraska; Carolina National Bank of Columbia, South Carolina; the Princeton National Bank of Princeton, New Jersey; State National Bank of Raleigh, North Carolina; being in number, 10.

Failed before June 30, 1865; money realized from sale of stocks	1
Failed before June 30, 1867; securities yet held in part	7
Failed in last fiscal year; securities yet held in part	6
Deposited money for amount of circulation, before June 30, 1867	2
Deposited money for amount of circulation, in fiscal year	1
Securities withdrawn, having had no circulating notes	10
Banks in operation June 30, 1868, according to the books of this office	1,655
Total number of national banks that have been organized	1,682

NATIONAL BANKS THAT HAVE FAILED.

In 1865.	First National Bank of Attica, New York		1
In 1866.	Merchants' National Bank of Washington, D. C	1	
In 1866.	Venango National Bank of Franklin, Pennsylvania	1	
			2
In 1867.	First National Bank of Medina, New York	1	
In 1867.	Tennessee National Bank of Memphis, Tennessee	1	
In 1867.	First National Bank of Newton, Newtonville, Massachusetts	1	
In 1867.	First National Bank of New Orleans, Louisiana	1	
In 1867.	First National Bank of Selma, Alabama	1	
			5
In 1868.	National Unadilla Bank of Unadilla, New York	1	
In 1868.	Farmers' and Citizens' National Bank of Brooklyn, New York	1	
In 1868.	Croton National Bank of New York, New York	1	
In 1868.	First National Bank of Bethel, Connecticut	1	
In 1868.	First National Bank of Keokuk, Iowa	1	
In 1868.	National Bank of Vicksburg, Mississippi	1	
			6
	Total number of banks that have failed		14

N. B.—The circulating notes of the First National Bank of Newton, Newtonville, Massachusetts, are assumed by the National Security Bank of Boston, Massachusetts, which has reimbursed the United States for former redemptions.

BANKS THAT HAVE VOLUNTARILY RETIRED AND DEPOSITED FUNDS TO REDEEM THEIR CIRCULATION.

October 13, 1865. First National Bank of Columbia, Missouri........	1
August 1, 1866. First National Bank of Carondelet, Missouri........	1
June 16, 1868. Farmers' National Bank of Waukesha, Wisconsin.....	1
	3

The circulating notes of these three banks, and of 13 of the 14 banks that have failed, are redeemed in lawful money on presentation.

The circulating notes so redeemed in the fiscal year were as follows:

First National Bank of Columbia, Missouri..	$4,620 00	
First National Bank of Carondelet, Missouri..	10,609 50	
		$15,229 50
First National Bank of Attica, New York....	16,303 50	
Venango National Bank of Franklin, Pennsylvania..................................	37,424 00	
Merchants' National Bank of Washington, D. C..................................	73,879 75	
First National Bank of Medina, New York...	19,043 00	
Tennessee National Bank of Memphis, Tennessee..................................	43,359 25	
First National Bank of Selma, Alabama.....	40,182 75	
First National Bank of New Orleans, Louisiana..................................	97,257 25	
National Unadilla Bank of Unadilla, New York.	53,538 50	
Farmers and Citizens' National Bank of Brooklyn, New York..........................	111,573 65	
Croton National Bank of New York, N. Y...	83,923 25	
First National Bank of Keokuk, Iowa.......	8,157 75	
First National Bank of Bethel, Connecticut..	110 00	
		584,752 65
Total redemptions in fiscal year....................		599,982 15

Banks having no circulating notes that have withdrawn their securities.

Prior to June 30, 1866:

First National Bank of Penn Yan, New York..................	1
Second National Bank of Ottumwa, Iowa......................	1

In the fiscal year closing with June 30, 1867:

National Bank of Crawford County, Meadville, Pennsylvania....	1	
City National Bank of Savannah, Georgia....................	1	
Pittston National Bank of Pittston, Pennsylvania...............	1	
	—	3

In the fiscal year closing with June 30, 1868:

The Kittanning National Bank, Kittanning, Pennsylvania	1	
	—	1
Total having no circulation that have withdrawn their securities...		12

Securities held in trust to assure the prompt redemption of the circulating notes of all the national banks.

The amount held at the date of the last report, in United States stocks pledged for the redemption of the circulating notes of all the national banks, was................		$340,607,500
Deposited during fiscal year..................	$10,050,900	
Withdrawn during fiscal year	9,162,500	
		888,400
Amount held June 30, 1868......................		341,495,900
Add to this for securities held to insure the prompt payment of public moneys with national bank depositaries, as per statement......................................		38,517,950
Total amount held in trust for national banks.....		380,013,850

The number of national banks qualified to act as depositaries of public money and fiscal agents of the government, as per last report, was..		385
Since then discontinued....................................	21	
Designated since then......................................	6	
	—	15
Number of depositary banks June 30, 1868..................		370

All the national banks whose designation as depositaries of public money has been revoked during the fiscal year have voluntarily withdrawn from their fiscal agencies, and have paid over the public funds in their custody, except the National Bank of the Metropolis, at Washington, District of Columbia, whose securities are still held for deposits, the bank having gone into liquidation. There are still unsettled claims for government funds against the Venango National Bank, at Franklin, Pennsylvania; the Merchants' National Bank of Washington, District of Columbia; the First National Bank of Selma, Alabama, and the First National Bank of New Orleans, Louisiana, which banks are in the hands of receivers, and their securities pledged for public deposits are yet in my hands.

The stocks held for the safe-keeping and prompt payment of government deposits on the 30th of June, 1867, were..		$39, 177, 950
Withdrawn during the fiscal year..........	$16, 156, 300	
Received during the fiscal year...........	15, 496, 300	
		660, 000
Total so remaining on deposit June 30, 1868.......		38, 517, 950

The securities held in trust for national banks in this office at the close of the fiscal year consisted of the following, viz:

Held for redemption of circulating notes.

Registered coin interest six per cents.....	$244, 103, 100	
Coupon coin interest six per cents........	53, 850	
Registered coin interest five per cents.....	90, 758, 950	
Coupon coin interest five per cents........	10, 000	
Registered currency interest six per cents..	6, 570, 000	
		$341, 495, 900

Held to assure the payment of public deposits.

Registered coin interest six per cents.....	$23, 714, 600	
Coupon coin interest six per cents........	2, 514, 500	
Registered coin interest five per cents.....	5, 659, 600	
Coupon coin interest five per cents........	2, 357, 750	
Registered currency interest six per cents..	3, 295, 000	
Seven-thirty treasury notes...............	946, 500	
Personal bond..........................	30, 000	
		38, 517, 950
Total amount of securities held in trust for banks..		380, 013, 850

The 25th section of the act entitled, "An act to provide a national currency," passed June 3, 1864, makes it the duty of every banking association having bonds deposited in the office of the Treasurer of the United States, once or oftener in each fiscal year, to examine and compare the bonds so pledged with the books of the Comptroller and the accounts of the association, and, if found correct, to execute to the Treasurer a certificate, setting forth that and other facts. Within the fiscal year these examinations have been made by 1,498 banks, and the required certificates made and delivered by their proper officers or attorneys. One hundred and fifty-seven others of these banks, although notified in writing to do so, which is not required by the law, have entirely neglected this their duty. It is to be regretted there is no legal penalty provided whereby this office has the authority to compel a compliance with the provisions of the act and a performance of the duty. A fine of fifty dollars, to be withheld from the interest on their stocks, would force compliance.

Interest accrued upon stocks held in the Treasury has been remitted to the banks entitled to receive the same by drafts for coupons, to wit:

237 currency drafts, amounting to	$370, 004 15
440 coin drafts, amounting to	281, 998 50
677 drafts for coupon interest, amounting to............	652, 002 65

Interest on registered stocks, deposited in trust by the national banks with the Treasurer, has been drawn by the various banks entitled to receive the same, at the offices where it was, at their request, made payable, during the fiscal year, amounting in the aggregate to the sum of....................................	$21, 481, 889 50
Add, as before stated, on coupons....................	652, 002 65
Total amount paid to banks for interest on stocks.	22, 133, 892 15

Semi-annual duty has been collected from national banks since the last report as follows:

For the term of six months preceding July 1, 1867.

On circulation	$1,464,459 32	
On deposits	1,278,515 52	
On capital	157,476 55	
		$2,900,451 39

For the term of six months preceding January 1, 1868.

On circulation	$1,470,226 31	
On deposits	1,240,265 13	
On capital	157,422 87	
		2,867,914 31
Total duty collected from banks for the year		5,768,365 70

There has been refunded to national banks during the last fiscal year, in compliance with a "resolution in relation to national banking associations," approved March 2, 1867, for duty claimed to have been paid in excess by certain of those banks to the Treasurer, as follows:

Collected in the six months preceding January 1, 1865	$87 10
Collected in the six months preceding July 1, 1865	290 46
Collected in the six months preceding January 1, 1866	1,453 19
Collected in the six months preceding July 1, 1866	3 61
Collected in the six months preceding January 1, 1867	424 22
Collected in the six months preceding July 1, 1867	25 00
	2,283 58

Which duty had been collected on—

Undivided profits	$1,932 32
Capital	250 00
Deposits	47 25
Circulation	54 01
Whole amount refunded during the fiscal year	2,283 58

Whole amount of duty collected for year preceding January 1, 1868	$5,768,365 70
Less amount refunded as above stated	2,283 58
Net duty for the year	5,766,082 12
Net duty for the preceding year	5,598,430 53
Increase of duty this year over the preceding year	167,651 59

Statement of national banks that have voluntarily retired, and also of such banks as have failed, with the respective dates of such retiring or failures, and the amount of outstanding notes of each on the day of closing business.

Names of banks.	Date of closing.	Outstanding circulation.
First National Bank of Columbia, Mo., voluntary	October 13, 1865	$11,990
First National Bank of Carondelet, Mo., voluntary	August 1, 1866	25,500
Farmer's National Bank of Waukesha, Wis., voluntary	June 16, 1868	90,000
First National Bank of Attica, N. Y., failed	April 14, 1865	44,000
Venango National Bank of Franklin, Pa., failed	May 5, 1866	85,000
Merchants' National Bank of Washington, D. C., failed	May 8, 1866	180,000
First National Bank of Medina, N. Y., failed	March 9, 1867	40,000
Tennessee National Bank of Memphis, Tenn., failed	March 21, 1867	90,000
First National Bank of Selma, Ala., failed	April 30, 1867	85,000
First National Bank of New Orleans, La., failed	May 20, 1867	180,000
National Unadilla Bank of Unadilla, N. Y., failed	August 6, 1867	100,000
Farmers & Citizens' National Bank of Brooklyn, N. Y., failed	September 5, 1867	253,900
Croton National Bank of New York, N. Y., failed	October 7, 1867	180,000
First National Bank of Keokuk, Iowa, failed	March 6, 1868	90,000
First National Bank of Bethel, Conn., failed	March 6, 1868	26,300
National Bank of Vicksburg, Miss., failed	April 24, 1868	25,500
Total		1,507,190

Statement of funds of national banks that have gone into voluntary liquidation, and of all such banks as have failed, together with the amounts deposited in the treasury for the purpose of redeeming the circulating notes of such banks respectively.

Names of banks.	Funds deposited.	Notes redeemed.
First National Bank of Carondelet, Mo., voluntary	$25,500 00	$14,889 50
First National Bank of Columbia, Mo., voluntary	11,990 00	5,940 00
First National Bank of Keokuk, Iowa, failed		8,157 75
First National Bank of Attica, N. Y., failed	44,000 00	29,988 50
First National Bank of Medina, N. Y., failed	27,329 25	23,043 00
First National Bank of New Orleans, La., failed	104,742 00	97,257 25
First National Bank of Selma, Ala., failed	41,247 20	40,182 75
First National Bank of Bethel, Conn., failed		110 00
Venango National Bank of Franklin, Pa., failed	61,871 00	58,994 00
Tennessee National Bank of Memphis, Tenn., failed	53,372 00	51,859 25
Merchants' National Bank of Washington, D. C., failed	139,095 02	113,354 75
Croton National Bank of New York, N. Y., failed	72,181 90	83,923 25
Farmers and Citizens' National Bank of Brooklyn, N. Y., failed	106,504 10	111,573 05
Farmers' National Bank of Waukesha, Wis., voluntary	90,000 00	
National Unadilla Bank of Unadilla, N. Y., failed	53,183 50	53,538 50
Total	831,015 97	692,812 15

Destruction of notes of national banks that have gone into liquidation.

First National Bank of Attica, New York, voluntary	$26,774 75
First National Bank of Carondelet, Missouri, voluntary	11,694 50
First National Bank of Columbia, Missouri, failed	4,230 00
First National Bank of Medina, New York, failed	18,878 50

First National Bank of Newton, Massachusetts, failed....	$2,198 25
First National Bank of New Orleans, Louisiana, failed....	64,224 50
First National Bank of Selma, Alabama, failed	30,272 75
First National Bank of Keokuk, Iowa, failed	20 00
Merchants' National Bank of Washington, D. C., failed ...	98,284 75
Venango National Bank of Franklin, Pennsylvania, failed.	50,694 00
Farmers and Citizens' National Bank of Brooklyn, New York, failed	78,717 00
Croton National Bank of New York, New York, failed.....	57,515 40
Tennessee National Bank of Memphis, Tennessee, failed...	39,489 25
Unadilla National Bank of Unadilla, New York, failed....	40,608 50
Discount for mutilation on above redemptions	12 85
Total	523,615 00
Amount destroyed before July 1, 1867	$30,330 00
Amount destroyed during the fiscal year	493,285 00
Total	523,615 00

NATIONAL BANK DEPOSITARIES.

The national banks that have been designated as depositaries and financial agents have paid in various ways, but at points and in the manner directed by this office, into the various offices of the treasury, and in most cases without any expense to the government, within the year in the aggregate.......... $237,872,495 36
And they held balances that aggregated June 30, 1868. 23,057,167 07

Total amount of payments and balances..........	260,929,662 43

The above balances were, on October 17, 1868, reduced to $14,295,637.03. For security for the prompt payment of this balance the treasurer holds United States stocks of the par value of $38,096,350. The payments were made by these banks as follows, viz.:

Free of any charge whatever to the treasury	$219,852,495 36
Through expresses at government expense	18,020,000 00
Total payments during the year, as above.....	237,872,495 36

MONEY COLLECTIONS BY NATIONAL BANKS FOR THE GOVERNMENT.

The business transactions between the treasury of the United States and the 373 national banks that have been designated as depositaries of the public moneys and financial agents of the government have been during the fiscal year as follows, to wit:

Balance brought from last year's account..........		$26,122,322 61
On account of stock subscription.....	$59,151,800 00	
On account of internal revenue.......	154,899,154 95	
On account of fractional currency.....	9,312,678 77	
From miscellaneous sources	11,443,706 10	
Total receipts..........		234,807,339 82
Total balance and receipts..........		260,929,662 43

All these collections have been promptly paid, as required; and the balance of last year has been reduced over $3,000,000 in this year.

The foregoing statement shows, that while these banks had deposited in the treasury of the United States, to insure the prompt payment of all moneys belonging to the government, stocks of the United States, the par value of which exceeded $38,000,000, they held to the credit of the Treasurer on the 30th day of June last a little over $23,000,000, and on the 17th day of October it was less than $14,300,000. The interest on the first named amount at six per cent. per annum would be about $1,383,000, and on the last named amount about $857,000, making the average interest about $1,120,000.

As an offset to this, it also appears that these banks collected for the United States, and remitted the same free of charge to the government to various offices of the treasury, as directed by the Treasurer, about $220,000,000. If a commission of one-half of one per cent. had been charged for making these collections and remittances, it would have cost the government about $1,100,000; thus about balancing the benefits to the banks and to the government.

COLLECTION OF DUTY AND TAXES

On referring to a preceding table it will be seen that the Treasurer has collected from the national banks during the fiscal year, for "duty" on the three items of "capital," "deposits," and "circulation," $5,768,365 70, without any expense to the government.

The Commissioner of Internal Revenue has also collected from these banks, on these identical three items for "taxes," an amount that cannot be with accuracy ascertained, because the collections of taxes from national banks are not kept separate from those collected from State banks and private bankers. But as the whole amount so collected from national banks, State banks, and private bankers, is but $1,858,739 67, it is obvious that the part collected from national banks as tax, by the collectors of internal revenue, must be less than one-quarter that collected from these banks for *duty* on these same items by the Treasurer.

The collections from national banks for "duty" are by law made semi-annually. They cost nothing. The collections from these banks for "taxes" are made by the collectors of internal revenue, and are by law assessed on "circulation" at one twelfth of one per cent. per month, and on "capital" and on "deposits" one twenty-fourth of one per cent. per month. For these trifling monthly collections of taxes the collectors receive a percentage. The aim of the government no doubt is, to make the collection of all taxes as cheaply as may be, and with as little annoyance as possible. The monthly appearance of the tax-gatherer cannot be otherwise than offensive. To avoid this vexation, to simplify the machinery, and to save the expense of collection, it is most respectfully suggested that the law should be so amended as to give the collection of duty that is now paid to the Treasurer, to the collectors of internal revenue, or to permit the national banks whose securities are held by the Treasurer and from the interest of which securities he can enforce the collection, to pay all their taxes semi-annually, in the same manner and at the same times as they now by law pay their duty, to the Treasurer of the United States

TRUST FUNDS.

The following is a descriptive list of stocks on deposit in this office, held in trust by the Secretary of the Treasury, belonging to the Chickasaw national fund:

State of Arkansas 6 per cent. bonds, due in 1868	$90,000 00
State of Indiana 6 per cent. bonds, due in 1867	141,000 00
State of Maryland 6 per cent. bonds, due in 1870	6,149 57
State of Maryland 6 per cent. bonds, due in 1890	8,350 17
Nashville and Chattanooga railroad 6 per cent. bonds, due in 1881	512,000 00
Richmond and Danville railroad 6 per cent. bonds, due in 1876	100,000 00
State of Tennessee 6 per cent. bonds, due in 1890	104,000 00
State of Tennessee 5¼ per cent. bonds, due in 1861	66,666 66
United States 6 per cent. bonds, loan of 1847, due in 1867	61,050 00
United States 6 per cent. bonds, loan of 1848, due in 1868	37,491 80
United States 6 per cent. bonds, loan of 1862, due in 1882	61,000 00
United States 6 per cent. bonds, loan of 1865, due in 1885	104,100 00
Total	1,291,808 20

State of Illinois 6 per cent. bonds due in 1860 to the amount of $17,000, have been redeemed by the State, and the amount paid into the Treasury.

All the other stocks above-named have, since the 30th June, 1868, been transferred to the Secretary of the Interior, in accordance with instructions of the Secretary of the Treasury contained in his letter bearing date August 7, 1868.

Descriptive list of stocks on deposit in this office held in trust by the Secretary of the Treasury belonging to the Smithsonian fund.

State of Arkansas 6 per cent. bonds, due in 1868	$538,000 00
United States 6 per cent. bonds, due in 1868	33,400 00
Redeemed and money paid into the treasury	104,061 64
Total reported last year	675,461 64

The redemptions and payments into the treasury during the fiscal year were as follows:

January 29, 1868, United States stocks, loan of 1842		$48,061 64
February 17, 1868, Illinois State stock	$10,000	
February 27, 1868, Illinois State stock	13,000	
March 14, 1868, Illinois State stock	33,000	
		56,000 00
Total redeemed and paid into the treasury in the fiscal year		104,061 64
Redeemed and paid into the treasury since, United States 6 per cent. stocks		33,400 00
Total redeemed and paid into the treasury since June 30, 1867		137,461 64
This leaves on deposit only the first named amount		538,000 00
Total amount as stated in last year's report, and as above		675,461 64

ISSUES OF NEW CURRENCY.

United States legal-tender notes and fractional-currency notes have been issued, during the fiscal year, of the numbers and denominations, and for the several amounts, as follows:

Numbers.	Denominations.	Amounts.	Totals.
8,112	of one thousand dollars is	$8,112,000	
4,064	of five hundred dollars is	2,032,000	
1,755,348	of two dollars is	3,510,696	
2,483,348	of one dollar is	2,483,348	
	Legal-tender notes		$16,138,044
19,097,364	of fifty cents is	9,548,682	
39,864,000	of twenty-five cents is	9,966,000	
55,300,000	of ten cents is	5,530,000	
	Fractional-currency notes		25,044,682
118,512,236	pieces.		
	Total issue of new currency		41,182,726

UNITED STATES SEVEN AND THREE-TENTH NOTES.

Statement of issues.

First series, August 15, 1864:		
363,952 of fifties is	$18,197,600	
566,039 of one hundreds is	56,603,900	
171,666 of five hundreds is	85,833,000	
118,528 of one thousands is	118,528,000	
4,166 of five thousands is	20,830,000	
		$299,992,500
Second series, June 15, 1865:		
182,926 of fifties is	9,146,300	
338,227 of one hundreds is	33,822,700	
175,682 of five hundreds is	87,841,000	
179,965 of one thousands is	179,965,000	
4,045 of five thousands is	20,225,000	
		331,000,000
Third series, July 15, 1865:		
343,320 of fifties is	17,166,000	
472,080 of one hundreds is	47,208,000	
108,654 of five hundreds is	54,327,000	
71,879 of one thousands is	71,879,000	
1,684 of five thousands is	8,420,000	
		199,000,000
Total issues by series		829,992,500

Recapitulation of all the issues.

890,198 of fifties is	$44,509,900
1,376,346 of one hundreds is	137,634,600
456,002 of five hundreds is	228,001,000

370,372 of one thousands is	$370,372,000
9,895 of five thousands is	49,475,000
Total issue as above	829,992,500

REDEMPTION OF SEVEN AND THREE-TENTH NOTES.

The amount of seven and three-tenth per cent. United States treasury notes of the issues of the years 1864 and 1865 converted into United States stocks, or redeemed in money during the fiscal year ending with June 30, 1868, was as follows:

First series, August 15, 1864	$84,342,100
Second series, June 15, 1865	244,576,500
Third series, July 15, 1865	121,798,450
Total redemptions during the fiscal year	450,717,050

Denominations.

431,697 of fifties	$21,584,850
724,142 of one hundreds	72,414,200
246,976 of five hundreds	123,488,000
206,110 of one thousands	206,110,000
5,424 of five thousands	27,120,000
Total, as above stated, for the year	450,717,050

Statement of redemptions.

FIRST SERIES, AUGUST 15, 1864.

Redeemed previous to July 1, 1866	$5,489,250
In year ending with June 30, 1867	209,386,500
In year ending with June 30, 1868	84,342,100
	299,217,850

SECOND SERIES, JUNE 15, 1865.

Redeemed previous to July 1, 1866	$6,881,900
In year ending with June 30, 1867	67,500,450
In year ending with June 30, 1868	244,576,500
	318,958,850

THIRD SERIES, JULY 15, 1865.

Redeemed previous to July 1, 1866	$11,379,500
In year ending with June 30, 1867	40,846,950
In year ending with June 30, 1868	121,798,450
	174,024,900

RECAPITULATION BY YEARS.

Redeemed previous to July 1, 1866	$23,750,650
In year ending with June 30, 1867	317,733,900
In year ending with June 30, 1868	450,717,050

Statement by series of the numbers, denominations, and amounts of the seven-thirty treasury notes that were outstanding on the 30th of June, 1868.

FIRST SERIES.

3,851 notes of fifty dollars is		$192,550
3,081 notes of one hundred dollars is		308,100
294 notes of five hundred dollars is		147,000
92 notes of one thousand dollars is		92,000
7 notes of five thousand dollars is		35,000
		774,650

SECOND SERIES.

14,487 notes of fifty dollars is		$724,350
25,538 notes of one hundred dollars is		2,553,800
7,634 notes of five hundred dollars is		3,817,000
4,616 notes of one thousand dollars is		4,616,000
66 notes of five thousand dollars is		330,000
		12,041,150

THIRD SERIES.

52,616 notes of fifty dollars is	$2,630,800	
76,518 notes of one hundred dollars is	7,651,800	
14,251 notes of five hundred dollars is	7,125,500	
6,787 notes of one thousand dollars is	6,787,000	
156 notes of five thousand dollars is	780,000	
		$24,975,100
Total outstanding		37,790,900

THE THREE SERIES COMBINED.

70,954 notes of fifty dollars is	$3,547,700
105,137 notes of one hundred dollars is	10,513,700
22,179 notes of five hundred dollars is	11,089,500
11,495 notes of one thousand dollars is	11,495,000
229 notes of five thousand dollars is	1,145,000
Total outstanding	37,790,900

Currency destroyed during the year as follows, to wit:

Demand notes	$64,520 50
Legal-tender notes	25,855,156 20
One-year 5 per cent. notes	336,130 00
Two-year 5 per cent. notes	208,547 50
Two-year coupon notes	65,000 00
Three-year 6 per cent. compound-interest notes	80,166,751 00
Gold certificates	79,046,020 00
Fractional currency, 1st issue	616,443 66
Fractional currency, 2d issue	1,051,751 86
Fractional currency, 3d issue	19,101,143 03
Discounts on the above	31,671 54

Certificates of indebtedness	$15,000 00	
Interest on the same	713 43	
		$15,713 43
Bonds, certificates, notes, and fractional currency, that had not been issued		563,623,866 87
Balance to new account		337,139 45
Total amount destroyed		770,519,855 04

REDEMPTION AND DESTRUCTION ACCOUNT.

Cash, Dr.

To balance from 1867	$504,861 42
To redeemed during fiscal year	206,343,741 78
	206,848,603 20

Cash, Cr.

By destroyed in fiscal year	$206,511,463 75
Balance to new account	337,139 45
	206,848,603 20
Discount for mutilations on above redemptions	31,671 54
Certificates of indebtedness and interest thereon	15,713 43
Statistical matter destroyed	563,623,866 87
Total amount destroyed	770,519,855 04
Last year the above statement footed	$529,104,757 94
Increase this year over the last year is	241,415,097 10
	770,519,855 04

These destructions have involved the separate examination of 117,229,939 distinct pieces of paper, each representing a money value.

Statement of the receipt for redemption, and of the destruction of the major part thereof, of all kinds of United States paper moneys and other government securities, and of the notes of all the national banks that have gone into liquidation, and that have been received for destruction, from the beginning and including June 30, 1868.

United States moneys destroyed—		
Before July 1, 1867	$786,548,239 78	
Within the fiscal year	206,511,463 75	
Discount on same	99,369 88	
		$993,159,073 41
Broken national bank notes destroyed—		
Before July 1, 1867	30,330 00	
Within the fiscal year	493,272 15	
Discount on same	12 85	
		523,615 00
Certificates of indebtedness—		
Before July 1, 1867	582,455,094 87	
Within the fiscal year	15,713 43	
		[illegible]

Statistical securities of the United States—

Before July 1, 1867	$882, 950, 738 50½	
Within the fiscal year	563, 623, 866 87½	
		$1, 446, 574, 605 38
There was remaining on hand on the 30th June, 1868		337, 139 45
Total amount received from the beginning to date		3, 023, 065, 241 54

STATEMENT OF REDEMPTIONS OF CURRENCY, ETC., FROM THE COMMENCEMENT.

Cash, Dr.

For United States notes and fractional currency	$993, 496, 212 86
For national bank notes of broken banks	523, 615 00
For certificates of indebtedness	582, 470, 808 30
For statistical matter	1, 446, 574, 605 38
For total amount received for destruction	3, 023, 065, 241 54

Cash, Cr.

By United States notes and fractional currency destroyed	$993, 059, 703 53
By discount for mutilations on same	99, 369 88
By notes of broken national banks destroyed	523, 602 15
By discount for mutilations on same	12 85
By certificates of indebtedness destroyed	582, 470, 808 30
By statistical matter destroyed	1, 446, 574, 605 38
By balance of money on hand, carried to new account	337, 139 45
Total amount destroyed, discounted and on hand	3, 023, 065, 241 54

These destructions required the separate examination, scrutiny and count of 442,137,927 pieces of money and other securities.

Discounts on mutilations have been made on the various kinds of currency and for amounts as follows:

Demand notes	$2, 084 50
Legal-tender notes	54, 518 30
One-year 5 per cent. notes	217 00
Two-year 5 per cent. notes	152 50
Two-year 5 per cent. coupon notes	2 50
Three-year compound interest notes	480 00
Postage currency, 1st issue	12, 215 87
Fractional currency, 2d issue	7, 430 12
Fractional currency, 3d issue	16, 008 68
Money redeemed, but not destroyed	6, 260 41
Total discounts from the beginning by kinds	99, 369 88

Discounts in year 1863	$615 27
Discounts in year 1864	11, 393 93
Discounts in year 1865	13, 108 09

Discounts in year 1866	$17,813 36
Discounts in year 1867	24,767 69
Discounts in year 1868	31,671 54
Total discounts from the beginning by years as above	99,369 88

Statements exhibiting, by denominations, the amount paid, the amount discounted for mutilations, and the total amount retired of all kinds of currency from the beginning up to and including June 30, 1868.

Denominations.	Amounts paid.	Amounts discounted.	Total retired.
OLD ISSUE DEMAND NOTES.			
Five dollars	$21,746,865 75	$471 75	$21,747,337 50
Ten dollars	19,979,542 75	432 25	19,979,975 00
Twenty dollars	18,159,679 50	1,180 50	18,160,860 00
Totals	59,886,088 00	2,084 50	59,888,172 50
NEW ISSUE LEGAL-TENDER NOTES.			
One dollar	$9,155,607 40	$15,238 60	$9,170,846 00
Two dollars	10,109,633 55	10,600 45	10,120,234 00
Five dollars	33,266,349 50	11,193 00	33,277,542 50
Ten dollars	25,852,851 75	7,688 25	25,860,540 00
Twenty dollars	11,399,222 00	6,558 00	11,405 780 00
Fifty dollars	2,013,270 00	1,380 00	2,014,650 00
One hundred dollars	2,616,540 00	1,260 00	2,617,800 00
Five hundred dollars	11,356,700 00	300 00	11,357,000 00
One thousand dollars	70,340,700 00	300 00	70,341,000 00
Totals	176 110,874 20	54,518 30	176,165,392 50
ONE-YEAR FIVE PER CENT. NOTES.			
Ten dollars	$6,117,349 00	$31 00	$6,117,380 00
Twenty dollars	16,212,224 00	116 00	16,212,340 00
Fifty dollars	8,166,105 00	45 00	8,166,150 00
One hundred dollars	13,565,675 00	25 00	13,565,700 00
Unknown	90 00	....	90 00
Totals	44,061,443 00	217 00	44,061,660 00
TWO-YEAR FIVE PER CENT. NOTES.			
Fifty dollars	$6,703,987 50	$62,50	$6,704,050 00
One hundred dollars	9,587,610 00	90 00	9,587,700 00
Totals	16,291,597 50	152 50	16,291,750 00
TWO-YEAR FIVE PER CENT. COUPON NOTES.			
Fifty dollars	$5,885,247 50	$2 50	$5,885,250 00
One hundred dollars	14,458,500 00	....	14,458,500 00
Five hundred dollars	40,293,500 00	....	40,293 500 00
One thousand dollars	89,283,000 00	....	89,283,000 00
Unknown	10,500 00	....	10,500 00
Totals	149,930,747 50	2,50	149,930,750 00

Statement—Continued.

Denominations.	Amounts paid.	Amounts discounted.	Total retired.
THREE-YEAR SIX PER CENT. COMPOUND INTEREST NOTES.			
Ten dollars	$21, 850, 663 00	$137 00	$21, 850, 800 00
Twenty dollars	24, 478, 107 00	133 00	24, 478, 240 00
Fifty dollars	46, 088, 970 00	180 00	46, 089, 150 00
One hundred dollars	33, 154, 470 00	30 00	33, 154, 500 00
Five hundred dollars	57, 327, 000 00	....	57, 327, 000 00
One thousand dollars	29, 088, 000 00	....	29, 088, 000 00
Totals	211, 987, 210 00	480 00	211, 987, 690 00
POSTAGE CURRENCY—FIRST ISSUE.			
Five cents	$1, 156, 882 74	$1, 374 56	$1, 158, 257 30
Ten cents	2, 736, 264 45	1, 877 35	2, 738, 141 80
Twenty-five cents	4, 035, 573 18	5, 315 32	4, 040, 888 50
Fifty cents	7, 405, 819 36	3, 648 64	7, 409, 468 00
Totals	15, 334, 539 73	12, 215 87	15, 346, 755 60
FRACTIONAL CURRENCY—SECOND ISSUE.			
Five cents	$1, 979, 134 41	$1, 612 09	$1, 980, 746 50
Ten cents	5, 000, 726 36	2, 937 94	5, 003, 664 30
Twenty-five cents	6, 671, 118 14	1, 403 61	6, 672, 521 75
Fifty cents	5, 589, 429 52	1, 476 48	5, 590, 906 00
Totals	19, 240, 408 43	7, 430 12	19, 247, 838 55
FRACTIONAL CURRENCY—THIRD ISSUE.			
Three cents	$470, 922 67	$109 13	$471, 031 80
Five cents	451, 317 48	275 62	451, 593 10
Ten cents	6, 876, 148 16	3, 464 54	6, 879, 612 70
Twenty-five cents	14, 441, 885 26	5, 267 24	14, 447, 152 50
Fifty cents	16, 242, 881 60	6, 892 15	16, 249, 773 75
Totals	38, 483, 155 17	16, 008 68	38, 499, 163 85

UNITED STATES CURRENCY.

The following tables exhibit under their appropriate heads the whole amount of paper money that has been issued by the government of the United States, from the commencement of such issues, under the act of July 17, 1861, and several other acts since passed, up to and including June 30, 1868, the amount during that time redeemed, and the amount at the last named date outstanding by kinds and denominations ranging from three-cent to five-thousand dollar notes:

United States demand notes.

Denominations.	Issued.	Redeemed.	Outstanding.
Five dollars	$21,800,000	$21,746,865 75	$53,134 25
Ten dollars	20,030,000	19,979,542 75	50,457 25
Twenty dollars	18,200,000	18,159,679 50	40,320 50
Totals	60,030,000	59,886,088 00	143,912 00
Deduct for discount for mutilations			2,084 50
Total of actual amount outstanding			141,827 50

This balance is receivable for customs and redeemable in gold coin at the treasury.

United States legal-tender notes.

Denominations.	Issued.	Redeemed.	Outstanding.
One dollar	$22,829,348	$9,155,607 40	$13,673,740 60
Two dollars	26,070,696	10,109,633 55	15,961,062 45
Five dollars	96,103,795	33,266,349 50	62,837,445 50
Ten dollars	108,685,040	25,852,851 75	82,832,188 25
Twenty dollars	74,999,680	11,399,222 00	63,600,458 00
Fifty dollars	27,508,800	2,013,270 00	25,495,530 00
One hundred dollars	29,654,000	2,616 540 00	27,037,460 00
Five hundred dollars	44,048,000	11,356,700 00	32,691,300 00
One thousand dollars	122,084,000	70,340,700 00	51,743,300 00
Totals	551,983,359	176,110,874 20	375,872,484 80
Deduct for new notes not issued			19,872,484 80
Amount authorized to be issued			356,000,000 00
Deduct discounts for mutilations			54,518 30
Real amount outstanding			355,945,481 70

Fractional currency—first issue.

Denominations.	Issued.	Redeemed.	Outstanding.
Five cents	$2,242,869	$1,156,882 74	$1,086,006 26
Ten cents	4,115,378	2,736,264 45	1,379,113 55
Twenty-five cents	5,225,692	4,035,573 18	1,190,118 82
Fifty cents	8,631,672	7,405,819 36	1,225,852 64
Totals	20,215,631	15,334,539 73	4,881,091 27
Deduct for discount for mutilations			12,215 87
Total of actual amount outstanding			4,868,875 40

Fractional currency—second issue.

Denominations.	Issued.	Redeemed.	Outstanding.
Five cents	$2,776,128 60	$1,979,134 41	$796,994 19
Ten cents	6,223,584 30	5,000,726 36	1,222,857 94
Twenty-five cents	7,618,341 25	6,671,118 14	947,223 11
Fifty cents	6,546,429 50	5,589,429 52	956,999 98
Totals	23,164,483 65	19,240,408 43	3,924,075 22
Deduct for discounts for mutilations			7,430 12
Total of actual amount outstanding			3,916,645 10

Fractional currency—third issue.

Denominations.	Issued.	Redeemed.	Outstanding.
Three cents	$601,923 90	$470,922 67	$131,001 23
Five cents	657,002 75	451,317 48	205,685 27
Ten cents	12,018,560 10	6,876,148 16	5,142,411 94
Fifteen cents	1,352 40	(*)	1,352 40
Twenty-five cents	23,291,699 75	14,441,885 26	8,849,814 49
Fifty cents	25,835,358 25	16,242,881 60	9,592,476 65
Totals	62,405,897 15	38,483,155 17	23,922,741 98
Deduct for discounts for mutilations			16,008 68
Real amount outstanding			23,906,733 30

* Specimens.

Two-year five per cent. notes.

Denominations.	Issued.	Redeemed.	Outstanding.
Fifty dollars	$6,800,000	$6,703,987 50	$96,012 50
One hundred dollars	9,680,000	9,587,610 00	92,390 00
Totals	16,480,000	16,291,597 50	188,402 50
Deduct for discounts for mutilations			152 50
Total of actual amount outstanding			188,250 00

Two-year five per cent. coupon notes.

Denominations.	Issued.	Redeemed.	Outstanding.
Fifty dollars	$5,905,600	$5,885,247 50	$20,352 50
One hundred dollars	14,484,400	14,458,500 00	25,900 00
Five hundred dollars	40,302,000	40,293,500 00	8,500 00
One thousand dollars	89,308,000	89,283,000 00	25,000 00
Totals	150,000,000	149,920,247 50	79,752 50
Deduct for redeemed, denominations unknown		10,500 00	
Deduct for discounts for mutilations		2 50	
			10,502 50
Total actual amount outstanding			69,250 00

One-year five per cent. notes.

Denominations.	Issued.	Redeemed.	Outstanding.
Ten dollars	$6,200,000	$6,117,349	$82,651
Twenty dollars	16,440,000	16,212,224	227,776
Fifty dollars	8,240,000	8,166,105	73,895
One hundred dollars	13,640,000	13,565,675	74,325
Totals	44,520,000	44,061,353	458,647
Deduct for redeemed, denominations unknown		90	
Deduct for discounts for mutilations		217	
			307
Total actual amount outstanding			458,340

United States six per cent. compound-interest notes.

Denominations.	Issued.	Redeemed.	Outstanding.
Ten dollars	$23,285,200	$21,850,663	$1,434,537
Twenty dollars	30,125,840	24,478,107	5,647,733
Fifty dollars	60,824,000	46,088,970	14,735,030
One hundred dollars	45,094,400	33,154,470	11,939,930
Five hundred dollars	67,846,000	57,327,000	10,519,000
One thousand dollars	39,420,000	29,088,000	10,332,000
Totals	266,595,440	211,987,210	54,608,230
Deduct discounts on mutilations			480
Total actual amount still outstanding			54,607,750

Certificate of indebtedness—statement of amounts issued, redeemed, and outstanding

OLD ISSUE.

Numbers 1 to 153,662, of $1,000	$153,662,000 00	
Numbers 1 to 69,268, of $5,000	346,340,000 00	
Numbers 1 to 13, various amounts	1,591,241 65	
		$501,593,241 65
Less 100 numbers intermitted, of $5,000 each	500,000 00	
Less 500 numbers, of $5,000 each, destroyed	2,500,000 00	
		3,000,000 00
Total of first series issued		498,593,241 65

NEW ISSUE.

Numbers 1 to 15,145, of $1,000	$15,145,000 00	
Numbers 1 to 9,603, of $5,000	48,015,000 00	
		63,160,000 00
Total issues of both series from commencement		561,753,241 65

Redeemed to June 30, 1867	$561,715,241 65
Redeemed since, to June 30, 1868	15,000 00
Still outstanding, to June 30, 1868	23,000 00
	561,753,241 65

Of the $23,000 remaining unredeemed, $15,000 has been caveated.

Interest paid on redemption up to June 30, 1867	$20,739,853 22
Interest paid in this fiscal year	713 43
	20,740,566 65
For principal redeemed as above stated	561,730,241 65
Total principal and interest paid to July 1, 1868	582,470,808 30

There were issued by the government during the rebellion 13 distinct kinds of paper money. Eleven of these kinds have ceased to be used as currency. The following table shows the amount of each outstanding:

OUTSTANDING CIRCULATION.

Legal-tender notes		$355,945,481 70
Fractional currency		32,692,253 80
Total in use as a circulating medium		388,637,735 50
Demand notes	$141,827 50	
One-year 5 per cent. notes	458,340 00	
Two-year 5 per cent notes	188,250 00	
Two-year five per cent. coupon notes	69,250 00	
Three-year 6 per cent. compound interest notes	54,607,750 00	
Seven and three-tenths interest notes	37,790,900 00	
Gold certificates	17,678,640 00	
Three per cent. certificates	65,230,000 00	
Certificates of indebtedness	23,000 00	
Total out of use as a circulating medium		176,187,957 50
Total amount of all kinds outstanding		564,825,693 00

The payments for the army, less repayments in each year, for the eight years from 1861 to 1868, both inclusive, were in the years and for the amounts as follows, to wit:

In 1861	$22,981,150 44
In 1862	394,368,407 36
In 1863	599,298,600 83
In 1864	690,791,842 97
In 1865	1,031,323,360 79
In 1866	284,449,701 82
In 1867	95,224,415 63
In 1868	123,246,648 62
Total actual payments in the eight years	3,241,684,128 46

The payments for the army in 1860 were	$16,409,737 10	
Multiplied by 8 for the eight years	8	
Would have made the payments in ordinary times only		$131,277,896 80
Leaves an excess on account of the rebellion of		3,110,406,231 66

The payments on account of the navy for eight years, from 1861 to 1868, both inclusive, less the repayments, were for the years and for the amounts as follows, to wit:

In 1861		$12,420,887 89
In 1862		42,668,277 09
In 1863		63,221,963 64
In 1864		85,725,994 67
In 1865		122,612,945 29
In 1866		43,324,118 52
In 1867		31,034,011 04
In 1868		25,775,502 72
Total actual payments in the eight years		426,783,700 86
The payments for the navy in 1860	$11,514,964 96	
Multiply by 8 for the eight years	8	
Would have made the payments as ordinarily		92,119,719 68
Leaves an excess on account of the rebellion		334,663,981 18

The payments on account of military pensions in each year of the eight years from 1861 to 1868, both inclusive, were for the years and for the amounts as follows, viz:

In 1861		$758,150 16
In 1862		803,289 73
In 1863		932,886 29
In 1864		4,902,651 01
In 1865		9,191,187 02
In 1866		13,483,665 19
In 1867		19,448,088 69
In 1868		23,987,469 14
Total actual payments in the eight years		73,507,387 23
The payments in 1861 were	$758,150 16	
Multiplied by 8 for eight years	8	
Would have made the payments in ordinary times only		6,065,201 28
Leaves the excess caused by the rebellion		67,442,185 95

The payments on account of naval pensions in each year of the eight years, from 1861 to 1868, both inclusive, were in the years and for the amounts as follows, to wit:

In 1861	$162,932 95
In 1862	122,798 54
In 1863	185,188 36
In 1864	184,755 04
In 1865	7,222,424 59
In 1866	3,371,058 33
In 1867	3,328,795 46
In 1868	890,828 69
Total actual payments in the eight years	15,468,781 96

The payments were in 1861	$162,932 95	
Multiplied by 8 for the eight years	8	
Would have made these payments in ordinary times only		1,303,463 60
Leaves the excess caused by the rebellion at		14,165,318 36

Statement made from the four foregoing tables, showing the actual payments in money raised by taxation, over and above the present public debt, for the purposes of the army and navy, in excess of the ordinary expenditures for those two branches of the public service for the eight years preceding July 1, 1868.

Paid to the army in excess of ordinary times	$3,110,406,231 66
Paid to the navy in excess of ordinary times	334,663,981 18
Paid for army pensions in excess of ordinary times	67,442,185 95
Paid for naval pensions in excess of ordinary times	14,165,318 36
Paid for loss of horses in the military service in 1865, 1866 and 1867	1,781,548 46
Total payments to the army and navy in 8 years	3,528,459,265 61
For public debt, March 4, 1861	68,482,686 19
Total debt before the war and for the military since	3,596,941,951 80

Public debt on the 1st August, 1868		$2,633,588,756 81
Less Pacific railroad bonds	$32,210,000 00	
Less cash in treasury	110,054,276 14	
		142,264,276 14
Actual debt of the United States on the 1st of August, 1868		2,491,324,480 67
Money raised by taxation for the army and navy in eight years from June 30, 1861, to June 30, 1868		1,105,617,471 13
Total amount expended on army and navy in 8 years		3,596,941,951 80

Having in the foregoing pages devoted much space to tables of comparison of the business of the treasury of the United States, between the fiscal year that closed June 30, 1868, and the year preceding it, and with other fiscal years going back to June 30, 1861, when the office

ness transactions of the treasury then and now, the suggestion presented itself that it might be interesting to compare the whole business transactions of the office for the year closing with June 30, 1860, only eight years since, and the last before the rebellion, with the year for which this report is made. For the purpose of doing this most effectually, the whole report of my rebel predecessor is herein reproduced in the words and figures as follows:

TREASURY OF THE UNITED STATES,
November 30, 1860.

SIR: In compliance with your instructions, I have the honor to submit the following summary of the business of this office during the fiscal year ending June 30, 1860.

The amount covered into the treasury during the year by 3,335 warrants was:

From customs, lands, and miscellaneous sources	$77,050,867 94
From Interior Department	251,950 98
From War Department	1,539,073 82
From Navy Department	1,701,412 97
Total	80,543,305 71

Which includes repayments of previous advances and amounts transferred from one appropriation to another in adjusting the balances of settled accounts.

The payments during the same period on 12,924 warrants and by 13,275 drafts were:

For civil, diplomatic, public debt, and miscellaneous	$45,796,058 95
For Interior Department	4,304,068 47
For War Department	17,948,810 92
For Navy Department	13,216,377 93
Total	81,265,316 27

Which also includes payments for transfers of balances in adjusting settled accounts.

The amount received at the several offices of the treasury for the use of the Post Office Department was	$11,340,805 04
And the amount of 6,600 post office warrants	10,360,824 05

Balance at the credit of the said department, subject to draft at the close of the year, $1,022,293 06.

The sum of $15,895,400, has been removed from one depository to another during the year, for the purpose of being coined, or for making disbursements for the public service.

Nine hundred and eighty-four transfer drafts were issued to authorize the movement of this amount, part of which was effected by actual transportation, and the remainder by the common practice of exchange, whereby much expense was avoided and a premium obtained on a considerable portion.

The practice of holding moneys drawn from the treasury at the credit of and subject to the orders of disbursing officers, continues to work satisfactorily, and has been extended considerably ever since the report of last year.

The receipts in the money branch of this office on treasury account proper, from all sources during the year, amounted to $7,884,737 98, of which $5,026,000, was transferred to it without expense by means of 2,606 checks given in exchange for coin paid in advance. Treasury drafts amounting to $7,377,200 42 have been satisfied, either with coin or by being entered to the credit of disbursing officers. Sixty-five accounts have been kept with disbursing officers, and at least 16,000 of their checks paid, amounting to $7,191,000.

In addition to the ordinary business of the office, we issued during the year 22,787 treasury notes, amounting to $19,345,200.

My recent connection with this office, and consequent want of personal knowledge of the operations set forth above, disqualify me from speaking of them decidedly, but I am satisfied, by what I have seen since my accession, that all the duties were performed before, as they have been since, with highly commendable despatch and accuracy.

W. C. PRICE,
Treasurer United States.

Hon. HOWELL COBB, *Secretary of the Treasury.*

SPECIMEN FRACTIONAL CURRENCY.

There has been sold at full face-value prices, of the various kinds o fractional currency, for specimens, with faces and backs printed sep arately, and little, if any, of which will ever be returned for payment $20,317 05.

EXCHANGE.

There has been received into the treasury, since a separate accoun has been kept thereof, for premiums on the sale of bills of exchange, a follows:

Prior to July 1, 1867	$66,410 3
In fiscal year closing with June 30, 1868	24,148 3
Total receipts for exchange	90,558 6

CONSCIENCE FUND.

There has been received into the treasury in various ways, from vari ous unknown persons, and in various sums, from a single cent upward since November, 1863, from which time a separate account has been kep thereof, as follows, to wit:

Prior to July 1, 1867	$47,578 4
In fiscal year closing with June 30, 1868	49,114 1
Total received since separate account has been kept	96,692 6

POST OFFICE DEPARTMENT.

The receipts and expenditures for and on account of the Post Offic Department for the fiscal year have been as follows:

Cash, Dr.

Balance brought forward from last year's account		$2,003,345 2
Received at Washington, D. C.	$269,100 02	
Received at Boston, Mass.	673,616 61	
Received at New York, N. Y.	4,202,691 01	
Received at Philadelphia, Pa.	534,054 00	
Received at St. Louis, Mo.	327,145 07	
Received at San Francisco, Cal.	1,110,832 26	
Received at Charleston, S. C.	188,291 90	
Received at New Orleans, La.	435,729 94	
Received at Denver, Col.	5,212 12	
Received at Buffalo, N. Y.	729 66	
Received at Chicago, Ill.	20,000 00	
Received at Olympia, W. T.	18 00	
Received at Louisville, Ky.	656 22	
Received at Pittsburg, Pa.	1,299 22	
Received at Cincinnati, Ohio	15 90	
Received at Des Moines, Iowa	242 50	
Received at St. Paul, Minn.	1,818 00	

eceived at Little Rock, Ark	$1,083 84	
eceived at Raleigh, N. C.	2,657 24	
eceived at Galveston, Texas	19 99	
eceived at Portland, Oregon	775 62	
eceived at Norfolk, Va.	719 71	
eceived at Dubuque, Iowa	58 84	
eceived at Savannah, Ga.	784 79	
eceived at Nashville, Tenn	440 52	
eceived at Concord, N. H.	20 00	
eceived at Cleveland, Ohio	194 43	
eceived at Richmond, Va.	28 67	
eceived at Westchester, Pa.	45 00	
eceived at San Antonio, Texas	104 00	
eceived at Knoxville, Tenn.	190 50	
eceived at First Nat'l Bank, Washington	2,168 95	
		$7,780,744 53
or amount of old warrants cancelled		1,420 00
Total		9,785,509 78

Warrants were issued on the various offices, and for the aggregate ıounts, as follows:

Cash, Cr.

ı Treasurer of the United States, Washington	$308,719 46
ı assistant treasurer at Boston	674,943 64
ı assistant treasurer at New York	5,572,756 40
ı assistant treasurer at Philadelphia	637,821 15
ı assistant treasurer at St. Louis	450,213 93
ı assistant treasurer at San Francisco	393,143 92
ı assistant treasurer at Charleston	236,964 53
ı assistant treasurer at New Orleans	546,668 23
ı assistant treasurer at Denver	829 47
ı designated depositary at Baltimore	620 14
ı designated depositary at Buffalo	3,426 65
ı designated depositary at Chicago	16,424 12
ı designated depositary at Louisville	1,136 89
ı designated depositary at Pittsburg	3,498 14
ı designated depositary at St. Paul	1,135 14
ı First National Bank of Des Moines	242 50
ı First National Bank of Washington	1,945 50
ı Merchants' National Rank of Little Rock	53 41
City National Bank of Grand Rapids	364 60
Raleigh National Bank of Raleigh	524 05
	8,851,431 87
id for suspended warrants on New Orleans	2,261 57
lance in cash to new account	931,816 34
Total	9,785,509 78

RECAPITULATION.

Cash, Dr.

To cash balance from year ending June 30, 1867	$2,003,345
Receipts from postmasters, government of the United States, and others	7,780,744
Warrants cancelled and money redeposited	1,420
Total	9,785,509

Cash, Cr.

By 5,192 warrants paid by drafts	$8,851,431
Suspended warrants on New Orleans paid	2,261
Balance to new account	931,816
Total	9,785,509

MONEYS DRAWN FROM THE TREASURY.

The following is a statement of moneys drawn from the treasury th were not receipts from the Post Office Department, but were appropriat for its use by Congress under the several laws as specified, and at t times and for the amounts as follows:

Under chapter 41 of the laws of 1867, passed February 18, 1867:

July 11, 1867, Treasury warrant No. 704	$225,000
October 5, 1867, Treasury warrant No. 1068	225,000
January 11, 1868, Treasury warrant No. 33	225,000
April 1, 1868, Treasury warrant No. 380	225,000
	900,000
For overland mail and marine transportation to California under the same act for mail steamship service between San Francisco and Japan and China, October 24, 1867, Treasury warrant No. 1156	$41,666
Under the same act for mail steamship service between United States and Brazil November 2, 1867, by Treasury warrant No. 1227	150,000
Under acts of Congress passed March 3, 1847, and March 3, 1851, for compensation for mail service performed for the two houses of Congress and other departments and offices of the government November 6, 1867, Treasury warrant No. 1237, accumulation of years	1,000,000
Under the act of July 30, 1867, for carrying the mails on roads established by the 39th Congress, 1st session, for year ending June 30, 1867—January 25, 1868, Treasury warrant No. 99	486,525
Under the acts of Congress passed March 3, 1847, and March 3, 1851, for compensation for mail service performed for the two houses of Congress and other departments and offices of the government—April 2, 1868, Treasury warrant No. 385	1,400,000
Total received from the government	3,978,191

The last named sum, received from the government of the United States for various services performed for it by the Post Office Department, is a part of the receipts, and also of the expenditures, as stated in the foregoing tables.

In addition to the amounts of receipts into the treasury as aforestated, there has been received by postmasters on account of letter postage, newspapers and pamphlets, registered letters, emoluments, stamps, dead letters, internal revenue, fines and miscellaneous; and there has been paid out again on the orders of the Post Office Department drawn on postmasters for compensation to postmasters, ship, steamboat and way letters, transportation of mails, wrapping paper, office furniture, advertising, mail bags, blanks, agents and assistants, mail locks, keys and stamps, mail depredations and special agents, clerks for office, postage stamps and stamped envelopes, letter carriers, dead letters, foreign mails, and miscellaneous, a like amount for the aggregate sums, and for and in the quarters in the fiscal year as follows:

For the quarter ending September 30, 1867	$3, 293, 665 42
For the quarter ending December 31, 1867	3, 344, 164 92
For the quarter ending March 31, 1868	3, 459, 914 84
For the quarter ending June 30, 1868	3, 586, 164 85
Total of such receipts and expenditures in fiscal year	13, 683, 910 03

MONEY LETTERS FROM POSTMASTERS.

In order to facilitate the return of worn-out and defaced fractional currency to the treasury, the Post Office Department has issued instructions to postmasters, requiring them to receive all such currency, and to forward it, in sums of three dollars or more, to the treasury of the United States.

The number of money packages received by mail, during the fiscal year, averaged over one hundred to every executive day; and the number is constantly on the increase. Complaints reach this office almost daily of the loss of such money letters. These alleged losses have been, with but a single exception, of letters that were not registered, and in that case the letter was traced to the post office in this city. The law, as it now stands, permits all communications by mail, including these money packages, to come free of postage to the Treasurer of the United States. But it does not authorize a postmaster to register such letters, except on the payment of the extra charge for its registration. Now, as it is desirable that this defaced currency should be returned to the treasury, and as it is made compulsory on postmasters to so return it, and as they are obliged to do this at their own risk of loss, and without pay for the service, it seems but fair that they should be permitted to register all money letters from themselves to the Treasurer or the treasury of the United States without charge. The passage of a law authorizing such free registration of their money letters is, therefore, most respectfully recommended.

OFFICIAL CORRESPONDENCE.

There were received during the fiscal year, through the mails, 99,150 official letters. Of this number 31,075 contained money or bonds. There were received by express in the cash division 3,872, and in the redemption division 18,636 packages containing money. There were sent by mail 87,905 letters, of which copies were kept. Of these 6,680 were in manuscript, and the remainder were partially printed and partially written in 42 different kinds of blank forms, many of these containing checks or money, and copies of all of them are preserved in bound books; 34,022 additional contained drafts payable to order, and no other enclosure. There were sent by express 16,462 money-packages. The account stated in figures stands thus:

Received by express containing money in cash division	3,872
Received by express containing money in redemption division	18,636
Received by mail containing money or bonds	31,075
Received by mail containing no money	68,075
Total of letters and money packages received	121,658

There were transmitted as follows:

By mail, in manuscript	6,680
By mail, drafts payable to order	34,022
By express, money-packages	16,462
By mail, printed forms filled up	81,225
Total of letters and money packages sent	138,389

Most of the printed-form letters contained money or checks.

UNCLAIMED INTEREST ON GOVERNMENT REGISTERED STOCKS.

From year to year, for a quarter of a century, beginning in 1843, and coming down to the present time, there has accumulated for unclaimed dividends belonging to a large number of unknown persons for interest due on registered United States stocks, which amounted in the aggregate, excluding such as had not been due over one year, and such as the parties in whose name it stood knew of, an amount aggregating $65,551,04 in coin. This is an amount not much in excess of that received in the fiscal year just closed, to the credit of the "Conscience fund." There seemed to be no good reason why the government should not be at least as just and honest to those of its citizens to whom money is due from it, as the repentant individuals had proved themselves who had made this restitution to the government. The Secretary will recollect that on stating these facts to him, and the further fact that certain persons, claim agents and others, outside of the department, had somehow obtained knowledge of these dues, and were procuring powers of attorney from the persons entitled to receive this money, and that these attorneys had commenced collecting the same, at a charge of from 10 to 50 per cent. to their principals for the service, that he verbally instructed the treasurer to give the fact that this interest remained due and unclaimed, to the public. In compliance with these, your instructions, the reporters for the newspapers were furnished with the statement, and it was very generally published that notice would in some way be given the parties interested. This notice effectually and at once closed the business of the 50 per cent. speculating attorneys. A clerk was then specially assigned to the duty to ascertain, if possible, the places of th residence of all the parties entitled to receive any dividend on stocks that had been standing to their credit for one year or more.

Letters have been addressed to 358 individuals, corporations and firms; 317 such have responded, and there has already been paid to these nearly one-half of the amount that remained so unclaimed, viz.: $32,362 08, in gold. There is still a list containing 809 names of persons whose residence cannot be ascertained, to whom there is due the balance remaining unpaid of $33,188 96. The knowledge that this interest is due would, no doubt, reach most of the persons entitled to receive the same, if a full list of the names and the amounts due each respectively should be published. But this would require an expenditure of money for which there is no appropriation by law.

It is, therefore, most respectfully suggested that Congress be asked to pass a law authorizing and directing the publication annually, on a day to be named in the law, in one or more of the leading newspapers of the country, a full list of the names to whom due, and the amounts of all such dividends that have remained due and unclaimed for one year or more. So long as the government shall be obliged to pay interest for the use of money, the interest on these unclaimed dividends would, no doubt, be sufficient to cover the cost and expense of the advertising. All dividends that should remain unclaimed for one year after three consecutive annual publications thereof, might be covered into the treasury. This course would certainly indemnify the government for all the cost of advertising.

OUTSTANDING LIABILITIES ACCOUNT.

Under the act entitled "An act to facilitate the settlement of the accounts of the Treasurer of the United States," passed May 2, 1866, there has been covered into the treasury to the proper appropriation, and to the credit of the persons entitled to receive the various amounts so covered in, at the times and from the sources as follows, viz:

Treasurer's drafts in 3d quarter of 1866	$87,472 75
Treasurer's drafts in 4th quarter of 1866	68,756 16
Treasurer's drafts in 1st quarter of 1867	7,017 00
Treasurer's drafts in 2d quarter of 1868	8,857 03
	172,102 94
Disbursing officers' checks in 4th quarter of 1867	940 01
Total amount covered in since the passage of the law	173,042 95

It will be observed that of the large amount so covered in nearly the whole was on unclaimed amounts due on drafts payable to various persons, that were issued by the Treasurer of the United States, and that the amounts so covered in that were due individuals on the checks of disbursing officers were insignificantly small, aggregating less than $1,000.

The statement of the account is as follows, to wit:

Covered in on drafts issued by the Treasurer	$172,102 94
Covered in on checks issued by disbursing officers	940 01
Total amount covered in to June 30, 1868	173,042 95

There has been paid to persons entitled thereto	$3,970 73
Remaining unclaimed in treasury June 30, 1868	169,072 22
Total as above stated as covered in	173,042 95

It is a noticeable fact that of the large amount that has been covered into the treasury, but a comparatively small amount has since, although nearly two years have elapsed, been drawn out and paid to the persons to whom it belonged.

It is believed that if an efficient system should be inaugurated, whereby all government disbursing officers should be compelled strictly to comply with the requirements of the law, large sums would be covered into the treasury for the benefit of the persons entitled thereto, and that in default of being claimed by such persons, would innure to the benefit of the whole people of the United States.

If a regulation were to be established compelling all government disbursing officers to remit to the proper officer of the treasury, with their vouchers and statements of their accounts, a detailed schedule setting forth the number, date, amount, on what particular office drawn, and to whom, and for which particular voucher given, of all checks issued by such officer; and then, if all depositaries and agents of the government, be they the Treasurer, assistant treasurers, designated depositaries, or national banks acting as such, should be required at stated periods to forward all the checks of government disbursing officers that had been paid by them, and charged to the account of such disbursing officer, to the proper officer of the Treasury Department; in order that each check might be put on file with the voucher for which it was given, there would then be a perfect check on all government officers, and it is believed that large sums that are now lost would, under such regulations, be saved to the true owners of the same, or to the people. The present law works well so far as it goes. With the additional requirements as suggested, and with the change recommended in my last report, so that any outstanding liability may be covered into the treasury at the end of one year, instead of three years as now, it will accomplish all the benefits that were anticipated from its passage.

MODES OF DESTRUCTION OF UNITED STATES NOTES AND NATIONAL BANK NOTES.

As Congress failed to act upon my suggestions in regard to the destruction of national bank notes, and as I consider them of great importance to the banks and to the government, and especially to the latter, I desire to again say what I said in my last annual report. No more specific mode for the destruction of any United States notes that had become mutilated, or otherwise unfitted for use, occurs in any one of the acts authorizing the issue of such notes, than that "they shall be cancelled

The mutilated securities, after cancellation by punching and cutting, are placed in a large revolving iron cylinder, which is then securely locked with three locks, the keys to the respective locks being kept one each by the three members of the committee appointed to witness their destruction. While so locked in the cylinder, they are treated through a flexible tube and an opening in the gudgeon with chemicals and steam, until they are thoroughly macerated and reduced to a fine pulp. The committee then unlock the cylinder, and certify to the total destruction of the securities. The daily product of this operation is worth between $300 and $400 dollars in money.

By the "Act to provide a national currency," which was passed while the practice of burning United States notes was still in vogue, and copying after the treasury regulations then in force, it was provided by the 32d section of that act, in reference to the retiring of mutilated national bank notes, that they "shall be burned to ashes." The same reasons that existed for the change from burning to maceration as to United States securities, apply with equal force to the notes of the national banks, and in an especial manner to those of the banks that have failed, and for the redemption of whose notes the government has thereby become liable. Such a change would do away with the necessity for two separate committees and two distinct establishments now kept up for the destruction of two kinds of currency.

A change in the national currency act, to make it conform, in regard to the destruction of their mutilated circulating notes, to the practice of the Treasury Department, would be safer and would save much money, and would be otherwise beneficial to both the banks and to the government.

So, too, if the national banks should be permitted to cut off, say one quarter, longitudinally from the bottom of all their notes, including the signatures of the president and the cashier, leaving the corporate name of the bank, the denomination, the numbers, and the seal intact, before sending them to the Treasury Department for destruction, all danger from loss on such notes while *in transitu* and while here would be wholly avoided. This last suggestion, if carried into effect, would save the banks the necessity, and the consequent expense, of employing an agent, or being here by one of their officers to witness the destruction of their notes. It is hoped that Congress may give these suggestions favorable consideration.

DUPLICATE CHECKS.

A very large proportion of the payments of this office, and nearly, if not quite, all those by disbursing officers are made through the medium of checks on this and the various other offices of the treasury that keep agency accounts. This mode of transacting the public business has become an absolute necessity, and it cannot now be dispensed with. It not unfrequently happens that these checks are lost in transit or otherwise. Whenever this is the case with checks of disbursing officers, the persons entitled to receive pay thereon, under present arrangements, have no remedy; and although the check may be payable to order, and therefore not payable without the proper endorsement of the person entitled to receive pay thereon, yet the payee or his assignee is forever precluded from receiving pay on any such lost check.

This is certainly a very great hardship, and the evil should be remedied. To some extent this has been done by the third section of the act entitled "An act to facilitate the payment of soldiers' bounties under the act of 1866," passed March 19, 1868. By that statute it is enacted "that the assistant treasurers at New York and San Francisco be and are hereby directed to pay duplicate checks for bounties granted under said act, upon notice and proof of the loss of the original check or checks, under such regulations as the Secretary of the Treasury may direct."

This act, it will be noticed, applies to only two of the many offices on which checks of government officers are drawn, and to but a single kind of checks, and that the kind, too, that will soon cease to be issued at all. With regard to the more numerous kinds, and which will probably always be issued, treasury officers refuse to pay on the *duplicate* checks of disbursing officers, and disbursing officers refuse to issue a second *original* check for the same payment, each of these officers claiming that it would not be safe for them to deviate in that regard from their respective rules. So the payee or assignee of a lost check has no remedy but to find the check. Even where such check is known to be totally destroyed there is no redress. Now, in the case of lost drafts that were issued in payment of warrants there is no such difficulty. In such an event, upon proof of the loss of any such draft, and upon the delivery of a bond executed in double the amount of the lost draft, made in favor of the United States by the payee or assignee, with two sureties, and approved by the Comptroller of the Treasury, a duplicate is at once issued to the party entitled thereto. There seems to be no good reason why the Comptroller of the Treasury should not in like manner be authorized to approve of bonds that he may deem sufficient when executed as aforesaid in cases of checks of any officer whose accounts are finally adjusted by him, that have been or that may be lost, as he now does in the case of lost drafts.

Nor is there any apparent good reason why the Second Comptroller should not be authorized in like manner to approve, if by him deemed sufficient, of such bonds to be so given, in the case of lost checks of government disbursing officers, issued in exchange for vouchers, the final settlement and adjustment of which pertain to his office. In view of the great hardships to which government creditors who may be so unfortunate as to have lost such checks are now subjected, it is most respectfully suggested that the passage of a law, in conformity with the views herein expressed, be recommended to Congress.

PERSONNEL OF THE OFFICE.

The number of appointments during the year was		51
Reduced by resignations	22	
Reduced by removals	14	
Reduced by transfers	5	
Reduced by decease	4	
		45
Increase during the year		6
In the office at the commencement of the year		272
In the office at the close of the year, June 30, 1868		278

The amount disbursed for salaries to the above number of employés during the year was as follows, to wit:

On regular roll	$173,476 77	
On temporary roll	156,482 55	
Total payments during the year was		$329,959 32
Less income tax retained from salaries		3,793 11
Net amount paid for salaries		326,166 21

Being for each person a little less than $1,173 per annum.

REORGANIZATION OF THE OFFICE.

More time and reflection have greatly strengthened my convictions of the correctness of the suggestions made in my reports for former years in regard to the reorganization of the office of the Treasurer, and of the pay of the persons employed therein. I am now fully persuaded that all that has heretofore been said on these subjects has been too mildly put, and understated. Fearing that the suggestions heretofore presented failed, from that cause and reason, to attract the attention that they deserved, they are reproduced and repeated with the emphasis and urged with the earnestness that it is believed their justness justifies.

Having these convictions, I feel sure of pardon for their reiteration.

It therefore again becomes my duty to present to you, and through you to the Congress of the United States, the great difficulty in the way of the proper conduct and management of this office, on account of the utterly inadequate pay awarded by law to its officers, clerks, and other employés. It is exceedingly difficult to procure the services of persons of the ability, capacity, and proved integrity of character required for places of such great responsibility; and when procured, it is still more difficult to retain them.

Banks and business men find it for their interest to pay rates nearly, if not quite, double those paid by the government for like services, of persons possessing the requisite talent, experience, application, and honesty, to fit them for the constant handling of and accounting for the millions of dollars that must necessarily pass through the hands of the employés of this office daily.

Poor men—and none other than poor men, will take these places—who have the requisite talents to perform such labors accurately and with despatch, and who have the integrity to deal honestly with a government that pays them barely enough for their valuable services to support themselves and their families in the plainest manner, and by the practice of the most rigid economy, can hardly be expected to remain in their places, especially when they are eagerly sought after by banking and other corporations and business men, who appreciate and find it their interest to secure the services of such persons by the payment of much higher salaries. Few men under such circumstances, now that the country is again at peace, feel it their duty so to sacrifice themselves and their families upon the altar of patriotism. Several, however, from motives of public spirit and duty, and a hope that Congress would, in the end, do them justice, and from personal persuasion from me, have been induced to remain in their places.

The chiefs of division in this office now hold much more responsible positions than were those occupied by the heads of bureaus before the rebellion. The chief of the division of national banks holds government securities the present cash value of which exceeds $400,000,000, being more than ten times the amount formerly held by the superintendent of the banking department of the State of New York. Yet his salary is only $2,200, while that of the superintendent of the New York banks, holding less than one-tenth of the securities, was $5,000.

The present system of compensation of the employés in the departments of the government is wrong, unwise, unjust, and very demoralizing. Although so to a degree in all the branches of the public service, it is particularly so with respect to the females so employed. Some of these are in places of great pecuniary responsibility, and incur great risks. This is especially true of such as are employed in the redemption of the national currency, where a loss of notes, an error in the count, or the overlooking of counterfeits, makes each clerk so engaged personally liable to respond in money to the amount of any errors so made. These amounts are deducted from the salaries of such clerks regularly at the end of each month.

Banks and business firms pay their tellers and others, who are responsible for money errors, higher salaries than those who perform mere routine office business.

It would be hard to find a reason why the same rules should not obtain in the government offices, or why clerks here, performing like duties and incurring like risks, should not be paid according to their individual merits, and the risks and liabilities that they severally incur.

Then again, where the labor and responsibility is of like character, the difference in the manner of doing the work, and the amount done, between two individuals, is very great. It is well known that some clerks are able to and do perform three times, and more, the labor of some others, and that they do it, too, with more skill and every way better; and yet it is insisted by legal enactment that the very poorest of such clerks shall receive the compensation of the very best. Who will say that this is right, or that it is not unjust? A change should be made that would tend to stimulate all to well-doing, by the hope of promotion and better pay; that would bring the poorer classes up to a higher standard, and not as is now done, under the sanction of law, inevitably drag the better classes down to the level of the very poorest.

So, too, the rule that has been so long in use that it seems to have the sanction of law, by which leaves of absence are granted for a month in each year, is claimed by all alike as a prescriptive right. In these cases, as in those of leaves of absence on account of ill health, or for sickness in family, or for other cause, the poorer clerks, whose absence is of little account to the business of the office, more readily obtain these leaves, while those who do their whole or more than their duty are necessarily denied the privilege, because their better services cannot be spared.

To remedy these evils it is suggested that the law should be so changed as to authorize a more perfect classification of the various employés of the department. This could be so done as to do justice to all, without increasing the aggregate amount of money now paid for salaries. The loss of time by reason and on account of regular leaves of absence, sickness, and from other causes, is believed to be more than 20 per cent. A law authorizing an increase of that percentage to the pay of each employé, and forbidding the payment for lost time for any cause whatever, would procure much more and better service than is now had.

The following plan for the reorganization of this office is most respectfully submitted:

	Per annum.
An assistant treasurer	$4,000
A cashier	3,500
An assistant cashier	3,000
A chief of division of banks	2,800
A chief of division of redemptions	2,800
A chief of division of issues	2,800
A chief of division of general accounts	2,800
A chief of division of treasurer's accounts	2,600
A chief of division of loans	2,600
A chief of division of correspondence	2,600
A paying teller	2,600
A receiving teller	2,600
An assistant paying teller	2,400
An assistant receiving teller	2,400
Two principal bookkeepers, each	2,400
Fifteen fifth class clerks, each	2,000
Fifteen fourth class clerks, each	1,800
Fifteen third class clerks, each	1,600
Fifteen second class clerks, each	1,400
Five first class clerks, each	1,200
One engineer	1,200
Nine messengers, each	1,000
Nine assistant messengers, each	800
Seven laborers, each	700
Fifteen female clerks, each	1,200
Fifteen female clerks, each	1,100
Fifteen female clerks, each	1,000
Seventeen female clerks, each	900
Seventeen female clerks, each	800
Seventeen female clerks, each	700
Seven female messengers, each	600
Seven female assistant messengers, each	500
Nine female laborers, each	400

Even under this arrangement it would for a time be necessary to employ additional clerks, but it is hoped that after a short time, with the return of specie payments, not only all extra or additional clerks, but some of the regular force as above recommended, might from time to time be dispensed with.

The experiment of employing females as clerks has been, so far as this office is concerned, a complete success. Indeed, in many kinds of office work, like the manipulating of fractional currency, and in all kinds of counting, and in detecting counterfeits, they excel, and, in my opinion, are to be preferred to male clerks.

There is as much difference in point of ability between the female clerks as there is between the several classes of male clerks. Some of the former incur great risks, being responsible for all mistakes in count, or in overlooking counterfeits. Restitution for these errors sometimes takes, during a month, more than one-half of the month's salary. It not unfrequently happens that a number unite to make up the loss of the unfortunate ones, thus detracting something from the salaries of each. All such as are subject to these risks should be paid accordingly.

These and other considerations have satisfied me that all should be better paid than they now are, and that the female clerks should be brought up nearer to the pay level of the male clerks.

The truth is that many of the former now do as much work, if not more, and do it as well, if not better, for $900 per annum, than some of the latter are able to do, who receive a yearly salary of just twice that amount.

It is true that these remarks apply more especially to one kind of work, but they apply to a kind of work that must be done so long as the issue of paper currency shall be continued.

The amount of fractional currency now in circulation exceeds $33,000,000. This saves to the people $2,000,000 in interest yearly. About $22,000,000—being nearly two-thirds of the entire circulation—is returned every year. As a like amount is issued it requires the preparing, counting and issuing, and the redemption, counting and destruction of $44,000,000 of this small currency annually. So long as this is continued, the services of female clerks cannot be dispensed with, save by replacing them by male clerks, whose salaries would cost the government nearly double the amount now paid for this service. The female clerks, with but few exceptions, are subject to greater risks of loss by reason of miscounts or by passing counterfeits, for which each one is pecuniarily liable and responsible, than nine-tenths of the male clerks, whose principal occupations are books and accounts, are subject to.

Right and fair dealing, therefore, demand that their pay should be assimilated more nearly than it now is to that of the other sex for like services and responsibilities. Impressed by these and other good considerations, I have been induced to make some changes from the plan submitted in my last annual report for the reorganization of this office. The principal change is one higher grade for female clerks. This additional grade of the *female clerks* fixes the pay of that, the *best class*, just as high as that paid to the *lowest class* of the *male clerks*. It does seem that no right-thinking mind can find reasonable objections to such a plan.

While candor required that this statement should be made in behalf of a certain class of meritorious clerks, justice demands that it should be stated that nearly all the employés of this office are underpaid. Their salaries, as a general rule, are fixed just above starvation prices. Were it not that this office is considered as a kind of business school, from which young men may after a time graduate and then obtain situations elsewhere where the pay for like services is better, it would be next to impossible to obtain or to retain the services of persons competent to manage the business transactions of this office, which exceed that of any moneyed institution in the world. Just so soon as young men become properly educated to the correct understanding and proper management of the public business they receive invitations to go elsewhere, to become bookkeepers, tellers and cashiers, at salaries largely in advance of those paid by the government. This draft upon the most competent men in the office is in constant progress. The policy of permitting this seems to be penny-wise and pound-foolish economy. Instead of educating men to manage other men's business, the government should employ only such persons as had already a good business education. It should pay such salaries as would command the best required talent, and that would retain the services of such as it had itself educated.

BASE METAL TOKENS.

The proposition that a government should not do anything that the law or the moral sense of the people would denounce as dishonest in an individual will scarce be denied by any right-thinking man. No community would for a day submit to having imposed upon it by individuals, inside or outside of the community, false, irredeemable and almost valueless tokens, wherewith to redeem and replace their promises to pay lawful money. Yet this is precisely what the general government has done and is still doing.

After the general suspension of specie payments by the moneyed institutions of the country, and by the government of the United States as well, all the silver fractional parts of a dollar simultaneously disappeared from all the business channels of the whole country. A substitute must be had. Ordinary postage stamps were at once, for the want of a better, used for the purpose. These were soon found to be very inconvenient and entirely inadequate.

Congress then authorized the Secretary of the Treasury to substitute paper bills representing the fractional parts of the dollar. The Secretary, under this authority, issued such bills of the denominations of 50 cents, 25 cents, 10 cents, 5 cents, and 3 cents. All these issues were by law made receivable to any amount for United States stamps, and they were all exchangeable for United States notes by the assistant treasurers and the designated depositaries of the United States, in sums of not less than $3; and they were further made receivable in payment of all dues to the United States for less than $5, except for customs, which are payable in gold. Congress has passed laws by which successively first the three cent and then the five cent notes were inhibited from being issued.

These are now almost entirely withdrawn from circulation. This convenient small change, that was in various ways receivable for public dues, and at the same time convertible into lawful money of the United States, has been replaced, under the specious plea of a "speedy return to specie payments," by an almost worthless, irredeemable, poisonous, and stinking copper and nickel token currency. The five cent tokens are made a legal tender for $1, and are redeemable in sums of not less than $100. All the others, including the one cent, the two cent, and the three cent tokens, and whether made of copper alone or of copper and nickel, are entirely irredeemable, and, as an irredeemable currency, have already become a nuisance by their great accumulations in the hands of small dealers.

Officers engaged in government collections, especially those connected with the Post Office Department, suffer in consequence. Postmasters are by law compelled to receive these government tokens in payment for postage stamps, and are then immediately liable to the government for the amounts of such sales in good money. But the government that sold these tokens at par for their face value, or paid them as money to its creditors, now turns round and refuses to receive them back in payment from its own officers, who were by law compelled to receive them on account of the government.

Postmasters who were so obliged to receive these tokens have offered them by the bagful in payment of their post office receipts at the counter of the treasury, and have been compelled to carry them home again, because the Treasurer cannot receive over 60 cents in three-cent pieces, nor over four cents in one or two-cent pieces, in any one payment. Was there ever an act of the government of a respectable people that, for meanness, can compare with this? An individual that would practice such a confidence game would be branded as a two-penny thief, and would soon be consigned to a house of correction. A government that practices such frauds upon the people cannot hope long to retain the respect of anybody. It has been intimated, and there are those that are uncharitable enough to believe the story, that the ownership of an unprofitable nickel mine had something to do in influencing the passage of these "speedy-return-to-specie-payment" laws.

A government that has the meanness to openly repudiate the payment or redemption of its one and two-cent issues will soon be suspected of being none too good to repudiate payment of the larger obligations of the nation. He that is not faithful in small things will scarcely be trusted in large ones. Congress can prevent this danger and save the reputation of the government only by making immediate provision for the prompt redemption of these, its smallest, obligations in lawful money.

The business and money transactions of the office, although steadily on the decrease, still continue to be of enormous proportions. The tables show that the aggregate of the necessary entries in the year closing with June 30, 1865, amounted to the sum of $9,117,855,012 58; in the year closing with June 30, 1867, to only $5,930,467,941 90; and in the year closing with June 30, 1868, to $5,522,361,160 05; being a falling off in the latter year of $408,106,781 85 from that of the preceding year. For the eight years beginning with July 1, 1860, and ending with June 30, 1868, the aggregate of these business transactions amounted to the almost inconceivable sum of $41,777,840,607 13. These figures would be read in the countries of continental Europe, forty-one billion seven hundred and seventy-seven million eight hundred and forty thousand six hundred and seven dollars and thirteen cents. But in Great Britain and its dependencies it would be more correctly expressed forty-one thousand seven hundred and seventy-seven million eight hundred and forty thousand and six hundred and seven dollars and thirteen cents. This last statement is not made for you, nor for Congress, but for the persons who almost every day inquire, *what is a billion?*

All this immense amount entered upon the books of this office, and the sum of $21,004,748,179 54, being very nearly one-half of the whole amount, originated in and belongs to the office in Washington exclusively.

When it is taken into consideration that nearly 300 persons are engaged in this office, and that two-thirds of the number are daily employed in the handling and charge of money, it is really a subject for wonder, and of gratulation as well, to all, inside and outside of the office, that not a single dollar has been lost to the people of the United States. This is no doubt due to kind fortune, and a kinder overruling Providence; but the honesty, fidelity, watchfulness, and efficiency of those associated with me in the discharge of the arduous duties and fearful responsibilities of the office should not be overlooked; neither should I, nor do I forget, the kind assistance always extended me by the chiefs and others of other bureaus, and especially the generous support received at your hands.

I am, sir, very respectfully, yours,

F. E. SPINNER,
Treasurer of the United States.

Hon. HUGH MCCULLOCH,
Secretary of the Treasury.

SCHEDULE A.

United States treasury, New York, receipts and payments for the fiscal year ending June 30, 1868.

RECEIPTS.	
On account of customs	$113, 242, 494 87
On account of internal revenue	4, 260, 302 90
On account of miscellaneous	458, 654, 921 51
On account of patent fees	52, 574 85
On account of Post Office Department	4, 877, 691 01
On account of coin certificates	77, 924, 910 00
On account of transfers	113, 741, 466 26
On account of temporary loan	50, 000, 000 00
PAYMENTS.	
On account Treasury Department	862, 109, 583 77
On account Post Office warrants	5, 584, 159 97
Amount credited to disbursing officers' account	169, 255, 148 73
Amount checks paid on disbursing officers' account	165, 013, 127 23
Amount paid for interest on public debt, (gold)	71, 619, 531 18¼
Amount paid for interest on public debt, (currency)	6, 024, 214 94½
Amount paid on temporary loan	6, 274, 735 33

SCHEDULE B.

Statement of the receipts and disbursements of the office of the assistant treasurer of the United States at Boston for the fiscal year ending June 30, 1868.

	Receipts.	Disbursements.
Customs	$17, 698, 816 66	....
Transfers	34, 432, 082 25	....
Temporary loan	250, 000 00	$976, 000 00
Internal revenue stamps	766, 105 00	....
Patent fees	40, 908 25	....
Fractional currency redeemed	....	1, 329, 130 00
Legal-tender notes redeemed	....	838, 000 00
Post Office Department	673, 616 61	675, 189 47
Disbursing officers	14, 611, 209 41	14, 187, 981 91
Fishing bounties	691 39	2, 719 96
Treasurer's general account	....	52, 172, 082 23
Interest account	15, 286, 158 53	17, 765, 259 80
Miscellaneous	1, 035, 383 28	....
Fractional currency	....	1, 200, 000 00

F. HAVEN, JR., *Assistant Treasurer U. S.*

SCHEDULE C.

U. S. TREASURY, PHILADELPHIA, PA., *July* 1, 1868.

SIR: I herewith submit a report of the receipts and disbursements of this office during the fiscal year ending June 30, 1868.

The receipts which were placed to the credit of the Treasurer of the United States during the fiscal year were as follows, viz:

From transfer orders	$23, 860, 000 00
From customs	8, 526, 129 87
From internal revenue tax	37 50
From internal revenue stamps	517, 055 00
From patent fees	19, 180 50
From semi-annual duty	53, 572 39
From miscellaneous	4, 012, 226 58
From United States moieties	32, 139 45
From Post Office	534, 151 00
Total	37, 554, 395 29
From similar sources previous year	$68, 671, 142 87
Deduct	37, 554, 395 29
Decrease of receipts this year	31, 116, 747 58

The disbursements from the office during the same term were as follows:

On general treasury	$38, 484, 244 00
On post office	621, 581 74
Total	39, 105, 825 74
Similar payments previous year	$71, 650, 335 77
Deduct	39, 105, 825 74
Decrease of payments this year	32, 544, 510 03
The payments made on disbursers' checks, numbering 26,418, including those drawn by the treasurer on his transfer account, amount to	$13, 971, 746 36
Similar payments previous year	11, 565, 614 07
Increase of payments this year	2, 406, 132 29
The amount standing to the credit of disbursing officers on the morning of July 1, 1867, was	$973, 382 96
Credits during fiscal year ending June 30, 1868	13, 826, 061 71
Total credits	14, 799, 444 67
Deduct total disbursements	13, 971, 746 36
Balance to credit disbursers June 30, 1868	827, 698 31
The amount of fractional currency redeemed during the fiscal year ending June 30, 1868, was	$2, 385, 377 00

The payments on account of interest on the public debt were as follows, viz:

On registered loans, (coin)	$4, 342, 268 25
On coupon loans, (coin)	4, 943, 647 61
On temporary loans, (L. M)	161, 641 02
On Pacific railroad loans, (L. M)	115, 142 97
Total	9, 563, 699 85
Similar payments previous year	7, 770, 683 24
Increase of payments this year	1, 793, 016 61

The payments of the coupons detached from the 7.30 notes, the interest on the compound interest notes and 7.30 notes redeemed, and on one and two-year notes, are not included in the foregoing, as they constitute a part of the disbursements from the general treasury.

SCHEDULE D.

Receipts and disbursements at the office of the assistant treasurer at St. Louis for the fiscal year ending June 30, 1868.

Receipts	$47, 192, 950 65
Disbursements	44, 812, 849 99

SCHEDULE E.

Receipts and disbursements at the office of the assistant treasurer at New Orleans for the fiscal year ending June 30, 1868.

Receipts*	$15, 389, 094 47
Disbursements	18, 972, 193 33

* Balance on hand in July, 1867, not given.

SCHEDULE F.

Receipts and disbursements at the office of the United States depositary at Baltimore for the fiscal year ending June 30, 1868.

Receipts	$16,366,185 26
Disbursements	13,323,422 02

SCHEDULE G.

Receipts and disbursements at the office of the United States depositary at Chicago, Illinois, for the fiscal year ending June 30, 1868.

Receipts	$11,493,775 65
Disbursements	10,648,622 22

SCHEDULE H.

Receipts and disbursements at the office of the United States depositary at Pittsburg, Pennsylvania, for the fiscal year ending June 30, 1868.

Receipts	$2,731,821 93
Disbursements	1,990,497 20

SCHEDULE I.

Receipts and disbursements at the office of the assistant treasurer at Charleston, South Carolina, for the fiscal year ending June 30, 1868.

Receipts	$10,875,254 08
Disbursements	9,724,170 91

SCHEDULE K.

Receipts and disbursements at the office of the assistant treasurer at Denver, Colorado, for the fiscal year ending June 30, 1868.

Receipts	$2,300 00
Disbursements	2,235 00

SCHEDULE L.

Receipts and disbursements at the United States depositary at Cincinnati, Ohio, for the fiscal year ending June 30, 1868.

Receipts	$23,674,405 25
Disbursements	20,908,414 79

SCHEDULE M.

Receipts and disbursements at the United States depositary at Louisville, Kentucky, for the fiscal year ending June 30, 1868.

Receipts	$6,882,527 83
Disbursements	6,882,527 83

REPORT OF THE REGISTER OF THE TREASURY.

TREASURY DEPARTMENT, REGISTER'S OFFICE,
November 11, 1868.

SIR: I have the honor to submit a statement of the business of the Register's office for the fiscal year ending June 30, 1868.

RECEIPTS AND EXPENDITURES.

The force employed in the division of receipts and expenditures comprises twenty-three (23) male clerks; its records consist of nine (9) legers, for personal accounts, eight (8) appropriation legers, five (5) journals, and a large number of auxiliary books, in which accounts, warrants, and drafts are registered. In addition to this, the annual statement of receipts and expenditures, in detail, is made up and condensed for printing, and the proof-sheets examined and corrected. A list of all "receipts and expenditures," warrants issued during each quarter, is prepared for quarterly settlement with the Treasurer; copies of records and accounts required in the prosecution of suits are prepared in this division and authenticated by the Register.

The custody of the files and their arrangement are also intrusted to this division. In addition to this, there is a large amount of miscellaneous work done, which cannot be detailed in this report.

With the exception of warrants issued for payments and repayments in the War, Navy, and Interior (Pension and Indian) Departments, the business of this division shows an increase over the preceding year, while the force employed has been diminished.

The number of warrants issued during the year for civil, diplomatic, miscellaneous, internal revenue, and public debt expenditures, was	22, 231
In the preceding year	21, 955
Increase	276
The number of warrants issued for receipts from customs, lands, direct tax, internal revenue, and miscellaneous sources was	9, 018
In the preceding year	8, 498
Increase	520
The number of warrants issued for payments and repayments in the War and Interior (Pension and Indian) Departments, was	9, 104
In the preceding year	10, 428
Decrease	1, 324
The number of journal pages required for the entry of accounts relating to the civil, diplomatic, internal revenue, miscellaneous and public debt receipts and expenditures, was	4, 114
In the preceding year	3, 705

The number of drafts registered was	39,684
In the preceding year	37,398
Increase	2,286

The number of certificates furnished for settlement of accounts was	6,380
In the preceding year	6,280
Increase	100

The number of accounts received from the offices of the First and Fifth Auditors, and Commissioner of the General Land Office, was	25,273
In the preceding year	23,340
Increase	1,933

LOAN BRANCH.

This branch of the Register's office is charged with the preparation of the bonds to be issued by the government, all of which are signed by the Register, the assistant register, or other officer specially authorized for that purpose; after which they are issued by the Register in accordance with the direction of the Secretary of the Treasury.

The magnitude of the trust necessarily reposed in the officers in charge of this work demands the strictest fidelity and efficiency. When it is observed that the direct issues of government securities for the last fiscal year exceeded four hundred and sixty-two millions (462,000,000) of dollars, the importance of thorough system and absolute accuracy of detail in the management of this business cannot be over-estimated.

To this end I have from time to time adopted such additional checks and safeguards as would, in my judgment, tend to prevent the possibility of error or mistake, and I am of opinion that there is, under the present system of management, no possible contingency for inaccuracy, that would not be detected in ample time to prevent injury or loss.

The following exhibits the number and amount of bonds issued during the fiscal year ending June 30, 1868:

Whole number of coupon bonds issued was 788,922, amount $375,879,900; of this amount, $373,204,600 were direct issues, $2,335,300 were issued on transfers, and $340,000 on exchange.

Whole number of registered bonds issued was 75,758, amount $201,473,650. Of this amount $88,658,800 were direct issues, $86,148,600 were issued for assignments, and $26,666,250 in exchange for coupon bonds.

Total number of bonds (coupon and registered) issued during the year was 864,680, amount $577,353,550. The following tabular statement exhibits the character, number, and amounts of the different issues, classified by their respective loans:

Statement showing the number of cases, number of bonds issued, and amount of direct issues, number of cases and number and amount of coupon and registered bonds issued and cancelled of the following loans, during the year ending June 30, 1868.

Loan.	DIRECT ISSUES.			EXCHANGES.				TRANSFERS.			
	Number of cases.	Bonds issued.	Amount.	Number of cases.	Bonds issued.	Bonds cancelled.	Amount.	Number of cases.	Bonds issued.	Bonds cancelled.	Amount.
1847								45	153	234	$800, 950
1848				13	28	73	$88, 000	61	194	235	972, 050
1858				5	682	80	746, 000	75	336	336	1, 680, 000
1860				2	15	19	23, 000	81	534	462	1, 849, 000
1861, act February 8				48	221	237	368, 000	175	406	503	955, 000
1861, act July 17	14	36	$1, 800	337	1, 291	5, 222	2, 850, 200	678	2, 732	3, 048	8, 473, 900
1862				134	1, 300	1, 439	1, 244, 500	1, 119	4, 661	5, 503	11, 350, 500
1863				178	481	1, 839	942, 700	322	1, 390	1, 324	5, 009, 300
1864, act March 3, 6 per cent								1	4	4	800
1864, act March 3, 5 per cent	128	19, 390	23, 298, 600	526	2, 846	11, 429	6, 021, 800	869	3, 201	3, 811	11, 108, 750
1864, act June 30				200	809	2, 588	2, 204, 300	442	1, 657	1, 328	4, 158, 600
1865, act March 3	25	16, 780	16, 350, 060	160	707	1, 781	1, 475, 700	510	2. 459	2, 461	6, 330, 600
1865, act March 3, consols	351	44, 872	30, 819. 150	915	3, 605	9, 452	6, 886, 200	1, 480	7, 954	6, 347	12, 111, 000
1867, act March 3, consols	14 481	699, 958	360, 623, 900	823	3, 693	7, 803	6, 491, 150	730	3, 826	3, 081	6, 576, 150
1868, act March 3, consols	196	33, 402	17, 648, 950								
Central Pacific Railroad	3	326	2, 432, 000					58	378	455	2, 458, 000
Union Pacific Railroad	9	1, 431	6, 877, 000					152	1, 038	1, 678	5, 761, 000
Union Pacific Railway, eastern division	7	337	2, 720, 000					130	906	845	4, 448, 000
Western Pacific Railroad								3	18	20	103, 000
Central Branch Union Pacific Railroad	1	65	320, 000					49	179	164	954, 000
Sioux City and Pacific Railroad	2	202	1, 112, 000					28	177	168	1, 048, 000
Total	15 217	816, 799	462, 203, 400	3, 341	15, 678	41, 962	29, 341, 550	7, 010	32, 203	31, 607	86, 148, 600

REDEMPTIONS.

Loan.	Number of cases.	Bonds cancelled.	Amount.
1847	32	266	$6, 429, 050
1848	19	280	678, 450
Total	51	546	7, 107, 500

RECAPITULATION.

Number of cases:		
Direct issues	15, 217	
Exchanges	3, 341	
Transfers	7, 010	
Redemptions	51	
		25, 619
Number of bonds issued:		
*Coupon, direct issue	785, 759	
Coupon, transfers	2, 823	
Coupon, exchanges	340	
Registered, direct issue	31, 040	
Registered, transfers	32, 203	
Registered, exchanges	12, 515	
		864, 680
Number of bonds cancelled:		
Coupon, exchanged	41, 962	
Registered, transfers	31, 607	
Redeemed	546	
		74, 115
Amount of bonds issued:		
Coupon, direct issue	$373, 204, 600	
Coupon, transfers	2, 335, 300	
Coupon, exchanges	340, 000	
Registered, direct issue	88, 658, 800	
Registered, transfers	86, 148, 600	
Registered, exchanges	26, 666, 250	
		$577, 353, 550
Amount of bonds redeemed:		
Coupon	181, 000	
Registered	6, 926, 500	
		7, 107,500

* These bonds were counted, examined, and the blank strips and cancelled coupons cut off by the ladies of the division.

Delivered to the Treasurer for destruction, defaced and cancelled bonds received from Mr. Clark, 76,191; coupons cancelled and cut from bonds, 344,381; strips cut from coupon bonds, 386,153; number of letters written, copied and mailed, or sent by express, 28,720. Schedules of interest have been made out, copied, and sent to government agents of 3,338 pages and 84,742 names. To facilitate the payment of interest at New York, the accounts have been vowelized and transferred to 32 new ledgers.

It will be observed that of the $201,473,650 registered bonds issued during the last fiscal year, $26,666,250 were issued in exchange for coupon bonds.

On the 30th of June, 1868, the market value of five-twenty coupon bonds loan of 1862 was 113, while registered bonds of the same loan, bearing the same rate of interest, were worth 109½.

The comparative value of these securities varies according to the estimate of the holders.

It will be observed that while four-fifths of the securities issued during the last fiscal year were coupon bonds, yet more than 13 per centum of the entire issue of registered stock was issued in exchange for coupon bonds. From which it would seem, that while a majority of holders prefer coupon bonds, a large number have surrendered coupon for registered bonds, notwithstanding the depreciation of the latter as compared with the former in the stock markets of this country and Europe. I am convinced that there is no substantial reason for this difference in the value of these stocks, except that coupon bonds are convertible into registered bonds, at the option of the holder, while the conversion of the latter into coupon bonds is prohibited.

Aside from this, I am convinced that the characteristics which distinguish these securities do not account for the difference in their market value.

Coupon bonds are transferred by delivery, registered bonds by assignment; in this respect the former are more desirable; but as coupon bonds are transferable by delivery, there is no remedy by which their owners may be reimbursed for their loss; while registered bonds are worthless except in the hands of their owners, and in this respect are more desirable than coupon.

The remaining difference applies to the manner in which the interest is paid. In the one case, the interest is paid on the presentation of the coupon; in the other, on demand at the depository which the party himself has selected.

I have taken the liberty of inviting your attention to this subject, because I believe that if these securities were placed on equal footing as regards conversion, the cause for the discrepancy in their values would be removed, and as it could in no event decrease the value of the one, it would necessarily, in my opinion, appreciate the other.

NOTE AND COUPON DIVISION.

The work performed in this branch of the Register's office consists in assorting, arranging, counting and registering treasury notes, compound interest notes, gold certificates, 7.30 treasury notes, and the coupons of all United States loans. In addition to this, all redeemed and exchanged bonds are examined, registered and filed by this division.

I.—*Treasury notes, comprising—*

One-year five (5) per cents., act March 3, 1863.
Two-year five (5) per cents., act March 3, 1863.
Two-year five (5) per cents., (coupon,) act March 3, 1863.

II.—*Compound interest notes, comprising—*

Three-year six (6) per cents., act March 3, 1863.
Three-year six (6) per cents., act June 30, 1864.

These notes are received from the office of the First Comptroller; the count of that office is verified, and they are then delivered to the Treasurer, in whose office they are again counted and cut in halves. The Treasurer returns the upper halves to this office, and delivers the lower to the loan branch of the Secretary's office.

The upper halves are carefully counted in this office, and arranged according to their letters (A, B, C, D,) and again counted in their respective letters, then arranged numerically, each note according to its number and denomination, after which they are registered in the records of this office, and then delivered to a committee composed of members representing the offices of the Secretary and Register, for final examination. If upon examination it is found that the books of the Secretary's office and Register's office agree in every particular, the notes are turned over to another committee for destruction.

III.—*Gold certificates.*

Gold certificates are received from the Treasurer's office. Like the

fully counted, they are arranged numerically, and entered upon the records of this office, according to their numbers and denominations. The count of the Secretary's and the Register's office is then compared, and if found to agree, the certificates are destroyed.

IV.—*Seven-thirty treasury notes.*

These notes are received from the office of the First Comptroller; they are first arranged according to their series and denominations, then according to their number, then counted and entered upon the records of the office, according to their series, numbers, and denominations, after which they are deposited in the files-room to await the redemption of those outstanding. Having been mutilated in the process of cancellation, there is no risk on account of their non-destruction; while their preservation is the means of detecting counterfeit notes or duplicates should any be presented.

V.—*Coupons.*

The coupons of all United States loans are received from the office of the First Comptroller. They are first assorted into their respective loans, series, and denominations; then carefully counted, in order to verify the schedule of the Comptroller's office; they are then arranged numerically, after which they are re-counted and entered upon the records of the office, according to their numbers, denominations, series, and loans, and then deposited in the files-room of this office.

VI.—*Redeemed and exchanged bonds.*

Redeemed and exchanged bonds having been cancelled, are sent from the loan branch division of this office to the note and coupon division, where they are arranged, counted, and registered.

Their registration is then compared with the records of the loan branch division of the Secretary's and Register's offices, and if it is found to be correct they are delivered to a committee representing the offices of the Secretary, Treasurer, and Register for destruction. Schedules containing a complete description of each security are made out in duplicate, one of which is delivered to the committee and the other retained in this office. The record of this division contains the evidence by which error, mistake, or fraud in the issue, redemption, or exchange of the national securities, or in the payment of their interest, may be instantly detected. It contains a pertinent description of each bond redeemed or exchanged, and each coupon that has been paid; and the arrangement and classification is such that each particular bond and coupon may be at once identified by reference to the record.

The public interest requires not only that this record be accurately made up, but that it be made up to the latest possible period; and for this reason the force employed should be always adequate to the current business, so as to prevent an accumulation of unfinished work.

The record discloses the history of these transactions only up to the period to which it is completed, and its value is increased as it approximates the period of the transaction which it records; and if instead of showing the actual condition of these securities—how much has been redeemed or exchanged, how much interest paid, or the amount of notes outstanding—the present record only gave their condition one, two, or more years ago, its value as a means of detecting error and preventing loss would be to a great extent destroyed.

If mistake or fraud had been committed in 1866, and the record of the transaction in which it occurred were not made up until 1868, it is evident that the opportunity for correction would be limited, if not completely lost.

At the date of my appointment as Register the conversions of the seven-thirties were in rapid progress, and were continued until after the expiration of the fiscal year 1867. The labor incident to these conversions demanded the instant attention of a large clerical force, which was supplied by relieving the employés engaged in counting and registering other securities, which resulted in a large accumulation of back work.

I found upon examination that this accumulation amounted to over four millions (4,000,000) of coupons, besides a large number of treasury notes, gold certificates, and compound interest notes.

For the reason before stated I deemed it important that this back work should be brought up; and for that purpose I requested the appointment of an additional number of female clerks, which was granted, (A.)

The whole number of clerks employed in this division on the 30th of June, 1867, was 67; the average number employed during the fiscal year ending June 30, 1868, was 87—an increase of thirty (30) per cent.

The detailed statements of the work performed during the fiscal year 1868, embraced in this report, show an increase equal to the increase of force, in addition to a careful recount of thirteen (13) millions of coupons which had been counted in 1865 and 1866.

In addition to this the entire amount of redeemed and exchanged bonds which had been received at this office prior to the date of my appointment had accumulated in the loan branch division, all of which has since been transferred to the note and coupon division, where it has been examined, arranged, counted, and registered—which labor required the services of seven (7) clerks, in addition to the number necessary for the current work of that particular branch of business.

The following tabular statements show in detail the amount of labor performed by the note and coupon division for the present fiscal year:

Statement of five per cent. treasury notes—upper halves.

Counted, assorted, arranged, registered, and examined.	Authorizing acts.	Number of pieces.	Amount.	Coupons attached.
One-year treasury notes	March 3, 1863	16,219	$336,150	
Two-year treasury notes	March 3, 1863	3,117	208,550	
Two-year treasury notes, (coupon)	March 3, 1863	745	65,000	261
Gold certificates	March 3, 1863	61,841	79,123,320	
Total		81,922	79,733,020	261
A decrease on the preceding year of		98,133	$45,154,560	1,081

NOTE, (A.)—At the date of this report, November 11, 1868, the entire work for which the additional force was employed has been brought up, and so much of the force as was not required for the current business of the office has been recommended for discharge.

Statement of six per cent. treasury notes—whole.

	Authorizing acts.	Number of pieces.	Amount.	Coupons attached.
Received from the First Comptroller:				
Whole notes, 5 and 6 per cent..	Mar. 3, 1863 & June 30, 1864	194, 064	$6, 878, 630	....
Delivered to the United States Treasurer:				
Whole notes, 5 and 6 per cent..	Mar. 3, 1863 & June 30, 1864	124, 100	3, 596, 840	....

Statement of six per cent. treasury notes—upper halves.

	Authorizing acts.	Number of pieces.	Amount.	Coupons attached.
Counted, assorted, and arranged:				
Compound-interest notes	Mar. 3, 1863	102, 185	$8, 330, 150	....
Compound-interest notes	June 30, 1864	1, 731, 106	70, 692, 940	....
Total................	....	1, 833, 291	79, 023, 090	....
An increase on the preceding year	....	822, 407	$34, 283, 950	....
Registered:				
Compound-interest notes	Mar. 3, 1863	102, 185	$8, 330, 150	....
Compound-interest notes	June 30, 1864	1, 507, 636	64, 654, 710	....
Total................	....	1, 609, 821	72, 984, 860	....
An increase on the preceding year	....	598, 937	$28, 245, 720	....
Examined and compared:				
Compound-interest notes	Mar. 3, 1863	103, 079	$8, 383, 550	....
Compound-interest notes	June 30, 1864	1, 460, 008	63, 458, 000	....
Total................	....	1, 563, 087	71, 841, 550	....
An increase on the preceding year	....	552, 203	$27, 102, 410	....

Statement of seven-thirty coupon treasury notes.

	Authorizing acts.	Number of pieces.	Amount.	Coupons attached.
Counted, assorted, and arranged:				
Issues dated August and October, 1861, and on warrants ..	July 17, 1861	135	$15, 900	....
1st series, dated Aug. 15, 1864.	June 30, 1864	646, 043	146, 502, 300	10, 905
2d series, dated June 15, 1865..	Mar. 3, 1865	439, 637	162, 587, 100	208, 841
3d series, dated July 15, 1865..	Mar. 3, 1865	444, 193	85, 762, 050	316, 279
Total................	....	1, 530, 008	394, 867, 350	536, 025
An increase on the preceding year	....	616, 765	$151, 485, 600	....

Statement of seven-thirty coupon treasury notes—Continued.

	Authorizing acts.	Number of pieces.	Amount.	Coupons attached.
Registered:				
Issues dated August and October, 1861, and on warrants ..	July 17, 1861	135	$15,900	....
1st series, dated Aug. 15, 1864..	June 30, 1864	734,228	167,833,350	11,418
2d series, dated June 15, 1865..	Mar. 3, 1865	402,079	152,585,450	239,584
3d series, dated July 15, 1865 ..	Mar. 3, 1865	400,917	79,507,400	351,562
Total..................	....	1,537,359	399,942,100	602,564
An increase on the preceding year	....	752,593	$187,713,650	....
Examined and compared:				
Issues dated August and October, 1861, and on warrants ..	July 17, 1861	135	$15,900	....
1st series, dated Aug. 15, 1864..	June 30, 1864	956,615	224,678,150	101,883
2d series, dated June 15, 1865..	Mar. 3, 1865	411,329	159,600,500	425,228
3d series, dated July 15, 1865..	Mar. 3, 1865	413,676	83,704,600	462,588
Total..................	....	1,781,755	467,999,150	989,699
An increase on the preceding year	....	1,295,368	$337,797,600	....

Statement of exchanged and redeemed bonds.

Registered, examined, scheduled, and delivered to the committee.	Authorizing acts.	Number of pieces.	Amount.	Coupons attached.
Exchanged bonds	July 17, 1861	73,345	$58,703,600	2,266,045
Exchanged bonds	Mar. 3, 1864	116,299	$75,439,250	7,601,553
Redeemed bonds	Mar. 3, 1864	1,998	1,501,500	145,717
Total..................	....	118,297	76,940,750	7,747,270
Exchanged bonds	June 30, 1864	58,147	$47,495,450	2,227,290
Exchanged bonds, 1st series...	Feb. 25, 1862	23,175	$15,660,400	764,676
Redeemed bonds, 1st series....	Feb. 25, 1862	1,242	315,100	37,475
Total..................	....	24,417	15,975,500	802,151
Exchanged bonds, 2d series....	Feb. 25, 1862	22,969	$14,609,300	759,768
Redeemed bonds, 2d series.....	Feb. 25, 1862	1,769	474,150	53,359
Total..................	....	24,738	15,083,450	813,127
Exchanged bonds, 3d series....	Feb. 25, 1862	18,683	$12,844,000	616,387
Redeemed bonds, 3d series	Feb. 25, 1862	898	159,650	27,019
Total..................	....	19,581	13,003,650	643,406
Exchanged bonds, 4th series...	Feb. 25, 1862	29,239	$19,244,150	967,943
Redeemed bonds, 4th series....	Feb. 25, 1862	1,659	492,600	50,169
Total..................	....	30,898	19,736,750	1,018,112
Total exchanged and redeemed bonds	....	349,423	$199,443,700	13,290,111

FRACTIONAL CURRENCY DIVISION.

In this division the redeemed fractional currency is examined, counted, and destroyed, together with United States notes, and the national bank notes of such banks as have suspended business and have settled their accounts with the Treasurer.

These securities consist of postal currency, fractional currency, (old and new issues,) United States demand notes, legal-tender notes, national bank notes, and statistical matter, consisting of notes and securities that have been mutilated in the process of manufacture, or that have not been carried into the cash account of the Treasurer, and all bonds that have been exchanged for other securities; all of which are returned to this division to be destroyed by maceration. An average of 3,500 pounds of legal-tender notes and fractional currency are destroyed by maceration once in 10 days.

The following statement exhibits the amount of labor performed in this division:

Statement showing the number of notes and amount of fractional currency, (old and new issues,) postal currency, and United States notes examined, counted, and destroyed during the year ending June 30, 1868; also, the number and amount of coupons examined, arranged, and counted during the same period.

	No. of notes.	Amount.
Fractional currency, old issue	8,000,944	$1,003,255 00
Fractional currency, new issue	87,530,104	18,680,584 00
Postal currency	3,600,094	608,555 00
United States notes, new issue	7,947,975	27,508,679 00
United States demand notes	7,762	64,480 00
National bank notes	21,281	129,797 15
Coupons	7,563,813	98,878,693 40

The whole number of notes examined, counted, and destroyed during the year ending June 30, was	114,671,973
In the preceding year	113,074,782
Increase	1,597,191
To this add coupons counted, assorted, and arranged	7,563,813
Total increase	9,161,004

TONNAGE DIVISION.

In this division a title record of property in "ships and vessels of the United States" is preserved, together with statistical information touching the merchant marine—embracing vessels in the foreign trade, coasting trade, and fisheries; steam vessels, sailing vessels, yachts, barges, and canal boats; also, vessels built, lost at sea, abandoned, or decayed. For many years this branch of the office has not received the attention which, in my judgment, its importance demanded.

The force employed does not seem to have been commensurate to the increase of business, and the system adopted at an early period of the government was not varied to meet the changes required by the rapid growth of the commercial enterprise of the country.

This condition resulted mainly, I presume, from two causes: first, the work performed being statistical in character, involving no settlement nor test of accuracy, it was not remarkable that more important duties should absorb the attention to which it was entitled; and, second, the natural reluctance with which our veteran functionaries abandon or modify the business routine to which they have been so long accustomed —a fact, I may observe, which is not peculiar to this office.

In order to reorganize the division I applied for the services of a competent officer who was familiar with the subject and its details, and Mr. Joseph Nimmo, jr., who had given much attention to it, and who had visited the different ports and districts for the purpose of instructing officers of the customs in regard to their duties relating to this business, was assigned to me for duty, and placed in charge of the division. An intelligent classification of the tonnage statistics has been adopted, and appropriate blank forms have been distributed to officers of the customs, with instructions in regard to making correct returns.

The following information, which has not been presented in former reports, will hereafter be furnished:

1. A statement showing the shipping of the Atlantic and Gulf coasts; of the Pacific coast; of the northern lakes, and of the western rivers.
2. Statements of the tonnage of the country by States.
3. The separation of sailing vessels and ocean steamers from barges, canal-boats, and other inland vessels.
4. Separate statements of the cod and mackerel fisheries and whale fishery by States and districts.
5. The number of vessels in each classification.
6. Statement of iron vessels, steam and sail.
7. Statement of yachts, steam and sail.

The foregoing embraces the entire transactions of this bureau for the fiscal year. It is due to the subordinate officers and employés of the bureau to add, in conclusion, that, with but few and slight exceptions, their duties have been performed with signal industry and fidelity.

Very respectfully, your obedient servant,

N. L. JEFFRIES, *Register.*

Hon. HUGH MCCULLOCH,
Secretary of the Treasury.

Statement of payments made during the year ending June 30, 1868, out of the appropriation for "claims not otherwise provided for," rendered in pursuance of act of March 3, 1809.

Date of payment.	Name and object.		Amount.
July 3, 1867	Commercial Advertiser Association: For advertising sale of government warehouses on Atlantic dock, Brooklyn, N. Y....		$32 40
	New York Times: For advertising sale of government warehouses on Atlantic dock, Brooklyn, N. Y....		40 50
	James Gordon Bennett, proprietor New York Herald: For advertising sale of government warehouses on Atlantic dock, Brooklyn, N. Y....		123 20
	Lawrence & Foulke, auctioneers, New York:		
	For advertising sale of government warehouses on Atlantic dock, Brooklyn, N. Y....	$58 56	
	For advertising sale of government stores at Atlantic dock....	2 50	
	For printing bills for sale of government stores at Atlantic dock....	11 00	
	For posting bills for sale of government stores at Atlantic dock....	6 75	
	For commission on $70,500 at 1 per cent....	705 00	
			783 81
May 15, 1868	G. S. Hillard, United States attorney for the district of Mass.:		
	For commissions on proceeds of land sold at South Boston....	$62 57	
	Cash paid for recording four mortgages....	5 00	
			67 57
	Total....		1,047 48

N. L. JEFFRIES, *Register.*

TREASURY DEPARTMENT, *Register's Office, November* 13, 1868.

Statement of the number of persons employed in each district of the United States for the collection of customs during the fiscal year ending June 30, 1868, with their occupation and compensation, per act 3d March, 1849.

Number.	District.	No. of persons employed.	Occupation.	Compensation.
1	Passamaquoddy, Me.	1	Collector....	$3,258 51
		1	Surveyor....	2,000 00
		1	Deputy collector....	1,600 00
		1	....do....	1,460 00
		6	Inspectors....	6,570 00
		5	....do....	4,562 00
		1	Aid to the revenue....	1,095 50
		3	....do....	2,737 50
		5	....do....	3,650 00
		1	....do....	945 00
		1	....do....	534 00
		1	Special inspector....	1,100 00
		1	....do....	860 00
		1	Special aid to the revenue....	486 00
		4	Watchmen....	2,920 00
		2	....do....	656 00
		1	Weigher and measurer....	1,500 00
		1	Special inspector....	273 00
		1	Boatman....	360 00

Statement of the number of persons employed, &c.—Continued.

Number.	District.	No. of persons employed.	Occupation.	Compensation.
2	Machias, Me	1	Collector	$2,248 04
		1	Inspector and deputy	1,006 00
		1	Inspector	792 00
		3	....do	2,196 00
		1	Inspector and deputy	639 50
		1	Inspector	250 00
		1	....do	244 00
		1	Boatman	45 50
3	Frenchman's Bay, Me	1	Collector	1,646 45
		1	Special deputy collector and inspector	1,152 00
		1	Deputy collector and inspector	1,098 00
		2	Deputy collectors and inspectors	900 00
		1	Inspector	793 00
		1	....do	914 00
		1	....do	65 00
		1	....do	54 17
		1	....do	117 00
		1	Boatman	548 00
4	Bangor, Me	1	....do	302 00
		1	Collector	3,000 00
		1	Deputy collector	1,500 00
		1	....do	1,095 00
		1	Inspector	1,460 00
		1	Deputy collector, weigher, and gauger	1,143 76
		1	Weigher, gauger, measurer	850 02
		2	Aids to the revenue	2,190 00
		1	....do	912 00
		1	....do	983 98
		1	....do	730 00
		1	Night-watchman	730 00
		1	Janitor	296 68
		1	Clerk	72 00
5	Castine, Me	......	No returns.	
6	Belfast, Me	1	Collector of customs	1,687 18
		1	Deputy collector	1,215 45
		2	Dep'y col'rs, insp'rs, w'ghers, gaugers, &c	2,190 00
		1	....do.... ......do..........do.....	1,134 12
		1	....do...... ....do..........do.....	857 00
		1	....do.... ......do..........do.....	481 97
		1	Temporary inspector	500 00
		1	....do	200 00
7	Waldoboro', Me	2	Deputy col'rs, insp'rs, weighers, &c	2,196 00
		1	....do...... ....do..........do.....	1,218 78
		1	....do...... ....do..........do.....	936 00
		1	....do...... ....do..........do.....	300 00
		1	....do...... ....do..........do.....	600 00
		1	....do...... ....do..........do.....	915 00
		1	....do...... ....do..........do.....	748 00
8	Wiscasset, Me	1	Collector	752 45
		3	Inspectors	3,294 00
		1	....do	916 00
		2	....do	700 00
9	Bath, Me	1	Collector	2,255 52
		1	Deputy col'r, inspectorr, weigher, &c	1,500 00
		1	Deputy collector and inspector	1,464 00
		1	Inspector	1,464 00
			....do	1,218 78
		1	Aid to the revenue	1,098 00
		1	Inspector	732 00

Statement of the number of persons employed, &c.—Continued.

Number.	District.	No. of persons employed.	Occupation.	Compensation.
9	Bath, Me.—Cont'd..	1	Inspector	$700 00
		1	....do	600 00
		1	....do	350 00
		1	....do	250 00
10	Portland and Falmouth, Me.	1	Collector	6,400 00
		3	Deputy collectors	9,000 00
		1	Inspector and clerk	1,800 00
		4	Clerks	5,200 00
		2	....do	2,400 00
		1	....do	1,100 00
		2	....do	1,716 49
		5	Special inspectors	7,300 00
		15	Inspectors	18,974 50
		6	Temporary inspectors	6,570 00
		2	Night inspectors	2,190 00
		2	Temporary inspectors	1,460 00
		1	....do........do	1,095 00
		2	Boatmen	1,186 00
		25	Temporary inspectors	3,604 00
		2	Weighers, gaugers, and measurers	4,000 00
		2	Occasional gaugers and measurers	3,431 22
		1	Surveyor	2,282 62
		1	Deputy surveyor	1,786 70
		1	Appraiser	2,722 53
		1	Assistant appraiser	2,500 00
		1	Examiner	1,300 00
		2	Store-keepers	2,920 00
		1	Porter	500 00
11	Saco, Me	1	Collector	250 00
		1	Deputy collector	782 00
		1	Inspector	500 00
		1	....do	100 00
		1	Special aid	252 00
12	Kennebunk, Me	1	Collector	272 66
		1	Inspector	600 00
		3	....do	468 00
13	York, Me	1	Collector	262 01
		2	Inspectors	200 00
14	Portsmouth, N. H.	......	No report.	
15	Vermont, Vt	1	Collector	2,500 00
		1	Deputy collector and inspector	2,000 00
		1	....do......do........do	1,800 00
		1	....do......do........do	1,400 00
		1	....do......do........do	1,324 00
		2	....do......do........do	2,000 00
		2	....do......do........do	1,200 00
		7	....do......do........do	3,500 00
		2	....do......do........do	1,830 00
		2	....do......do........do	1,400 00
		1	....do......do........do	151 00
		1	....do......do........do	1,467 00
		1	....do......do........do	1,267 00
		3	....do......do........do	3,201 00
		1	Inspector	1,400 00
		1	....do	1,200 00
		11	....do	10,065 00
		2	....do	1,300 00
		1	....do	840 00
		1	....do	768 00

Statement of the number of persons employed, &c.—Continued.

Number.	District.	No. of persons employed.	Occupation.	Compensation.
15	Vermont, Vt.—Continued.	1	Inspector	$585 00
		1	....do	290 00
		1	....do	308 00
		1	....do	605 00
		1	....do	240 00
		1	....do	615 00
		1	....do	876 00
		1	....do	963 00
		2	....do	2,196 00
		1	....do	702 00
		1	....do	414 00
		1	....do	732 00
		1	....do	360 00
		2	....do	1,000 00
		1	....do	100 00
		1	....do	243 00
		2	....do	532 00
		1	....do	285 00
		1	....do	176 00
		2	....do	1,098 00
		2	....do	2,928 00
		1	....do	241 00
		3	....do	582 00
		2	....do	382 00
		1	....do	197 00
		1	....do	828 00
		1	....do	745 00
		1	....do	625 00
		5	....do	765 00
		1	....do	178 00
		1	....do	138 00
		1	....do	44 00
		1	....do	38 00
		1	....do	58 00
		1	Revenue aid	564 00
		1	....do	834 00
		1	....do	184 00
		2	....do	1,830 00
		1	....do	1,000 00
		1	....do	586 00
		1	....do	150 00
		2	....do	1,464 00
		1	Revenue boatman	209 00
		1	....do.....do	622 00
		1	....do.....do	540 00
		1	....do.....do	383 00
		2	Night watchmen	1,464 00
		1	Porter	480 00
16	Newburyport, Mass.	1	Collector	1,984 00
		1	Surveyor (at Newburyport)	557 00
		1	Deputy collector and inspector	1,095 00
		1	Weigher, gauger, &c., and inspector	1,095 00
		1	Inspector	1,095 00
		1	Surveyor (at Ipswich)	250 00
17	Gloucester, Mass.	1	Collector	3,000 00
		1	Surveyor	932 27
		1	Deputy collector and inspector	1,500 00
		1	Clerk	1,000 00
		2	Inspectors	2,928 00

Statement of the number of persons employed, &c.—Continued.

Number.	District.	No. of persons employed.	Occupation.	Compensation.
17	Gloucester, Mass.—Continued.	1	Inspector	$300 00
		2	Aids to revenue	1,464 00
		1	....do	52 00
		1	....do	36 00
		1	Boatman	355 00
		1	Janitor	271 67
		1	Keeper of custom-house	225 00
18	Salem and Beverly, Mass.	1	Collector	311 98
		1	Deputy collector and inspector	915 00
		1	....do......do.......do	366 00
		1	Inspector, weigher, gauger, and measurer	324 00
		1	....do......do......do.........do	307 76
		1	Inspector	102 00
		1	Surveyor	114 99
		1	Boatman	150 00
		1	....do	100 00
19	Marblehead, Mass	1	Collector	1,454 69
		1	Deputy collector and inspector	1,098 00
		1	....do......do.......do	400 00
		1	....do......do.......do	300 00
		1	....do......do.......do	200 00
20	Boston and Charlestown, Mass.	......	No report.	
21	Plymouth, Mass	......	No report.	
22	Barnstable, Mass	1	Collector	1,395 00
		1	Deputy collector and inspector	1,095 00
		2	....do......do.......do	800 00
		1	....do......do.......do	600 00
		2	....do......do.......do	1,000 00
		1	....do......do.......do	900 00
		1	Aid to the revenue	300 00
		1	Inspector	1,460 00
		1	Keeper of the custom-house	350 00
23	New Bedford, Mass	1	Collector	3,000 00
		1	Deputy collector and inspector	1,460 00
		1	Inspector, weigher, gauger, and measurer	,460 00
		1	Inspector	1,400 00
		1	Aid to revenue	1,000 00
		1	Boatman	600 00
		1	Inspector	125 00
		1	....do	300 00
		1	....do	120 00
		2	....do	160 00
		1	Inspector and weigher	500 00
		1	Admeasurement clerk	116 00
		1	Temporary clerk	132 00
24	Fall River, Mass	1	Collector	773 00
		1	Dep'y collector, inspector, weigher, &c.	1,184 00
		1	Inspector, weigher, and measurer	1,173 00
		1	....do..........do..........do	1,098 00
25	Edgartown, Mass	1	Collector	1,126 24
		1	Deputy collector and inspector	1,350 00
		1	....do...............do	1,095 00
		2	Temporary inspectors	1,460 00
		1	....do......do	500 00
		2	Night inspectors	1,200 00
		1	Revenue boatman	420 00
		1	.... do	240 00
26	Nantucket, Mass	......	No report	3,000 00

Statement of the number of persons employed, &c.—Continued.

Number.	District.	No. of persons employed.	Occupation.	Compensation.
27	Providence, R. I....	1	Collector	$3,000 00
		1	Surveyor at Providence	979 71
		1	Surveyor at East Greenwich	251 50
		1	Surveyor at Pawtuxet	200 00
		2	Coastwise inspectors	1,460 00
		3	Foreign inspectors	2,380 00
		1	Inspector	1,460 00
		1	Inspector and measurer	1,500 00
		1	Inspector and weigher	1,500 00
		1	Inspector and gauger	1,092 00
		1	Inspector of measurement of lumber	308 00
		1	Secret inspector	915 00
		1	Inspector and messenger	1,500 00
		1	Inspector at Pawtuxet	1,095 00
		1	Inspector at East Greenwich	300 00
		1	Weigher	1,500 00
		1	Measurer	1,272 00
		1	Boatman	600 00
28	Bristol and Warren, R. I.	1	Collector	751 42
		1	Inspector	1,004 00
		1	....do	188 00
		3	Temporary inspectors	75 00
		1	Gauger	27 84
		1	Boatman	216 00
		1	Surveyor	382 20
		1	....do	252 13
29	Newport, R. I......	1	Collector, &c	1,325 51
		1	Surveyor at Newport	418 63
		1	Surveyor at North Kingston	250 00
		1	Surveyor at Tiverton	200 00
		1	Deputy collector	1,200 00
		2	Inspectors at $3 per day, Newport	2,196 00
		1	Inspector at Dutch island	600 00
		1	Inspector at North Kingston	224 76
		1	Inspector at North Shoreham	200 00
		4	Inspectors, occasional, $4 per day	968 00
		1	Gauger	154 32
		1	Measurer	146 07
		1	Boatman	500 00
30	Stonington, Conn...	1	Collector	600 00
		1	Inspector	500 00
		1	....do	400 00
		1	Boatkeeper	144 00
		1	Surveyor	150 00
31	New London, Conn.	1	Collector	2,098 09
		1	Clerk, deputy collector, &c	1,800 00
		1	Inspector at New London	600 00
		1	Temporary inspector	978 00
		1	Inspector, &c., at Norwich	916 51
		1	Inspector at Black Point	200 00
32	Middletown, Conn..	1	Collector	931 04
		1	Surveyor	288 75
		1	....do	288 50
		1	....do	278 24
		1	Inspector, deputy collector, gauger, &c.	650 00
		1	....do..........do..........do.	478 00
		1	....do..........do..........do.	284 00
33	New Haven, Conn..	1	Collector	3,000 00
		1	Deputy collector, inspector, and clerk	2,000 00

Statement of the number of persons employed, &c.—Continued.

Number.	District.	No. of persons employed.	Occupation.	Compensation.
33	New Haven, Conn.—Continued.	1	Inspector and clerk	$1,500 00
		1	....do..........do	876 38
		2	Weighers and gaugers	3,000 00
		3	Inspectors	3,832 50
		1	....do	1,095 00
		1	....do	60 00
		1	....do	72 00
		1	....do	48 00
		1	Night inspector	1,095 00
		1	Aid to revenue	459 00
		1	Messenger and porter	500 00
		2	Boatmen and temporary inspectors	800 00
34	Fairfield, Conn	1	Collector	3,330 37
		1	Inspector, weigher, measurer, &c.	1,776 63
		1	Inspector	200 00
		1	....do	125 00
		1	Night watch	294 00
35	Sag Harbor, N. Y	1	Collector	716 38
		1	Deputy collector	300 00
		1	Surveyor	317 25
		1	Inspector	180 00
		1	....do	120 00
		1	....do	27 00
36	New York, N. Y	1	Collector	6,400 00
		1	Assistant collector	5,000 00
		1	Auditor	7,000 00
		1	Assistant auditor	5,000 00
		1	....do.....do	2,500 00
		9	Deputy collectors	27,000 00
		1	Cashier	5,000 00
		1	Assistant cashier	3,500 00
		1	Clerk	3,500 00
		3	....do	9,000 00
		1	....do	2,700 00
		14	....do	35,000 00
		1	....do	2,200 00
		29	....do	58,000 00
		40	....do	72,600 00
		31	....do	49,600 00
		33	....do	49,500 00
		57	....do	79,800 00
		4	....do	5,200 00
		83	....do	99,600 00
		47	....do	47,000 00
		1	....do	1,281 00
		1	....do	1,098 00
		1	....do	942 00
		16	....do	14,400 00
		3	....do	2,400 00
		2	....do	1,500 00
		1	Superintendent of custom-house	2,400 00
		1	Assistant superintendent custom-house	1,500 00
		1	Usher	1,200 00
		3	....do	2,700 00
		3	Messengers	3,000 00
		10	....do	9,000 00
		7	....do	5,600 00
		26	....do	19,500 00
		14	Porters	10,080 00

Statement of the number of persons employed, &c.—Continued.

Number.	District.	No of persons employed.	Occupation.	Compensation.
36	New York, N. Y.—Continued.	4	Messengers	$2,800 00
		1	Janitor, (at No. 23 Pine street)	800 00
		2	Messengers	1,000 00
		1	Carpenter	1,281 00
		1	Engineer	1,200 00
		3	Firemen	2,160 00
		8	Watchmen	8,000 00
		2	Sunday watchmen	260 00
		1	Special deputy and act'g naval officer	2,500 00
		2	Deputies	5,000 00
		1	Auditor	2,500 00
		4	Entry clerks	10,000 00
		1	Surveyor	4,651 44
		3	Deputy surveyors	7,500 00
		1	....do............(for five months)	1,041 67
		19	Weighers	47,500 00
		8	Gaugers	16,000 00
		230	Inspectors	336,720 00
		7	....do....female	7,686 00
		125	....do....night	137,250 00
		1	....do....at Troy	1,464 00
		1	Captain night watch	1,600 00
		2	Lieutenants night watch	2,400 00
		1	Appraiser	4,000 00
		1	Appraiser at large	3,000 00
		10	Assistant appraisers	30,000 00
		30	Appraisers' clerks	75,000 00
		8	....do	16,000 00
		10	....do	18,000 00
		1	....do	1,600 00
		10	....do	15,000 00
		34	....do	40,800 00
		3	....do	3,000 00
		1	Warehouse superintendent	3,000 00
		120	Storekeepers	175,000 00
		1	Assistant storekeeper	1,000 00
		2	....do........do	1,600 00
		1	Captain of watchmen	1,464 00
		9	Watchmen	8,235 00
		1	Debenture clerk	1,400 00
		22	....do	28,600 00
		1	Measurer of marble	2,000 00
		9	Inspectors for measuring vessels	13,176 00
		3	Asst. inspectors for measuring vessels	3,294 00
		1	Surveyor at Troy	250 00
37	Albany, (port of) N. Y.	2	Deputy collectors and inspectors	2,250 00
		3	Deputy collectors and assistant clerks	3,400 00

Statement of the number of persons employed, &c.—Continued.

Number.	District.	No. of persons employed.	Occupation.	Compensation.
40	Cape Vincent, N. Y.—Continued.	2	Inspectors	$1,824 00
		1	....do	730 00
		6	Secret inspectors	4,380 00
		4	Temporary inspectors	602 00
41	Oswego, N. Y	1	Collector	2,500 00
		2	Deputy collectors and inspectors	3,000 00
		3	Clerks	3,300 00
		1	Deputy collector	1,000 00
		2	....do	1,875 00
		1	Inspector	1,460 00
		3	Clerks	3,000 00
		1	Clerk	730 00
		5	Inspectors	5,475 00
		2	....do	1,458 00
		3	....do	821 25
		3	Inspectors, and measurers of lumber	3,285 00
		2	....do ....do	1,093 76
		1	....do ....do	791 00
		1	Janitor	547 50
42	Genesee, N. Y	......	No report.	
43	Niagara, N. Y	......	No report.	
44	Buffalo Creek, N. Y.	......	No report.	
45	Dunkirk, N. Y	1	Collector	1,000 00
		1	Deputy collector	915 00
		4	Inspectors	3,660 00
46	Newark, N. J	1	Collector	620 79
		1	Deputy collector	1,095 00
		1	Inspector	939 00
		1	....do	1,460 00
47	Perth Amboy, N. J	1	Collector	2,228 78
		1	Deputy collector	700 00
		1	Surveyor	150 00
		3	Inspectors	1,800 00
		1	....do	500 00
		1	....do	400 00
48	Little Egg Harbor, N. J.	4	....do	1,128 00
		1	Boatman	681 00
49	Great Egg Harbor, N. J.	1	Collector	611 85
		1	Inspector	549 00
50	Burlington, N. J	1	Collector	521 36
51	Bridgeton, N. J	......	No report.	
52	Philadelphia, Pa	1	Collector	6,340 00
		2	Deputy collectors	6,000 00
		1	Cashier	2,500 00
		1	Assistant cashier	2,000 00
		1	Assistant collector at Camden	1,500 00
		1	Surveyor at Chester	500 00
		1	Naval officer	4,950 00
		1	Deputy naval officer	2,500 00
		1	Surveyor	4,445 00
		1	Deputy surveyor	2,500 00
		1	General appraiser	3,000 00
		1	Appraiser	3,000 00
		2	Deputy appraisers	5,000 00
		1	Examiner	1,800 00
		3	Clerks	5,400 00
		3	....do	4,800 00
		1	Clerk	1,500 00

Statement of the number of persons employed, &c.—Continued.

Number.	District.	No. of persons employed.	Occupation.	Compensation.
52	Philadelphia, Pa.—Continued.	17	....do	23,800 00
		14	....do	18,200 00
		1	....do	1,200 00
		2	Admeasurement clerks	2,190 00
		1	....do........do	1,460 00
		2	Examiners	3,000 00
		2	....do	2,800 00
		1	Storekeeper	1,500 00
		12	Assistant storekeepers	17,520 00
		1	Examiner of drugs	1,000 00
		1	Superintendent of warehouse	1,300 00
		61	Inspectors	89,060 00
		1	Lieutenant of night inspectors	1,200 00
		26	Night inspectors	28,470 00
		5	Night watchmen	4,562 50
		2	Inspectors	1,095 00
		1	....do	500 00
		1	Weigher	2,000 00
		1	....do	1,200 00
		1	....do	4,380 00
		1	First foreman to weighers	912 50
		1	Second foreman to weighers	912 50
		2	Gaugers	2,970 00
		6	Beamsmen	6,570 00
		4	Temporary beamsmen	4,380 00
		4	Bargemen	3,650 00
		8	Messengers	7,300 00
		8	....do	8,030 00
		1	....do	900 00
		1	Marker	912 50
		9	....do	8,100 00
		1	Assistant sampler	821 25
		1	Janitor	821 25
		1	Laborer	821 25
53	Erie, Pa	1	Collector	1,000 00
		1	Deputy collector and inspector	1,400 00
		1	Inspector	1,082 50
		2	Temporary inspectors	1,098 00
		3	....do........do	1,921 50
		1	Lumber measurer	423 00
54	Port of Pittsburg, Pa.	1	Deputy surveyor and clerk	1,400 00
		1	Surveyor's clerk	900 00
55	Delaware, Del	1	Collector	2,828 54
		1	Deputy collector and inspector	1,200 00
		1	....do........do	54 44
		1	....do........do	800 00
		1	Inspector	800 00
		1	....do	500 00
		2	Messengers	732 00
		4	Oarsmen	400 00
56	Baltimore, Md	......	No report.	
57	Annapolis, Md	1	Collector	374 95
		1	Surveyor	269 25
		1	....do	210 25
		1	....do	150 00
		2	Boatmen	160 00
58	Town Creek, Md	......	No report.	
59	Eastern Maryland	1	Collector	1,200 00

Statement of the number of persons employed, &c.—Continued.

Number.	District.	No. of persons employed.	Occupation.	Compensation.
59	Eastern Maryland—Continued.	1	Deputy collector	$796 00
		1	Clerk	400 00
60	Georgetown, D. C	1	Collector	2,306 19
		2	Deputy collectors and inspectors	2,400 00
		1	Aid to revenue	1,200 00
		1	Deputy inspector	200 00
		1	Laborer	628 00
61	Alexandria, Va	1	Collector	502 23
		1	Deputy collector and inspector	1,500 00
		2	Inspectors	2,190 00
		1	Surveyor	300 00
62	Tappahannock, Va	1	Collector	382 15
		1	Deputy collector and inspector	350 00
		1	Deputy coll'r and inspector, Yeocomico	96 00
		1	Boatman	300 00
63	Richmond, Va	1	Collector	1,671 52
		1	Deputy collector	1,800 00
		1	....do	1,460 00
		3	Inspectors	4,380 00
		1	Clerk	1,460 00
		1	Janitor	912 50
		1	Watchman	730 00
64	Yorktown, Va	1	Collector	429 83
		1	Deputy collector	1,772 00
65	Petersburg, Va	1	Collector	536 94
		1	Deputy collector and clerk	1,550 00
		1	Inspector	1,292 00
		1	....do	1,189 00
		1	....do	424 00
66	Norfolk and Portsmouth, Va.	1	Collector	3,000 00
		1	Deputy collector	1,800 00
		1	Marine clerk	1,500 00
		1	Warehouse clerk	1,500 00
		1	Temporary clerk	65 00
		3	Inspectors	4,380 00
		1	....do	1,348 00
		1	....do	1,348 00
		1	....do	828 00
		1	....do	108 00
		1	....do	912 50
		1	Inspector, temporary	36 00
		1	....do.......do	16 00
		1	Watchman	912 50
		1	....do	180 00
		1	Temporary watchman	30 00
		1	....do.......do	30 00
		1	....do.......do	20 00
		1	....do.......do	6 00
		1	Boatman	480 00
		1	....do	400 00
		1	....do	400 00
		1	....do	434 34
		1	....do	45 16
		1	Weigher and gauger	44 53
		1	Measurer	478 58
67	Cherrystone, Va	1	Collector	725 41
		1	Surveyor	380 00
		1	Inspector	1,610 50
		3	Revenue boatmen	1,080 00

Statement of the number of persons employed, &c.—Continued.

Number.	District.	No. of persons employed.	Occupation.	Compensation.
68	Wheeling, W. Va...	1	Surveyor	$1,150 34
		1	Janitor	471 66
69	Parkersburg, W. Va.	......	No report.	
70	Albemarle, N. C	1	Deputy collector and inspector	1,464 00
		1	Special deputy collector and inspector..	1,221 00
		1	Inspector	1,221 00
		1	....do	492 00
		1	....do	182 00
71	Pamlico, N. C	1	Collector	2,167 17
		2	Deputy collectors and inspectors	2,928 00
		1	....do......do........do	1,392 00
		1	....do......do........do	928 00
		1	Inspector	1,448 00
		1	....do	360 00
		3	Revenue boatmen	900 00
		1	....do......do	250 00
72	Beaufort, N. C......	1	Collector	1,494 93
		1	Inspector	747 08
		1	Boatman	300 00
73	Wilmington, N. C...	1	Collector	2,000 00
		1	Clerk	1,200 00
		1	Storekeeper, gauger, and weigher	1,460 00
		5	Inspectors	7,300 00
		2	Revenue boatmen	720 00
		1	Messenger	600 00
74	Georgetown, S. C...	1	Collector	805 83
		1	Special inspector	184 00
		1	Inspector	1,005 00
		2	Revenue boatmen	660 00
75	Charleston, S. C	1	Collector	5,754 03
		1	Deputy collector and cashier	2,200 00
		1	Auditor	2,000 00
		2	Clerks	3,200 00
		2	....do	2,800 00
		1	....do	1,300 00
		2	Appraisers	3,000 00
		3	Porters	2,190 00
		12	Inspectors	17,520 00
		7	Night inspectors	6,387 50
		2	Night watchmen	1,460 00
		4	Boatmen	3,650 00
		1	Weigher and measurer	1,500 00
		1	Gauger	1,048 70
		1	Messenger	1,000 00
		1	Porter	600 00
		1	Naval officer	1,060 83
		1	Deputy naval officer	1,400 00
		1	Surveyor	1,903 81
		1	Deputy surveyor	1,460 00
76	Beaufort, S. C......	1	Collector	1,291 00
		1	Inspector	1,281 00
		2	Boatmen	600 00
77	Savannah, Ga......	1	Collector	4,000 00

Statement of the number of persons employed, &c.—Continued.

Number.	District.	No. of persons employed.	Occupation.	Compensation.
77	Savannah, Ga.—Continued.	8	Inspectors	$11,680 00
		1	Storekeepers	900 00
		1	Assistant storekeeper	1,095 00
		3	Night watchmen	2,737 50
		1	Porter and night watch	840 00
		6	Boat hands	4,320 00
		1	Appraiser's porter	360 00
78	Brunswick, Ga.	......	No report.	
79	St. Mary's, Ga.	......	No report.	
80	Fernandina, Fla.	1	Collector	1,126 67
		1	Deputy collector	1,200 00
		1	Inspector	636 00
		1	....do	1,098 00
		1	....do	732 00
		3	Boatmen	1,620 00
		1	....do	366 00
81	St. John's, Fla.	2	Inspectors	2,139 00
		1	Inspector and deputy	1,464 00
		4	Boatmen	1,440 00
82	St. Augustine, Fla.	......	No report.	
83	Key West, Fla.	1	Collector	1,722 89
		1	Deputy collector and inspector	1,464 00
		1	Inspector	1,464 00
		1	Clerk	942 00
		1	Temporary inspector and night watch	399 00
84	St. Mark's, Fla.	1	Dep. collector and inspect'r, Cedar Keys	1,460 00
		1	Deputy collector and inspector, Tampa	1,460 00
		1	Acting inspector	294 00
85	Apalachicola, Fla.	1	Collector	1,424 00
		1	Inspector	1,220 00
		1	Temporary inspector	60 00
		1	Weigher and gauger	1,284 00
		4	Revenue boatmen	1,200 00
		1	Captain revenue cutter	2,500 00
		1	First lieutenant revenue cutter	1,800 00
		1	Second lieutenant revenue cutter	1,500 00
		1	Third lieutenant revenue cutter	1,200 00
		3	Seamen	1,620 00
		1	....do	480 00
		6	....do	2,520 00
		6	....do	2,160 00
		1	....do	240 00
		2	....do	360 00
		3	....do	432 00
86	Pensacola, Fla.	1	Collector	2,916 38
		1	Inspector and deputy collector	1,098 00
		1	....do......do........do	594 00
		1	....do......do........do	66 00
		2	Revenue boatmen	720 00
87	Mobile, Ala.	1	Collector	6,000 00

Statement of the number of persons employed, &c.—Continued.

Number.	District.	No. of persons employed.	Occupation.	Compensation.
87	Mobile, Ala.—Cont.	1	Bargeman	$600 00
88	Selma, Ala	1	Collector (salary not reported.)	
89	Pearl River, Miss	1	Collector	62 50
90	Vicksburg, Miss	1	Collector (salary not reported.)	
91	Natches, Miss	......	No report.	
92	New Orleans, La	......	No report.	
93	Teché, La	......	No report.	
94	Galveston, Texas	1	Collector	2,500 00
		1	Deputy collector and special deputy	2,000 00
		1	Deputy collector and chief clerk	1,800 00
		5	Clerks	8,000 00
		1	Deputy collector and boarding inspector	1,800 00
		1	Weigher, gauger, &c	1,800 00
		1	Deputy collector and inspector	1,500 00
		1	Surveyor	1,000 00
		2	Inspectors	2,920 00
		8	....do	11,680 00
		2	Night inspectors	2,920 00
		1	Messenger	730 00
		1	Porter	730 00
		1	Night watchman	1,095 00
		6	Revenue boatmen	4,800 00
		1	Storekeeper	1,600 00
		1	Laborer	1,252 00
		3	....do	2,700 00
		1	....do	626 00
95	Saluria, Texas	1	Collector	2,500 00
		1	Surveyor	600 00
		1	Deputy collector and clerk	1,500 00
		1	Deputy collector	1,000 00
		1	Deputy collector and storekeeper	1,168 48
		1	Mounted inspector	1,095 00
		1	Inspector	437 00
		1	Inspector and clerk	1,168 00
		1	Inspector	436 00
		1	Special inspector	1,460 00
		1	Inspector	360 00
		1	Boatman	600 00
96	Corpus Christi, Tex	......	No report.	
97	Brazos Santiago, Texas.	......	No report.	
98	Passo del Norte, Tex.	......	No report.	
99	Memphis, Tenn	1	Surveyor	1,678 59
		2	Inspectors	1,800 00
		1	Messenger	600 00
		1	Clerk	550 00
100	Nashville, Tenn	1	No report.	
101	Paducah, Ky	......	No report.	
102	Louisville, Ky	1	Clerk	1,300 00
		1	Measurer	1,300 00
		1	Temporary inspector	1,095 00
		1	Porter and rewarehouseman	720 00
103	Cincinnati, Ohio	......	No report	
104	Cuyahoga, Ohio	1	Collector	2,891 46

Statement of the number of persons employed, &c.—Continued.

Number.	District.	No. of persons employed.	Occupation.	Compensation.
104	Cuyahoga, Ohio.—Continued.	1	Special night deputy collector	$205 00
		1	Weigher, gauger, and measurer	915 00
		1	Temporary inspector	912 00
		1	Measurer and inspector	1,098 00
		1	Inspector	760 00
		1	Deputy collector	480 00
		3	....do....do	900 00
		1	Janitor	732 00
105	Sandusky, Ohio	1	Collector	2,600 00
		1	Deputy collector	1,000 00
		1	....do....do	925 00
		1	....do....do	600 00
		1	....do....do	300 00
		3	....do....do	600 00
		1	Clerk	600 00
106	Miami, Ohio	1	Collector	1,000 00
		1	Deputy collector	1,285 00
		1	Deputy collector and inspector	1,266 94
		1	Night deputy	694 35
		4	Inspectors	3,862 00
		1	Messenger	300 00
		1	Temporary inspector	90 00
107	Detroit, Mich	1	Collector	2,900 00
		1	Chief deputy collector	2,083 33
		1	Clerk	1,500 00
		1	Deputy collector and cashier	1,500 00
		1	Deputy collector and clerk	1,400 00
		1	Deputy collector and inspector	1,300 00
		1	....do............do	1,200 00
		1	....do............do	1,095 00
		4	....do............do	4,015 00
		1	....do............do	1,000 00
		1	....do............do	950 00
		2	....do............do	1,825 00
		1	....do............do	300 00
		3	....do............do	600 00
		1	....do............do	120 00
		1	....do............do	90 00
		1	Deputy collector	176 00
		1	....do	55 00
		1	....do	200 00
		1	Inspector	1,460 00
		1	....do	1,095 00
		4	....do	4,000 00
		2	....do	1,898 00
		3	....do	2,737 50
		1	....do	895 00
		1	....do	772 00
		2	....do	1,606 00
		2	....do	1,400 00
		1	....do	500 05
		1	....do	250 00
		1	....do	240 00
		2	Inspectors	240 00
		1	Female inspector	240 00
		1	Porter, messenger, and watchman	900 00
		7	Insp'rs (pd. by R. R. co.'s thro' cust. ho.)	7,000 00
108	Port Huron, Mich	1	Special deputy	1,779 13
		1	Cashier and bookkeeper	1,500 00

Statement of the number of persons employed, &c.—Continued.

Number.	District.	No. of persons employed.	Occupation.	Compensation.
106	Port Huron, Mich.—Continued.	1	Bond and entry clerk	$1,200 00
		1	Vessel papers clerk	1,095 00
		1	General clerk	1,015 50
		1	Secret detective	1,132 00
		1	Deputy at Grand Trunk crossing	1,299 00
		3	....do............do	3,285 00
		1	....do............do	453 00
		2	....do............do	1,642 50
		1	Night deputy, &c	774 00
		1	Deputy at Great Western crossing	772 50
		3	Secret detectives	3,285 00
		1	....do.....do	453 00
		5	....do.....do	4,562 50
		1	....do.....do	537 50
		1	Watchman	730 00
		1	Female inspector	386 00
		1	Deputy at Bay City	686 00
		1	....do.. at Algona	450 00
		1	....do.. at St. Clair	552 66
		1	....do.. at East Saginaw	550 00
		1	....do.. at Marine City	535 00
		1	....do.. at Alpena	520 00
		1	....do.. at Lexington	190 00
		1	....do.. at Sand Beach	173 33
109	Michilimackinac, Mich.	1	Deputy collector and inspector	1,200 00
		4	....do..........do....at $2 50 per day	2,252 50
		1	....do..........do	732 00
		3	....do..........do....at $2 per day	1,422 00
		1	....do..........do....at $100 per ann	100 00
		2	....do..........do....at $400 per ann	800 00
		2	....do..........do....at $300 per ann	300 00
		1	Female inspector	100 00
		3	Aids to the revenue at $2 50 per day	2,745 00
		1	....do........do	395 00
		1	....do........do	915 00
		1	Deputy collector and inspector	300 00
110	Michigan, Mich	......	No report.	
111	Madison, Ind	......	No report.	
112	New Albany, Ind	......	No report.	
113	Evansville, Ind	1	Surveyor	350 00
		1	Deputy surveyor	....
114	Chicago, Ill	......	No report.	1,185 64
115	Galena, Ill	1	Surveyor	
116	Quincy, Ill	1	....do	350 00
117	Alton, Ill	......	No report.	
118	Cairo, Ill	1	Surveyor	1,132 94
		1	Inspector	939 00
119	Milwaukee, Wis	1	Collector	2,900 00
		2	Deputy collectors	3,000 00
		1	....do......do	600 00
		3	....do......do	1,200 00
		1	....do......do	300 00
		1	....do......do	200 00
		3	Inspectors	3,285 00
		1	Watchman and janitor	730 00
120	Minnesota, Minn	......	No report.	
121	Dubuque, Iowa	1	Surveyor	1,007 56
		1	Janitor	600 00
122	Burlington, Iowa	......	No report.	

Statement of the number of persons employed, &c.—Continued.

Number.	District.	No. of persons employed.	Occupation.	Compensation.
123	Keokuk, Iowa......	1	Surveyor..........	$350 00
		1	Inspector..........	110 00
		1	Deputy surveyor..........	....
124	St Louis, Mo.......	1	Surveyor..........	6,348 48
		1	Clerk and deputy..........	2,083 33
		1	Clerk and cashier..........	2,000 00
		1	Clerk..........	1,333 33
		2	....do..........	2,533 32
		1	....do..........	1,021 90
		1	Porter..........	850 00
		1	Warehouseman..........	850 00
		1	Inspector..........	1,460 00
		1	Janitor, (appointed by Secretary).....	912 50
125	Montana and Idaho.	......	No report.	
126	Puget Sound, W. T.	1	Collector..........	3,000 00
		1	Deputy collector..........	2,000 00
		1	....do..........	1,800 00
		1	Record clerk..........	1,600 00
		3	Inspectors, $3 75 per day..........	3,376 25
		6	....do..........	9,760 00
		1	Waterman..........	900 00
		4	Revenue boatmen..........	3,600 00
127	Oregon, Or.........	1	Collector..........	3,765 02
		1	Deputy collector and clerk..........	1,800 00
		1	Deputy collector and inspector..........	1,394 02
		1	....do..........do..........	263 73
		1	Permanent inspector..........	1,200 00
		1	Secret special inspector..........	808 00
		1	....do..........do..........	1,440 00
		1	....do..........do..........	352 00
		......	Several sp'l insp's, a few days at a time.	848 00
		5	Temporary inspectors..........	5,000 00
		1	....do..........do..........	1 54
		......	Travelling and incidental exp. of insp'rs.	1,124 37
128	San Francisco, Cal..	1	Collector..........	6,400 00
		1	Auditor and deputy collector..........	4,000 00
		2	Deputy collectors..........	7,158 30
		1	Cashier..........	3,000 00
		1	Adjuster of duties..........	3,000 00
		6	Clerks..........	13,200 00
		1	....do..........	2,100 00
		5	....do..........	10,000 00
		6	....do..........	11,280 00
		13	....do..........	23,400 00
		1	....do..........	1,750 00
		1	....do..........	1,700 00
		7	....do..........	11,200 00
		1	Cashier and assistant treasurer..........	3,000 00
		1	Bookkeeper and assistant treasurer....	2,500 00
		8	Messengers..........	8,640 00
		5	Watchmen..........	5,400 00
		1	Porter..........	1,080 00
		1	Deputy collector and storekeeper......	3,579 15
		9	Ass't storekeepers (pd. by bonded stores)	....
		2	Superintendents of laborers..........	2,400 00
		18	Laborers..........	14,440 00
		2	Appraisers..........	6,000 00
		2	Assistant appraisers..........	2,500 00
		1	Examiner of merchandise..........	2,250 00

Statement of the number of persons employed, &c.—Continued.

Number.	District.	No. of persons employed.	Occupation.	Compensation.
128	San Francisco, Cal.—Continued.	1	Examiner of drugs	$2,000 00
		2	Laborers, at $3 50 per day	2,191 00
		1	Surveyor	4,000 00
		2	Deputy surveyors	7,158 30
		4	District officers	7,200 00
		21	Inspectors	32,760 00
		13	....do	13,000 00
		1	Captain night watch	1,560 00
		1	Lieutenant night watch	1,400 00
		17	Night inspectors	20,400 00
		4	Weighers and measurers	8,000 00
		1	Gauger	2,000 00
		2	Boarding officers	3,200 00
		6	Bargemen	6,480 00
		1	Special agt. Treas. Dept., $9 per day	3,285 00
		1	Ass't spec. agt...do......$6 per day	2,190 00
		5	Inspectors, special service	7,300 00
		1	Special agent, Arizona	1,460 00
		1	Naval officer	4,500 00
		1	Deputy naval officer	3,125 00

N. L. JEFFRIES, *Register.*

TREASURY DEPARTMENT, *Register's Office, November* 13, 1868.

Statement showing the amount of moneys expended at each custom-house in the United States previous to June 30, 1868, *not heretofore reported, per act of March* 3, 1849.

District or port.	Period reported.	Amount.
Passamaquoddy, Maine	From December 31, 1866, to June 30, 1868	$96,358 78
Machias, Maine	From June 30, 1867, to June 30, 1868	5,646 01
Frenchman's Bay, Maine	..........do.................do	7,218 35
Bangor, Maine	From November 4, 1866, to June 30, 1868	22,704 48
Castine, Maine	From June 30, 1867, to June 30, 1868	58,497 99
Belfast, Maine	..........do.................do	8,161 07
Waldoboro', Maine	..........do.................do	16,299 23
Wiscasset, Maine	..........do.................do	6,389 91
Bath, Maine	..........do.................do	11,899 79
Portland and Falmouth, Maine	..........do.................do	284,748 56
Saco, Maine	From September 30, 1865, to June 30, 1868	4,541 92
Kennebunk, Maine	From June 30, 1867, to June 30, 1868	1,127 79
York, Maine	..........do.................do	504 62
Portsmouth, New Hampshire	From March 31, 1867, to June 30, 1868	15,712 49
Vermont, Vermont	..........do.................do	112,118 85
Newburyport, Mass	From June 30, 1867, to June 30, 1868	5,361 23
Gloucester, Mass	..........do.................do	10,835 94
Salem and Beverly, Mass	From March 31, 1867, to June 30, 1868	24,311 91
Marblehead, Mass	From June 30, 1867, to June 30, 1868	2,483 60
Boston and Charlestown, Mass	From October 8, 1866, to August 31, 1867	376,594 55
Plymouth, Mass	From June 30, 1867, to June 30, 1868	3,940 23

Statement showing the amount of moneys expended, &c.—Continued.

District or port.	Period reported.	Amount.
Barnstable, Mass	From June 30, 1867, to June 30, 1868	$8,019 92
New Bedford, Mass	do do	31,433 16
Fall River, Mass	do do	4,045 61
Edgartown, Mass	do do	9,870 99
Nantucket, Mass	do do	2,005 81
Providence, R. I	do do	21,566 62
Bristol and Warren, R. I	do do	2,466 60
Newport, R. I	do do	33,644 80
Stonington, Conn	do do	1,616 38
New London, Conn	do do	32,146 06
Middletown, Conn	do do	3,237 95
New Haven, Conn	do do	43,518 49
Fairfield, Conn	do do	4,189 31
Sag Harbor, N. Y	do do	1,213 89
New York, N. Y	From Dec. 31, 1866, to Sept. 30, 1867	1,923,950 15
Albany, N. Y	From June 30, 1867, to June 30, 1868	6,236 56
Champlain, N. Y	From March 31, 1867, to June 30, 1868	45,276 18
Oswegatchie, N. Y	do do	84,400 32
Cape Vincent, N. Y	From March 4, 1867, to June 30, 1868	34,688 82
Oswego, N. Y	From June 30, 1867, to June 30, 1868	52,796 07
Genesee, N. Y	From March 7, 1867, to June 30, 1868	38,409 89
Niagara, N. Y	From June 30, 1867, to June 30, 1868	33,775 44
Buffalo creek, N. Y	do do	65,383 67
Dunkirk, N. Y	do do	5,843 91
Newark, N. J	From March 31, 1867, to June 30, 1868	4,971 03
Perth Amboy, N. J	From June 30, 1867, to June 30, 1868	4,376 69
Little Egg Harbor, N. J	do do	2,147 58
Great Egg Harbor, N. J	do do	1,268 34
Burlington, N. J	do do	295 77
Bridgeton, N. J	do do	513 32
Philadelphia, Pa	From August 31, 1866, to June 30, 1867	324,276 90
Erie, Pa	From June 30, 1867, to June 30, 1868	22,317 61
Pittsburgh, Pa	do do	9,280 18
Delaware, Del	do do	20,464 94
Baltimore, Md	From March 31, 1867, to December 31, 1867	252,162 31
Annapolis, Md	From June 30, 1867, to June 30, 1868	1,075 26
*Vienna, Md	From March 31, 1867, to final account	127 25
Town Creek, Md	From December 31, 1866, to June 30, 1868	231 80
*Oxford, Md	From March 31, 1867, to final account	53 33
Eastern, Md	From June 30, 1867, to June 30, 1868	1,647 60
*Havre de Grace, Md	From January 1, 1865, to March 31, 1865	42 56
Georgetown, D. C	From June 30, 1867, to June 30, 1868	5,603 18
Alexandria, Va	do do	4,866 83
Tappahannock, Va	do do	1,116 00
Richmond, Va	From December 31, 1866, to June 30, 1868	18,574 48
Yorktown, Va	From June 30, 1867, to June 30, 1868	2,944 08
Petersburg, Va	From March 31, 1867, to December 31, 1867	1,957 00
Norfolk and Portsmouth, Va	From Dec. 31, 1866, to Dec. 31, 1867	55,222 52
Cherrystone, Va	From June 30, 1867, to June 30, 1868	3,731 20
Wheeling, West Va	do do	1,089 61
Parkersburg, West Va	From Jan. 20, 1866, to Dec. 31, 1867	666 31
Albemarle, N. C	From May 14, 1867, to December 31, 1867	4,363 67
*Camden, N. C	From Sept. 19, 1865, to March 31, 1867	388 89
Pamlico, N. C	From April 5, 1867, to December 31, 1867	27,459 29
Washington, N. C	From December 1, 1866, to March 31, 1867	361 44
Beaufort, N. C	From June 30, 1867, to June 30, 1868	13,769 13
*Newbern, N. C	From September 7, 1866, to April 4, 1867	8,577 81
Wilmington, N. C	From Dec. 31, 1866, to Dec. 31, 1867	42,261 10
*Ocracoke, N. C	From March 31, 1867, to final account	3 81
*Plymouth, N. C	From May 13, 1867, to final account	605 97
Georgetown, S. C	From December 31, 1866, to June 30, 1868	3,247 74
Charleston, S. C	do do	150,326 66

* Abolished.

Statement showing the amount of moneys expended, &c.—Continued.

District or port.	Period reported.	Amount.
Beaufort, S. C	From June 30, 1867, to June 30, 1868	$3,982 10
Savannah, Ga	From January 31, 1867, to June 30, 1867	49,574 22
Brunswick, Ga	No reports.	
St. Mary's, Ga	From September 1, 1866, to June 30, 1868	631 79
Fernandina, Fla	From June 30, 1867, to March 31, 1868	18,304 16
St. John's, Fla	From June 30, 1867, to June 30, 1868	6,979 35
St. Augustine, Fla	From April 27, 1867, to June 30, 1867	87 89
Key West, Fla	From June 30, 1866, to December 31, 1867	47,609 87
St. Mark's, Fla	From June 30, 1867, to June 30, 1868	9,423 87
Appalachicola, Fla	From February 28, 1867, to March 31, 1868	21,021 89
Pensacola, Fla	From March 31, 1867, to June 30, 1868	7,108 43
Mobile, Ala	From June 30, 1867, to June 30, 1868	60,286 66
Selma, Ala	No reports.	
Pearl River, Miss	From July 11, 1866, to June 30, 1868	527 91
Vicksburg, Miss	From June 30, 1867, to June 30, 1868	1,184 40
Natchez, Miss	From June 30, 1867, to March 31, 1868	403 05
New Orleans, La	From February 28, 1867, to March 31, 1868	876,653 31
Teche, La	No reports.	
Texas, Texas	From September 30, 1866, to June 30, 1868	143,211 35
Saluria, Texas	From June 30, 1867, to June 30, 1868	12,271 38
Corpus Christi, Texas	From January 19, 1867, to March 4, 1867	426 96
Brazos de Santiago, Texas	From Dec. 31, 1866, to Sept. 30, 1867	8,157 16
Paso del Norte, Texas	From December 31, 1866, to June 30, 1868	26,069 30
Memphis, Tenn	From December 31, 1860, to March 3, 1866	11,982 25
Nashville, Tenn	From November 30, 1866, to June 30, 1868	3,759 97
Paducah, Ky	From June 30, 1864, to November 15, 1866	728 99
Louisville, Ky	From Sept. 17, 1866, to Dec. 31, 1867	16,545 55
Cincinnati, Ohio	From March 3, 1867, to June 30, 1867	14,978 81
Cuyahoga, Ohio	From December 31, 1866, to June 30, 1868	60,092 04
Sandusky, Ohio	From June 30, 1867, to June 30, 1868	4,206 63
Miami, Ohio	do do	5,712 33
Detroit, Mich	From March 31, 1867, to June 30, 1868	100,196 74
Port Huron, Mich	From June 30, 1867, to June 30, 1868	34,680 58
Michilimackinack, Mich	do do	23,913 75
Michigan, Mich	do do	5,273 03
*Madison, Ind	From June 30, 1867, to October 31, 1867	127 01
New Albany, Ind	From March 14, 1866, to March 31, 1868	796 56
Evansville, Ind	From September 30, 1866, to June 30, 1868	1,007 31
Chicago, Ill	From June 30, 1866, to June 30, 1868	113,200 18
Galena, Ill	From June 30, 1867, to June 30, 1868	558 71
Quincy, Ill	From September 30, 1866, to June 30, 1868	290 12
Alton, Ill	From June 30, 1867, to June 30, 1868	592 30
Cairo, Ill	do do	2,168 09
Milwaukee, Wis	From March 31, 1867, to June 30, 1868	45,321 73
Minnesota, Minn	From March 31, 1867, to December 31, 1867	9,325 95
Dubuque, Iowa	From June 30, 1867, to December 31, 1867	247 93
Burlington, Iowa	From April 1, 1867, to March 31, 1868	521 32
Keokuk, Iowa	From June 30, 1867, to June 30, 1868	2,120 86
St. Louis, Mo	From June 30, 1866, to June 30, 1868	77,695 36
Montana and Idaho	No reports.	
Puget Sound, W. T	From June 30, 1867, to September 30, 1867	10,159 41
Oregon, Oregon	From May 24, 1867, to December 31, 1867	28,323 90
San Francisco, Cal	From June 30, 1867, to December 31, 1867	289,046 12
Total		6,715,071 67

* Abolished.

N. L. JEFFRIES, *Register.*

TREASURY DEPARTMENT,
Register's Office, November 16, 1868.

Statement of the public debt on the 1st day of January in each of the years from 1791 *to* 1842, *inclusive, and at various dates in subsequent years to July* 1, 1867.

Date	Year	Amount
January 1	1791	$75,463,476 52
	1792	77,227,924 66
	1793	80,352,634 04
	1794	78,427,404 77
	1795	80,747,587 38
	1796	83,762,172 07
	1797	82,064,479 33
	1798	79,228,529 12
	1799	78,408,669 77
	1800	82,976,294 35
	1801	83,038,059 80
	1802	80,712,632 25
	1803	77,054,686 30
	1804	86,427,120 88
	1805	82,312,150 50
	1806	75,723,270 66
	1807	69,218,398 64
	1808	65,196,317 97
	1809	57,023,192 09
	1810	53,173,217 52
	1811	48,005,587 76
	1812	45,209,737 90
	1813	55,962,827 57
	1814	81,487,846 24
	1815	99,833,660 15
	1816	127,334,933 74
	1817	123,491,965 16
	1818	103,466,633 83
	1819	95,529,648 28
	1820	91,015,566 15
	1821	89,987,427 66
	1822	93,546,676 98
	1823	90,875,877 28
	1824	90,269,777 77
	1825	83,788,432 71
	1826	81,054,059 99
	1827	73,987,357 20
	1828	67,475,043 87
	1829	58,421,413 67
January 1	1830	$48,565,406 50
	1831	39,123,191 68
	1832	24,322,235 18
	1833	7,001,032 88
	1834	4,760,081 08
	1835	351,289 05
	1836	291,089 05
	1837	1,878,223 55
	1838	4,857,660 46
	1839	11,983,737 53
	1840	5,125,077 63
	1841	6,737,398 00
	1842	15,028,486 37
July 1	1843	27,203,450 69
	1844	24,748,188 23
	1845	17,093,794 80
	1846	16,750,926 33
	1847	38,956,623 38
	1848	48,526,379 37
December 1	1849	64,704,693 71
	1850	64,228,238 37
November 20	1851	62,560,395 26
December 30	1852	65,131,692 13
July 1	1853	67,340,628 78
	1854	47,242,206 05
November 17	1855	39,969,731 05
November 15	1856	30,963,909 64
July 1	1857	29,060,386 90
	1858	44,910,777 66
	1859	58,754,699 33
	1860	64,769,703 08
	1861	90,867,828 68
	1862	514,211,371 92
	1863	1,098,793,181 37
	1864	1,740,690,489 49
	1865	2,682,593,026 53
	1866	2,783,425,879 21
	1867	2,692,199,215 12
	1868	2,636,320,964 67

N. L. JEFFRIES, *Register*.

TREASURY DEPARTMENT,
Register's Office, November 16, 1868.

Statement of the revenue collected from the beginning of the government to the 30th of June, Lands, and Miscellaneous sources, with the receipts

	From customs: Duties, imposts, and tonnage.	From internal revenue.	From direct tax.	From postage.
From March 4, 1789, to Dec. 31, 1791	$4,399,473 09			
1792 (for the year)	3,443,070 85	$208,924 81		
1793	4,255,306 56	337,705 70		$11,020 51
1794	4,801,065 28	274,089 62		29,478 49
1795	5,588,461 26	337,755 36		22,400 00
1796	6,567,987 94	475,289 60		72,909 84
1797	7,549,649 65	575,491 45		64,500 00
1798	7,106,061 93	644,357 95		39,500 00
1799	6,610,449 31	779,136 44		41,000 00
1800	9,080,932 73	809,396 55	$734,223 97	78,000 00
1801	10,750,778 93	1,048,033 43	534,343 38	79,500 00
1802	12,438,235 74	621,898 89	206,565 44	35,000 00
1803	10,479,417 61	215,177 69	71,879 20	16,427 26
1804	11,098,565 33	50,941 29	50,198 44	26,500 00
1805	12,936,487 04	21,747 15	21,883 91	21,342 50
1806	14,667,698 17	20,101 45	55,763 86	41,117 67
1807	15,845,521 61	13,051 40	34,732 56	3,614 73
1808	16,363,550 58	8,210 73	19,159 21	
1809	7,296,020 58	4,044 39	7,517 31	
1810	8,583,309 31	7,430 63	12,448 68	
1811	13,313,222 73	2,295 95	7,666 66	37 70
1812	8,958,777 53	4,903 06	859 22	85,039 70
1813	13,224,623 25	4,755 04	3,805 52	35,000 00
1814	5,998,772 08	1,662,984 22	2,219,497 36	45,000 00
1815	7,282,942 22	4,678,059 07	2,162,673 41	135,000 00
1816	36,306,874 88	5,124,708 31	4,253,635 09	149,787 74
1817	26,283,348 49	2,678,100 77	1,834,187 04	29,371 91
1818	17,176,385 00	955,279 20	264,333 36	20,070 00
1819	20,203,608 76	229,593 63	83,650 78	71 32
1820	15,005,612 15	106,260 53	31,586 82	6,465 95
1821	13,004,447 15	69,027 63	29,349 05	516 91
1822	17,589,761 94	67,665 71	20,961 56	602 04
1823	19,088,433 44	34,242 17	10,337 71	110 69
1824	17,878,325 71	34,663 37	6,201 96	
1825	20,098,713 45	25,771 35	2,330 85	469 56
1826	23,341,331 77	21,589 93	6,638 76	300 14
1827	19,712,283 29	19,885 68	2,626 90	101 00
1828	23,205,523 64	17,451 54	2,218 81	20 15
1829	22,681,965 91	14,502 74	11,335 05	86 60
1830	21,922,391 39	12,160 62	16,980 59	55 13
1831	24,224,441 77	6,933 51	10,506 01	561 02
1832	28,465,237 24	11,630 65	6,791 13	244 95
1833	29,032,508 91	2,759 00	394 12	
1834	16,214,957 15	4,196 09	19 80	100 00
1835	19,391,310 59	10,459 48	4,263 33	893 00
1836	23,409,940 53	370 00	728 79	10 91
1837	11,169,290 39	5,493 84	1,687 70	
1838	16,158,800 36	2,467 27		
1839	23,137,924 81	2,553 32	755 22	
1840	13,499,502 17	1,682 25		
1841	14,487,216 74	3,261 36		
1842	18,187,908 76	495 00		
1843 (half year to June 30)	7,046,843 91	103 25		
1844 (fiscal year ending June 30)	26,183,570 94	1,777 34		
1844–'45	27,528,112 70	3,517 12		
1845–'46	26,712,667 87	2,897 26		
1846–'47	23,747,864 66	375 00		
1847–'48	31,757,070 66	375 00		
1848–'49	28,346,738 82	375 00		
1849–'50	39,668,686 42			
1850–'51	49,017,567 92			
1851–'52	47,339,326 62			
1852–'53	58,931,865 52			
1853–'54	64,224,190 27			
1854–'55	53,025,794 21			
1855–'56	64,022,863 50			
1856–'57	63,875,905 05			
1857–'58	41,789,620 96			
1858–'59	49,565,824 38			
1859–'60	53,187,511 87			
1860–'61	39,582,125 64			
1861–'62	49,056,397 62		1,795,331 73	
1862–'63	69,059,642 40	37,640,787 95	1,485,103 61	
1863–'64	102,316,152 99	109,741,134 10	475,648 96	
1864–'65	84,928,260 60	209,464,215 25	1,200,573 03	
1865–'66	179,046,651 58	309,226,813 42	1,974,754 12	
1866–'67	176,417,810 88	266,027,537 43	4,200,233 70	
1867–'68	164,464,599 56	191,087,589 41	1,788,145 85	

TREASURY DEPARTMENT, REGISTER'S OFFICE, *November* 16, 1868.

1867, *under the several heads of Customs, Internal Revenue, Direct Tax, Postage, Public from loans and treasury notes, and the total receipts.*

From public lands.	From bank stocks, dividends, and bonds.	From miscellaneous sources.	Total, exclusive of loans and treasury notes.	From loans and treasury notes.	Total receipts.
....	....	$19,440 10	$4,418,913 19	$5,791,112 56	$10,210,025 75
....	$8,028 00	9,936 65	3,669,960 31	5,070,806 46	8,740,766 77
....	38,500 00	10,390 37	4,652,923 14	1,067,701 14	5,720,624 28
....	303,472 00	23,799 48	5,431,904 87	4,609,196 78	10,041,101 65
....	162,000 00	5,917 97	6,114,534 59	3,305,268 20	9,419,802 79
$4,836 13	1,240,000 00	16,506 14	8,377,529 65	362,800 00	8,740,329 65
83,540 60	385,220 00	30,379 29	8,688,780 99	70,135 41	8,758,916 40
11,963 11	79,920 00	18,692 81	7,900,495 80	308,574 27	8,209,070 07
....	71,040 00	45,187 56	7,546,813 31	5,074,646 53	12,621,459 84
443 75	71,040 00	74,712 10	10,848,749 10	1,602,435 04	12,451,184 14
167,726 06	88,800 00	266,149 15	12,935,330 95	10,125 00	12,945,455 95
188,628 02	1,327,560 00	177,905 86	14,995,793 95	5,597 36	15,001,391 31
165,675 69	....	115,518 18	11,064,097 63	....	11,064,097 63
487,526 79	....	112,575 53	11,826,307 38	9,532 64	11,835,840 02
540,193 80	....	19,039 80	13,560,694 20	128,814 94	13,689,509 14
765,245 73	....	10,004 19	15,559,931 07	48,897 71	15,608,828 78
466,163 27	....	34,935 69	16,398,019 26	....	16,398,019 26
647,939 06	....	21,802 35	17,060,661 93	1,822 16	17,062,484 09
442,252 33	....	23,638 51	7,773,473 12	....	7,773,473 12
696,548 82	....	84,476 84	9,384,214 28	2,759,992 25	12,144,206 53
1,040,237 53	....	60,068 52	14,423,529 09	8,309 05	14,431,838 14
710,427 78	....	41,125 47	9,801,132 76	12,837,900 00	22,639,032 76
835,655 14	....	236,571 00	14,340,409 95	26,184,435 00	40,524,844 95
1,135,971 09	....	119,399 81	11,181,625 16	23,377,911 79	34,559,536 95
1,287,959 28	....	150,282 74	15,696,916 82	35,264,320 78	50,961,237 60
1,717,985 03	....	123,994 61	47,676,985 66	9,494,436 16	57,171,421 82
1,991,226 06	202,426 00	80,389 17	33,099,049 74	734,542 59	33,833,592 03
2,606,564 77	525,000 00	37,547 71	21,585,180 04	8,765 62	21,593,945 66
3,274,422 78	675,000 00	57,027 10	24,603,374 37	2,291 00	24,605,665 37
1,635,871 61	1,000,000 00	54,872 49	17,840,669 55	3,040,824 13	20,881,493 68
1,212,966 46	105,000 00	152,072 52	14,573,379 72	5,000,324 00	19,573,703 72
1,803,581 54	297,500 00	452,355 15	20,232,427 94	....	20,232,427 94
916,523 10	350,000 00	141,019 15	20,540,666 26	....	20,540,666 26
984,418 15	350,000 00	127,603 60	19,381,212 79	5,000,000 00	24,381,212 79
1,216,090 56	367,500 00	129,982 25	21,840,858 02	5,000,000 00	26,840,858 02
1,393,785 09	402,500 00	94,288 52	25,260,434 21	....	25,260,434 21
1,495,845 26	420,000 00	1,315,621 83	22,966,363 96	....	22,966,363 96
1,018,308 75	455,000 00	65,106 34	24,763,629 23	....	24,763,629 23
1,517,175 13	490,000 00	112,561 95	24,827,627 38	....	24,827,627 38
2,329,356 14	490,000 00	73,172 64	24,844,116 51	....	24,844,116 51
3,210,815 48	490,000 00	583,563 03	28,526,820 82	....	28,526,820 82
2,623,381 03	659,000 00	101,165 66	31,867,450 66	....	31,867,450 66
3,967,682 55	610,285 00	334,796 67	33,948,426 25	....	33,948,426 25
4,857,600 69	586,649 50	128,412 32	21,791,935 55	....	21,791,935 55
14,757,600 75	569,280 82	696,279 13	35,430,087 10	....	35,430,087 10
24,877,179 86	328,674 67	2,209,891 32	50,826,796 08	....	50,826,796 08
6,776,236 52	1,375,965 44	5,625,479 15	24,954,153 04	2,992,989 15	27,947,142 19
3,081,939 47	4,542,102 22	2,517,252 42	26,302,561 74	12,716,820 86	39,019,382 60
7,076,447 35	....	1,265,088 91	31,482,749 61	3,857,276 21	35,340,025 82
3,292,683 29	1,744,513 80	911,733 82	19,480,115 33	5,589,547 51	25,069,662 84
1,365,627 42	672,769 38	331,285 57	16,860,160 27	13,659,317 38	20,519,477 65
1,335,797 52	....	440,807 97	19,965,009 25	14,808,735 64	34,773,744 89
897,818 11	....	296,235 99	8,241,001 26	12,541,409 19	20,782,410 45
2,059,939 80	....	1,075,419 70	29,320,707 78	1,877,847 95	31,198,555 73
2,077,022 30	....	333,201 78	29,941,853 90	....	29,941,853 90
2,694,452 48	....	274,139 44	29,684,157 05	....	29,684,157 05
2,498,355 20	....	284,444 36	26,531,039 22	28,870,765 36	55,401,804 58
3,328,642 56	....	627,021 13	35,713,109 65	21,293,780 00	57,006,889 65
1,688,959 55	....	338,233 70	30,374,307 07	29,422,585 91	59,796,892 98
1,859,894 25	....	706,059 12	42,234,639 79	5,435,126 96	47,669,766 75
2,352,305 30	266,072 09	921,933 24	52,557,878 55	203,400 00	52,761,278 55
2,043,239 58	1,021 34	438,580 76	49,822,168 30	46,300 00	49,868,468 30
1,667,084 99	....	1,188,104 07	61,787,054 58	16,350 00	61,803,404 58
8,470,798 39	....	1,105,352 74	73,800,341 40	1,950 00	73,802,291 40
11,497,049 07	....	827,731 40	65,350,574 68	800 00	65,351,374 68
8,917,644 93	....	1,116,190 81	74,056,699 24	200 00	74,056,899 24
3,829,486 64	....	1,259,920 88	68,965,312 57	3,900 00	68,969,212 57
3,513,715 87	....	1,352,029 13	46,655,365 96	23,717,300 00	70,372,665 96
1,756,687 30	....	2,163,953 96	53,486,465 64	28,287,500 00	81,773,965 64
1,778,557 71	....	1,088,530 25	56,054,599 83	20,786,808 00	76,841,407 83
870,658 54	....	1,023,515 31	41,476,299 49	41,895,340 65	83,371,640 13
152,203 77	....	931,787 64	51,935,720 76	529,692,460 50	581,628,181 26
167,617 17	....	4,344,139 82	112,687,290 95	776,682,361 57	889,379,652 52
583,333 29	....	51,505,502 26	264,626,771 60	1,121,131,842 98	1,385,758,614 58
996,553 31	....	37,125,002 89	333,714,605 08	1,472,224,740 85	1,805,939,345 93
665,031 03	....	67,119,369 91	558,032,620 06	712,851,553 05	1,270,884,173 11
1,163,575 76	....	42,824,852 50	490,634,010 27	640,426,910 29	1,131,060,920 16
1,348,715 41	....	46,949,033 09	405,638,083 32	625,111,433 20	1,030,749,516 52

N. L. JEFFRIES, *Register.*

Statement of expenditures from the beginning of the government to June 30, 1868, under the Indian department, and Miscellaneous, with

[The years 1862, 1863, and 1864 are from the account of warrants on the treasury

	Civil list.	Foreign intercourse.	Navy Department.	War Department.	Pensions.
From Mar. 4, 1789, to Dec. 31, 1791	$757,134 45	$14,733 33	$570 00	$632,804 03	$175,813 88
1792 (for the year)	380,917 58	78,766 67	53 02	1,100,702 09	109,243 15
1793	358,241 08	89,500 00	....	1,130,249 08	80,017 81
1794	440,946 58	146,403 51	61,408 97	2,629,097 59	81,399 24
1795	361,633 36	912,685 12	410,562 03	2,480,910 13	68,673 22
1796	447,139 05	184,859 64	274,784 04	1,260,263 84	100,843 71
1797	483,233 70	669,788 54	382,631 89	1,039,402 66	92,256 97
1798	504,605 17	457,428 74	1,381,347 76	2,009,522 30	104,845 33
1799	592,905 76	271,374 11	2,858,081 84	2,466,946 98	95,444 03
1800	748,688 45	395,288 18	3,448,716 03	2,560,878 77	64,130 73
1801	549,288 31	295,676 73	2,111,424 00	1,672,944 08	73,533 37
1802	596,981 11	550,925 93	915,561 87	1,179,148 25	85,440 39
1803	526,583 12	1,110,834 77	1,215,230 53	822,055 85	62,902 10
1804	624,795 63	1,186,655 57	1,189,832 75	875,423 93	80,092 80
1805	585,849 79	2,798,028 77	1,597,500 00	712,781 28	81,854 59
1806	684,230 53	1,760,421 30	1,649,641 44	1,224,355 38	81,875 53
1807	655,524 65	577,826 34	1,722,064 47	1,288,685 91	70,500 00
1808	691,167 80	304,992 83	1,884,067 80	2,900,834 40	82,576 04
1809	712,465 13	166,306 04	2,427,758 80	3,347,772 17	87,833 54
1810	703,994 03	81,367 48	1,654,244 20	2,294,323 94	83,744 10
1811	644,467 27	264,904 47	1,965,566 39	2,032,828 19	75,043 88
1812	826,271 55	347,703 29	3,959,365 15	11,817,798 24	91,402 10
1813	780,545 45	209,941 01	6,446,600 10	19,662,013 02	86,989 91
1814	927,424 23	177,179 97	7,311,290 60	20,350,806 86	90,164 36
1815	852,247 16	290,892 04	8,660,000 25	14,794,294 22	69,656 06
1816	1,208,125 77	364,620 40	3,908,278 30	16,012,096 80	188,804 15
1817	994,556 17	281,995 97	3,314,598 49	8,004,236 53	297,374 43
1818	1,109,559 79	420,429 90	2,953,695 00	5,622,715 10	*890,719 90
1819	1,142,180 41	284,113 94	3,847,640 42	6,506,300 37	2,415,939 85
1820	1,248,310 05	253,370 04	4,387,990 00	2,630,392 31	3,208,376 31
1821	1,112,292 64	207,110 75	3,319,243 06	4,461,291 78	242,817 25
1822	1,158,131 58	164,879 51	2,224,458 98	3,111,981 48	1,948,199 40
1823	1,058,911 65	292,118 56	2,503,765 83	3,096,924 43	1,780,588 52
1824	1,336,266 24	†5,140,099 83	2,904,581 56	3,340,939 85	1,498,326 59
1825	1,330,747 24	371,666 25	3,049,083 86	3,659,913 18	1,308,810 57
1826	1,256,745 48	232,719 08	4,218,902 45	3,943,194 37	1,556,593 83
1827	1,228,141 04	659,211 87	4,263,877 45	3,938,977 88	976,148 86
1828	1,455,490 58	1,001,193 66	3,918,786 44	4,145,544 56	850,573 57
1829	1,327,069 36	207,765 85	3,308,745 47	6,250,230 28	949,594 47
1830	1,579,724 64	294,067 27	3,239,428 63	6,752,688 66	1,363,297 31
1831	1,373,755 99	298,554 00	3,856,183 07	4,846,405 61	1,170,665 14
1832	1,800,757 74	325,181 07	3,956,370 29	5,446,131 23	1,184,422 40
1833	1,562,758 28	955,395 88	3,901,356 75	6,705,022 95	4,589,152 40
1834	2,080,601 60	241,562 35	3,956,260 42	5,698,517 51	3,364,285 30
1835	1,905,551 51	774,750 28	3,864,939 06	5,827,948 57	1,954,711 32
1836	2,110,175 47	533,382 65	5,807,718 23	11,791,208 02	2,882,797 96
1837	2,357,035 94	4,603,905 40	6,646,914 53	13,731,172 31	2,672,162 45
1838	2,688,708 50	1,215,095 52	6,131,580 53	13,088,169 69	2,156,057 29
1839	2,116,982 77	987,667 92	6,182,294 25	9,227,045 90	3,142,750 50
1840	2,736,769 31	083,278 15	6,113,896 89	7,155,204 99	2,603,562 17
1841	2,556,471 79	428,410 57	6,001,076 97	9,042,749 92	2,388,434 51
1842	2,905,041 65	563,191 41	8,397,242 95	6,658,137 16	1,378,931 33
1843 (six months ending June 30)	1,222,422 48	400,566 04	3,727,711 53	3,104,638 48	839,041 12
1844 (fiscal year ending June 30)	2,454,958 15	636,079 66	6,498,199 11	5,192,445 05	2,032,008 99
1844–'45	2,369,652 79	702,637 22	6,297,177 89	5,819,888 50	2,398,867 29
1845–'46	2,532,232 92	409,292 55	6,455,013 92	10,362,374 36	1,809,739 62
1846–'47	2,570,338 44	405,079 10	7,900,635 76	35,776,495 72	1,742,820 85
1847–'48	2,645,802 87	448,593 01	9,408,476 02	27,838,374 80	1,226,500 92
1848–'49	2,865,196 91	6,908,996 72	9,786,705 92	16,563,543 33	193,695 87
1849–'50	3,027,454 39	5,990,858 81	7,904,724 66	9,687,924 58	1,866,886 02
1850–'51	3,481,219 51	6,256,427 16	8,880,581 38	12,161,965 11	2,293,377 22
1851–'52	3,439,923 22	4,196,321 59	8,918,842 10	8,521,506 19	2,401,858 78
1852–'53	4,265,861 68	950,871 30	11,067,789 53	9,910,498 49	1,736,262 45
1853–'54	4,621,492 24	§7,763,812 31	10,790,096 32	11,722,282 97	1,369,009 47
1854–'55	6,350,875 88	997,007 26	13,327,095 11	14,648,074 07	1,542,255 40
1855–'56	6,452,256 35	3,642,615 39	14,074,834 64	16,963,160 51	1,344,027 70
1856–'57	7,611,547 27	999,177 65	12,651,694 61	19,159,150 87	1,423,770 85
1857–'58	7,116,339 04	1,396,508 72	14,053,264 64	25,679,121 63	1,221,163 14
1858–'59	5,913,281 50	981,946 87	14,690,927 90	23,154,720 53	161,190 66
1859–'60	6,077,008 95	1,146,143 79	11,514,649 83	14,472,202 72	1,100,802 32
1860–'61	6,074,141 83	1,147,786 91	12,387,156 52	23,001,530 67	1,034,599 73
1861–'62	5,939,009 29	1,339,710 35	42,674,569 69	394,468,407 36	879,583 23
1862–'63	6,350,618 78	1,231,413 06	63,211,105 27	599,298,600 83	3,140,194 44
1863–'64	8,059,177 23	1,290,691 92	85,733,292 77	690,791,842 97	4,979,633 17
1864–'65	10,833,944 87	1,260,818 08	122,567,776 12	1,031,323,360 79	9,291,610 48
1865–'66	12,287,828 55	1,338,388 18	43,324,118 52	284,449,701 82	15,605,352 35
1866–'67	15,585,489 55	1,548,589 26	31,034,011 04	95,224,415 63	20,936,551 71
1867–'68	11,950,156 58	1,441,344 05	25,775,502 72	123,246,648 62	23,782,386 78

* The first revolutionary pensions. † Purchase of Florida. ‡ Actual payments

§ Includes seven millions of Mexican indemnity. The years 1849 to 1852 also embrace large sums paid to Mexico.

several heads of Civil List, Foreign Intercourse, Navy Department, War Department, Pensions, the interest and principal of the public debt.

issued; all previous years are from the account of warrants paid.]

Indians.	Miscellaneous.	Total of ordinary expenditures.	Interest on public debt.	Principal of public debt.	Total debts and loans.	Total expenditures.
$27,000 00	$311,533 83	$1,919,589 52	$2,349,437 44	$2,938,512 06	$5,287,949 50	$7,207,539 02
13,648 85	194,572 32	1,877,903 77	3,201,628 23	4,062,037 76	7,267,665 90	9,141,569 67
27,282 83	24,709 46	1,710,070 26	2,772,242 12	3,047,263 18	5,819,505 29	7,529,575 55
13,042 46	118,248 30	3,500,546 65	3,490,292 52	2,311,285 57	5,801,378 09	9,302,124 74
23,475 69	92,718 50	4,350,658 04	3,189,151 16	2,895,260 45	6,084,411 61	10,435,069 65
113,563 98	150,476 14	2,531,930 40	3,195,054 53	2,640,791 91	5,835,846 44	8,367,776 84
62,396 38	103,880 82	2,833,590 96	3,300,043 06	2,492,378 76	5,792,421 82	8,626,012 78
16,470 09	149,004 15	4,623,223 54	3,053,281 28	937,012 86	3,990,294 14	8,613,517 68
20,302 19	175,111 81	6,480,166 72	3,186,287 60	1,410,589 18	4,596,876 78	11,077,043 50
31 22	193,636 59	7,411,369 77	3,374,704 72	1,203,665 23	4,578,369 95	11,989,739 92
9,000 00	269,803 41	4,981,669 90	4,412,912 93	2,878,794 11	7,291,707 04	12,273,376 94
94,000 00	315,022 36	3,737,079 91	4,125,038 95	5,413,965 81	9,539,004 76	13,276,084 67
60,000 00	205,217 87	4,002,824 44	3,848,828 00	3,407,331 43	7,256,159 43	11,258,983 67
116,500 00	379,558 23	4,452,858 91	4,266,582 85	3,905,204 90	8,171,787 45	12,624,646 36
196,500 00	384,720 19	3,737,079 91	4,148,998 82	3,220,890 97	7,369,889 79	13,727,124 41
234,200 00	445,485 18	6,080,209 36	3,723,407 88	5,266,476 73	8,989,884 61	15,070,093 97
205,425 00	464,546 52	4,984,572 89	3,369,578 48	2,938,141 62	6,307,720 10	11,292,292 99
213,575 00	427,124 98	6,504,338 85	3,428,152 87	6,832,092 48	10,260,245 35	16,764,584 20
337,503 84	337,032 62	7,414,672 14	2,866,074 90	3,586,479 26	6,452,554 16	13,867,226 30
177,625 00	315,783 47	5,311,082 28	2,845,427 53	5,163,476 93	8,098,994 46	13,319,986 74
151,875 00	457,919 66	5,592,604 86	2,465,733 16	5,543,470 89	8,009,204 05	13,601,808 91
277,845 00	509,113 37	17,829,498 70	2,451,272 57	1,998,349 88	4,449,622 45	22,279,121 15
167,358 28	738,949 15	28,082,396 92	3,599,455 22	7,505,668 22	11,108,123 44	39,190,520 36
167,394 86	1,103,425 50	30,127,686 38	4,593,239 04	3,307,304 90	7,900,543 94	38,028,230 32
530,750 00	1,755,731 27	26,953,571 00	5,754,568 63	6,874,353 71	12,628,922 35	39,582,493 35
274,512 16	1,416,995 00	23,373,432 53	7,213,258 69	17,657,804 24	24,871,062 93	48,244,495 51
319,463 71	2,242,384 62	15,454,609 92	6,389,209 81	19,041,826 31	25,423,036 12	40,877,646 04
505,704 27	2,305,849 82	13,808,672 78	6,016,446 74	15,279,754 88	21,296,201 62	35,104,875 40
463,181 39	1,640,917 06	16,300,273 44	5,163,538 11	2,540,388 18	7,703,926 29	24,004,199 73
315,750 01	1,090,341 85	13,134,530 57	5,126,097 20	3,502,397 08	8,628,494 28	21,763,024 85
477,005 44	903,718 15	10,723,479 07	5,087,274 01	3,279,821 61	8,367,093 62	19,090,572 69
575,007 41	644,985 15	9,827,643 51	5,172,578 24	2,676,370 88	7,848,949 12	17,676,592 63
380,781 82	671,063 78	9,784,154 55	4,922,684 60	607,331 81	5,530,016 41	15,314,171 00
429,987 90	678,942 74	15,330,144 71	4,996,562 08	11,571,831 68	16,568,393 76	31,898,538 47
724,106 44	1,046,131 40	11,490,459 94	4,366,769 08	7,728,575 70	12,095,344 78	23,585,804 72
743,447 83	1,110,713 23	13,062,316 27	3,973,480 54	7,067,601 65	11,041,082 19	24,103,398 46
760,624 88	826,123 67	12,653,095 65	3,486,071 51	6,517,596 88	10,003,668 39	22,656,764 04
705,084 24	1,219,368 40	13,296,041 45	3,098,800 59	9,064,637 48	12,163,438 07	25,459,479 52
576,344 74	1,565,679 66	12,660,400 62	2,542,843 23	9,841,024 55	12,383,867 78	25,044,358 40
622,262 47	1,363,624 13	13,229,533 33	1,913,533 40	9,442,214 82	11,355,748 22	24,585,281 55
926,167 98	1,392,336 11	13,864,067 80	1,383,582 95	14,790,795 27	16,174,378 22	30,038,446 12
1,352,323 40	2,451,202 64	16,516,388 77	772,561 50	17,067,747 79	17,840,309 29	34,356,698 06
1,801,977 08	3,198,091 77	22,713,755 11	303,796 87	1,239,746 51	1,543,543 38	24,257,298 49
1,002,625 07	2,082,565 00	18,425,417 25	202,152 98	5,974,412 21	6,176,565 19	24,601,982 44
1,637,652 80	1,549,396 74	17,514,950 28	57,863 08	328 20	58,191 28	17,573,141 56
4,993,160 11	2,749,721 60	30,868,164 04	†63,389 85	†3,140 32	66,500 17	30,934,664 21
4,299,594 68	2,932,428 93	37,243,214 24	....	21,822 91	21,822 91	37,265,037 15
5,313,245 81	3,256,868 18	32,849,718 08	14,997 54	5,590,722 73	5,605,720 27	39,455,438 35
2,218,967 18	2,621,340 20	26,496,948 72	399,834 24	10,718,153 19	11,117,967 43	37,614,936 15
2,271,857 10	2,575,351 50	24,139,929 11	174,635 77	3,911,977 93	4,086,613 70	28,226,533 81
2,273,697 44	3,505,999 09	26,196,840 29	288,063 45	5,312,626 29	5,600,689 74	31,797,530 03
1,151,400 54	3,307,391 55	24,361,336 59	778,550 06	7,796,989 88	8,575,539 94	32,936,876 53
382,404 47	1,579,724 48	11,256,508 60	528,584 57	333,011 98	861,596 55	12,118,105 15
1,282,271 00	2,554,146 05	20,650,108 01	1,874,863 66	11,117,039 18	12,991,902 84	33,642,010 85
1,467,774 95	2,839,470 97	21,895,369 61	1,066,985 04	7,528,054 06	8,595,039 10	30,490,408 71
1,080,047 80	3,769,758 42	26,418,459 59	843,228 77	370,594 54	1,213,523 31	27,632,282 90
1,496,008 69	3,910,190 81	53,801,569 37	1,117,830 22	5,601,452 15	6,719,282 37	60,520,851 74
1,103,251 78	2,554,455 37	45,227,454 77	3,391,652 17	13,036,036 25	15,457,688 42	60,655,143 19
509,263 25	3,111,140 61	39,933,542 61	3,554,419 40	12,898,460 73	16,452,880 13	56,386,422 74
1,663,591 47	7,025,450 16	37,165,990 09	3,884,406 95	3,554,321 22	7,438,728 17	44,604,718 26
2,829,801 77	8,146,577 33	44,049,949 48	3,711,407 40	714,947 43	4,426,154 83	48,476,104 31
3,043,576 04	9,867,926 64	40,389,954 56	4,002,014 13	2,320,640 14	6,322,654 27	46,712,608 83
3,900,537 87	12,246,335 03	44,078,156 35	3,666,905 24	6,832,000 15	10,498,905 35	54,577,061 74
1,413,995 08	13,461,450 13	51,142,138 42	3,074,078 33	21,256,902 33	24,335,980 66	75,473,119 08
2,708,347 71	16,738,442 29	56,312,097 72	2,315,996 25	7,536,681 99	9,852,678 24	66,164,775 96
2,596,465 92	15,260,475 94	60,533,836 45	1,954,752 34	10,437,772 78	12,392,505 12	72,726,341 57
4,241,028 60	18,946,180 91	65,032,559 76	1,594,845 44	4,647,182 17	6,242,027 61	71,274,587 37

No. 17.—*Statement exhibiting the amount of tonnage of the United States annually, from 1789 to 1868, inclusive; also the registered, enrolled, and licensed tonnage employed in steam navigation in each year.*

Year ending—	Registered sail tonnage.	Registered steam tonnage.	Enrolled and licensed sail tonnage.	Enrolled and licensed steam tonnage.	Total tonnage.
	Tons.	*Tons.*	*Tons.*	*Tons.*	*Tons.*
Dec. 31, 1789	123, 893	....	77, 669	....	201, 562
1790	346, 254	....	132, 123	....	274, 377
1791	362, 110	....	139, 036	....	502, 146
1792	411, 438	....	153, 019	....	564, 457
1793	367, 734	....	153, 030	....	520, 764
1794	438, 863	....	189, 755	....	628, 618
1795	529, 471	....	218, 494	....	747, 965
1796	576, 733	....	255, 166	....	831, 899
1797	597, 777	....	279, 136	....	876, 913
1798	603, 376	....	294, 952	....	898, 328
1799	662, 197	....	277, 212	....	939, 409
1800	559, 921	....	302, 571	....	972, 492
1801	632, 907	....	314, 670	....	947, 577
1802	560, 380	....	331, 724	....	892, 104
1803	597, 157	....	352, 015	....	949, 172
1804	672, 530	....	369, 874	....	1, 042, 404
1805	749, 341	....	391, 027	....	1, 140, 368
1806	808, 265	....	400, 451	....	1, 208, 716
1807	848, 307	....	420, 241	....	1, 268, 584
1808	759, 054	....	473, 542	....	1, 242, 596
1809	910, 059	....	440, 222	....	1, 350, 281
1810	984, 269	....	449, 515	....	1, 424, 748
1811	768, 852	....	463, 650	....	1, 232, 502
1812	760, 624	....	509, 373	....	1, 269, 997
1813	674, 853	....	491, 776	....	1, 666, 629
1814	674, 633	....	484, 577	....	1, 159, 210
1815	854, 295	....	513, 833	....	1, 368, 128
1816	800, 760	....	571, 459	....	1, 372, 219
1817	800, 725	....	590, 187	....	1, 399, 912
1818	606, 089	....	619, 096	....	1, 225, 185
1819	612, 930	....	647, 821	....	1, 260, 751
1820	619, 048	....	661, 119	....	1, 280, 167
1821	619, 896	....	679, 062	....	1, 298, 958
1822	628, 150	....	696, 549	....	1, 324, 699
1823	639, 921	....	671, 766	24, 879	1, 336, 566
1824	669, 973	....	697, 580	21, 610	1, 389, 163
1825	700, 788	....	699, 263	23, 061	1, 423, 112
1826	737, 978	....	762, 154	34, 059	1, 534, 191
1827	747, 170	....	833, 240	40, 198	1, 620, 608
1828	812, 619	....	889, 355	39, 418	1, 741, 392
1829	650, 143	....	556, 618	54, 037	1, 260, 798
1830	575, 056	1, 419	552, 248	63, 053	1, 191, 776
1831	619, 575	877	613, 827	33, 568	1, 267, 847
1832	686, 809	181	661, 827	90, 633	1, 439, 450
1833	749, 482	545	754, 819	101, 305	1, 606, 151
1834	857, 098	340	778, 995	122, 474	1, 758, 907
Sept. 30, 1835	885, 481	340	816, 645	122, 474	1, 824, 940
1836	897, 321	454	839, 226	145, 102	1, 822, 103
1837	809, 343	1, 104	932, 576	153, 661	1, 896, 684
1838	819, 801	2, 791	982, 416	190, 632	1, 995, 640
1839	829, 096	5, 149	1, 062, 445	199, 789	2, 096, 479
1840	895, 610	4, 155	1, 082, 815	198, 154	2, 180, 764
1841	945, 057	746	1, 010, 599	174, 342	2, 130, 744
1842	970, 658	4, 701	892, 072	224, 960	2, 092, 391
June 30, 1843	1, 003, 932	5, 373	917, 804	231, 494	2, 158, 603
1844	1, 061, 856	6, 909	946, 060	265, 270	2, 280, 095

No. 17.—*Statement exhibiting the amount of tonnage, &c.*—Continued.

Year ending—	Registered sail tonnage.	Registered steam tonnage.	Enrolled and licensed sail tonnage.	Enrolled and licensed steam tonnage.	Total tonnage.
	Tons.	*Tons.*	*Tons.*	*Tons.*	*Tons.*
June 30 1859	2, 414, 654	92, 748	1, 961, 631	676, 005	5, 145, 038
1860	2, 448, 941	97, 296	2, 036, 990	770, 641	5, 353, 868
1861	2, 540, 020	102, 608	2, 122, 589	774, 596	5, 539, 813
1862	2, 177, 253	113, 998	2, 224, 449	596, 465	5, 112, 165
1863	1, 892, 899	133, 215	2, 660, 212	439, 755	5, 126, 081
1864	1, 475, 376	106, 519	2, 550, 690	853, 816	4, 986, 401
1865, old admeasurement	1, 022, 465	69, 539	1, 794, 372	630, 411	3, 516, 787
1865, new admeasurement	482, 110	28, 469	730, 695	338, 720	1, 579, 994
1866, old admeasurement	341, 619	42, 776	443, 635	114, 269	942, 299
1866, new admeasurement	953, 018	155, 513	1, 489, 194	770, 754	3, 368, 479
1867, old admeasurement	182, 203	32, 593	95, 869	36, 307	346, 972
1867, new admeasurement	1, 187, 714	165, 522	1, 646, 820	957, 458	3, 957, 514
1868, old admeasurement	33, 449	....	....	....	33, 449
1868, new admeasurement	1, 310, 344	221, 939	1, 808, 550	977, 476	4, 318, 309

N. L. JEFFRIES, *Register.*

TREASURY DEPARTMENT, *Register's Office, Nov.* 17, 1868.

Statement exhibiting a condensed view of the tonnage of the several States and customs districts of the United States on the 30th day of June, 1868.

Customs districts.	Registered.		Enrolled.		Licensed under 20 tons.		Total.	
	Number of vessels.	Tonnage.	Number of vessels.	Tonnage.	Number of vessels.	Tonnage.	Number of vessels.	Tonnage.
MAINE.								
Passamaquoddy	62	14, 359. 14	128	11, 255. 72	23	298. 24	213	25, 912. 70
Machias	40	7, 757. 16	154	7, 485. 62	22	65. 75	216	15, 308. 53
Frenchman's bay	8	1, 310. 78	226	15, 024. 17	46	559. 31	282	16, 894. 26
Castine	14	4, 409. 71	348	19, 686. 25	109	1, 652. 33	471	25, 748. 29
Bangor	44	14, 622. 71	191	17, 487. 28	6	74. 76	241	32, 184. 75
Belfast	68	25, 079. 26	223	23, 829. 79	80	1, 221. 89	371	50, 130. 94
Waldoboro'	44	23, 960. 77	316	27, 316. 18	108	1, 403. 19	468	52, 680. 14
Wiscasset	6	2, 190. 09	113	6, 519. 16	49	632. 02	168	9, 341. 27
Bath	65	52, 925. 96	102	12, 056. 40	37	460. 76	204	65, 443. 12
Portland and Falmouth	160	58, 125. 07	162	18, 261. 23	66	872. 32	388	77, 258. 62
Saco	2	1, 860. 87	10	1, 149. 91	4	44. 89	16	3, 055. 67
Kennebunk	5	2, 791. 79	21	1, 248. 95	3	20. 66	29	4, 061. 40
York	.....	....	12	673. 77	3	32. 51	15	706. 28
	518	209, 393. 31	2, 008	161, 994. 03	556	7, 338. 63	3, 082	378, 725. 97
NEW HAMPSHIRE.								

Statement exhibiting a condensed view of the tonnage of the several States, &c.—Continued.

Customs districts.	Registered.		Enrolled.		Licensed under 20 tons.		Total.	
	Number of vessels.	Tonnage.	Number of vessels.	Tonnage.	Number of vessels.	Tonnage.	Number of vessels.	Tonnage.
MASSACHUSETTS—Con.								
Barnstable	59	5, 390. 98	480	40, 521. 23	50	608. 83	589	46, 521. 04
Nantucket	6	933. 70	20	1, 931. 01			26	2, 864. 71
Edgartown	14	2, 987. 88	15	946. 08	5	58. 92	34	3, 992. 88
New Bedford	204	49, 693. 96	61	5, 781. 15	32	320. 22	297	55, 795. 33
Fall River	9	1, 355. 42	92	10, 379. 63	14	162. 26	115	11, 897. 31
	804	315, 651. 08	1, 806	157, 904. 29	320	4, 381. 85	2, 930	477, 937. 22
RHODE ISLAND.								
Providence	15	3, 455. 57	86	20, 049. 66	8	82. 45	109	23, 587. 68
Bristol and Warren	6	1, 135. 06	14	8, 442. 65	10	109. 85	30	9, 687. 56
Newport	7	1, 064. 31	46	12, 507. 75	31	404. 16	84	13, 976. 22
	28	5, 654. 94	146	41, 000. 06	49	596. 46	223	47, 251. 46
CONNECTICUT.								
Stonington	7	2, 092. 86	88	16, 156. 16	37	553. 94	132	18, 802. 96
New London	32	4, 296. 07	102	17, 185. 98	50	694. 73	184	22, 176. 78
Middletown	1	229. 21	120	17, 395. 37	19	202. 40	140	17, 826. 98
New Haven	31	6, 221. 35	109	14, 970. 30	21	256. 27	161	21, 447. 92
Fairfield	4	762. 98	118	13, 437. 03	45	532. 43	167	14, 732. 44
	75	13, 602. 47	537	79, 144. 84	172	2, 239. 77	784	94, 987. 68
NEW YORK.								
New York	920	648, 378. 01	3, 321	485, 841. 32	507	5, 686. 10	4, 748	1, 139, 905. 43
Sag Harbor	6	1, 140. 81	101	8, 778. 14	73	850. 67	180	10, 769. 62
Champlain			670	42, 937. 83	2	23. 89	672	42, 961. 72
Oswegatchie			17	2, 168. 82	4	54. 66	21	2, 223. 48
Cape Vincent			20	3, 105. 03	6	72. 34	26	3, 177. 37
Oswego			1, 064	114, 006. 37	6	67. 32	1, 070	114, 073. 69
Genesee			180	21, 342. 65	4	57. 27	184	21, 399. 92
Niagara			24	3, 089. 84	1	18. 85	25	3, 108. 69
Buffalo Creek			635	131, 769. 63			635	131, 769. 63
Dunkirk			9	5, 799. 34	1	5. 45	10	5, 804. 79
	926	649, 518. 82	6, 041	816, 838. 97	604	6, 836. 55	7, 571	1, 475, 194. 34
NEW JERSEY.								
Newark			66	6, 614. 80	9	98. 78	75	6, 713. 58
Perth Amboy	15	2, 344. 91	239	35, 005. 89	88	1, 024. 19	342	38, 374. 99
Little Egg Harbor	1	183. 16	45	7, 057. 89	9	57. 10	55	7, 298. 15
Great Egg Harbor			115	18, 819. 82	29	331. 03	144	19, 150. 85
Bridgeton			164	13, 309. 00	111	1, 391. 70	275	14, 700. 70
Burlington			108	11, 372. 42	5	72. 19	113	11, 444. 61
	16	2, 528. 07	797	92, 179. 82	251	2, 974. 99	1, 004	97, 682. 88
PENNSYLVANIA.								
Philadelphia	125	63, 438. 34	1, 154	235, 518. 62	40	1, 528. 19	1, 319	300, 485. 15
Erie	4	1, 132. 94	232	11, 403. 77	7	63. 80	243	12, 600. 51
Pittsburg			612	93, 152. 03			612	93, 152. 03
	129	64, 571. 28	1, 998	340, 074. 42	47	1, 591. 99	2, 174	406, 237. 69
DELAWARE.								
Delaware	13	2, 275. 95	157	22, 624. 55	28	348. 23	198	25, 248. 73
MARYLAND.								
Baltimore	132	52, 013. 63	739	69, 224. 75	183	3, 135. 20	1, 054	124, 373. 58
Annapolis	1	12. 00	59	2, 288. 21	52	467. 22	112	2, 767. 43
The Eastern District	2	32. 27	316	12, 340. 01	224	2, 533. 34	542	14, 905. 62
	135	52, 057. 90	1, 114	83, 852. 97	459	6, 135. 76	1, 708	142, 046. 63

Statement exhibiting a condensed view of the tonnage of the several States, &c.—Continued.

Customs districts.	Registered.		Enrolled.		Licensed under 20 tons.		Total.	
	Number of vessels.	Tonnage.	Number of vessels.	Tonnage.	Number of vessels.	Tonnage.	Number of vessels.	Tonnage.
DISTRICT OF COLUMBIA.								
Georgetown	43	4, 178. 96	345	23, 539. 93	49	547. 17	437	28, 266. 06
VIRGINIA.								
Alexandria	21	7, 739. 95	62	2, 673. 06	54	700. 71	137	11, 113. 72
Tappahannock	1	53. 08	8	386. 72	19	155. 69	28	595. 49
Yorktown	4	145. 11	44	1, 617. 96	34	378. 42	82	2, 141. 49
Richmond	7	846. 55	18	1, 068. 00	2	25. 38	27	1, 939. 93
Petersburg	2	361. 44	1	43. 18	1	10. 11	4	414. 73
Norfolk and Portsmouth	40	5, 373. 11	114	6, 852. 70	229	1, 915. 94	383	14, 141. 75
Cherrystone	1	3, 231	105	3, 687. 89	143	1, 505. 00	249	5, 225. 20
	76	14, 551. 55	352	16, 329. 51	482	4, 691. 25	910	35, 572. 31
NORTH CAROLINA.								
Albemarle	7	405. 83	23	1, 505. 66	23	265. 94	53	2, 177. 43
Pamlico	5	775. 29	24	1, 193. 98	78	810. 75	107	2, 780. 02
Beaufort	5	224. 71	14	518. 58	59	604. 68	78	1, 347. 97
Wilmington	45	8, 494. 60	15	1, 343. 80	15	205. 09	75	10, 043. 49
	62	9, 900. 43	76	4, 562. 02	175	1, 886. 46	313	16, 348. 91
SOUTH CAROLINA.								
Georgetown	13	1, 807. 02	5	421. 77	.....	....	18	2, 228. 79
Charleston	24	5, 282. 74	84	5, 852. 85	77	1, 101. 91	185	12, 237. 50
Beaufort	2	313. 52	1	28. 75	5	30. 80	8	373. 07
	39	7, 403. 28	90	6, 303. 37	82	1, 132. 71	211	14, 839. 36
GEORGIA.								
Savannah	8	2, 566. 56	5	624. 00	6	65. 01	19	3, 255. 57
Brunswick	.....	....	.....	....	.....	....	.....	....
St. Mary's	.....	....	.....	....	.....	....	.....	....
	8	2, 566. 56	5	624. 00	6	65. 01	19	3, 255. 57
FLORIDA.								
Fernandina	3	1, 145. 55	.....	....	2	25. 94	5	1, 171. 49
St. John's	11	1, 485. 75	10	901. 21	7	73. 97	28	2, 460. 93
St. Augustine	.....	....	.....	....	.....	....	.....	....
Key West	46	5, 795. 56	4	221. 24	62	667. 16	112	6, 683. 96
St. Mark's	1	152. 06	.....	....	8	90. 55	9	242. 61
Appalachicola	2	260. 83	15	2, 568. 93	9	105. 41	26	2, 935. 17
Pensacola	37	5, 518. 53	25	2, 060. 25	27	215. 40	89	7, 794. 18
	100	14, 358. 28	54	5, 751. 63	115	1, 178. 43	269	21, 288. 34
ALABAMA.								
Mobile	21	6, 782. 24	149	24, 181. 05	63	598. 33	233	31, 561. 62
MISSISSIPPI.								
Pearl River	.....	....	22	984. 20	35	444. 00	57	1, 428. 20
Natchez	.....	....	2	158. 22	.....	....	2	158. 22
Vicksburg	.....	....	13	2, 238. 11	.....	....	13	2, 238. 11
	.....	....	37	3, 380. 53	35	444. 00	72	3, 824. 53
LOUISIANA.								
New Orleans	110	51, 436. 12	399	72, 503. 24	271	2, 775. 18	780	126, 714. 54
Teche	.....	....	.....	....	.....	....	.....	....
	110	51, 436. 12	399	72, 503. 24	271	2, 775. 18	780	126, 714. 54
TEXAS.								
Texas	30	7, 562. 51	76	10, 534. 31	72	773. 21	178	18, 870. 03

Statement exhibiting a condensed view of the tonnage of the several States, &c.—Continued.

Customs districts.	Registered.		Enrolled.		Licensed under 20 tons.		Total.	
	Number of vessels.	Tonnage.	Number of vessels.	Tonnage.	Number of vessels.	Tonnage.	Number of vessels.	Tonnage.
TEXAS—Continued.								
Saluria	7	732.12	6	660.40	34	501.86	47	1,894.38
Corpus Christi								
Brazos de Santiago	14	1,341.38			3	34.86	17	1,376.24
	51	9,636.01	82	11,194.71	109	1,309.93	242	22,140.65
TENNESSEE.								
Memphis			45	10,412.62			45	10,412.62
Nashville			18	3,000.21			18	3,000.21
			63	13,412.83			63	13,412.83
KENTUCKY.								
Louisville			79	25,764.66			79	25,764.66
Paducah			10	1,608.21			10	1,608.21
			89	27,372.87			89	27,372.87
MISSOURI.								
St. Louis			308	112,123.18			308	112,123.18
IOWA.								
Keokuk			9	810.74			9	810.74
Burlington			9	827.73			9	827.73
Dubuque			38	3,363.82			38	3,363.82
			56	5,002.29			56	5,002.29
MINNESOTA.								
St. Paul			145	18,982.01			145	18,982.01
WISCONSIN.								
Milwaukee			239	40,627.01			239	40,627.01
ILLINOIS.								
Chicago	10	3,313.61	645	97,193.53	21	246.57	676	100,753.71
Galena			121	16,342.81	4	54.30	125	16,397.11
Alton			5	1,845.23			5	1,845.23
Quincy			11	1,093.83	1	19.28	12	1,113.11
Cairo			29	7,968.20			29	7,968.20
	10	3,313.61	811	124,443.60	26	320.15	847	128,077.36
INDIANA.								
Evansville			26	5,293.88			26	5,293.88
New Albany								
			26	5,293.88			26	5,293.88
MICHIGAN.								
Michigan			102	12,520.56	31	367.99	133	12,888.55
Superior			29	2,807.37	20	204.37	49	3,011.74
Huron	1	36.00	144	20,313.93	29	346.66	174	20,696.59
Detroit	2	369.56	400	80,855.57	75	1,018.18	477	82,243.31
	3	405.56	675	116,497.43	155	1,937.20	833	118,840.19
OHIO.								
Miami			197	17,084.30	8	191.26	205	17,275.56
Sandusky	2	200.90	72	10,720.27	16	214.97	90	11,136.14
Cuyahoga	7	1,096.20	378	63,657.35	17	251.30	402	65,004.85
Cincinnati			490	98,714.45			490	98,714.45
	9	1,297.10	1,137	190,176.37	41	657.53	1,187	192,131.00

Statement exhibiting a condensed view of the tonnage of the several States, &c.—Continued.

Customs districts.	Registered.		Enrolled.		Licensed under 20 tons.		Total.	
	Number of vessels.	Tonnage.	Number of vessels.	Tonnage.	Number of vessels.	Tonnage.	Number of vessels.	Tonnage.
WEST VIRGINIA.								
Wheeling	......	....	121	20,774.68	11	149.23	132	20,923.91
Parkersburg	......	....	12	1,191.51	......	....	12	1,191.51
	......	....	133	21,966.19	11	149.23	144	22,115.42
CALIFORNIA.								
San Francisco	136	76,840.42	469	62,608.60	170	2,215.30	775	141,673.32
OREGON.								
Oregon	1	214.94	39	8,536.40	13	252.78	53	9,004.12
WASHINGTON TER'TORY.								
Puget sound	39	4,711.75	31	11,075.86	6	47.30	76	15,834.91
Total	3,367	1,532,283.10	20,439	2,733,166.49	4,312	52,850.91	28,118	4,318,309.50

N. L. JEFFRIES, *Register.*

TREASURY DEPARTMENT, *Register's Office November* 17, 1868.

REPORT OF THE SOLICITOR.

TREASURY DEPARTMENT,
Solicitor's Office, November 17, 1868.

SIR: I have the honor to transmit herewith six tabular statements, exhibiting the amount, character, and results of the litigation under the direction of this office for the year ending June 30, 1868, so far as the same are shown by the reports received from the United States attorneys of the several districts.

These tables embrace respectively:

1. Suits on transcripts of accounts of defaulting public officers, contractors, &c., adjusted by the accounting officers of the Treasury Department.
2. Suits for the recovery of fines, penalties, and forfeitures under the customs, revenue, and navigation laws.
3. Suits on custom-house bonds.
4. Suits against collectors of customs for refund of duties.
5. Suits in which the United States were interested, not embraced in any of the before-mentioned tables.
6. A general summary or abstract of all the other tables.

An examination of this summary will show that the whole number of suits brought within the year was 2,004, of which—

39 were of class 1, for the recovery of	$1,414,253 12
662 were of class 2, for the recovery of	2,430,217 85
692 were of class 3, for the recovery of	4,428,376 63
379 were of class 4	
232 were of class 5, for the recovery of	2,697,399 99
Making a total sued for of	10,970,147 59

so far as shown by these tables. Of the total number of suits brought 669 were disposed of within the year as follows, to wit: 417 were decided for the United States; 40 were adversely decided; 193 were settled and dismissed, and 19 were remitted by the Secretary of the Treasury, leaving 1,335 still pending. Of the suits pending at the commencement of the year, 130 were decided for the United States, 48 were decided adversely, and 238 were settled and dismissed. The entire number of suits decided or otherwise disposed of during the year was 1,085; the entire amount for which judgments were obtained, exclusive of judgments *in rem*, was $473,871 36; the whole amount collected from all sources was $644,517 42.

The following tables exhibit a comparative view of the litigation of the last year and of the next preceding one.

In suits commenced during the fiscal year ending—

	June 30, 1867.	June 30, 1868.
Total amount reported sued for .... dollars..	13,582,619 22	10,970,147 59
Total amount of judgments for the United States .... dollars..	430,616 36	345,740 67
Total amount reported collected .... dollars..	728,007 30	449,608 44
Decided for the United States .... number.	1,785	417
Decided against the United States .... number.	50	40
Settled and dismissed .... number.	257	193
Remitted .... number.	21	19
Pending .... number.	1,760	1,335
Total number of suits brought	3,873	2,004

In suits commenced prior to the fiscal year ending—

	June 30, 1867.	June 30, 1868.
Amount of judgments in old suits .... dollars..	224,144 73	128,130 69
Decided for the United States .... number.	408	130
Decided against the United States .... number.	215	48
Settled and dismissed .... number.	424	238
Amount collected in old suits .... dollars..	1,892,659 39	194,908 98
Total number of suits disposed of	3,160	547
Whole number of judgments in favor of United States	2,193	1,085
Whole amount of judgments in favor of United States during the fiscal year .... dollars..	654,761 09	473,871 36
Whole amount collected from all sources during the fiscal year... dollars..	2,620,696 69	644,517 42

These tables show a large decrease in the aggregate amounts for the last year as compared with the next preceding one, owing to the omission therefrom of suits arising under the internal revenue laws, and the cessation of proceedings under the confiscation acts, and in prize cases. By the third section of the act of Congress approved March 2, 1867, to amend existing laws relating to internal revenue, it was made the duty of district attorneys, instead of reporting to the Solicitor, to make report to the Commissioner of Internal Revenue; consequently no record of such suits is now kept in this office, and no statement thereof appears in the present report. In those classes of cases, however, which are included in the tables for the past fiscal year, a considerable increase is shown in the aggregate amount of business over that of the year next preceding.

Since the submission of my last annual report settlements have been made of a considerable number of the suits which were then pending arising out of the seizure of wines and other merchandise for violations of the revenue laws. The terms upon which these settlements have been made, if they have not been all that the government could have desired, have nevertheless, it is believed, been such as substantially to attain the chief end for which all such proceedings should be adopted, viz.: the effectual admonition of the delinquent parties and others who might be tempted to follow their example, and a consequent diminution in the number and flagrancy of frauds upon the revenue.

Experience, however, having shown the difficulty of procuring at the hands of juries verdicts of condemnation in such cases, when the amounts are large and the interests involved extensive, it has been deemed expedient to prosecute the inquiries which have been conducted through agents of the department in foreign countries less with a view to such seizures and proceedings for condemnation, than to the information of the local officers of the revenue, and the advancement of the value declared in the invoice to the actual dutiable value of the merchandise in cases of undervaluation. I entertain no doubt of the importance of the service which may be rendered by such agents in the manner indicated, and therefore recommend an adherence to the system of measures of which they are an essential part.

The operations of the secret service division, under my general direction, have continued throughout the past year to be conducted by its efficient head with great energy, ability, and success.

Very considerable progress has been made in the final settlement of the class of old claims which have been placed in the care of Mr. W. P. Mellen, and a handsome amount has already been realized therefrom, a large portion of which would doubtless never have been collected but for the special efforts put forth by him. I anticipate, in the future, still more satisfactory results from the same source, as the fruits of much of Mr. Mellen's intelligent, judicious, and very assiduous labors are now apparently just beginning to be realized.

I have the honor to be, very respectfully,

EDWARD JORDAN,
Solicitor of the Treasury.

Hon. HUGH MCCULLOCH,
Secretary of the Treasury.

Statistical summary of business arising from suits in which the United States is a party or has an interest, under charge of the Solicitor of the Treasury during the fiscal year ending June 30, 1868.

Judicial districts.	SUITS BROUGHT DURING THE FISCAL YEAR ENDING JUNE 30, 1868.												
	Suits on treasury transcripts.		Fines, penalties, and forfeitures under the customs revenue laws, &c.		Suits on custom-house bonds.		Suits against collectors of customs and agents or officers of the United States.		Miscellaneous suits.		Aggregate amount reported sued for.	Aggregate amount reported in judgment in favor of the United States.	Aggregate amount reported collected.
	No.	Amount.	No.	Amount.	No.	Amount.	No.	Amount.	No.	Amount.			
Maine			141	$61,400 00	1	$5,000 00					$66,400 00	$7,249 70	$6,910 36
New Hampshire			3				1		2	$500 00	500 00	500 00	325 00
Vermont			17									700 00	
Massachusetts	1	$9,114 78	26	100 00			6		7	2,300 00	11,514 78		9,114 78
Connecticut	1	2,486 54							1	600 00	3,086 54		
Rhode Island			1						2	3,500 00	3,500 00	2,500 00	
New York, northern district	4	16,910 04	33	454,255 39	1	20,000 00			58	47,892 72	539,058 15	15,790 00	11,610 60
New York, eastern district					19	34,994 40			6	5,500 00	40,494 40		
New York, southern district	1	2,751 14	132	1,759,606 76	571	3,903,102 98	370		19	1,595,700 00	7,261,160 88	10,991 13	311,249 18
New Jersey	1	1,466 34							3	1,200 00	2,666 34	1,272 00	1,609 93
Pennsylvania, eastern district	4	56,193 99					2		3	29,500 00	85,693 99	25,000 00	
Pennsylvania, western district	2	3,533 16							3	11,000 00	14,533 16	11,000 00	
Delaware													
Maryland	1	219 80									219 80		100 00
District of Columbia													
Virginia													
West Virginia													
North Carolina			1										
South Carolina			5	25,000 00	1	1,952 00			3	8,797 30	35,749 30	450 00	
Georgia, northern district													
Georgia, southern district			1										
Florida, northern district	2	7,495 13	2						1	16,487 00	23,982 13	16,587 00	100 00
Florida, southern district													
Alabama, northern district													

Mississippi, northern district									1				
Mississippi, southern district			9	900 00							900 00	700 00	
Texas, eastern district	1	4,983 14	6		23	109,432 00					114,415 14		355 33
Texas, western district													
Arkansas, eastern district													
Arkansas, western district									16	51,600 00	51,600 00	4,560 00	
Missouri, eastern district			4	27,000 00					1	1,900 00	28,960 00		
Missouri, western district	1	583 11							9	4,050 00	4,633 11	500 00	
Tennessee, eastern district									9	145,020 00	145,020 00	145,020 00	
Tennessee, middle district	2	1,907 54									1,907 54		
Tennessee, western district													
Kentucky	2	47,836 44							10	14,838 77	62,675 21	600 00	1,434 69
Ohio, northern district			1										
Ohio, southern district	3	95,424 97	18	4,200 00					4	4,390 00	104,014 97	5,725 00	617 50
Indiana	1	6,205 72	21	500 00							6,705 72	500 00	483 49
Illinois, northern district			6		1	32,000 00			1		32,000 00	277 00	377 00
Illinois, southern district	1	768 46							2	1,800 00	2,568 46		
Michigan, eastern district			178	36,830 70	6	21,096 00			23	12,750 00	70,676 70	34,761 84	40,130 19
Michigan, western district	2	6,143 46									6,143 46		
Wisconsin			2						1			1,000 00	1,068 10
Iowa			1		1	437 00			5	5,063 00	5,500 00	2,937 00	
Minnesota			1										447 75
Kansas	1	1,130 41	1						5		1,130 41	10 00	
California	1	32,860 52	32	48,725 00	7	77,740 00			1	411 20	159,736 72	32,500 00	62,759 79
Oregon			5	8,000 00					1	3,000 00	11,000 00	4,500 00	
Nevada	1	31,691 22							2	500 00	32,191 22	20,000 00	
Nebraska									2				
Washington Territory			1						1	500 00	500 00	100 00	300 00
New Mexico									28	13,500 00	13,500 00	10 00	12 50
Dakota			1						1				
Idaho	1	33,000 00									33,000 00		
Total	39	1,414,253 12	662	2,430,217 85	692	4,428,376 63	379		232	2,697,399 99	10,970,147 59	345,740 67	449,608 44

Statistical summary of business arising from suits in which the United States is a party, &c.—Continued.

Judicial districts.	SUITS BROUGHT DURING THE FISCAL YEAR ENDING JUNE 30, 1868.						IN SUITS BROUGHT PRIOR THERETO.					Whole number of judgments returned in favor of the United States during the year.	Number of suits disposed of.	Aggregate amount of judgments (reported) in favor of the United States during the year.	Aggregate of collections from all sources during the year.
	Decided for the United States.	Decided against the United States.	Settled, discontin'd, &c.	Remitted.	Pending.	Total number of suits commenced.	Amount of judgments (reported) in old suits.	Decided for the United States.	Decided against the United States.	Settled, discontin'd, &c.	Amount (reported) collected in all old suits.				
Maine	26	13	33	......	70	142	$12,857 74	17	1	16	$6,502 53	43	108	$20,107 44	$13,412 89
New Hampshire	2	1	......	......	3	6	600 00	1	1	3	2,300 00	3	8	1,100 00	2,625 00
Vermont	7	......	......	......	10	17	518 00	6	......	3	7,000 07	13	16	1,218 00	7,000 07
Massachusetts	7	......	1	......	32	40	7,450 29	6	2	3	14,487 92	13	19	7,450 29	23,602 70
Connecticut	......	......	......	......	2	2	......	......	......	......	216 44	......	......	......	216 44
Rhode Island	2	......	......	......	1	3	50 00	3	......	......	6,079 54	5	5	2,550 00	6,079 54
New York, northern district	32	2	14	......	48	96	4,742 30	10	7	11	19,418 69	42	76	20,532 30	31,029 29
New York, eastern district	......	......	2	......	23	25	......	......	......	......	......	......	2	......	......
New York, southern district	53	6	96	6	932	1,093	200 00	13	17	99	41,393 73	66	290	11,191 13	352,642 91
New Jersey	3	......	1	......	......	4	......	2	......	......	1,050 00	5	6	1,272 00	2,659 93
Pennsylvania, eastern district	1	......	1	......	7	9	......	......	......	......	......	1	2	25,000 00	......
Pennsylvania, western district	3	......	......	......	2	5	......	......	......	......	......	3	3	11,000 00	......
Delaware	......	......	......	......	......	......	......	......	......	......	......	......	......	......	......
Maryland	1	......	......	......	......	1	......	......	......	......	......	1	1	......	400 00
District of Columbia	......	......	......	......	......	......	24,833 12	4	......	1	19,466 45	4	5	24,833 12	19,466 45
Virginia	......	......	......	......	......	......	......	......	......	1	1,500 00	......	1	......	1,500 00
West Virginia	......	......	......	......	......	......	......	......	......	......	......	......	......	......	......
North Carolina	......	......	......	......	1	1	3,400 24	3	......	1	2,702 09	3	4	3,400 34	2,702 09
South Carolina	2	......	2	......	5	9	1,169 50	1	......	......	......	3	5	1,619 50	......
Georgia, northern district	......	......	......	......	......	......	......	......	......	......	......	......	......	......	......
Georgia, southern district	......	......	......	......	1	1	......	......	......	......	......	......	......	......	......
Florida, northern district	2	......	......	......	3	5	......	......	......	5	2,909 29	2	7	16,587 00	3,009 29
Florida, southern district	......	......	......	......	......	......	......	......	......	......	3,712 65	......	......	......	3,712 65
Alabama, northern district	......	......	......	......	......	......	5,318 02	13	......	18	......	13	31	5,318 02	......
Alabama, middle district	......	......	......	......	......	......	......	2	......	......	225 00	2	2	......	225 00
Alabama, southern district	......	......	1	......	......	1	......	......	......	......	......	......	1	......	......
Louisiana	2	1	13	1	62	79	......	4	......	15	1,111 50	6	36	......	1,593 75
Mississippi, northern district	......	......	......	......	1	1	......	......	......	......	......	......	......	......	......
Mississippi, southern district	6	2	......	1	......	9	......	......	......	......	......	6	9	700 00	......
Texas, eastern district	4	2	......	......	24	30	200 00	3	4	3	191 82	7	16	200 00	547 15
Texas, western district	......	......	......	......	......	......	......	......	......	......	......	......	......	......	......

Arkansas, western district	14				2	16	30 00	3			437 58	17	17	4,590 00	437 58
Missouri, eastern district	1				4	5			1	6	2,910 75	1	8		2,910 75
Missouri, western district	1				9	10	200 00	1			2,050 00	2	2	700 00	2,050 00
Tennessee, eastern district	9					9		18	5			27	32	145,020 00	
Tennessee, middle district					2	2				1			1		
Tennessee, western district															
Kentucky	10		1		1	12	100 00	1	1	3		11	16	700 00	1,434 69
Ohio, northern district					1	1	2,000 00	2		2	23,340 80	2	4	2,000 00	23,340 80
Ohio, southern district	10		2		13	25	500 00	1		5	440 00	11	18	6,225 00	1,057 50
Indiana	2		1		19	22	100 00			17	1,662 44	2	20	600 00	2,145 93
Illinois, northern district	3		2	1	2	8				5	4,713 61	3	11	277 00	5,090 61
Illinois, southern district			1		2	3				3			4		
Michigan, eastern district	176	1	4	3	23	207	234 93	4	8	7	18,240 56	180	203	34.996 77	58,370 75
Michigan, western district					2	2									
Wisconsin	1	1			1	3				1	750 00	1	3	1,000 00	1,838 10
Iowa	6				1	7	950 00	3				9	9	3,887 00	
Minnesota	1					1				1	2,150 00	1	2		2,597 75
Kansas	5				2	7						5	5	10 00	
California	19		4	7	11	41	1,556 11	2		6	6,460 07	21	38	34,056 11	69,219 86
Or-go-	1				5	6	200 00	1			1,585 45	2	2	4,700 00	1,585 45
Nevada	1				2	3						1	1	20,000 00	
Nebraska					2	2									
Washington Territory	1		1			2						1	2	100 00	300 00
New Mexico	1	11	13		3	28						1	25	10 00	12 50
Dakota	2					2						2	2		
Idaho					1	1									
Total	417	40	193	19	1,335	2,004	128,130 69	130	48	238	194,908 98	547	1,085	473,871 36	644,517 42

REPORT OF THE LIGHT-HOUSE BOARD.

[Light-house Board of the United States, organized in conformity to the act of Congress approved August 31, 1852.]

LIST OF MEMBERS.

Hon. Hugh McCulloch, Secretary of the Treasury, *ex officio* President.
Rear-Admiral W. B. Shubrick, U. S. Navy, Chairman.
Professor Joseph Henry, LL.D., Secretary Smithsonian Institution.
Brevet Brigadier General Hartman Bache, colonel corps of engineers.
Brevet Major General Richard Delafield, brigadier general corps of engineers.
Rear-Admiral C. K. Stribling, U. S. Navy.
Professor B. Peirce, LL.D., Superintendent Coast Survey.
Commodore A. A. Harwood, U. S. Navy, Naval Secretary.
Brevet Brigadier General O. M. Poe, major of engineers, U. S. A., Engineer Secretary.

COMMITTEES.

FINANCE.

General Delafield. | Admiral Stribling.

ENGINEERING.

General Bache. | General Delafield.

LIGHTING.

Professor Peirce. | General Bache.

LIGHT-VESSELS, BUOYS, ETC.

Admiral Stribling. | Professor Henry.

EXPERIMENTS.

Professor Henry. | Professor Peirce.

The chairman and secretaries are *ex officio* members of all committees.

TREASURY DEPARTMENT,
OFFICE LIGHT-HOUSE BOARD,
Washington, D. C., November 6, 1868.

SIR: I have the honor respectfully to submit for your consideration and for the information of Congress a report of the operations of the light-house establishment during the past year.

It will be seen that particular attention has been given to the important subject of ear-signals as aids to navigation, and to the not less important investigation of the question as to the best means for light-house illumination, with a view to economy and power.

Nothing indicates the liberality, prosperity or intelligence of a nation more clearly than the facilities which it affords for the safe approach of the mariner to its shores.

The introduction and improvement of these facilities are every year becoming more and more important, since the number of lives and the amount of property exposed to the dangers of the sea are increasing with time in a geometrical ratio; and notwithstanding the aids which have been afforded navigation and the perfection of the art itself, the number of marine disasters which are annually reported is truly frightful.

Our own government has given special attention to this important subject, and though our coast line far exceeds in extent that of any other nation, yet it is second to none in the means which it offers for the safety of the mariner. The provisions afforded by accurate maps of the marine topography of our coast, and the system of lights, beacons, buoys and signals which have been established, indicate the liberal views which are held and have been acted upon in regard to this matter. The idea is no longer entertained that expenditures on aids to navigation are confined in their effects to the prosperity of the maritime portions of our country. It is now well understood that whatever affects the commerce of the nation affects all its interests, those of the interior as well as those of the immediate vicinity of the sea.

It need scarcely be stated that the facilities afforded by maps and signals, to be of real value and not delusions as to danger, must be founded upon precise principles of science and well established facts of experience. The maps furnished by the government surveys are characterized by an accuracy which leaves nothing to be desired, and it has been, from the first, the design of the Light-house Board not only to adopt the best methods of illumination and signals already in use, but also by original experiments and researches to improve the system itself, in which the prosperity and common humanity of the world are interested.

We may be allowed to say that the proper discharge of the duties of the Light-house Board involves acquirements, if not talents, of no ordinary character, such as skill in seamanship, practical knowledge of engineering, the abstract principles of mathematics, of physics and chemistry. In accordance with these requirements the organization of the board includes two officers of the navy, two officers of the engineer corps of the army, two civilians of a scientific character, well versed in original investigation, and two executive secretaries, one an officer from the navy, and the other from the engineering department of the army. In order that these may work in harmony they are placed under the direction of the department having the care of commerce.

The result of this organization, and the manner in which the board, in accordance with it, has discharged its duty, are evinced by the history of the operations connected with this service. Since its establishment the number of lights has been more than doubled, the old system of reflectors, which was previously in use, has been replaced by the more effective apparatus of Fresnel, and the efficiency and economy of every part of the service have materially been advanced. At the commencement of the operations of the board the only material used for illumination was sperm oil, but the gradual diminution of the supply of this substance induced the board to attempt the introduction into this country of the cultivation of colza, and the production of oil from this plant. For this purpose a quantity of rape seed was imported and distributed through the Agricultural Department to farmers in the western States, but the supply of colza oil produced was not more than sufficient for domestic use, and by no means enough for general adoption in the light-house service. In consideration of this condition of affairs a series of investigations were undertaken by the board in regard to different materials for illumination, which has resulted in the introduction of lard oil, as not only a much cheaper material, and one to which there is scarcely any limit of supply in this country, but also as better adapted to burning in light-house lamps than any other illuminating fluid which has, as yet, been proposed. The principal objection to the use of this material at first was its tendency to solidify at a slight reduction of temperature; but this has been effectually overcome by an arrangement of the lamps, in which the heat evolved at the point of combustion is applied to keep the oil in a liquid condition. The introduction of lard oil was gradual, being first used in the larger lamps, while the smaller ones were still supplied with sperm or colza; but during the last year it has been successfully introduced into lamps of all sizes, and in every position in which lights are required along our seaboard.

Various propositions have been urged upon the board for the introduction of kerosene and other forms of petroleum; but, after a careful series of experiments in regard to this substance, its use has been discarded, with a single exception, namely, that in which a small quantity of it is mingled with lard oil, for burning during cold weather on the light-ships; but even this application is not approved, and will be discontinued as soon as lamps of a form better adapted for this service can be constructed.

The reason for not using pretroleum is the danger arising from its highly inflammable character, and the explosiveness of its vapor when mingled with atmospheric air. In the larger lamps of the light-house service a degree of heat is evolved sufficient to cause the ignition at once of the whole mass of the liquid, instead of confining the combustion to that part which is drawn up into the wick. In the smaller lamps danger principally arises from the vapor evolved from kerosene by the heat of the lamp, added to the ordinary temperature of the room. Ten per cent. of this vapor, of a given density, diffused through the air in the space above the oil in the reservoir, produces a detonating compound, which is capable of exploding with the violence of gunpowder, and of thus causing accidents of the most serious character. When an explosion of this kind takes place, the reservoir is usually broken in pieces, the oil ignited, and, while in a state of intense combustion, is projected in every direction. The danger is enhanced from the fact that the burning oil cannot be extinguished by water, but floats and burns on the surface of this liquid. Even the mixture of five or ten per cent. of kerosene with lard oil is not free from danger; the two ingredients of this compound do not enter into a chemical combination, and the explosive vapor is evolved with almost as much readiness from the mixture as from kerosene alone.

One difficulty in the way of the introduction of lard oil was the want of some definite means by which the illuminating quality of the samples could be determined. This difficulty, as stated in a previous report, has been overcome, and a system of scientific precision introduced, by which the board is always assured that the article accepted is in strict conformity with the terms of the contract. For making the test of the oil, and other experiments connected with materials used in the light-house service, a photometric room and laboratory have been established at the depot at Staten island. At this place, also, for the better preservation of the oil, and to facilitate the inspection, a large vault, furnished with five tanks, each capable of containing 10,000 gallons of oil, has been constructed. The tanks, which are kept at a nearly uniform temperature during the whole year, preserve the oil from deterioration due to chemical changes, prevent the loss by leakage, and facilitate the precise measurement of the quantity which has been received, as well as that

The board has also introduced important improvements in the lamps usually supplied by the makers of the Fresnel apparatus. These are of two classes, the mechanical lamp and the moderator lamp. In the former the oil is pumped up to the burner from a reservoir below by clock-work, impelled by the descent of a heavy weight. This apparatus is of a complicated character, and is subject to derangement; the valves must be renewed from time to time and the clock-work cleaned. The proper performance of these operations is beyond the skill of an ordinary keeper, and requires the frequent aid of a trained lampist. The *moderator* lamp is less complicated, and was invented to obviate the difficulties just mentioned. In this lamp the oil is forced up from a cylindrical reservoir below by the descent of a loaded piston, and the supply to the burner, which would otherwise diminish as the weight of oil, added to that of the piston, becomes less, is regulated by increasing the size of an opening in withdrawing from it a wire slightly tapering. This apparatus, however, is liable to irregularity on account of derangement of the supplying apparatus, the varying friction of the packing of the piston, as well as the change in the flow of the quantity of oil, owing to its less liquidity on account of a diminution of temperature. The improvement consists in substituting for these lamps one of constant level, invented by Mr. Joseph Funck, the foreman of the workshop at the light-house depot, Staten Island. In this lamp the reservoir containing the oil is placed above the burner, and the flow of oil necessary for perfect combustion regulated by a floating piston placed in an enlarged portion of the supply tube, and carrying on its upper surface a conical projection, which increases or diminishes the size of the supplying orifice in accordance with the rapidity of combustion. This lamp is not only free from the objections mentioned as pertaining to the other lamps, but is less expensive and better adapted to the burning of lard oil. It affords a freer combustion, and consequently a more intense light, though at the cost of a larger amount of the burning material. This is principally due to passing the heated air and products of combustion from the lamp through a cylindrical opening in the reservoir of the oil, forming, as it were, a prolongation of the chimney, and thus keeping the oil at a temperature which prevents freezing in the coldest weather, and supplies it to the burner in the best condition for combustion. Moreover, the lamp is so simple in its construction as to seldom need repair, and can be kept clean and in good condition by any keeper of ordinary intelligence. The superiority of this lamp has now been established by the trial of a number of years, there being at present in actual use 1 of the 1st order; 14 of the 3d order; 7 of the 3½ order.

They are much liked by the keepers, as they give less trouble in attendance, and it is the intention of the board to adopt them in all cases in which new apparatus is supplied to light-houses, or in which lamps of the old form are to be replaced.

Not only has a series of experiments been made on the different illuminating liquids, but also on light of different character, viz.: the electrical light, the oxy-hydrogen lime lights, and the magnesium lights. In order to study experimentally the peculiarities of the electric lights, one of the latest electro-magnetic machines, that invented by Mr. Wilde, of Liverpool, has been purchased. The committee on experiments have, however, found difficulty in procuring an engine with the requisite gearing to obtain the rotary motion of the armature necessary to produce the maximum effect of this machine. From the observations, however, which have been made in regard to it, it is, in its present form, not well adapted to light-house purposes. It requires a speed of 2,500 revolutions per minute to develop its maximum effect, but a velocity of revolution as great as this must soon destroy the parts connected with the centres of motion, and require their frequent renewal. Besides this, the problem is not alone what machine of a given size will produce the greatest amount of electricity without regard to the powers expended, but that which will produce the greatest amount of electricity with a given expenditure of power. This problem, we think, has scarcely yet been solved.

Furthermore, from the investigations which have been made by the committee on experiments, it would appear that the penetrating power of light in absorbing media depends principally upon the number of rays which are emitted from a given luminous space; and hence, if the absorbing power of fog be similar to that of colored glass, with which the experiments have been made, the penetrating power of a beam of electric light may be equalled by one from the combustion of lard oil. This opinion is founded upon the fact that flame is transparent, and that the penetrating power of two separate flames is increased by bringing them together, as has been proved by experiments on lamps with concentric wicks.

Experiments have also been made upon the application of the oxy-hydrogen lime light, but the labor and danger connected with the production of the gases, the expensive apparatus, and the liability of the lime to become deranged, far outweigh any advantages in the way of superior illumination which can be derived from it.

The light from the combustion of magnesium has also been examined, and from the results it would appear that if this metal could be procured in sufficient quantities, and at a reasonable cost, it would probably supersede all other materials which have been proposed for light-house illumination. A flattened wire, weighing 3⅓ grains to the foot, gave a light while burning in the air, without a lamp, equivalent to 206 candles. In the present state of supply of the substance, however, it is only applicable to a casual use by the photographer, or for illuminating during a brief period illustrations in the lecture room.

The subject of fog signals, as stated in previous reports, has received the special attention of the board. The sounding instruments which have been employed are bells, steam whistles, trumpets, sirenes, and in some instances cannon. The sound from a bell of ordinary size, viz., of 2,000 lbs., or under, has less penetrating power, or can be heard to a less distance than that from either of the other instruments above enumerated. It is, however, used in cases in which the danger to be signalized is at a small distance from the direct channel. For ringing the bell, an automatic apparatus, borrowed from the French system, was first employed. This was afterwards improved, and during the past year has received another modification which greatly diminishes the amount of muscular power expended in producing the desired effect. In the old form of the machine, the descent of the moving weight was regulated by a fly-wheel, which, being in constant revolution, expended a large portion of the motive power in giving velocity to the air. In the improved apparatus, the intervals of striking are governed by a pendulum and clock escapement, which is kept in motion by a small extra weight, and which, unlocking at a given moment a detent, allows the large weight, during a brief descent, to give motion to the hammer. By this arrangement, the same number of blows, of equal intensity, are struck in the descent through the same distance of a weight of one-fourth or one-fifth the magnitude of that used in the previous form of the machine.

The ordinary steam whistle on the eastern part of our coast is a favorite instrument, it having been successfully applied as a fog signal for a number of years at Partridge island, in New Brunswick. In proportion to the power applied, the sound produced with this instrument, as measured by the distance at which it can be heard, is less than that from the trumpet or the sirene. The sound is given off in every direction, and therefore, as in the case of the light from an ordinary lamp, without reflectors or lenses, but a small portion of the sound is utilized for signalizing in a given direction. If, however, the amount of steam expended is not taken into consideration, a sound sufficient for any purpose may be obtained. But the large amount of power required to produce a given effect is not the only objection to the general use of this instrument, since it also involves the employment of a steam boiler and other apparatus not entirely free from danger, on account of explosions, and necessitating the supply of fresh water in some places where this liquid is not readily obtainable. A fog signal of this kind has, however, been ordered for West Quoddy Head, near the extreme eastern portion of Maine.

The fog trumpet is an ordinary horn of large dimensions, in which the vibrations are produced by a steel tongue put in motion by a blast of air from a reservoir in which it is condensed by a hot-air engine. When the steel reed is properly attuned so as to vibrate in unison with the column of air contained in the trumpet, the sound produced is greater than that of any other instrument with the same expenditure of power, though the absolute quantity of sound obtained may perhaps be exceeded by other instruments.

The sirene, as is well known, consists of a revolving disk perforated with holes or openings, and made to revolve with great rapidity before the head of a drum of the same diameter, also perforated with the same number of holes, and terminating the pipe leading from a steam boiler. The currents of steam issuing from the holes in the end of the drum being suddenly stopped and again allowed to move, thus alternately give rise to a sound of which the pitch varies with the rapidity of motion of the revolving plate. This instrument, to which is also attached a large horn or trumpet, affords admirable facilities for determining the penetrating power of sounds of different pitch. The sound it produces in proportion to the power expended is intermediate to that produced by the steam whistle and the trumpet. In comparing the sound of a large horn in which the vibrations were produced by a sirene with that of another in which a similar office was performed by a steel tongue, the result was in favor of the sirene, though, after improving the unison of the steel tongue in the case of the horn, the effect of the latter was increased so as to be heard, under circumstances not the most favorable, from Sandy Hook to the light-house depot on Staten island, New-York, a distance of 15 miles. A final comparison was not made at the time on account of the accidental burning of the shanty erected for the protection of the sirene, and the consequent derangement of the instrument.

Investigations in reference to fog-signals, as well as the methods of illumination, are still in progress. They involve, however, no small degree of labor and of original thought. In case of the former it is necessary not only to ascertain the instrument best adapted for producing sound at different localities, but also the proper motive power to be employed.

These investigations will be very much facilitated by the laboratory, photometrical room and other accommodations for experimental purposes, now being provided in the new building at the light-house depot on Staten island.

The operations of the Light-house establishment since the last annual report, and the requirements of the next year, are presented in detail by

FIRST DISTRICT.

The first light-house district extends from the northeastern boundary of the United States to Hampton harbor, New Hampshire. There are in this district—

Light-houses and lighted beacons	46
Light-vessels	None.
Beacons unlighted	41
Buoys actually in position	303
Spare buoys to supply losses	234
Tenders, (steam)	1
Tenders, (sailing	None.

The following is a statement of operations, condition, and requirements:

1. *West Quoddy Head.*—A copper base for dome of ventilator; new cooking-stove and fixtures; new lantern stove, and call-bell for watch room, have been supplied. The illuminating apparatus has been examined and repaired where necessary. A cylindrical tank, 11 feet inside diameter and 8 feet 3 inches deep, with a well in the centre 4 feet in diameter and 3 feet 3 inches deep below the bottom of the tank, has been dug and walled. It is estimated that a supply of about 4,500 gallons will be obtained. The tower is reported to be leaky. The joints of the stone gallery around the parapet wall require raking out and thorough repointing with cement mortar. The tower wall, which is of brick, should be cement washed outside two coats, and the interior wall, iron stairs, window frames, and oil butts, repainted. A road from the westerly line of the government property at this place to the light-house, a distance of about three-fourths of a mile, would add much to the convenience of the station in transporting supplies. The fog-signal, a trumpet operated by a hot-air engine, established in 1866 at this station, having been found to be defective in power, the establishment of a steam apparatus designed to blow an 8-inch whistle in blasts of 10 seconds duration, with intervals of 50 seconds, is in progress. This whistle may be operated at a presure of 100 pounds per square inch. The necessary supply pipe, &c., is now being laid. The present engine house and coal shed will be enlarged to suit the new machinery.

2. *Little river.*—The roof of the keeper's dwelling has been reshingled; new saddleboards provided; zinc placed around four windows; cooking stove renovated; lantern stove and fixtures supplied; floors painted; revolving machinery and clock cleaned; burners resoldered; and new packing and valves put in house pump; new cellar door and window shutters provided; plank supports placed under cellar stairs, and new door at head of stairs; plastering of all rooms repaired; boat-house reboarded, renailed, and roof reshingled.

3. *Libby island.*—Boat-slip repaired; new boat with sails, oars, &c., completely supplied; old boat repaired and sent to Franklin island light station; lantern stove and fixtures supplied; cooking stove refitted; floors and lantern outside painted; illuminating apparatus overhauled and new inside cover for lantern dome ventilator supplied. The fog-bell machinery, which had been broken by the blowing down of the bell tower last year, has been readjusted.

4. *Moosepeak.*—Revolving machinery cleaned; burners repacked; watch room call-bell and fixtures set; lantern door refitted; lightning conductor reset; cooking stove renovated.

5. *Nash's island.*—Cooking and lantern stoves refitted; floors painted; illuminating apparatus examined and adjusted.

6. *Narraguagus.*—Dwelling and wood-shed painted outside; cooking stove refitted; illuminating apparatus examined; burners and accessories repaired; cistern pump repaired.

7. *Petit Menan.*—Dwelling, wood-shed, and boat-house painted outside; plastering in three rooms repaired; doors refitted and floors patched; cooking and lantern stoves refitted; floors painted; 28 panes of glass set; illuminating apparatus examined; revolving machinery cleaned; burners, lamp-cover, and other accessories repaired; watch room call-bell and fixtures set; lantern painted inside. New hammer, screw-bolt, and springs for fog-bell machine supplied. The bell at this station having been cracked a new one has been provided. A new boat, with sails, oars, &c., complete, has been furnished.

8. *Winter harbor.*—Iron spindle for lantern dome ventilator; cast-iron smoke-pipe for lantern provided; cooking stove and fixtures supplied; inside wood-work of dwelling painted; illuminating apparatus examined. A new boat is required for this station, the one now in use being worn out and unworthy of repairs.

9. *Mount Desert.*—Inside wood-work of dwelling painted; 30 panes of glass set; two galvanized buckets for tower and coal shovel supplied; boat slips repaired, and doors of boat-house refitted; water-closets repaired; new boat and fixtures supplied.

10. *Baker's island.*—Dwelling painted outside; new door furnished to boat-house; cooking stove and fixtures supplied; ventilator for lantern and smoke-pipe provided; seven panes of glass set; inside wood-work of tower painted; two lens covers supplied; illuminating apparatus examined.

11. *Bear island.*—Roof of dwelling reshingled; valley releaded; chimneys and underpinning of dwelling and tower repointed with cement mortar; exterior wood-work of dwelling painted; cooking stove and fixtures supplied; illuminating apparatus examined and new tubes fitted in burners; glass set where required; new boat, with sails, oars, &c., complete, supplied.

12. *Bass Harbor Head.*—Dwelling painted outside; covering stone put on kitchen chimney; cistern pump and fixtures for cooking stove supplied; illuminating apparatus examined and burner retubed.

13. *Edgemoggin.*—Plastering in kitchen repaired; side of dwelling in wood-shed ceiled with plank; new door-latches fitted; back doorsteps rebuilt and windows reputtied; cooking stove fixtures; hinges, hooks and staples for boat-house doors; two conductor dippers and a 6-inch ventilator for lantern smoke-pipe supplied; new boat and accessories supplied.

14. *Saddleback Ledge.*—Wooden addition to tower painted outside; floors painted; 24 panes of glass set; lantern, stove fixtures, and 6-inch ventilator for tower supplied. A new boat, with masts, oars, &c., has been furnished.

15. *Heron Neck.*—Exterior and interior wood-work of dwelling painted; two doors for cellar bulkhead, with hinges and hooks provided; glass set where required; fixtures for cooking stove supplied; illuminating apparatus, burners and accessories repaired; new valves fitted in cistern pump and pipe soldered; timepiece cleaned; new boat and accessories supplied.

16. *Deer Island Thoroughfare.*—New privy built; stove fixtures and hardware supplied; illuminating apparatus examined. The boat at this station is old and worn out, and a new one, as well as a suitable boat-

18. *Pumpkin island.*—Wood-shed underpinned with stone, and floor partially renewed; old wooden cistern removed and a new one, also of wood, resting on stone piers, built in its place; water conductors repaired; floors and interior iron-work painted; cooking stove fixtures supplied, and 24 panes of glass set; illuminating apparatus examined and burners retubed; new boat and accessories furnished.

19. *Matinicus Rock.*—Door latches refitted; interior wood-work of dwellings repainted; 24 panes of glass set; a lantern, stove and fixtures, and 15 fathoms rope for fog-bell supplied; illuminating apparatus examined; watch room call-bell set; leak in lantern dome repaired; lanterns painted outside; pipe to pump repaired.

20. *White Head.*—Illuminating apparatus examined and repaired; new cistern pump provided; stove fixtures supplied; new boat and equipments furnished. A watch-room call-bell is required.

21. *Owl's Head.*—A frame wood-shed, 15 feet square in plan, has been built; plank steps at back door renewed, and storm house built over door; cooking stove, cistern pump, and copper ventilator for lantern dome supplied; illuminating apparatus examined; burners retubed, and timepiece cleaned.

22. *Brown's Head.*—Inside wood-work painted; roof of work room reshingled; fixtures for cooking stove; cast-iron stove-pipe for lantern supplied; glass set where required; illuminating apparatus examined.

23. *Negro island.*—Dwelling cleansed throughout; all broken glass reset, and sashes repainted two coats; outside wood-work painted, walls repointed, and leaks about window-frames and chimneys stopped; door latches repaired or renewed, as required; storm-houses constructed over back and front doors; kitchen floors relaid; walls and ceilings partially replastered; chimney flue repaired; new cast-iron sink, pump, and pipe put in, and inside wood-work painted two coats; three rooms and passage partially replastered, and walls repapered; three closets built; all inside wood-work of dwelling painted; tower porch whitewashed inside and furnished with a service closet; privy moved to the rear of the dwelling, and plank to it laid; new wood-shed, 10 x 14 in plan, built; boat-house reboarded and reshingled, and fitted with new sills, doors, and fastenings. The boat slip has been repaired with new timbers, rollers, and fastenings. The wharf has been repaired with new planking and cap sills, and a flight of plank steps supplied. Illuminating apparatus examined and repaired; timepiece cleaned.

24. *Grindel's Point.*—Lantern, stove and fixtures, and two lens covers supplied; illuminating apparatus examined and repaired.

25. *Dice's Head.*—Cooking stove fixtures; new step-ladder supplied; floors and tower stairs painted.

26. *Fort Point.*—New lantern, stove and fixtures; accessories for cooking stove; two lens covers supplied; lantern railing painted; glass set where required; illuminating apparatus examined.

27. *Tenant's Harbor.*—Cooking stove and accessories supplied; set of revolving trucks made and adjusted; revolving machinery cleaned and burners repaired.

28. *Marshall's Point.*—New cooking stove and accessories supplied; illuminating apparatus examined.

29. *Manheigin island.*—Wooden dwelling painted outside, roof of dwelling, work room and covered walk to tower reshingled, walls of dwelling repointed, glass set where required, floors painted, cistern pump and fix-

split keys, washers, and 8 fathoms of rope supplied, revolving machinery cleaned, lamps repaired, new set of jack-screws for lens made; top of bell tower resheathed and painted, deck sheathed and painted and water conductors supplied, new doors and steps made; privy repaired; new sill put under cellar floor.

30. *Franklin island.*—Cooking stove fixtures, new clock cord, dripping butt, cast-iron smoke pipe, spikes for boat slip supplied, glass set where required, illuminating apparatus examined and repaired.

31. *Pemaquid Point.*—Illuminating apparatus examined and repaired, 42 feet man rope and stove fixtures supplied, glass set where required.

32. *Burnt island.*—New pumps furnished, fixtures for lantern stoves and plank for cellar floor supplied; illuminating apparatus examined and repaired.

33. *Hendrick's Head.*—New cooking stove and accessories and two lens covers supplied; floors painted, glass set where required; illuminating apparatus examined and revolving machinery cleaned; new sails and painter for boat supplied. The exterior wood-work of the dwelling requires repainting.

34. *Pond island.*—New pump furnished, floors and tower stairs painted; illuminating apparatus examined and repaired. The cistern in cellar of dwelling leaks and requires re-cementing.

35. *Seguin.*—The exterior and interior woodwork of dwelling, interior of tower, iron stairs, watch room deck, exterior of lantern, balustrades, &c., have been thoroughly repainted; paint closet built in cellar, two storm-house doors furnished, two pumps and 16 feet of lead pipe, tool chest and full set of tools, fixtures for cooking and lantern stoves, a 35-foot ladder supplied, glass set where required; illuminating apparatus examined and adjusted, watch room call bell set, burners and lamps repaired; cover made for fog bell machinery. The boat has been thoroughly repaired and new oars supplied.

Halfway Rock.—An estimate of appropriation required to mark with a light-house this dangerous rock was submitted to Congress at its last session, but no appropriation having been made, the estimate is again submitted, a larger amount than was at first estimated having been found necessary. The corresponding increase has been provided for.

36. *Cape Elizabeth.*—The towers have been repointed with cement mortar and red stripes recolored, covered walks clapboarded, and two woodsheds 10 by 14 feet built; an oven stove and a cooking stove have been supplied, revolving machinery cleaned, lens cowl repaired, watch-room call-bells set, new smoke stack for lamp made and adjusted, wick-holders and lamps repaired.

37. *Portland Head.*—Cooking stove fixtures provided, new spring for timepiece, two new weight-blocks and stud for fog bell machinery supplied; illuminating apparatus examined and watch room call bell set, tower whitewashed, dwelling and interior iron-work painted.

38. *Portland Breakwater.*—Cast-iron smoke-pipe for lantern supplied; illuminating apparatus examined, cowl repaired.

39. *Wood island.*—Boat house and slip 150 feet long built, illuminating apparatus examined, revolving machinery and timepiece cleaned, new boat and equipments supplied.

40. *Goat island.*—New cooking stove and fixtures supplied, interior of dwelling and tower painted and walls of one room papered, illuminating apparatus examined and repaired, new boat and equipments supplied.

41. *Boon island.*—Exterior and interior finish of dwelling painted, also floors and tower stairs; two new cooking stoves and fixtures, new lens cowl, new pump and rope for boat windlass supplied; glass set where

required, boat-house renovated and boat slip partially repaired, illuminating apparatus examined, watch-room call-bell set, valves put in cistern pump; new boat and equipments supplied. The boat-slip requires additional string-pieces, straps and bolts.

42. *Whale's Back.*—The top of the pier has been repointed with cement mortar, and two of the iron straps rebolted, two 22-gallon water casks and fixtures for cooking stove supplied; a new boat and equipments and new fall for the same has been furnished. This tower is reported to leak badly.

43. *Portsmouth harbor.*—Enclosure fence and gate repaired, two rooms papered, pump spear and box, lantern stove and fixtures supplied.

44. *Isle of Shoals.*—Hinges, hooks, and staples for boat-house and walk doors and two lamp covers supplied, tower stairs painted; illuminating apparatus examined, revolving machinery cleaned, watch-room call-bell set; boat overhauled and repaired and new sails, oars, &c., supplied.

BEACONS UNLIGHTED.

Sharp's Rock, entrance to Saco river. This spindle, iron, was broken off some months since and a spar buoy has been placed temporarily to mark the danger. The necessary repairs to the spindle are in progress.

Trott's Rock, entrance to Portland harbor. The top of the shaft, iron, has been bent, but otherwise is in good condition.

Black Jack Rock, entrance to Kennebec river. During last winter this spindle was carried away by ice; will be renewed.

Lee's Rock, Kennebec river, carried away by ice on its breaking up last spring. The work of renewing and resetting this spindle is in progress.

Ram Island Ledge, carried away by ice; renewal and resetting in progress.

Carlton Ledge and Lime Rock, beacons finished and set.

Merrill's Ledge, Clough's Rock, beacons finished and set.

Outer Rock and Middle Ground Shoals, entrance Castine harbor. The monuments formerly marking these shoals were overthrown by the ice on its breaking up last spring. Inasmuch as spars will answer all the requirements of a commerce which has much diminished since the monuments were erected, it is not deemed advisable to rebuild these expensive structures.

Lower Middle Ground, Lubec Narrows. The wooden beacon which formerly marked this station was thrown down some years since, and its place has been supplied with a spar buoy.

The beacons in the district which have not been specially referred to in this report are in good condition.

BUOYS.

The following buoys have been placed to supply losses during the past year, viz: First class nun on South Breaker; first class can twice replaced on Broad Cove Rock, entrance to Portland harbor; second class can on Old Anthony or Vapor Rock; second class nun on Witch Rock, entrance to Portland harbor; third class nuns on Fort Point Reef, Bay Ledge and Bell Rock, and third class cans on Sheep Island bar, Upper Gangway Ledge, Muscle Ridge channel.

Spar buoys replaced as follows; Pond Island reef, Old Man, Green Island reef, Bunker's ledge, Seal ledge, Boon Island ledge, Old Prince ledge, Mark Island ledge, Heron Island ledge, Petit Menan bar, Prospect Harbor ledge, Seguin ledge, Halftide ledge, Green Island reef, Turnip

Island ledge, Mark Island ledge, Eastern and Western ledges, Catfish rock, Sharp's rocks, Janceberry ledge, Outer bar and Inner bar, Saco river, Negro Island ledge, Gangway ledge, Cow and Calf, Otter Rock shoal, and Middle Ground shoal, entrance to Castine harbor.

The following new buoys have been placed in Hurl Gate passage, from Kennebec to Sheepscot rivers: Approaches to Sheepscot river; entrance to Pemaquid new harbor; eastern end of Northeast ledge; Camden harbor; entrance to isle au Haut harbor; Half-tide ledge; Low-water rock in Sullivan's harbor; Petit Menan reef, approach to harbor of Narraguagus; Nova's rock, and Little ledge to mark deep water channel to Seguin passage; Pembroke river, from Eastport to Pembroke.

Care has been taken to provide and keep on hand a full supply of spare buoys and appendages, a precaution peculiarly important in this district, wherein occur such frequent losses of buoys and their moorings from ice.

TENDERS.

The steam tender Iris has been constantly employed in carrying supplies to the several light stations; transporting workmen and materials for repairs and renovations, and in raising, cleaning, painting, and replacing buoys, &c.

The boiler of this vessel being found to be defective and unworthy of further repairs, a new one has been contracted for, and will be completed and placed in the course of a few weeks.

DEPOTS.

The buoy depot of the district is located partly upon a ledge, and the depth of water close to is insufficient to allow the tender to lie alongside except at high water. The building is, moreover, objectionable from the fact that it extends beyond (about one-third its length) the limit of the ground at the disposal of the light-house establishment. It is recommended that the building be taken down and rebuilt with enlarged accommodations, and greater depth of water close to.

SECOND DISTRICT.

The second light-house district extends from Hampton harbor, New Hampshire, to include Gooseberry Point, Massachusetts. There are in this district—

Light-houses and lighted beacons	54
Light-vessels	9
Beacons unlighted	47
Buoys actually in position	468
Spare buoys to supply losses	578
Tenders, steam,	1
Tenders, sailing	1

LIGHT-HOUSES, LIGHT-VESSELS, AND LIGHTED BEACONS.

45. *Newburyport harbor and beacon.*—New pipe and two boxes for cistern pump supplied; one room papered; kitchen chimney taken down to the roof and retopped; defective joints of two chimneys repointed with cement mortar, and tops painted two coats; large fireplace in kitchen bricked up, and hearth partially relaid; the privy, which had been blown down, has been righted and repaired. The inspector reports that in consequence of the great change of position of the bar at the entrance of this

harbor, these lights would be better guides to navigation if placed nearer to the northern extremity of the island.

46. *Ipswich harbor and beacon.*—Dwelling thoroughly repaired, with new windows, cistern, and well-pumps; stove fixtures, door latches, cellar case, shelving in cellar; exterior wood-work repainted; porch reshingled; and space enclosed from porch to privy; illuminating apparatus examined; revolving machinery cleaned; a set of new lens trucks of bronze supplied; burners repaired; new cooking-stove and accessories supplied. The plank walk leading from the dwelling to the range light, 989 feet in length, requires renewal.

47. *Annisquam.*—Two rooms and entry of dwelling papered; leaks around chimney stopped; shingling on roof of barn patched, and lamp-heater supplied; new gate at entrance to grounds built, and eight fathoms rope for well furnished; burner repaired.

48. *Straitsmouth.*—A brick cistern built in cellar of dwelling, and new pump and lead pipe furnished; 20 lineal feet of wood conductors put up; plastering of one room repaired; one chimney retopped, and interior of dwelling painted; lamp heater supplied; burners repaired; cooking and lantern stoves supplied. The east end of the dwelling leaks; attempts to find the leaks have been unsuccessfully made.

49. *Cape Ann.*—Boat-ways repaired; cistern of new dwelling enlarged; chimney retopped; ventilator reset; wood-shed enlarged, roof renewed, and sides shingled; ledge removed by blasting; old stone-house reshingled and walls repointed; stove fixtures, lamp covers, boat compass supplied, and boat repaired; the scow used for landing fog-signal engine has been redecked; cistern and oil-butt stands recovered with boards, and board partition built in attic of wooden dwelling for clothes press; illuminating apparatus examined; burners repaired; interior of both towers and exterior of wooden dwelling painted two coats; 37 sets window blinds and trimmings for both dwellings provided, painted, and hung; two new cistern pumps supplied; one room and two entries papered; the fog-signal engine has been repaired and repacked throughout, in April, July, and September.

50. *Eastern Point.*—Old porch removed, and new porch built; cistern ventilator and filtering box supplied; house roof partially reshingled and repaired; water conductors, threshold, and sill of outer door renewed; partition built in chamber for a clothes press; cistern pump renewed and cistern recemented; barn repaired with new sills, floor, and side boarding; exterior trimmings of dwelling repainted; also kitchen floor and bell tower; ventilator for kitchen chimney supplied; stove fixtures and chest of tools furnished; two rooms papered; illuminating apparatus examined and repaired. A new bell weighing about 1,120 pounds was provided with the proceeds of sale of the old bell and a condemned bell, which had long been in store in the first district. In February last a set of Stevens's improved striking apparatus, including weight, for the fog bell was erected, and the old machinery properly cared for. The cellar at this station is damp and requires attention. The top of bell

52. *Baker's island.*—Bell tower and lanterns of both towers painted; new window frames, packed with paint cement, set in eastern tower; lantern and cooking stoves refitted; illuminating apparatus examined and repaired; fog-bell machine repaired and adjusted; timepiece cleaned; new boat with sails, &c., complete, and chest of tools supplied.

53. *Marblehead.*—Kitchen hearth relaid in concrete on stone foundation; ceiling of one room replastered; glass set where required; sashes reputtied and painted; shed door repaired; boat-house repaired with new sills, floor, saddle-boards, and roof reshingled; outside trimmings of dwelling repainted; illuminating apparatus examined; burners repaired; timepiece cleaned and oiled; new ensign and halyards for boat; chest of tools supplied; the covered walk to the tower is reported to be leaky and requires reshingling.

54. *Egg Rock.*—New floor laid in wood-shed and roof repaired; junction of tower and roof releaded; weather strips fitted to doors and iron plates to sills; frame of one door repaired and latch fitted; tin water conductors supplied; boat repaired; illuminating apparatus examined, repaired, and adjusted.

55. *Minot's ledge.*—Entrance ladder repaired; stove fixtures supplied; also ensign and halyards, hand lamps for watch-room, new boat moorings, and boats repaired.

56. *Boston.*—A plank platform, 40 feet long by four feet wide, has been built from the kitchen door to the wood-shed, with a close board fence instead of hand-rail; new cistern pipe fitted; new folding outside cellar doors made; glass set where required; wood-shed reshingled and weather-boarding partially renewed; part of bank wall near tower relaid in cement mortar; two new sink drains, each 20 feet long, laid, and a well cover of joist and plank made. Boat-house repaired with new cleat door and two-hinge pintles, and useless door boarded up; double doors restripped and hinges refastened. A new sill has been put in coal-shed and one end of shed reboarded. The inner side of the south pier has been replanked vertically on an area of 36 feet by eight feet, and the tops of the same repaired by renewal of defective plank. The inshore corner has been refilled with 15 hundred weight of stone, and broken planking renewed. The outer side of the north pier has been repaired with 160 superficial feet of planking and 35 cubic yards of stone filling, the caps having previously been studded up with posts and stone blocking, and 152 tons of heavy stones have been placed outside a distance of 60 feet in length, and extending from the planking about four feet.

The sloop Billow, in delivering this stone, was caught between the piers—the passage in and out having been safely made in a previous trip—was left by the tide and fell about eight feet, having 80 tons of stone on board. She was damaged beyond the possibility of extrication in a whole condition, and was stripped and abandoned by her owners. As she laid at the entrance of the only landing at the station her immediate removal was a necessity, and a contract was therefore made to cut off her bow, fill both parts with casks and tow her to Quincy, where she was sold at auction. Four fender piles split by the sloop have been renewed and securely fastened.

The brick lining of the tower has been pointed, also stairs and watch-room walls; two storm windows for dwelling built; glass set where required; call-bell fixtures, stove fixtures, lamp smoke-stack for watch-room, and iron pipe to lead from smoke-stack to lantern ventilator, also damper for the same supplied; illuminating apparatus examined; revolving machinery cleaned and oiled; fan regulator and rod lamp repaired; new oars and boat moorings supplied and boat repaired; tool chest fur-

57. *Narrows.*—Ice-breaker painted; flight of wooden landing steps renewed; galvanized ventilators on two chimneys having rusted out, were removed at the roof and chimneys retopped with brick, with an arch turned on each and painted; illuminating apparatus examined, repaired, and adjusted; new stove fixtures, oars, boat-falls and moorings, and chest of tools, supplied.

58. *Long Island Head.*—One side of roof of dwelling addition reshingled; door latch renewed; service closet built and privy rebuilt; roof of boat house reshingled and plank walk repaired; exterior of tower repainted; globe ventilator set; plank walk to boat house rebuilt a distance of 35 feet; new sill put in boat house platform; illuminating apparatus examined and repaired; new burner and lamp heater, stove fixtures, supplied.

60. *Plymouth.*—Illuminating apparatus examined and repaired.

The exterior and interior of the dwelling and 18 pairs of blinds require repainting and blinds to be repaired. New flight of steps to outside extrance of cellar required.

61. *Race Point.*—Cistern pump, cooking stove and appendages, chest of tools and hand lantern for use at fog bell supplied; illuminating apparatus examined and timepiece cleaned.

62. *Long Point.*—Roof of dwelling patched and renailed, and all leaks stopped. New stove and cistern pump required.

63. *Mayo's Beach.*—Leak in tower stopped with paint cement; tower and exterior trimmings of dwelling repainted; glass set where required; illuminating apparatus examined and adjusted; burners repaired; cooking stove and chest of tools supplied.

64. *Billingsgate.*—Plank platforms around the buildings renewed with joists and planks; walk from dwelling to landing relaid; arch turned over top of kitchen chimney; roof of shed patched; tower stairs, pedestal, &c., painted; stove fixtures, lamp heater, supplied.

65. *Sandy Neck.*—One room papered; new sail boat supplied; lamps repaired. Tin cowl required in lantern; also leaks in east gable of dwelling and around tower windows to be repaired.

66. *Cape Cod.*—Roof valley releaded and shingling renailed; saddle-boards and window frames packed with paint cement; storm doors repaired; floor of covered walk repaired, and rebuilt 300 feet of enclosure fence; a plank sink drain and cesspool laid; one chimney arched in place of ventilator blown off; call bell fixtures set; tie rods fitted around parapet wall outside, the lower end of each having a cross head bolted to the gallery stone with wedge bolts, and the upper end going through the projecting iron deck of lantern with a nut turned on; three rooms papered; lantern glass set; tower stairs and decks painted; illuminating apparatus examined and lamps, &c., repaired; rope for white-washing tackle, wick rings, stove fixtures supplied, and oil butts repaired.

67. *Nausett.*—Ten new window frames provided and set; chimney pieces in two rooms repaired; glass set where required; old windows repaired; new sink drain of plank laid and plank cesspool built; new sill put in end of barn and boarding and battening repaired; top of one chimney from which ventilator had been blown, built up with brick three feet, braced to roof with four iron braces, and arch of galvanized iron put on top; partition of matched boards, with door built in assistant's room and painted; windows and frames painted, three coats; lock fitted to tower door; lamp repaired; oil carrier and chest of tools supplied.

68. *Chatham.*—Defective plastering of tower walls renewed; two chimneys of dwelling rebuilt from the roof; repointed one chimney top and cement-washed the cistern; roofs of dwelling reshingled and patched; front door cased and door blind hung; new gutters set; exterior trim-

mings and chimneys painted; covered walk and fences repaired; arch turned on kitchen chimney; two new windows and frames in tower made, set and painted; new frame made for cellar door and painted; one room papered; illuminating apparatus examined and repaired; timepiece cleaned and oiled; two lucernes, two lamp heaters, new oil cloth, new cooking stove and fixtures supplied.

69. *Pollock Rip light-vessel No.* 2.—This vessel was run into by the steamer Neptune on the 21st December, 1867, and very badly damaged. She was taken to New Bedford and thoroughly repaired at an expense of $5,000, and returned to her station March 9; the Relief occupying the station during her absence. The papers have been placed in the hands of the United States district attorney to commence suit against the owners of the Neptune. Whilst in New Bedford for repairs, the lantern was taken off and thoroughly overhauled and repaired; reflectors cleaned and polished, new rack socket supplied; glass set, top puttied and ventilator repaired, apparatus generally repaired.

70. *Monomoy Point.*—Wash boiler set in cellar of dwelling; brick oven repaired and oven door and cellar window supplied; iron sink set in kitchen and lead spout connected; new window and frame; a painter for boat supplied; illuminating apparatus examined and repaired.

71. *Shovelful Shoal light-vessel No.* 3.—This vessel was taken to New Bedford in August, 1868, and supplied with a new hawse pipe; 30 fathoms new chain cable; belfry; windlass purchase, tiller, try-sail mast, outer jib; plate glass for lantern; paint and oil for painting; lantern house repaired; deck under lantern house calked and sheathed; 30 sheets new metal put on bottom; illuminating apparatus repaired.

72. *Handkerchief light-vessel No.* 4.—This vessel was taken to Hyannis in July, 1868, and 12 feet of false stem put in; metal on bottom repaired; new chock for step of lantern mast; extra purchase for windlass; some new rigging; new bedding; new foresail and jib and lightning conductor supplied; bell recast and old sails repaired; illuminating apparatus examined, and spare lamps and accessories supplied.

73. *Nantucket* (*Great Point.*)—One chimney rebuilt above the roof and braced, one repointed and one cleaned and retopped and ventilator reset; ceiling of portico plastered; window frames packed; roof patched and renailed; top of cistern repaired and cover made; sink drain relaid and barn repaired; new cooking and lantern stoves supplied.

74. *Sankaty Head.*—Iron sink, cistern pump and lead pipe supplied; lantern dome ventilator renewed; illuminating apparatus examined and repaired.

75. *Nantucket new south shoals light-vessel No.* 1.—Spare anchor; try and square sails; spare chain; leather hose; set of scales; new bedding supplied; old sails repaired; lamps cleansed; new burners fitted; two burners repaired, and 10 wick racks resoldered.

76. *Gay Head.*—Lantern and tower stairs painted; parapet doors repaired; barn repaired; illuminating apparatus examined; revolving machinery cleaned; lamps centred and levelled; burners repaired, and tinware resoldered.

77 and 78. *Brant Point and Beacon.*—All plank platforms and walks around the premises renewed; privy braced with joists; enclosure fence repaired; new pump, 5 panes lantern glass, new sail boat, and chest of tools supplied; illuminating apparatus examined; timepiece cleaned and oiled; lamps repaired. The dwelling and tower are leaky and require repairs. The range light requires new posts, repairs to boarding around the eaves and covering inside overhead.

79. *Nantucket Cliff Beacons.*—Plank walks renewed; illuminating ap-

paratus examined and adjusted; timepiece oiled and cleansed; lamps repaired; two lamps refitted with new burners; chest of tools supplied.

80. *Bass River.*—Illuminating apparatus examined; timepiece oiled and cleaned; burners repaired; chest of tools supplied.

81. *Bishop and Clerks.*—New boat fender built and fitted; protecting stones around the tower pier replaced, laid in cement mortar and tied together with iron dogs and backed with heavy stones laid in cement; iron entrance ladder to tower provided and door set at foot of lower stairway of tower; glass set where required; illuminating apparatus examined; revolving machinery cleaned; burner repaired; lamp heater and tools supplied.

82. *Hyannis.*—New box and spear furnished for yard pump; new box for cistern pump; bolt for door, canvass cover for folding doors of cellar, and chest of tools supplied; enclosure fence repaired; illuminating apparatus examined and burners repaired.

83. *Cross Rip light-vessel No. 5.*—This vessel was taken to Hyannis in July and the metal on bottom repaired; part of deck calked; tin and crockery ware and cordage supplied; boat repaired.

84. *Cape Poge.*—Chimney ventilator set; chest of tools supplied; burners repaired. The inspector reports that the bluff upon which this light is situated is rapidly wearing away and the light will soon require removal further inland.

85. *Succonnesset Shoal light-vessel No. 6.*—New bedding, new awning, and boat sails, tin and crockery ware supplied; two panes of glass set in lantern; lamps repaired; pumps and davits repaired and bulwarks partially replanked. A set of new lamps (8) is required.

86. *Edgartown.*—Roof of dwelling, tower, wall, and corner boards renailed and leaks stopped; two rooms and entry repapered; storm house and store shed built; sink, gate, and planking of bridge repaired; illuminating apparatus examined; timepiece oiled and cleaned, lamps and burners repaired.

The two large wooden cisterns in dwelling require to be taken down and the stone foundation repaired. About 30 feet in length of the stone protecting wall of the causeway leading to the light-house, at a point on the seaward side where the northeast winds and tide strike, have settled so that they afford no protection from the sea, and require to be replaced. It is believed that there is a sufficient quantity of stone lying at the inshore end of the causeway. These renovations have been ordered.

87. *Holmes's Hole, West Chop.*—Illuminating apparatus examined, burners and tin-ware repaired. An iron sink in place of the wooden one, nearly worn out, is required; also three new doors and repair of three others; roof of dwelling needs patching; new privy and one pane of lantern glass required.

88. *Nobsque Point.*—Corner boards of tower packed with paint cement; walls of dwelling repointed; plastering renovated; cistern recemented; nailed studding in one room and reset base boards; sink built in kitchen; one window renewed, all others repaired and blinds repainted; new weather boards on east end of tower fitted; wooden addition and exterior trimmings repainted, two coats; new yard gate set; illuminating

The boat-house is very much out of repair, and it is proposed to build a new one next year. A covered walk from the tower to the dwelling is also needed.

90. *Vineyard Sound light-vessel No. 7.*—New bedding, hoods for hatches, new boat sails, blocks, metal on bows, supplied; bulwarks repaired; lamps refitted and repaired.

91. *Hen and Chickens light-vessel No. 8.*—This vessel was taken to New Bedford, decks resheathed and other necessary repairs made; caboose, deck light for cabin, new windlass purchase, new boat, new trysail mast, signal lantern, stove fixtures, blocks, &c., supplied; illuminating apparatus examined and lantern glass set.

92. *Cuttyhunk.*—Illuminating apparatus examined and repaired.

93. *Dumpling Rock.*—Lower end of boat-slip refastened; new boat-house built, sides and roof boarded and shingled, and painted, two coats; double-board floor, and attic single-board; four windows, double doors in one end and single door in side, tongued and grooved; sills bolted to rock. Platform renewed, 40 feet in length 9 feet 6 inches wide, and 60 feet in length 5 feet wide, of 2-inch plank, on sills 6 by 6 bolted to the rock; roof of shed reshingled on tarred paper; new floor laid in one room; pawl to crane repaired; sliding strips to shed door renewed; tower and all exterior trimmings of dwelling painted one coat, new storm blinds three coats; one skid in boat-slip renewed; walls repapered; illuminating apparatus examined and burners repaired; new blocks for boat-falls, new sail-boat and accessories, supplied.

94. *Clark's Point.*—Illuminating apparatus examined and burner repaired; stove fixtures supplied. This light-house is about one-fourth mile from the dwelling and stands directly under a face of the fort which is building, and in the certainty of its proposed speedy discontinuance in that site, has not received the attention in the way of repairs which it requires. Steps are in progress for its removal to a position upon the fortification works.

95. *Palmer's island.*—Illuminating apparatus examined, lamps repaired and brackets provided; new boat moorings supplied and boat repaired. Interior of dwelling requires painting.

96. *Ned's Point.*—A section of the stone wall protecting this site has been entirely relaid a distance of 37 feet in length, 7 feet high, and 3 feet wide, and well backed with stone; the top of the wall, for an additional length of 123 feet, has been relaid; new porch built against south side of dwelling, enclosing yard pump; leaks in dwelling stopped with paint cement; pump boxes releathered; new platform of plank built over well; new floor timbers set in one side of dwelling, beam 8 by 8 inches, with brick pier under centre; other timbers 3 by 8 inches and 3 by 9 inches, and three new sills 3 by 8 inches alongside of old sills in the other side of the dwelling. An outside entrance to cellar has been built, 3 feet 8 inches wide, with seven stone steps, with an outside shed covering opening from covered walk. The large chimney in the kitchen, including a brick oven and large fireplace, taken down and rebuilt, and galvanized iron ventilator from old chimney reduced in size at base and reset; the sink, which interfered with a window, removed to side with the chimney; closet set and shelved; ceiling and walls of kitchen replastered; new stove-pipe thimble and pine mantel shelf set; pantry built, shelved, lathed and plastered; closet provided; door-way from pantry to east front room made; in east front room, floor taken up, timbers renewed, and floor replaced, base boards partly renewed, plastering renewed, mantel shelf removed and reset on iron brackets, closet built under stairs, room papered and painted; dormer window built; inside of curbing floored with brick

from chimney. Unfinished entry at head of stairs lathed and plastered; scuttle window set in roof of kitchen; east roof of dwelling reshingled; 10 pairs of blinds and outside front door repainted one coat, and exterior trimmings and new work of interior two coats; two new doors and trimmings furnished; illuminating apparatus examined and repaired.

97. *Bird island.*—Tower parapet sheathed outside with matched pine boards, joints packed with white lead and painted two coats; sea-wall rebuilt for a length of 220 feet from the bottom average 7 feet high, 4 feet thick, and well backed; boat-ways repaired with seven new rollers; distance between landing piers increased; boat cradle fitted to receive new boat; boat-house and well-curb painted; new hook for head of boat cradle, new stove fixtures, new sail-boat and accessories, supplied; illuminating apparatus examined; revolving machinery and timepiece cleaned.

The work of relaying the sea-wall, refastening sections of landing piers, building close board fence, and painting the dwelling, is in progress.

98. *Wing's Neck.*—Roof valleys reshingled; gutters worked down at ends and all leaks stopped with paint cement; three chimney tops repointed and chimneys painted two coats; repainted two rooms, exterior trimmings, tower (on roof of dwelling,) cellar doors, and well-curb; three rooms repapered; inside cellar door rehung; one pane of glass set in lantern.

Relief light-vessel No. 9.—New windlass purchased; four panes of glass for lantern supplied; sails, blocks, pump, and decks repaired.

This vessel has been kept in readiness to occupy a station at any moment when the withdrawal of a light-vessel for repairs was necessary, or when the light-vessel had been driven from her station by any casualty.

The inspector reports that the light-vessels have all been put in excellent condition and all necessary articles supplied. Two spare bells have been cast, and are kept in readiness to be hung in case of accident to those now in use.

UNLIGHTED BEACONS.

Spindle Rock.—The small iron spindle which marked this rock was carried away by ice and has been replaced.

Bird island.—This stone beacon, which had capsized, was righted up and filled around with 40 tons of riprap stone.

Sunken island.—The spar and cage which had been carried away have been reset.

Half-tide Rock.—This beacon, stone with a wooden spindle, was carried away by the sea. Its renewal is now in progress.

Little Aquavitæ.—This wooden spindle was carried away by the sea last spring. It has been renewed and replaced.

Hardy's Rock.—The spar which had been carried away by the sea has been renewed and replaced and supported by four iron rod braces one inch diameter.

Bowditch beacon.—Several supporting stones near the base of this spindle have been knocked out of position and the spindle is out of plumb. No present repair is contemplated.

Halfway Rock.—This beacon was demolished several years ago, and as it stood upon a rock large and high enough to afford a sufficiently prominent mark, no attempt has been made to rebuild it.

Ram's Horn.—The top of the beacon, which had been carried away by ice, has been relaid and mast and day-mark renewed.

The beacons in this district not herein specifically referred to are in good condition.

BUOYS.

In this district during the past year, 103 buoys have been carried away or moved from their true positions. About one-third of this number have been recovered and replaced, and the deficiency made up from spare buoys on hand. Only five buoys are now known to be out of positions, and these the tenders are now engaged in replacing. All the other buoys have been shifted and painted; moorings examined.

The bell-boat off Harding's ledge has been taken ashore, her bottom cleaned and painted, and her moorings put in good order.

A spar buoy has been placed to mark a detached rock south of the extremity of East Chop Holmes's Hole, and a similar buoy placed to mark another rock at the entrance to Edgartown harbor.

Of the spare nun and can buoys on hand, 123 are new buoys of original faulty construction, which after alteration and strengthening are still found unreliable. Several have been again altered by repacking the tompions with vulcanized rubber, and some of them have been for some time in use and appear to stand well. Sixty new stone sinkers have been contracted for, to be delivered at Gulf island in October, ironed ready for use.

Some additional new spar buoys will soon be required. A large part of the old spar buoys reported on hand are at Wood's Hole, and are duplicates of those in position. A considerable number, the tops of which have been broken off, can be redressed and fitted for short buoys at small expense.

TENDERS.

The buoy tender Wave (schooner,) employed in the northern part of the district, was carefully examined and an estimate of required repairs submitted. After the commencement of these repairs, the vessel was found to be much more decayed than was anticipated. She had to be nearly entirely new topped as well as partially new planked below the water line, and new caulked and metalled throughout. This vessel is now as well adapted to the service as a sailing vessel can be, and is believed to be stronger and more efficient than ever before.

The steam-tender Cactus having been constantly employed during the winter in attending upon the light-vessels and buoys in the southern part of the district, authority was given to have her taken upon the railway and her planking and metal, which had been considerably injured by ice, repaired. Before, however, there was an opportunity to attend to these repairs, the vessel took fire, (probably from the hair-felt about the head of the boiler,) and was only preserved from total destruction by the energy and presence of mind of her master. The damages, with the other repairs authorized, were promptly attended to; the boiler protected from a like occurrence by being covered with galvanized sheet iron, and an iron bulkhead substituted for one of wood near the forward end of the boiler. The vessel is now in excellent condition.

The supply vessel Guthrie was reported by her master, on his return from his summer cruise of 1867, as giving unmistakable signs of weakness. A survey was held upon her and she was found to be in need of very extensive repairs. The vessel was put in the hands of ship-builders for repairs under contract, and she has been put in a condition of complete efficiency.

During the progress of these repairs the schooners J. Bender, jr., and Mary Willey were chartered temporarily to perform the duties belonging

The repairs to the supply vessel Pharos, which were in progress at the date of the last annual report, were duly completed, and this vessel has been regularly engaged in carrying supplies to light-stations.

DEPOTS.

The buoy depot at Gulf island, where the buoys and appurtenances are kept for the part of the district north of Cape Cod, is in good order, except that some of the sheds for storing articles are in need of slight repairs.

During the past year a valid title to the buoy depot at Wood's Hole having been obtained, plans and specifications have been prepared for increasing the wharf facilities; enlarging the area devoted to storage of buoys and appurtenances; removal of present buildings to more convenient sites, and erection of coal-sheds and water tanks; also, a building to contain blacksmith's shops, cooperage, paint room, and office.

It is proposed to obtain the requisite earth-filling by dredging the channel across the bar at the entrance to the harbor, so as to insure the passage of the relief light-vessel which it is designed to station at this place instead of in Great Harbor, as heretofore.

THIRD DISTRICT.

The third district embraces all aids to navigation from Gooseberry Point, Massachusetts, to include Squam Inlet, New Jersey, as well as Lake Champlain and Hudson river. There are in the third district—

Light-houses and lighted beacons	94
Light-vessels, (one being a relief)	8
Beacons, (unlighted)	40
Buoys actually in position	340
Spare buoys, to supply losses	379
Tenders, (steam)	1
Tenders, (sailing)	1

The operations in the district, as reported for the present year, and as proposed for the coming year, are as follows:

99. *Brenton's Reef light-vessel No.* 11.—A new lantern and repairs to another have been authorized, and the requisite materials have been provided; but owing to the absence of suitable mechanics the work has been delayed. Repairs to boats, caboose, &c., have been made during the year.

100. *Beaver Tail light-house.*—The present condition of this station is not very good. The tower leaks and is quite damp. The paint on the iron-work, stairs, &c., is worn off.

It is proposed to cover the brick-work inside the tower with several coats of cement wash; to repoint the granite work, and repaint the iron-work; also, to repaint the wood-work of the keeper's dwelling, and raise the floor of the cellar.

The fog-signal is a Daboll horn, operated by an Ericsson hot-air engine. It has recently been repaired; but the keeper reports difficulty in getting heat sufficient to start it in less than thirty minutes after lighting the fire, and that even sixty minutes are required when the weather is very cold. It may be necessary to substitute some other engine before the difficulty is entirely removed.

101. *Lime Rock light-house.*—This station is in good condition, with the exception of the cellar walls. The leaks in the floor, as proposed in

the last annual report, having been stopped by concrete, the water sometimes forces its way through the cellar walls. The walls, which are of brick, are not sufficient to resist the pressure of the water coming from the seams and cracks in the rock out of which the cellar is cut. It is proposed to line the sides with a brick wall, of four inches thick, leaving a space of three-quarters of an inch between it and the old wall, and then fill up this space with asphaltum.

102. *Newport harbor.*—The old building has been removed. It is proposed to fill up the old cellar and level off the grounds.

Rose island.—By act of Congress approved July 20, 1868, the sum of $7,500 was appropriated for the establishment of a light on the south end of this island. The work of constructing the requisite buildings will be commenced early in the ensuing spring.

103. *Dutch island.*—The wood-work requires painting, which will be attended to; otherwise this station is in good condition.

104. *Poplar Point.*—The keeper's dwelling is built of rubble masonry, one story high, with an attic. An octagonal tower of wood rises from the eastern gable, and is crowned by a lantern of old and discarded style, the deck and roof of which leak badly. The entrance to the tower is through a bedroom, of which it forms a part. It is not lined inside, and in winter freely admits cold and snow. No provision is made for keeping the stores and supplies. All the wood-work needs repainting, and the well requires a new chain.

The wall which was built along the greater portion of the water front is in a dilapidated condition, caused principally by frost. It has been in this condition for a number of years, and from observation it is evident that no serious damage will result if left in its present condition. As it would require a considerable amount of money to rebuild the wall, it is recommended that it be not done at present.

It is proposed to replace the present lantern by a new one of the beacon pattern, with iron deck-plate; to separate the tower from the bedroom by a partition; to line the inside of the tower with ceiling boards, and to provide closets and shelves for properly keeping the stores and supplies; to light and ventilate the bedroom thus separated by a dormer window; to repaint the wood-work, and to provide a new chain for the well.

105. *Prudence island.*—The dwelling requires repairs and thorough repainting, both inside and out. A suitable room should be arranged, with closets, shelves and hooks, for proper keeping of the stores, which are now unprovided for. A new stove and ladder are needed for the tower.

106. *Bristol ferry.*—This station consists of a square brick tower, attached to the keeper's dwelling. It is built without any furring or air-space, and is therefore damp. It is proposed to have those rooms in the tower which are used for store and watch rooms furred off and lined. A new ladder is also required.

107. *Warwick Neck.*—All the wood-work requires repainting, and the ceilings in several rooms need repairing; gates need renewing, and the out-buildings considerable repairs.

108. *Nayatt Point.*—The transfer of this light to Connimicut Point beacon having been authorized, the requisite preparations have been made, and the transfer will take place on the 1st November, 1868. It is proposed to retain the dwelling for the use of the keeper of Connimicut Point beacon. A small boat landing will have to be built, and slight repairs to the dwelling will have to be made.

Connimicut beacon.—This was formerly an unlighted beacon, was built of granite, and very substantial. An appropriation for the purpose having been made by Congress, it was prepared for the reception of a lantern and lens by increasing its height, and arranging the necessary watch and store rooms. The work is nearly completed, and the station will be lighted for the first time on the night of November 1, 1868, at which time the light at Nayatt Point will be discontinued, it being no longer required.

109. *Point Judith.*—The tower at this station is now being thoroughly repaired. The fog-signal, a trumpet operated by a Wilcox hot-air engine, is in good order, and according to the statement of the keeper can be sounded in from five to ten minutes after the fires are started.

110. *Block island.*—A new dwelling, with lantern attached, has been been built on a more eligible site than that occupied by the old one, and on the night of the 15th September a light was for the first time exhibited from the new structure. Workmen are now engaged in taking down the old buildings, the materials of which will be used for the protection of the site against the destructive action of the wind.

111. *Watch Hill.*—The condition of this station remains as when last reported upon. The repairs and improvements then recommended have been delayed by other and more pressing requirements elsewhere.

112. *Montauk Point.*—The copper wire rope, which served as a lightning conductor on the tower, has again broken to pieces. The floor beams and floor of the dining room are badly decayed. It is proposed to provide a new lightning conductor, to renew the floor beams and floor, and to provide for ventilation under the same.

113. *Stonington.*—Is in good condition, and will not require anything in the way of repairs during the coming year.

114. *Eel grass shoal light-vessel No. 12.*—Repairs to caboose, &c., have been made, and new rope for boat's tackles has been furnished—all at small cost.

115. *Morgan's Point.*—An appropriation for repairs and renovations at this station having been made, the work has been so far advanced during the present season as to admit of the occupation of the new buildings. The old dwelling remains to be taken down, the cellar filled and the grounds graded. The wooden addition to the old dwelling will be removed to the southern boundary of the grounds and will be fitted up for a stable. The present outbuildings, which are in a dilapidated condition, will be removed, the stone fences repaired, and new gates provided.

116. *North Dumpling.*—By act of Congress approved July 20, 1868, the sum of $10,000 was appropriated for repairs and renovations at this station, Watch Hill, and Saybrook. This amount, but little more than one-third the estimate submitted to Congress, is barely sufficient for the necessary repairs, &c., at the two stations last named. It is recommended to rebuild this station, and an estimate of the cost thereof is again submitted for consideration.

across the light-house grounds upon condition that they should keep it fenced. Heretofore they have failed to comply with the condition, but now promise to attend to the matter at once.

Race Rock.—The subject of the construction of a beacon to mark this danger has been under consideration by the board for some years, and by the act approved July 28, 1866, the sum of $90,000 was appropriated by Congress for the purpose. Detailed plans for the construction of a tower of granite have been adopted by the board. It was proposed to lay the foundation upon the bed-rock, twelve feet below low water, by means of a coffer dam. This proposition was based upon soundings made at different times, which indicated that the area required for the proposed structure around the boulder known as Race Rock was very nearly flat, there being a slight inclination outwards from the boulder, this deviation from a horizontal plane not being at any point more than twelve inches. With difficulty these soundings were obtained, by means of an iron rod, from a vessel's boat, the current running at a very rapid rate.

In view of all the difficulties of the proposed construction, it was not deemed safe to rely upon the information gained in the foregoing manner, and a much more careful examination of the site was therefore made. An apparatus was contrived by means of which more reliable soundings could not only be made for the moment, but located and retaken if desired. The soundings could be, and were, referred to a bench mark, and were, therefore, independent of variations in the plane of either high or low water. This apparatus disclosed the fact that the former soundings were insufficient and unreliable for the purpose of a work requiring so much accuracy, and that the area required for the base of the proposed tower was made up of an aggregation of boulders of smaller size than Race Rock itself, and of such number and size as to make the use of a coffer dam impracticable. The project which contemplated the use of one has therefore been abandoned. New plans are now in course of preparation, and it is hoped that ere long something satisfactory may be designed, when the work will be immediately commenced.

118. *Bartlett's reef light vessel No.* 13.—The injuries which this vessel received by the ice during the past winter have been repaired, the decks and upper works have been calked, and boats repaired, the vessel having been taken to New London for the purpose, her place being supplied by the relief light vessel No. 17. A new riding-chain cable has been furnished, and the proper workmen are now engaged in putting the lamps in good order for the winter.

119. *Little Gull island.*—The works of repair and renovation at this station have been carried on during the past season, but have been limited by the appropriation heretofore available for the specific purpose. A wharf for the landing of building materials was constructed, a bell-frame, which stood upon the site selected for the new buildings, removed and prepared for the reception of a lens, from which to show the light during the course of the renovations, and the old tower taken down and the materials composing it prepared for use in rebuilding. In order to get a good foundation for the new tower, it was found necessary to extend the excavation to a depth of 19 feet below the coping of the protecting pier.

These preliminary works, together with the lack of room for the employment of more than a small force of workmen, and the exposed position of the station, which renders the landing of materials difficult, have tended to protract operations, and it will require the greater part, if not all, of next season to complete the work.

An estimate of the amount necessary to complete the work is submitted.

120. *Gardiner's island.*—This station is in good condition, and requires nothing at present.

121. *Plum island.*—Both the tower and keeper's dwelling are in bad condition and should be rebuilt. The tower, built in 1827, leaks badly; the masonry is soft and crumbling; the lantern is of the old pattern and with small lights and large astragals, and it leaks badly. It is thought that the old buildings are not worth the money which would be required to put them in good order, and it is therefore proposed to rebuild them. An estimate of the amount which will be required to do this is herewith submitted.

122. *Cedar island.*—The rebuilding of this station, as authorized by act of Congress approved March 2, 1867, is now in progress and will be completed before the close of the season.

123. *Saybrook.*—By act of Congress approved July 20, 1868, means are provided for making the repairs and renovations required at this station. They will consist of an iron deck plate for the lantern; brick lining to the tower; iron stairway; suitable storerooms; rebuilding the foundation walls of the north and west sides of the platform on which the buildings stand; a coal and wood-house and other outbuildings; and will soon be taken in hand.

124. *Calves island.*—Nothing required.

125. *Brockway's Reach.*—It is proposed to rebuild the protecting pier at this station before the close of the present season, the requisite funds being now available.

126. *Devil's Wharf.*—Nothing required.

127. *Cornfield Point light vessel No.* 14.—The injuries caused by running ice have been repaired; a new boat, new jib, and new bell have been furnished. This vessel broke from her moorings on the 18th of March; was discovered adrift and a tug sent to her assistance from New London, which towed her to that place. On the 20th she was returned to her station, anchored with a single anchor, and remained until June, when she was taken to New London for repairs. The moorings which had been lost in March were recovered, and after the completion of the repairs to the vessel and her return to the station, were again used in mooring her.

128. *Horton's Point.*—This station is in bad condition. The lantern deck (of stone) leaks badly and the water filters through the wall at the base, making the rooms for the storage of oil and other supplies very damp. The roof of the dwelling leaks and the walls and floors need repairs, and all the woodwork requires painting. It is proposed to cover the stone deck of the tower with a cast-iron deck plate; to repair the roof; to provide a proper storeroom, by enclosing a portion of the passage-way from the dwelling to the tower; to repair the barn and fences, and to repaint all the woodwork. The necessary estimates are submitted.

129. *Faulkner's island.*—Since the last annual report, the repairs then proposed have been made.

The tower at this station is built of cut sandstone with rough stone backing, all laid in lime mortar. It is octagonal in plan, and on the west side has four windows with wooden frames and sashes. The stairway and landings are of wood and are decaying. The tower leaks in many places and requires repointing. The lantern and lantern deck are of iron and in good condition.

The dwelling is built of wood, is one and half stories high, with a kitchen attached. The kitchen is conneeted with the tower by a covered passage-way. Under the south room of the dwelling there is a cellar, walled with brick, which has an entrance from the outside of the dwelling. The dwelling has, besides the kitchen, dining room, and sitting room, three bedrooms, that over the kitchen having an entrance door of only four feet in height. Since an assistant keeper has been appointed to this station the dwelling is too small for the accommodation of both. The roof of the dwelling is of shingles, nailed to strips two inches wide, and from five to six inches apart. During the winter large quantities of snow drive in, injuring the ceilings, floors, and the health of the occupants. The barn and boat house are in a dilapidated condition.

It is proposed to substitute iron stairs, landings, and windows for those of wood in the tower; to raise the roof of the main part of the dwelling so as to admit another story of two rooms; to reshingle the roof over matched boards and tarred paper; to provide an inside entrance to the cellar, and a storeroom for the supplies, &c., for the tower, and to repair the barn and out-houses; and for these repairs and renovations the requisite estimate of the cost is submitted.

130. *New Haven.*—The tower requires new windows; in every other respect it is in good condition. The dwelling and kitchen, the adjoining sheds, and the oil vault, are unfavorably located, and not properly drained, in consequence of which the surface water accumulates there and causes the rotting of the floor beams and floors, besides dampness in the dwelling. At times the oil-vault has as much as eight inches of water on the floor. The cistern leaks. The stable and barn are in very bad condition, and the fence requires attention.

It is proposed to put new windows in the tower; to use a part of the passage-way, between the tower and house, for a storeroom; to lay suitable drains under the dwelling and adjoining buildings; to renew the floors and floor timbers; repair the plastering and repaint the wood-work; to repair the engine-house, rebuild the stable and barn, and thoroughly repair the fences. An estimate of the cost is submitted.

131. *New Haven, Long Wharf.*—Requires nothing.

132. *Stratford Point.*—This station is in bad condition. The tower is of wood, shingled outside, but without ceiling or lining inside; it is old, leaks badly, and is very frail; the lantern is too small; the dwelling is old, and repairs upon it are frequently required and made. It is not deemed good economy to expend any more money upon the old buildings, and after reference to the remarks concerning this station, in the annual report of last year, the recommendation therein made is renewed, as well as the estimate of the required appropriation.

133. *Stratford Shoals, light-vessel No.* 15.—A new boat and new hawse pipe have been furnished, and injuries to copper and hull by ice have been repaired, for which purpose the vessel was in June last taken to New Haven, taken out of the water and closely examined, after which she was returned to her station. She was driven from her station by ice three times during the past winter; once in February and twice in March. Upon the last occasion she dragged her anchors into deep water, where one of them became fouled in such a way that, with all the power and purchases which could be used, both on board the vessel and the tender, it was impossible to lift it. An attempt will be made to recover it, together with the 15 fathoms of chain cable attached to it, but if the attempt is not successful within a reasonable time, another anchor, with the needful length of cable, will be sent from the store on hand, and the vessel remoored, in preparation for the winter.

134. *Bridgeport Beacon.*—During last winter this iron-pile beacon was

badly injured by the ice, and although it has been repaired, it is not regarded as secure, and should the ice be as heavy this winter as last, it will probably be carried away. In view of this, and the frequent and expensive repairs to the structure, its exposed position and importance as a guide to the harbor, and the apparent steady increase of the commerce of Bridgeport, it is recommended that a stone structure, similar to those lately built upon the Hudson river, be substituted for the present beacon, and an estimate of the requisite appropriation therefor is submitted.

135. *Old Field Point.*—The reconstruction of the buildings at this station has been commenced by the delivery of the materials therefor; but owing to other and more pressing operations nothing further has been done, and it is not now probable that the work can be pushed forward before next spring.

136. *Black Rock.*—By act of Congress approved March 2, 1867, the sum of $3,400 was appropriated for repairs and renovations at this station. The greater portion of the materials required were delivered, and it was expected, as reported last year, that the work would be completed before the close of the season. However, before the work was commenced, the buildings were once more subjected to a careful examination, and it was found that the condition of the tower had become such that any money spent upon it in the way of repairs would be wasted.

The dwelling is separated from the tower by a marsh of considerable width, crossed by a narrow pathway and bridge of planks, which in easterly gales are often covered by water. This makes the attendance of the light in severe storms not only uncertain but dangerous.

Black Rock harbor is much frequented in stormy weather, and the light is of great importance, and therefore should be perfectly reliable.

It is recommended to rebuild this station, placing the tower and dwelling in close connection, on the site of the present tower, an estimate of the cost of doing which is submitted.

—. *Penfield Reef.*—It is recommended to establish a light upon this reef, the proposition being based upon the recommendation of both the inspector and engineer of the 3d district, as well as of the committee on lighting of the board, at the head of which is the Superintendent of the Coast Survey. It is proposed to build the station in five feet of water, and to pursue the same plan as heretofore carried out in rebuilding certain stations on the Hudson river. An estimate of the probable cost of such a structure is submitted.

137. *Eaton's Neck.*—The repairs and renovations at this station, for which provision was made by act of Congress approved March 2, 1867, were commenced and carried to completion during the present season.

The parapet of the tower has been covered with cast-iron panels, and a cast-iron deck-plate put around the lantern. The wooden stairway in the tower has been replaced by iron steps and landings built inside of a cylindrical brick wall. Iron window frames and sashes were substituted for those of wood; an oil-room of brick, provided with closets and shelves, built in connection with the tower; the passage-way between the tower and dwelling rebuilt. The dwelling was repaired and repainted, and an addition built to it, with a cellar underneath. That portion of the dwelling not worth repair was removed and connected with the barn, which was put in repair. A new cistern was built, and the old one repaired; the fences around the garden were partly renewed, and the whole repaired. A powerful fog-signal has been authorized for this station, and will be soon placed there.

138. *Lloyd's Harbor.*—The slight repairs required at this station have

139. *Norwalk island.*—The repairs and renovations authorized by act of Congress approved March 2, 1867, were commenced in September, and it is expected they will be completed before the close of the season.

140. *Great Captain's island.*—At this station the repairs and renovations provided for by act of Congress approved March 2, 1867, are in progress, and it is hoped they will be completed during the month of November.

141. *Execution Rocks.*—The repairs and renovations authorized by act of Congress approved March 2, 1867, are in progress, and are in a forward condition. They consist of the construction of a protecting pier of stone, with an entirely new keeper's dwelling thereon, together with a complete overhauling and improvement of the tower, providing it with a new lantern and iron deck-plate, and iron windows. The fog-bell will be replaced by a trumpet operated by a hot-air engine.

142. *Sand's Point.*—Repairs and renovations were authorized by act of Congress approved March 2, 1867; they are now completed, and consist of a new dwelling, placed in connection with the tower; iron stairways and windows in place of those of wood in the tower; the construction of a barn and outhouses from the materials of the old dwelling, and the repair of the fences.

—. *Hart island.*—By act of Congress approved April 7, 1866, the sum of $6,600 was appropriated "for a new light-house on Hart island, New York, or vicinity." Negotiations for the purchase of a site were opened, but it was found impossible to come to an agreement with the owner, and proceedings were instituted for the condemnation of the land required. The award of the appraisers, for an area of five acres, was $25,000—a sum which not only largely exceeded the appropriation, but was considered so very much greater than the real value of the land that the award would have been declined on the latter ground, even had the appropriation been ample. It is recommended that no further steps be taken in this matter at present. However, should it be deemed best to make further effort to meet the wants of navigation in the vicinity, it can be done by the further appropriation of the sum of $15,000, which, with the former appropriation, will suffice for the construction of a screw pile light-house off the point of the island, and below low water mark.

143. *Throgg's Neck.*—The tower is of wood, is old, leaky and shakey, and requires immediate and thorough repairs. The lantern is of inferior pattern, with small lights of glass, with leaky roof and deck. There is no room fit for the storage of the supplies. The dwelling also requires thorough overhauling and repainting. On account of the position of this station, immediately under the walls of Fort Schuyler, no structure of more than a temporary character can be placed there. To remedy the defects referred to above, it is proposed to replace the present lantern with a new one of the beacon pattern, with an iron deck-plate; to line the inside of the tower with matched ceiling; to arrange the lower compartment of the tower for the storage of oil and other supplies; to repair and repaint the keeper's dwelling, and to build a new cistern.

horizontally in a line with the air registers, caused, it is thought, by the oscillation of the tower," and it was "proposed to cover the deck with an iron plate, and encase the parapet with cast-iron plates which will be fastened to the parapet and lantern deck." The repointing of the deck in the summer of 1867 has stopped the leakage, and a coating of cement wash applied to the parapet at the same time has served to remove all anxiety concerning the stability of the parapet and lantern of this fine structure. Notwithstanding the heavy gales of last winter, the cracks in the parapet wall have reappeared in but slight degree, and only on the northwest side of the parapet, and may have been caused by the shrinkage of the cement wash, rather than by the oscillation of the tower. Considering these facts, the estimate of the cost of the repairs heretofore recommended is respectfully withdrawn.

145. *Fire island.*—Nothing required except some small articles of supply, which will be furnished.

146. *Sandy Hook light-vessel No.* 16.—A new riding chain cable is required, and will be supplied as soon as a suitable one can be found. Repairs to boats, caboose, &c., have been made to the extent required.

—. *Wreck of the Scotland, light-vessel No.* 20.—Under authority of the joint resolution of Congress approved March 2, 1868, the light-vessel No. 20, transferred from the fourth district, was fitted up, and on the 15th of April, 1868, was moored to mark the obstruction to navigation caused by the wreck of the steamship Scotland.

147. *Highlands of Navesink.*—The stone work requires partial repointing. The slate roof of the keeper's dwelling has been damaged by gales; the tin roofs need repainting, and the barn and stable need rebuilding. This being a station much visited by citizens from all parts of the country, it is proposed, after the completion of the repairs, &c., indicated above, to give some attention to the ornamentation of the grounds.

148. *Sandy Hook main light.*—The station would be improved by placing earth, clay, or some other suitable material around the buildings to keep the sand from blowing away.

149. *East beacon, Sandy Hook.*—The new buildings at this station were completed and the light exhibited from them on the 1st of April last. On the 16th June they caught fire from the smoke stack of the engine-house and were consumed; the apparatus and fog-signal were saved, though the latter was in a somewhat damaged condition. The buildings were entirely reconstructed upon the original plan, with slight modification noted below, within thirteen weeks after their destruction.

The fog-signal at this station is a siren, operated by taking the steam directly from a 15 horse-power boiler. The damage to the signal by the fire referred to has been repaired, and in the reconstruction of the station, the buildings covering it have been detached from the others, and greater security against fire obtained at the point where the smoke stack passes through the roof.

150. *West beacon, Sandy Hook.*—The beacon is still in danger of being washed away, and before long it may have to be moved inward. The

151. *Conover beacon.*—The tower is very frail and skaky. Some three years ago it had become necessary to stay it by iron guys; the bottom timbers have decayed, and the tower has settled. The tower is higher than necessary, and the lantern is so small that it does not afford sufficient room in which to properly care for the illuminating apparatus. It is proposed to renew the timbers which have decayed, and to remove ten feet from the top of the tower, which will not only increase the room in the lantern, but render the tower itself much more stable.

152. *Chapel Hill beacon.*—Requires nothing.

153. *Point Comfort beacon.*—A working party is now engaged in raising this building, filling up the grounds around it, and in making other needed repairs.

154. *Waackaack beacon.*—Repairs will be made to the cistern and cistern pump, to the steps to the entrance to the hall and kitchen, and to the copper on the lantern deck, when the station will be in good order.

—. *Cliffwood Point.*—A petition for a small light on this point, in Raritan bay, having been sent to this office, due examination into the subject was made, and the board deeming the request of the petitioners reasonable, recommend the establishment of a light of the sixth order, and submit an estimate of the probable cost thereof.

155. *Elm Tree beacon.*—Nothing required.

156. *New Dorp beacon.*—Requires nothing.

157. *Princess' bay.*—The reconstruction of the keeper's dwelling and the renovation of the out-buildings are going on, and will be completed this season.

158. *Fort Tompkins.*—Slight repairs to the dwelling have been made. The whole station will have to be rebuilt, as soon as the fortifications are far enough advanced to permit the selection of the proper site.

159. *Robbins's Reef.*—Requires nothing.

160. *Bergen Point.*—Requires nothing.

161. *Corner Stake beacon.*—Requires nothing.

162. *Passaic.*—The buildings need repainting and the masonry of the foundation needs repointing.

Elbow beacon.—Requires nothing.

163. *Stony Point.*—The dwelling needs repairing and the outhouses need rebuilding.

164. *West Point.*—Repairs to the ladder and foundations were made by the mechanics of the post during the summer. It requires nothing.

165. *Esopus Meadows.*—As reported last year, this station is in exceedingly bad condition, and should be rebuilt as soon as possible. The estimate of last year is accordingly renewed.

A new boat has been supplied.

166. *Rondout.*—The rebuilding of this station has been completed.

167. *Saugerties.*—The reconstruction of this station is in progress. The pile foundation is finished and a part of the stone work of the protecting pier laid. It is expected that the pier will be completed and the house carried up and roofed before the close of the season, leaving the inside work to be completed next spring.

168. *Four Mile Point.*—Repairs to cistern, to chimney, to one room, and to the barn are required, and when made the station will be in good condition.

169. *Coxsackie.*—This station is now in process of reconstruction, and will be completed this season. The old buildings will be then taken down, and whatever stone is in them will be placed around the new pier.

170. *Stuyvesant.*—This station is now being reconstructed, and the work will be completed this season.

171. *New Baltimore stake light.*—The stake has been protected by stone, and is now in good condition.

172. *Five Hook Island stake light.*—This light hasbeen removed to the dike which was built in front of it.

173. *Coeyman's Bar stake light.*—A dike has been built in front of the former position of the light, and the light has been transferred to the dike.

174. *Schodaok Channel stake light.*—This light has also been transferred to the dike built in front of its former position.

175. *Cow Island stake light.*—In good condition.

176. *Van Wie's Point.*—Nothing required.

LAKE CHAMPLAIN LIGHTS.

1. The nine structures of heavy timber, filled with stone, which have taken the place of the former stake lights in Whitehall Narrows, have stood the test of the breaking up of the ice during another winter, and remain in good condition.

It is proposed that the government assume the care of the four stake lights in the Narrows, now kept by the steamboat companies, and an estimate of the necessary appropriation therefor is submitted.

—. *Middle Grounds.*—Upon the Middle Grounds at the mouth of Whitehall river it is proposed to build a station similar to those constructed upon the Hudson river, and an estimate of the probable cost is submitted.

2. *Crown Point.*—When a barn and stable shall have been built at this station, and the buildings repainted, it will be in good condition.

—. *Barber's Point.*—It is recommended that a light be established upon this point, and the requisite estimate therefor is submitted.

3. *Split Rock.*—A boat having been supplied this station, nothing further is required.

4. *Juniper island.*—Requires nothing.

5. *Burlington beacons.*—A light on each end of the breakwater constitute the station known by this name. They have been recently built and are in good condition.

Owing to the extension of the northern end of the breakwater, the corresponding beacon no longer marks the extremity; consequently it is extinguished, and a light from an ordinary mast-head lantern is shown from the proper point, and will be maintained as the work progresses. Upon its completion the present north beacon will be moved to the end of the breakwater and relighted.

—. *Bluff Point, Valcour island.*—It is proposed to establish a light-house at this point, and an estimate of the requisite appropriation is submitted.

6. *Plattsburg beacons.*—The repairs to the north end of the breakwater having been completed by the engineer department, the corresponding beacon has been erected, and a light will be exhibited from it before the close of navigation. The station will then be in efficient condition.

7. *Cumberland Head.*—The tower and keeper's dwelling have been rebuilt upon a more eligible site, and the light will be exhibited from the new tower on the night of November 1, 1868.

8. *Point au Roche.*—Repairs to the house, the building of a barn and stable, and the continuation of the fences around the whole site are now in progress, and will be completed before the close of the season.

9. *Ile la Motte.*—This light is exhibited from the top of a stone pyramid, and is kept by a farmer who lives in the neighborhood. The

supplies are kept in his private dwelling. In stormy nights it is not to be relied on, though it is one of considerable importance.

It is proposed to build a dwelling with a lantern on top, from which to exhibit the light. The land necessary for the site is now in possession of the government, and an estimate of the cost of the requisite structure is submitted.

10. *Windmill Point.*—The lantern deck and roof of dwelling leak, and together with the ceilings need repairing, and all the wood-work requires painting.

UNLIGHTED BEACONS, INCLUDING SPINDLES.

South Point, Rose island.—Granite structure, surmounted by a spindle and cage; in good condition.

Half-way Rocks.—Spindle with square cage; in good condition.

Connimicut Point.—Granite beacon. It has been properly prepared for the reception of a lantern and lens, and on and after November 1, 1868, will appear as a lighted beacon, taking the place of Nayatt Point light-house, which will be simultaneously discontinued.

Bullock's Point.—Of granite; in good condition.

Pawtuxet beacon.—Of stone, and in good condition.

Saben's Point.—It is proposed to erect a stone beacon, and the requisite estimate is submitted for one upon the plan of that at Bullock's Point.

Punham beacon.—A stone beacon, with vane and ball on top; is in good condition.

Fuller's Rocks, Providence river.—It is proposed to construct a stone beacon, and an estimate of the cost is submitted.

East Lime Rock.—A granite structure, surmounted by an iron spindle and cage.

Muscle bed, Bristol ferry.—A stone beacon; in good condition.

Borden's flats, opposite Fall River.—A stone beacon, in bad condition. An appropriation for rebuilding it is now available, and the work will receive attention.

Castle island.—A stone beacon, surmounted by a black ball. It is situated between Papoose, Squaw, and Hog islands, and guards the west channel.

Allen's Rocks, Warren river.—Is a stone beacon; in good condition.

Spindle Rock, west channel of Narraganset bay.—Is an iron spindle, 25 feet high, with square wooden cage, painted black; in good condition.

White Rock spindle, channel into Wickford harbor.—A rock, bare at low water, surmounted by an iron spindle; in good condition.

Spindle Rock, Greenwich harbor.—An iron spindle, bearing a square cage; in good condition.

Hen and Chickens, Long Island sound.—An iron spindle, bearing a square cage; painted black; in good condition.

Branford Reef beacon.—Circular beacon of gray granite, surmounted by an iron shaft, bearing a black day-mark. It is built on Branford reef; its base being bare at low water, and is now in good condition.

Black Rock beacon.—An iron pile beacon, with cage on top. It stands on the end of a shoal which extends from Fairfield, Connecticut, about two miles into the sound. It is in good condition.

Watch Hill spindle.—Stands on a rock which is bare at low water, and is surmounted by a cage; in good condition.

Sugar Reef beacon.—Is erected on the north end of the reef, (which resembles a horseshoe in shape.) It is an iron pile beacon, with cage-work day-mark in the form of a cone; in good condition.

Lord's channel.—Iron spindle; square cage-work day-mark; in good condition.

Catumb reef.—Iron pile beacon 25 feet in height, with square cage-work day-mark; in good condition. It stands on a reef running off to the eastward of Wicoposset island.

Latimer's Reef spindle.—Stands near the west point of the reef, which is bare at low water. It is an iron spindle, bearing a square cage-work, and is in good condition.

Ellis's Reef spindle.—On the north end of the reef is an iron spindle with a square cage-work; in good condition.

Groton Long Point beacon.—Stands on a large boulder at the extreme outer end of the reef off Groton Long Point. It consists of an iron pile structure, bearing a cage-work in the form of an inverted cone; it is in good condition.

Sea Flower or Potter's Reef beacon.—The reef is rocky; of about 150 feet in diameter. The beacon stood on the west side of the reef, and consisted of an iron spindle set into the largest boulder on the reef, and bearing a diamond-shaped cage-work day-mark. Under the pressure of the running ice at its breaking up last spring the boulder was overturned, the spindle acting as a lever. The spindle, which is still in the rock, was not broken, but was somewhat bent, and can easily be recovered and repaired. It is proposed to build a granite structure for the purpose of upholding the spindle and cage of the old beacon. An estimate of the cost is submitted.

Black Ledge beacon.—The reef is rocky, and about 200 feet in diameter; the beacon, consisting of an iron shaft, bearing a cage-work day-mark, formed by two cones connected at the vertices, stands on the northwest end; in good condition.

Whale Rock beacon.—This beacon is of iron, 24 feet high, and bears a globe cage-work day-mark. It stands upon the ledge, which is 50 feet long, formed of loose boulders, bare at low water; in good condition.

Crook's spindle.—Is an iron spindle with a keg on top; in good condition.

Spindle on the Whale, entrance to the Mystic river.—Was an iron spindle bearing a square cage-work and marked the sharp elbow at the narrow part of the channel. It has been carried away by ice; and since a good and reliable structure is much needed, particularly at night, it is proposed to erect in its stead a lighted beacon, of granite, as suggested in the last annual report, and the estimate is again submitted.

Saybrook beacon.—Is built of stone. It stands on Saybrook bar, and is in good condition.

Quixie's ledge.—An iron spindle with a cask on top. Stands on a rock that is dry at half tide. It is in good condition.

Stratford River beacon.—A wooden crib filled with stone supporting a spar surmounted by a cask. It stands on the west side of the channel at the entrance to Stratford river. The crib-work is old, and is breaking up under the action of the ice. It is proposed to build a new beacon, using granite in its construction. An estimate of the cost is submitted.

Outer beacon, Inner beacon, Bridgeport harbor.—Both beacons have been raised and improved, and now form very satisfactory aids to navigation.

Southport beacon, Southport Breakwater beacon.—These beacons, marking the entrance into Southport creek, are new and substantial structures of rock-faced granite laid in cement, the outer beacon bearing a shaft, crowned with a day-mark of iron, and in excellent condition.

Norwalk beacon.—Stands on the western end of Long Beach island and guides into Norwalk river. Is a new structure, of rock-faced granite laid

Sand Spit.—Is on the south point of Sand Spit, Sag Harbor. It is an iron frame-work beacon with a cage at the top, and in good condition.

Long Beach bar, entrance to Greenport.—A petition for a beacon at this point has been presented and favorably reported upon by the inspector of the district. If built, it should be upon the plan recently carried out at Connimicut Point, Providence river; and, if authorized, will require an appropriation of the amount indicated in the estimate.

Romer beacon.—Stands on the west side of Romer shoal, entrance to the Bay of New York, and is an excellent guide to vessels passing up or down the swash channel. It is conical in shape, built of stone, and supports a square cage-work at a height of 30 feet above the sea level.

Mill reef.—Is an iron beacon supporting an iron cage upon a mast 22 feet in height. It marks a rocky reef extending from the north point of the entrance to Kill Van Kull.

Success Rock, Long Island sound.—An appropriation for a beacon on this rock is available, and plans for its erection are now under consideration.

BUOYS.

Buoys have been place to mark the entrance to Napeague harbor, east end of Long island; the entrance to Stratford or Housatonic river, Connecticut; a rock in Harlem river, New York; and the wreck of the Scotland. Contracts have been made for keeping the buoys in Lake Champlain and Pawtucket river; and the usual arrangements for placing the buoys in the Hudson river, on the opening of navigation in the spring, have been made at the customary rates with the parties who have performed the service for many years. All the rest of the buoy service has been performed by the buoy tenders.

New London buoy depot.—For the storage of 100 tons of coal for the use of the steam tender, and the supply required for the light-houses and light-vessels, a coal bin has been put up on the buoy wharf at New London. This wharf is small, and its accommodations insufficient. It is intended to extend the wharf a distance of 140 feet, when there will be sufficient room to take care of the buoy tender and relief light-vessel without trespassing upon private property, as is now done.

Norwalk island buoy depot.—The removal of the spare buoys for the supply of the district extending from Great Captain's island eastward to New Haven, which have hitherto been kept on private land at Norwalk island, to the public land at Black Rock light-house, is now under consideration. If the removal be determined upon, a small wharf for landing the buoys, with a close shed for the storage of a small quantity of coal for the use of the tender, and a small building for the storage of paints, tools, small buoy appendages, and other articles which must be kept under lock and key, will be required. It is the opinion of the inspector that such a depot is necessary, not only to facilitate the changing of the buoys in the spring of the year, but to economize both the time and fuel now expended by the tender in returning from Long Island sound to Staten island, for a new supply of coal every time she needs it.

Goat island, Newport harbor, buoy wharf is in good condition, except that a small building for the storage of paints and other small stores is required.

A large portion of the buoys and appendages enumerated in the tabular statement are subject to transfer to other districts, and shipments of them are frequently made. A portion of the materials required for the repair of damaged iron buoys has been procured, and the work of repairing will soon be commenced.

TENDERS.

In November, 1867, the tender *General Putnam*, while lying at anchor in the Delaware river, in a fog, was run into and sunk by the steamer Reybold, plying between Wilmington and Philadelphia. A contract for raising her was entered into with the Atlantic Submarine Company, and operations were soon commenced, but it was not until the spring was far advanced that she was floated. Upon examination she was found to be so badly injured that she could only be made again serviceable by the most extensive repairs. The vessel was needed so badly that they were undertaken at once at Wilmington, Delaware, and will be completed before the 1st December, when she will be substantially a new vessel. Meanwhile the steam-tug *Martha Washington* was chartered and fitted for the service of the district by adding suitable hoisting apparatus, &c., and will be retained until the completion of the repairs of the General Putnam. All the apparatus, outfits and supplies being the property of the United States, will be removed from her when the vessel is discharged from the light-house service.

The schooner *Sunbeam* is stationed at New London, and her principal duty is to attend upon the light-vessels, beacons, and buoys from New Haven eastward. She has had small repairs made to her hull, boats, &c., on several occasions, and has had a new jib, rope, and other small articles to replace those worn out.

The vessel is old and needs a thorough overhauling, but her services have been so necessary that it has not been found practicable to withdraw her from her duties for a length of time sufficient to make the requisite examination and repair. It is hoped that with care she may be made to do service until the busy season of next year is over, when she can be attended to.

Both tenders are kept constantly busy, either in attending to buoys, beacons and light-vessels, or in transporting materials and supplies for light stations in course of construction or repair, and the work which they have to perform seems to be steadily upon the increase.

STATEN ISLAND LIGHT-HOUSE DEPOT.

In December last, the inspector's office in New York city was broken up and removed to this depot, greatly to the advantage of the service, because that portion of the duties of the inspector of the district relating to the receipt, overhauling, repairing, and shipment of illuminating apparatus and stores for general use has been brought directly under his supervision. The change has given him a better control of the tender, as well as brought him more directly in contact with the whole light-house system.

There are employed in the workshop for the manufacture and repair of lamps, apparatus, implements, and all accessories of light stations, one foreman, seven lampists, one machinist, one laborer, and for the general work of the depot in the receipt, packing and delivery of stores, keeping the grounds in order and caring for the public property, one foreman, two watchmen, eleven laborers.

The services of these persons being frequently required for discharging or loading vessels, in making repairs and much other duty out of the usual working hours,they are employed by the month at the rates which prevail in the neighborhood.

Some idea of the magnitude of the operations at this depot can be gathered from the following statements, viz.:

Statement of boxes, packages, bundles, cans, &c., received at and shipped from the United States light-house depot, Staten island, N. Y., from October 1, 1867, to September 30, 1868, inclusive.

	Boxes.	Packages, bundles, cans, &c.	Barrels and kegs.	Total.
Received	899	1,616	742	3,257
Shipped	851	622	851	2,324
Total	1,750	2,238	1,593	5,581

Statement of lens apparatus and lanterns received at and shipped from the United States light-house depot, Staten island, N. Y., from October 1, 1867, to September 30, 1868, inclusive.

	Lens apparatus.								Lanterns.		
	First order.	Second order.	Third order.	Fourth order.	Fifth order.	Sixth order.	Steamer lens.	Range-light apparatus.	Light-house.	Light-vessel.	Total.
Received	5	1	......	5	7	3	13	4	......	2	40
Shipped	4	2	4	12	5	6	16	1	1	3	54
Total	9	3	4	17	12	9	29	5	1	5	94

Statement of buoys and appendages received at and shipped from the United States light-house depot, Staten island, N. Y., from October 1, 1867, to September 30, 1868, inclusive.

	Can buoys, (iron.)			Nun buoys, (iron.)				Sinkers.				Ballast balls.				
	1st class.	2d class.	3d class.	1st class.	2d class.	3d class.	Spar buoys.	1st class—iron.	2d class—iron.	3d class—iron.	Stone.	1st class.	2d class—cans.	2d class—nuns.	3d class.	Total.
Received	26	....	....	15	45	....	25	28	45	....	120	28	25	70	....	427
Shipped	3	18	13	3	26	28	....	11	20	25	......	21	27	27	38	260
Total	29	18	13	18	71	28	25	39	65	25	120	49	52	97	38	687

Articles manufactured or repaired in the lamp shop at the United States light-house depot, Staten island, N. Y., from October 1, 1867, *to September* 30, 1868, *inclusive.*

	Pressed glass lenses.	Lenses.	Lamps.	Burners.	Miscellaneous articles.	Total.
Manufactured	12	....	185	181	145	523
Repaired	....	4	87	10	10	111
Total	12	4	272	191	155	634

The purchase of a strip of land 49 feet 7 inches wide, extending along the whole length of the south side of the depot grounds, as contemplated at the date of the last annual report, has been effected, and a patent therefor obtained from the State of New York.

The street on the north side of the grounds, access to which was obtained under authority of a special act of Congress, appropriating the amount necessary for the purchase from the State of New York of the strip of ground, 29 feet 1½ inches wide, and extending the entire length of the grounds, has recently been fenced in by C. K. Hamilton. The United States district attorney (Hon. B. F. Tracey) was instructed to take the necessary steps to secure the government in its rights in this street, but as yet little progress seems to have been made.

The following will show more in detail the operations for the improvement of the depot, carried on during the past year, and what is proposed and recommended for the ensuing year.

Oil Vaults.—The entire completion of these vaults upon the original design is expected at an early day. The depot will then afford facilities for the storage in the best manner, and the necessary handling in the most convenient way, of 85,000 gallons of oil, of which 50,000 gallons will be stored in five large tanks of cast-iron lined with tin, and the remainder in barrels, piled in rows, in shallow iron troughs. It may be safely said that not a single drop of oil can by any chance be wasted. The entire leakage is led to a single tank, out of which it may be pumped and disposed of in whatever manner may be best. It is doubtful whether there is in the whole world an oil cellar better adapted to the purpose.

Sea-wall.—The sea-wall in front of that portion of the depot grounds extending from the former revenue wharf to the northern boundary line, and along this line to the shore, to connect with the brick wall built thereon, has been completed in a very substantial manner of large blocks of coursed granite, backed by rubble masonry, the whole being bonded in the best manner and laid in cement. Every alternate stone is a header extending through the entire thickness of the wall. As this depot will be required as long as there are light-houses to build or maintain, no pains is spared to make the construction as durable as the materials used. It is proposed, at some future time, to extend this sea-wall along the remainder of the water front.

Dredging of basin.—The basin in front of the depot, having through a long series of years become filled to such an extent that it afforded landing facilities only to vessels of the lightest draught, has been dredged out to a depth of eight feet at low water, and a large portion of the material thus obtained used in filling in behind the sea-wall. Soundings are taken every month to ascertain the probable change of the bottom of the basin. Up to the present time there is no indication of any filling in, nor was it expected that there would be any until winter, when the heavy gales which then prevail will doubtless cause a different showing.

Building for workshops.—It was proposed to take down the two old buildings acquired by transfer from the revenue branch of the Treasury Department, and to use the materials in the construction of new workshops, but upon a closer examination it was found that one of the buildings could be profitably used for a few years longer. The construction of a fire-proof building for workshops for the manufacture of lamps and illuminating apparatus; for testing oils and other supplies purchased by contract; and for experimenting with lamps and illuminating apparatus, has been commenced, and has now reached the second story. Contracts have been made for the iron-work required, including floor-beams, stairways, roof, &c., and it is hoped that the entire building will be enclosed before winter and completed next spring. As was stated in the last annual report, no appropriation will be asked for specially applicable to this work, but the cost of its construction will be defrayed from the funds appropriated for the general maintenance of the light-house establishment, of which this building is so necessary an adjunct.

Office building.—At present the offices connected with the service of this depot, and of the 3d district, are located in the storehouse, a building which is not fire-proof, and wherein is usually stored something like a half million dollars' worth of light-house supplies and apparatus, besides records which could not be replaced. No fire should ever be permitted in or about this building, and to avoid the necessity which now exists, a fire-proof building for offices, and for the preservation of archives, should be built after the design long since approved as a part of this establishment. For this building the foundation has been laid, and the walls carried up to the water table, where the work will probably stop for a year, unless an appropriation for its continuance is specially made, as it is not thought the general fund for the support of the light-house establishment during this year and the next can afford a larger draft upon it than that required for the completion of the workshops.

Filling in and grading.—A large quantity of earth obtained from the bank at the depot grounds has been used in filling in behind the sea-wall, and for properly raising and grading the grounds. By permission, about 2,690 cubic yards of earth were obtained from the quarantine grounds, without charge, taken to the depot grounds, and used for filling in. A large quantity of earth is yet required to complete the filling. The high bank behind the depot buildings has been graded and sodded.

Landing wharf.—This wharf broke down under a load of less than 50 tons. It is scarcely necessary, in view of the character of the constructions made at this depot since it came under the control of the board, as well as those contemplated, to add that the wharf was built before the property became a part of the light-house establishment. The requisite repairs to fit it for use until a better one can be built have been made.

Basins for light vessels, supply vessels, and tenders.—During gales from the north, by the east around to the south, the basin at the depot affords no security to vessels. The subject of the construction of a suitable basin has been carefully considered by the board, both on account of the cost of the work and the difficulty of making a harbor which will not require very frequent dredging. A plan has finally been approved, and if the necessary appropriation is made the work will be carried into effect. The plan is of such a character that, if not successful, it will form a necessary part of any alternative plan.

Condition of the depot.—From the foregoing it will be seen that a great deal of work has been done during this season, and that much remains to be done to make the depot all that it ought to be, and secure all the benefits which its establishment have rendered apparent. Its economy is of daily demonstration, and its convenience so great as to cause surprise that it was possible to get along without it. The fact that the estimates of the cost of maintaining the light-house establishment for the next fiscal year are much below what they were in this is in no small degree due to this depot. And with this decrease of expense a greater degree of efficiency is obtained, through the better quality and more uniform character of all kinds of apparatus and supplies sent out for the support of the light-houses and other aids to navigation.

FOURTH DISTRICT.

The fourth light-house district extends from Squam inlet, New Jersey, to include Metomkin inlet, Virginia, as well as Delaware bay and its tributaries. There are in this district—

Light-houses and lighted beacons	18
Light-vessels	2
Beacons, (unlighted)	None.
Buoys actually in position	78
Spare buoys to supply losses	60
Tenders, (steam)	None.
Tenders, (sailing)	1

177. *Barnegat light-station.*—The work of constructing jetties of brushwood, and depositing stone along the beach between high and low water, was continued last year until the close of the season, at which time a number of jetties had been constructed, and 331½ tons of stone deposited. Many of the jetties were damaged by storms and others swept away by running ice, leaving enough, however, to give material protection to the beach.

On the 1st of August of the present year, shortly after the necessary appropriation had been made by Congress, operations were resumed; the damaged jetties have since been repaired, a number of new ones constructed, and 670 tons of stone deposited up to the 30th of September. The engineer of the district reports the result, so far, as satisfactory.

The base of the sand-hills along the light-house lot, which is also, to a great extent, the high-water line on the beach, has not been disturbed in the least. The beach is gaining in height and extent, the water is shoaling along the outer or channel edge of the work, and continues to shoal as the work is extended to the southward. It is therefore confidently expected that, before the close of the present season, the site will be perfectly secure. The tower and oil-house have been washed with brick-colored cement from the top half way down, and the lower half whitewashed; the pump in the assistant keeper's dwelling, and the water-conductor from the roof of the oil-house, have been repaired.

A suitable boat for the station, and a boat-house and ways, have been provided. Two panes of heavy plate glass, for the lantern, have been supplied, also drip-buckets for the oil butts.

The keeper's dwelling requires painting inside and out.

178. *Tucker's beach.*—The sand-fence constructed along the beach, in front of the buildings, is in good order, and answers the purpose for which it was constructed. The cement work put on the tower and keeper's dwelling last year has been effective in keeping the walls dry. Two panes of heavy plate glass have been furnished for the lantern.

179. *Absecum.*—Semi-monthly admeasurements of the beach, in the

vicinity of the light-house at this station, have been taken during the year.

On the ocean front several changes are noted, but, so far, none of a character to affect the safety of the light-house. The channel, from the inlet seaward, runs nearly straight. A survey to ascertain the exact course and strength of the currents will be made as soon as the more pressing duties of the engineer of the district will permit.

During the year the following repairs have been made to the buildings at the station: New wooden steps at the back doors of the principal keeper's dwelling; brick pavement repaired; new door frame in the covered way between dwelling and tower; new door from watch-room into gallery, hung on three heavy wrought-iron, galvanized hinges; repairs to porch door of principal keeper's dwelling; the tower has received two coats of cement wash, brick color; both keeper's dwellings, including the tin roofs, stairway of tower outside of lantern, watch-room gallery, and picket fence, require painting, the inside of the tower washing fawn color. A small sum will also be required for the purchase of gravel, and for repairing curb around the building.

180. *Five-Fathom Bank light-vessel No.* 18 has been thoroughly repaired and supplied.

181. *Cape May.*—During the last year the fence, bridge and roadway, referred to in the last annual report, as having been damaged by storms, have been thoroughly repaired. The spindle of the governor of the revolving machinery has been supplied with new friction rollers, and copper wire furnished to secure the wire fenders or screen to the lantern. The keepers have painted the lantern and watch-room on the outside, with materials furnished them for the purpose. The tower has been washed with cement of gray or granite color. Sponge, lens cover, and stove-pipe have been supplied for use in the lantern.

182. *Cape Henlopen.*—The only work done at this station has been in placing brushwood to prevent the sand around the buildings from being blown away. Examinations conducted by the light-house engineer of the district, for a series of years, show that the dune at this station, called the "big sand-hill," situated at the north of the tower, and formed by drifting sand, had moved to the southward at the rate of 11 feet a year. The height of this hill in 1863 was 73 feet, since which it has lowered and widened at the base. At the period just referred to the old keeper's dwelling had to be abandoned, the sand having banked up to the second-story windows. Fears were entertained that a similar drift would obstruct the tower. So far, however, an effectual remedy has been found in the application of brushwood to exposed places. The keeper's dwelling requires painting inside and out; the pumps in the water cisterns need some repairs.

183. *Cape Henlopen beacon.*—The building has been painted inside and out, and the steps leading from the platform to the ground have been repaired. The double terra cotta pipes used for chimney flues, having been found to crumble, are considered unsafe, and fire-brick flues, surrounded by a wall of the same material, will be substituted for the pipes without delay. New brass faucets for the water tanks and an iron water sink have been supplied.

184. *Delaware breakwater.*—At this station a new floor for the fog-bell machinery has been laid; the roof has been repaired temporarily, the pathway around the building and from the boat landing repaired, and the building painted throughout. The changes and repairs in progress and nearly completed, are the removal of the old lantern and putting on a new one, and a new roof on the building.

185. *Brandywine shoals.*—The wooden platform around the structure, and the platform and ladders, have been repaired.

186. *Maurice river.*—A lens cover and boat have been supplied. During the coming year repairs will be required to the wooden platform, and in painting.

187. *Egg island.*—At this station the old buildings have been taken down, and the screw-pile light-house referred to in the last annual report has been erected; a new boat-house and ways built; the boat reserved at the sale of the sloop Granite put in order and fitted with centre-board, oars and sails, for the use of the station; new lens covers, lantern curtains, and oil measures have been supplied. The light was exhibited for the first time from the new lantern on the night of July 24, and the structure was completed on the 21st of August last.

188. *Cross Ledge light-vessel No.* 19 has been thoroughly repaired and supplied.

189. *Mahon's river.*—The brick water cistern, which leaked, has been repaired, and new lantern covers have been supplied at this station.

190. *Cohansey.*—During the past year the frame oil-house has been furnished with new cover posts, and the plank platform and plastering in the kitchen have been repaired. The work of putting on a new roof, new gutters and conductors, is nearly finished. A set of lantern curtains has been supplied.

191. *Bombay Hook.*—At this station the following operations are nearly completed: new roof on the building; repair to plastering; new pumps; repair of fences enclosing building and garden.

192. *Reedy island.*—The extensive repairs to the bank around the buildings, referred to in the last annual report, were completed in October, 1867. During the past year the pathway to boat-house and the plank platform around the house have been repaired; a new pump with check valve has been placed in the water cistern, and two sets of lantern curtains have been supplied.

193. *Christiana.*—The cement of the water cistern having been loosened by frost, has been renewed. The building requires painting.

194. *Fort Mifflin.*—Repairs during the last year have been made to the corner of the pier upon which the building is founded. The sheet-iron top upon the chimney having blown away, the chimney has been carried up and arched over with brick; two panes of plate-glass and three foundation lamps have been supplied.

195. *Fenwick's island.*—Repairs made; a galvanized iron weight-tube, with the necessary fixtures for the weight of the flashing machinery, has been placed in the tower; sill of the wash-room window renewed; fireplace in the kitchen repaired. Repairs required: To keeper's dwelling, painting inside and out; to fence enclosing the light-house.

196. *Assatcague.*—The works in construction at this place, referred to in the last annual report, have been completed; the tower and keeper's dwelling on the 31st of October, 1867. During the year now closing the iron hand-rail has been put up in the tower, the tower and oil-house washed with brick-colored cement, and the brass tablet plate placed on the tower.

BUOYS IN POSITION.

The buoys at the following *inlets* are attended to and kept in position by contractors:

Barnegat, *Little Egg harbor*, including *Tucker's cove*, *Absecum*, *Great Egg harbor*, and *Chincoteague.*—This service is reported to have been performed in a satisfactory manner at all these places with the exception of

Barnegat inlet, respecting the buoyage of which complaints have been made, which are now under investigation; and any neglect or defect which may be found will be promptly corrected.

The buoys in Delaware bay and river have been in charge of the master of the buoy tender belonging to district, and have been kept in serviceable condition.

Spar buoys, forty feet long, painted, have been placed to mark two wrecks in Delaware bay; notices in regard to which have been published.

CONDITION OF SPARE BUOYS.

Barnegat inlet.—One wooden can under repair. Depot requires repair.

Little Egg Harbor inlet.—Depot has been built since the last annual report. One first-class iron sinker and ballast ball are required.

Absecum inlet.—A new depot has been built. Four stone sinkers required.

Great Egg Harbor inlet.—A new depot has been built. Four stone sinkers are required.

Delaware bay and river.—There are on hand 67 logs in the rough for making spar buoys, as they are called for.

BUOY TENDERS.

The sailing tender *Spray* has been engaged during the year in attending to the buoyage of Delaware bay and river, and in supplying the light-house and light-vessels of the district. The Spray had become so rotten as to require extensive repairs; in May last, therefore, she was taken in hand and is now in good working order.

The steam-tender General Putnam is attached to the third light-house district. In November, 1867, she was sent to tow a second-class light-vessel to Cross Ledge light-station, to take the place of No. 19, and bring her to Wilmington for repair. This service performed, the Putnam, while on her way to resume her station, anchored in the Delaware, above New Castle, in a thick fog, and was run into by the steamer Major Reybold, and so much injured that she was with difficulty dragged out of the channel to the Jersey shore by the revenue cutter Seward.

Late in November, 1867, a contract was made with the Atlantic Submarine Company to raise the Putnam; but the season being too far advanced, and the condition of the vessel such as to render the operation difficult, it was not accomplished until last July, when the Putnam was transferred to the railway of Messrs. E. & C. Moore, of Wilmington; and, after a close examination of the condition of the vessel, a contract was made with Messrs. Moore to repair her hull and engines and place her in serviceable condition. The renovation and equipment of the Putnam will be finished and the vessel restored to her station within the limits of the contract.

FIFTH DISTRICT.

The fifth light-house district embraces the coast from Metomkin inlet, Virginia, to include New River inlet, North Carolina, as well as Chesapeake bay and tributaries, and Albemarle and Pamlico sounds.

There are in this district—

Light-houses and lighted beacons	65
Light-vessels	3
Beacons unlighted	89

Buoys actually in position.. 472
Spare buoys to supply losses.. 297
Tenders, steam.. 2
Tenders, sailing..None.

(NOTE.—In this summary are embraced the light-house stations at Bogue Banks and Bodies island, which have not been re-established since their extinction in 1861.)

LIGHT-HOUSES, LIGHT-VESSELS, AND LIGHTED BEACONS.

197. *Hog island.*—Window frames and sashes in tower repaired; a door and frame supplied; all wood-work painted; lantern painted inside and out; an enclosure, picket fence, 40 feet square, built around the tower, and a similar fence built, 80 feet square, for garden; new set of blinds for windows of dwelling house fitted, hung, and painted; in the dwelling, doors, windows, and floors repaired; hearths relaid; plastering in all the rooms repaired; all wood-work painted two coats; house, tower, and fences whitewashed two coats; new glass set where required, and landing wharf repaired; cistern put in good order.

It is recommended that the present lamp (fountain) be removed and a Franklin lamp substituted in its place. Slight repairs to the roof of the dwelling are also reported to be necessary.

198. *Cape Charles.*—A few minor articles required for the proper maintenance of this station have been supplied.

199. *Cape Henry.*—Plate glass; five plates have been supplied for use in the lantern whenever it should be required.

200. *Willoughby Spit light-vessel No.* 21.—From the effects of the severe storm of January 21, 1868, this vessel parted her moorings at a defective shackle, and on the morning of the 23d of the same month, while endeavoring to reach a harbor, was taken in tow by the revenue cutter Northerner, and anchored in Hampton Roads. On the 24th of January she was, with the assistance of the revenue cutter Nemaha, replaced on her station, having been supplied with new moorings. The old moorings, embracing anchor and 75 fathoms of chain, were subsequently recovered by the tender Heliotrope. A new shackle was substituted for the broken one, and the end of the chain having been passed into the vessel, she has since lain at her original moorings. During the past summer it was found that during heavy weather the vessel leaked to a considerable extent above her copper. The sides have been calked, and are now in good condition. The deck inside the lantern house is rotten, as is also the lantern mast at the partners; these defects have been temporarily remedied. The vessel has been painted, and a new bowsprit provided to replace one broken off by collision with an outward-bound steamer December 6, 1867. A new main deck awning has been supplied. Light-vessel No. 23, recently marking Smith's Point light-station, is now being repaired, preparatory to being placed on this station; when No. 21 will be withdrawn and sent to Windmill Point.

201. *Old Point Comfort.*—No repairs to this station have been found necessary during the year.

202. *Craney Island shoal.*—Iron work of foundation and outside of superstructure painted two coats; tin roof repaired; lantern painted inside and out, and wood-work of two rooms inside, two coats; new glass set in windows.

203. *Naval Hospital.*—This structure has been rebuilt and enlarged, and the lantern raised about nine feet higher, thus increasing the range of the light.

204. *White shoal.*—Iron-work of foundation and tin roof painted two coats; railing around gallery repaired; new glass set in windows. It is recommended that a Franklin lamp be substituted for the constant level lamp now in use.

205. *Point of Shoals.*—Framework of house wherever decayed repaired; also railing around gallery repaired; iron-work, tin roof, and lantern, inside and out, painted two coats. It is recommended that the present constant level lamp be replaced by a Franklin lamp.

206. *Deep Water shoals.*—The new light-house at this place, which at the date of the last annual report was under construction, was completed and lighted on the evening of January 15, 1868.

207. *Jordan's Point.*—No repairs required.

208. *Cherrystone.*—New cooking stove supplied, and boat repaired.

209. *Back river.*—Entrance doors refitted with new locks and hinges; steps to porch repaired; new glass set in windows; lantern and wood-work painted inside and out two coats; house and tower whitewashed; rip-rap stone collected and placed around the tower to serve as a break-water; old guard-house on the beach moved up to the dwelling for use as an outbuilding.

210. *York Spit light-vessel No.* 24.—New main deck, awning, and bedding for crew supplied. This vessel is now in good condition, except the lantern mast, which is defective at the partners. This mast has been securely stayed to answer temporarily. New water casks and crotch for the main boom have been supplied. The vessel has been thoroughly painted.

211. *New Point Comfort.*—Window frames and sashes in tower repaired; all wood-work and lantern painted inside and out two coats; roof of dwelling re-shingled, and new rain-water gutters supplied; doors, locks, and hinges repaired; porches and inside of dwelling painted two coats; new pump to cistern provided; house, tower, and fences whitewashed, and the latter rebuilt; new glass set in windows.

212. *Wolf Trap light-vessel No.* 22.—Vessel thoroughly painted. There is reason to believe that the bottom of this vessel is in want of repairs, and so soon as the services of a relief vessel are available to take her place, she will be withdrawn for examination and repair; above water she appears to be in good order.

213. *Stingray Point.*—Iron foundation and the superstructure painted two coats; locks and hinges repaired; lantern painted inside and out two coats; new glass set in windows where required.

214. *Windmill Point light-vessel.*—This vessel was removed by the rebels in 1861, and has not since been restored. Instructions have been given to re-establish the light so soon as a suitable vessel is available. Light-vessel No. 21, after being withdrawn from Willoughby Spit, where she now is, will be placed to mark this station.

215. *Watts's island.*—Revolving machinery of illuminating apparatus repaired.

216. *Jane's island.*—In good condition.

217. *Somers's cove.*—In good condition.

218. *Smith's Point.*—A screw pile light-house has been erected to take the place of the light-vessel formerly marking this station, and the light was exhibited for the first time on the evening of September 9, 1868.

219. *Fog Point.*—In good condition.

220. *Clay island.*—In good condition.

221. *Point Lookout.*—In good condition.

222. *Hooper's straits.*—In good condition.

223. *Cove Point.*—A large portion of the tower has been re-cemented

and whitewashed two coats; sashes and frames in tower repaired and painted; lantern painted inside and out; shingling on roof of dwelling repaired; doors, sashes and hardware in dwelling repaired; wood-work in same painted: fire-hearths and walks around house re-set; new pump provided for cistern; new glass in windows set where required; new fog bell frame erected in place of old structure, found to be entirely decayed.

224. *Sharp's island.*—Iron-work of foundation painted two coats; also dwelling and lantern two coats inside and out; new glass set where required, and tin on roof thoroughly painted.

225. *Thomas's Point.*—Window frames and sashes in tower repaired; wood-work and lantern painted inside and out, two coats; doors, sashes and window-shutters in dwelling, also locks and hinges, repaired; plastering in all rooms repaired; fire-hearths relaid, and dwelling painted inside two coats; cistern house rebuilt and new pump supplied; gutters and conductors to roof repaired; small smoke-house eight feet square built; new glass set where required; fences repaired, and, as well as the tower and dwelling, whitewashed two coats.

Bloody Point and Love Point, on Kent island.—Numerously signed petitions for the establishment of lights to mark these points in Chesapeake bay having been forwarded to the Board, with a report as to their necessity from the inspector and engineer of the district, the subject received careful consideration, which resulted in an approval of the objects asked for. Estimates to cover the cost are submitted.

226. *Greenbury Point.*—Doors, sashes, window-shutters, also locks and hinges, repaired; new porch to front door built; all wood-work and the lantern painted inside and out, two coats; plastering in all the rooms repaired; rain-water gutters and conductors renewed; new pump for cistern supplied; picket fence 600 feet to boundary of lot erected, and whitewashed two coats; boat belonging to the station repaired.

227. *Sandy Point.*—Cistern re-cemented and pump repaired; new cellar steps and door supplied; lantern painted inside and out; also brick walls of dwelling painted one coat; wood-frame of bell tower and fences whitewashed and repaired; the old boat having, by reason of long use, become unfit for further service, has been replaced by a new one; Franklin lamp substituted for constant level.

228. *Seven-foot Knoll.*—Slight temporary repairs made to boats. One of these boats is represented to be too badly damaged to warrant the expense of repairs, and a new one will be required.

229. *North Point.*—In good condition.

230. *Fort Carroll.*—Platform, steps of tower and bell-frame repaired; lantern and dwelling painted inside and out; new glass set where required; a Franklin lamp has been substituted for the constant level lamp heretofore in use.

231. *Brewerton channel.*—The work on the lights to mark this channel in Patapsco river, which was under progress at the date of the last annual report, has been completed, and the lights will be exhibited for the first time on the evening of November 1, 1868. These two structures, one near Hawkins's Point, the other on Leading Point, are distant apart 1½ mile, bearing N. W. and S. E. from each other, both being exactly in range with the axis of Brewerton channel. The front light, Hawkins's Point, is built in six feet water, upon a screw pile foundation, with a frame superstructure to accommodate two lights, one above the other, at heights respectively of 28 and 70 feet above ordinary tides, the space between them being open. The rear light, Leading Point, is built on the bluff point, and consists of a brick dwelling surmounted by a lantern, showing one light at an elevation of 40 feet above the ground, and 70

feet above ordinary tides. When a vessel is on the true course coming up or going down the channel, the three lights will be seen in line, one above the other; but whenever this course is departed from, however slightly, to port or starboard, a corresponding change in the positions of the lights will be observed.

232. *Pool's island.*—In good condition.

233. *Turkey Point.*—A Franklin lamp has been substituted in place of the constant level or fountain lamp heretofore in use.

234. *Fishing Battery.*—Franklin lamp substituted for constant level lamp. The boat belonging to this station being old and no longer fit for service, has been replaced by another in good condition.

235. *Havre de Grace.*—In good condition.

236. *Piney Point.*—In good condition.

237. *Blackiston's island.*—In good condition.

238. *Lower Cedar Point.*—In good condition.

239. *Upper Cedar Point.*—In good condition.

240. *Fort Washington.*—In good condition.

241. *Jones's Point.*—In good condition.

242. *Bowler's Rock.*—A screw-pile light-house has been erected to take the place of the light-vessel formerly marking this station, and the light was exhibited for the first time on the evening of June 10, 1868.

243. *Bodies island.*—This light-house was totally destroyed by the rebels during the war, and the board does not recommend its re-establishment; but, instead, it is recommended to build between Cape Henry and Cape Hatteras—a distance of 120 miles of dangerous coast, now unmarked by any light—three light-houses of the fourth order, and an estimate of the cost is submitted.

244. *Cape Hatteras.*—An appropriation is available for rebuilding this important light-house, and the requisite materials therefor are now being collected. Contracts for the brick have been entered into, a tram road of the Peteler pattern has been contracted for, and every other necessary preparation will be made looking to the commencement of work early in the ensuing season.

Since the estimate for this work was submitted to Congress it has been found that the interests of commerce require a tower of much greater elevation than was provided for. At the time of making the estimate it was supposed that a tower of 150 feet in height (the ordinary altitude of first-order towers) would answer every requirement, but it is now deemed necessary to erect a structure having a focal plane of 180 feet. This increased height will augment the cost of the structure, and an estimate of the additional amount required is submitted.

To the present tower new plate glass for lantern and window glass to dwelling have been supplied.

245. *The Beacon* light requires repairs.

246. *Ocracoke.*—A large portion of the tower has been recemented, and whitewashed two coats. Lantern and all wood-work in keeper's dwelling and tower painted inside and out two coats; lantern deck and sashes and frames repaired; stairway renovated extensively, putting in 33 feet of newel 14 inches diameter; one side of roof of keeper's dwelling reshingled and other side repaired; fire-hearths and brick walks around the house relaid; plastering repaired in every room; also doors, sashes, and hardware; floors repaired where necessary, and dwelling whitewashed.

247. *Southwest Point of Royal Shoals.*—Iron-work of foundation painted two coats and the outside of superstructure one coat; lantern painted inside and out; new glass set where required.

248. *Northwest Point of Royal Shoals.*—Painted iron-work of founda-

tion and dwelling two coats, also lantern inside and out; new glass set where required; gallery railing repaired, and tin roof extensively; new water casks supplied; also new locks and hinges.

249. *Harbor island.*—Iron-work of foundation painted two coats, dwelling one coat, and lantern inside and out two coats.

250. *Brant island.*—Iron-work of foundation painted two coats, outside of dwelling one coat, and lantern painted inside and out two coats; locks and hinges to doors repaired and new glass set where required; new cooking stove and fixtures supplied.

251. *Neuse river.*—Iron-work of foundation painted two coats, outside of dwelling one coat, and lantern inside and out two coats; new glass set where required; new cooking stove and fixtures supplied.

252. *Pamlico Point.*—New boat supplied.

253. *Long shoal.*—Iron-work of foundation painted two coats, lantern inside and out two coats, also two rooms inside; new glass set where required.

254. *Roanoke marshes.*—Iron-work and outside of dwelling painted two coats; gallery railings and tin roof repaired; new glass set where required; new cooking stove and fixtures supplied and new boat furnished.

255. *Croatan.*—Iron-work of foundation painted two coats; also outside of dwelling, and lantern inside and out; new glass set where required; a new cooking stove and fixtures—also materials for boat falls—supplied.

256. *North river.*—Iron-work of foundation painted two coats; also lantern inside and out; new glass set where required; new cooking stove and fixtures; also materials for boat sails supplied.

257. *Wade's Point.*—Iron-work of foundation painted two coats; also lantern inside and out; landing platform raised two feet higher; new boat falls supplied.

Laurel Point.—Several petitions, numerously signed, asking for the establishment of a light at this point, to facilitate the navigation of Albemarle sound, having been forwarded to the Board by the inspector of the district, with his report as to the necessity for the light, the subject received careful consideration, and the Board is of opinion that a light at or near that point is desirable. An estimate of appropriation required is submitted.

258. *Roanoke river.*—Iron-work of foundation and outside of dwelling painted two coats; lantern painted inside and out; new glass set where required.

259. *Cape Lookout.*—In good condition. The old tower at this place is old and dilapidated, but answers very well as a day mark for passing vessels.

260. *Bogue Bank light-house and beacon.*—These lights were entirely destroyed by the rebels, and have not yet been re-established.

At the date of the last annual report the appearance of the ground at Lazaretto Point light-station led to the belief that the yield of iron ore would be equal to that of previous years; but as the work of excavation progressed it was found that whatever amount of ore remained unexcavated was within the garden lot and running toward the keeper's dwelling. It was not deemed advisable to disturb the garden lot, especially as the quantity of ore to be obtained thence would be inconsiderable. On making his last payment the contractor proposed a cancellation of the lease, but this has been deferred until he shall have filled in the excavations and properly levelled the ground.

Since the last annual report 156 tons of ore have been excavated, for which the sum of $243 84 has been received.

Upon the withdrawal of light-vessel No. 23 from Smith's Point, Chesapeake bay, (upon the completion of the new screw-pile light-house at that place,) she was towed to Norfolk by the buoy tender Heliotrope and placed on the railway for examination and repair preparatory to taking the place of the light-vessel at present marking Willoughby Spit, which, having but one lantern, does not suitably mark the station. The repairs are now in progress.

Light-vessel No. 25 has been thoroughly overhauled, necessary repairs made, and placed to mark Deep Water Shoals, James river, during the construction of the light-house at that place. Upon the completion of the light-house she was taken to Norfolk and securely moored. She is kept in readiness for service as a relief vessel.

Light-vessel No. 28 is the regular relief vessel of the district. She has been repaired where necessary, and has rendered valuable service in marking temporarily Bowler's Rock in Rappahannock river and Smith's Point in Chesapeake bay, during the progress of construction of light-houses at those points. While at Smith's Point, and during a gale of wind, the main boom was broken. A new one has been supplied and she is now in good condition.

The old iron vessel formerly marking Willoughby Spit, being worn out and unfit for further service, was, after having been stripped of all articles of value to the light-house service, sold at public auction for the net sum of $2,113 73 and the proceeds turned into the treasury.

UNLIGHTED BEACONS.

The general condition of the beacons and stakes of the district is reported to be good, and these aids to navigation have received such attention as the exigencies of the service would permit.

At North Landing river four beacons, consisting each of a spar surmounted by a barrel, have been placed, and are found to materially assist in the navigation of the river.

One of the beacons off Bell's island is reported to have disappeared from its station. A new one has been prepared and will be placed at the first opportunity.

Core sound.—Beacons and stakes marking the channel through the sound replaced.

Blair's channel.—It has recently been learned, that all the beacons have disappeared from their proper places in this channel, excepting the first beacon, which still remains. Whenever the services of the buoy tender can be spared she will be sent to attend to the duty of replacing these beacons.

The other beacons of the district are in good condition.

BUOYS.

The buoys in Metomkin, Watchapreague, Hog island, Matchapungo and Sand Shoal inlets, on the eastern coast of Virginia, have been properly attended by contract. A new contract for this service for the year ending 30th July, 1869, has been entered into.

The buoys in Cape Henry channel, Hampton Roads, Norfolk channel, Hampton creek, Elizabeth river, James river, York river, Mobjack bay, Piankatank river, Rappahannock river, Great Wicomico river, Potomac river and tributaries, have been carefully attended during the year by the steam tender of the district.

In Chesapeake bay, from the Capes of Virginia to Havre de Grace, Maryland, the buoys have been regularly attended to. Two new buoys have been placed to mark wrecks, viz., one to mark the wreck of the schooner Mary E. Killinger, which lies in three fathoms water west by south half south from Cape Charles light-house, distant seven miles, and one to mark the wreck of the revenue cutter Nemaha, lying in five and a half fathoms water off the mouth of the Great Wicomico river, Windmill Point bearing south by west half west, distant nine and a half miles. The buoys in West river, Annapolis Roads, Bodkin Swash, Patapsco river, North Point creek, Swan Point channel, Cherrystone inlet, Hooper's straits, Kedge's channel, Tangier sound, Little Annamessix river, Wicomico river, Pocomoke sound, Great Choptank river, Eastern bay, St. Michael's river, Wye river, Chester river, Little Choptank river, have been visited by the tender and the buoys overhauled and replaced.

The buoys in Hatteras inlet, Ocracoke inlet and bar, Neuse river, Pamlico sound and river, Hyde county landings, and Bell's bay, Croatan sound and Albemarle sound, up Roanoke river to Plymouth, have been kept in good order.

In Alligator river, the spar buoys heretofore marking the channel have been replaced by iron nun-buoys of the third class, and an additional spar buoy placed off Sandy Point, about two and three-fourths miles above the mouth of the river.

In Core sound the buoys have been properly replaced by the buoy tender.

Care has been taken to provide the district with a large number of spare buoys and accessories, and a lot (290 pieces) of kentledge removed from the condemned iron vessel from Willougby spit were appropriated to use as buoy moorings and fitted accordingly.

An additional number of spars for buoys has been contracted for.

TENDERS.

During the year the buoy tender *Heliotrope* has been constantly employed in the work of replacing buoys and carrying supplies to light-stations. On the 1st February last, while in North Carolina, the cross-head of the air-pump broke, which accident compelled the vessel to remain inactive for 12 days, when a new cross-head was procured and fitted.

Upon the return of the vessel from the sounds of North Carolina she was taken on the railway and her copper repaired and hull caulked above water mark, needful repairs have also been made to the engine, deck planking, canvas covering of hurricane deck.

The steamer *J. N. Seymour* has been steadily employed in connection with the engineering branch of the service.

The great extent of this district seems to render it necessary to provide another vessel, a sailing vessel of small size, to attend exclusively upon the buoys in the lower part of the district, including Albemarle and Pamlico sounds, and the Board hopes to be able in the course of the coming season to make such arrangements as will enable it to detail a vessel for this duty.

DEPOTS.

A suitable storehouse for the security of supplies, sails, buoy accessories, boats, and other valuable property, is much needed in this district, and it has been found necessary to store certain articles of spare property on hand in the hold of an unemployed light-vessel, and in the event of that vessel being required for duty a transfer of these articles must be made to some other vessel, or have them placed on private stor-

SIXTH DISTRICT.

The sixth light-house district extends from New River inlet, North Carolina, to include Cape Canaveral, Florida. There are in this district—

Light-houses and lighted beacons	50
Light-vessels	6
Beacons, unlighted	3
Buoys actually in position	130
Spare buoys, to supply losses	35
Tenders, steam	None
Tenders, sailing	2

261. *Federal Point light station.*—Nothing has been done at this station during the year, and having been erected in 1866 it is believed that only incidental repairs will be required next year. The flues at this station are of terra-cotta pipes, which at other localities have been found objectionable, and it may be necessary to remove them and substitute other material.

When this light-house was built the site occupied came within the limits of Fort Fisher and was in possession of the government. The land was owned by a private individual and has recently been restored to him by the government. Compensation being asked for the land occupied by the light-house establishment, steps are now in progress for its purchase.

262. *Frying-pan Shoals light-vessel No.* 29.—This vessel was relieved June 29, 1868, by the Relief and brought to Charleston, and after having been thoroughly repaired was returned to her station.

263. *Cape Fear light station.*—Discontinued in 1866 and not since re-established.

264. *Oak island.*—Range lights for crossing the bar western entrance to Cape Fear river in good condition, and it is thought that only incidental repairs will be required during next year.

265. *Price's creek.*—Not yet re-established; examinations have been made as to the necessity of changes in the positions of these ranges.

266. *Horseshoe shoal.*—The screw-pile structure, reported at the date of the last annual report as being on hand, was erected at this station and lighted for the first time on the evening of March 9, 1868. On February 25, the work being well advanced, signs of settlement were first discovered, and the opposite side was weighted to make the settlement equal if possible. On the 23d of March the work suddenly settled three feet, and in the precarious state of the structure the light was discontinued, and the light-house, as far as practicable, removed and placed in store at Newbern, North Carolina. The parts left standing on the shoal are the piles, with five-feet screws, sleeves and lower tension rods.

267. *Orton's Point.*—The materials for re-establishing this station have been procured and are stored at Wilmington, North Carolina.

268. *Campbell's island.*—This station has not been re-established since its discontinuance in 1861.

269. *Upper jettee.*—These range lights were extinguished by the rebels in 1861, and the structures entirely destroyed.

270. *Georgetown.*—As this station was re-established and placed in complete condition in 1867, and a new keeper's dwelling erected at the same time, no repairs have been required, and it is thought that only incidental renovation will be necessary during the next year.

271. *Fort Point*, near Georgetown, South Carolina.—This light was extinguished and building destroyed in 1861. Its re-establishment at this time is not deemed necessary.

272. *Cape Romain.*—During the year general repairs have been made to the keeper's dwelling as follows: joints of wall raked out and repointed and cement washed; flashings around chimneys examined and replaced; roof repaired; chimneys cement-washed; cistern built; gutters to eaves and conductors to cistern furnished; plastering repaired; new door and frame made for porch. To the assistant keeper's house: new roof built; porch made in front; plastering repaired; joints of wall raked out and repointed; cistern built; gutters and conductors provided; doorway cut through wall and frame, and door to back kitchen furnished; an old brick one-story building in a dilapidated condition, formerly used as an oil-house, has been torn down and the brick used for cisterns; all new work painted; boat-house 13′ × 30′ erected and suitable tackle furnished.

The tower is in good condition with the exception of the exuding and wasting of the mortar on the inside. But few if any repairs will be required next year.

273. *Bull's bay.*—This station has been re-established, and the light was exhibited for the first time on the evening of August 31. A new lantern and apparatus have been placed; dwelling furnished with new inside doors, walls furred, lathed and plastered; outside walls repointed and cement-washed; roof repaired; wood-work painted; conductors furnished to cistern and general renovation made; boat-house built and new boat with sails, &c., furnished.

274. *Rattlesnake Shoal light-vessel No.* 30.—This vessel has continued during the year at her station to mark Charleston bar; no repairs were necessary.

275. *Weehawken light-vessel No.* 31.—This vessel needs general repairs; her deck is too old to admit of calking, and it is proposed to cover it with some water-proof material as a temporary expedient. It is feared that it may be found necessary to entirely remove her and substitute another vessel.

276. *Charleston.*—This station was extinguished by the rebels in 1861, and the structure destroyed. An examination of the locality has been made with a view to the location of range lights. A final decision upon the subject has been deferred to await the completion of new and detailed surveys rendered necessary by change of channels since 1861.

277. *Sullivan's island.*—The temporary light marking this station is located upon private property, and negotiations for the purchase of the land required for the sites of the range lights authorized at the last session of Congress are in progress.

278. *Fort Sumter.*—In good condition.

279. *Castle Pinckney.*—In good condition.

280. *Battery beacon.*—In good condition. Fence built around base of shaft.

281. *Hunting island.*—This station was discontinued and the buildings destroyed in 1861.

282. *Combahee bank.*—A screw-pile light-house has been erected in place of the light-vessel formerly marking this station; and light exhibited for the first time on the evening of February 22, 1868.

283. *Martin's Industry light-vessel* No. 32.—This vessel is in good condition. No repairs have been required during the year.

284. *Bay Point.*—When the sale of public property belonging to the Navy Department at this place was made, the building heretofore occupied as a keeper's dwelling was reserved from sale and turned over to the light-house establishment. It required considerable repairs to roof, &c. The tower is but temporary in its character, and is in good condition.

No steps have yet been taken towards building the light-house authorized by act of Congress approved July 28, 1866; and it is doubtful whether the light will ever be required.

285. *Hilton Head.*—Range lights for entrance into Port Royal harbor; in good condition.

286. *Fishing Rip light-vessel* No. 33.—This vessel (formerly the relief light-vessel) left Charleston May 27, to relieve the light-vessel No. 34, then at Fishing Rip station; previous to being sent down she was thoroughly overhauled.

287. *Braddock's Point, Calibogue sound.*—Negotiations are now in progress for procuring title to the requisite land at this locality, preparatory to the erection of a light-house in place of the light-vessel formerly stationed in Calibogue sound. An appropriation is available for this object, and according to the terms of the law, the work will be done by contract.

288. *Tybee.*—In good condition.

289. *Tybee Island knoll.*—Discontinued in 1861, and not re-established. An appropriation of $15,000 for a light-house to mark this knoll was made March 2, 1867, and by the terms of the law the work is to be done by contract. The necessary preliminary steps have been taken.

290. *Cockspur island.*—A substantial boat-landing has been erected; piles cased with yellow metal; tower whitewashed; station in good condition.

291. *Oyster Beds.*—Boat-landing erected; piles cased with yellow metal; tower whitewashed; station in good condition. The keeper's dwellings for this and the preceding station have been re-boarded, new roofs supplied, and conductors supplied; fence constructed.

292. *Fig island.*—In good condition.

293. *The bay, Savannah.*—In good condition.

294. *Sapelo.*—This station has been re-established, and was lighted for the first time on the evening of April 15, 1868. The keeper's dwelling has been almost entirely rebuilt, except the walls; new roofs, sash, doors, porch in front, plastering, stairs, and painted. New lantern and apparatus placed in tower; new window frames and sash; new door frames and door; and steps largely renewed. Tower red and whitewashed; fence built.

A skeleton frame beacon 50 feet in height, on a tramway of 100 feet, has been erected in front of the tower, and distant therefrom 660 feet. The light was exhibited April 15.

295. *Wolf island—two beacon lights.*—During the year a substantial dwelling of frame for the keeper has been erected, with tower and lantern on top; the work is not yet completed. The foundation of the building consists of 11 wooden piles 12 inches in diameter, driven to a depth of 28 feet, cut off below the surface of the marsh and cased with an iron cylinder three feet below the surface, and extending four feet above to receive the caps for sills; there is a platform 10 feet wide built on wooden piles extending along the entire front, and on one side back to and in front of the kitchen. A cistern also is placed in front of the

tions have been prepared, and bids called for, to be opened November 6, 1868.

297. *Little Cumberland island.*—In good condition.

298. *Amelia island.*—The repairs in progress at this station at the date of the last annual report have been completed and a fence constructed. A plank walk 840 yards in length has been made across the marsh to the beacon light in front, and a roadway, 680 yards, cleared.

299. *North beacons, Amelia island.*—This station has not been re-established.

300. *St. John's river.*—In good condition.

301. *Dame's Point light-vessel.*—This light-vessel, in St. John's river, was discontinued during the war and has not been re-established. The interests of commerce do not require a light at this place, and upon the recommendation of the Board, the honorable the Secretary of the Treasury has directed that the station be discontinued.

302. *St. Augustine.*—In good condition.

303. *Cape Canaveral.*—The iron light-house which, at the date of the last annual report, was in course of construction has been completed, and the light therefrom exhibited for the first time on the evening of May 10, 1868. The illuminating apparatus is a lens of the first order, revolving, showing a white light which attains its greatest brilliancy once every 60 seconds. Its elevation is 139 feet above sea level, and the light should be visible from the deck of a vessel at a distance of 18 nautical miles. Upon the exhibition of the new light, the fourth order fixed light which had been shown was discontinued.

LIGHT-VESSELS.

The relief light-vessel No. 34, belonging to this district, has been completely repaired. She is now in good condition, excepting mast, in which defects have recently been found to exist; these will be promptly remedied.

Light-vessel No. 35, formerly marked Martin's Industry. She was sunk by the rebels in Savannah river, was raised, repaired and fitted for service. Evidence of serious decay being observed, a thorough survey was held upon her and resulted in her condemnation. It was found that nearly every part of her hull was pervaded by dry rot, and to such an extent as rendered her unworthy of repair. She was accordingly stripped of every appurtenance which could be of service to the light-house establishment, and sold at auction September 25, 1868.

BEACONS, (UNLIGHTED.)

Two substantial day beacons have been erected on the oyster rocks opposite to Cockspur island.

They are built on four iron piles driven 10 feet and extending eight feet above the surface of the rock. An enclosed framework is placed on the tops of the piles 9 feet 7¼ inches square at the base, 12 feet high, and 6 feet square at the top. As these beacons are on the port side of the channel in entering, they are painted black.

A skeleton frame day beacon has been erected on the south end of Elba island, to take the place of one destroyed by decay.

BUOYS.

with the exception of one buoy at St. Augustine bar, Florida, which has recently dragged from its position, and will be replaced as soon as possible.

A buoy has been placed to mark a sunken wreck just above Cockspur, in Savannah river; and a buoy has been placed to mark the position formerly occupied by the Dame's Point light-vessel in St. John's river.

An adequate number of spare buoys and appurtenances has been kept on hand to supply losses.

TENDERS.

The light-house and buoy vessel *Maggie*, a sailing schooner of 80 tons burden, provided in February last for this district, has been constantly employed in buoying out the different harbors and channels, and in transporting supplies to light-vessels.

On the 20th September she was docked at Charleston; was calked outside, from the water-line up; her spar and cabin decks were also calked; new bowsprit and jibboom supplied. She is now in good order, and ready for further duty.

The *Narraganset* (schooner) has been employed during the year upon engineer duty. In October last a new foremast was placed in her, and all of her spars shortened and sails reduced, thus materially increasing her usefulness. Her general condition is good.

The small schooner *Dupont* was employed as a tender upon the works at Cape Canaveral light-house, and, upon their final completion, was taken to Charleston and securely cared for. Her small size renders her incapable of performing any but minor service.

DEPOTS.

A substantial shed building, 70 feet by 25 feet, for the storage of spare buoys and accessories, and other articles kept on hand, has been erected on James island, near Fort Johnson. The wharf, however, is in a dilapidated condition, and will soon require extensive renovation.

SEVENTH DISTRICT.

The seventh light-house district embraces the coast from Cape Canaveral to include Cedar Keys. There are in this district—

Light-houses and lighted beacons	11
Light-vessels	None.
Beacons, unlighted	6
Buoys actually in position	63
Spare buoys to supply losses	43
Tenders, steam	None.
Tenders, sailing	1

304. *Jupiter inlet.*—Illuminating apparatus examined; revolving machinery and timepiece cleaned and oiled; chimney-holders enlarged.

The walls of this tower are damp during the rainy season, causing the plastering to fall off. The proper remedies will be applied. A gutter around porch roof is needed.

305. *Cape Florida.*—A new iron door has been fitted in the tower; door locks repaired; four new blinds furnished to dwelling; new boat with appurtenances and new cooking stove supplied; tripod of lamp

306. *Carysfort Reef.*—New hinges fitted on storm doors; new revolving trucks fitted and rod lamp repaired; revolving machinery oiled and cleaned.

The necessity for a new boat being urgent, and none being available, a boat belonging to the buoy tender was altered, sloop-rigged, air-tight cases of galvanized iron fitted under the thwarts, and new boat falls fitted. New curtains supplied. Iron-work above needs painting, and below scraping and painting; new ladder and boat davits required.

Alligator Reef.—An estimate was submitted at the last session of Congress of appropriation required towards the erection of a first-class light at Alligator reef, being a part of the system for lighting the Florida reefs. No appropriation having been made, and the necessity for this light being deemed of great urgency, the estimate is again submitted.

307. *Dry Bank.*—New clamps fitted on braces; new hinges provided for tower windows; glass set where required; three new dampers for lens chimney supplied. The large accumulation of rubbish on the platform has been cleared off, giving thereby more space for the storage of fuel and necessary occupations.

The solidity of this tower, like Carysfort, seems to be perfect, though requiring a general painting above and scraping and painting below.

An iron davit for hoisting in stores is much needed. The wooden beam across the braces just above the roof, heretofore used for this purpose, has had the effect of causing a leak. Three clamps of diagonal braces below have been broken by the force of the sea; new ones are needed. A new boat is also required.

308. *Sand Key.*—Carelessness in winding up the revolving machinery having caused a displacement and consequent irregularity, the machine has been overhauled, adjusted, cleaned and oiled; timepiece cleaned and oiled. One of the old water tanks having been found unworthy of repairs, a new one was supplied. A new set of tanks on a different plan seems to be required. A new sail boat of a large size is required.

309. *Key West.*—Lightning conductor renovated; new platinum point required.

The lantern is very old and defective; the door cannot be made to shut properly. It is found that this light is frequently obscured by myriads of insects about the lantern, sometimes getting into the lamp itself.

310. *Northwest Passage.*—This station begins to show the effects of the climate. The roof of the dwelling leaks, and the station needs a general overhauling and repairs.

311. *Dry Tortugas.*—The old and rusty iron lightning conductor has been replaced by a new one of copper with horn insulators; supply pipes of burners repaired; eight panes glass set in the lantern.

This tower also shows the effects of the heavy rains in this climate. Much of the mortar on the south and southwest sides is washed out, in some places to the depth of nearly half an inch. These walls should be repointed with cement. The plastering of the oil room and kitchen has fallen down and needs repairs. A suitable enclosure fence is recommended.

312. *Dry Tortugas harbor.*—The flooring of the balcony around the lantern is much worn, and the seams in some places open, which admits rain-water inside the tower, and causes dampness and injury to the walls. The necessary remedy will be applied.

313. *Egmont.*—The dwelling has been repaired, leaks in roof stopped, and an almost entirely new porch put up. The old kitchen has been newly roofed and is now used as a storeroom; new cooking stove and accessories supplied. A suitable enclosure fence is recommended.

BEACONS, (UNLIGHTED.)

Of the fifteen day-marks along the Florida reefs from Fowey rocks to Eastern Sambo, as originally established, but five now remain, the others having been lost.

Those which remain are Long Reef beacon, letter N; Elbow beacon, letter J, about 5½ miles southeast from Carysfort reef light house; Grecian shoal beacon, letter H, on the outer edge of Grecian shoal; French reef beacon, letter G, on reef of same name; and Conch reef beacon, letter E, on Conch reef.

They are placed on the most projecting and dangerous points of the Florida reef, and within half a mile in every case of the edge of the Gulf Stream. They may be approached from seaward within a few hundred yards, but in bad weather a wider berth should be given.

These beacons are composed each of an iron shaft 36 feet in height, erected upon iron screw foundations, distinguished by a vane upon which a letter of the alphabet is painted.

The re-establishment of those which have been lost is pressed upon the Board as a measure of great importance to the navigating interests.

The day beacon at Coffin's Patches consists of an iron shaft, 6 inches in diameter and 40 feet high, surmounted at the height of 25 feet above the water by two ellipses at right angles to each other, of open lattice work, eight feet by five feet, presenting the appearance of a ball; and at the height of 33 feet by a cross of open lattice work, with arms nine inches wide and extending three feet from the shaft, and on the top a ball 15 inches in diameter. This beacon is in good order, though inclining a few degrees from the perpendicular.

BUOYS.

The buoys of the district have all been examined, cleaned, and painted; sinkers, chains, and ballast balls renewed where necessary.

The following additional buoys are recommended:

A first-class buoy on the south end of Tortugas shoal.

A first-class buoy on Rebecca shoals in place of the second-class buoy now there.

A second-class buoy off the south end of Pine island, Charlotte harbor, to guide vessels bound up Pease creek.

All the spare buoys on hand have been kept scraped and painted ready for immediate service.

TENDERS.

The buoy tender *Florida*, sailing vessel, has been thoroughly repaired, recalked, recoppered, and nearly all of her iron-work renewed. She now only requires new awnings to be as good and efficient as ever. A new suit of sails was put on her. New stern boat required. She has been constantly employed in attending upon the buoys and in carrying supplies to stations. It being found that these duties were greater than could be performed by one vessel, by the courtesy of the Coast Survey the schooner George M. Bache, belonging to that service, was temporarily employed, and has rendered valuable aid. Her duty being completed she was returned to the Coast Survey on September 15, after having been used for three months in buoy service.

EIGHTH DISTRICT.

The eighth light-house district comprises the coast from Sea Horse Key, Florida, to Rio Grande, Texas.

There are in this district—

Light-houses and lighted beacons	59
Light-vessels	None.
Beacons unlighted	2
Buoys actually in position	73
Spare buoys to supply losses	116
Tenders, steam	1
Tenders, sailing	3

LIGHT-HOUSES AND LIGHTED BEACONS.

315. *St. Mark's.*—In good condition.

316. *Dog island.*—The attention of the Board has been called to the dangerous exposure of this tower in heavy gales, being situated on a low spit, liable to be washed away in the first hurricane that may sweep over that part of the coast. The new dwelling on screw piles situated on a sand-hill about 15 feet above sea level will afford secure refuge to the keepers and their families in case of loss of tower. The ground is highly favorable for the construction of a new light-house on high ground at a moderate cost, the secure harbor, "Pilot's Cove," affording conveniences of landing materials at all times unsurpassed by any station in the district, except those in the Mississippi.

The eventual destruction of the present tower, under the circumstances stated, cannot be doubted, resulting in the extinction of one of the important lights on the Gulf coast, the destruction of public property, and involving danger to the lives of the attendants. In view of these facts the early construction of a new iron light-house, and, by reason of its position, an increase in the order of the light, is recommended.

317. *Cape St. George.*—In fair condition.

318. *Cape St. Blas.*—In fair condition. There is no dwelling provided for the keeper, who is now obliged to live in the watch room. A dwelling on screw piles within a short distance of the tower and connected therewith by a plank walk or bridge, is recommended. A bridge would seem to be requisite, as the place is overflowed in heavy gales to an extent rendering communication between tower and proposed dwelling difficult if not dangerous.

319. *Pensacola.*—In good condition. The temporary light which has been exhibited from this station since 1862 is a fourth-order lens. An appropriation for general repairs and for building a keeper's dwelling is now available, and so soon as the works have sufficiently progressed, it is proposed to fit up a first-order apparatus similar to the one in use before the war. The lantern is in perfect order for its reception.

Sand Island beacons Nos. 1 *and* 2.—These beacons were entirely destroyed during the war, and it is proposed to re-establish them when the new light is built.

321. *Mobile Point.*—An appropriation is available for the construction of a new light-house at this place, which work will be taken in hand at the same time with Sand island. The facility of communication between the two stations will enable one foreman with a suitable assistant to execute both works at the same time.

Mobile Point beacons Nos. 1 *and* 2.—These were entirely destroyed during the war. Cheap wooden structures are quite sufficient and will be erected during the progress of the new building for main light.

322. *Choctaw Point.*—As stated in the last annual report, the old site is probably ineligible by reason of changes in the channel induced by artificial obstructions. A detailed survey will be required before any conclusion as to proper site or character of structure can be arrived at.

Choctaw Pass.—These range beacons in connection with the foregoing light-house were entirely destroyed during the war. Their re-establishment as to location and time will necessarily depend upon the result of investigations concerning the main light.

323. *Round island.*—In good condition. Some trifling repairs are required, such as rendering water-tight the gallery deck, which leaks from unequal expansion of the cast iron and cement of which the deck is composed. The lantern and gallery are cast in one; the gallery being found too small was widened by building out the brick cornice, and the portion outside of the iron gallery is cemented. Various expedients have been tried to remedy the defect, but without more than partial success.

324. *East Pascagoula river.*—Renovated and put in complete order during the year and the light exhibited for the first time since 1861 on the evening of April 20, 1868.

The growing importance of Pascagoula river, which penetrates far into the rich pine forests bordering the northern shore of the Mississippi sound, the artificial deepening of the bar of the river and the natural deepening of the entrance called Horn Island Pass, have induced the Board to recommend, after thorough examination of the subject, the erection of a new light-house on *Horn island.* The ground is very favorable, being hard sand, and more elevated than Ship island. The surrounding country affords lumber and brick of excellent quality, and a brick structure is recommended as less costly than any other of sufficiently permanent character. Vessels of 14 feet draught of water can find safe anchorage in storms under the lee of this island.

An appropriation of $20,000 will be required for this light-house, and the necessary estimate will be submitted.

325. *Ship island.*—In good condition.

326. *Biloxi.*—In consequence of difficulty in making this light-house by day, through reason of the tower being painted black and shown against a background of dark pine woods immediately adjoining, the color of the tower has been changed to white. Station in good condition.

327. *Cat island.*—The buildings at this place were destroyed during the hurricane of 1860. The screw-pile dwelling on the land was burnt at the commencement of the war. The lantern was subsequently taken possession of and applied to Tchefuncti light station.

This light is important as a guide to vessels through the south pass of Cat island, through Pass Marianne, and to the entrance into Cat island harbor, into which 16 feet may be carried at low tide, giving complete shelter in all kinds of weather, especially the dreaded "northers."

This light will be re-established so soon as time and opportunity

328. *Pass Christian.*—In good condition.

329. *Merrill's Shell Bank.*—In good condition.

330. *St. Joseph's island.*—This island had washed away to considerable extent and it was found necessary to move the structure further back, about 25 feet from its former position. Nine piles were driven to a depth of nearly 60 feet in the positions to be occupied by the new piers. The ground around these piles was excavated as far as practicable and surrounded by brick masonry, thus completely protecting the wooden piles from the influence of the atmosphere and damage by worms. The piers are two and a half feet square and connected by diagonal tension rods of two and a half inch iron. Outside the foundation of the light-house a breakwater was built to protect it from the wash of the sea in southeast winds, which are the only ones capable of doing any damage. The space under the house between and around the piers was filled up with concrete. The station is now being painted and at the same time five panes of lantern glass will be put in, some of which may have been broken during the operation of moving the house back to its present position.

The work done is of the most substantial character and will probably preserve the light-house for a long time.

331. *Rigolets, (Pleasanton's island.)*—Tower in good condition. The keeper's dwelling requires repairs to roof and galleries, which have been authorized but not executed.

332. *Proctorsville.*—Destroyed in the hurricane of 1860 and not re-established. This station is comparatively unimportant, and a wooden structure, of an inexpensive character, would answer every requirement.

333. *West Rigolets.*—In good condition.

334. *Bon Fouca.*—Destroyed in 1862 and not re-established.

The important point in this vicinity seems to be Pointe aux Herbes, directly opposite, on the south shore of the lake, forming the principal landmark for all steamers and sailing vessels trading in the lakes. The abandonment of the present site and the erection of a light-house on Pointe aux Herbes is recommended, and an estimate of appropriation necessary will be submitted.

335. *Port Pontchartrain.*—The breakwater around the tower, which was in progress at the date of the last annual report, was completed in December, 1867. It is a solid and substantial work. The station has been thoroughly painted and a new cistern built.

336. *Bayou St. John.*—The work of erecting the beacon-light upon the old screw-piles of the former structure at this place is actively progressing. The iron work has been made by contract and transported to the site. The structure will be finished in a few days.

337. *New Canal.*—The work of rebuilding the breakwater at this place, and of general repairs to the station, is in progress.

338. *Tchefuncti river.*—The new light-house, which was in course of construction at the date of the last annual report, was completed and the light exhibited for the first time on the evening of December 1, 1867. A recent inspection found this station in perfect order.

339. *Pass Manchac.*—In good condition.

340. *Chandeleur.*—In good condition.

Grand Grozier.—An appropriation for the construction of a light-house at this place was asked of Congress at its last session, but not granted. The estimate will be again submitted.

341. *Pass à Loutre.*—The dwelling at this section, of frame resting upon nine brick piers, has settled down very uniformly and equally about three feet, so that the sills are at present only about 18 inches above the

ground. It is proposed to raise this structure to about its former level, and at the same time surround it with a fence of piling, to protect it from drift-logs, which, being afloat at high water and drifting against the piers, would endanger them.

342. *South Pass.*—Slight repairs are required to the sills of the house gallery, rain-gutters, reshingling, &c.

In view of the great importance of this light, which is the first one made by all vessels coming from the northern ports and the West India islands, and frequently by those coming from the western and southern coast of the Gulf, the insufficiency of the present third order light, and the perishable nature of the present structure, which is entirely of wood and surrounded by high swamp cane, readily set on fire by malicious or careless persons; and in consideration of the fact that the present light-house is getting old, and therefore likely to be a constant source of expense for repairs—it is deemed important to provide for the early erection at this place of a new structure, which should be of the first order. Every facility is offered for the landing and safety of materials, with deep water close up to the bank, and well sheltered.

343. *Head of the Passes.*—The work of building a breakwater in front of this light-house, which was in progress at the date of the last annual report, has been completed, and the good effects anticipated have been fully realized. The current of the river being checked by the piles, a rapid deposition of sediment has taken place, raising the ground between one and two feet during the year. A growth of willow is springing up, which will still further increase the deposition, and it seems reasonable to expect that by these means the stability of the light-house will be assured.

344. *Southwest Pass.*—The old light-house remains in the same condition as was reported last year, but the site is being rapidly encroached upon from the west by the wash of the sea. Some slight repairs have been made during the year. An appropriation is available for the construction of a new light-house at this place, and the subject has received the careful consideration of the Board; but in view of the difficulty of securing an adequate foundation no definite conclusion has been arrived at.

Barrataria bay.—In good condition.

345. *Timbalier bay.*—In the last annual report the necessity for building a new screw-pile light-house in shoal water, inside the island, was urged. The remarks then made are again called to the attention of the Department.

346. *Ship Shoal.*—In good condition. In October of last year the centre of a severe cyclone passed very near this light-house; the pyramidal sea caused such a vibration of the tower that the oil was thrown out of the reservoirs, and all efforts to relight the lamps were unavailing for six hours. The structure, however, was uninjured. Since the application of coal-tar for painting the tower, in order to ameliorate the dreadful sanitary condition of the station, the health of the keepers has been uninterruptedly good, and there can no longer be any doubt that the red-lead paint, with which the structure was painted, washing into the rain-water tanks was the cause of the sickness.

347. *Southwest Reef.*—This screw-pile structure was much damaged by the hurricane of October, 1867. The necessary repairs were promptly commenced, and are now in active progress. The chief features of the work consist in levelling and straightening the screw-piles, adapting the diagonal tension braces in the direction of southeast to northwest—the direction of prevailing and damaging winds. There were no braces previously—a very serious omission in so exposed a structure. A new gal-

lery of boiler-plate, on wrought-iron girders, on two sides of the structure, is now nearly finished. The interior was repaired, nearly all the wood-work of the tower having been broken up.

348. *Shell Keys.*—This structure was entirely destroyed in the hurricane of 1867, and has not been rebuilt—the appropriation asked for at the last session of Congress not having been granted. The absence of this light is very much felt by vessels trading between Berwick's bay and the Texas coast, and its early reconstruction is strongly recommended.

Calcasieu.—Among the few inlets on the Gulf coast west of the Mississippi, the bay of Calcasieu, some years before the war, acquired considerable importance on account of the extensive lumber trade carried on in that bay and in the river of the same name. This business has much increased since the close of the war, and bids fair to assume very large proportions. The depth of water on the bar is about six feet. The soil bordering the entrance is low salt marsh, subject to inundation during heavy gales.

349. *Sabine Pass.*—In good condition.

350. *Bolivar Point.*—Though the present temporary structure, with 4th order lens, suffices for the present necessities of the harbor of Galveston, yet the importance of the Texas trade seems to require that a permanent structure be erected. The third order iron tower, which was totally destroyed during the war, was found in every respect satisfactory for the exhibition of a light powerful enough for the locality, and the reconstruction of a similar tower and illuminating apparatus is recommended. An estimate of appropriation required will be submitted.

Bolivar beacon.—This structure was destroyed during the war. It was situated on a reef nearly awash in ordinary high tides, running parallel to the beach and 200 or 300 yards distant from it. It is highly probable that the exposed position of this beacon prevented its being lit when most wanted. As it only served for a range with the principal light, the necessity or expediency of its re-establishment will depend upon the location assigned to the main light.

351. *Pelican Spit.*—The necessity for re-establishing these range lights can only be decided upon after examination of the recent work of the coast survey. At all events the simplest contrivances will answer the purpose if it be determined to re-establish the range.

352. *Galveston range beacon.*—The remarks made in the case of Pelican Spit apply equally to this station.

353. *Half-moon shoal.*—The exigencies of the service have prevented any steps toward re-establishing this station, beyond ascertaining its condition.

354. *Red-fish bar.*—Of this structure the iron screw piles only remained, the rest having been burned during the war. A force was sent there in July last with the necessary materials, and the reconstruction of the light-house is progressing rapidly. The lantern is nearly finished and will shortly be sent down. It is expected that the work will be completed in about a month. A temporary light was established May 8, 1868.

355. *Clopper's bar.*—This light-house escaped destruction, though discontinued during the war. A temporary light-house was established and the light exhibited May 8, 1868. The station is in a satisfactory condition except that it needs painting, which will be attended to in a few weeks.

356. *Matagorda.*—The broken sections of this iron tower have been re-cast and are now ready for shipment. The work of putting up the tower is at present delayed in consequence of the undetermined state of the negotiations with the authorities of the State of Texas for the sale

and cession of a new site, the old one having been rendered valueless by the encroachment of the sea, which at the present time is nearly up to the spot formerly occupied. There is, however, a good prospect of an early and favorable action on the application for a new site, when there need be no further delay in the completion of the work.

357. *Saluria.*—This structure was entirely destroyed during the war, and there seems to be no very pressing necessity for its immediate reconstruction.

358. *Half-moon reef.*—This structure has been thoroughly repaired, and the light re-exhibited on the evening of February 20, 1868. The station is now in perfect order.

359. *Swash.*—Of the former structure only the screw-piles of iron remain, and which will answer for a new superstructure, an estimate of the cost of which will be submitted.

360. *Aransas Pass.*—In good condition.

361. *Brazos Island beacon.*—In good condition.

362. *Point Isabel.*—In good condition.

UNLIGHTED BEACONS.

Pass à l'Outre.—This beacon is a triangular skeleton pyramid of wood, constructed in 1863. It is topped with a circle of open slat-work, about eight feet in diameter. Although of simple and cheap construction, it has lasted well considering that very severe gales have visited the locality since its establishment. The structure is 45 feet high, and forms a range with the light-house for crossing the bar in the best water. Two similar structures about 30 feet high are on hand at the depot and await application.

Galveston.—This beacon is an iron screw-pile structure near the outer edge of the bar. It was constructed prior to 1853. It is about 20 feet above the surface of the water and forms a very conspicuous and useful sea-mark. Nothing has been done to it since its original construction, and it bids fair to last for many years more.

BUOYS.

The buoyage of the district has received especial attention and is now in as good condition as at any time before the war, with the exception of St. Andrew's bay and the South Pass of Cat island, which have not yet been buoyed.

A buoy which had been adrift was picked up and brought to New Orleans. An examination disclosed the fact that it did not belong to the United States light-house establishment, and that it was of English manufacture. The facts have been stated to the Department in a special communication, with a view to ascertain the ownership of the buoy and its return accordingly.

TENDERS.

The steam tender *Geranium* has been almost constantly occupied during the past year in placing, changing, and painting bouys, and has moreover performed occasional and valuable service in the engineering branch.

Notwithstanding the smallness of this steamer, the defects in her hull and boiler, she has performed a vast deal of service, and has demonstrated the advantage of steam over sailing vessels for buoy duty.

Her boiler was repaired in May last, at an expense of $1,547 80, and the total cost of all repairs to her hull, boiler and machinery during the year amounted to $2,509 03.

The inspector reports that the present condition of this vessel is by no means satisfactory; her hull being very weak, bends up fore and aft when in a sea-way, and her boiler cannot be considered safe with a pressure exceeding 22 pounds to the square inch. She is next to unseaworthy, and another vessel should be substituted for her as soon as possible. This vessel was purchased from the Navy Department at the close of the late war. An estimate of the appropriation required to provide a new vessel is submitted.

The schooner *Florida* has been used during the past year in transporting men and materials to the several stations undergoing repairs. Both masts have been renewed; some rotten timbers have been discovered in her and will require repair. The vessel not having been hauled out for about four years, it is desirable to do so at an early day, and at that opportunity make such repairs as may be required. Her sails are about half worn out and may last another year.

The launch *Susan* was thoroughly repaired during the past year, and is in very good condition. The dingey belonging to her, and which was saved from the wreck of the tender Chaos, 1866, is nearly worn out and not worth repairs. A new one is required.

The launch *Pharos* requires some repairs, which have been authorized.

Both of these launches have done excellent service during the past year in carrying materials and workmen and in attending upon stations. Their great efficiency was so evident that the construction of a third vessel has been commenced and is now near completion.

DEPOTS.

Depot at the Head of the passes.—A substantial wharf was built last year, and is in excellent condition. From a flat-boat loaded with coal, purchased last year, planks were obtained for building a fence around the coal pile and laying a platform. The buildings consist of an enclosed shed, 20 feet by 40 feet, and an old small tool-house built in 1862. The necessity which exists for suitably extending this depot by the construction of proper buildings and accessories, which was reported in the last annual report, still exists, and the estimate of last year is again submitted.

TENTH DISTRICT,

Extending from the north of the St. Regis river to include the Grassy Island light-house, in Detroit river. There are in this district—

Light-houses and lighted beacons	44
Light-vessels	None.
Beacons unlighted	None.
Buoys actually in position	69
Spare buoys to supply losses	21
Tenders, steam	1

One steam tender, the *Haze*, is common to the tenth and eleventh districts, and is also used by the engineer of those districts after the light stations have been inspected and supplied.

LIGHT STATIONS.

The numbering of stations is according to the light-house list for the lakes, January 1, 1867.

level of the river; when the waters are high the floors are damp. Repairs are required to the roof, which leaks, and the plastering, which is falling.

12. *Crossover island.*—Balcony of lantern leaks badly in several places. The chimneys of the dwelling require rebuilding, above the roof. Outside shutters to the windows are recommended, on account of the exposed position of the dwelling. This building requires repairs, having been constructed of that inferior material known as "soft brick," portions of which have fallen out in many places.

The wood-shed adjoining the keeper's dwelling also requires repair.

There is no boat shed, which, in point of economy, is indispensable.

Sisters' islands, St. Lawrence river.—No progress has been made in establishing the beacon at this point since the last annual report. The papers for perfecting the title of the site are still in the hands of the district attorney.

13. *Sunken Rock.*—In progress, painting of tower and lantern. A new boat, to supply the place of one damaged beyond repair.

14. *Rock island.*—New steps to the front entrance of the keeper's dwelling have been ordered.

15. *Tibbett's Point.*—At this station the roof of the keeper's dwelling, which leaks, the barn, and the plastering of the brick belt on which the lantern rests, require repair. Ventilators are much needed for the lantern, which sweats continually.

16. *Galloo island.*—Repairs to the roof and replastering inside are required for the old dwelling occupied by the assistant keeper; the barn to be entirely reshingled. A boat-house is needed.

17. *Horse island.*—The roof leaks and the plastering is off of the keeper's dwelling in many places. The barn and out-houses are in a dilapidated condition. A small boat-house is required.

18. *Stony Point.*—The dwelling, tower, and out-houses are very old, and considered not worthy of repair. New buildings are recommended.

19. *Oswego.*—At this station the authorized change of light from a fourth order fixed to a third order fixed is in progress. The deck plate and lantern are nearly completed, and other materials are being collected; it is not expected, however, that the cut stone can be obtained in time to finish the work before the close of navigation. The keeper's dwelling is reported as requiring considerable, and the cistern and fences slight repairs; the well has partly caved in, and is useless in its present condition. A new boat is required.

20. *Big Sodus bay.*—New range light lanterns have been put in the place of old ones, which were broken.

The keeper's dwelling is of stone, and the walls apparently good; the walls require furring and replastering. A new roof is recommended by the inspector of the district.

The tower, also of stone, leaks and is very damp.

21. *Genesee.*—Authority has been given to rebuild the walk from the shore to the beacon, which stands at the end of the West Harbor pier, which work will be finished before the close of navigation.

22. *Niagara Fort.*—The wooden tower stands in the old block-house now used for officers' quarters, and is so old and out of repair as to let in the snow and rain in stormy weather. Last winter the roof of the building took fire from a spark from one of the four chimneys which surround the tower. The danger of having the valuable lens destroyed by an accident of this kind, and the inconvenience of using the stairway and passages of the officers' quarters as a thoroughfare for the supply of

the light, make it expedient to erect a new tower, (the old one not being worth repairing,) in a safer and more convenient position.

The floors and plastering of the keeper's dwelling and the fences require repair. The barn is in a ruinous state, and should be removed or rebuilt.

23. *Black Rock beacon.*—In very good order, requiring nothing.

24. *Horse-shoe beacon.*—The pier for the protection of this beacon was begun last fall, but, owing to the inclemency of the weather, had to be suspended. It was resumed this summer, and is now complete. Slight repairs of the flooring of the balcony and the floor and ceiling of the oil-room are required.

25. *Buffalo.*—Slight repairs are needed to the fences.

26. *Dunkirk.*—The keeper's dwelling leaks and the plastering is out of order. The roof leaks and the sills of the covered way which connects the dwelling with the tower are rotten. The main tower is cracked, and the fence enclosing a portion of the grounds is of indifferent quality. The beacon tower is decayed and leaks. The alterations and improvements in progress at Dunkirk, under the direction of the engineer department of the army, afford an appropriate occasion for renovating and perfecting the aids to navigation at this station.

27. *Presque Isle, (Erie.)*—The new tower authorized to be built at this station was finished in the autumn of 1867, but casually omitted in the last annual report. The plastering of the dwelling house inside needs repair, also the window frames and other wood-work.

Presque Isle beacon.—The iron tower needs painting; the roof of the keeper's dwelling, which leaks, requires repair; the house, painting and whitewashing.

28. *Conneaut beacon.*—No repairs of importance have been made or required.

29. *Ashtabula.*—Station in good working order; no repairs made during the past year, and none required for the coming season.

30. *Grand River.*—The light-house at this station is a duplicate of the tower at Presque Isle, Erie, Pennsylvania, which being in a dangerous condition was taken down and rebuilt in 1867. The soil at both stations is of the same nature, and the Grand River tower in about the same condition that the tower at Erie (station No. 27) was found in by the committee of the Light-house Board who examined it. Iron bands have been resorted to to hold the tower together, one of which, unable to withstand the heavy strain put upon it, has fallen off. The keeper's dwelling, built in 1825, is in a very dilapidated condition.

Estimates are submitted for rebuilding the tower, like that recently erected at station No. 27, and a suitable keeper's dwelling. A railing is required on the pier to enable the keeper to reach the beacon in bad weather, in order to light it.

31. *Cleveland.*—Station in order.

At Cleveland beacon a change of light from a sixth order, white, fixed, to a fifth order, fixed, varied by red flashes, has been authorized and will be made as soon as the lens is received.

32. *Black River.*—The tower, which was built of brick of inferior quality, is cracked, owing to the action of the waves on the crib-work. It is proposed to make the necessary repairs in both.

33. *Vermillion beacon.*—The tower, a small structure of wood, has been forced out of perpendicular by the action of the waves in gales of wind and requires repair.

34. *Huron beacon.*—A proper store-room for the supplies is required for this station.

35. *Cedar Point beacon.*—In good condition.

36. *Cedar Point range.*—In good condition.

37. *Sandusky.*—Repair of plastering of keeper's dwelling has been authorized; a store-room for wicks, chimneys, paints and oils, is required. These articles are now kept in the kitchen.

38. *Port Clinton.*—Repairs are required to the tower, which leaks. A well or cistern, slight repairs to the plastering of the keeper's dwelling, thorough repair of fences.

39. *Green island.*—Some slight repairs required to the plastering of the walls inside.

40. *West Sister.*—The tower at this station has been renovated and the keeper's dwelling rebuilt.

41. *Turtle island.*—A new tower and keeper's dwelling, of Milwaukee brick, were finished last year, but not included in the annual report for 1867.

New Maumee ranges.—Three sets of ranges for the navigation of Maumee bay and river have been erected, and will be lighted before the close of the season.

42. *Monroe.*—The wooden tower requires repainting. The lantern (ot the old pattern) leaks in the roof and around the base. The deck leaks also. There is no covered passage between the tower and dwelling, though close to each other.

The dwelling, also of wood, needs extensive repairs; the planking of the pier to be removed. An estimate of the cost of putting this station in proper repair is submitted.

43. *Gibraltar.*—Extensive repairs are reported as necessary at this station. The tower leaks, and it is with difficulty that the main door of the tower can be opened, the pressure above the sill having caused it to settle. The lantern leaks, and lantern doors do not close tightly. The roof of the dwelling leaks, and the house is thoroughly wet in rainy weather. The ceilings need replastering. Fences and well are out of order.

44. *Mamajuda.*—In very good condition.

45. *Grassy island.*—The house and tower of this station are of wood and stand upon a pile foundation on a shoal in Detroit river. The roof of the dwelling is in a very leaky condition, in consequence of which much of the plastering has fallen off. The tower and dwelling require painting inside and out. The lantern, of the old pattern, should be replaced by a fifth order lantern of modern style. An estimate of the cost of the necessary repair and improvements is submitted.

BEACONS, (UNLIGHTED.)

None.

BUOYS ACTUALLY IN POSITION.

There has been no change in the buoyage of the 10th district since the last annual report; the system has elicited no complaint, and the service, under contract, has been performed in a satisfactory manner. The buoys in position, as well as "spare," are in serviceable condition.

TENDERS.

The steam tender *Haze*, after supplying the 10th district, was turned over to the inspector of the 11th district.

As an evidence of the superior efficiency of a tender like the Haze, whose engine occupies a comparatively small space, and is very economical in the consumption of fuel, it is worthy of record that this vessel visited and supplied every station on Lake Erie in *five* days, and the whole

ELEVENTH DISTRICT.

The eleventh district includes all of the lake region above Grassy Island light-house, Detroit river. There are in the district—

Light-houses and lighted beacons	69
Light-vessels	None.
Beacons (unlighted)	1
Buoys actually in position	94
Spare buoys to supply losses	38
Tenders (steam, common to 10th and 11th districts)	1
Tenders (sailing, upon Waugoshance works)	1

The operations in the district during the past year, and those proposed for the next fiscal year, are as follows: The numbering of the stations is, according to the light-house list for the lakes, 1st January, 1868—

46. *Windmill Point.*—Is in good condition.

47. *St. Clair flats and beacon.*—The crib-work on which the structures are situated needs some minor repairs; also the plastering of the dwelling, and the boat.

It is probable that the new channel across the flats, now being dredged under the direction of the engineer department of the army, will be completed by the close of navigation of 1869; and it is proposed to commence the construction of range lights to mark it, under the appropriation of $60,000 now available for the purpose, sufficiently early next season to secure their completion by the time the channel can be used.

48. *Fort Gratiot.*—The change of the distinctive characteristics of this light from fixed to fixed varied by flashes, made necessary a flue for the descending weight of the revolving machinery, and it was constructed. The tower is in good condition, except a small leak at the base of the lantern. The dwelling is quite old, but in tolerable repair. A fence to enclose the premises is needed.

An additional coast light between Fort Gratiot and Point aux Barques, Lake Huron, is very much needed. The distance between the two places is 75 miles, for the whole of which vessels keep the shore well aboard while going in either direction.

An estimate of the probable cost of such a structure as is required is submitted.

49. *Point aux Barques.*—The buildings at this station are in fair condition, and will probably require no repairs during the coming season. As reported last year, the trees on a point to the southward and eastward interfere with the range of the light in that direction.

50. *Tawas (Ottawa) Point.*—It has not been found practicable to make the repairs which last year were reported as necessary, and the condition of the station is not improved.

51. *Charity island.*—In the keeper's dwelling the plastering has fallen in many places, and, together with the kitchen floor, requires repairing. New sails and oars for the boat, and blocks and falls for hauling it out of the water, are needed.

52. *Saginaw bay.*—The station is in fair condition. Nothing is required for the tower. The dwelling is old, but can be made comfortable for some time yet by repairing the plastering, which has fallen in many places, refitting the doors, which now fit badly and permit storms to beat in and injure the floors, and renewing the floor in one of the rooms.

The boat requires repairing and calking, and new sails and oars.

Sturgeon Point.—An appropriation of $15,000 for the construction of a light-house at this point is available. The land needed for the site has been purchased, and the title-papers are now in the hands of the United States district attorney for examination, preliminary to submitting them to the Attorney General for his opinion concerning the validity of the title proposed to be conveyed to the United States.

Trowbridge Point, (Alpena.)—By act of Congress, approved July 20, 1868, the Board was authorized to change the site formerly proposed for this light-house. The proper site is at the mouth of Thunder Bay river, the entrance to which will thus be marked, and the station subserve a much better purpose than it would on Trowbridge Point, a mile distant.

A company, chartered under the laws of the State of Michigan, is now engaged in building piers at the mouth of Thunder Bay river, and if the works are properly constructed, and the right of way can be secured, the best place for the light will be at the end of one of the piers, where it will answer both as a guide into Thunder bay and into the mouth of the river to the town and harbor of Alpena. A dwelling on shore will have to be built for the keeper.

It is proposed to wait until the piers referred to are completed, before any further steps are taken in the matter.

53. *Thunder Bay island.*—The dwelling at this station has been entirely rebuilt since the last annual report, the cost thereof being borne by the appropriation approved March 2, 1867, specially applicable to the work. The station is now in good condition.

54. *Presque Isle.*—The appropriation, approved March 2, 1867, for rebuilding the keeper's dwelling has not been expended. After due consideration of the subject, it was determined to recommend the removal of this light to a site about one mile north of the present one, so as to make it answer the purposes of a much needed coast light, instead of being a mere harbor light as it now is. Owing to the character of the entrance to the harbor, the light is of little value to guide vessels into it. If the removal of the light is made as contemplated, its power must be increased, which involves the necessity for an additional appropriation, which should also provide for the establishment of range lights to guide into the harbor. With the arrangement now proposed, this fine harbor of refuge will become available, and the requirements of commerce for a coast light on the point of the peninsula will be at the same time fully met.

Spectacle reef is a very dangerous shoal in Lake Huron, ten miles to the eastward of Bois Blanc light-house. It is in the way of all vessels beating through Lake Huron, and is probably more dreaded by navigators than any other danger now unmarked throughout the entire chain of lakes, and a light-house there would be scarcely second in importance to Waugoshance. The Board has recently authorized placing a buoy of the first class upon it. But this, of course, is of use only in the daytime. The reef is composed of boulders, and is exposed to the whole sweep of Lake Huron; therefore, the construction of a light-house upon it would be both difficult and expensive. It would cost probably not less than three hundred thousand dollars to build a proper structure. Large as this sum is, the wreck upon it last fall of two vessels at *one* time involved a loss greater than required to mark the danger, and it is not unlikely that the aggregate of all the losses which have occurred here would build several such light-houses. In view of the great commerce upon the lakes, and its prospective increase, the Board feels that they are justified in now bringing the matter to the attention of Congress, and in submitting an estimate for an appropriation to begin the work.

55. *Bois Blanc.*—The new tower and dwelling in course of construction

at the date of the last annual report was completed and lighted a expected. The station is now in excellent condition.

56. *Cheboygan.*—The necessary repairs to the foundation of the buildin have been made, but it requires protection by paving or sodding to pr vent the sand again drifting from under it. Otherwise the station is i good condition.

Straits of Mackinac.—Attention is respectfully directed to remarks i the last annual report concerning the necessity of a light to mark th passage between the island of Mackinac and Round island, known a the North Channel, and the estimate then made is renewed.

57. *Detour.*—Nothing required, the station being in good condition.

McGulpin's Point.—A valid title to the requisite site for a light-hous at this point having been vested in the United States by the proceed ings in condemnation, last year reported as in progress, the work wa commenced this season, and it is expected that the light will be show for the first time on or before the 15th November, 1868.

58. *Waugoshance.*—It was necessary at the close of operations las season to leave the work of excavation for the face wall of the new pie of protection at this station in a somewhat critical condition. The exca vation had been carried down through the old crib work, and to a dept of six and a half feet below the surface of the water. However, ever precaution was taken, the iron dam being filled with water and wel shored to the surrounding pier, and the machinery being entirely cov ered in with timber and plank. A reliable man was left in charge, wh remained there during the winter, and early in the spring made th gratifying report that nothing at the station had been injured by the ic and gales of the season. At that time a portion of the pier was stil covered with piles of ice twenty feet in thickness, but one of the air locks of the dam was free, and there was but little ice on the engine room, and none inside of it, so that the work of setting up the machin ery and getting ready for this season's operations could be at once begun One month was consumed in this preliminary work, and in erecting a der rick of sufficient power to handle the heavy stone to be laid in the wall. A portion of time was also devoted to strengthening the dam by putting a large number of stay braces in the space occupied by the two uppe courses of the boiler iron composing it. These were to prevent th springing of the dam under the heavy load (nearly seven hundre pounds to the square foot) to which it was subjected while being sunk as the excavation proceeded.

Meanwhile a force of stonecutters was organized at Marblehead, Ohio, for the purpose of cutting that portion of the stone which had been contracted for in the rough, and comprising all the even-numbered courses in the wall. The odd-numbered courses had been contracted for to be cut to the net dimensions by the contractors; and all were to be delivered at Waugoshance pier by the contractors free of expense to the United States.

On the 23d of May, everything being in readiness, the operation of sinking the dam was resumed, and, from this time until the 20th of June, was continued both night and day. The material excavated consisted of limestone and granitic boulders, packed in sand and gravel. Some of these boulders weighed from three to four tons each, and were situated partly within and partly without the dam. Such had to be either undermined and drawn into the dam, or drilled and split, to allow the dam to pass them in sinking. As the stones were excavated from the bottom, they were deposited upon the top of the dam in timber cribs built to receive them, and by their weight assisted in sinking it. During the process of excavation, nearly three times the cubic contents of the material displaced by the dam were removed, this great excess arising from the materials which either fell in from the outside, or were drawn in to make way for the dam. At one time the dam became so tightly jammed by the pressure against it of the boulders on the outside that it was necessary to raise it to permit the stones and gravel to roll inwards, and afterwards pass them out through the air-locks.

The excavation continued until the evening of the 20th June, when it was stopped at the depth below the water surface of twelve feet two inches. From the bottom of the excavation at this depth, holes were sunk three feet deeper into the reef without finding rock in place. The material reached (boulders, gravel, and sand) was so compact that it was with difficulty it could be broken up with crowbars, and it was finally determined to carry the excavation no further.

The bed-rock is in full view on three sides of the pier, and distant from it only a couple of hundred feet, at a depth of 10 feet below the surface of the water. Not finding bed-rock at the exact site of the tower, at 15 feet below the water surface, it is inferred that the tower stands upon a reef which has formed within the horseshoe-like rock seen from the pier.

As bed-rock had not been reached, the difficulty of making a cement bottom for the dam, which would be capable of resisting the buoyant effort of the water when the dam was opened to the external air, was greatly increased. To distribute this buoyant effort equally over the whole bottom, a floor was made of Norway pine plank, six inches in thickness, laid as closely together as possible, and extending beyond the sides of the dam all around to a distance of three inches. This floor was completed on the 3d of July, and, between that time and the close of the month, the workmen were engaged in filling in with concrete the space between the dam and the foundation of the tower, and in building a railway around the dam, so as to distribute the stone for the wall by means of a truck.

During the months of August and September repeated attempts were made to close the bottom of the dam with cement and concrete. Twice the bottom was made so strong that it stood until the pressure underneath it was within one pound to the square inch of that required, and each time it failed. A large valve was then cut in the top of the dam, and a few stone for the bottom course passed through it into the dam, then full of water. Air was then forced into the dam until the water was expelled, and afterwards the stone were laid in their places. More stone were then passed through the valve and laid in the same way. The work is now progressing finely, and it is expected that two entire courses of stone will be laid before operations are suspended for the winter.

It is hoped that next season will be sufficient for the entire completion of this very important work.

St. Helena island.—For the reasons given in the last annual report a light to mark the anchorage at this island is deemed necessary, and the estimate then submitted is respectfully renewed.

59. *Skillagalee*, (Isle au Galets.)—The work of rebuilding and improving this light station, suspended at the close of last season, was resumed in the spring, and has been completed. Formerly a light of the sixth order was exhibited from a height of 35 feet. Since the 19th of July last a light of the third order, elevated 106 feet above the water, marks this station. The improvement was greatly needed and has already proven of great benefit to navigators.

60. *Beaver Island harbor.*—An appropriation of $5,000 approve July 20, 1868, for repairs and renovations at this station, is available. In addition to the thorough renovation of the dwelling, it may possibly b necessary to rebuild the tower and supply it with a new deck plate an lantern. It is proposed to make the necessary renovations and improve ments during the course of next season.

61. *Beaver island.*—The tower and dwelling are in good repair, excep that some of the shutters have been blown off the dwelling. The should be replaced, and a good cistern should be built.

62. *South Fox island.*—This station is new and in good condition The inside of the dwelling and the iron stairway of the tower requir painting.

63. *Grand Traverse.*—Tower and dwelling in good condition; a boat house and ways are required.

Mission Point—the point dividing Grand Traverse bay. An appro priation of $6,000, approved March 3, 1859, is available for building a light-house upon this point. The necessity for the construction of th light-house never having been at all urgent, the money has not bee expended. Further examination into the matter will be made, and if i does not appear that the station is required the appropriation will b transferred to the surplus fund.

64. *South Manitou island.*—This station requires extensive repairs The house is of brick, surmounted by a wooden tower. New plastering i required throughout, as well as painting. New eaves troughs and con ductors are needed, also a new cistern. The house which protects th fog signal is in bad condition and requires general repairs. An estimat of the probable cost of putting the station in good condition is submit ted.

65. *Point Betsey.*—This station is greatly in need of repairs; the plas tering has fallen in many places, and the floors are considerably decayed Some of the foundation stones of the tower have become displaced; the should be replaced and the entire foundation repointed.

66. *Grand Point au Sable.*—This station is new and in good condition The drifting of the sand threatens the stability of the tower.

Manistee.—The requisite site has been purchased, and the title approve by the Attorney General. It is proposed to build the light-house durin next season.

White river.—The harbor works at this place are not yet sufficientl advanced to warrant a final decision concerning the character of th requisite buildings and their exact site.

67. *Muskegon.*—An appropriation of $8,000 approved March 2, 1867 "for rebuilding keeper's dwelling at Muskegon light station," is available As the light was exhibited from the keeper's dwelling, the rebuilding o the latter involved the necessity of rebuilding the whole station. Plan for a structure of wood were prepared, as none other could be built for th amount of the appropriation, and early in the last spring the work wa commenced. A temporary building was erected from which the ligh was exhibited; the old buildings were taken down and the timber frame for the new building. At this stage, it was represented that a fram building upon the old site would be exposed to great danger of fire from piles of combustibles (lumber, slabs, sawdust and shavings) which sur round it. It was found upon examination that these representation were well founded, and, moreover, that the lake front of the site was no owned by the United States, and that the description of the site as give in the deed was very indefinite. The work was consequently suspende and steps taken to secure a proper site on the north side of the river

One of the owners of this site being absent from the country, nothing further can be done in the matter until his return, which is expected at an early day.

Because of the close proximity of so much that will readily take fire, the new building ought to be as near fire-proof as circumstances will permit, and in order to make it so a small appropriation in addition to the former one is required.

68. *Grand river.*—This light station has been put in thorough repair; the tower has been raised four feet and provided with a new lantern, for which a special appropriation has been made, approved March 2, 1867.

South Haven.—The south pier at this harbor is now completed and a light similar to the one established on Kenosha pier should be placed upon it. It is proposed to purchase the necessary site for a keeper's dwelling in time to begin the construction of the buildings during next season.

69. *Kalamazoo.*—The station and all about it are in good condition.

70. *St. Joseph's and beacon.*—The light-house at this station consists of a wooden dwelling surmounted by a wooden tower. They require repainting, and the cellar needs draining. A cistern is wanted, and the house should be provided with eaves gutters and conductors. A new fence is required.

71. *Michigan City.*—The dwelling leaks badly where the tower joins the roof; eaves troughs and conductors are needed; the roof requires repairs, and a cistern and new outbuildings are wanted.

72. *Chicago.*—This station is in good condition so far as repairs are concerned. A cistern is needed and will be built.

73. *Waukegan.*—New outbuildings and repairs to roof of dwelling and to the cistern and well are required, and a pump is wanted for the latter.

74. *Kenosha and beacon.*—This station is in excellent condition in every respect.

75. *Racine.*—It is proposed to put into this light-house a new lens, illuminating 225° of the horizon, instead of 180°, as at present.

76. *Milwaukee.*—This station has been put in thorough repair. The tower has been raised four feet and supplied with a new and improved lantern, much to the benefit of those for whose use it is intended.

77. *North Cut beacon.*—The tower and dwelling are in good condition.

78. *Port Washington.*—In good condition; small repairs have been made to the cistern and well.

79. *Sheboygan.*—After some slight repairs to the cistern and fence have been made, the station will be in good condition.

80. *Manitowoc.*—Tower old, but in fair condition. The dwelling requires general repairs.

81. *Bayley's harbor.*—By act of Congress, approved March 2, 1867, the sum of $15,000 was appropriated for "repairs and renovations" at this station. Upon examination it was deemed best not to expend this money at Bayley's harbor, but to remove the light to Cana island, a short distance to the northward, and making it a lake coast light, and to build range lights to mark the channel into Bayley's harbor. Upon making this apparent to Congress the requisite authority for the change was given.

Bayley's harbor range lights.—An appropriation of $6,000 for range lights to mark the entrance to and channel into the harbor has been made and the title to the land required for the sites has been vested in the United States. The work will be commenced upon the opening of next season, and before its close this fine harbor of refuge will be made available, which has never before been the case.

Cana island.—Under authority of a provision of the act of Congres approved July 20, 1868, the light heretofore located on the island : the entrance to Bayley's harbor is to be removed to Cana island. A the position proposed will give to the new light much greater importanc and make it a lake coast light, it should be increased from the fifth ord to the third to correspond with the other lake coast lights. This increa of power and efficiency will, of course, cause an increase of cost, and a estimate of the amount which will be required in addition to the $15,0(now available is submitted.

North bay.—This excellent harbor of refuge, situated to the northwa of Cana island, is now without a light. To render it available a sing set of range lights, of inexpensive character, is required, and an estima of the cost thereof is submitted. With these ranges, taken in connectic with the coast light on Cana island and the ranges for Bayley's harbo this portion of the coast of Lake Michigan, now so much dreaded i stormy weather, will be made almost perfectly safe.

82. *Port du Morts.*—The dwelling requires replastering and paintin; The tower and fog-signal house also require painting. The fire-clay li ing to the furnace of the engine, which operates the fog signal, nee renewing.

83. *Pottawatomie.*—Tower and dwelling in good condition. Nothin required, except some trifling repairs to the plastering of the dwelling.

Poverty island.—The recommendation and estimates for a light-hou on Poverty island, northern entrance to Green bay, contained in th report of last year, is, for the reasons there given, respectfully renewe

84. *Point Peninsula.*—The front wall of the dwelling is cracked, an the cellar is wet. When these are attended to and corrected the statio will be in good condition.

85. *Escanaba.*—The light at this new station was exhibited, as expecte at the date of the last annual report.

Chambers's island, (Manomah.)—This new light station was complete during the season, and the light exhibited for the first time on the nig of October 1st.

86. *Green island.*—In good condition. Some small supplies for the bo are needed.

Eagle bluff.—This light station (a new one) was entirely constructe during the season, and a light was exhibited from it for the first time o the night of October 15, 1868.

87. *Tail Point.*—This station is in good condition.

Fox river.—By acts of Congress approved July 2, 1864, and April 1866, the sum of $11,000 is available for the purpose of building a beaco light at the mouth of Fox river. A cut is now being dredged throug Grassy island; it is about half done, but work upon it is now suspende it is understood, for want of funds. There is now sufficient water i the cut to permit steamers of light draught to pass through. It is recon mended that no steps be taken toward lighting this channel until i completion, and that no attempts be made to light the old channel which are crooked, and would be difficult to light satisfactorily.

88. *Round island.*—This station is in such a condition that it probabl requires rebuilding, but the question cannot be definitely determine until a more thorough examination is made. Meanwhile, it is propose to make such temporary repairs as are required.

89. *Point Iroquois.*—The condition of this station is such that it may po sibly require rebuilding, a question which must remain in doubt unt the structures are examined by competent persons. The necessa repairs of a temporary nature will meanwhile be made.

90. *White Fish Point.*—Tower and illuminating apparatus are in excellent condition. Slight repairs are required to the plastering of the dwelling, and a cistern and cellar are much needed.

A coast light between White Fish Point and Grand Island harbor, Lake Superior.—Attention is respectfully directed to the recommendation concerning and estimate for this work, contained in the annual report of the Board for last year. The necessity for this light is great, and the recommendation and estimate are repeated.

Grand Island harbor, eastern entrance, range lights.—These range lights were completed during this season, and lighted for the first time on the night of the 15th August.

91. *Grand island.*—Tower and dwelling new, and in good condition.

Grand Island harbor, western entrance, range lights.—Were completed during the season, and lighted for the first time on the night of August 15th, 1868.

92. *Marquette.*—Tower and dwelling are in good condition; some repairs to the cistern are required.

Granite island.—By the proceedings in condemnation last year reported in progress, a valid title to the whole island (which only contains a couple of acres) has been vested in the United States, and a working party is now engaged in the construction of the buildings, and it is expected that they will be completed before the close of the season. The landing of the materials at this place was accompanied by more than ordinary difficulty. The island (granite rock) rises almost perpendicularly out of Lake Superior, with deep water all around it. Whatever was landed had to be moved from the steamer to the top of the island, which is sixty feet above the water. At ten feet above the water a platform was erected, from which a track was laid to the summit of the island, where a portable steam engine was placed, for the purpose of hauling up a track upon which all the materials were carried.

The transportation from Detroit, Michigan, of the materials used in the buildings and accessories, was done by the steamer Haze, (belonging to the light-house establishment,) which rendered very valuable service in this way.

Much of the top of the rock had to be removed by blasting, in order to get a suitable place for the light-house buildings.

It will be necessary to construct suitable davits with which to hoist the light-house boat out of the way of the sea.

West Huron island.—The buildings are placed upon the highest part of the island, at an elevation of 163 feet above the lake. The island consists of granite, of which material both the house and the tower are built. A road had to be constructed from the foot of the island to its summit in order to transport the materials used, and the labor involved in the transportation was very great. Large quantities of rock had to be removed, both in constructing the road and in making a level site for the buildings.

The light will be exhibited for the first time on the night of the 20th October, 1868.

93. *Portage river.*—The buildings are in a dilapidated condition, described in detail as follows:

The tower is built of rubble stone, with solid walls which are very damp inside. The stairway is of wood, and badly decayed. The lantern leaks, and is too small for the apparatus, having an inside diameter

house is very damp throughout, in consequence of which the floors are so badly decayed as to be unsafe. The plastering has fallen off the ceilings and walls in many places. The eaves of the roof do not project beyond the walls.

It is recommended that the tower be provided with an interior brick cylinder, an iron stairway, and a lantern of modern style, with cast-iron deck plate; also, that a new dwelling be built, and that it be connected with the tower by a covered passage-way.

To make these repairs and renovations will require a special appropriation, for which an estimate is submitted.

Portage entry range lights.—These range lights were entirely built this season, and were lighted for the first time on the night of the 1st October, 1868.

Mendota—An appropriation of $14,000, approved March 2, 1867, is available for the purpose of establishing this light station. The act of Congress making the appropriation for this light-house provides that it shall be built by contract. A site has been purchased, and the title approved by the Attorney General of the United States. It is proposed to place a wooden tower at the end of the south pier, and to erect a keeper's dwelling on shore.

94. *Manitou.*—In good condition, except that the main band encircling the column at the southeast corner of the tower has been cracked by some unknown cause.

95. *Gull Rock.*—This station is new and in good condition.

96. *Copper Harbor.*—Except the cistern, which leaks badly, everything about this station is in good condition.

97. *Copper Harbor range lights.*—Under authority of the act of Congress approved July 20, 1868, appropriating the additional sum of $5,000 for a range of lights for Copper Harbor, a working party is now engaged in building the dwelling for the keeper of the range lights, rendered necessary by the circumstances detailed in the last annual report. It is expected that the dwelling will be completed before the close of the season.

98 *Eagle Harbor.*—The light-house buildings at this place are in very bad condition, and have been so for several years. The dwelling is built of rubble stone, laid together in the rudest manner. It is surmounted by an octagonal wooden tower, with a lantern of the oldest pattern, having small panes of glass, and heavy sash bars, which obstruct the light.

It is recommended that this station be rebuilt, and an estimate of the cost of doing this is submitted.

99. *Eagle river.*—At this station the buildings are situated on a sand hill, and the tower forms one corner of the dwelling. Owing to the character of the foundation the walls have cracked, and the crack has enlarged materially within the last year, showing that the destructive influences are still at work. The inspector reports that already there is danger that the corner of the dwelling supporting the tower will fall. Either very extensive repairs or a new structure are required, and believing that the latter would prove to be the most economical, an estimate of the cost is submitted.

100. *Ontonagon.*—The buildings at this station are new and in good condition.

101. *La Pointe.*—The work of protecting the foundation of the structure at this place has been somewhat delayed by the failure of the contractor to deliver the stone as agreed upon. Recently, about 50 cords of stone have been delivered, and will at once be broken up and placed. As the piers upon which the building rests extend downwards to the

102. *Raspberry island.*—The dwelling requires replastering throughout and repainting. A boat landing is needed; also steps to lead from the landing to the top of the bluff (40 feet high) upon which the buildings stand. An estimate of the cost of these improvements is submitted.

Michigan island.—During next season it is proposed to renovate and relight this station, in accordance with the provision of the act of Congress approved July 20, 1868.

103. *Minnesota point.*—The tower is in good condition. The dwelling leaks badly around the chimneys. The rain and soot have discolored the walls. The plastering has fallen in many places, and is loose in nearly all the rooms. It is proposed to replaster the house throughout, and to reflash the chimneys.

Beaver bay.—The act of Congress approved July 28, 1866, appropriating $15,000 for a light-house at this place, contains the following provision, "That the Light-house Board of the Treasury Department, after due examination, shall deem a light-house at that point necessary."

Under instructions from the board, Beaver bay was visited by General William F. Raynolds, corps of engineers, engineer of the district, who, under date of August 19, 1868, submitted a report, the substance of which is as follows:

"The light is not needed for local purposes, nor is it required by the general wants of commerce. Its erection at present could only be justified by the anticipation of trade, which will no doubt spring up in this region of Lake Superior upon the completion of the St. Paul railroad."

The Board does not deem a light-house at that point necessary at present.

Pigeon river.—An appropriation of $15,000, approved March 2, 1867, is now available for a light-house at this point. By the terms of the act it is provided that the work shall be done by contract. Nothing has yet been done in the matter beyond the selection of the required site. The engineer of the district reports that in his opinion the light-house is not required, and unless otherwise directed the Board, acting upon this opinion, will not establish the light until the more important requirements of the district are attended to.

BEACONS, (UNLIGHTED.)

Stannard's rock.—This day-beacon was erected during the season. It consists of a stone pyramid in the form of a frustum of a right cone of nine feet base; eight feet at the top; composed of three courses of stone, each being two feet in thickness and made up of three stones of equal size. This frustum is capped by one large stone of five feet three inches in diameter, and 21 inches in thickness. To prevent slipping along any of the horizontal joints, offsets are cut in the rock and on each horizontal face of each course, these offsets fitting into corresponding projections on the adjacent stones. For further security all the courses are dowelled to each other and to the rock by iron dowells of five feet in length and two and a half inches in diameter; the lower dowells penetrating the rock to the depth of two feet, and all wedged in place. The stones of each course are also fastened to each other with clamps. A shaft of eight inches in diameter and 18 feet 6 inches in length is stepped through the pyramid, and rests directly upon the rock. It bears at its top a spherical cage of iron six feet in diameter, the centre of the cage being elevated 25 feet above the surface of the water.

This rock, being more than 20 miles from the nearest land, of small area at the surface of the water, and rising only a couple of feet above it, was awash, even in the most moderate weather, and it was therefore necessary to provide a vessel to serve the purpose of quarters for the workmen and storage for the materials. A steam barge, chartered for the purpose, answered admirably.

A day-beacon on Whale's Back, Green bay.—Near the middle of Green bay is a dangerous reef of boulders, known as Whale's Back, having only one foot of water upon it. It lies nearly in the line of all commerce to and from points at or near the head of the bay, and is much dreaded by navigators.

A beacon should be built upon it, somewhat like that on Stannard's rock, to do which will require a special appropriation of the amount specified in the estimate submitted.

Beacon on Peshtigo shoal.—After the completion of the light-house on Chambers's island, a balance of about $10,000 will remain from the appropriation, approved July 28, 1866, of $25,000 for "additional aids to navigation in Green bay, including a light-house on Chambers's island and a beacon on Peshtigo shoal." It is proposed to apply this balance to the purpose intended by Congress, as soon as satisfactory plans have been made, which will probably be in time to secure the completion of the beacon during next season.

BUOYS.

St. Clair flats.—The present channel over the St. Clair flats is marked by 11 spar-buoys, all in good condition. When the channel now being dredged is completed, a new arrangement of the buoys will be required. The buoys are attended to by contract.

Saginaw river.—The entrance to Saginaw river has recently been improved by dredging, and there is now 11 feet of water in the cut. The channel is marked by nine spar-buoys. The buoys are attended to by contract.

Spectacle reef.—After this season this dangerous reef, heretofore unmarked, will be designated by an iron can buoy of the first class, placed in 18 feet water, between the two shoals forming the reef.

Garden city reef.—Upon the opening of navigation next spring a first-class iron can buoy will be placed to designate this shoal, heretofore unmarked. The loss of the steamer "Garden City" upon this shoal gave to it the name by which it is now known.

Graham shoals.—A survey of these shoals has been made, with a view to marking them with buoys of the proper class. The result is now before the Board, and appropriate action will be taken.

Lake Muskegon, Michigan.—Since the last annual report, a change has been made in the buoyage of this place by the discontinuance of the buoy off Pillsbury Point—the channel being sufficiently defined by the booms now there.

Grand river, Michigan.—The completion of the south pier at this place has materially increased the depth of the water in the channel, and has also changed the character of the channel so much as to render unnecessary all the buoys formerly marking it, except a single spar.

Chicago river.—The entrance to this river is designated by one spar buoy.

Racine reef.—An examination of this reef, with a view to properly marking it with buoys, has been made, and the result is now before the

Point Peninsula.—During this season two spar buoys have been placed at this point—one to mark the end of the "spit" making off from Point Peninsula, and the other to mark a dangerous spot, having on it 10½ feet water, laying off the point at a distance of about two and a half miles from the light-house.

Sand Point, (Escanaba,) Green bay.—Upon the opening of navigation in the spring, a third-class iron can-buoy, heretofore used to mark Whale's Back, is to be placed at this point.

Whale's Back shoal, Green bay.—During the present season a second-class iron can-buoy has been substituted for the third-class buoy previously marking this shoal. The locality is a dangerous one, and by reference to a previous part of this report it will be seen that the Board has recommended the construction of a beacon, to mark it more distinctly.

Horseshoe reef, Green bay.—During the present season a second-class can-buoy was placed to mark this reef. In one of the recent severe gales the buoy broke from its moorings, and was picked up by the light-keeper at Chambers's island. Steps have been taken to return it to its station.

Peshtigo reef, Green bay.—The inspector of the district recommends buoying the seven-foot channel inside the outer end of this reef with four spar buoys. It is proposed during the coming season to build a day-beacon to mark the reef itself.

Green bay entrance to Fox river.—No change has been made in the buoyage at this point. The cut through Green island is somewhat advanced, but is not of sufficient depth or width for the general purposes of commerce. It may be advisable to mark this cut in a manner different from the old channel, (which must be used for a long time yet,) either by piles driven into the ground or some other simple and inexpensive method.

The old channel is now marked by 11 spar buoys, which are attended to by contract.

Sault Ste. Marie river.—The buoyage of this river is now represented by 47 spar buoys and eight stakes. In case the proposed improvement of the West Neebish channel is made, a change in that portion of the buoyage will be required. The buoys are attended to by contract.

TENDERS AND SUPPLY VESSELS.

The steamer *Haze*, which is used as a supply vessel for the entire lake region, and as tender upon such works of construction as may be deemed advisable, left Detroit on the 18th of May last, after taking on the supplies necessary for distribution in the 10th district. After supplying that district, she was turned over to the inspector of the 11th, who placed on board the supplies for his district, and on the 26th of June left Detroit for the purpose of distributing them. This duty being completed, the steamer returned to Detroit on the 5th of August, having up to that time steamed, in the 11th district alone, a distance of nearly 4,000 miles, at an expense of less than $800 for fuel, and nothing for repairs or delays. In addition to distributing the supplies, she transported and delivered the several sets of illuminating apparatus for the new light stations in process of construction, and was employed, in accordance with the orders of the Board, in examining certain reefs in Lakes Huron and Michigan.

On the 10th of August she was turned over to the engineer of the district, for use in transporting workmen, materials, and supplies for the light-house works in progress under his direction. She was at once despatched with a full load for Granite Island light-house, Lake Superior, which she delivered, and then, returning to Lake Huron and proceeding to Eagle bluff, Green bay, removed the working party which had been engaged upon that light station to McGulpin's Point, Straits of Mackinac; after which she delivered at the same point 20 cords of stone, obtained at Drummond's island. She then returned to Detroit, to again load with materials, &c., for McGulpin's Point. In addition to the points named, she had, up to the 1st of October, also visited the following places, on general duty with reference to the work of the light-house engineer, viz: Thunder bay, Lake Huron, Grand island, Marquette, Huron island, Portage entry, Portage light-house, Lac la Belle and Copper Harbor, Lake Superior; Bois Blanc island, Cheboygan, and Mackinac, in the Straits of Mackinac; Skillagalee, Bayley's harbor, and Cana island, in Lake Michigan; Chambers's island, Whale's Back, and Escanaba, in Green bay. On the 1st of October she was at Milwaukee, loading with brick for McGulpin's Point. It is expected that she will also deliver this season the brick required for Cana island and Presque Isle light-houses.

The sailing tender *Belle* has been constantly in attendance upon the Waugoshance works, transporting materials (except stone) and supplies, as well as serving as quarters for a portion of the force connected with that work. She is a fine vessel of her size, and is in good condition.

TWELFTH DISTRICT,

Embracing the Pacific coast, from the southern boundary of California to the forty-first parallel of latitude. There are in this district—

Light-houses and lighted beacons	9
Light-vessels	None.
Beacons unlighted	None.
Buoys actually in position	4
Spare buoys to supply losses	Not reported.
Tenders, steam	1
Tenders, sailing	None.

Reports in relation to the various light-house stations in this district, though not as full as expected, contain the following information:

363. *Point Loma.*—In good condition. A small boat for this station has been ordered.

Point Hueneme—Anacapa island.—These two points, among others on the coast, have been visited by the engineer of the district, for the purpose of selecting the best site for a light-house. For the reasons which follow he gives the preference to Anacapa.

Point Hueneme is at the southern entrance of the Santa Barbara channel, where the direction of the coast changes considerably, and where for more than 10 miles the land is very low—in fact, not much above the level of the sea. The position of the point, therefore, would be good, but for the disadvantages of low ground, drifting sands, and the neighborhood of a number of lagoons, which make it difficult to build and not desirable to live there.

Anacapa island, the eastern end of which is but 12 miles to the southward and westward of Hueneme, is believed to be at that point about 250 feet above the sea, and a light there would not only command the Santa Barbara channel, but the waters to the south, southeast, and southwest of it, with an arc of visibility of nearly 360°. Anacapa is rocky and destitute both of wood and water. Its sides, which are bluff, and the want of a harbor, will make building difficult and expensive there.

These disadvantages, however, are not greater than those which exist at Point Hueneme, while in respect to situation that point is decidedly inferior. It is therefore recommended that instead of a fourth-order light at Point Hueneme, as contemplated, a first or second-order light be established at Anacapa, estimates for which purpose are accordingly submitted. Anacapa island belongs to the general government, while the title to Point Hueneme must be acquired. It is proper to add that the owners of the point have offered to give to the United States a piece of land suitable for a light-house.

364. *Santa Barbara.*—Extensive repairs have been made at this station. In the cellar a new floor has been made of bricks laid on edge in cement, in place of the old floor, which, being composed of bricks laid flat in ordinary mortar, was flooded by heavy rains. A drain leading outside from the cellar floor has also been constructed. A brick chimney has been substituted for the stove-pipe which passed through the roof and was considered unsafe. The tower and chimneys, where they pass through the roof, have been repointed with cement mortar. A storm-house has been built over and in front of the kitchen door, to keep out the rain. Slight repairs to the kitchen have been made.

San Miguel.—A light-house at this island, which is situated at the southern entrance of the channel of Santa Barbara, 35 miles from Point Arguello and 25 from Point Conception, is of immediate importance, and would be especially useful to the Panama steamers and vessels coming up the coast from Mexico. The island has a very commanding position, a good harbor, and though there is no water there in summer, the difficulties of building a light-house there are fewer than those usually encountered on this coast. Estimates for the erection of a suitable light-house on San Miguel are submitted.

365. *Point Conception.*—Some repairs have been made at this station. The cistern, two sides of which were comprised in the walls of the house, would not hold water, those walls being cracked. To make the cistern tight a portion of the brick-work was removed, a new floor laid, and the inside coated with cement plaster. All the cracks in the outer walls have been pointed with cement. The caps and lintels of the doors and windows of the house were found to be rotten, and new ones have been put in. A wood-house and a small stable for a mule and a shed for the cart have been built. The fence around the light-house grounds has been repaired. The light station is now reported in good condition.

366. *Point Pinos.*—No recent account of the condition of this station has been received. The title of the United States to the property on which the light-house at this station is built is in dispute.

Santa Cruz.—An appropriation has been made and the preliminary steps have been taken for establishing a light at this point, which is situated at the northern extremity of the bay of Monterey, opposite Point Pinos. The title has been examined and its validity confirmed, and the work will be taken in hand with as little delay as possible.

Point Año Nuevo.—An appropriation has been made, also, for a first-order light at Point Año Nuevo. The site selected is an island about a quarter of a mile distant from the main land, and has been reserved for light-house purposes by the President of the United States. Nevertheless, the owners of the rancho claim the title to the island to be vested in them. Whenever this question is settled the building will be commenced.

367. *Farrallon.*—At this station a new roof has been put on the keeper's dwelling, and repairs have been made in the gutters and down-pipes

368. *Point Bonita.*—When inspected was found to need no repair.

369. *Fort Point.*—During the past year the glass of the lantern has been reset, (the India-rubber in which it was set having become rotten;) the iron tower has been scraped and repainted. The fog-signal structure and machinery, which were badly damaged by the salute fired on the 4th of July last, have been repaired. Application has been made in the proper quarter to prevent the recurrence of this accident.

370. *Alcatras.*—On examining this station quite extensive repairs were found necessary, and have been accordingly made, viz: The gallery floor and its iron fastening have been taken up; the brick-work of the tower, from where it passes through the roof of the keeper's dwelling, has been repointed; a coat of cement has been given to the coping of the tower; a new gallery floor has been laid; the boiler iron covering of the lower part of the lantern has been removed, straightened and refitted, the glass-work of the lantern reset, chimneys repointed and plastered; the tower has received a coat of mortar; a drain for the cellar has been constructed.

Point Reyes.—Instructions have been given to the engineer of the district to institute legal proceedings for the condemnation, according to the laws of California, of sufficient land for a light-house at this point, with a landing at Drake's bay, and a right of way. The exorbitant price for a spot valueless for any other purpose, which has been demanded by the owners of the rancho on which the point is situated, has been for several years the sole obstacle in the way of establishing a light-house there.

Point Arenas.—A reservation has been made of the site for a light-house at this point, and an appropriation by Congress for the purpose is available. The construction of the work will be commenced as soon as practicable.

Cape Mendocino.—The iron light-house and the keeper's dwelling for this station were completed in San Francisco in September, 1867; but the lens and lantern not arriving in time, the shipment of the tower, lantern and lens was delayed until July last, when they were shipped to Eureka, in Humboldt bay, about thirty miles to the northward of the cape, to avoid the difficulty and risk of landing them there. All the materials for the keeper's dwelling were shipped to the cape during August and September of 1867, a portion of them on board of sailing vessels, and some on board of the steam tender Shubrick. The wreck of that vessel and the probable loss of those materials were mentioned in the annual report of last year. The hull of the Shubrick has since been recovered, but the light-house materials were lost.

The nature of the ground at Cape Mendocino makes it difficult to secure a good foundation. The excavation for the foundation of the keeper's dwelling was made during the summer in ground as hard as rock, and apparently of equal consistency and durability. In the rainy season, however, this ground becomes soft, and on many parts of the coast, near

and a little larger in circumference than the bed-plate of the tower, with concrete.

By the last advices it was expected that the tower would be finished in October of this year.

The dwelling is 29 by 31, with two additions for kitchens, 12 by 14, and is built of the best materials. The walls are of brick, with an air space between; the roof is covered with galvanized iron. In consequence of the great difficulty in landing materials on the open sea-shore, the cost of transportation has exceeded that of the materials.

371. *Humboldt.*—Has been visited and found in good condition.

BUOYS ACTUALLY IN POSITION.

Two conical buoys have been placed to mark the entrance of Petaluma inlet, head of San Francisco bay.

After a careful examination, and a consultation with pilots, the following buoys were placed at Humboldt: One first-class iron outside of the bar at the entrance of the harbor, and one third-class iron inside, and directly opposite the entrance on Howard spit.

The inspector reports that no more buoys are required in the bay, as the bar is constantly changing, and vessels never go in or out without a steam-tug and a pilot.

SPARE BUOYS TO SUPPLY LOSSES—NOT REPORTED.

Tenders steam.—In the last annual report it was stated that the steam tender Shubrick attached to the 12th and 13th districts had been wrecked on the coast, about 30 miles below Cape Mendocino.

Prompt measures were taken to save all movable articles, and the engine and machinery were taken out and brought to San Francisco. The boiler, which had been long in use, was taken out and abandoned, not being worth the expense of repair. When the vessel was hauled on shore for repairs, it was found that she had been driven with such force upon a sunken boulder, as to fix it in her port bow so firmly that recourse was had to blasting to extricate it. The hole left was eight feet long and seven wide. The hull, after being taken up on the beach out of reach of the sea, where the leak was stopped, was successfully launched in May, 1868, and brought to San Francisco, and by the courtesy of the Navy Department placed at the navy yard, Mare island, for repair. Upon a careful survey, repairs amounting almost to an entire renewal of the hull were found necessary, a fact by no means surprising, considering that the vessel had been in constant service for upward of ten years, with comparatively slight repairs, and the extraordinary shock she received when she was wrecked. According to the latest information received at this office the Shubrick is expected to be ready for service early in November of the present year. At the time of sending in the estimates for light-house purposes for the current year, it was supposed that the Shubrick was a total loss, and an appropriation was asked of Congress to build a vessel to supply her place. This appropriation was granted; meanwhile the Shubrick having been recovered, and the estimated cost of her repair nearly reaching that required for building a new vessel, it became a question how the sum granted by Congress ought to be applied. The Secretary of the Treasury, to whom the subject was referred, was of opinion that the appropriation having been made with a view to supply a deficiency caused by the loss of the only tender on the Pacific coast, it would be most properly used in defraying the expenses of her repairs, which were too large to be met by the general fund appropriated for the maintenance of the light-house establishment.

THIRTEENTH DISTRICT,

Embracing the Pacific coast belonging to the United States north of the 41st parallel of latitude. There are in this district—

Light-houses and lighted beacons	9
Light-vessels	None.
Beacons unlighted	None.
Buoys actually in position	21
Spare buoys to supply losses	7
Tenders, steam, (common to 12th and 13th districts)	1
Tenders, sailing (a sailing schooner has been chartered during the repair of the steam tender Shubrick)	None.

LIGHT STATIONS.

372. *Crescent City.*—Station found in good condition, excepting that the floor timbers in the south end of the house, where they join the walls, are much decayed; they may still last, however, for a number of years.

Cape Blanco.—A piece of land has been purchased as a site for a light station at this cape. It is hoped that the light-house will be built, and a first-order light exhibited next year. The land purchased by the United States is bounded by a bluff bank, rising abruptly from the sea, and by a meridian line, and is inaccessible except by passing through the adjoining private property. Materials for making and burning brick are found on this property, and not on the land owned by the United States; consequently it has been necessary to purchase a right of way with privilege of taking water, sand, clay, and wood; a contract has also been entered into for making the bricks and for clearing the light-house site on the Cape.

373. *Cape Gregory.*—In good condition, and supplied for the year. No repairs are required to the dwelling. The tower required repointing, which was ordered.

374. *Cape Hancock.*—Was found to require extensive repairs. The building has been repainted, a new wood-shed erected, the foundation of the storehouse and cistern repaired, besides some slight repairs to the inside of the dwelling. Supplied for the year.

375. *Shoalwater bay.*—The engineer of the district reports the following repairs in progress: Reshingling the roof of keeper's dwelling; building a bulkhead around the foundation to keep the sand in place. House, tower, and lantern in good condition, and station supplied for the year.

376. *Cape Flattery.*—The keeper's dwelling, which is of stone, was found, on inspection, to be very damp, and the walls, discolored by moisture, causing illness among the keepers. The walls have been thoroughly oiled and painted, an extra amount of fuel has been furnished the keepers for the purpose of drying the house, and the engineer of the district has been requested to devise a permanent remedy for the defect. Station supplied for the year.

377. *New Dungeness.*—The light-house and tower were found in good condition. Sufficient lumber was furnished to the keeper to make new covers to the cistern. Station supplied for the year.

378. *Smith's island.*—In good condition; no repairs required; supplied for the year.

379. *Admiralty Head.*—Buildings in good condition, generally. Orders have been given to repaint the outside of the keeper's dwelling; also, a stormhouse, for the protection of the kitchen door against wind and rain. As there was no cistern to the house, and the supply of water, obtained from a pool at some distance from it, being small, a cistern has been ordered to be constructed. Station supplied for the year.

380. *Ediz Hook.*—At this station no other repair was found necessary than to repaint the keeper's dwelling. Material has been sent for that purpose.

BUOYS ACTUALLY IN POSITION.

North channel of Columbia river, marked by four iron buoys, has changed so much within the past year that it is no longer safe, except for vessels of very light draught, handled by experienced persons. It is contemplated, whenever a suitable vessel shall have been provided for the district, to take up all these buoys.

South channel of Columbia river is marked by five iron buoys, and two spar buoys.

Woody Island channel of Cathlamet bay is marked by six spar buoys.

Gray's Harbor entrance is marked by four iron buoys. The inspector of the district reports that this channel, though well buoyed, has not been used by any but the supply vessel, since the buoys were placed.

In *Puget sound* there are no buoys, but the inspector recommends that a buoy be placed off New Dungeness spit, which has within two years made out more than a mile.

TENDERS.

There has actually been none, except a chartered schooner. The extent of the thirteenth district, recently increased by the acquisition of Alaska, together with the impossibility of properly performing the light-house and buoy service with a sailing vessel, even if the board had one, makes it absolutely necessary that a steam tender should be provided, and the required estimate therefor is submitted. Without the steam tender it may be considered certain that the service cannot be efficiently attended to.

ALASKA.

After the treaty for the purchase of this territory had been ratified by Congress, the Board ordered that the expenses of the light at Sitka, previously maintained by the Russian government, should be defrayed by the United States light-house establishment.

It was previously known to the Board that an expedition to Alaska had been ordered by the Secretary of the Treasury, which would be accompanied by a coast-survey party for the purpose of making a geographical reconnoissance. The Superintendent of the Coast Survey was therefore requested to instruct the assistant in charge of the party to examine and report upon the aids to navigation required in Sitka sound and the approaches to the harbor of New Archangel or Sitka.

The following memoranda, gleaned from Mr. Davidson's valuable report, will greatly assist the Board in properly marking those approaches. (See Appendix L, p. 307, Ex. Doc. No. 177.)

Heads forming the entrance to Sitka sound.—These are the south point of Kuxczor island, called Cape Edgecumbe, and the northwest point of Biorka (Beech) island. Biorka bears E. by S. ½ S. by compass, and is distant 11 miles from Cape Edgecumbe. The cape is the rocky bluff shore of the flooded plateau making out from the base of the extinct volcano, Mount Edgecumbe, which is situated about four and a half miles north-northeast from the cape. It has an extended horizontal summit, the rim of the crater 2,800 feet above the ocean, with regular sloping sides, and forms a most characteristic landfall for the port. The navigators of the Russian American Company regard it as the most recognizable headland along the coast, being readily known 50 miles at sea. Mr. Davidson remarks that "if a complete system of lights were warranted by the commercial importance of the sound, a light should be put upon Cape Edgecumbe and one on Biorka island; but under present circumstances thinks the inner lights and aids to navigation he recommends are sufficient and first needed. These are as follows:

On Vitskari Rock, (Sitka sound,) a light of the second order, to be about 100 feet above the sea, and thus be visible from a ship's deck about 16 miles in clear weather. It would command an arc of the horizon of 70° from southwest by west to south-southeast, of which a few degrees would be intercepted by the island of St. Lazaneff. A vessel from the southward would thus open it by Biorka island, when well in with the coast. The tower should be painted black, that it may be more readily made out in thick weather, especially when the water breaks around it. According to the present arrangement, vessels approaching in thick weather, or at night, fire a gun, and are answered by a gun and light from the governor's house. If found practicable it may be well to provide a gun at Vitskari to answer the signal from vessels. Mr. Davidson found it impossible to land upon Vitskari during his stay at Archangel, on account of bad weather, and could not, therefore, measure the extent or ascertain the nature of the rocks, and the difficulties of working them; but from examination of the rocks on the adjacent islands he thinks there is no doubt that an ample and secure foundation may be had. Vitskari is preferred as a light-house site to the Kulichoff Rock, (which rises 20 feet from the water, with adjacent reefs,) Vitskari being the more dangerous locality, and on that side of the sound navigators would prefer, as the southern and eastern shores are broken up by innumerable islets and rocks.

On the island of Mochnati it is recommended to establish a light of the fifth order about 80 feet above the water. In approaching the islets which lie outside of the anchorage of New Archangel in thick weather, the navigators of the Russian American Company endeavor to make Mochnati. It is five miles distant from Vitskari rock, from which it bears NW. by N. ¼ N., is from 20 to 30 feet high, rocky and covered with a thick growth of spruce, whose dark foliage, with the black rocks beneath, brought out in sharper relief by the surf breaking round it, makes it discernible through the fog when the other islands cannot be recognized. To increase this relief, the buildings of Mochnati should be white, except that part of the tower which is higher than the tops of the trees, which should be painted black. It is obvious that the background

of the west end of Japonski island and NE. ½ E. from the west end of Battery island, bare at half tides, he proposes a beacon to be built of dark stone with a base of about 20 feet diameter and an elevation of 20 feet, in the form of a frustum of a cone. This would save the expense of repairing buoys and keeping them in place, and be a much more distinguishable mark in thick weather.

Other rocks are mentioned which it may be necessary to mark; among these is the Zenobia rock, described by a captain of the Russian American Company as a bayonet rock, the position of which is not accurately known and can only be determined in good smooth weather. It will be necessary to make a detailed examination for the position of a buoy.

Aids to navigation necessary for the approaches to the harbor of St. Paul, Kodiak island.—This station, formerly the chief depot of the Russian American Company, now ranks next in importance to that of Sitka. The two entrances to St. Paul's harbor generally adopted are round the north and south end of Wooded island and designated respectively the northern and southern channels. To the eastward of Wooded island and separated by a channel one mile wide lies Long or Barren island, which is nearly four miles long, north-northeast and south-southwest, averaging a mile in width. It has extensive reefs off its north and south points. The north point of the island is about 200 or 250 feet high, with bold rocky shore. Mr. Davidson passed close to it when entering St. Paul by the south channel, and had a fair opportunity to judge of its availability and importance as a site for a light-house. In leaving by the north channels his first impressions were confirmed. A light there would be seen by vessels coming out of Narrow strait to the west-northwest, and from Rabbit bay, when clear of Spruce island. A reef with a small islet makes off three-quarters of a mile from the point, while a reef and islet lie half a mile southeast of the south end.

Both channels have dangers in their approaches; the northern channel has a sunken ledge called "William's bank" lying three miles north of the north end of Long island. It has deep water round it. Upon it were formerly two buoys, red and blue. Mr. Davidson recommends as a second light-house site, Near island, from which station he obtained bearings of the breakers on William's bank which placed it half a mile nearer the northwest point of Long island than it is laid down in the charts. It bears from Near island north 44° 12′ east, (by compass.) Between William's bank and the reef off the northwest point lies a sunken, sharp, isolated rock, having but 10 feet of water over it at low water, with very deep water around it, and no breaker seen upon it. The Russian American Company's vessel the Kodiac struck upon it, had her bottom pierced and was lost. Its position has since been determined to be two miles north-northwest from the northwest point of Long island, and, with William's bank and the reef off the point, lies on the prolongation of the shore of the west side of Long island. One mile north-northeast from White Fir cape is a rock and reef.

In the southern approaches to the harbor, there are the Humpback, 18 feet above water, and other dangers near the entrance of the harbor. To avoid these dangers and to give a vessel's position by cross-bearings upon two objects, to avoid William's bank and the Humpback, a harbor light is recommended to be established upon the high ridge at the northern end of Rocky island abreast of the town. This light would be seen up to the anchorage off the ice company's wharf by both channels, and also for the whole bay of Chinyak and the channel to the south and east.

A buoy is needed on the north end of the reef which makes nearly half a mile northward from the extremity of Topaskoff inlet, with seven fathoms water close to its extremity.

A buoy should also mark the extremity of the reef making north from the north point of Near island, and forming one side of the entrance to the narrow harbor of St. Paul.

All the approaches and entrances to this harbor need extensive and detailed examination.

The two lights recommended are considered amply sufficient to mark the approaches and entrances to St. Paul's, however important it may become. The light on Long island is the most important of the two. The materials for this light can be safely landed in the land-locked bay on the west side of the island and thence transported to the island about a mile distant. Upon Near island a roadway would have to be made along the steep sides of the island, for carrying up stone and other materials. The stone of which the island is composed, and which crops out at the summit of the island, may be found fit for building purposes.

In some places in the harbor of St. Paul a highly metamorphic sandstone may be found available for building. No limestone was known to exist there.

Aids to navigation for Unalaska bay.—Unalaska bay lies on the north side of the island of the same name, one of the group of Fox islands.

The general direction of the bay is about south-southwest for 11 miles, contracting to a small harbor called Captain's harbor, and about halfway inside the entrance is divided by a bold high island called Ahmaknok, rising precipitously to an elevation of 1,800 feet and sloping southward to Captain's harbor so as to form Illoolook harbor on its eastern side eight miles inside Kaleochla cape.

Illoolook harbor is a mile wide, with a depth of water from 20 to 7 fathoms over irregular bottom.

A point on the outer face of the precipitous head of Ahmaknock. On the outer face of this head the light would have an arc of visibility extending from north 70° west (compass) tangent to Cape Cheerful round by the north to north 24° east tangent to Cape Kaleochta. In this situation it would have the advantage of guiding vessels into Captain's harbor, on the west side of Ahmaknock island, and would be seen after passing seven or eight miles westward through Akatan strait.

A position should be selected about 100 or 150 feet above the water, where the wall-like cliff begins to slope inward. The tower should be painted white so as to contrast with the dark rocky mass behind it. To reach the position that would open Cape Cheerful a roadway would have to be made for about half a mile from the lowland at the head of Polucha bay, where a vessel can anchor in 10 fathoms water, rocky bottom close to the shore. The dwelling could be built here, where some of the Aleutians have small patches of garden for raising turnips and potatoes.

This bay may become an important point for the curing of codfish caught in this vicinity. It is sometimes visited by whalers, but at present is deficient in the kind of supplies which would induce them to touch there. The Coast Survey party passing eastward through the narrow Strait of Unalga counted 10 sperm whales within an hour. Upon entering it a week before, they saw nearly as many to the east-southeast of the straits.

All of which is respectfully submitted.

W. B. SHUBRICK,
Chairman.

ANDREW A. HARWOOD, *Naval Secretary.*
O. M. POE, *Engineer Secretary.*

REPORT OF SUPERINTENDENT OF THE COAST SURVEY.

TREASURY DEPARTMENT,
Coast Survey Office, Washington, October 26, 1868.

SIR: I have the honor to submit estimates for expenditure in the survey of the coast of the United States during the fiscal year 1869-'70. Like those of the last year from which they are somewhat diminished, they exceed the appropriations of the preceding years. The estimate is, as nearly as possible, that which is required to maintain the most economical action, without any augmentation of the scale of the work. It is the least amount that will keep the parties steadily at work, and preserve this service in a constant state of useful activity.

The laying out of the work is carefully adjusted to meet the commercial wants of the whole country, and in strict accordance with the plan of progress which has hitherto prevailed.

In the following brief statement a general view is given of the distribution of the parties of the survey on the coast, in applying the appropriation of the present fiscal year.

The advance made, considering the means that were available, has been satisfactory.

During the year ending with the present month, progress has been made in the regular operations of the survey at Penobscot entrance, and on the group known as the Fox islands in Penobscot bay, including also the Thoroughfare passage; in the completion of work on the St. George river, and on Medomak river; in the completion of soundings in Muscongus bay, and near Kennebec entrance; in extension of the survey of the Kennebec between Merrymeeting bay and Augusta; in the detailed topography of islands in Casco bay; in a minute survey of the vicinity of Munjoy Hill (Portland) for the city authorities; in a development of the vicinity of Half-way Rock (Casco entrance;) and in general progress in Saco bay, coast of Maine. On the sea-coast and inside of Cape Cod peninsula, outstanding work has been completed by three parties; changes affecting navigation have been developed off Monomoy Point, Massachusetts; and two parties have continued the detailed survey of Narragansett bay, in Rhode Island. In New York harbor a special examination has been made between Governor's island and the Narrows, for the city authorities; and a survey is in progress to develop facilities for navigation at Rondout, on Hudson river. Progress has been made in the coast topography of New Jersey, at Barnegat bay. Two parties have been employed in defining and sounding the smaller estuaries of Chesapeake bay, and of the lower part of the Potomac; and a special examination has been made of shoals obstructing the navigation of the Rappahannock river. The primary triangulation has been in progress connecting stations near Washington city with others on the Blue Ridge. The off-shore hydrography has been prosecuted north of Cape Hatteras towards the Virginia line. In North Carolina the detailed survey of the Neuse river has been completed, and triangulation and hydrography have been continued in Pamplico sound. The triangulation south of Charleston has been connected with stations on the Savannah river; and progress has been made in the detailed survey of the branches of Port Royal sound. On the coast of Georgia, St. Catharine's sound, St. Andrew's sound, and Doboy sound have been surveyed, and soundings have been completed at the last named entrance. Outstanding work in the vicinity of Barnes's sound, Florida, has been nearly completed, and investigations of great interest have been prosecuted in the Florida strait. Two parties have continued the survey of St. Joseph's bay, north, and a third has been employed on the Gulf coast between Perdido bay and Mobile Point. On the coast of Louisiana the triangulation of Isle au Breton sound has been completed, and soundings have been made in the bays and lagoons between the Mississippi passes. Last island has been connected by triangulation with the coast; and the true position has been determined of Ship Shoal light-house, off Last island. At Galveston, Texas, the longitude has been determined by the telegraphic method, in continuation of a series of observations terminating in a previous year at New Orleans. Soundings have been continued in Galveston bay. At Lavaca, latitude, azimuth, and the magnetic elements have been determined, and the hydrographic survey has been continued in Corpus Christi bay.

On the coast of California the survey has been in progress between Point Conception and Buenaventura, and on the peninsula near San Francisco; on the coast of Oregon at the Yaquina river; at Nehalem river entrance, and at Columbia river; and in the waters of Washington Territory at Port Madison.

ESTIMATES IN DETAIL.

For general expenses of all the sections, namely, rent, fuel, materials for drawing, engraving, and printing, and for transportation of instruments, maps, and charts; for miscellaneous office expenses, and for the purchase of new instruments, books, maps, and charts.......................... $20,000

SECTION I. *Coast of Maine, New Hampshire, Massachusetts, and Rhode Island.—Field-work.*—To continue the triangulation of *Passamaquoddy bay* and its branches, and to extend the work so as to include the northeastern boundary along the *St. Croix river;* to continue the topography of *Frenchman's bay;* that of the islands and shores of *Penobscot bay;* that of *Saco bay;* and of the shores and islands of *Narragansett bay;* to continue off-shore soundings along the *coast of Maine,* and the hydrography of *Frenchman's bay, Goldsborough bay, Penobscot bay,* and *Isle au Haut bay;* to continue tidal and magnetic observations. *Office-work.*—To make the computations from field observations; to continue the engraving of general coast chart No. 1, *(Seal island to Cape Cod,)* and complete that of No. 2, *(Cape Cod to Gay Head;)* to continue the drawing and engraving of No. 4, *(Naskeag Point to White Head light, including Penobscot bay;)* that of charts No. 5 and No. 6, *(White Head light to Wood Island light;)* that of No. 7 and No. 8, *(Seguin light to Cape Porpoise light,)* and of coast chart No. 13, *(from Cuttyhunk to Point Judith, including Narragansett bay;)* and to continue the drawing and engraving of the harbor and river charts of the *coast of Maine,* and of *Narragansett bay,* will require....... 80,000

SECTION II. *Coast of Connecticut, New York, New Jersey, Pennsylvannia, and part of Delaware.—Field-work.*—To make supplementary astronomical observations; to continue verification work on the coast of *New Jersey;* to continue the topography of the shores of the *Hudson river;* to execute such supplementary hydrography as may be required in *New York bay and Delaware bay;* to continue the tidal observations. *Office-work.*—To make the computations and reductions; to continue the drawing and engraving of a chart of *New York harbor*, on a large scale; also, of coast chart No. 21, *(from Sandy Hook to Barnegat,)* and of No. 22, *(from Barnegat bay to Absecom inlet,)* will require......... $15,000

SECTION III. *Coast of part of Delaware and that of Maryland and part of Virginia.*—*Field-work.*—To continue astronomical and magnetic observations in this section; to continue the primary triangulation parallel to the coast, from *Washington city* southward, along the *Blue Ridge;* to continue the topography of the eastern shore of *Virginia* and of the shores of *James river*, and triangulation requisite therefor; to make the hydrographic survey of estuaries and inlets remaining unsurveyed in this section; to continue tidal observations, and to make observations for determining the longitude of the *Pacific coast.* *Office-work.*—To make the computations from field-work; to continue the drawing and engraving of coast charts No. 29 and No. 30, *(from Chincoteague inlet to Cape Henry,)* and of general coast chart No. 4. *(approaches to Delaware and Chesapeake bays,)* and to engrave supplementary work, on the charts heretofore published, will require... 35,000

SECTION IV. *Coast of part of Virginia and part of North Carolina.*—*Field-work.*—To complete, if practicable, the primary triangulation of *Pamplico sound*, and to make the requisite astronomical and magnetic observations; to continue the triangulation and topography of the western shores and estuaries of *Pamplico sound;* to complete the topography of the outer coast of *North Carolina, between Bogue sound and New River inlet;* to continue the in-shore and off-shore hydrography of this section; to continue soundings in *Currituck and Pamplico sounds and their estuaries*, and to make observations on the tides and currents. *Office-work.*—To make the computations and reductions; to continue the drawing and engraving of general coast chart No. 5, *(from Cape Henry to Cape Lookout;)* of coast charts No. 38 and No. 39, *(coast from Currituck banks to Cape Hatteras;)* of Nos. 42, 43, and 44, *(Pamplico sound and estuaries;)* of No. 45 and No. 46, *(coast from Cape Hatteras to Cape Lookout;)* and of charts of the *Neuse river* and *Pamplico river*, will require... 35,000

SECTION V. *Coast of South Carolina and Georgia.*—*Field-work.*—To make the requisite astronomical and magnetic observations on the *coast of Georgia;* to extend the topography from *Winyah bay to Cape Romain;* to complete the topography from *St. Simon's sound* southward to the *St. Mary's river*, and to sound the interior water passages among the sea islands from *Sapelo sound* southward, and continue off-shore hydrography and the tidal observations. *Office-work.*—To make the computations; to continue the drawing and engraving of the general coast chart, No. VII, *(from Cape Romain to St. Mary's river;)* of coast charts No. 56 and No. 57, *(from Savannah river to St. Mary's river;)* and of charts of *Altamaha sound, St. Andrew's sound*, and the inland tide water communication on the coast of *Georgia*, will require.. 40,000

SECTION VI. *Coast, keys and reefs of Florida.—Field-work.*—To determine the longitnde of several points on the west coast of *Florida;* to continue the triangulation and topography from *Matanzas inlet* southward to *Mosquito inlet;* to complete the survey of the keys and sounds between *Key Largo* and *Cape Sable;* to commence the survey of *Tampa bay;* to continue the hydrography of the *Florida reef* between the *Marquesas* and the *Tortugas*, and that of the *Strait of Florida;* to complete the hydrography of the *Bay of Florida*, and to make tidal and magnetic observations. *Office-work.*—For computing from field observations; to continue the drawing and engraving of off-shore chart No. XI, *(western part of Florida reef, including the Tortugas;)* of coast charts No. 75 and No. 76, *(from Caloosa entrance to Tampa entrance;)* and of coast charts No. 70 and No. 71, *(Key West to Tortugas,)* will require $35,000

SECTION VII. *Western coast of Florida peninsula, north of Tampa bay, and coast of West Florida.—Field-work.*—To continue the triangulation from *Cedar Keys* towards the *Suwanee river;* from *St. Andrew's bay* towards *Chattahoochee bay;* and to make such astronomical and magnetic observations as may be required; to continue the topography to the westward of *St. Andrew's bay*, and that of the *Gulf coast* adjacent to *Santa Rosa sound;* to survey and sound the entrance to the *Suwanee river;* to complete the hydrography of *St. George's sound;* and to make soundings off *Cape San Blas;* and continue the tidal observations. *Office-work.*—To make the computations from field-work; to continue the drawing and engraving of coast charts No. 82 and No. 83, *(from Ocilla river to Cape San Blas;)* and of No. 89, *(from Pensacola to Mobile Point;)* and to prepare a chart of the approaches and entrance to the *Suwanee river*, will require 30,000

SECTION VIII. *Coast of Alabama, Mississippi, and part of Louisiana.—Field-work.*—To continue the triangulation from the *Mississippi delta* westward, and to make the astronomical and magnetic observations required in this section; to commence triangulation for the survey of the *Mississippi* and its tributaries in the vicinity of *St. Louis*, *Cincinnati*, and such other points as may be practicable; to complete the survey of the shores of *Isle au Breton sound*, and of the adjacent banks of the Mississippi; to continue the hydrography within the same limits; and that of *Lake Borgne* and *Lake Pontchartrain;* and to make tidal observations. *Office-work.*—To make the computations pertaining to field-work; to continue the drawing and engraving of the general chart No. XIV, *(Gulf coast, between Mobile Point and Vermillion bay;)* of coast charts No. 91, *(Lake Borgne* and *Lake Pontchartrain;* No. 92 and No. 93, *(Chandeleur islands to Southwest Pass;)* and No. 94, *(Mississippi delta,)* will require ... 50,000

SECTION IX. *Coast of part of Louisiana and coast of Texas.—Field-work.*—To measure a primary base line; to continue the triangulation and topography of *Madre Lagoon* from *Corpus Christi* bay southward; to complete the hydrography of *Aransas, Copano, and Espiritu Santo bays*; to continue the off-shore hydrography and to make the required tidal obser-

vations. *Office-work.*—To make the office computations; to complete the engraving of coast chart No. 107, (*Matagorda and Lavaca bays;*) to continue the drawing and engraving of No. 108 and No. 109, (*Gulf coast from Matagorda to Corpus Christi bay;*) to engrave the resurvey of *Galveston entrance;* and to continue the drawing and commence the engraving of general chart No. XVI, (*Gulf coast from Galveston to the Rio Grande,*) will require	$30,000
Total for Atlantic coast and Gulf of Mexico..........	370,000

The estimates for the *Pacific coast* of the United States are intended to provide for the following progress in the survey:

SECTION X. *Coast of California.*—*Field-work.*—To make the required observations for latitude, longitude, and azimuth at stations of the primary triangulation; and to make magnetic observations; to connect the islands *Santa Cruz, Santa Rosa,* and *San Miguel,* with the coast triangulation; to execute the topography of the same and continue the topography of the coast from *Buenaventura* to *Santa Barbara* and from *Pt. Conception* northward; to continue the off-shore hydrography of the coast of *California,* and the tidal observations. *Office-work.*—To make the computations of observations, and to continue the drawing and engraving of the maps and charts made in the field; also for the operations in—	
SECTION XI. *Coast of Oregon and Washington Territory.*—*Field-work.*—To continue the astronomical and magnetic observations in this section, and the triangulation, topography, and hydrography in *Washington sound* and in *Puget sound;* to continue the survey of the mouth of the *Columbia river,* and to make such special surveys as may be called for by public interests, on the coast of *Oregon* and *Washington Territory,* and to continue the drawing and engraving dependent on the field-work and hydrography, will require	$175,000
For publishing the observations made in the progress of the survey of the coast of the United States, per act March 3, 1843	5,000
For repairs and maintenance of the complement of vessels used in the survey of the coast, including the purchase of new vessels to replace those too old for repairs, per act of March 2, 1853	60,000
For pay and rations of engineers for the steamers used in the hydrography of the coast survey, no longer supplied by the Navy Department, per act of June 12, 1858	5,000

The annexed table shows, in parallel columns, the appropriations made for the fiscal year 1868–'69, *and the estimates now submitted for the fiscal year* 1869–'70.

Object.	Estimated for 1869–'70.	Appropriated for 1868–'69.
For survey of the Atlantic and Gulf coasts of the United States, including compensation of civilians engaged in the work, per act March 3, 1843	$370,000	$275,000
For continuing the survey of the Pacific coast of the United States, including compensation of civilians engaged in the work, per act of September 30, 1850	175,000	130,000
For publishing the observations made in the progress of the survey of the coast of the United States, including compensation of civilians engaged in the work, per act of March 3, 1843	5,000	5,000
For the repairs and maintenance of the complement of vessels used in the survey of the coast, per act of March 2, 1853	60,000	30,000
For pay and rations of engineers for the steamers used in the hydrography of the coast survey, no longer supplied by the Navy Department, per act of June 12, 1858	5,000	10,000
Total	615,000	450,000

Respectfully submitted:

BENJAMIN PEIRCE,
Superintendent United States Coast Survey.

Hon. HUGH MCCULLOCH,
Secretary of the Treasury.

ANNUAL REPORT OF THE DIRECTOR OF THE BUREAU OF STATISTICS.

BUREAU OF STATISTICS, TREASURY DEPARTMENT,
Washington, D. C., November 18, 1868.

SIR: I have the honor to submit herewith the second (nominally the third*) annual report of this bureau.

It will be recollected that this organization resulted from a division of the functions of the Register of the Treasury. It was created as a separate bureau by act of July 28, 1866. At the time this separation took place, the number of clerks employed upon the work transferred from the Register's office, namely, the compilation of the various custom-house accounts relating to our foreign trade, tonnage, &c., was 24; but experience seemed to prove that with this limited number of clerks these vast accounts could not be correctly kept; and as the law, besides transferring these functions from the Register to the Director of the Bureau of Statistics, also provided for the performance of other functions—for example, that the Director should prepare a registry of the merchant marine of the United States, and provide a system for numbering each vessel and award numbers to all of them—a necessity was created for the employment of additional clerks. Accordingly the clerical force of this bureau was increased to 45 clerks; and although at times the number of clerks employed has been greater, (the present number is 53,) this has been less on account of the exigencies of the bureau than for other reasons connected with the economical disposition of the clerical force employed in the department. This force is employed as follows:

In compiling the various accounts of import entries, imports, duties, warehouse transactions, re-exports, indirect trade, and *in transitu* commerce, 13 clerks; in compiling the accounts of domestic exports, 6 clerks; in compiling the accounts of navigation, tonnage, emigration and immigration, 3 clerks; in registering the merchant marine of the United States, and awarding numbers and signal letters to the same, 11 clerks; in analyzing, checking and preparing the accounts of collectors of customs, before depositing them with the compiling divisions, 6 clerks; in arranging classifications, preparing forms, and superintending the library of the bureau, 4 clerks; on miscellaneous statistics, and in copying, registering, and drafting statistical tables and letters of instructions to officers of the revenue, 8 clerks; in superintending the publication of reports, and in receiving and distributing the mails, 2 clerks. Total: 53 clerks.

Some important changes have recently been made in the system of accounts; the principal quarterly accounts, for example, having been superseded by monthly accounts. When these changes shall have been completely accomplished, which it is expected will be the case in the course of another month, the clerical force of the bureau may be still further reduced; but it is respectfully recommended that in making such reduction, care be taken that no essential portion of the work now performed in the bureau be dispensed with.

The work of the past year has already been alluded to in previous reports, and in this place it needs only to be briefly summarized. The commerce and navigation accounts are completed for the year ended June 30, 1868, and summary tables are respectfully submitted herewith, showing the course of our foreign trade and the foreign tonnage movement. (They will be found on another page of this volume.) Detailed transcripts of the records are now being prepared for the public printer to form the annual volume of tables on commerce and navigation.

In accordance with the practice inaugurated in the year 1866, a census of the population of the United States was obtained by this bureau during the year 1867, by means of inquiries instituted through the internal revenue organization, the jurisdiction of whose numerous officers covers the entire area of the country. The results of the census of 1867 are respectfully submitted herewith:

	Whites.	Colored.	Total.
Six New England States*	3,480,397	30,701	3,511,098
Five middle States †	9,072,647	352,469	9,425,116
Thirteen southern States ‡	6,764,928	3,884,532	10,649,460
Thirteen western and Pacific States §	12,356,081	311,493	12,667,574
Nine Territories ‖	435,774	54,176	489,950
Total United States	32,109,827	4,633,371	36,743,198

* Maine, New Hampshire, Vermont, Massachusetts, Rhode Island, and Connecticut.

† New York, New Jersey, Pennsylvania, Delaware, and Maryland.

‡ Virginia, West Virginia, North Carolina, South Carolina, Georgia, Alabama, Florida, Mississippi, Louisiana, Texas, Arkansas, Kentucky, and Tennessee.

§ Ohio, Indiana, Illinois, Michigan, Wisconsin, Minnesota, Iowa, Missouri, Kansas, Nebraska, Nevada, California, and Oregon.

‖ Arizona, Colorado, Dakota, Idaho, Montana, New Mexico, Utah, Washington, and District of Columbia.

Compared with those of the preceding year, and with the census of 1860, they present the following comparison:

	Population in 1860; preliminary census, page 131.			Population in 1866; returns to Bureau of Statistics.	Population in 1867; returns to Bureau of Statistics.		
	White.	Colored.	Total.	Total.	White.	Colored.	Total.
Six New England States*	3, 110, 572	24, 711	3, 135, 283	3, 440, 881	3, 480, 397	30, 701	3, 511, 098
Five Middle States†	7, 934, 202	323, 948	8, 258, 150	9, 221, 225	9, 072, 647	352, 469	9, 425, 116
Thirteen Southern States‡	6, 368, 980	3, 890, 037	10, 259, 017	a9, 568, 709	6, 764, 928	3, 884, 532	10, 649, 460
Thirteen Western and Pacific States§	9, 329, 974	203, 079	9, 533, 053	11, 869, 440	12, 356, 081	311, 493	12, 667, 574
Nine Territories‖	231, 847	27, 730	259, 577	405, 627	435, 774	54, 176	489, 950
Total United States	26, 975, 575	4, 469, 505	31, 445, 080	a 34, 505, 882	32, 109, 827	4, 633, 371	36, 743, 198

* Maine, New Hampshire, Vermont, Massachusetts, Rhode Island, and Connecticut.
† New York, New Jersey, Pennsylvania, Delaware, and Maryland.
‡ Virginia, West Virginia, North Carolina, South Carolina, Georgia, Alabama, Florida, Mississippi, Louisiana, Texas, Arkansas, Kentucky, and Tennessee.
§ Ohio, Indiana, Illinois, Michigan, Wisconsin, Minnesota, Iowa, Missouri, Kansas, Nebraska, Nevada, California, and Oregon.
‖ Arizona, Colorado, Dakota, Idaho, Montana, New Mexico, Utah, Washington, and District of Columbia.

a Imperfect; some of the sub-district returns having omitted the colored population.

A similar census for the year 1868 is now being made, and while it is not claimed that these tables are absolutely correct, yet they furnish approximate results that cannot but prove valuable in the absence of more precise information. There has been no expense involved in obtaining them, beyond the partial employment of the services of one clerk.

Through similar means, a census of the cotton crop was obtained in 1867, the result of which was published on the 14th of November of that year. Similar data are being obtained for the present year's crop, but they are not yet sufficiently complete for publication.

Original statistics of the railroads of the United States, their length, cost, quantity of rolling stock in use, the amount of their annual earnings and expenses, number of passengers, the quantity and value of freight transported, &c., and statistics of the domestic manufactures of the country, are being obtained and compiled for the use of the department.

It was intended, had occasion permitted, to have suggested a reform in the present system of obtaining the statistics of our foreign commerce. Experience has proved that the plan now pursued cannot be continued successfully without a large expenditure of labor, and of labor of a much more technical and critical character than can readily be secured under the existing provisions of law as to salaries. The statistics of the past two years are believed to contain but few of the numerous forms of error that vitiated those which preceded them; but these advantages have only been secured by such extra exertion and care as is hardly to be looked for under ordinary circumstances. The clerks of this bureau have been prompted to make these extra exertions from the desire to so improve upon the statistics previously prepared in the department, as to reflect credit upon and give character to the new organization with which they had become identified. But the discouragements have been so great, and the accounts received from the collectors of customs continue to be so erroneous and perplexing, that I fear the failure of a stimulus already too long maintained, and consequently that unless a change is made in the system, our commercial statistics will gradually relapse again into the deplorable condition from which it has taken so much exertion to extricate them. The reform intended to be suggested was that of requiring the collectors of customs no longer to transmit accounts of the business of their offices to the bureau, but to substitute therefor duplicates of the original entries, manifests, clearances, &c., deposited with them, and from these original data to compile the statistics required by Congress. By this means not only would the many errors of classification and arrangement which now distort and vitiate the collectors' accounts as they are received at this bureau, and before correction, be obviated; but a more complete and direct surveillance of the transactions of the various custom-houses be exercised by the department. This is the system understood to be practised in Great Britain, France, Canada and other foreign countries, and it is hoped that measures may be taken at some future time to effect its realization. The secondary advantage of these important transactions was secured of late, when, under the Director's supervision, the compilation of warehouse and *in transitu* statistics was inaugurated in this bureau; but under the present system the details are not sufficient for critical purposes.

As, besides this report and the accompanying tables, it is made the duty of the Director to publish a monthly statistical report and an annual volume of statistical tables, it is not deemed advisable to extend these observations any further than to refer with gratitude to the hearty and intelligent co-operation to which he is indebted to the clerks of this bureau for the successful performance of his labors and in their preparation for publication, and more particularly to the several chiefs of divisions, Messrs. C. S. Mixter, Thomas Clear, J. N. Whitney, J. H. McIlvaine, H. Marix, J. W. De Krafft, and James Ryan.

Justice also demands that mention be again made of the value of the services performed by the female clerks employed in the bureau, who are mostly engaged in compiling the warehouse accounts, and in the preparation of statistical tables connected therewith. In these respects as in others they have exhibited clerical abilities of a high order. As the law at present stands, they receive but half the salaries of the higher grade of male clerks, and there does not appear to me to be any sound reason why, as government clerks, if they prove capable of performing equally arduous and difficult services, they should not be equally remunerated.

I have the honor to be, sir, very respectfully, your obedient servant,

ALEXANDER DELMAR,
Director.

Hon. HUGH MCCULLOCH,
Secretary of the Treasury.

No. 1.—*Statement exhibiting the imports and exports of coin and bullion from 1821 to 1868, inclusive.*

Years ended—	Imports.	Exports.		
		Domestic exports.	Foreign re-exports.	Total.
September 30 1821	$8,064,890	....	$10,478,059	$10,478,059
1822	3,369,846	....	10,810,180	10,810,180
1823	5,097,896	....	6,372,897	6,372,897
1824	8,379,835	....	7,014,552	7,014,552
1825	6,150,765	....	8,797,055	8,797,055
1826	6,880,966	$605,855	4,098,678	4,704,533
1827	8,151,130	1,043,574	6,971,306	8,014,880
1828	7,489,741	693,037	7,550,439	8,243,476
1829	7,403,612	612,886	4,311,134	4,924,020
1830	8,155,964	937,151	1,241,622	2,178,773
1831	7,305,945	2,058,474	6,956,457	9,014,931
1832	5,907,504	1,410,941	4,245,399	5,656,340
1833	7,070,368	366,842	2,244,859	2,611,701
1834	17,911,632	400,500	1,676,258	2,076,758
1835	13,131,447	729,601	5,748,174	6,477,775
1836	13,400,881	345,738	3,978,598	4,324,336
1837	10,516,414	1,283,519	4,692,730	5,976,249
1838	17,747,116	472,941	3,035,105	3,508,046
1839	5,595,176	1,908,358	6,868,385	8,776,743
1840	8,882,813	2,235,073	6,181,941	8,417,014
1841	4,988,633	2,746,487	7,287,846	10,034,333
1842	4,087,016	1,170,754	3,642,785	4,813,539
Nine months to June 30 1843	22,390,559	107,429	1,413,362	1,520,791
June 30 1844	5,830,429	183,405	5,270,809	5,454,214
1845	4,070,242	844,446	7,762,049	8,606,495
1846	3,777,732	423,851	3,481,417	3,905,268
1847	24,121,289	62,620	1,844,404	1,907,024
1848	6,360,284	2,700,412	13,141,204	15,841,616
1849	6,651,240	956,874	4,447,774	5,404,648
1850	4,628,792	2,046,679	5,476,315	7,522,994
1851	5,453,592	18,069,580	11,403,172	29,472,752
1852	5,505,044	37,437,837	5,236,298	42,674,135
1853	4,201,382	23,548,535	3,938,340	27,486,875
1854	6,939,342	38,062,570	3,218,934	41,281,504
1855	3,659,812	53,957,418	2,289,925	56,247,343
1856	4,207,632	44,148,279	1,597,206	45,745,485
1857	12,461,799	60,078,352	9,058,570	69,136,922
1858	19,274,496	42,407,246	10,225,901	52,633,147
1859*	7,434,789	57,502,305	6,385,106	63,887,411
1860*	8,550,135	56,946,851	9,599,388	66,546,239
1861*	46,339,611	23,799,870	5,991,210	29,791,080
1862*	16,415,052	31,044,651	5,842,305	36,886,956
1863*	9,584,105	55,993,562	8,163,049	64,156,611
1864*	13,115,612	100,321,371	4,922,979	105,244,350
1865*	9,810,072	64,618,124	3,025,102	67,643,226
1866*	10,700,092	82,643,374	3,400,697	86,044,071
1867*	22,070,475	54,976,196	5,892,176	60,868,372
1868*	13,702,928	83,746,161	10,038,127	93,784,288

* From the manuscript records.

ALEX. DELMAR, *Director.*

BUREAU OF STATISTICS,
Treasury Department, November 16, 1868.

No. 2.—*Statement exhibiting the domestic exports of merchandise and specie from the Atlantic and Pacific ports from 1860 to 1868, inclusive.*

Years ended—	Atlantic ports.		Pacific ports.		Total merchandise.	Total specie.	Total exports.	Total exports (including specie) with merchandise reduced to gold values.
	Merchandise.	Specie.	Merchandise.	Specie.				
June 30 .... 1860*	$311, 480, 020	$53, 207, 734	$3, 762, 403	$3, 739, 117	$316, 242, 423	$56, 946, 851	$373, 189, 274	$373, 189, 274
1861*†	352, 378, 497	19, 918, 292	6, 658, 107	3, 881, 578	359, 036, 604	23, 799, 870	382, 836, 474	382, 836, 474
1862*†	175, 695, 241	25, 773, 062	6, 553, 796	5, 271, 589	182, 249, 037	31, 044, 651	213, 293, 688	213, 253, 580
1863*†	242, 768, 777	53, 404, 902	7, 468, 377	2, 588, 660	250, 235, 154	55, 993, 562	306, 228, 716	240, 407, 512
1864*†	209, 870, 923	59, 386, 586	7, 726, 586	40, 934, 785	217, 597, 509	100, 321, 371	317, 919, 880	241, 967, 048
1865*	252, 515, 313	42, 395, 251	6, 609, 750	22, 222, 873	259, 125, 063	64, 618, 124	323, 743, 187	196, 235, 455
1866*	458, 462, 372	64, 287, 837	9, 578, 531	18, 355, 537	468, 040, 903	82, 643, 374	550, 684, 277	417, 142, 084
1867*	371, 645, 085	42, 822, 014	11, 956, 031	12, 154, 182	383, 601, 116	54, 976, 196	438, 577, 312	334, 350, 653
1868*‡	356, 365, 184	73, 462, 297	14, 077, 245	10, 283, 864	370, 442, 429	83, 746, 161	454, 188, 590	352, 788, 202

* From the manuscript records.
† As amended by the incorporation of back returns from southern ports, received during the year 1868, of no material account except in 1861.
‡ The values for 1868 are taken from the records before they are balanced, and will probably differ slightly from those to be published in the Director's Annual Report on Commerce and Navigation.

ALEX. DELMAR, *Director.*

BUREAU OF STATISTICS,
Treasury Department, November 16, 1868.

No. 3.—*Statement exhibiting the value of foreign merchandise imported and re exported, and net imports, from 1821 to 1868, inclusive.*

Years ended—		Import entries.			Re-exports.				Net imports.
		Specie.	Merchandise.	Total.	Merchandise.		Specie.	Total.	
					From warehouse.	Not from warehouse.			
September 30	1821	$8,064,890	$54,520,834	$62,585,724			$10,478,059	$21,302,488	$41,283,236
	1822	3,369,846	79,871,695	83,241,541			10,810,180	22,286,202	60,955,339
	1823	5,097,896	72,481,371	77,579,267			6,372,897	27,543,622	50,035,645
	1824	8,379,835	81,169,172	89,549,007			7,014,552	25,337,157	64,211,850
	1825	6,150,765	90,189,310	96,340,075			8,797,055	32,590,643	63,749,432
	1826	6,880,966	78,093,511	84,974,477			4,098,678	24,530,612	60,443,865
	1827	8,151,130	71,332,938	79,484,068			6,971,306	23,403,136	56,080,932
	1828	7,489,741	81,020,083	88,509,824			7,550,439	21,595,017	66,914,807
	1829	7,403,612	67,088,915	74,492,527			4,311,134	16,658,478	57,834,049
	1830	8,155,964	62,720,956	70,876,920			1,241,622	14,387,479	56,489,441
	1831	7,305,945	95,885,179	103,191,124			6,956,457	20,033,526	83,157,598
	1832	5,907,504	95,121,762	101,029,266			4,245,399	24,039,473	76,989,793
	1833	7,070,368	101,047,943	108,118,311			2,244,859	19,822,735	88,295,576
	1834	17,911,632	108,609,700	126,521,332			1,676,258	23,312,811	103,208,521
	1835	13,131,447	136,764,295	149,895,742			5,748,174	20,504,495	129,391,247
	1836	13,400,881	176,579,154	189,980,035			3,978,598	21,746,360	168,233,675
	1837	10,516,414	130,472,803	140,989,217			4,692,730	21,854,962	119,134,255
	1838	17,747,116	95,970,288	113,717,404			3,035,105	12,452,795	101,264,609
	1839	5,595,176	156,496,956	162,092,132			6,868,385	17,494,525	144,597,607
	1840	8,882,813	98,258,706	107,141,519			6,181,941	18,190,312	88,951,207
	1841	4,988,633	122,957,544	127,946,177			7,287,846	15,469,081	112,477,096
	1842	4,087,016	96,075,071	100,162,087			3,642,785	11,721,538	88,440,549
9 months to June 30	1843	22,390,559	42,363,240	64,753,799			1,413,362	6,552,697	58,201,102
Years ended June 30	1844	5,830,429	102,604,606	108,435,035			5,270,809	11,484,867	96,950,168
	1845	4,070,242	113,184,322	117,254,564			7,762,049	15,346,830	101,907,734
	1846	3,777,732	117,914,065	121,691,797			3,481,417	11,346,623	110,345,174
	1847	24,121,289	122,424,349	146,545,638	$786,967	$5,379,787	1,844,404	8,011,158	138,534,480
	1848	6,360,284	148,638,644	154,998,928	2,869,941	5,116,865	13,141,204	21,128,010	133,870,918
	1849	6,651,240	141,206,199	147,857,439	3,692,363	4,948,728	4,447,774	13,088,865	134,768,574
	1850	4,628,792	173,509,526	178,138,318	5,261,291	4,214,202	5,476,315	14,951,808	163,186,510
	1851	5,453,592	210,771,340	216,224,932	5,666,706	4,628,415	11,403,172	21,698,293	194,526,639
	1852	5,505,044	207,440,398	212,945,442	6,855,770	5,197,314	5,236,298	17,289,382	195,656,060
	1853	4,201,382	263,777,265	267,978,647	8,036,551	5,583,569	3,938,340	17,558,460	250,420,187
	1854	6,939,342	297,623,039	304,562,381	9,244,448	11,285,132	3,218,934	23,748,514	280,813,867
	1855	3,659,812	257,808,708	261,468,520	13,975,795	12,182,573	2,289,925	28,448,293	233,020,227
	1856	4,207,632	310,432,310	314,639,942	7,566,890	7,214,482	1,597,206	16,378,578	298,261,364
	1857	12,461,799	348,428,342	360,890,141	5,195,960	9,721,027	9,058,570	23,975,617	330,914,524

No. 3.—*Statement exhibiting the value of foreign merchandise imported and re-exported, &c.*—Continued.

Years ended—		Import entries.			Re-exports.				Net imports.
		Specie.	Merchandise.	Total.	Merchandise.		Specie.	Total.	
					From warehouse.	Not from warehouse.			
Years ended June 30	1858	$19, 274, 496	$263, 338, 654	$282, 613, 150	$7, 747, 930	$12, 912, 311	$10, 225, 901	$30, 886, 142	$251, 727, 008
	1859	7, 434, 789	331, 333, 341	338, 768, 130	4, 385, 870	10, 124, 101	6, 385, 106	20, 895, 077	317, 873, 053
	1860*	8, 550, 135	353, 616, 119	362, 166, 254	6, 414, 036	10, 919, 598	9, 599, 388	26, 933, 022	335, 233, 232
	1861*†	46, 339, 611	306, 399, 776	352, 739, 387	6, 661, 337	7, 992, 880	5, 991, 210	20, 645, 427	*332, 093, 960
	1862*†	16, 415, 052	259, 031, 887	‡275, 446, 939	7, 239, 941	1, 063, 043	5, 842, 989	14, 145, 973	261, 300, 966
	1863*†	9, 584, 105	243, 335, 815	252, 919, 920	7, 928, 205	10, 032, 330	8, 163, 049	26, 123, 584	226, 796, 336
	1864*†	13, 115, 612	316, 449, 522	329, 565, 134	10, 979, 251	4, 354, 710	4, 922, 979	20, 256, 940	309, 308, 194
	1865*	9, 810, 072	238, 745, 580	248, 555, 652	17, 205, 561	11, 883, 494	3, 025, 102	32, 114, 157	216, 441, 495
	1866*	10, 700, 092	434, 812, 066	445, 512, 158	8, 073, 166	3, 268, 254	3, 400, 697	14, 742, 117	430, 770, 041
	1867*	22, 070, 475	389, 662, 834	411, 733, 309	12, 895, 560	1, 823, 772	5, 892, 176	20, 611, 508	391, 121, 801
	1868*§	13, 702, 928	359, 706, 520	373, 409, 448	10, 825, 626	1, 331, 665	10, 038, 127	22, 195, 438	351, 214, 010

* From manuscript records.

† The amount of import entries each year has been amended by the incorporation of back returns from southern ports received during the year 1868, of no material account except in 1861.

‡ $275,357,051 is the amount stated in ink on the manuscript records as the footing, by articles, of the imports of 1862; though the correct addition, as the figures stand, appears to be $197,867,937. Owing to the confused condition of the work, however, it is by no means certain which amount, if either, is correct. The erroneous character of the commerce and navigation statistics from 1862 to 1865, inclusive, are alluded to in the annual report of the Director of the Bureau of Statistics for 1867.

§ The values for 1868 are taken from the records before they are balanced, and will probably differ slightly from those to be published in the Director's Annual Report on Commerce and Navigation.

ALEX. DELMAR, *Director.*

BUREAU OF STATISTICS, *Treasury Department, November 16, 1868.*

DOMESTIC EXPORTS, 1868—DETAILS.

No. 4.—*Summary statement from returns of collectors of customs, of commodities, the growth, produce, and manufacture of the United States, exported from the United States during the twelve months ended June 30, 1868.*

NOTE.—This statement is taken from the records before they are balanced, and, both in details and total, will probably differ slightly from the statement to be published in the Director's Annual Report on Commerce and Navigation.

Commodities.	Quantity.	Value.
1. Agricultural implements		$702, 188
2. Animals, living, of all kinds		739, 432
3. Ashes, pot and pearl ..lbs..	2, 491, 066	256, 076
4. Breadstuffs:		
Barley ..bush..	25, 747	$25, 956
Bread and biscuit ..lbs..	8, 512, 748	649, 652
Indian corn ..bush..	11, 156, 943	13, 068, 738
Indian meal ..bbls..	335, 784	2, 064, 902
Oats ..bush..	133, 696	104, 821
Rice ..lbs..	1, 474, 500	168, 807
Rye ..bush..	501, 350	836. 838
Rye flour ..bbls..	10, 643	91, 443
Wheat ..bush..	15, 981, 110	30, 341, 600
Wheat flour ..bbls..	2, 073, 798	20, 804, 338
Potatoes ..bush..	368, 764	473, 025
Maccaroni, vermicelli, and all other preparations from breadstuffs used as food		154, 228
Total		68, 784, 348
5. Books, pamphlets, maps, and engravings, and other publications		$337, 368
6. Brooms and brushes of all kinds		147, 495
7. Cordage, ropes, and twines of all kinds ..cwt..	29, 003	425, 977
8. Candles ..lbs..	2, 916, 789	533, 697
9. Carriages, and parts of		377, 701
10. Children's carriages, and parts of		4, 013
11. Clocks, and parts of		537, 255
12. Clothing, cut and sewed together		472, 660
13. Coal ..tons..	277, 068	1, 513, 332
14. Coffee, cocoa, and spices, including ginger, pepper, and mustard		33, 226
15. Copper, and manufactures of:		
Copper ore ..cwt..	74, 354	$194, 533
Copper ..lbs..	2, 576, 056	586, 453
Manufactures of		123, 887
Total		904, 873
16. Cotton:		
Sea island ..lbs..	5, 836, 388	$3, 236, 599
Upland ..lbs..	777, 161, 010	149, 546, 211
Total	782, 997, 398	152, 782, 810
17. Cotton, manufactures of		$4, 929, 310
18. Drugs and dyes not specified		1, 491, 315
19. Fruits of all kinds		255, 635
20. Furs and fur skins		1, 151, 060
21. Glass and glassware		551, 442
22. Gunpowder ..lbs..	991, 663	236, 651

No. 4.—*Statement from returns of collectors of customs, &c.*—Continued.

Commodities.	Quantity.	Value.
23. Gold and silver:		
Gold bullion		$23,984,021
Silver bullion		12,865,147
Gold coin		44,358,637
Silver coin		2,538,356
Total		83,746,161
24. Hides and skins, other than fur		$563,478
25. Hops ... lbs..	509,290	258,639
26. India rubber and gutta percha manufactures		144,151
27. Iron and steel, and manufactures of:		
Pig iron ... cwt..	7,331	$14,022
Castings ... cwt..	5,112	18,815
Bar iron ... cwt..	3,580	22,515
Nails and spikes ... lbs..	6,044,896	371,317
Railroad bars or rails ... cwt..	189	1,304
Hardware		1,196,623
Muskets, pistols, rifles, and sporting guns		2,611,778
Machinery, other than sewing machines		2,534,326
Steel ingots, bars, sheets, and wire; cutlery, files, saws, and tools		229,944
Manufactures of iron and steel not specified		1,948,766
Total		8,949,410
28. Jewelry and other manufactures of gold and silver		$48,869
29. Lamps		114,854
30. Leather and leather goods:		
Leather of all kinds		$593,465
Boots and shoes ... pairs..	388,466	579,892
Boots and shoes, second-hand ... pairs..	4,488	1,560
Saddlery and harness		97,536
Manufactures of leather not specified		139,522
Total		1,411,975
31. Naval stores:		
Rosin ... bbls..	405,525	$1,815,375
Turpentine ... bbls..	44,109	232,139
Spirits of turpentine ... galls..	2,992,604	1,626,528
Tar and pitch ... bbls..	22,735	94,470
Total		3,768,512
32. Oil cake ... lbs..	100,266,536	$2,754,341
33. Coal oils and petroleum:		
Coal oil, crude ... galls..	337,044	$113,073
Coal oil, refined ... galls..	617,379	210,439
Petroleum, crude ... galls..	8,459,767	1,342,290
Petroleum, refined ... galls..	67,518,576	19,775,198
Benzine ... galls..	1,513,498	267,483
Total	78,446,264	21,708,483
34. Whale and fish oils:		
Spermaceti oil ... galls..	668,612	$1,382,190
Whale and fish oil ... galls..	701,257	500,843
Total	1,368,869	1,883,033

No. 4.—*Statement from returns of collectors of customs, &c.*—Continued.

Commodities.	Quantity.	Value.
35. Provisions and tallow:		
Beef .... lbs..	21,831,606	$2,697,597
Butter .... lbs..	2,126,906	582,025
Cheese .... lbs..	51,058,079	7,010,188
Fish, fresh	....	76,973
dried and smoked .... cwt..	132,804	598,941
pickled .... bbls..	24,272	205,810
other cured	....	124,614
Hams and bacon .... lbs..	43,913,632	5,473,445
Lard .... lbs..	65,078,795	9,417,956
Pork .... lbs..	28,034,637	3,263,188
Tallow .... lbs..	22,461,963	2,529,947
Vegetables, fresh or preserved	....	189,058
Total	....	32,169,742
36. Quicksilver .... lbs..	2,885,768	$1,182,254
37. Salt .... bush..	622,252	$286,441
38. Sewing machines .... number..	85,896	1,647,433
39. Soap of all kinds .... lbs..	7,094,627	629,633
40. Spirits, distilled:		
From grain .... galls..	601,866	$332,395
From molasses .... galls..	1,212,568	521,183
From other materials .... galls..	1,020,341	577,739
Total	2,834,775	1,431,317
41. Starch .... lbs..	2,301,056	$199,634
42. Sugars and molasses:		
Brown .... lbs..	13,541	$1,427
Refined .... lbs..	2,158,164	315,928
Molasses .... galls..	42,764	22,697
Candy and confectionery .... lbs..	30,062	10,194
Total	....	350,246
43. Tobacco:		
Leaf .... lbs..	199,133,361	$22,948,148
Cigars .... M..	1,914	71,423
Snuff .... lbs..	11,123	8,650
Other manufactures	....	3,042,238
Total	....	26,070,459
44. Vessels sold to foreigners:		
Steamers .... tons..	2,165	$198,800
Sailing vesels .... tons..	1,623	139,694
Total	3,788	338,494
45. Whalebone .... lbs..	708,588	$587,303
46. Wood, and manufactures of:		
Boards, clapboards, deals, planks, joists, and scantling .... *M ft..	118,164	$2,564,860

* Board measure.

No. 4.—*Statement from returns of collectors of customs, &c.*—Continued.

Commodities.	Quantity.	Value.
46. Wood, and manufactures of—Continued.		
Laths, palings, pickets, curtain sticks, broom handles, and bed slats .... M..	5,177	$11,835
Shingles .... M..	32,747	140,223
Box shooks	....	692,080
Other shooks, and staves and headings	....	5,793,588
All other lumber	....	1,346,649
Fire-wood .... cords..	4,532	12,675
Hop, hoop, telegraph and other poles	....	691,746
Logs, masts, spars, and other whole timber	....	266,265
Timber, sawn and hewn .... *M..	48,157	908,898
All other timber	....	119,488
Household furniture	....	1,154,345
Boxes, coopered wares, and turnery	....	280,308
All other manufactures of wood not specified	....	1,038,235
Total	....	15,021,195
47. Wool, raw and fleece .... lbs..	546,533	$182,437
48. Wool, manufactures of	....	266,404
49. All other unmanufactured articles	....	2,804,690
50. All other manufactured articles	....	8,501,138
Total domestic exports, value as returned	....	$454,188,590
Total domestic exports, value reduced to American gold	....	$352,788,202

* Board measure.

ALEX. DELMAR, *Director.*

BUREAU OF STATISTICS,
Treasury Department, November 16, 1868.

FOREIGN RE-EXPORTS, 1868.—DETAILS.

No. 5.—*Summary statement from returns of collectors of customs, of foreign commodities re-exported from the United States during the twelve months ended June* 30, 1868.

NOTE.—This statement is taken from the records before they are balanced, and, both in details and total, will probably differ slightly from the statement to be published in the Director's Annual Report on Commerce and Navigation.

Commodities.	Quantity.	Value.
FREE OF DUTY.		
1. Articles in a crude state used in dyeing and tanning	....	$1,931
2. Bolting cloths	....	560
3. Cochineal .... lbs..	4,769	3,993
4. Dyewoods in sticks .... cwt..	178,607	203,040
5. Gold and silver:		
Gold bullion	....	$94,508
Silver bullion	....	566,439
Gold coin	....	4,070,678
Silver coin	....	5,306,502
Total	....	10,038,127

No. 5.—*Statement from returns of collectors of customs, &c.*—Continued.

Commodities.	Quantity.	Value.
6. Gypsum, or plaster of Paris, unground ....tons..	....	....
7. Horsehair, used for weaving, cleaned or uncleaned, drawn or undrawn ....lbs..	....	....
8. Household and personal effects and wearing apparel, old and in use, of persons arriving from foreign countries....	....	$4,612
9. Indigo ....lbs..	22,247	18,955
10. Madder:		
Ground or prepared ....lbs..	....	....
Root ....lbs..	....	....
Total	....	....
11. Rags of cotton or linen for the manufacture of paper ..lbs..	....	....
12. Silk, raw, or as reeled from the cocoon ....lbs..	32,519	$245,657
13. Guano, except from American islands ....tons..	1,864	71,793
14. Wood, all cabinet, unmanufactured	....	98,248
15. All other articles	....	22,091
Total free of duty	....	10,709,007
DUTIABLE.		
16. Animals, living, of all kinds	....	$10,794
17. Articles, the growth, produce, and manufacture of the United States, exported, brought back, and re-exported ..	....	....
18. Argols, or crude tartar ....lbs..	3,912	340
19. Brass, and manufactures of	....	6,820
20. Breadstuffs:		
Barley ....bush..	813	$1,047
Bread and biscuit ....lbs..	....	....
Indian corn ....bush..	2,264	1,800
Indian meal ....bbls..	....	....
Oats ....bush..	36,821	22,664
Rice ....lbs..	10,271,499	346,988
Rye ....bush..	58,670	61,056
Rye flour ....bbls..	100	883
Wheat ....bush..	193,319	320,585
Wheat flour ....bbls..	6,531	78,838
Potatoes ....bush..	8,572	6,442
Maccaroni, vermicelli, and all other preparations from breadstuffs used as food	....	95,875
Total	....	936,178
21. Books, pamphlets, maps, and engravings, and other publications	....	$5,235
22. Buttons of all kinds	....	2,685
23. Cordage, ropes, and twines of all kinds ....lbs..	268,428	30,965
24. Chiccory, ground or prepared, and root ....lbs..	13,799	442
25. Chloride of lime, or bleaching powder ....lbs..	....	....
26. Clothing, except when of silk:		
Cut and sewed together	....	$9,616
Articles of wear not specified	....	39,051
Total	....	48,667
27. Coal, bituminous ....tons..	308	$3,074
28. Cocoa ....lbs..	1,109,108	132,458
29. Coffee ....lbs..	7,622,875	824,489

No. 5.—*Statement from returns of collectors of customs, &c.*—Continued.

Commodities.	Quantity.	Value.
30. Copper:		
Ore .... cwt..	53,073	$266,811
Copper .... lbs..	49,284	8,327
Manufactures of	....	121,408
Total	....	396,546
31. Cotton and manufactures of:		
Cotton, raw .... lbs..	651,593	$118,630
Bleached and unbleached .... sq. yds..	1,992,914	164,918
Printed, painted, or colored .... sq. yds..	3,074,260	378,299
Jeans, denims, drillings, &c .... sq. yds..	91,876	15,152
Manufactures not specified	....	175,659
Total	....	852,658
32. Cutch, catechu or terra japonica and gambier .... lbs..	189,227	$12,405
33. Chemicals, drugs, and dyes not specified	....	338,256
34. Earthen, stone, and China ware	....	9,120
35. Fancy goods, invoiced by dozens, gross, or hundreds	....	11,962
36. Fish, fresh and cured, not of American fisheries	....	332,839
37. Flax and manufactures of:*		
Flax, raw .... tons..	....	....
By yard .... sq. yds..	174,981	$44,386
Other manufactures	....	107,291
Total	....	151,677
38. Fruits of all kinds	....	$86,064
39. Furs and fur skins	....	106,201
40. Glass and glassware:		
Cylinder, crown, or common window .... lbs..	....	....
Cylinder and crown, polished .... sq. ft..	....	....
Fluted, rolled, or rough plate .... sq. ft..	714	$357
Cast polished plate, not silvered .... sq. ft..	600	272
Cast polished plate, silvered .... sq. ft..	....	....
Manufactures not specified	....	17,492
Total	....	18,121
41. Gums .... lbs..	85,950	$23,639
42. Gunpowder .... lbs..	....	....
43. Hemp and manufactures of:†		
Raw .... tons..	2,713	$218,211
Manufactures of, by yards .... yds..	86,352	20,245
Other manufactures of	....	37,276
Total	....	275,732
44. Hides and skins, other than furs	....	$566,264
45. India-rubber and gutta-percha;		
Unmanufactured .... lbs..	416,033	$222,633
Manufactures of	....	2,869
Total	....	225,502

* Including brown hollands, burlaps, canvas, coatings, crash, diaper, duck, handkerchiefs, huckabacks lawns, paddings, and all like manufactures of which flax, jute, or hemp, shall be the material of chief value.

No. 5.—*Statement from returns of collectors of customs, &c.*—Continued.

Commodities.	Quantity.	Value.
46. Iron and steel, and manufactures of:		
Pig iron .... cwt..	....	....
Castings .... cwt..	....	$1,035
Bar iron .... cwt..	746	1,755
Boiler iron .... lbs..	4,680	291
Band, hoop, and scroll iron .... lbs..	2,240	97
Railroad bars or rails .... tons..	700	20,097
Sheet iron .... lbs..	56,183	2,022
Old and scrap iron .... lbs..	....	....
Hardware	....	6,459
Anchors, cables, and chains of all kinds .... lbs..	3,494	8,046
Machinery	....	842
Muskets, pistols, rifles, and sporting guns	....	11,088
Steel ingots, bars, sheets, and wire	....	31,851
Cutlery	....	5,921
Files	....	2,123
Saws and tools	....	534
Manufactures of iron and steel not specified	....	73,169
Total	....	165,330
47. Jewelry and other manufactures of gold and silver	....	$2,917
48. Jute and other grasses, and cocoa fibre, and manufacture of:*		
Raw .... tons..	90	$12,806
Manufactures of, by yard .... yds..	....	....
Gunny cloth and gunny bags, and other manufactures of, used for bagging	102,912	7,186
Other manufactures	....	33,080
Total	....	53,072
49. Lead and manufactures of:		
Pigs, bars, and old .... lbs..	125,629	$7,662
Manufactures of	....	232
Total	....	7,894
50. Leather and leather goods;		
Leather of all kinds .... lbs..	47,290	$30,622
Gloves of kid and cheveril .... doz. prs..	107	790
All other gloves of skin or leather .... doz. prs..	37	164
All other manufactures of	....	8,671
Total	....	40,247
51. Oils:		
Whale and fish, not of American fisheries .... galls..	11,111	$16,708
Olive, salad .... galls..	4,869	9,062
Olive, not salad .... galls..	2,023	2,108
All other fixed oils .... galls..	86,701	116,928
Volatile or essential .... lbs..	2,790	10,268
Total	....	155,074
52. Opium and extract of .... lbs..	65,142	$472,808
53. Paints:		
White and red lead, and litharge .... lbs..	30,281	$1,914
Whiting and Paris white .... lbs..	1,000	16
All other paints and painter's colors	....	9,231
Total	....	11,161

No. 5.—*Statement from returns of collectors of customs, &c.*—Continued.

Commodities.	Quantity.	Value.
54. Paper and manufactures of:		
Printing paper .... lbs..	....	$697
Writing paper .... reams..	....	110
Other paper	....	4,383
Papier maché, and all other manufactures of paper, and including parchment	....	2,108
Total	....	7,298
55. Precious stones	....	$1,655
56. Perfumery	....	17,890
57. Provisions and tallow	....	199,439
58. Saltpetre, (nitrate of potash) .... lbs..	100	18
59. Salt .... lbs..	17,694,443	68,684
60. Silk, manufactures of:		
Dress and piece goods .... yds..	1,299	$1,259
Manufactures not specified	....	132,884
Total	....	134,143
61. Soda and salts of:		
Bicarbonate .... lbs..	32,732	$1,174
Carbonate, including sal soda, soda ash, barilla, and kelp .... lbs..	308,320	18,530
Caustic soda .... lbs..	56,813	2,211
Nitrate, acetate, sulphate, phosphate, and all other salts of soda .... lbs..	3,197	204
Total	....	22,119
62. Spices of all kinds, including ginger, pepper, and mustard .... lbs..	1,379,775	$109,499
63. Sugar and molasses:		
Brown .... lbs..	11,712,007	$527,700
Refined .... lbs..	271,523	32,506
Molasses .... galls..	512,456	115,289
Melado and sirup of sugar cane .... lbs..	1,014,302	29,397
Candy and confectionary .... lbs..	380	252
Total	....	705,144
64. Sulphur or brimstone, crude or refined .... tons..	....	....
65. Tea .... lbs..	2,172,013	$699,196
66. Tin and manufactures of:		
In bars, blocks, or pigs .... cwt..	1,622	$45,436
In plates .... cwt..	628	5,445
Manufactures of	....	653
Total	....	51,534
67. Tobacco, and manufactures of:		
Leaf .... lbs..	1,373,205	$463,556
Cigars .... lbs..	185,694	286,638
Snuff .... lbs..	11,295	4,374
Other manufactures	....	24,541
Total	....	779,109
68. Watches, and watch movements and materials	....	$3,094

Summary statement from collectors of customs, &c.—Continued.

Commodities.	Quantity.	Value.
69. Wines, spirits, and cordials:		
Spirits and cordials in casks .... Pf. galls..	180, 374	$156, 077
Spirits and cordials in bottles .... doz..	10, 229	15, 771
Wine in casks .... galls..	228, 448	119, 288
Wine in bottles .... doz..	11, 557	45, 835
Total	....	336, 971
70. Wood and manufactures of, (except cabinet wood, for which see "articles free of duty," and except "produce of forests of State of Maine")	....	$235, 237
71. Wool, sheep, goats' and camel's hair, and manufactures of:		
Raw and fleece .... lbs..	2, 792, 161	$446, 470
Cloths and cassimeres	....	73, 974
Woollen rags, shoddy, mungo, waste and flocks.... lbs..	133, 814	11, 557
Shawls	....	23, 893
Blankets	....	4, 988
Carpets .... yds..	....	4, 157
Dress goods .... yds..	1, 138, 513	262, 760
Manufactures not specified	....	209, 330
Total	....	1, 037, 129
72. Zinc, spelter, or teutenegue, and manufactures of:		
In blocks or pigs .... lbs..	8, 982	$902
In sheets .... lbs..	72, 601	4, 566
Total	81, 583	5, 468
73. All articles not enumerated	....	$955, 168
Total of dutiable kinds	....	$11, 486, 431
Total free of duty	....	10, 709, 007
Total re-exports	....	22, 195, 438
From warehouse	....	$10, 825, 626
Not from warehouse	....	11, 369, 812

ALEX. DELMAR, *Director*

BUREAU OF STATISTICS,
Treasury Department, November 16, 1868.

FOREIGN IMPORTS, 1868.—DETAILS.

No. 6.—*Summary statement from returns of collectors of customs of the import entries of foreign commodities into the United States during the twelve months ended June 30, 1868.*

NOTE.—This statement is taken from the records before they are balanced, and both in details and total will probably differ slightly from the statement to be published in the Director's annual report on commerce and navigation.

Commodities.	Quantity.	Value.
FREE OF DUTY.		
1. Articles in a crude state used in dyeing and tanning		$486,545
2. Bolting cloths		159,911
3. Cochineal ... lbs	1,306,052	1,071,585
4. Dyewoods, in sticks ... cwt	1,187,256	842,226
5. Gold and silver:		
Gold bullion		$1,565,956
Silver bullion		85,891
Gold coin		7,051,439
Silver coin		4,999,642
Total		13,702,928
6. Gypsum, or plaster of Paris, unground ... tons	97,249	$85,838
7. Horsehair, used for weaving, cleaned or uncleaned, drawn or undrawn ... lbs	3,028,276	579,987
8. Household and personal effects and wearing apparel, old and in use, of persons arriving from foreign countries		839,844
9. Indigo ... lbs	854,257	775,187
10. Madder:		
Ground or prepared ... lbs	13,838,438	$1,135,258
Root ... lbs	356,750	37,573
Total	14,195,188	1,172,831
11. Rags of cotton or linen for the manufacture of paper, lbs	49,091,047	$1,944,972
12. Silk, raw, or as reeled from the cocoon ... lbs	509,167	2,520,348
13. Guano, except from American islands ... tons	44,634	1,153,255
14. Wood, all cabinet, unmanufactured		595,254
15. All other articles		3,873,436
Total free of duty		29,804,147
DUTIABLE.		
16. Animals, living, of all kinds		$2,290,679
17. Articles, the growth, produce, and manufacture of the United States, brought back		63,675
18. Argols, or crude tartar ... lbs	1,890,239	257,923
19. Brass, and manufactures of		243,950
20. Breadstuffs:		
Barley ... bush	3,730,509	$3,107,690
Bread and biscuit ... lbs	18,716	6,129
Indian corn ... bush	43,042	30,399
Indian meal ... bbls	135	497
Oats ... bush	709,258	305,225
Rice ... lbs	47,197,801	1,353,637
Rye ... bush	227,802	236,476
Rye flour ... bbls	222	1,035
Wheat ... bush	1,612,572	2,727,559

No. 6.—*Summary statement of the import entries, &c.*—Continued.

Commodities.	Quantity.	Value.
20. Breadstuffs—Continued.		
Wheat flour .... bbls..	77,309	$562,260
Potatoes .... bush..	194,905	120,853
Macaroni, vermicelli, and all other preparations from breadstuffs used as food	....	233,805
Total	....	8,685,565
21. Books, pamphlets, maps, and engravings, and other publications	....	$1,358,525
22. Buttons of all kinds	....	1,400,805
23. Cordage, ropes, and twines of all kinds .... lbs..	1,394,994	143,032
24. Chiccory, ground or prepared, and root .... lbs..	2,409,082	79,827
25. Chloride of lime, or bleaching powder .... lbs..	23,937,753	643,641
26. Clothing, except when of silk:		
Cut and sewed together	....	$735,769
Articles of wear not specified	....	542,036
Total	....	1,277,805
27. Coal, bituminous .... tons..	402,299	$1,274,261
28. Cocoa .... lbs..	4,924,770	543,402
29. Coffee .... lbs..	252,198,459	24,986,669
30. Copper:		
Ore .... cwt..	122,538	$440,699
Copper .... lbs..	286,436	35,524
Manufactures of	....	37,328
Total	....	513,551
31. Cotton and manufactures of:		
Cotton, raw .... lbs..	496,562	$96,196
Bleached and unbleached .... sq. yds..	19,771,339	2,792,301
Printed, painted, or colored .... sq. yds..	16,394,932	2,488,422
Jeans, denims, drillings, &c. .... sq. yds..	5,266,285	722,978
Manufactures not specified	....	11,211,173
Total	....	17,311,070
32. Cutch, catechu or terra japonica and gambier .... lbs..	1,720,551	$102,168
33. Chemicals, drugs, and dyes not specified	....	$4,575,542
34. Earthen, stone, and China ware	....	4,071,710
35. Fancy goods, invoiced by dozens, gross, or hundreds ..	....	2,845,153
36. Fish, fresh and cured, not of American fisheries	....	1,584,591
37. *Flax and manufactures of:		
Flax, raw .... tons..	1,626	$613,412
By yard .... sq. yds..	....	10,256,941
Other manufactures	....	3,044,323
Total	....	13,914,676
38. Fruits of all kinds	....	$5,047,968
39. Furs and fur skins	....	2,142,048
40. Glass and glassware:		
Cylinder, crown, or common window .... lbs..	29,325,991	$1,238,239
Cylinder and crown, polished .... sq. feet..	309,857	105,236
Fluted, rolled, or rough plate .... sq. feet..	1,281,152	137,318

* Including "brown hollands, burlaps, canvas, coatings, crash, diaper, duck, handkerchiefs, huckabacks,

No. 6.—*Summary statement of the import entries, &c.*—Continued.

Commodities.	Quantity.	Value.
40. Glass and glassware—Continued.		
Cast polished plate, not silvered............sq. feet..	886,685	$344,031
Cast polished plate, silvered.................sq. feet..	1,360,232	368,577
Manufactures, not specified........................	....	858,740
Total..	....	3,052,141
41. Gums..lbs..	10,083,646	$1,085,511
42. Gunpowder...................................lbs..	10,945	6,045
43. *Hemp, and manufactures of:		
Raw..tons..	21,155	$3,470,414
Manufactures of by yards......................yds..	1,629,535	252,147
Other manufactures of..............................	....	323,063
Total..	....	4,045,624
44. Hides and skins, other than furs..................	....	$10,562,726
45. India-rubber and gutta percha:		
Unmanufactured...............................lbs..	....	2,079,348
Manufactures of....................................	....	663,505
Total..	....	2,742,853
46. Iron and steel, and manufactures of—		
Pig iron....................................cwt..	2,107,905	$1,810,482
Castings....................................cwt..	....	32,674
Bar iron....................................cwt..	1,185,412	2,906,231
Boiler iron.................................lbs..	1,999,533	73,221
Band, hoop, and scroll iron.................lbs..	31,756,702	672,264
Railroad bars or rails......................tons..	203,819	4,781,575
Sheet iron..................................lbs..	31,642,085	1,187,644
Old and scrap iron..........................lbs..	145,816,983	1,283,269
Hardware...	....	185,460
Anchors, cables, and chains of all kinds.......lbs..	8,611,864	315,183
Machinery..	....	609,820
Muskets, pistols, rifles, and sporting guns.........	....	291,440
Steel ingots, bars, sheets, and wire................	....	1,705,337
Cutlery..	....	1,248,877
Files..	....	578,941
Saws and tools.....................................	....	121,990
Manufactures of iron and steel not specified........	....	5,692,427
Total..	....	23,496,835
47. Jewelry and other manufactures of gold and silver.....	....	$677,212
48. Jute and other grasses, and cocoa fibre, and manufactures of:*		
Raw..tons..	4,054	$304,098
Manufactures of, by yard......................yds..	338,432	73,443
Gunny cloth and gunny bags, and other manufactures of, used for bagging..............lbs..	33,155,872	1,112,504
Other manufactures..................................	....	1,617,105
Total..	....	3,107,150
49. Lead, and manufactures of—		
Pigs, bars, and old..........................lbs..	68,202,558	$2,851,403
Manufactures of....................................	....	78,871
Total..	....	2,930,274

No. 6.—*Summary statement of the import entries, &c.*—Continued.

Commodities.	Quantity.	Value.
50. Leather and leather goods:		
Leather of all kinds.......lbs..	....	$3,400,419
Gloves of kid and cheveril.......doz. pairs..	195,395	1,164,338
All other gloves of skin or leather.......doz. pairs..	240,174	727,863
All other manufactures of............	....	434,335
Total............	....	5,726,955
51. Oils:		
Whale and fish, not of American fisheries....galls..	136,812	$74,642
Olive, salad.......galls..	121,649	227,821
not salad.......galls..	48,413	60,048
All other fixed oils.......galls..	1,099,883	547,559
Volatile or essential.......lbs..	172,325	315,649
Total............	....	1,225,719
52. Opium and extract of.......lbs..	218,386	$984,573
53. Paints:		
White and red lead, and litharge.......lbs..	9,405,478	$555,288
Whiting and Paris white.......lbs..	3,852,400	19,078
All other paints and painter's colors............	....	477,424
Total............	....	1,051,790
54. Paper and manufactures of—		
Printing paper.......lbs..	....	$199,496
Writing paper.......reams..	....	213,027
Other paper............	....	482,517
Papier maché, and all other manufactures of paper, and including parchment............	....	280,158
Total............	....	1,175,198
55. Precious stones............	....	$1,062,433
56. Perfumery............	....	365,373
57. Provisions and tallow............	....	1,743,495
58. Saltpetre (nitrate of potash).......lbs..	5,173,120	159,043
59. Salt.......lbs..	636,041,262	1,390,962
60. Silk, manufactures of:		
Dress and piece goods.......yds..	....	$7,887,697
Manufactures not specified............	....	10,153,653
Total............	....	18,041,350
61. Soda and salts of:		
Bicarbonate.......lbs..	19,221,883	$591,228
Carbonate, including sal soda, soda ash, barilla, and kelp.......lbs..	125,888,003	2,511,885
Caustic soda.......lbs..	13,798,162	502,561
Nitrate, acetate, sulphate, phosphate, and all other salts of soda.......lbs..	16,193,039	279,259
Total............	175,101,087	3,884,933
62. Spices of all kinds, including ginger, pepper, and mustard.......lbs..	8,794,950	$671,204

No. 6.—*Summary statement of the import entries, &c.*—Continued.

Commodities.	Quantity.	Value.
63. Sugar and molasses:		
Brown .... lbs..	1,093,284,541	$49,616,827
Refined .... lbs..	149,086	11,173
Molasses .... galls..	57,396,071	12,218,103
Melado and sirup of sugar cane .... lbs..	5,372,437	155,672
Candy and confectionery .... lbs..	71,312	15,475
Total	....	62,017,250
64. Sulphur or brimstone, crude or refined .... tons..	14,092	$352,062
65. Tea .... lbs..	37,615,685	11,075,908
66. Tin and manufactures of:		
In bars, blocks, or pigs .... cwt..	92,575	$1,633,077
In plates .... cwt..	1,208,088	6,913,633
Manufactures of	....	75,666
Total	....	8,622,376
67. Tobacco, and manufactures of—		
Leaf .... lbs..	3,836,972	$1,302,426
Cigars .... lbs..	321,784	887,410
Snuff .... lbs..	19,821	6,040
Other manufactures	....	14,187
Total	....	2,210,063
68. Watches, and watch movements and materials	....	$1,777,035
69. Wines, spirits, and cordials:		
Spirits and cordials in casks .... pf. galls..	1,141,947	$1,016,484
Spirits and cordials in bottles .... doz..	11,318	60,271
Wine in casks .... galls..	5,154,684	2,048,938
Wine in bottles .... doz..	214,075	1,515,616
Total	....	4,641,309
70. Wood and manufactures of, (except cabinet wood, for which see "articles free of duty," and except "produce of forests of State of Maine")	....	$7,594,246
71. Wool, sheep, goats', and camel's hair, and manufactures of:		
Raw and fleece .... lbs..	24,474,327	$3,868,137
Clothes and cassimers	....	6,956,449
Woollen rags, shoddy, mungo, waste, and flocks. lbs..	568,040	47,125
Shawls	....	1,559,999
Blankets	....	28,196
Carpets .... yds..	2,797,199	2,766,291
Dress goods .... yds..	55,379,889	15,196,233
Manufactures not specified	....	5,902,591
Total	....	36,325,021
72. Zinc, spelter, or teutenegue, and manufactures of:		
In blocks or pigs .... lbs..	7,033,163	$329,005
In sheets .... lbs..	5,032,452	270,830
Total	12,065,615	599,835
73. All articles not enumerated	....	$23,842,552

No. 6.—*Summary statement of the import entries, &c.*—Continued.

Commodities.	Quantity.	Value.
Total paying duty		$343, 605, 301
Total free of duty		29, 804, 147
Total import entries		$373, 409, 448
Entered for consumption		208, 106, 454
Entered warehouse		165, 302, 994

ALEX. DELMAR, *Director.*

BUREAU OF STATISTICS,
Treasury Department, November 16, 1868.

No. 7.—*Statement exhibiting the tonnage of American and foreign vessels which entered and cleared at each collection district of the United States, from and to foreign countries, during the fiscal year ended June 30, 1868.*

Districts.	ENTERED—			CLEARED—		
	American vessels.	Foreign vessels.	Total.	American vessels.	Foreign vessels.	Total.
	Tons.	*Tons.*	*Tons.*	*Tons.*	*Tons.*	*Tons.*
Passamaquoddy	105, 488	10, 953	116, 441	115, 004	11, 327	126, 331
Frenchman's bay	148	686	834	1, 772	99	1, 871
Machias	1, 240	348	1, 588	14, 518	1, 832	10, 350
Castine	1, 775	674	2, 449	1, 252	81	1, 333
Waldoborough		204	204	1, 105	164	1, 269
Wiscasset				2, 204	257	2, 461
Bath	2, 502	1, 683	4, 185	1, 179	1, 472	2, 651
Portland and Falmouth	72, 712	97, 929	170, 641	117, 192	105, 442	222, 634
Kennebunk		138	138	195	138	333
Belfast	720	905	1, 625	3, 770	1, 067	4, 837
Bangor	2, 081	4, 088	6, 169	14, 645	8, 262	22, 907
Portsmouth	692	4, 143	4, 835	2, 806	3, 806	6, 612
Vermont	4, 686	65, 581	70, 267	4, 243	81, 231	85, 474
Newburyport	1, 330	1, 797	3, 127	2, 082	1, 803	3, 885
Gloucester	6, 156	6, 763	12, 919	4, 382	6, 500	10, 882
Salem and Beverly	1, 810	11, 171	12, 981	3, 163	10, 776	13, 939
Marblehead		2, 630	2, 630	102	2, 682	2, 784
Boston and Charlestown	237, 613	404, 865	642, 478	230, 769	364, 249	595, 018
Plymouth, Mass		450	450	64	450	514
Fall River	158	586	744	687	586	1, 273
Barnstable	291	212	503	541	212	753
New Bedford	17, 257	3, 613	20, 870	16, 133	4, 145	20, 278
Edgartown	9, 940	3, 961	13, 901	1, 398		1, 398
Nantucket				57		57
Providence	1, 580	17, 146	18, 726	2, 642	14, 281	16, 923
Bristol and Warren	246		246	1, 619		1, 619
Newport	664	450	1, 114	1, 468	450	1, 918
Middletown	323		323			
New London	2, 955	2, 372	5, 327	1, 812	1, 994	3, 806
New Haven	10, 034	4, 395	14, 429	8, 077	4, 816	12, 893
Fairfield	1, 035	8, 339	9, 374	218	7, 576	7, 794
Stonington		117	117			
Genesee	12, 088	62, 773	74, 861	47, 939	58, 339	106, 278
Oswego	206, 088	376, 611	582, 699	183, 687	375, 176	558, 863
Niagara	928	51, 765	52, 693	1, 174	51, 866	53, 040
Buffalo Creek	296, 362	88, 078	384, 440	293, 640	89, 786	383, 426
Oswegatchie	9, 247	29, 479	38, 726	17, 367	19, 622	36, 989
Champlain	44, 364	104, 899	149, 263	30, 455	85, 428	115, 883
Cape Vincent	104, 661	83, 935	188, 596	103, 325	84, 153	187, 478
Dunkirk	86	1, 493	1, 579	43	1, 493	1, 536
Sag Harbor	708		708			
New York	1, 064, 263	1, 800, 989	2, 865, 252	932, 682	1, 820, 133	2, 752, 815
Perth Amboy		73	73	3, 765	2, 117	5, 882
Newark	312	2, 883	3, 195		2, 883	2, 883
Philadelphia	188, 318	90, 122	278, 440	156, 854	140, 235	297, 089
Erie	14, 635	15, 611	30, 246	3, 678	18, 126	21, 804
Delaware	207	262	469		208	208

No. 7.—*Statement exhibiting the tonnage of American and foreign vessels, &c.*—Continued.

Districts.	ENTERED—			CLEARED—		
	American vessels.	Foreign vessels.	Total.	American vessels.	Foreign vessels.	Total.
	Tons.	*Tons.*	*Tons.*	*Tons.*	*Tons.*	*Tons.*
Georgetown, D. C	105	114	219	....	114	114
Richmond	449	2, 170	2, 619	5, 077	7, 132	12, 209
Petersburg	....	270	270	....	270	270
Norfolk and Portsmouth	5, 344	10, 220	15, 564	10, 402	11, 968	22, 370
Alexandria	1, 047	1, 026	2, 073	....	....	....
Albemarle	186	....	186	625	....	625
Pamlico	253	....	253	389	....	389
Beaufort, N. C	....	136	136	629	....	629
Wilmington, N. C	1, 237	862	2, 099	4, 369	10, 780	15, 149
Charleston	18, 578	25, 212	43, 790	23, 796	25, 385	49, 181
Georgetown, S. C	528	....	528	2, 788	321	3, 109
Beaufort, S. C	....	....	....	138	474	612
Savannah	24, 161	60, 027	84, 188	53, 499	81, 006	134, 505
St. Mary's	....	1, 423	1, 423	3, 027	4, 839	8, 466
Mobile	22, 665	65, 879	88, 544	49, 202	60, 676	109, 878
Pensacola	5, 022	35, 471	40, 493	8, 266	41, 784	50, 050
Key West	25, 053	3, 404	28, 457	28, 641	1, 294	29, 935
St. Mark's	122	218	340	585	218	803
St. John's	764	862	1, 626	3, 834	865	4, 699
Appalachicola	448	....	448	30	....	30
Fernandina	1, 063	449	1, 512	3, 359	3, 276	6, 635
Pearl River	....	....	....	258	200	458
New Orleans	161, 615	164, 601	326, 216	225, 216	174, 324	400, 133
Galveston	1, 882	21, 772	23, 654	9, 410	19, 706	29, 116
Saluria	86	156	242	358	150	508
Brazos de Santiago	109	525	634	109	192	301
Miami	11, 334	14, 083	25, 417	5, 506	13, 342	18, 848
Sandusky	2, 184	3, 312	5, 496	2, 005	3, 382	5, 387
Cuyahoga	41, 442	36, 435	77, 877	27, 045	39, 323	66, 368
Detroit	189, 445	117, 410	306, 855	189, 502	117, 730	307, 232
Port Huron	130, 186	266, 070	396, 256	124, 566	267, 274	391, 840
Superior	....	15, 220	15, 220	....	14, 950	14, 950
Chicago	15, 231	33, 148	48, 379	47, 514	35, 978	83, 492
Milwaukee	1, 888	23, 736	25, 624	11, 236	17, 661	28, 897
Oregon	6, 564	1, 576	8, 140	7, 057	1, 576	8, 633
Puget sound	39, 729	8, 040	47, 769	40, 420	20, 081	60, 501
San Francisco	299, 676	113, 997	413, 673	386, 203	93, 835	480, 038
Alaska	1, 305	888	2, 193	734	2, 746	3, 480
Total	3, 550, 550	4, 495, 465	8, 046, 015	3, 717, 956	4, 561, 060	8, 279, 016

ALEX. DELMAR, *Director.*

TREASURY DEPARTMENT, *Bureau of Statistics, November* 16, 1868.

No. 8.—*Statement exhibiting the tonnage of American and foreign vessels which entered from and cleared to foreign countries, into and from the United States, during the fiscal year ended June* 30, 1868.

Countries.	ENTERED—			CLEARED—		
	American vessels.	Foreign vessels.	Total.	American vessels.	Foreign vessels.	Total.
	Tons.	*Tons.*	*Tons.*	*Tons.*	*Tons.*	*Tons.*
Russia on the Baltic and White seas	7, 217	1, 651	8, 868	5, 804	10, 302	16, 106
Russia on the Black sea	....	4, 459	4, 459	....	176	176
Asiatic Russia	....	....	....	1, 036	1, 012	2, 048
Russian possessions in North America*	3, 385	1, 268	4, 653	3, 633	598	4, 231
Prussia	....	834	834	806	11, 707	12, 513
Sweden and Norway	3, 958	12, 449	16, 407	....	1, 839	1, 839
Swedish West Indies	....	....	....	133	....	133
Denmark	436	....	436	....	1, 537	1, 537
Danish West Indies	11, 678	8, 906	20, 674	18, 747	7, 640	26, 387
Greenland	2, 327	2, 728	5, 055	995	1, 891	2, 886
Hamburg	....	155, 888	155, 888	1, 894	144, 842	146, 736
Bremen	30, 971	242, 324	273, 295	31, 586	271, 057	302, 643
Lubeck	....	....	....	....	142	142

* These transactions took place before the territory was formally taken possession of by the United States.

No. 8.—*Statement exhibiting the tonnage of American and foreign vessels, &c.*—Continued.

Countries.	ENTERED—			CLEARED—		
	American vessels.	Foreign vessels.	Total.	American vessels.	Foreign vessels.	Total.
	Tons.	*Tons.*	*Tons.*	*Tons.*	*Tons.*	*Tons.*
Holland	4, 305	16, 205	20, 510	5, 991	41, 790	47, 781
Dutch West Indies	9, 159	8, 309	17, 468	5, 135	3, 890	9, 025
Dutch Guiana	2, 240	4, 559	6, 799	1, 247	3, 477	4, 724
Dutch East Indies	3, 873	2, 558	6, 431	4, 988	1, 864	6, 852
Belgium	9, 745	34, 287	44, 032	12, 417	74, 461	86, 878
England	412, 718	1, 234, 987	1, 647, 705	416, 271	1, 259, 906	1, 676, 177
Scotland	9, 800	126, 924	136, 724	11, 236	100, 719	111, 955
Ireland	1, 705	15, 021	16, 726	14, 468	101, 660	116, 128
Gibraltar	1, 413	806	2, 219	9, 943	18, 126	28, 069
Malta	....	....	....	326	1, 265	1, 591
Canada	1, 084, 963	1, 391, 099	2, 476, 062	1, 094, 173	1, 398, 011	2, 492, 184
Other British North American possessions on the Atlantic	246, 330	357, 318	603, 648	268, 884	490, 638	759, 522
British American possessions on the Pacific	68, 538	9, 660	78, 198	75, 352	16, 060	91, 412
British West Indies	63, 379	68, 772	132, 151	65, 978	56, 285	122, 263
British Honduras	8, 679	3, 273	11, 952	8, 757	3, 176	11, 933
British Guiana	11, 401	16, 177	27, 578	12, 905	12, 653	25, 558
British possessions in Africa	4, 277	6, 362	10, 639	7, 108	3, 672	10, 780
British East Indies	29, 678	46, 575	76, 253	18, 906	2, 818	21, 724
Australia	9, 962	9, 799	19, 761	21, 169	15, 465	36, 634
France on the Atlantic	64, 923	74, 678	139, 601	114, 513	73, 523	188, 036
France on the Mediterranean	11, 563	9, 158	20, 721	25, 648	4, 086	29, 734
French North American possessions	....	982	982	317	4, 054	4, 371
French West Indies	3, 334	9, 908	13, 242	11, 726	2, 903	14, 629
French Guiana	447	....	447	549	140	689
French possessions in Africa	3, 505	1, 597	5, 102	2, 244	1, 622	3, 866
Spain on the Atlantic	11, 481	6, 049	17, 530	19, 140	18, 917	38, 057
Spain on the Mediterranean	16, 499	14, 832	31, 331	9, 591	31, 487	41, 078
Canary islands	285	1, 655	1, 940	2, 741	2, 768	5, 509
Philippine islands	18, 894	8, 904	27, 798	2, 539	300	2, 839
Cuba	665, 210	218, 683	883, 893	648, 481	110, 453	758, 934
Porto Rico	47, 807	27, 169	74, 976	44, 421	7, 952	52, 373
Portugal	2, 476	5, 963	8, 439	5, 695	6, 055	11, 750
Madeira	703	....	703	1, 825	130	1, 955
Cape de Verde islands	2, 820	5, 350	8, 170	1, 484	827	2, 311
Azores	1, 176	2, 494	3, 670	2, 505	4, 282	6, 787
Italy	26, 213	18, 748	44, 961	19, 228	21, 290	40, 518
Sicily	33, 930	30, 517	64, 447	3, 557	4, 579	8, 136
Austria	....	5, 994	5, 994	718	4, 873	5, 591
Greece	....	1, 273	1, 273	....	....	....
Ionian islands	....	593	593	....	....	....
Turkey in Europe	1, 088	....	1, 088	2, 225	696	2, 921
Turkey in Asia	3, 005	2, 652	5, 657	2, 369	855	3, 224
Egypt	....	....	....	377	....	377
Liberia	2, 846	184	3, 030	3, 246	280	3, 526
Other ports in Africa	5, 357	2, 762	8, 119	3, 382	155	3, 537
Hayti	12, 949	16, 249	29, 198	14, 643	15, 712	30, 355
San Domingo	3, 710	4, 068	7, 778	360	652	1, 012
Mexico	44, 749	24, 054	68, 803	59, 382	17, 676	77, 058
Nicaragua	37, 953	1, 215	39, 168	34, 084	1, 621	35, 705
Costa Rica	590	2, 623	3, 213	612	1, 214	1, 826
Guatemala	372	808	1, 180	41	531	572
Honduras	212	....	212	....	117	117
Salvador	....	290	290	....	874	874
United States of Colombia	287, 216	7, 150	294, 366	316, 769	5, 307	322, 076
Venezuela	2, 764	11, 488	14, 252	2, 417	14, 217	16, 634
Brazil	55, 695	88, 367	144, 062	50, 439	27, 014	77, 453
Uruguay	4, 653	6, 105	10, 758	21, 485	31, 087	52, 572
Buenos Ayres, or Argentine Republic	15, 845	11, 624	27, 469	18, 543	25, 653	44, 196
Chili	4, 093	16, 043	20, 136	7, 636	21, 306	28, 942
Peru	28, 248	14, 681	42, 929	21, 704	13, 796	35, 500
Ecuador	116	....	116	116	....	116
Hawaiian islands	19, 483	6, 143	25, 626	21, 350	6, 627	27, 977
Other islands of the Pacific	2, 008	1, 762	3, 770	5, 338	1, 844	7, 182
China	15, 093	41, 068	56, 161	39, 381	12, 342	51, 723
Japan	29, 220	6, 941	36, 161	38, 509	2, 564	41, 073
Other ports in Asia	728	1, 443	2, 171	....	....	....
Whale fisheries	19, 064	....	19, 064	16, 738	....	16, 738
Total	3, 550, 550	4, 495, 465	8, 046, 015	3, 717, 956	4, 561, 060	8, 279, 016

ALEX. DELMAR, *Director.*

TREASURY DEPARTMENT, *Bureau of Statistics, November* 16, 1868.

No. 9.—*Monthly summary of warehouse transactions from the fiscal years 1866 to 1868, inclusive, from the records of the Bureau of Statistics*, (000's *omitted*.)

[NOTE.—The total in warehouse at the beginning of the month, with the amount received during the month, less the amount withdrawn during the same period, should agree with the total in warehouse as shown at the foot of each monthly table. In many instances throughout the following tables previous to the fiscal year 1867, when the Bureau of Statistics was first organized, this is not the case. No explanation of these discrepancies having been furnished at the time, and none being attainable now, the figures can only be given as they were originally published in the back numbers of the finance reports.]

Merchandise.	July, 1866.	August, 1866.	Septe'ber, 1866.	October, 1866.	Nove'ber, 1866.	Dece'ber, 1866.	January, 1867.	Febru'ry, 1867.	March, 1867.	April, 1867.	May, 1867.	June, 1867.
	Amount.	Amount.	Amount.	Amount.	Amount.	Amount.	Amount.	Amount.	Amount.	Amount.	Amount.	Amount.
In warehouse on the first day of each month	$46,540	$47,485	$44,643	$39,426	$36,746	$38,132	$46,774	$43,790	$41,949	$36,111	$41,881	$43,741
Received from foreign ports	15,455	12,214	10,722	11,450	13,387	14,206	} 13,342	16,237	14,347	21,572	18,882	16,520
Received from other districts	673	787	610	846	1,711	1,530						
Total	62,669	60,487	55,976	51,724	51,844	53,869	60,117	60,028	56,296	57,684	60,763	60,261
Withdrawn for consumption	13,201	14,179	14,674	12,481	9,370	6,899	14,144	15,565	17,312	13,371	14,549	12,330
Withdrawn for transportation	924	670	890	1,487	2,806	1,256	917	1,029	811	809	1,127	1,088
Withdrawn for exportation	1,052	883	1,078	1,007	1,512	1,274	1,040	1,484	2,061	1,675	1,343	1,025
Total	15,178	15,733	16,643	14,976	13,689	9,431	16,102	18,078	20,184	15,856	17,020	14,444
In warehouse at the close of each month	47,490	44,753	39,331	36,747	38,155	44,438	44,014	41,949	36,112	41,827	43,742	45,817

Merchandise.	July, 1867.	August, 1867.	Septe'ber, 1867.	October, 1867.	Nove'ber, 1867.	Dece'ber, 1867.	January, 1868.	Febru'ry, 1868.	March, 1868.	April, 1868.	May, 1868.	June, 1868.
	Amount.	Amount.	Amount.	Amount.	Amount.	Amount.	Amount.	Amount.	Amount.	Amount.	Amount.	Amount.
In warehouse on the first day of each month	$48,034	$50,763	$48,396	$43,434	$42,017	$41,655	$41,674	$40,372	$39,994	$42,880	$42,867	$43,404
Received from foreign ports	} 16,989	13,947	11,658	13,520	13,040	10,695	10,799	14,185	19,932	17,927	17,924	17,340
Received from other districts												
Total	65,025	64,711	60,055	56,955	55,058	52,351	52,473	54,559	59,927	60,807	60,792	60,744
Withdrawn for consumption	12,527	14,649	14,593	12,161	10,214	8,564	10,290	12,838	15,004	16,119	13,717	11,002
Withdrawn for transportation	865	954	1,214	1,767	2,106	1,050	988	1,152	1,040	944	1,614	1,120
Withdrawn for exportation	868	712	813	1,009	1,081	1,061	822	573	1,057	874	1,005	831
Total	14,261	16,315	16,620	14,938	13,402	10,676	12,101	14,564	17,102	17,939	16,337	12,954
In warehouse at the close of each month	50,763	48,396	43,435	42,017	41,655	41,675	40,372	39,994	42,825	42,867	44,455	47,790

REPORT OF THE DIRECTOR OF THE MINT.

MINT OF THE UNITED STATES,
Philadelphia, October 31, 1868.

SIR: I have the honor to submit the following report of the operations of the mint and branches for the fiscal year ending June 30, 1868.

The deposits of bullion at the mint and branches during the fiscal year were as follows: gold, $25,472,894 82; silver, $1,693,423 88; total deposits, $27,166,318 70. Deducting from this total the redeposits of bullion or bars made at one branch of the mint and deposited at another for coinage, the amount will be $24,591,325 84.

The coinage for the same period was as follows: gold coin, pieces, 976,539; value, $18,114,425. Unparted and fine gold bars, $6,026,810 06. Silver coin, pieces, 3,321,067; value, $1,136,750. Silver bars, $456,236 48. Nickel, copper, and bronze coinage, pieces, 45,438,000; value, $1,713,385. Total number of pieces struck, 49,735,840. Total value of coinage, $27,447,606 54.

The distribution of the bullion received at the mint and branches was as follows: at Philadelphia, gold deposited, $4,043,048 63; gold coined, $3,864,425; fine gold bars, $98,848 03; silver deposits and purchases, $342,635 72; silver coined, $314,750; silver bars, $6,729 94; nickel, copper, and bronze coinage, value, $1,713,385; total deposits of gold and silver, $4,385,684 35; total coinage, $5,892,560. It is proper to remark that coinage operations were suspended at the mint during the first three months of the fiscal year for the purpose of making extensive repairs of the machinery, furnaces, and fixtures, which had become absolutely necessary. The coinage, therefore, of nickel, copper, and bronze represents, in point of fact, only nine months' operations.

At the branch mint, San Francisco, the gold deposits were $14,979,558 52; gold coined, $14,250,000; silver deposits and purchases, $713,867 66; silver coined, $822,000; total deposits and purchases, $15,693,426 18; total coinage, $15,072,000.

The assay office in New York received during the year, in gold bullion, $6,092,352 56; silver bullion, including purchases, $631,837 83; number of fine gold bars stamped, 4,084; value, $5,567,082 77; silver bars, 3,992; value, $449,506 54; total, $6,016,589 31.

At the branch mint, Denver, Colorado, the deposits for unparted bars were, gold, $357,935 11; silver, $5,082 67; total, $363,017 78. The deposits at this institution during the preceding fiscal year amounted to $130,559 70.

The branch mint at Charlotte, North Carolina, has been in operation for several months as an assay office, deposits being received, assayed, and returned to depositors in the form of unparted bars. The business at this institution is quite limited, requiring the services only of the assayer and one assistant.

appear to be no reason for reviving coinage operations at either of the three branch mints formerly in operation in the southern States. They could only be put in condition for coinage at a heavy expense, and to carry them on afterwards would require an annual outlay out of proportion to any accommodation that would be conferred on the people of the States in which they are respectively located. I therefore recommend that those establishments be disposed of to the best advantage.

The machinery and fixtures for the new branch mint at Carson City, Nevada, has nearly all been shipped, and will be put up during the coming winter.

A new branch mint edifice is about to be erected at San Francisco on a scale commensurate with the demand of the important bullion interests of the Pacific States. As the mint at that point will be called on to execute a large coinage in the future, I recommend that it be fitted up with new and improved machinery. When this institution shall have been completed, it will, with the mint at Philadelphia, be sufficient for the prompt execution of the coinage of our country. No other mints for coinage will, therefore, be necessary. The public interests may occasionally require the establishment of assay offices at other points. They should be on a scale sufficient for the receipt, refining, but not parting, assay, and return to depositors of the identical bullion deposited by the owners respectively. For these purposes an edifice need not be more than one-third the size and cost of a branch mint, and an assayer and a few assistants would be all the force required.

A few months since a contract for separating and refining bullion was entered into by the superintendent of the branch mint at San Francisco with a private refining company in that city, under the terms of which the cost of those operations would have been reduced about three cents per ounce; but being found to conflict with a recent act of Congress on the subject, it was, by your direction, cancelled. I respectfully recommend the repeal of the law referred to, and that such contracts be authorized to be made, with the approval of the Secretary of the Treasury, whenever required by the public interests.

In my last report I recommended, for reasons therein stated, that provision should be made for the reduction and redemption of the inferior coins by creating a fund for redemption out of the profits of such coinage. I beg to again call your attention to the subject, and recommend that a section something like the following may be submitted to the committees on coinage and finance:

Be it enacted, That the Secretary of the Treasury is hereby required to ascertain the amount which has been paid into the treasury by the mint of the United States, beginning with the year 1857, as profits accruing from the coinage of nickel, copper, and bronze pieces, which amount is hereby set apart and appropriated as a fund for the purpose hereinafter mentioned; and to this fund shall be added all similar profits accruing from and after the passage of this act. And it shall be the duty of the treasurer of the mint, under regulations made by the director of the mint, and approved by the Secretary of the Treasury, to receive any such coins that may be offered in sums not less than ——— dollars, and to pay for the same out of the fund herein created; and the metal thus received may be worked into new coin or otherwise disposed of to the best advantage; and any gain or loss thereby is to be set to the account of said fund.

If it should be thought best to avoid retroaction, and begin with the present time, then the section may read thus: That the amount of profits accruing from the coinage of nickel, copper, and bronze pieces, from and after the passage of this act, is hereby set apart and appropriated as a fund for the redemption of such coins; and it shall be the duty of the treasurer of the mint, under regulations made by the director of the mint, and approved by the Secretary of the Treasury, to receive any such coins that may be offered in sums not less than ——— dollars, and to pay for the same out of the fund herein created, as soon as such fund shall have sufficiently accumulated; and the metal thus received, &c., (as before.)

The inferior coinage consists of two different alloys, namely: a one and two cent piece of bronze (copper 95 per cent., 3 per cent. tin, 2 per cent. zinc) and a three and five cent piece of nickel and copper, (25 per cent. nickel and 75 per cent. copper.) There is no reason for continuing the coinage of the two cent piece, and the law authorizing its issue should be repealed. The net profits arising from the minor coinage and paid into the treasury of the United States during the fiscal year amounts to $1,300,000.

The purchase of the nickel copper cents, composed of 88 per cent. copper and 12 per cent. nickel, still continues, payment being made in the three and five cent nickel coins. The amount purchased to the close of the fiscal year was $260,482 04. This operation results in a small profit to the United States and serves to reduce the redundancy of cent coins.

CHARGES FOR COINAGE.

Whether it is according to propriety a good policy to make a charge for the coinage of bullion, and so far to make a difference of value between coin and bullion, has often been a matter of debate; and it has been variously decided in different countries and in our own at different times.

It is not necessary here to enter into the discussion; but it may be well, as it is certainly interesting, to take note of an argument which, so far as I know, has never been used before, going to sustain the rule upon which our laws of minting have settled. It is to be found in the "Report addressed to the Lords Commissioners of the Treasury (British) by the master of the mint (Professor Thomas Graham) and Mr. C. R. Wilson," delegates from England to the monetary conference at Paris. The paragraph reads as follows:

It is well known that all gold brought to the mint is returned in the form of sovereigns without deduction or charge; and there is no doubt that our practice is correct in principle, for the metal which, like gold, is adopted as the measure of value. But it is at the same time undeniable that some additional value is imparted to the metal by the work applied to it in coining, and a small charge to cover, or partially cover, the mint expenses is on that account generally imposed upon coin in the countries of the continent under the name of *brassage*. In France, the charge thus borne by the holders of bullion amounts to 6 francs 70 centimes on a kilogram of gold, which is coined into 155 napoleons, or 3,100 francs, being equivalent to 4.32 centimes on a 20-franc piece. The system of free mintage has also, since 1853, been abandoned in the United States, where, in addition to the charge for refining, a charge of one-half per cent. (50 cents on $100) is now taken upon all gold brought for conversion into coin. A small mint charge does not appear to be complained of anywhere. The charge acts usefully for the preservation of the coin by removing any inducement to melt it down for any ordinary technical purpose, or even to supply bullion to foreign mints. We have never reason to fear, from what we learned from professional members of the monetary conference, that the British gold coinage is liable to suffer heavily in this way. London is the entrepôt for the precious metals from which other countries draw their supplies. Now, gold may be procured from London either in the form of bars or sovereigns at the same price; while to the foreign purchaser, if a mint contractor, sovereigns offer the following advantages: the assay may be safely relied upon; the gold is already alloyed with copper, and, more than all, the suitability of the metal for coining is insured. Further, sovereigns are taken by number, and the aggregate weight may be, as nearly as possible, correct. But that is not true of the weight of individual pieces, which, from the unavoidable imperfection of manufacture, are some heavy and some light, within a certain small range, recognized as the *tolerance* in coining. There is reason to believe that large masses of new British sovereigns are occasionally treated so as to separate out the heavy pieces, and these are disposed of as bullion; while the lighter pieces, which may still be all of legal weight, are preserved and put into circulation. This fact will not surprise those persons who are aware of the small margin of profit upon which bullion transactions are often conducted. A small mint charge on the British sovereign thus appears to be called for, as the necessary means of preservation to the coin; while the measure is further recommended as an equitable repayment to the country of the cost of coinage.

The paragraph just cited affords an excellent and convincing summary of arguments in favor of a coinage charge, not a little strengthened by stating the sordid practice of sorting out the "lights" and "heavies."

At the same time it may be acknowledged, and indeed urged as a matter of reform, that our charge of one-half per cent. is twice as much as it ought to be. The French charge is rather less than one-quarter per cent.; our charge being two and one-third times as much as theirs. It is therefore recommended to lower the mint charge, by law, to one-fourth of one per cent. This rate would increase the tendency to turn gold bars into coin, and to prepare for a gold currency.

CHANGE IN THE FRENCH COINAGE.

Although not a matter of prime importance, it should be generally known that the silver coins of France, as also those of Italy, Switzerland, and Belgium, of the size of two francs and less, are no longer issued at the same fineness as the five-franc piece. This change took place in 1866, in pursuance of a monetary convention between those nations, agreeing to reduce the fineness from 900 to 835 thousandths.

This reduction of about seven per cent. was no doubt owing to the advanced value of silver as against gold, rendering it impossible to keep up the supply of money "*d'appoint*," for which we need a more definite English word than "change." This reduction brings the silver coin to a parallel with that of England, which has long been coined at such a rate as to keep it out of the reach of fluctuations in market price—that is, to keep it safe from being melted down or exported, being worth more as a legal currency than it would be if turned into bars. And here it may well be remarked that if we had now a silver currency, or any near prospect of it, it would be a necessary act of legislation to make a reduction in *our* silver coins; not merely to correspond with England and France, but to comply with the oscillations of the silver market, and to prevent the coins from being withdrawn, whether for export or for manufacture of plate. The provision to reduce the half-dollar from 192 to 179 grains, in the bill lately reported by the Finance Committee, was based upon the introduction of a general international gold currency, by which our gold dollar would be lightened, and consequently the silver must be also, even in greater proportion, for although it is but a home currency, there ought to be very nearly a parity in relative valuation. If our gold coin is not to be changed, then our silver should not be reduced farther than to 186 grains for the

This is not an example worthy to be followed. The change ought not to be in the hidden quality which no one but an assayer can determine, but in that which is tangible, and can be tried in a moment. The common mind understands *weight*, but is not so well skilled in fineness; yet it is uneasy at debasement, covered up by a good surface. Moreover, it is a departure from simplicity of proportion to put 835 thousandths in the stead of nine-tenths. We are urged to embrace the French metrical system on account of its easy decimalization; but France does not hesitate to drop the short fraction for a long one. And in the gold coinage, which is of much greater importance, no attention is paid to simple numbers; in fact, the exact weight of the napoleon or twenty-franc piece can only be expressed by a difficult vulgar fraction; the line of decimals is endless. It is still further to be noted that they continue the five-franc silver piece at full weight and fineness, although it can never be kept current at those rates. In this they repeat the mistake made in coining our silver dollar at a different rate from the lesser pieces, or rather in having any silver dollar.

INTERNATIONAL COINAGE.

On this interesting subject, belonging to mint affairs, a few remarks will be offered. There is a question in it on which men of science and men of business are totally at variance; the main question, whether there should be a unification of currency; and there are weighty arguments on each side. But there is one view of the matter which has not been duly considered.

In this proposed unity every country is called upon to make a concession, except France, and those already in conformity with her. If we take part it must be at the expense of a great recoinage, and so with England. But France is supposed to be right already, because her coin, the 20-franc piece, is of such a weight that it cannot be expressed in decimals. It is precisely $6\frac{14}{31}$ grams, a most impracticable and unscientific figure. Nor would the 25-franc piece, the counterpart of the proposed pound sterling and half eagle, make any better show. It is not fit to be measured, either by grams or grains. The history of this matter, how it came to be so, offers no apology for perpetuating such an awkwardness.

It has, therefore, been well suggested to take for the proposed 25-franc piece, or half eagle, or pound sterling, the neat and concise standard of 81 decigrams, (or 8.1 grams,) which has also the merit of being exactly equal to 125 grains. This would make so small a difference from the present French standard that it would probably avoid the necessity of a recoinage there; and so the difference of value in the British sovereign would be so slight as to obviate a recoinage, were it not that the present standard of fineness, eleven-twelfths, is out of the line of unification.

This small change would not affect the earth's quadrant, nor any point of science. It would certainly tend to consummate the business; and it is little enough to ask that France, Belgium, and Italy should do something towards simplicity and uniformity of standards. Indeed, without a spirit of concession all around, the scheme seems not likely to be carried through.

The British commission on international coinage have recently made their report to Parliament, and it is important to note the conclusions at which they arrive after a careful and able investigation.

They say, "we entertain no doubt that a uniform system of coins, as well as a uniform system of weights and measures, would be productive of great general advantage;" and further, "we do not consider it necessary that any measures for the assimilation of the currencies should be postponed until steps are also taken for the assimilation of weights and measures."

But upon full view of the circumstances they "do not recommend that this country should merely adopt a gold coin, of the value of 25 francs, to be substituted for the sovereign." In fine, they think the whole matter should receive further consideration in a general monetary conference.

The report, with testimonies and documents annexed, makes up a large volume, and is a storehouse of valuable information and discussion, chiefly upon this subject, but also upon existing monetary laws in other nations. Such a state paper does honor to the country, and to the commission in particular.

COMMERCIAL CURRENCY OF CHINA.

Our silver dollar is not received by the Chinese except at a discount. This is owing to the fact that while it is of equal fineness with the Spanish or Mexican dollar, it is about one per cent. less in weight. This rejection seems to take away the last plea for continuing to coin this piece.

We have some interesting details on this subject from the master of the British mint at Hong-Kong, established there a few years since for the purpose of furnishing a silver currency, with the Mexican dollar as its basis. The mint has recently been discontinued; but while it lasted its issues were acceptable to the Chinese traders, although the chief part of the coinage found its way to Singapore and the region thereabouts. Fractional parts of the dollar were also struck, both in silver and copper, and it is curious to observe that they followed our centesimal notation, issuing pieces of ten cents, five cents, one cent, and other denominations.

In concluding this report it is proper that I should express my acknowledgment to the officers, clerks, and employés of the mint, for the faithful and efficient manner in which they have performed their respective duties.

The statistics relating to the coinage will be found in the tabular statements hereto annexed; also a statement of the weight, fineness and value of certain foreign coins.

Very respectfully, your obedient servant,

H. R. LINDERMAN,
Director of the Mint.

Hon. HUGH MCCULLOCH,
Secretary of the Treasury, Washington, D. C.

A.—*Statement of deposits at the mint of the United States, the branch mint, San Francisco assay office, New York, and branch mint, Denver, during the fiscal year ending June 30, 1868.*

Description of bullion.	United States mint, Philadelphia.	Branch mint, San Francisco.	Assay office, New York.	Branch mint, Denver.	Total.
GOLD.					
Fine bars	$2, 142, 337 12	$8, 693, 399 01	....	....	$10, 835, 736 13
Unparted bars	....	....	....	....	....
United States bullion	1, 300, 338 53	6, 156, 718 83	$5, 409, 996 53	$357, 935 11	$13, 224, 989 02
United States coin	95, 452 90	....	54, 074 20	....	149, 527 10
Jewellers' bars	157, 418 38	....	269, 598 30	....	427, 016 68
Foreign coins	14, 789 73	73, 098 15	25, 127 27	....	113, 015 15
Foreign bullion	332, 711 97	56, 342 53	333, 556 24	....	722, 610 74
Total gold	4, 043, 048 63	14, 979, 558 52	6, 092, 352 56	357, 935 11	25, 472, 894 82
SILVER.					
Bars	$219, 727 08	$397, 341 00	....	....	$617, 068 08
United States bullion	67, 700 78	253, 898 05	$262, 312 96	$5, 082 67	588, 994 46
United States coin	7, 587 81	....	99, 935 77	....	107, 523 58
Jewellers' bars	26, 320 77	....	85, 807 05	....	112, 327 82
Foreign coin	17, 907 72	53, 671 87	142, 215 87	....	213, 795 46
Foreign bullion	3, 191 56	8, 956 74	41, 566 18	....	53, 714 48
Total silver	342, 635 42	713, 867 66	631, 837 83	5, 082 67	1, 693, 423 88
Total gold and silver	$4, 385, 684 35	$15, 693, 426 18	$6, 724, 190 39	$363, 017 78	$27, 166, 318 70
Less redeposits at different institutions: gold, $2, 355, 128 38; silver, $219, 864 48					2, 574, 992 86
Total deposits					24, 591, 325 84

B.—*Statement of the coinage at the mint of the United States, the branch mint, San Francisco, assay office, New York, and branch mint, Denver, during the fiscal year ending June* 30, 1868.

Denomination.	United States mint, Philadelphia.		Branch mint, San Francisco.		Assay office, New York.	Branch mint, Denver.	Total.	
	Pieces.	Value.	Pieces.	Value.	Value.	Value.	Pieces.	Value.
GOLD.								
Double eagles	188, 540	$3, 770, 800 00	696, 750	$13, 935, 000			885, 290	$17, 705, 800 00
Eagles	3, 050	30, 500 00	12, 500	125, 000			15, 550	155, 500 00
Half eagles	5, 750	28, 750 00	25, 000	125, 000			30, 750	153, 750 00
Three dollars	4, 900	14, 700 00					4, 900	14, 700 00
Quarter eagles	3, 650	9, 125 00	26, 000	65, 000			29, 650	74, 125 00
Dollars	10, 550	10, 550 00					10, 550	10, 550 00
Fine bars	151	98, 848 03			$5, 567, 082 77			5, 665, 930 80
Unparted bars						$360, 879 26		360, 879 26
Total gold	216, 591	3, 963, 273 03	760, 250	14, 250, 000	5, 567, 082 77	360, 879 26	976, 690	24, 141, 235 06
SILVER.								
Dollars	54, 800	$54, 800 00					54, 800	$54, 800 00
Half dollars	411, 500	205, 750 00	1, 482, 000	$741, 000			1, 893, 500	946, 750 00
Quarter dollars	29, 900	7, 475 00	120, 000	30, 000			149, 900	37, 475 00
Dimes	423, 150	42, 315 00	310, 000	31, 000			733, 150	73, 315 00
Half dimes	85, 800	4, 290 00	400, 000	20, 000			485, 800	24, 290 00
Three-cent pieces	4, 000	120 00					4, 000	120 00
Bars	83	6, 729 94						456, 236 48
Total silver	1, 009, 233	321, 479 94	2, 312, 000	822, 000	449, 506 54		3, 321, 150	1, 592, 986 48
COPPER.								
Five-cent pieces	28, 902, 000	1, 445, 100 00					28, 902, 000	$1, 445, 100 00
Three-cent pieces	3, 613, 000	108, 390 00					3, 613, 000	108, 390 00
Two-cent pieces	3, 066, 500	61, 330 00					3, 066, 500	61, 330 00
One-cent pieces	9, 856, 500	98, 565 00					9, 856, 500	98, 565 00
Total copper	45, 438, 000	1, 713, 385					45, 438, 000	1, 713 385 00

C.—*Statement of gold and silver of domestic production deposited at the mint of the United States, the branch mint, San Francisco, assay office, New York, and branch mint, Denver, during the fiscal year ending June 30, 1868.*

Description of bullion.	United States mint, Philadelphia.	Branch mint, San Francisco.	Assay office, New York.	Branch mint, Denver.	Total.
GOLD.					
Alabama	$153 13				$153 13
Arizona	115 01	$77, 620 62	$293 25		78, 028 88
California	25, 640 20	4, 446, 139 27	2, 308, 861 39		6, 780 640 86
Colorado	65, 410 70		657, 694 35	$357, 935 11	1, 081, 040 16
Georgia	36, 675 88		15, 889 05		52, 564 93
Idaho	90, 035 17	867, 845 45	40, 656 38		998, 537 00
Maryland	150 53				150 53
Montana	985, 061 53	268, 059 64	2, 087, 756 32		3, 340, 877 49
Nebraska	2, 231 00				2, 231 00
Nevada	860 97	37, 414 56	338 36		38, 613 89
New Mexico	16, 001 14		21, 299 18		37, 300 32
North Carolina	51, 199 64		38, 706 38		89, 906 02
Oregon	6, 680 39	337, 183 04	5, 225 14		349, 088 57
South Carolina	1, 019 11		587 81		1, 606 92
Tennessee			273 64		273 64
Utah			4, 783 30		4, 783 30
Vermont			898 66		898 66
Virginia	10, 235 21		970 18		11, 205 39
Mint bars			212, 791 26		212, 791 26
Parted from silver	8, 868 92	122, 456 25	12, 971 90		144, 297 07
Fine bars		8, 693, 399 01			8, 693, 399 01
Total gold	1, 300, 338 53	14, 850, 117 84	5, 409, 996 55	357, 935 11	21, 918, 388 03
SILVER.					
Arizona	$249 70	$5, 877 32	$584 27		$6, 711 29
California	406 57	2, 517 45	6, 272 92		9, 195 94
Colorado	16, 163 15		25, 635 31	$5, 082 67	46, 881 13
Idaho		37, 293 70	308 86		37, 602 56
Lake Superior	13, 095 94		13, 499 78		26, 595 72
Minnesota			73 75		73 75
Montana			23, 547 73		23, 547 73
Nevada	18, 197 87	151, 791 92	120, 425 72		290, 415 51
New Mexico			473 56		473 56
Oregon					
Bars		397, 341 00	137 40		397, 478 40
Parted from gold	19, 587 55	56, 417 66	71, 353 66		147, 358 87
Total silver	67, 700 78	651, 239 05	262, 312 96	5, 082 67	986, 335 46
Total gold and silver of domestic production	$1, 368, 039 31	$15, 501, 356 89	$5, 672, 309 51	$363, 017 78	$22, 904, 723 49

D.—*Coinage of the mint and branches from their organization to the close of the fiscal year ending June 30, 1868.*

1. MINT OF THE UNITED STATES, PHILADELPHIA.

Period.	GOLD COINAGE.							SILVER COINAGE.				
	Double eagles.	Eagles.	Half eagles.	Three dolls.	Qr. eagles.	Dollars.	Fine bars.	Dollars.	Half dolls.	Qr. dolls.	Dimes.	Half dimes.
	Pieces.	*Pieces.*	*Pieces.*	*Pieces.*	*Pieces.*	*Pieces.*	*Value.*	*Pieces.*	*Pieces.*	*Pieces.*	*Pieces.*	*Pieces.*
1793 to 1817	....	132, 592	845, 909	....	22, 197	....	....	1, 439, 517	13, 104, 433	650, 280	1, 007, 151	265, 543
1818 to 1837	....	....	3, 087, 925	....	879, 903	....	....	1, 000	74, 793, 560	5, 041, 749	11, 854, 949	14, 463, 700
1838 to 1847	....	1, 227, 759	3, 269, 921	....	345, 526	....	....	879, 873	20, 203, 333	4, 952, 073	11, 387, 995	11, 093, 235
1848 to 1857	8, 122, 526	1, 970, 597	2, 260, 390	223, 015	5, 544, 900	15, 348, 608	$33, 612, 140 46	350, 250	10, 691, 088	41, 073, 080	35, 172, 010	34, 368, 520
1858 to 1867	5, 740, 871	179, 745	795, 075	66, 381	1, 609, 749	2, 360, 834	1, 078, 168 51	758, 700	12, 632, 830	22, 955, 730	6, 042, 330	12, 995, 330
1868	188, 540	3, 050	5, 750	4, 000	3, 650	10, 550	98, 849 03	54, 800	411, 500	29, 900	423, 150	85, 900
Total	14, 051, 937	3, 513, 743	10, 264, 970	294, 296	8, 405, 925	17, 719, 992	34, 789, 157 00	3, 484, 149	131, 836, 744	74, 702, 812	65, 887, 585	73, 272, 128

Period.	SILVER COINAGE.		COPPER COINAGE.					TOTAL COINAGE.				
	Three cents.	Bars.	Five cents.	Three cents.	Two cents.	Cents.	Half cents.	No. of pieces coined.	Gold.	Silver.	Copper.	Total value.
	Pieces.	*Value.*	*Pieces.*	*Pieces.*	*Pieces.*	*Pieces.*	*Pieces.*		*Value.*	*Value.*	*Value.*	
1793 to 1817	....	....	....	....	....	29, 316, 272	5, 235, 513	52, 019, 407	$5, 610, 957 50	$8, 268, 295 75	$319, 340 28	$14,198,593 53
1818 to 1837	....	....	....	....	....	46, 554, 830	2, 205, 200	158, 882, 876	17, 639, 382 50	40, 566, 897 15	476, 574 30	58,682,853 95
1838 to 1847	....	....	....	....	....	34, 967, 663	....	88, 327, 378	29, 491, 010 00	13, 913, 019 00	349, 676 63	43,753,705 63
1848 to 1857	37, 778, 900	$32, 355 55	....	....	....	51, 449, 979	544, 510	244, 898, 373	256, 950, 474 46	22, 365, 413 55	517, 222 34	279,873,110 35
1858 to 1867	4, 209, 330	73, 552 45	32, 574, 000	16, 987, 000	38, 245, 500	284, 909, 000	....	443, 061, 692	128, 169, 899 65	14, 263, 259 97	5, 752, 350 00	148,185,509 62
1868	4, 000	6, 729 94	28, 902, 000	3, 613, 000	3, 066, 500	9, 856, 500	....	46, 663, 590	3, 864, 425 00	314, 750 00	1, 713, 385 00	5,892,560 00
Total	41, 992, 230	112, 637 94	61, 476, 000	20, 600 000	41, 312, 000	457, 054, 244	7, 985, 223	1, 033, 853, 316	441, 726, 149 11	99, 691, 635 42	9, 128, 548 55	350,546,333 08

D.—*Coinage of the mint and branches, &c.*—Continued.

2. BRANCH MINT AT SAN FRANCISCO.

Period.	GOLD COINAGE.							
	Double eagles.	Eagles.	Half eagles.	Three dollars.	Quarter eagles.	Dollars.	Unparted bars.	Fine bars.
	Pieces.	*Pieces.*	*Pieces.*	*Pieces.*	*Pieces.*	*Pieces.*	*Value.*	*Value.*
1854	141, 468	123, 826	268	....	246	14, 632	$5, 641, 504 05	$5, 863 16
1855	859, 175	9, 000	61, 000	6, 600	....	....	3, 270, 594 93	68, 782 50
1856	1, 181, 750	73, 500	94, 100	34, 500	71, 120	24, 600	3, 047, 001 29	122, 136 55
1857	604, 500	10, 000	47, 000	5, 000	20, 000	....	....	....
1858	885, 940	27, 800	58, 600	9, 000	49, 200	20, 000	816, 295 65	....
1859	689, 140	2, 000	9, 720	....	8, 000	15, 000	....	19, 871 63
1860	579, 975	10, 000	16, 700	7, 000	28, 800	13, 000	....	....
1861	614, 300	6, 000	8, 000	....	14, 000	....	....	....
1862	760, 000	18, 000	18, 000	....	30, 000	....	....	....
1863	866, 423	9, 000	16, 500	....	4, 000	....	....	....
1864	947, 320	5, 000	10, 000	....	8, 800	....	....	....
1865	925, 160	8, 700	12, 000	....	6, 256	....	....	....
1866	876, 500	30, 500	53, 420	....	46, 080	....	....	....
1867	901, 000	2, 000	24, 000	....	26, 000	....	....	....
1868	696, 750	12, 500	25, 000	....	26, 000	....	....	....
Total	11, 529, 401	347, 826	454, 308	62, 100	340, 502	87, 232	12, 775, 395 92	236, 653 89

Period.	SILVER COINAGE.						TOTAL COINAGE.			
	Dollars.	Half dollars.	Quarter dollars.	Dimes.	Half dimes.	Bars.	No. of pieces.	Gold.	Silver.	Total value.
	Pieces.	*Pieces.*	*Pieces.*	*Pieces.*	*Pieces.*	*Value.*		*Value.*	*Value.*	
1854	....	....	....	....	....	....	280, 440	$9, 731, 574 21	....	$9, 731, 574 21
1855	....	121, 950	412, 400	....	....	....	1, 470, 125	20, 957, 677 43	$164, 075 00	21, 121, 752 43
1856	....	211, 000	286, 000	....	....	$23, 609 45	1, 976, 570	28, 315, 537 84	200, 609 45	28, 516, 147 29
1857	....	86, 000	28, 000	....	....	....	800, 500	12, 490, 000 00	50, 000 00	12, 540, 000 00
1858	....	218, 000	63, 000	30, 000	....	19, 752 61	1, 361, 540	19, 276, 095 65	147, 502 61	19, 423, 598 26
1859	15, 000	463, 000	172, 000	90, 000	....	29, 469 87	1, 463, 860	13, 906, 271 68	327, 969 87	14, 234, 241 55
1860	5, 000	693, 000	24, 000	40, 000	....	211, 411 52	1, 417, 475	11, 889, 000 00	572, 911 52	12, 461, 911 52
1861	....	350, 000	52, 000	100, 000	....	71, 485 61	1, 144, 300	12, 421, 000 00	269, 485 61	12, 690, 485 61
1862	....	1, 179, 500	120, 000	219, 500	....	1, 278 65	2, 345, 000	15, 545, 000 00	642, 978 65	16, 187, 978 65
1863	....	1, 542, 000	43, 000	291, 250	100, 000	224, 763 63	2, 872, 173	17, 510, 960 00	1, 040, 638 68	18, 551, 598 68
1864	....	648, 000	20, 000	140, 000	90, 000	120, 909 02	1, 869, 120	19, 068, 400 00	468, 409 02	19, 536, 809 02
1865	....	613, 000	22, 000	150, 000	36, 000	145, 235 58	1, 775, 116	18, 670, 840 00	474, 035 58	19, 144, 875 58
1866	....	490, 000	19, 000	210, 000	204, 000	442, 342 64	1, 929, 881	18, 217, 300 00	723, 292 64	18, 940, 592 64
1867	....	1, 216, 000	52, 000	130, 000	....	146, 048 54	2, 351, 133	18, 225, 000 00	780, 048 54	19, 005, 048 54
1868	....	1, 482, 000	120, 000	310, 000	400, 000	....	3, 072, 250	14, 250, 000 00	822, 000 00	15, 072, 000 00
Total	20, 000	9, 313, 450	1, 433, 400	1, 710, 750	830, 000	1, 436, 307 17	26, 129, 483	250, 474, 656 81	6, 683, 957 17	257, 158, 613 98

D.—*Coinage of the mint and branches, &c.*—Continued.

3. BRANCH MINT, NEW ORLEANS.

Period.	GOLD COINAGE.					
	Double eagles.	Eagles.	Half eagles.	Three dollars.	Quarter eagles.	Dollars.
	Pieces.	*Pieces.*	*Pieces.*	*Pieces.*	*Pieces.*	*Pieces.*
1838 to 1847		1,026,342	709,925		550,528	
1848 to 1857	730,500	534,250	108,100	24,000	546,100	1,004,000
1858	47,500	21,500	13,000		34,000	
1859	24,500	4,000				
1860	4,350	8,200				
1861	9,600	5,200				
Total	816,450	1,599,492	831,025	24,000	1,130,628	1,004,000

Period.	SILVER COINAGE.							TOTAL COINAGE.			
	Dollars.	Half dollars.	Qr. dollars.	Dimes.	Half dimes.	Three cents.	Bars.	No. of pieces.	Gold.	Silver.	Total coined.
	Pieces.	*Pieces.*	*Pieces.*	*Pieces.*	*Pieces.*	*Pieces.*	*Value.*		*Value.*	*Value.*	*Value.*
1838 to 1847	59,000	13,509,000	3,273,600	6,473,500	2,789,000			28,390,895	$15,189,365	$8,418,700 00	$23,608,065 00
1848 to 1857	40,000	21,406,000	4,556,000	5,690,000	8,170,000	720,000		43,528,950	22,934,250	12,881,100 00	35,815,350 00
1858		4,614,000	1,416,000	1,540,000	2,540,000		$334,996 47	10,226,000	1,315,000	2,942,000 00	4,257,000 00
1859	200,000	4,912,000	544,000	440,000	1,060,000		25,422 33	7,194,500	530,000	3,223,996 37	3,753,996 57
1860	280,000	2,212,000	388,000	370,000	1,060,060		16,818 33	4,322,550	169,000	1,598,422 33	1,767,422 33
1861	395,000	828,000						1,237,800	244,000	625,818 33	1,069,818 33
Total	974,000	47,481,000	10,177,600	14,513,500	15,619,000	720,000	377,237 13	94,890,695	40,381,615	29,890,037 03	70,271,652 03

4. BRANCH MINT, DENVER.

Period.	Unparted silver bars.	Unparted gold bars.
	Value.	*Value.*
1864		$486,329 97
1865		545,363 00
1866		159,917 76
1867		130,559 70
1868		360,879 26
Total		1,683,049 69

D.—*Coinage of the mint and branches, &c.*—Continued.

4. BRANCH MINT, DAHLONEGA, GEORGIA.

Period.	Gold coinage. Half eagles.	Three dollars.	Qr. eagles.	Dollars.	Total.	Total.
	Pieces.	*Pieces.*	*Pieces.*	*Pieces.*	*Pieces.*	*Value.*
1838 to 1847	576, 553		134, 101		710, 654	$3, 218, 017 50
1848 to 1857	478, 392	1, 120	60, 605	60, 897	601, 014	2, 607, 729 50
1858	19, 256		900	1, 637	21, 793	100, 167 00
1859	11, 404		642	6, 957	19, 003	65, 582 00
1860	12, 800		1, 602	1, 472	15, 874	69, 477 00
1861	11, 876			1, 566	13, 442	60, 946 00
Total	1, 110, 281	1, 120	197, 850	72, 529	1, 381, 780	6, 121, 919 00

5. BRANCH MINT, CHARLOTTE, N. C.

Period.	Gold coinage. Half eagles.	Qr. eagles.	Dollars.	Total.	Total.
	Pieces.	*Pieces.*	*Pieces.*	*Pieces.*	*Value.*
1838 to 1847	269, 424	123, 576		393, 000	$1, 656, 060 00
1848 to 1857	500, 872	79, 736	103, 899	684, 507	2, 807, 599 00
1858	31, 066	9, 056		40, 122	177, 970 00
1859	39, 500		5, 235	44, 735	202, 735 00
1860	23, 005	7, 469		30, 474	133, 697 50
1861	14, 116			14, 116	70, 580 00
Total	877, 983	219, 637	109, 134	1, 206, 954	5, 048, 641 50

6. ASSAY OFFICE, NEW YORK.

Period.	Fine gold bars.	Fine silver bars.	Total.
	Value.	*Value.*	*Value.*
1854	$2, 888, 059 18		$2, 888, 059 18
1855	20, 441, 813 63		20, 441, 813 63
1856	19, 396, 046 89	$6, 792 63	19, 402, 839 52
1857	9, 335, 414 00	123, 317 00	9, 458, 731 00
1858	21, 798, 691 04	171, 961 79	21, 970, 652 83
1859	13, 044, 718 43	272, 424 05	13, 317, 142 48
1860	6, 831, 532 01	222, 226 11	7, 053, 758 12
1861	19, 948, 728 88	187, 078 63	20, 135, 807 51
1862	16, 094, 768 44	415, 603 57	16, 510, 372 01
1863	1, 793, 838 16	158, 542 91	1, 952, 381 07
1864	1, 539, 751 27	173, 308 64	1, 713, 059 91
1865	4, 947, 809 21	165, 003 45	5, 112, 812 66
1866	8, 862, 451 00	459, 594 00	9, 322, 045 00
1867	11, 411, 258 26	425, 155 26	11, 836, 413 52
1868	5, 567, 082 77	449, 506 54	6, 016, 589 31
Total	163, 901, 963 17	3, 230, 514 58	167, 132, 477 75

8. SUMMARY EXHIBIT OF THE COINAGE OF THE MINT AND BRANCHES TO THE CLOSE OF THE FISCAL YEAR ENDING JUNE 30, 1868.

Mints.	Commencement of coinage.	Gold coinage.	Silver coinage.	Copper coinage.	Entire coinage.	
		Value.	*Value.*	*Value.*	*Pieces.*	*Value.*
Philadelphia	1793	$441, 904, 870 50	$90, 702, 984 74	$9, 128, 548 55	1, 033, 853, 686	$541, 736, 403 79
San Francisco	1854	250, 474, 656 81	6, 683, 957 17		26, 129, 483	257, 158, 613 98
New Orleans (Jan. 31, 1865)	1838	40, 381, 615 00	29, 890, 037 13		94, 890, 695	70, 271, 652 13
Charlotte (March 31, 1861)	1838	5, 048, 641 50			1, 206, 954	5, 048, 641 50
Dahlonega (Feb. 28, 1861)	1838	6, 121, 919 00			1, 381, 780	6, 121, 919 00
New York Assay Office	1854	163, 901, 963 17	3, 230, 514 58			167, 132, 477 75
Denver	1863	1, 683, 049 69				1, 683, 049 69
Total		909, 516, 715 67	130, 507, 493 62	9, 128, 548 55	1, 157, 462, 598	1, 049, 152, 757 84

E.—*Statement of gold of domestic production deposited at the mint of the United States and branches to the close of the year ending June 30, 1868.*

1. MINT OF THE UNITED STATES, PHILADELPHIA.

Period.	Parted from silver.	Virginia.	N. Carolina.	S. Carolina.	Georgia.	Tennessee.	Alabama.	New Mexico Territory.	California.	Nebraska.
1804 to 1827			$110,000 00							
1828 to 1837		$427,000 00	2,519,500 00	$327,500 00	$1,763,900 00	$12,400 00				
1838 to 1847		518,294 00	1,303,636 00	152,366 00	586,318 00	16,499 00	$45,493 00			
1848 to 1857		534,491 50	467,237 00	55,626 00	44,577 50	6,669 00	9,451 00	$48,397 00	$226,839,521 62	
1858 to 1867	$105,070 16	77,889 48	214,453 74	6,155 15	129,910 00	835 68	530 06	9,685 33	4,096,277 30	$3,645 08
1868	8,868 92	10,235 21	51,199 64	1,019 11	36,675 88		153 13	16,001 14	25,640 20	2,231 00
Total	113,939.08	1,567,910 19	4,666,026 38	542,667 26	2,541,409 38	36,403 88	55,627 19	74,083 47	230,961,439 12	5,876 08

Period.	Montana Territory.	Oregon.	Colorado Territory.	Arizona Territory.	Washington Territory.	Idaho Territory.	Utah Territory.	Nevada.	Other sources.	Total.
1804 to 1827										$110,000 00
1828 to 1837									$13,200 00	5,063,500 60
1838 to 1847									21,037 00	2,623,641 00
1848 to 1857		$54,285 00							7,218 00	228,067,473 62
1858 to 1867	$3,990,940 52	123,238 80	$5,855,150 23	$7,768 28	$26,127 55	$2,799,559 81	$4,327 11	$2,522 67	5,108 85	17,459,227 00
1868	985,061 53	6,680 39	65,410 70	115 01		90,035 17		860 97	150 53	1,300,338 53
Total	4,976,002 05	184,204 19	5,920,560 93	7,883 29	26,127 55	2,889,594 98	4,327 11	3,383 64	46,714 38	254,624,180 15

E.—*Statement of gold of domestic production, &c.*—Continued.

2. BRANCH MINT, SAN FRANCISCO.

Period.	Parted from silver.	California.	Colorado Territory.	Nevada.	Oregon.	Dakota Territory.	Washington Territory.	Idaho Territory.	Arizona Territory.	Montana Territory.	Refined gold.	Total.
1854		$10, 842, 281 23										$10, 842, 281 23
1855		20, 860, 437 20										20, 860, 437 20
1856		29, 209, 218 24										29, 209, 218 24
1857		12, 526, 826 93										12, 526, 826 93
1858		19, 104, 369 99										19, 104, 369 99
1859		14, 098, 564 14										14, 098, 564 14
1860		11, 319, 913 83										11, 319, 913 83
1861		12, 206, 382 64										12, 206, 382 64
1862	$822, 823 01	14, 029, 759 95	$680 00	$13, 000 00	$888, 000 00							15, 754, 262 96
1863	1, 108, 456 57	13, 045, 711 69	59, 472 00	11, 250 00	3, 001, 104 00	$5, 760 00	$12, 672 00					17, 244, 426 26
1864	220, 890 18	14, 863, 657 52			2, 139, 305 00			$1, 257, 497 50				18, 481, 350 20
1865	217, 935 98	11, 089, 974 52		5, 400 00	1, 103, 076 54		22, 460 94	3, 449, 281 14	$20, 369 48	$3, 000 00	$2, 598, 601 49	16, 510, 100 09
1866	374, 393 28	10, 034, 775 03		43, 497 28	858, 433 11			2, 880, 203 48	30, 430 68	549, 733 32	2, 665, 033 00	17, 436, 499 18
1867	395, 750 76	8, 179, 771 82		48, 677 09	975, 974 30			2, 020, 899 72	23, 437 51	576, 397 80	5, 715, 260 40	17, 936, 169 40
1868	122, 456 25	4, 446, 139 27		37, 414 56	337, 183 04			867, 845 45	77, 620 62	268, 059 64	8, 693, 399 01	14, 850, 117 84
Total	3, 262, 706 03	205, 857, 784 00	60, 152 00	159, 238 93	9, 303, 075 99	5, 760 00	35, 132 94	10, 475, 727 29	151, 858 29	1, 397, 190 76	19, 672, 293 90	250, 380, 920 13

3. BRANCH MINT, NEW ORLEANS.

Period.	North Carolina.	South Carolina.	Georgia.	Tennessee.	Alabama.	California.	Colorado Territory.	Other sources.	Total.
1838 to 1847	$741 00	$14, 306 00	$37, 364 00	$1, 772 00	$61, 903 00			$3, 613 00	$119, 699 00
1848 to 1857		1, 911 00	2, 317 00	947 00	15, 379 00	$21, 606, 461 54		3, 677 00	21, 630, 692 54
1858			1, 560 00	164 12		448, 439 84			450, 163 96
1859						93, 272 41			93, 272 41
1860					661 53	97, 135 00	$1, 770 39		99, 566 92
1861 (to January 31)						19, 932 10	1, 666 81		21, 598 91
Total	741 00	16, 217 00	41, 241 00	2, 883 12	77, 943 53	22, 265, 240 89	3, 437 20	7, 290 00	22, 414, 993 74

E.—*Statement of gold of domestic production, &c.*—Continued.

4. BRANCH MINT, DAHLONEGA.

Period.	Utah Terri'y.	N. Carolina.	S. Carolina.	Georgia.	Tennessee.	Alabama.	California.	Colorado Territory.	Other sources.	Total.
1838 to 1847		$64, 351 00	$95, 427 00	$2, 978, 353 00	$32, 175 00	$47, 711 00				$3, 218, 017 00
1848 to 1857		28, 278 82	174, 811 91	1, 159, 420 98	9, 837 42	11, 918 92	$1, 124, 712 82		$951 00	2, 509, 931 87
1858			32, 322 28	57, 891 45	107 33		5, 293 52			95, 614 58
1859		2, 656 88	4, 610 35	57, 023 12			699 19	$82 70		65, 072 24
1860		3, 485 70	2, 004 36	35, 588 92			1, 097 37	2, 490 86		44, 667 21
1861 (to February 28)	$145 14	812 79	2, 066 91	22, 182 14			4, 213 79	32, 772 28		62, 193 05
Total	145 14	99, 585 19	311, 242 81	4, 310, 439 61	42, 119 75	59, 629 92	1, 136, 016 69	35, 345 84	951 00	5, 995, 495 95

5. BRANCH MINT, CHARLOTTE, N. C.

Period.	N. Carolina.	S. Carolina.	California.	Total.
1838 to 1847	$1, 529, 777 00	$143, 941 00		$1, 673, 718 00
1848 to 1857	2, 503, 412 68	222, 754 17	$87, 321 00	2, 813, 487 85
1858	170, 650 33	5, 507 16		176, 157 49
1859	182, 489 61	22, 762 71		205, 252 32
1860	134, 491 17			134, 491 17
1861 (to March 31)		65, 558 30		65, 558 30
Total	4, 520, 820 79	460, 523 34	87, 321 00	5, 068, 665 13

E.—*Statement of gold of domestic production, &c.*—Continued.

6. ASSAY OFFICE, NEW YORK.

Period.	Parted from silver.	Virginia.	N. Carolina.	S. Carolina.	Georgia.	Alabama.	New Mexico Territory.	California.	Montana Territory.
1854		$167 00	$3,916 00	$395 00	$1,242 00			$9,221,457 00	
1855		2,370 00	3,750 00	7,620 00	13,100 00	$350 00		25,026,896 11	
1856		6,928 00	805 07	4,052 29	41,101 28	233 62		16,529,008 90	
1857		1,531 00	1,689 00	2,663 00	10,451 00	1,545 00		9,899,957 00	
1858		501 00	7,007 00	6,354 00	12,951 00	2,181 00		19,660,531 46	
1859		436 00	20,122 00	700 00	14,756 00	593 00		11,694,872 25	
1860		4,204 00	9,755 00		19,368 00			6,023,628 36	
1861		3,869 00	2,753 00	670 00	6,900 00	818 00	$6,714 00	19,227,658 14	
1862	$241,029 00	316 00	2,232 00	2,065 00	1,469 00		1,543 00	12,580,647 83	
1863	34,328 00		130 00				5,580 00	346,244 60	
1864	7,618 00							116,101 06	
1865	14,003 00				3,422 00	2,269 00	3,924 00	2,177,954 04	$1,217,518 00
1866	79,304 00	1,693 00	29,536 00		11,161 00	1,135 00		4,456,392 00	3,132,370 00
1867	42,935 50	700 74	27,354 50	713 93	8,084 31		9,616 33	5,103,602 24	4,246,410 00
1868	12,971 90	970 18	38,706 38	587 81	15,889 05		21,299 18	2,308,861 39	2,087,756 32
Total	432,189 40	23,685 92	147,755 95	25,821 03	159,894 64	9,124 62	48,676 51	144,373,812 38	10,684,054 32

Period.	Idaho Territory.	Colorado Territory.	Utah Territory.	Arizona Territory.	Orogon.	Nevada.	Vermont.	Other sources.	Total.
1854									$9,227,177 00
1855								$1,600 00	25,055,686 11
1856									16,582,129 16
1857									9,917,836 00
1858					$5,581 00			27,523 00	19,722,629 46
1859		$3,944 00			2,866 00			405 00	11,738,694 25
1860		248,981 00	$4,680 00	$1,190 00					6,311,806 36
1861		1,449,166 00	73,734 00	16,871 00	3,181 00				20,792,334 14
1862		912,403 00		391 00	205 00	$40,846 00		3,293 00	13,786,439 83
1863		937,535 00		391 00	7,813 00		$298 00		1,332,319 60
1864	$201,288 00	715,208 00		3,775 00	8,650 00	74 00		117,347 00	1,170,061 06
1865		938,593 00		707 00	9,876 00	949 00	316 00	364,857 00	4,734,388 04
1866	205,844 00	496,805 00			8,705 00	5,710 00		129,100 00	8,557,755 00
1867	108,467 43	657,390 69			4,377 32				10,209,652 99
1868	40,656 38	657,694 35	4,783 30	293 25	5,225 14	338 36	898 66	273 64	5,197,205 29
Total	556,255 81	7,017,720 04	83,197 30	23,618 25	56,479 46	47,917 36	1,512 66	644,398 64	164,336,114 29

E.—*Statement of gold of domestic production, &c.*—Continued.

7. BRANCH MINT, DENVER.

Period.	Colorado Territory.	Montana Territory.	Idaho Territory.	Oregon.	Arizona Territory.	Total.
1864	$486, 329 97					$486, 329 97
1865	375, 065 90	$93, 613 01	$71, 310 49	$1, 230 16	$339 48	541, 559 04
1866	96, 521 38	44, 134 13	19, 549 89	777 54		160, 982 94
1867	110, 203 82	13, 758 92	531 61	6, 065 35		130, 559 70
1868	357, 935 11					357, 935 11
Total	1, 426, 056 18	151, 506 06	91, 391 99	8, 073 05	339 48	1, 677, 366 76

8. SUMMARY EXHIBIT OF THE ENTIRE DEPOSITS OF DOMESTIC GOLD AT THE MINT OF THE UNITED STATES AND BRANCHES TO JUNE 30, 1868.

Mint.	Parted from silver.	Virginia.	N. Carolina.	S. Carolina.	Georgia.	Alabama.	Tennessee.	Utah Territory.	Nebraska.	Colorado Territory.	California.
Philadelphia	$113, 399 08	$1, 567, 910 19	$4, 666, 026 38	$542, 667 26	$2, 541, 409 38	$55, 627 19	$36, 403 88	$4, 327 11	$5, 876 08	$5, 920, 560 93	$230, 961, 430 12
San Francisco	3, 262, 716 03									60, 152 00	205, 857, 784 00
New Orleans			741 00	16, 217 00	41, 241 00	77, 943 53	2, 883 12			3, 437 20	22, 265, 240 89
Charlotte			4, 520, 730 79	460, 523 34							87, 321 01
Dahlonega			99, 585 19	311, 242 81	4, 310, 459 61	59, 629 92	42, 119 75	145 14		35, 345 84	1, 136, 016 69
N. Y. assay office	432, 189 40	23, 683 92	147, 755 95	25, 821 03	159, 894 64	9, 124 62	273 64	83, 197 30		7, 017, 720 04	144, 372, 812 38
Denver										1, 426, 056 18	
Total	3, 808, 844 51	1, 591, 594 11	9, 434, 839 31	1, 356, 471 44	7, 053, 004 63	202, 325 26	81, 680 39	87, 669 55	5, 876 08	14, 463, 272 19	604, 680, 605 09

Mint.	Montana Territory.	Arizona Territory.	New Mexico Territory.	Oregon.	Nevada.	Washington Territory.	Dakota Territory.	Vermont.	Idaho Territory.	Other sources.	Total.
Philadelphia	$4, 976, 001 78	$7, 883 29	$74, 083 47	$184, 474 19	$3, 383 64	$26, 127 56	$2, 198 88		$2, 889, 594 98	$44, 515 50	$254, 624, 440 88
San Francisco	1, 397, 190 76	151, 858 29		9, 303, 075 99	159, 238 93	35, 132 94	5, 760 00		10, 625, 727 29	19, 672, 293 90	250, 530, 930 13
New Orleans										7, 290 00	22, 414, 993 74
Charlotte											5, 068, 575 14
Dahlonega										951 00	5, 995, 495 95
N. Y. assay office	10, 684, 054 58	23, 618 25	48, 676 51	56, 479 46	47, 917 36			$1, 512 66	556, 255 81	644, 125 00	164, 335, 112 55
Denver	151, 506 66	339 48		8, 073 05					91, 391 99		1, 677, 366 76

F.—*Statement of the silver coinage at the mint of the United States and branches at San Francisco and New Orleans, under the act of February 21, 1853.*

Year.	United States mint, Philadelphia.	Branch mint, San Francisco.	Branch mint, N. Orleans, to Jan. 31, '61.	Total.
1853	$7,806,461 00		$1,225,000 00	$9,031,461 00
1854	5,340,130 00		3,246,000 00	8,586,130 00
1855	1,393,170 00	$164,075 00	1,918,000 00	3,475,245 00
1856	3,150,740 00	177,000 00	1,744,000 00	5,071,740 00
1857	1,333,000 00	50,000 00		1,383,000 00
1858	4,970,980 00	127,750 00	2,942,000 00	8,040,730 00
1859	2,926,400 00	283,500 00	2,689,000 00	5,898,900 00
1860	519,890 00	356,500 00	1,293,000 00	2,169,390 00
1861	1,433,800 00	198,000 00	414,000 00	2,045,800 00
1862	2,168,941 50	641,700 00		2,810,641 50
1863	326,817 80	815,875 00		1,142,692 80
1864	177,544 10	347,500 00		525,044 10
1865	278,279 66	474,635 58		752,915 24
1866	399,314 50	723,292 64		1,122,607 14
1867	352,871 00	780,048 54		1,132,919 54
1868	314,750 00	822,000 00		1,136,750 00
Total	32,893,089 56	5,961,876 76	15,471,000 00	54,325,966 32

G.—*Statement of the amount of silver and domestic production deposited at the mint of the United States and branches from January, 1841, to June 30, 1868.*

Year.	Parted from gold.	Oregon.	Arizona Territory.	Nevada.	Lake Superior.	Idaho Territory.	Georgia.	California.	Montana Territory.	N. Mexico Territory & Sonora.	North Carolina.	Colorado Territory.	Bars.	Total.
1841 to 1851	$768,509 00													$768,509 00
1852	404,494 00													404,494 00
1853	417,297 00													417,297 00
1854	328,199 00													328,199 00
1855	333,053 00													333,053 00
1856	321,938 38													321,938 38
1857	127,256 12													127,256 12
1858	300,849 36				$15,623 00									316,472 36
1859	219,647 34				30,122 13						$23,398 60			273,167 47
1860	138,561 70		$13,357 00	$102,540 57	25,880 58					$1,200 00	12,257 00			293,796 85
1861	364,724 73		12,260 00	213,420 84	13,372 72						6,233 00			610,011 29
1862	245,122 47		105 00	757,446 60	21,366 38			$824 00						1,024,864 45
1863	188,394 94			856,043 27	13,111 32									1,057,549 53
1864	166,791 55			311,837 01	8,765 77					45 00				487,439 33
1865	251,757 87			355,910 42	13,671 51			459 18		25 84				621,824 82
1866	271,888 51	$1,580 51	139 63	540,345 87	22,913 96	$38,859 49	$403 83	453 00				$419 00	$16,278 22	893,282 02
1867	265,932 64	183 68	3,212 26	579,931 76	18,535 35	160,269 24		310 25	$19,095 48		(*)	543 78	10,709 00	1,058,743 44
1868	147,358 87		6,711 29	290,415 51	26,595 72	37,602 56		9,196 94	23,547 73	473 56	73 75	46,881 13	397,478 40	986,335 46
Total	5,261,776 48	1,764 19	35,785 18	4,007,891 85	209,978 44	236,731 29	403 83	11,243 37	42,643 21	1,744 40	41,961 75	47,843 91	424,465 62	10,324,233 52

* Minnesota.

W.—*Silver coins.*

Country.	Denominations.	Weight.	Fineness.	Value.
		Oz. dec.	*Thous.*	
Austria	Old rix dollar	0. 902	833	$1 02. 3
	Old scudo	0. 836	902	1 02. 6
	Florin before 1858	0. 451	833	51. 1
	New florin	0. 397	900	48. 6
	New Union dollar	0. 596	900	73. 1
	Maria Theresa dollar, 1780	0. 895	838	1 02. 1
Belgium	Five francs	0. 803	897	98. 0
Bolivia	New dollar	0. 643	903. 5	79. 1
	Half dollar	0. 432	667	39. 2
Brazil	Double milreis	0. 820	918. 5	1 02. 5
Canada	Twenty cents	0. 150	925	18. 9
Central America	Dollar	0. 866	850	1 00. 2
Chili	Old dollar	0. 864	908	1 06. 8
	New dollar	0. 801	900. 5	98. 2
China, Hong Kong	Dollar (English) assumed	0. 866	901	1 06. 2
	Ten cents	0. 087	901	10. 6
Denmark	Two rigsdaler	0. 927	877	1 10. 7
England	Shilling, new	0. 182. 5	924. 5	21. 0
* England	Shilling, average	0. 178	925	22. 4
France	Five francs, average	0. 800	900	98. 0
	Two francs, 1867–'8	0. 320	835	36. 4
Germany, north	Thaler before 1857	0. 712	750	72. 7
	New thaler	0. 595	900	72. 9
Germany, south	Florin before 1857	0. 340	900	41. 7
	New florin, (assumed)	0. 340	900	41. 7
Greece	Five drachms	0. 719	900	88. 1
Hindostan	Rupee	0. 374	916	46. 6
Japan	Itzebu	0. 279	991	37. 6
	New itzebu	0. 279	890	33. 8
Mexico	Dollar, new	0. 867. 5	903	1 06. 6
	Dollar, average	0. 866	901	1 06. 2
	Péso of Maximilian	0. 861	902. 5	1 05. 5
Naples	Scudo	0. 844	830	95. 3
Netherlands	2½ guilders	0. 804	944	1 03. 3
Norway	Specie daler	0. 927	877	1 10. 7
New Granada	Dollar of 1857	0. 803	896	98. 0
Peru	Old dollar	0. 866	901	1 06. 2
	Dollar of 1858	0. 766	909	94. 8
	Half dollar, 1835–'38	0. 433	650	38. 3
	Sol	0. 802	900	98. 2
Prussia	Thaler before 1857	0. 712	750	72. 7
	New thaler	0. 595	900	72. 9
Rome	Scudo	0. 864	900	1 05. 8
Russia	Rouble	0. 667	875	79. 4
Sardinia	Five lire	0. 800	900	98. 0
Spain	New pistareen	0. 166	899	20. 3
Sweden	Rix dollar	0. 092	750	1 11. 5
Switzerland	Two francs	0. 323	899	39. 5
Tunis	Five piastres	0. 511	898. 5	62. 5
Turkey	Twenty piastres	0. 770	830	87. 0
Tuscany	Florin	0. 220	925	27. 6

* Less pieces in proportion.

Weight and value of United States silver coins.

				Weight in grains.
United States	Dollar, (legal)	0. 859. 375	900	412. 5
	Half dollar	0. 406.	900	192
	Quarter dollar	0. 200.	900	96
	Dime	0. 080.	900	38. 4
	Half dime	0. 040.	900	19. 2
	Three cents	0. 024.	900	11. 52

X.—*Gold coins.*

Country.	Denominations.	Weight.	Fineness.	Value.	Value after deduction.
Australia	Pound of 1852	0. 281	916. 5	$5 32. 4	$5 29. 7
	Sovereign of 1855-'60	0. 256. 5	916	4 85. 7	4 83. 3
Austria	Ducat	0. 112	986	2 28. 3	2 27
	Sovereign	0. 363	900	6 75. 4	6 72
	New Union crown, assumed	0. 357	900	6 64. 2	6 60. 9
Belgium	Twenty-five francs	0. 254	899	4 72	4 69. 8
Bolivia	Doubloon	0. 867	870	15 59. 3	15 51. 5
Brazil	Twenty milreis	0. 575	917. 5	10 90. 6	10 85. 1
Central America	Two escudos	0. 209	853. 5	3 68. 8	3 66. 9
	Four reals	0. 027	875	48. 8	48. 6
Chili	Old doubloon	0. 867	870	15 59. 3	15 51. 5
	Ten pesos	0. 492	900	9 15. 4	9 10. 8
Denmark	Ten thaler	0. 427	895	7 90	7 86. 1
Ecuador	Four escudos	0. 433	844	7 55. 5	7 51. 7
England	Pound or sovereign, new	0. 256. 7	916. 5	4 86. 3	4 83. 9
	Pound or sovereign, average	0. 256. 2	916	4 85. 1	4 82. 7
France	Twenty francs, new	0. 207. 5	899	3 85. 8	3 83. 9
	Twenty francs, average	0. 207	899	3 84. 7	3 82. 8
Germany, north	Ten thaler	0. 427	895	7 90	7 86. 1
	Ten thaler, Prussian	0. 427	903	7 97. 1	7 93. 1
	Krone, (crown)	0. 357	900	6 64. 2	6 60. 9
Germany, south	Ducat	0. 112	986	2 28. 2	2 27. 1
Greece	Twenty drachms	0. 185	900	3 44. 2	3 42. 5
Hindostan	Mohur	0. 374	916	7 08. 2	7 04. 6
Italy	Twenty lire	0. 207	898	3 84. 3	3 82. 3
Japan	Old cobang	0. 362	568	4 44	4 41. 8
	Old cobang	0. 289	572	3 57. 6	3 55. 8
Mexico	Doubloon, average	0. 867. 5	866	15 53	15 45. 2
	Doubloon, new	0. 867. 5	870. 5	15 61. 1	15 53. 3
	Twenty pesos, (Max)	1. 086	875	19 64. 3	19 54. 5
Naples	Six ducati, new	0. 245	996	5 04. 4	5 01. 9
Netherlands	Ten guilders	0. 215	899	3 99. 7	3 97. 6
New Granada	Old doubloon, Bogata	0. 868	870	15 61. 1	15 53. 3
	Old doubloon, Papayan	0. 867	858	15 37. 8	15 30. 1
	Ten pesos	0. 525	891. 5	9 67. 5	9. 62. 7
Peru	Old doubloon	0. 867	868	15 55. 7	15 47. 9
	Twenty soles	1. 035	898	19 21. 3	19 11. 7
Portugal	Gold crown	0. 308	912	5 80. 7	5 77. 8
Prussia	New Union crown, assumed	0. 357	900	6 64. 2	6 60. 9
Rome	Two-and-a-half scudi, new	0. 140	900	2 60. 5	2 59. 2
Russia	Five roubles	0. 210	916	3 97. 6	3 95. 7
Spain	One hundred reals	0. 268	896	4 96. 4	4 93. 9
	Eighty reals	0. 215	869. 5	3 86. 4	3 84. 5
Sweden	Ducat	0. 111	975	2 23. 7	2 22. 6
Tunis	Twenty-five piastres	0. 161	900	2 99. 5	2 98. 1
Turkey	One hundred piastres	0. 231	915	4 36. 9	4 34. 8
Tuscany	Seguin	0. 112	999	2 31. 3	2 30. 1

Weight and value of United States gold coins.

					Weight in grains.
United States	Dollar legal	0. 053. 75	900	$1 00	25. 8
	Quarter eagle	0. 134. 37	900	2 50	64. 5
	Three dollar	0. 161. 25	900	3 00	77. 4
	Half eagle	0. 268. 75	900	5 00	129
	Eagle	0. 537. 5	900	10 00	258
	Double eagle	1. 075	900	20 00	516

Gold, silver, and copper coinage at the mint of the United States in the several years from its establishment in 1792, *the coinage at the branch mints and the assay office, New York, from their organization, to June* 30, 1867.

Years.	Gold.	Silver.	Copper.	Total.
1793-1795	$71, 485 00	$370, 683 80	$11, 373 00	$453, 541 80
1796	102, 727 50	79, 077 50	10, 324 40	192, 129 40
1797	103, 423 50	12, 591 45	9, 510 34	125, 524 29
1798	205, 610 00	330, 291 00	9, 797 00	545, 698 00
1799	213, 285 00	323, 515 00	9, 106 68	645, 906 68
800	317, 760 00	224, 296 00	29, 279 40	571, 335 40
	1, 014, 290 00	1, 44 , 454 75	79, 390 82	2, 534, 135 57

Gold, silver, and copper coinage at the mint of the United States, &c.—Continued.

Years.	Gold.	Silver.	Copper.	Total.
1801	$422, 570 00	$74, 758 00	$13, 628 37	$510, 956 37
1802	423, 310 00	58, 343 00	34, 422 83	516, 075 83
1803	258, 377 50	87, 118 00	25, 203 03	370, 698 53
1804	258, 642 50	100, 340 50	12, 844 94	371, 827 94
1805	170, 367 50	149, 388 50	13, 483 48	333, 239 48
1806	324, 505 00	471, 319 00	5, 260 00	801, 084 00
1807	437, 495 00	597, 448 75	9, 652 21	1, 044, 595 96
1808	284, 665 00	684, 300 00	13, 090 00	982, 055 00
1809	169, 375 00	707, 376 00	8, 001 53	884, 752 53
1810	501, 435 00	638, 773 50	15, 660 00	1, 155, 868 50
	3, 250, 742 50	3, 569, 165 25	151, 246 39	6, 971, 154 14
1811	$497, 905 00	$608, 340 00	$2, 495 95	$1, 108, 740 95
1812	290, 435 00	814, 029 50	10, 755 00	1, 115, 219 50
1813	477, 140 00	620, 951 50	4, 180 00	1, 102, 271 50
1814	77, 270 00	561, 687 50	3, 578 30	642, 535 80
1815	3, 175 00	17, 308 00	....	20, 483 00
1816	....	28, 575 75	28, 209 82	56, 785 57
1817	....	607, 783 50	39, 484 00	647, 267 50
1818	242, 940 00	1, 070, 454 50	31, 670 00	1, 345, 064 50
1819	258, 615 00	1, 140, 000 00	26, 710 00	1, 425, 325 00
1820	1, 319, 030 00	501, 680 70	44, 075 50	1, 864, 786 20
	3, 166, 510 00	5, 970, 810 95	191, 158 57	9, 328, 479 52
1821	$189, 325 00	$825, 762 45	$3, 890 00	$1, 018, 977 45
1822	88, 980 00	805, 806 50	20, 723 39	915, 509 89
1823	72, 425 00	895, 550 00	....	967, 975 00
1824	93, 200 00	1, 752, 477 00	12, 620 00	1, 858, 297 00
1825	156, 385 00	1, 564, 583 00	14, 926 00	1, 735, 894 00
1826	92, 245 00	2, 002, 090 00	16, 344 25	3, 110, 679 25
1827	131, 565 00	2, 869, 200 00	23, 577 32	3, 024, 342 32
1828	140, 145 00	1, 575, 600 00	25, 636 24	1, 741, 381 24
1829	295, 717 50	1, 994, 578 00	16, 580 00	2, 306, 875 50
1830	643, 105 00	2, 495, 400 00	17, 115 00	3, 155, 620 00
	1, 903, 092 50	16, 781, 046 95	151, 412 20	18, 835, 551 65
1831	$714, 270 00	$3, 175, 600 00	$33, 603 60	$3, 923, 473 60
1832	798, 435 00	2, 579, 000 00	23, 620 00	3, 401, 065 00
1833	978, 550 00	2, 759, 000 00	28, 160 00	3, 765, 710 00
1834	3, 954, 270 00	3, 415, 002 00	19, 151 00	7, 388, 423 00
1835	2, 186, 175 00	3, 443, 003 00	39, 489 00	5, 668, 667 00
1836	4, 135, 700 00	3, 606, 100 00	23, 100 00	7, 764, 900 00
1837	1, 148, 305 00	2, 096, 010 00	55, 583 00	3, 299, 898 00
1838	1, 809, 595 00	2, 315, 250 00	63, 702 00	4, 188, 547 00
1839	1, 375, 760 00	2, 098, 636 00	31, 286 61	3, 505, 682 00
1840	1, 690, 802 00	1, 712, 178 00	24, 627 00	3, 427, 607 61
	18, 791, 862 00	27, 199, 779 00	342, 322 21	46, 333, 963 21
1841	$1, 102, 107 50	$1, 115, 875 00	$15, 973 67	$2, 233, 957 17
1842	1, 833, 170 50	2, 325, 750 00	23, 833 90	4, 182, 754 40
1843	8, 302, 797 50	3, 722, 260 00	24, 283 20	12, 049, 330 70
1844	5, 428, 230 00	2, 230, 550 00	23, 977 52	7, 687, 757 51
1845	3, 756, 447 50	1, 873, 200 00	38, 948 04	5, 668, 595 54
1846	4, 034, 176 57	2, 558, 580 00	41, 208 00	6, 633, 965 50
1847	20, 221, 385 00	2, 374, 450 00	61, 836 69	22, 657, 671 60
1848	3, 775, 512 50	2, 040, 050 00	64, 157 99	5, 879, 720 49
1849	9, 007, 761 50	2, 114, 950 00	41, 984 32	11, 164, 695 82
1850	31, 981, 738 50	1, 866, 100 00	44, 467 50	33, 392, 306 00
	89, 443, 328 00	22, 226, 755 00	380, 670 83	112, 050, 753 83
1851	$62, 614, 492 50	$774, 397 00	$99, 635 43	$63, 488, 524 93
1852	56, 846, 187 50	999, 410 00	50, 630 94	57, 896, 228 44
1853	55, 213, 906 94	9, 077, 571 00	67, 059 78	64, 358, 537 72
1854	52, 094, 595 47	8, 619, 270 00	42, 638 35	60, 756, 503 82
1855	52, 795, 457 20	3, 501, 245 00	16, 030 79	56, 312, 732 99
1856	59, 343, 365 35	5, 196, 670 17	27, 106 78	64, 567, 142 30
1857, (Jan. 1 to June 30, inclusive)	25, 183, 138 68	1, 601, 644 46	63, 510 46	26, 848, 293 60
1858, fiscal year	52, 889, 800 29	8, 233, 287 77	234, 000 00	61, 357, 088 06
1859, fiscal year	30, 409, 953 70	6, 833, 621 47	307, 000 00	37, 550, 585 17
1860, fiscal year	23, 447, 283 35	3, 250, 636 26	342, 000 00	27, 039, 919 61
	470, 838, 180 98	48, 087, 763 13	1, 249, 612 53	520, 175, 55 64

Years.	Gold.	Silver.	Copper.	Total.
1861	$80, 708, 400 64	$2, 883, 706 94	$101, 660 00	$83, 693, 767 58
1862	61, 676, 576 55	3, 231, 081 51	116, 000 00	65, 023, 658 06
1863	22, 645, 729 90	1, 564, 207 22	478, 450 00	24, 688, 477 12
1864	23, 982, 748 31	850, 086 99	463, 800 00	25, 296, 635 30
1865	30, 685, 699 95	950, 218 69	1, 183, 330 00	32, 819, 248 64
1866	37, 429, 430 46	1, 596, 646 58	646, 570 00	39, 672, 647 04
1867	39, 838, 878 82	1, 562, 694 18	1, 879, 540 00	43, 281, 113 00
1868	24, 141, 245 06	1, 592, 986 48	1, 713, 385 00	27, 447, 616 54
	321, 108, 709 69	14, 231, 718 59	6, 582, 735 00	341, 923, 157 28

RECAPITULATION OF COINAGE FROM 1793 TO 1868, INCLUSIVE.

Years.	Gold.	Silver.	Copper.	Total.
1793-1800, 8 years	$1, 014, 290 00	$1, 440, 454 75	$79, 390 82	$2, 534, 135 57
1801-1810, 10 years	3, 250, 742 50	3, 569, 165 25	151, 246 39	6, 971, 154 14
1811-1820, 10 years	3, 166, 510 00	5, 970, 810 95	191, 158 57	9, 328, 479 52
1821-1830, 10 years	1, 903, 092 50	16, 781, 046 95	151, 412 20	18, 835, 551 65
1831-1840, 10 years	18, 791, 862 00	27, 199, 779 00	342, 322 21	46, 333, 963 21
1841-1850, 10 years	89, 443, 328 00	22, 226, 755 00	380, 670 83	112, 050, 753 83
1851-1860, 9½ years	470, 838, 180 98	48, 087, 763 13	1, 249, 612 53	520, 175, 556 64
1861-1868, 8 years	321, 108, 709 69	14, 231, 718 59	6, 582, 735 60	341, 923, 163 28
Total 75 years	909, 516, 715 67	139, 507, 493 62	9, 128, 548 55	1, 058, 152, 757 84

RECAPITULATION OF AVERAGES OF COINAGE FOR EACH DECADE FROM 1793 TO 1868, INCLUSIVE.

Years.	Gold.	Silver.	Copper.	Total.
1793-1800, 8 years	$126, 786 25	$180, 056 84	$9, 923 85	$316, 766 94
1801-1810, 10 years	325, 074 25	356, 916 52	15, 124 64	697, 115 41
1811-1820, 10 years	316, 651 00	597, 081 09	19, 115 86	932, 847 95
1821-1830, 10 years	190, 309 25	1 678, 104 69	15, 141 22	1, 883, 555 16
1831-1840, 10 years	1, 879, 186 20	2, 719, 977 90	34, 232 22	4, 633, 396 32
1841-1850, 10 years	8, 944, 332 80	2, 222, 675 50	38, 067 08	11, 205, 075 38
1851-1860, 9½ years	49, 561, 913 79	5, 061, 869 80	131, 538 16	54, 755, 321 75
1861-1868, 8 years	40, 138, 587 46	1, 778, 964 82	822, 840 62	42, 740, 392 90

Statement showing the present liabilities of the United States to Indian tribes under stipulations of treaties, &c.

Names of tribes.	Description of annuities, stipulations, &c.	Reference to laws; Statutes at Large.	Number of instalments yet unappropriated, explanations, remarks, &c.	Annual amount necessary to meet stipulations, indefinite as to time, now allowed, but liable to be discontinued.	Aggregate of future appropriations that will be required during a limited number of years to pay limited annuities incidentally necessary to effect the payment.	Amount of annual liabilities of a permanent character.	Amount held in trust by the United States on which five per cent. is annually paid; and amounts which, invested at five per cent., would produce permanent annuities.
Assinaboines	Twenty instalments to be made during the pleasure of Congress; to be expended at the discretion of the President in such articles, goods, and provisions as he may from time to time determine; $10,000 of which may be expended in the purchase of stock, animals, &c.	Not published	7th article treaty July 18, 1866, eighteen instalments unappropriated, estimated at $30,000 each.		$540,000 00		
Arickarees, Gros Ventres, and Mandans.	Twenty instalments to be made during the pleasure of Congress; to be expended in such goods, provisions, and other articles as the President may from time to time determine; $5,000 of which to be expended in stock, animals, &c.	...do	7th article treaty July 27, 1866, eighteen instalments unappropriated, estimated at $40,000 each.		720,000 00		
Apaches, Kiowas, and Comanches.	Thirty instalments provided to be expended under 10th article treaty Oct. 21, 1867.	...do	Twenty-nine instalments unappropriated at $30,000 each.		870,000 00		
Do	Purchase of clothing	...do	10th article treaty Oct. 21, 1867	$26,000 00			
Do	For construction of buildings for carpenter, farmer, blacksmith, miller, and engineer.	...do	4th article treaty Oct. 21, 1867, estimated at $2,000 each house.	10,000 00			
Do	For erection of steam circular saw-mill, with grist mill and shingle machine attached.	...do	4th article treaty Oct. 21, 1867	8,000 00			
Do	For pay of carpenter, farmer, blacksmith, miller, and engineer, physician and teacher.	...do	14th article treaty Oct. 21, 1867	7,700 00			
Do	For construction of school-house or mission building and dwelling house for Tosh-e-wa, (or Silver Brooch.)	...do	4th and 15th article treaty Oct. 21, 1867.	5,750 00			
Do	Three instalments to be expended in presents to the ten persons of said tribe who shall grow the most valuable crops.	...do	15th article treaty Oct. 21, 1867; three instalments unappropriated, at $500 each.		1,500 00		
Do	For transportation of goods, &c.	...do		7,000 00			
Calapooias, Molallas,	Five instalments of the 3d series of annuity for	Vol. 10, page 1144	2d article treaty Jan. 22, 1855; one		6,500 00		

Cheyennes and Arapahoes.	Thirty instalments provided to be expended under 10th article treaty Oct. 28, 1867.	Not published	Twenty-nine instalments unappropriated, at $20,000 each.		580,000 00		
Do	For the purchase of clothing	do	10th article treaty Oct. 28, 1867	20,000 00			
Do	For the construction of five buildings for carpenter, farmer, blacksmith, miller, and engineer; for erection of steam circular saw-mill, with grist mill and shingle machine attached, and for construction of school-house or mission building.	do	4th article treaty Oct. 28, 1867	23,000 00			
Do	Three instalments to be expended in presents to the ten persons of said tribe who may grow the most valuable crop.	do	14th article treaty Oct. 28, 1867; three instalments to be appropriated, at $500 each.		1,500 00		
Chasta, Scoton, and Umpquas.	$2,000 annually for fifteen years	Vol. 10, page 1122	3d article treaty Nov. 18, 1854; one instalment yet due.		2,000 00		
Do	Support of schools and farmer fifteen years	Vol. 10, page 1123	Same treaty 5th article; estimated for schools, $1,200, farmer, $1,000, one appropriation due.		2,200 00		
Chippewas of Saginaw, Swan creek, and Black river.	For this amount to be placed to the credit of the educational fund of the Chippewas of Saginaw, Swan creek, and Black river.	Vol. 14, page 657	4th article treaty Oct. 18, 1860	20,000 00			
Chippewas of Lake Superior.	Twenty instalments in coin, goods, implements, &c., and for education.	Vol. 10, page 1111	4th article treaty Sept. 30, 1854; six instalments unappropriated, estimated at $19,000.		114,000 00		
Do	Twenty instalments for six smiths and assistants, and for iron and steel.	do	5th article treaty Sept. 30, 1854; six instalments unappropriated, estimated at $6,360 each.		38,160 00		
Do	Twenty instalments for the seventh smith, &c	do	Eight instalments unappropriated, at $1,060 each.		8,480 00		
Do	For support of a smith and shop, and pay of two farmers during the pleasure of the President.	Vol. 11, page 1112, vol. 14, page 766	12th article treaty Sept. 30, 1854, and 3d article treaty April 7, 1866, estimated at $1,800 per annum.	1,800 00			
Do	For insurance, transportation, &c., of annuities and provisions.		Estimated at $5,762 63 per annum.	5,762 63			
Chippewas, Boise Forte band.	Twenty instalments for support of one blacksmith and assistant, and for tools, iron, &c.	Vol. 14, page 766	3d article treaty April 7, 1866; seventeen instalments unappropriated, estimated at $1,500 each.		25,500 00		
Do	Twenty instalments for the support of schools, and for the instruction of the Indians in farming and purchase of seed, tools, &c.	do	3d article treaty April 7, 1866; seventeen instalments unappropriated, estimated at $1,600 each.		27,200 00		
Do	Twenty instalments of annuity in money, goods, and other articles, in provisions, ammunition, and tobacco.	do	3d article treaty April 7, 1866; annuity, $3,500; goods, &c., $6,500; provisions, ammunition, and tobacco, $1,000; seventeen instalments unappropriated.		187,000 00		
Do	For transportation, &c., of annuity goods	do	6th article treaty April 7, 1866	1,500 00			
Chippewas of the Mississippi.	Money, goods, support of schools, provisions, and tobacco; 4th article treaty Oct. 4, 1842; 8th article treaty Sept. 30, 1854, and 3d article treaty May 7, 1864.	Vol. 7, page 592; vol. 10, page 1111; and page 86, sec. 3, pamphlet copy of laws.	Ten instalments of the second series, at $9,000 01; eight instalments to be appropriated.		72,000 08		

NOTE.—The reference mark thus (*) are to the pamphlet copy of Laws, 1st session 39th Congress.

Statement showing the present liabilities of the United States to Indian tribes, &c.—Continued.

Name of tribes.	Description of annuities, stipulations, &c.	Reference to laws; Statutes at large.	Number of instalments yet unappropriated, explanations, remarks, &c.	Annual amount necessary to meet stipulations, indefinite as to time, now allowed, but liable to be discontinued.	Aggregate of future appropriations that will be required during a limited number of years to pay limited annuities incidentally necessary to effect the payment.	Amount of annual liabilities of a permanent character.	Amount held in trust by the United States on which five per cent. is annually paid; and amounts which, invested at five per cent., would produce permanent annuities.
Chippewas of the Mississippi—Continued.	Two farmers, two carpenters, two smiths and assistants, iron and steel; same article and treaty.	Vol. 7, page 592; vol. 10, page 1111; pamphlet copy laws, 2d sess. 38th Congress, page 86, sec. 3.	Ten instalments of the second series, at $1,400; eight instalments unappropriated.	....	$11,200 00	....	....
Do............	Twenty instalments in money of $20,000 each..	Vol. 10, page 1167..	3d article treaty Feb. 22, 1855; six unexpended.	....	120,000 00	....	....
Do............	Twenty-six instalments of $1,000 each to be paid to the Chippewas of the Mississippi.	....do	3d article treaty Aug. 2, 1847, and 5th article treaty Mar. 19, 1867; four instalments unappropriated.	....	4,000 00	....	....
Do............	Ten instalments for support of schools in promoting the progress of the people in agriculture, and assist them to become self-sustaining, support of physician, and purchase of medicine.	Not published......	3d article treaty Mar. 19, 1867; nine instalments unappropriated, at $1,500.	....	103,500 00	....	....
Do............	For insurance, transportation, &c., of annuities and provisions.	....do	6th article treaty Mar. 19, 1867....	$5,000 00	....	....	....
Chippewas, Pillager and Lake Winnebagoshish bands.	Money, $10,666 66; goods, $8,000; and purpose of utility, $4,000; 3d article treaty of Feb. 22, 1855.	Vol. 10, page 1168..	Thirty instalments: sixteen instalments unappropriated, estimated at $22,666 66.	....	362,666 53	....	....
Do............	For purposes of education: same article and treaty.	....do	Twenty instalments of $3,000 each; six instalments yet due.	....	18,000 00	....	....
Do............	For support of smiths' shops: same article and treaty.	....do	Fifteen instalments of $2,120 each; one yet due.	....	2,120 00	....	....
Do............	For engineer at Leech lake: same article and treaty.	....do	Ten instalments of $600 each; one unappropriated.	....	600 00	....	....
Chippewas of the Mississippi, Pillager and Lake Winnebagoshish bands of Chippewa Indians in Minnesota.	Ten instalments of $1,500 each, to furnish said Indians with oxen, log chains, &c., 5th article treaty May 7, 1864.	Vol. 13, page 694...	Five instalments unappropriated.	....	7,500 00	....	....

Do	This amount to be applied for the support of a saw-mill, as long as the President may deem necessary.	...do	6th article treaty May 7, 1864; annual appropriation.	1,000 00			
Do	Pay of services and travelling expenses of a board of visitors, not more than five persons, to attend annuity payments to the Indians, &c.	...do	7th article treaty May 7, 1864	650 00			
Do	For pay of female teachers employed on the reservation.	Vol. 13, page 695	13th article treaty May 7, 1864	1,000 00			
Chippewas of Red Lake and Pembina tribe of Chippewas.	$10,000, as annuity, to be paid per capita to the Red Lake band, and $5,000 to the Pembina band, during the pleasure of the President.	Vol. 13, pages 668 and 689.	3d article treaty Oct. 2, 1863, and 2d article supplementary treaty April 12, 1864; annual appropriation required.	15,000 00			
Do	Fifteen instalments of $12,000 each, for the purpose of supplying them with gilling twine, cotton maitre, linsey, blankets, sheetings, &c.	Vol. 13, pages 689 and 690.	3d article supplementary treaty April 12, 1864; estimated for Red Lake band, $8,000; Pembina band, $4,000; ten instalments unappropriated.		120,000 00		
Do	One blacksmith, one physician, &c., one miller, one farmer, $3,900; iron and steel, and other articles, $1,500; carpentering, &c., $1,000.	Vol. 13, page 690	4th article supplementary treaty April 12, 1864; fifteen instalments, ten unappropriated, at $6,400 each.		64,000 00		
Do	To defray the expenses of a board of visitors, not more than three persons, to attend the annuity payments of said Chippewa Indians.	Vol. 13, page 668	6th article treaty Oct. 2, 1863; fifteen instalments of $390 each; ten unappropriated.		3,900 00		
Do	For insurance and transportat'n of annuity goods, &c., and material for building mill, &c., &c.		Estimated at $10,000 per annum	10,000 00			
Chickasaws	For permanent annuity in goods	Vol. 1, page 619	Act of Feb. 25, 1799; $3,000 per year.			$3,000 00	
Choctaws	Permanent annuities	Vol. 7, pages 99 and 614, and vol. 11, pages 213 and 236	2d article treaty Nov. 16, 1805, $3,000; 13th article treaty Oct. 18, 1820, $600; 2d article treaty Jan. 20, 1825, $6,000.			9,600 00	
Do	Provisions for smiths, &c	Vol. 7, page 212	6th article treaty Oct. 18, 1820, and 9th article treaty Jan. 20, 1825.			920 00	
Do	Interest on $390,257 92; articles 10 and 13 treaty Jan. 22, 1855.	Vol. 11, pages 613 and 614.	Five per cent. for educational purposes.			19,512 89	$390,257 80
Confederated bands and tribes in Middle Oregon.	For beneficial objects, at the discretion of the President; 2d article treaty June 25, 1855.	Vol. 12, page 964	Five instalments, of $6,000 each, of the 2d series, one unappropriated.		6,000 00		
Do	For farmer, blacksmith, and wagon and plough maker, for the term of fifteen years.	Vol. 12, page 965	4th article treaty June 25, 1855; six instalments unappropriated, estimated at $3,500 each.		21,000 00		
Do	For physician, sawyer, miller, superintendent of farming, and school teacher, twenty years.	...do	4th article treaty June 25, 1855; eleven instalments unappropriated, estimated at $5,600 each.		61,600 00		
Do	Salary of head chief of the confederated bands twenty years.	...do	4th article treaty June 25, 1855; eleven instalments unappropriated, estimated at $500 each.		5,500 00		
Creeks	Permanent annuities	Vol. 7, pages 36, 69, and 287, and vol. 11, page 700.	4th article treaty Aug. 7, 1790, $1,500; 2d article treaty June 16, 1802, $3,000; 4th article treaty Jan. 24, 1826, $20,000.			24,500 00	490,000 00

Statement showing the present liabilities of the United States to Indian tribes, &c.—Continued.

Names of tribes.	Description of annuities, stipulations, &c.	Reference to laws; Statutes at Large.	Number of instalments yet unappropriated, explanations, remarks, &c.	Annual amount necessary to meet stipulations, indefinite as to time, now allowed, but liable to be discontinued.	Aggregate of future appropriations that will be required during a limited number of years to pay limited annuities incidentally necessary to effect the payment.	Amount of annual liabilities of a permanent character.	Amount held in trust by the United States on which five per cent. is annually paid; and amounts which, invested at five per cent., would produce permanent annuities.
Creeks—Continued.	Smiths, shops, &c.	Vol. 7, page 287	8th article treaty Jan. 24, 1826; say $1,110.			$1,110 00	$22,200 00
Do	Wheelwright, permanent	Vol. 7, p. 287, and vol. 11, p. 700.	8th article treaty Jan. 24, 1826; say $600.			600 00	12,000 00
Do	Allowance during the pleasure of the President.	Vol. 7, pages 287 and 419.	5th article treaty Feb. 14, 1833, and 8th article treaty Jan. 24, 1826.	$4,710 00			
Do	Interest on $200,000, held in trust; 6th article treaty August 7, 1856.	Vol. 11, page 700	Five per cent. for education			10,000 00	200,000 00
Do	Interest on $775,168, held in trust; 3d article treaty June 14, 1866.	Vol. 14, page 786	Five per cent. to be expended under the direction of the Secretary of the Interior.			38,758 40	775,168 00
Do	For transportation of such articles as may be purchased for the Creek nation.		3d article treaty June 14, 1866	5,000 00			
Crows	Twenty instalments for pay of nineteen half-breeds, in goods or money, at the discretion of the President, $50 each.	Not published	7th article treaty July 16, 1866; eighteen instalments unappropriated, estimated at $950 each.		$17,100 00		
Do	This amount to be paid Pierre Chien, in consideration of the friendship and services rendered by him to the Crow Indians.	Not published	7th article treaty July 16, 1866	200 00			
Do	For construction of warehouse or storeroom, $2,500; agency building, $3,000; residence for physician, $3,000; five buildings for carpenter, farmer, blacksmith, miller, and engineer, $10,000; school-room or mission building, $2,500; and erection of steam circular saw mill, with grist mill and shingle machine attached, $8,000.	Not published	Estimated at $29,000	29,000 00			
Do	For pay of physician, carpenter, miller, engineer, farmer, and blacksmith.	Not published	Estimated at $6,600	6,600 00			
Delawares	Life annuity to chief		Private act to supplementary	100 00			

Dwamish and other allied tribes in Washington Territory.	For $150,000, under the direction of the President, in twenty instalments.	Vol. 12, page 928	6th article treaty Jan. 22, 1855; eleven instalments unappropriated.		82,500 00		
Do	Twenty instalments for an agricultural school and teacher; 14th article treaty Jan. 22, 1855.	Vol. 12, page 929	Eleven instalments unappropriated, estimated at $3,000 each.		33,000 00		
Do	Twenty instalments for smith and carpenter shops and tools; 14th article treaty Jan. 22, 1855.	do	Eleven instalments unappropriated, estimated at $500 each.		5,500 00		
Do	Twenty instalments for blacksmith, carpenter, farmer, and physician.	do	Eleven instalments unappropriated, estimated at $4,600 each.		50,600 00		
Flatheads and other confederat'd tribes.	Five instalments of the third series, for beneficial objects, under the direction of the President.	Vol. 12, page 976	4th article treaty July 16, 1855; five instalments unappropriated.		20,000 00		
Do	Twenty instalments for support of an agricultural and industrial school, providing necessary furniture, books, stationery, &c., and for the employment of suitable instructors therefor.	Vol. 12, page 977	5th article treaty July 16, 1855; agricultural and industrial school, &c., $300; pay of instructors, $1,800; eleven instalments unappropriated, estimated at $2,100 each.		22,100 00		
Do	Twenty instalments for two farmers, two millers, one blacksmith, one gunsmith, one tinsmith, carpenter and joiner, and wagon and plough maker, $7,400; and keeping in repair blacksmith's, carpenter's, and wagon and plough maker's shops, and furnishing tools therefor, $500.	do	5th article treaty July 16, 1855; eleven instalments unappropriated, estimated at $7,900 each.		86,900 00		
Do	Twenty instalments for keeping in repair flouring and saw mill, and supplying the necessary fixtures.	do	5th article treaty July 16, 1855; eleven instalments unappropriated, estimated at $500 each.		5,500 00		
Do	Twenty instalments for pay of physician, $1,400, and keeping in repair hospital and furnishing the necessary medicine, $300.	do	5th article treaty July 16, 1855; eleven instalments unappropriated, estimated at $1,700 each.		18,700 00		
Do	For keeping in repair the buildings of employés, &c., for twenty years.	do	5th article treaty July 16, 1855; eleven instalments unappropriated, estimated at $300 each.		3,300 00		
Do	For $500 per annum for twenty years for each of the head chiefs; 5th article treaty July 16, 1855.	do	Eleven instalments unappropriated, estimated at $1,500 each.		16,500 00		
Do	For insurance and transportation of annuity goods and provisions.	do	5th article treaty July 16, 1855	11,920 41			
Iowas	Interest on $57,000, being the balance of $157,500.	Vol. 10, page 1071	9th article treaty May 7, 1854			2,875 00	57,500 00
Kansas	Interest on $200,000, at 5 per cent	Vol. 9, page 842	2d article treaty Jan., 1846			10,000 00	200,000 00
Kickapoos	Interest on $100,000, at 5 per cent	Vol. 10, page 1079	2d article treaty May 18, 1854			5,000 00	100,000 00
Do	Gradual payment on $200,000	do	2d article treaty May 18, 1854; $173,000 heretofore appropr.ated due.		27,000 00		
Klamaths and Modocs.	Five instalments of $8,000, to be applied under the direction of the President.		2d article treaty Oct. 14, 1864; two instalments unappropriated.		16,000 00		

Statement showing the present liabilities of the United States to Indian tribes, &c.—Continued.

Names of tribes.	Description of annuities, stipulations, &c.	Reference to laws; Statutes at Large.	Number of instalments yet unappropriated, explanations, remarks, &c.	Annual amount necessary to meet stipulations, indefinite as to time, now allowed, but liable to be discontinued.	Aggregate of future appropriations that will be required during a limited number of years to pay limited annuities incidentally necessary to effect the payment.	Amount of annual liabilities of a permanent character.	Amount held in trust by the United States on which five per cent. is annually paid; and amounts which, invested at five per cent., would produce permanent annuities.
Klamaths and Modocs—Continued.	For keeping in repair saw and flouring mills and buildings for blacksmiths, carpenters, wagon and plough maker, manual labor school, and hospital for 20 years.		4th article treaty Oct. 14, 1864; 18 instalments unappropriated, estimated at $1,000 each.		$18,000 00		
Do	For purchase of tools and materials for saw and flouring mills, carpenter, blacksmith, wagon and plough maker's shops, and books and stationery for the manual labor school.		4th article treaty Oct. 14, 1864; 20 instalments of $1,500 each, 17 unappropriated.		25,500 00		
Do	For pay of superintendent of farming, farmer, blacksmith, sawyer, carpenter, and wagon and plough maker 15 years.		8th article treaty Oct. 14, 1864; 12 instalments of $6,000 each, unappropriated.		72,000 00		
Do	For pay of physician, miller, and two school teachers for 20 years.		5th article treaty Oct. 14, 1864; 17 instalments of $3,600 each, unappropriated.		61,200 00		
Makahs	Four instalments of $30,000, for beneficial objects, under the direction of the President, (being 4th series.)	Vol. 12, page 940	5th article treaty Jan. 31, 1855; one instalment of $1,500, unappropriated.		1,500 00		
Do	Twenty instalments for an agricultural and industrial school and teachers.	Vol. 12, page 941	11th article treaty Jan. 31, 1855; 11 instalments of $2,500 each, unappropriated.		27,500 00		
Do	Twenty instalments for smith, carpenter shops, and tools.	do	11th article treaty Jan. 31, 1855; 11 instalments of $500 each, unappropriated.		5,500 00		
Do	Twenty instalments for blacksmith, carpenter, farmer, and physician.	do	11th article treaty Jan. 31, 1855; 11 instalments of $4,600 each, unappropriated.		50,600 00		
Menomonees	Pay of miller for 15 years	Vol. 10, page 1065	3d article treaty May 12, 1854; two instalments of $600 each, unappropriated.		1,200 00		
Do	Fifteen instalments to pay $242,686 for cession of lands.	Vol. 10, page 1068	4th article treaty May 12, 1854, and Senate amendment thereto;		194,148 72		

Miamies of Kansas..	Permanent provision for smith's shop, &c., and miller.	Vol. 7, pages 191 and 194; vol. 10, page 1095.	5th article treaty Oct. 6, 1818, 5th article treaty Oct. 23, 1834, and 4th article treaty June 5, 1854; say $940 for shop and $600 for miller.	....	....	$1,540 00	$30,800 00
Do..........	Twenty instalments on $200,000; 3d article treaty June 5, 1854.	Vol. 10, page 1094..	$150,000 of said sum payable in 20 instalments of $7,500 each, 11 unappropriated.	....	82,500 00	....	....
Do..........	Interest on $50,000, at 5 per cent..........	....do..........	3d article treaty June 5, 1854.....	....	....	2,500 00	50,000 00
Miamies of Indiana..	Interest on $221,257 86, in trust..........	Vol. 10, page 1099..	Senate amendment to 4th article treaty June 5, 1854.	....	....	11,062 89	221,257 86
Miamies of Eel river.	Permanent annuities..........	Vol. 7, pages 51, 91, 146, and 116.	4th article treaty 1795, 3d article treaty 1805, and 3d article treaty Sept. 1809; aggregate.	....	....	1,100 00	22,000 00
Molels..........	For keeping in repair saw and flouring mill, and furnishing suitable persons to attend the same, for a period of 10 years.	Vol. 12, page 981...	2d article treaty Dec. 21, 1855; one instalment of $1,500 unappropriated.	....	1,500 00	....	....
Do..........	For pay of teacher to manual labor school, and for subsistence of pupils and necessary supplies.	....do..........	2d article treaty Dec. 21, 1855; amount necessary during the pleasure of the President.	$3,000 00	....	....	....
Do..........	For carpenter and joiner to aid in erecting buildings, making furniture, &c., for 10 years.	Vol. 12, page 982...	2d article treaty Dec. 21, 1855; one instalment of $2,000 unappropriated.	....	2,000 00	....	....
Nisqually, Puyallup, and other bands of Indians.	For payment of $32,500 in graduated payments.	Vol. 10, page 1133..	4th article treaty Dec. 26, 1854; still unappropriated.	....	5,250 00	....	....
Do..........	Pay of instructor, smith, physician, carpenter, &c., 20 years.	Vol. 10, page 1134..	10th article treaty Dec. 26, 1854; six instalments of $6,700 each, unappropriated.	....	40,200 00	....	....
Do..........	For support of an agricultural and industrial school, and support of smith and carpenter shops, and providing the necessary tools therefor.	....do..........	10th article treaty Dec. 26, 1854; six instalments of $1,500 each, unappropriated.	....	9,000 00	....	....
Navajoes..........	For such articles of clothing, or raw material in lieu thereof, for 8,000 Navajo Indians, not exceeding $5 per Indian; and for seeds, farming implements, work-cattle, and other stock, for 1,400 families.	Not published.....	7th and 8th articles treaty June 1, 1868; estimated for articles of clothing, or raw material in lieu thereof, $40,000; and for seeds, farming implements, work-cattle, &c., $140,000.	180,000 00	....	....	....
Do..........	For surveying the Navajo Indian reservation..	....do..........	5th article treaty June 1, 1868; estimated at $36,220.	36,220 00	....	....	....
Nez Percés..........	Five instalments of the second series, for beneficial objects, at the discretion of the President.	Vol. 12, page 958...	4th article treaty June 11, 1855, one instalment of $8,000 unappropriated.	....	8,000 00	....	....
Do..........	Twenty instalments for the support of two schools, &c., and pay of one superintendent of teaching, and two teachers.	Vol. 12, page 959...	5th article treaty June 11, 1855, eleven instalments of $3,700 each, unappropriated.	....	40,700 00	....	....
Do..........	Twenty instalments for one superintendent of farming, and two farmers, two millers, two blacksmiths, one tinner, one gunsmith, one carpenter, and one wagon and plough maker.	....do..........	5th article treaty June 11, 1855, eleven instalments of $9,400 each, unappropriated.	....	103,400 00	....	....

Statement showing the present liabilities of the United States to Indian tribes, &c.—Continued.

Names of tribes.	Description of annuities, stipulations, &c.	Reference to laws; Statutes at Large.	Number of instalments yet unappropriated, explanations, remarks, &c.	Annual amount necessary to meet stipulations, indefinite as to time, now allowed, but liable to be discontinued.	Aggregate of future appropriations that will be required during a limited number of years to pay limited annuities incidentally necessary to effect the payment.	Amount of annual liabilities of a permanent character.	Amount held in trust by the United States on which five per cent. is annually paid; and amounts which, invested at five per cent., would produce permanent annuities.
Nez Percés—Cont'd.	Twenty instalments for keeping in repair grist and saw mill, and providing the necessary tools.	Vol. 12, pape 959	5th article treaty June 11, 1855, eleven instalments of $500 each, unappropriated.		$5,500 00		
Do	Twenty instalments for pay of physician and keeping in repair hospital and furnishing necessary medicine, &c.	do	5th article treaty June 11, 1855, eleven instalments of $1,700 each, unappropriated.		18,700 00		
Do	Twenty instalments for keeping in repair buildings for employés.	do	5th article treaty June 11, 1855, eleven instalments of $300 each, unappropriated.		3,300 00		
Do	Twenty instalments for salary of head chief	do	5th article treaty June 11, 1855, eleven instalments of $500 each, unappropriated.		5,500 00		
Do	Twenty instalments for keeping in repair the blacksmith, tinsmith, gunsmith, carpenter, and wagon and plough maker's shops, and providing necessary tools therefor.	do	5th article treaty June 11, 1855, eleven instalments of $500 each, unappropriated.		5,500 00		
Do	Four instalments to enable the Indians to remove and locate upon the reservation, to be expended in ploughing land and fencing lots.	Vol. 14, page 649	4th article treaty June 9, 1863, one instalment of $20,000 unappropriated.		20,000 00		
Do	Sixteen instalments for boarding and clothing children who attend school, providing school and boarding houses with necessary furniture, purchase of wagons, teams, tools, &c.	do	4th article treaty June 9, 1863, thirteen instalments of $3,000 each, unappropriated.		39,000 00		
Do	For salary of two subordinate chiefs	Vol. 14, page 650	5th article treaty June 9, 1863	$1,000 00			
Do	Fifteen instalments for repairs of houses, mills, shops, &c., and providing necessary furniture, tools, &c.	do	5th article treaty June 9, 1863, thirteen instalments of $2,500 each, unappropriated.		32,500 00		
Do	For salary of two matrons to take charge of the boarding schools, two assistant teachers, one farmer, one carpenter, and two millers.	do	5th article treaty June 9, 1863	7,600 00			
Omahas	Fifteen instalments, being the third series, in	Vol. 10, page 1844	4th article treaty March 16, 1854,		280,000 00		

Do	Ten instalments, for pay of engineer and assistant, miller and assistant, farmer and blacksmith and assistant, and keeping in repair grist and saw mills, support of blacksmith shop, and furnishing tools for the same.	Vol. 10, page 1044, and Vol. 14, page 668.	8th article treaty March 16, 1864, and 3d article treaty March 16, 1865; estimated engineer and assistant, $1,800; miller and assistant, $1,200; farmer, $900; blacksmith and assistant, $1,200; keeping in repair grist and saw mills, and support of blacksmith shop, $600; seven instalments of $5,700 each, unappropriated.		39,900 00		
Osages	Interest on $69,120 at 5 per centum, for educational purposes.	Vol. 7, page 242	Senate resolutions January 19, 1838, 6th article treaty Jan. 2, 1825.			$3,456 00	$69,120 00
Do	Interest on $300,000 at 5 per centum, to be paid semi-annually, in money, or such articles as the Secretary of the Interior may direct.	Vol. 14, page 687	1st article treaty Sept. 29, 1865			15,000 00	300,000 00
Do	For transportation of goods, provisions, &c		do	3,500 00			
Ottawas and Chippewas of Michigan.	Four equal annual instalments, in coin, of the sum of $206,000, being the unpaid part of the principal sum of $306,000.	Vol. 11, page 624	2d article treaty July 31, 1855, three instalments of $51,500 each, unappropriated, to be distributed per capita, in the usual manner of paying annuities.		154,500 00		
Do	For interest on $103,000 at 5 per centum, being the balance of $206,000.	Vol. 12, page 624	2d article treaty July 31, 1855			5,150 00	103,000 00
Ottoes and Missourias.	Fifteen instalments, being the third series, in money or otherwise.	Vol. 10, page 1039	4th article treaty March 15, 1854, fourteen instalments of $9,000 each, unappropriated.		126,000 00		
Pawnees	For annuity goods and such articles as may be necessary for them.	Vol. 11, page 729	2d article treaty Sept. 24, 1857			30,000 00	
Do	For the support of two manual labor schools during the pleasure of the President, and pay of two teachers.	Vol. 11, page 730	3d article treaty Sept. 24, 1857	11,200 00			
Do	For purchase of iron, steel, and other necessaries for shops, and pay of two blacksmiths, one of whom to be gunsmith and tinsmith, and compensation of two strikers or apprentices.	do	4th article treaty Sept. 24, 1857; estimated for iron, steel, &c., $500; for two blacksmiths, &c., $1,200, and two strikers, &c., $480.	2,180 00			
Do	For farming utensils and stock during the pleasure of the President, and pay of farmer.	do	4th article treaty Sept. 24, 1857, estimated at $1,800.	1,800 00			
Do	For pay of miller and engineer, at the discretion of the President.	do	do	1,800 00			
Do	For compensation to apprentices to assist in working the mill and keeping in repair grist and saw mills.	do	4th article treaty Sept. 24, 1857, estimated at $800.	800 00			
Poncas	Ten instalments, of the second series, to be paid to them or expended for their benefit.	Vol. 12, page 997	2d article treaty March 12, 1858, five instalments of $10,000 each, unappropriated.		50,000 00		
Do	This amount to be expended during the pleasure of the President, for aid in agricultural and mechanical pursuits.	Vol. 12, page 999	2d article treaty March 12, 1858	7,500 00			

Statement showing the present liabilities of the United States to Indian tribes, &c.—Continued.

Names of tribes.	Description of annuities, stipulations, &c.	Reference to laws; Statutes at Large.	Number of instalments yet unappropriated, remarks, explanations, &c.	Annual amount necessary to meet stipulations, indefinite as to time, now allowed, but liable to be discontinued.	Aggregate of future appropriations that will be required during a limited number of years to pay limited annuities incidentally necessary to effect the payment.	Amount of annual liabilities of a permanent character.	Amount held in trust by the United States on which five per cent. is annually paid; and amounts which, invested at five per cent., would produce permanent annuities.
Pottawatomies	Life annuities to chiefs	Vol. 7, pages 379, 433.	3d article treaty Oct. 20, 1832, $200; 3d article treaty Sept. 26, 1837, $700.	$900 00			
Do	Permanent annuity in money	Vol. 7, pp. 51 and 114; vol. 11, pp. 185, 317, 320, and 855.	4th article treaty 1795, $724 77; 3d article treaty 1809, $362 39; 3d article treaty 1818, $1,811 93; treaty 1828, $1,449 54; 2d article treaty July, 1829, $11,596 33; 10th article treaty June, 1864, $217 43.			$16,162 39	$323,247 80
Do	Education during the pleasure of Congress	Vol. 7, pp. 296, 318, and 401.	3d article treaty Oct. 16, 1826; 2d article treaty Sept. 20, 1828, and 4th article treaty Oct. 27, 1832, $5,000.	5,000 00			
Do	Permanent provisions for three smiths	Vol. 7, pp. 296 and 318; vol. 11, p. 321.	2d article treaty Sept. 20, 1828; 3d article treaty Oct. 16, 1826.	2,042 94			
Do	Permanent provisions for furnishing salt	Vol. 7, page 320	2d article treaty July 29, 1829, estimated at $317 09.	317 09			
Do	Interest on $466,027 48 at 5 per centum	Vol. 9, page 854	7th article treaty June 8 and 17, 1846.			23,301 37	466,027 48
Pottawatomies of Huron.	Permanent annuities	Vol. 7, page 106	2d article treaty Nov. 17, 1807			400 00	8,000 00
Quapaws	Provision for education and for smith and farmer, and smiths' shops, during the pleasure of the President.	Vol. 7, page 425	3d article treaty May 13, 1833, $1,000 per year for education, and $1,660 for smith, farmer, &c., $2,660.	2,660 00			
Qui-nai-elts & Quel-leh-utes.	For $25,000, being the 4th series, to be expended for beneficial objects under the direction of the President.	Vol. 12, page 972	4th article treaty July 1, 1855, one instalment of $1,300 unappropriated.		$1,300 00		
Do	Twenty instalments for support of agricultural	Vol. 12, page 973	10th article treaty July 1, 1855,		27,500 00		

Do	Twenty instalments, for support of smith and carpenter shops and tools.	do	10th article treaty July 1, 1855, eleven instalments of $500 each, unappropriated.		5,500 00		
Do	Twenty instalments for employment of blacksmith, carpenter, farmer, and physician.	do	10th article treaty July 1, 1855, eleven instalments of $4,600 each, unappropriated.		50,600 00		
Rogue Rivers	Sixteen instalments, in blankets, clothing, farming utensils, and stock.	Vol. 10, page 1019	3d article treaty Sept. 10, 1853, one instalment of $2,500 unappropriated.		2,500 00		
Sacs and Foxes of Mississippi.	Permanent annuities	Vol. 7, page 85	3d article treaty Nov. 3, 1804			1,000 00	20,000 00
Do	Interest on $200,000, at 5 per centum	Vol. 7, page 541	2d article treaty Oct. 21, 1837			10,000 00	200,000 00
Do	Interest on $800,000, at 5 per centum	Vol. 7, page 596	2d article treaty Oct 11, 1842			40,000 00	800,000 00
Sacs and Foxes of Missouri.	Interest on $157,400, at 5 per centum	Vol. 7, page 543	2d article treaty Oct. 21, 1837			7,870 00	157,400 00
Seminoles	Interest on $500,000, per 8th article treaty August 7, 1856.	Vol. 11, page 702	$25,000 annuities			25,000 00	500,000 00
Do	Interest on $70,000, at 5 per centum	Vol. 14, page 757	3d article treaty March 21, 1866, for support of schools, &c.			3,500 00	70,000 00
Senecas	Permanent annuities	Vol. 7, pages 161 and 179.	4th article treaty Sept. 29, 1817, $500; 4th article treaty Sept. 17, 1817, $500.			1,000 00	20,000 00
Do	Provisions for smith and smiths' shop and miller during the pleasure of the President.	Vol. 7, page 349	4th article treaty Feb. 28, 1831, say $1,660.	$1,660 00			
Senecas of New York	Permanent annuities	Vol. 4, page 442	Act Feb. 19, 1841, $6,000			6,000 00	120,000 00
Do	Interest on $75,000, at 5 per centum	Vol. 9, page 35	Act June 27, 1846, $3,750			3,750 00	75,000 00
Do	Interest on $43,050, transferred from the Ontario Bank to the United States treasury.	do	Act June 27, 1846, $2,152 50			2,152 50	43,050 00
Senecas and Shawnees.	Permanent annuities	Vol. 7, page 119	4th article treaty Sept. 17, 1818			1,000 00	20,000 00
Do	Provisions for support of smiths and smiths' shop during the pleasure of the President.	Vol. 7, page 352	4th article treaty July 20, 1831	1,060 00			
Shawnees	Permanent annuities for education	Vol. 7, pages 51 and 100, and vol. 10, page 1056.	4th article treaty Aug. 3, 1795; 3d article treaty May 10, 1854; and 4th article treaty Sept. 29, 1817.			3,000 00	60,000 00
Do	Interest on $40,000, at 5 per centum	Vol. 10, page 1056	3d article treaty May 10, 1854			2,000 00	40,000 00
Shoshones—Eastern bands.	Twenty instalments of $10,000 each, to be applied under the direction of the President.	*Vol. 15, page 717	5th article treaty July 2, 1863; fifteen instalments unappropriated.		150,000 00		
Shoshones—Goship bands.	Twenty instalments of $1,000 each, to be applied under the direction of the President.	Vol. 13, page 682	7th article treaty Oct. 7, 1863; fifteen instalments unappropriated.		15,000 00		
Shoshones — Northwestern bands.	Twenty instalments of $5,000 each, to be expended under the direction of the President.	Vol. 13, page 663	3d article treaty July 30, 1863; fifteen instalments unappropriated.		75,000 00		
Shoshones — Western bands.	Twenty instalments of $5,000 each, to be expended under the direction of the President.	*Vol. 2, page 557	7th article treaty Oct. 1, 1863; fifteen instalments unappropriated.		75,000 00		
Sioux of Dakota—Blackfeet band.	Twenty instalments of $7,000 each, to be paid under the direction of the Secretary of the Interior.	Vol. 14, page 728	4th article treaty Oct. 19, 1865; seventeen instalments unappropriated.		119,000 00		

*Pamphlet copy of laws, 2d session, 38th Congress.

Statement showing the present liabilities of the United States to Indian tribes, &c.—Continued.

Names of tribes.	Description of annuities, stipulations, &c.	Reference to laws; Statutes at Large.	Number of instalments yet unappropriated, explanations, remarks, &c.	Annual amount necessary to meet stipulations, indefinite as to time, now allowed, but liable to be discontinued.	Aggregate of future appropriations that will be required during a limited number of years to pay limited annuities incidentally necessary to effect the payment.	Amount of annual liabilities of a permanent character.	Amount held in trust by the United States on which five per cent. is annually paid; and amounts which, invested at five per cent., would produce permanent annuities.
Sioux of Dakota—Lower Brulé band.	Twenty instalments of $6,000 each, to be expended under the direction of the Secretary of the Interior.	Vol. 14, page 700	4th article treaty Oct. 14, 1865; seventeen instalments unappropriated.		$102,000 00		
Do	Five instalments of $2,500 each, to be expended under the direction of the Secretary of the Interior.	Vol. 14, page 700	6th article treaty Oct. 14, 1865; three instalments unappropriated.		7,500 00		
Do	For pay of farmer, support of one blacksmith, and for tools, iron and steel, and other articles necessary for the shop.	Vol. 14, page 700	6th article treaty Oct. 14, 1865; estimated at $2,500.	$2,500 00			
Do	For pay of engineer, sawyer, and employés, and keeping in repair saw-mill, and purchase of tools therefor.		Estimated at $3,740	3,740 00			
Sioux of Dakota—Minneconjou band.	Twenty instalments of $10,000 each, under the direction of the Secretary of the Interior.	Vol. 14, page 696	4th article treaty Oct. 10, 1865; seventeen instalments unappropriated.		170,000 00		
Sioux of Dakota—Onk-pah-pah band.	Twenty instalments of $9,000 each, under the direction of the Secretary of the Interior.	Vol. 14, page 740	4th article treaty Oct. 20, 1865; seventeen instalments unappropriated.		153,000 00		
Sioux of Dakota—O'Gallalla band.	Twenty instalments of $10,000 each, under the direction of the Secretary of the Interior.	Vol. 14, page 748	4th article treaty Oct. 28, 1865; seventeen instalments unappropriated.		170,000 00		
Sioux of Dakota—Sans Arc band.	Twenty instalments of $8,400 each, under the direction of the Secretary of the Interior.	Vol. 14, page 732	4th article treaty Oct. 20, 1865; seventeen instalments unappropriated.		142,800 00		
Do	Five instalments of $950 each, to be expended in agricultural implements and for improvements.	Vol. 14, page 732	5th article treaty Oct. 20, 1865; three instalments unappropriated.		2,850 00		
Sioux of Dakota—Two Kettles' band.	Twenty instalments of $6,000 each, under the direction of the Secretary of the Interior.	Vol. 14, page 724	4th article treaty Oct. 19, 1865; seventeen instalments unappropriated.		102,000 00		
Do	Five instalments of $2,825 each, to be expended in agricultural implements and improvements.	Vol. 14, page 724	5th article treaty Oct. 19, 1865; three instalments unappropri-		8,475 00		

Do	For pay of farmer, support of one blacksmith, furnishing tools, iron and steel, and other articles necessary for the shop.	Vol. 14, page 724	6th article treaty Oct. 19, 1865; for farmer $1,000; support of one blacksmith, &c., $1,500.	2,500 00			
Do	For pay of engineer, sawyer, and employés, keeping in repair saw-mill, and purchase of tools therefor.		Estimated at $3,740	3,740 00			
Sioux of Dakota—Upper Yanctonai band.	Twenty instalments of $10,000 each, under the direction of the Secretary of the Interior.	Vol. 14, page 744	4th article treaty Oct. 28, 1865; seventeen instalments unappropriated.		170,000 00		
Sioux of Dakota—Yanctonai band.	Twenty instalments of $10,500 each, under the direction of the Secretary of the Interior.	Vol. 14, page 736	4th article treaty Oct. 20, 1865; seventeen instalments unappropriated.		178,500 00		
Do	Five instalments of $2,875 each, to be expended in agricultural implements and improvements.	Vol. 14, page 736	5th article treaty Oct. 20, 1865; three instalments unappropriated.		8,625 00		
Do	For pay of farmer, support of one blacksmith, furnishing tools, iron and steel, and other articles necessary for the shop.	Vol. 14, page 736	5th article treaty Oct. 20, 1865; for farmer $1,000; for one blacksmith, &c., $1,500.	2,500 00			
Sioux of Dakota	For transportation and delivering articles purchased for the several bands of Sioux Indians.		Amount required	20,000 00			
Six Nations of New York.	Permanent annuities in clothing, &c.	Vol. 7, page 46	6th article treaty Nov. 11, 1794			$4,500 00	$90,000 00
S'Klallams	Four instalments on $60,000, (being the fourth series,) under the direction of the President.	Vol. 12, page 934	5th article treaty Jan. 26, 1855; one instalment unappropriated.		3,000 00		
Do	Twenty instalments for support of an agricultural and industrial school and pay of teachers.	Vol. 12, page 934	11th article treaty Oct. 26, 1855; eleven instalments of $2,500 each unappropriated.		27,500 00		
Do	Twenty years' employment of blacksmith, carpenter, farmer, and physician.	Vol. 12, page 935	11th article treaty Oct. 26, 1855; eleven instalments of $4,600 unappropriated.		50,600 00		
Tabequache band of Utahs.	Ten instalments of $20,000 each.	Vol. 13, page 676	8th article treaty Oct. 7, 1863; (goods, $10,000; provisions, $10,000;) five instalments unappropriated.		100,000 00		
Do	For purchase of iron, steel, and tools for blacksmith shop, and pay of blacksmith and assistant.	Vol. 13, page 675	10th article treaty Oct. 7, 1863; iron and steel, $220; blacksmith and assistant, $1,100.	1,320 00			
Do	For insurance, transportation, &c., of goods, provisions, and stock.			5,000 00			
Umpquas and Calapooias of Umpqua valley, Oregon.	Five instalments of the third series of annuities for beneficial objects under the direction of the President.	Vol. 10, page 1126	3d article treaty Nov. 29, 1854; one instalment unappropriated.		1,700 00		
Do	Support of teachers, &c., twenty years.	Vol. 10, page 1127	6th article treaty Nov. 29, 1854; six instalments of $1,450 each unappropriated.		8,700 00		
Do	Support of physician fifteen years.	Vol. 10, page 1127	6th article treaty Nov. 29, 1854; one instalment unappropriated.		2,000 00		
Umpquas — Cow Creek band.	Twenty instalments of $550 each.	Vol. 10, page 1027	3d article treaty Sept. 19, 1853; five instalments unappropriated.		2,750 00		
Walla-Walla, Cayuse, and Umatilla tribes.	Five instalments of the second series, to be expended under the direction of the President.	Vol. 12, page 946	2d article treaty June 9, 1855; one instalment unappropriated.		$6,000 00		

Statement showing the present liabilities of the United States to Indian tribes, &c.—Continued.

Names of tribes.	Description of annuities, stipulations, &c.	Reference to laws; Statutes at Large.	Number of instalments yet unappropriated, explanations, remarks, &c.	Annual amount necessary to meet stipulations, indefinite as to time, now allowed, but liable to be discontinued.	Aggregate of future appropriations that will be required during a limited number of years to pay limited annuities incidentally necessary to effect the payment.	Amount of annual liabilities of a permanent character.	Amount held in trust by the United States on which five per cent. is annually paid; and amounts which, invested at five per cent., would produce permanent annuities.
Walla-Walla, Cayuse, and Umatilla tribes—Contin'd.	Twenty instalments for pay of two millers, one farmer, one superintendent of farming operations, two school teachers, one physician, one blacksmith, one wagon and plough maker, and one carpenter and joiner.	Vol. 12, page 947	4th article treaty June 9, 1855; eleven instalments of $11,200 each unappropriated.		$123, 200 00		
Do	Twenty instalments for mill fixtures, tools, medicines, books, stationery, furniture, &c.	do	4th article treaty June 9, 1855; eleven istalments of $3,000 each unappropriated.		33, 000 00		
Do	Twenty instalments of $1,500 each for the head chiefs of these bands, ($500 each.)	do	5th article treaty June 9, 1855; eleven instalments unappro'ated.		16, 500 00		
Do	Twenty instalments for salary of son of Pio-pio-mox-mox.	do	5th article treaty June 9, 1855; eleven instalments of $100 each unappropriated.		1, 100 00		
Winnebagoes	For interest on $1,000,000, at five per centum	Vol. 7, page 546, and vol. 12, page 628.	4th article treaty Nov. 1, 1837, and Senate amendment July 17, 1862.			$50, 000 00	$1, 000, 000 00
Do	Thirty instalments of interest on $85,000	Vol. 9, page 879	4th article treaty Oct. 13, 1846; eight instalments of $4,250 unappropriated.		34, 000 00		
Woll-pah-pe tribe of Snake Indians.	Five instalments of $2,000 each, under the direction of the President.	Vol. 14, page 684	7th article treaty Aug. 12, 1865; three instalments unappropriated.		6, 000 00		
Yakamas	Five instalments of the second series, for beneficial objects, at the discretion of the President.	Vol. 12, page 953	4th article treaty June 9, 1855; one instalment unappropriated.		8, 000 00		
Do	Twenty instalments for support of two schools, one of which to be an agricultural and industrial school, keeping them in repair, providing books, stationery, and furniture.	do	5th article treaty June 9, 1855; eleven instalments of $500 each unappropriated.		5, 500 00		
Do	Twenty instalments for one superintendent of teaching and two teachers.	do	5th article treaty June 9, 1855; eleven instalments of $3,200 each unappropriated.		35, 200 00		
Do	Twenty instalments for one superintendent of farming and two farmers, two millers, two	do	5th article treaty June 9, 1855; eleven instalments of $11,400		125, 400 00		

Do	Twenty instalments for keeping in repair hospital and furnishing medicine, &c., and pay of physician.	do	5th article treaty June 9, 1855; eleven instalments of $1,700 each unappropriated; (physician, $1,400; hospital, &c., $300.)		18,700 00		
Do	Twenty instalments for keeping in repair grist and saw mill, and furnishing the necessary tools therefor.	do	5th article treaty June 9, 1855; eleven instalments of $500 each unappropriated.		5,500 00		
Do	Twenty instalments for keeping in repair buildings for employés.	do	5th article treaty June 9, 1855; eleven instalments of $300 each unappropriated.		3,300 00		
Do	For salary of head chief for twenty years	do	5th article treaty June 9, 1855; eleven instalments of $500 each unappropriated.		5,500 00		
Do	Twenty instalments for keeping in repair blacksmith's, tinsmith's, gunsmith's, carpenter's, and wagon and plough-maker's shops, and furnishing tools therefor.	do	5th article treaty June 9, 1855; eleven instalments of $500 each unappropriated.		5,500 00		
Yancton tribe of Sioux.	Ten instalments of $40,000 each, of the second series, to be paid to them or expended for their benefit.	Vol. 11, page 744	4th article treaty April 19, 1858; ten instalments due.		400,000 00		
	Total			$538,223 07	8,846,725 33	396,321 44	7,056,028 94

DEPARTMENT OF THE INTERIOR,
Office of Indian Affairs, November 19, 1868.

REPORT OF THE COMMISSIONER OF INTERNAL REVENUE.

TREASURY DEPARTMENT,
OFFICE OF INTERNAL REVENUE,
Washington, November 20, 1868.

SIR: The first measure adopted by Congress after the outbreak of the rebellion, providing revenue from internal taxation, was approved August 5, 1861. From that date until the summer of 1865 the costs of the war were annually increasing, and these costs, coupled with the interest on the rapidly augmenting public debt, and the necessity of preserving the national credit, made constantly increasing taxation absolutely indispensable.

During all that period the attention of the Treasury Department and of Congress was continually employed in the discovery of new objects of taxation and additional sources of revenue. That the people carried the burdens thus imposed upon them so universally, and carried them, too, so uncomplainingly, will forever be evidence to their posterity of their power and their loyalty. It was not until the authority of the government had been fully established, its liabilities determined, and its financial capacity and responsibility thoroughly proven to the world, that any relief from tax was furnished or even generally desired.

The largest receipts of internal revenue were during the fiscal year 1866, when taxation had reached its highest limits. The estimates of the reductions since that period, made from time to time, with reference to proposed legislation, were—

	Annually.
By statute of July 13, 1866	$65,000,000
By statute of March 2, 1867	40,000,000
By statute of February 3, 1868	23,000,000
By statute of March 31, 1868 By statute of July 20, 1868	45,000,000
Total	173,000,000

The two statutes last named swept away the tax upon manufactures, mineral oils and petroleum, and the estimate is without reference to the reduction of the rates upon distilled spirits.

The receipts for the last fiscal year were from the statutes existing July 1, 1867, modified by the act of March 31, 1868.

The statute of February relates to cotton, and relieved only that grown after the year 1867.

From the accounts kept in this office, as required by law, I herewith transmit tabular statements, which it is the duty of the Secretary of the Treasury to lay before Congress. They are:

Table A, showing the receipts from each specific source of revenue, and the amounts refunded in each collection district, State, and Territory of the United States for the fiscal year ending June 30, 1868.

Table B, number and value of internal revenue stamps procured monthly by the Commissioner, and monthly receipts from purchasers of internal revenue stamps, the commissions allowed on the same, and the receipts from agents for the sale of stamps.

Table C, comparative table, showing the territorial distribution of internal revenue from various sources in the United States.

Table D, the ratio of the receipts from specific sources to the aggregate of all collections for the years 1865, 1866, 1867, and 1868.

Table E, the ratio of the gross collections from the several sources of revenue to the aggregate collections, exclusive of the receipts from passports, salaries, stamps, United States marshals, special agents of the treasury, and Solicitor of the Treasury, for the fiscal years ending June 30, 1864, 1865, 1866, 1867, and 1868, respectively.

Table F, total collections from each specific source of revenue for the fiscal years ending June 30, 1863, 1864, 1865, 1866, 1867, and 1868, respectively.

Table G, abstract of reports of district attorneys concerning suits and prosecutions under the internal revenue laws.

AGGREGATE RECEIPTS.

The aggregate receipts from internal revenue, exclusive of the direct tax upon lands and the duty upon the circulation and deposits of national banks, were for the year—

1866	$310,906,984 17
1867	265,920,474 65
1868	*191,180,564 28

These amounts include drawback upon goods exported and sums refunded as erroneously assessed and collected.

The amounts of drawback and sums refunded were as follows:

	Drawback.	Amounts refunded.
1866	$798,866 73	$514,844 43
1867	1,864,631 68	706,581 69
1868	1,379,980 01	1,018,334 81

The increase of drawback in 1867 was due to the increased exportation of cotton goods and of spirits of turpentine, and the presentation of claims for taxes upon articles exported prior to June 30, 1864, which presentation was stimulated by the statute of limitations barring their payment unless presented before October, 1866.

During the last year this large exportation continued, and claims were multiplied by a new statute of limitations. Since October 1, 1868, no drawback has been allowed, except upon goods manufactured exclusively of tax-paid cotton, upon beer, and proprietary articles to which stamps had been attached.

About $300,000 of amounts refunded in 1867 and 1868 arose from the refunding to wholesale dealers, under direction of the act of July, 1866, so much of their license tax as was due to the excess of their estimated over their actual sales.

In many districts railroads were taxed upon their gross receipts from freight long after the repeal of the law imposing such tax, and the amount has been refunded, as has been also the sum of $52,856 42, illegally assessed, in the opinion of the Attorney General, upon cotton grown on the Indian reservations.

* The difference between the amounts here stated and those reported by the Treasurer is due to the fact that the same receipts are not entered upon the books of the two offices on the same day. The statistics of this office are based almost entirely upon the current collections, while the accounts of the Treasurer include such collections only when they are covered into the treasury.

RECEIPTS FROM SEVERAL SOURCES.

Banks, trust companies, and savings institutions.

	1866.	1867.	1868.
Dividends and additions to surplus	$4,186,023 72	$3,774,975 32	$3,624,774 99
Circulation	990,328 11	208,276 07	26,901 99
Deposits	2,099,635 83	1,355,395 98	1,438,512 77
Capital	374,074 11	476,867 73	399,562 90

The tax upon the dividends and additions to surplus of all banks, trust companies, and saving institutions, is reported to this office through assessors and collectors, while that upon the circulation, deposits, and capital of national banks is paid to the Treasurer of the United States.

The reduction of receipts reported from capital and circulation is due to the conversion of State banks into national associations, and that from deposits is due to the same cause and to the relief by the act of July, 1866, to all sums of less than $500 deposited in the name of any one person in savings institutions having no capital stock. The receipts from capital are variable, as in determining the taxable capital of any institution its average investment in United States bonds is deductible.

Railroads.

	1866.	1867.	1868.
Dividends and profits	$2,205,804 45	$3,379,262 19	$2,630,174 08
Interest on bonds	1,255,916 98		1,259,155 80
Gross receipts	7,614,448 13	4,128,255 24	3,134,337 19

The collectors' monthly abstracts for 1867 did not give the receipts from interest upon bonds separate from those upon dividends and profits. During the fiscal year 1866 and two months of 1867 the tax collected was from assessments upon the gross receipts for the transportation of property as well as of persons.

Insurance companies.

	1866.	1867.	1868.
Dividends and additions to surplus	$767,231 12	$563,473 93	$605,489 78
Premiums and assessments	1,169,722 23	1,326,014 38	1,288,745 79

Dividends of insurance companies, railroads, and banks have been taxed five per cent. during the three years, while the tax upon premiums and assessments has been one and a half per cent.

Gross receipts of telegraph companies.

The receipts of the fiscal year 1866 were from the tax of five per cent., as were those of two months of 1867. After that time the rate was three per cent. The reduction in the rates of companies for the transmission of despatches has, it is believed, contributed to the reduction of receipts by the government.

Gross receipts of express companies.

1866	$645,769 02
1867	558,359 28
1868	671,949 62

The rate during the three years remained unchanged from three per cent.

Revenue stamps.

1866	$15,044,373 18
1867	16,094,718 00
1868	14,852,252 02

By the act of March 2, 1867, receipts for the delivery of property, affidavits, appeals, confessions of judgment, writs, and other original processes, canned and preserved meats and shell-fish, vegetables, and fruits, were exempted from stamp duty. Beer stamps are not included in the above.

In 1867 $1,927,117 56, and in 1868 $2,026,823, were received from the sale of one cent stamps.

The sum of $3,231,247 27 in 1867, and of $3,549,177 32 in 1868, was received for stamps from special dies for matches, perfumery, cosmetics, medicines, and other proprietary articles.

Legacies and successions.

1866	$1,168,765 59
1867	1,861,429 16
1868	2,813,751 97

Special attention during the past year has been devoted to the assessment of legacies and successions both on the part of this office and that of assessors and their assistants, and to this fact, in no small degree, is due the increase of receipts from these sources.

Income.

1866	$60,894,135 85
1867	57,040,640 67
1868	32,027,610 78

The amount collected in the fiscal year 1866, and four-fifths of that collected in 1867, were assessed at the highest war rates, and the increase of exemption appeared for the first time in the returns for 1868. The assessments on the incomes for the calendar year cannot all be collected in the same fiscal year, although great progress towards this end was made with the last annual list. The total amount thus far reported from the tax on incomes of the calendar year 1866 is $27,417,956 65, and from that of 1867 $22,236,381 79; of the former amount $9,773,858 were collected in the fiscal year 1867, and $17,644,098 in 1868. Of the tax on incomes of 1867 $14,389,781 were collected in the fiscal year 1868, and but $7,846,600 in 1869. There remain several districts from which full returns have not been received, and it is believed that the amount actually collected upon the incomes of 1867 exceeds $23,000,000.

The number of persons assessed for an income tax on the annual list

ber was 259,385, and in 1868 in 222 districts, from which reports have been received, the number was 222,775. In the 18 missing districts the number in 1867 was 20,948.

Articles in schedule A.

1866	$1,692,791 65
1867	2,116,495 22
1868	1,134,105 88

The change from May to March, in 1867, of the time for making the annual assessment of articles in schedule A, as in the case of income and special taxes, makes the collections of the fiscal year 1867 disproportionate to those of 1866 or 1868. The receipts during that year by this change embraced an unusual amount of two annual assessments.

For the last two years, yachts, piano-fortes, and musical instruments, and carriages of less value than $300, have not been taxed. The receipts from the annual list of 1867 were $939,654 71; and the total amount thus far reported from the list of 1868 is $804,437 92.

Special taxes.

1866	$18,015,743 32
1867	18,103,615 69
1868	15,966,313 26

The reduction in the receipts of the last fiscal year is only apparent, and arises from the change of the tax upon wholesale dealers from an annual one collected at the beginning of the year to a monthly tax upon sales.

The collections of special taxes, like those for income and articles named in schedule A, cannot all be made in the fiscal year of their assessment.

The receipts from the assessment of 1867 were $14,136,459 18; those already reported from the assessment of 1868 are $10,779,599 08, which amount will be considerably increased when the collectors' abstracts are all received.

The comparative receipts from several sources during the last three years are presented in the following table:

	1866.	1867.	1868.
Apothecaries	$43,712 86	$55,447 42	$58,377 46
Auctioneers	89,721 42	98,084 86	97,448 14
Bankers	1,262,649 05	1,433,715 79	1,490,383 95
Brewers	105,412 23	238,155 14	270,205 22
Brokers of various sorts	673,260 30	598,854 94	538,417 43
Claim agents	70,637 39	84,627 49	63,149 99
Dealers, retail	1,949,017 04	2,047,860 77	2,163,632 00
wholesale	5,428,344 86	3,880,281 13	1,854,387 80
retail liquor	2,807,225 59	2,966,683 73	3,242,915 31
wholesale liquor	801,531 32	982,134 94	592,045 72
Distillers, coal oil	17,350 12	21,809 32	19,629 66
spirituous liquors	81,295 06	174,445 71	121,868 92
apples, grapes or peaches	20,239 31	57,332 15	74,188 45
Hotels	580,021 56	663,656 32	656,795 41
Insurance agents	104,866 83	148,647 85	152,143 51
Lawyers	264,836 75	357,648 41	383,030 95
Manufacturers	1,043,030 78	1,296,487 27	1,427,688 52
Peddlers	679,013 63	708,113 28	724,210 29
Physicians and surgeons	425,596 66	549,368 64	580,566 31
Rectifiers	61,300 91	80,470 06	87,770 28

Under the law existing prior to that of July, 1866, brewers paid an annual tax of $25, and when their product was more than 500 barrels per year $25 additional. By the act of July, 1866, this tax was doubled, as was that upon distillers of spirituous liquors. The act of July, 1868, will very largely increase the receipts from rectifiers and distillers.

Cotton.

1866	$18,409,654 90
1867	23,769,078 80
1868	22,500,947 77

During the fiscal year 1866 the tax was two cents per pound. From August 1, 1866, until September 1, 1867, it was three cents, and after that date two and a half cents per pound. As the removal of cotton from the districts of its growth is limited during the months of July and August, and the tax for ten months of the last fiscal year was at the reduced rate, it is evident that the amount brought to charge during that year was greater than in any year preceding, and considerably in excess of two millions of bales.

Cigars, cigarettes, and cheroots.

1866	$3,476,236 86
1867	3,661,984 39
1868	2,951,675 26

During the fiscal year 1866 the tax upon cigars was $10 per thousand. From August 1, 1866, to March, 1867, the rate was partly specific and in part ad valorem. After the last-named date the tax was uniform, and at $5 per thousand. Since the act of 1862 the rate upon cigars has been frequently changed; but as their number has always been an element in determining the amount of tax, it has been practicable every year to compute from the returns of the local officers the number of cigars upon which the tax has been collected.

From these it appears that the number in the fiscal years

1863 was	199,288,284
1864 "	492,780,700
1865 "	693,230,989
1866 "	347,443,894
1867 "	483,806,456
1868 "	590,335,052

The act of June 30, 1864, taking effect at the beginning of the fiscal year 1865, had long been before Congress, and as it provided, among other things, a large increase of tax upon cigars, their manufacture for several months was very largely stimulated; and of the number which paid tax in 1865, 160,304,197 were returned to the assessors at the close of the year preceding, and paid the lower rates.

This increase of stock in the market accounts in some measure for the small returns in 1866. The reduction of the rate to $5 enhanced the production during 1868.

Chewing and smoking tobacco.

1866	$12,339,921 93
1867	15,245,477 81
1868	14,947,107 53

The receipts for 1866 were unfavorably affected by the accumulation of tobacco in the south before the close of the rebellion, much of which came to market untaxed. The amount received during the last fiscal year was somewhat prejudiced by the anticipation of reduced rates under the revenue bill for several months pending in Congress.

The product brought to charge in 1866 was 35,748,351 pounds; in 1867, 45,635,581 pounds; in 1868, 44,900,880 pounds.

The reduction of the consumption of tobacco during the past year is compensated by its increased use in the manufacture of cigars consequent upon their reduced taxation.

The amount stored in bonded warehouse on the 1st day of July, 1866, was 4,123,631 pounds; 1867, 7,625,001 pounds; 1868, 8,280,253 pounds.

The amount exported in bond during 1867 was 11,075,568 pounds; 1868, 11,962,670 pounds.

Fermented liquors.

1866	$5, 115, 140 49
1867	5, 819, 345 49
1868	5, 685, 663 70

The tax at $1 per barrel has been uniform during the year.

Distilled spirits and brandy.

	Distilled spirits.	Brandy.
1866	$29, 198, 578 15	$283, 499 84
1867	28, 296, 264 31	868, 145 03
1868	13, 419, 092 74	871, 638 24

The falling off of receipts in 1868 resulted in some degree from the general expectation that the tax would be reduced, and the consequent unwillingness to withdraw spirits from bond at the higher rate, but mainly from the frauds which made such reduction indispensably necessary. In my last annual report I discussed at so great length the nature and extent of these frauds, and that, too, after so long and so careful attention to the subject, that it is unnecessary for me further to discuss them. Their remedy lies in the improved character of the revenue and judicial officers, rather than in the increased stringency of the law or improved regulations and requirements of the department. The above figures do not include the receipts from forfeitures.

The amount of spirits in bonded warehouse July 1, 1866, was 6,081,551 gallons; in 1867, 17,887,272 gallons; in 1868, 27,278,420 gallons.

The quantity out of warehouse under transportation bonds at the beginning of the fiscal year 1867 and of 1868 was at each date considerably in excess of 3,000,000 gallons. There was none at the commencement of 1869. The quantity exported in bond in 1867 was 4,654,816 gallons, and in 1868, 4,128,188 gallons. The number of gallons removed to "Class 2 warehouses," in 1867, for the manufacture of cosmetics, medicines, cordials, &c., for exportation, was 892,727; while in 1868, allowed by law during only a portion of the time, it was 98,213 gallons.

EXPENSES OF COLLECTING THE REVENUE.

The major part of the cost of assessing and collecting the revenue is the compensation of local officers, including assistant assessors and assessors' clerks, who are paid a fixed and definite sum per day or year, regardless of the amount accruing to the treasury through their services.

Until the statute of March, 1868, and the close of the last fiscal year, it was found necessary to retain in most of the collection districts the full number of subordinate officers, and the effect of the reduction since that time will not appear until the next annual report of this office.

Expense of assessing and collecting internal revenue for the fiscal years ending June 30, 1866 1867, and 1868.

	1866.	1867.	1868.
Compensation and expenses to assessors and assistant assessors	$4, 034, 043 09	$4, 811, 665 62	$5, 181, 179 97
Compensation and expenses to collectors	2, 161, 710 14	2, 453, 050 89	2, 262, 231 69
Superintendents of exports	16, 714 00	15, 434 71	20, 385 97
Revenue agents	35, 455 79	45, 541 85	61, 210 32
Special agents to this office	17, 226 82	39, 812 00	94, 650 99
Revenue inspectors	121, 078 70	189, 271 84	374, 518 73
Special revenue commission	22, 080 60	1, 228 85	....
Officers and clerks of this bureau	277, 672 71	296, 909 75	316, 769 82
Stamps and cotton tags	177, 089 55	186, 234 61	139, 365 71
Other incidental expenses of this office	40, 093 02	87, 999 69	71, 349 85
Commissions on sale of stamps	786, 536 04	855, 536 22	805, 638 69
Total	7, 689, 700 46	8, 982, 686 03	9, 327, 301 74

These statements comprise the accounts adjusted and passed by the accounting officers of the department, and appear more in detail in the report of the Fifth Auditor.

The expenses for the year 1867, as presented in my last annual report, did not include unadjusted claims, amounting to $961,751 80 for assessing, and $308,845 21 for collecting.

These amounts in the above statement have been charged to their appropriate year. The increased cost for assessing for 1867 over that for 1866 arose from the increased number of collection districts in the south, and the employment of a larger number of officers. The excess of 1868 above the expenses of 1867 was occasioned mainly by the increase of the pay of assistant assessors from $4 to $5 per day. A much larger number of special agents and inspectors were in service during the last year than in any year preceding, but these were all retired by the act of July 20, 1868. The number of assistant assessors in commission on the 1st day of November, 1867, was 3,180. This number, with the sources of revenue diminished by the act of March last, has been largely reduced, and on the first day of the present month but 2,284 were in service. The allowance to assessors for clerical service is, under the terms of the statute, made by "the proper officers of the treasury." This language has been construed to mean the accounting officers, and the Commissioner has no voice in determining the amount; but it is understood that it is being gradually reduced.

The receipts of internal revenue for the fiscal years 1866, 1867, and 1868, respectively, and the ratio thereto of the expenses during the same periods, were as follows:

Years.	Gross collections.	Refunded.	Drawback.	Net collections.	Expenses.	Per cent. gross collections.	Per cent. net collections.
1866	$310, 906, 984 17	$514, 844 43	$798, 866 73	$309, 593, 273 01	$7, 689, 700 46	2. 47	2. 49
1867	265, 920, 474 65	706, 581 09	1, 864, 631 68	263, 349, 261 28	8, 982, 686 03	3. 38	3. 41
1868	191, 180, 564 28	1, 018, 334 81	1, 379, 980 01	188, 782, 249 46	9, 327, 301 74	4. 88	4. 94

The ratio of costs to collections has increased, of course, with the reduction of the latter. It has required the same machinery and the same number of officers to collect taxes at two or three per centum as at five per centum, and until the passage of the statutes of the present calendar year it was necessary to keep the officers substantially to their maximum number.

PROBABLE RECEIPTS FOR THE PRESENT FISCAL YEAR.

It has always been difficult to make any accurate estimate of the receipts for the future from internal taxation. The frequent modifications of the laws themselves, the varying condition of different manufacturing interests, the shifting values consequent upon paper currency, together with other disturbing elements, have materially affected the worth of data collected at this office from which otherwise the receipts for any fiscal year could be foreshadowed with considerable accuracy.

The reduction of the sources of revenue has now, however, somewhat diminished these embarrassments, and the collections for the current year can be calculated with reasonable certainty.

The following tabular statement presents the aggregate of certificates of deposits by collectors received at this office during July, August, September, and October, for the fiscal years 1867, 1868, and 1869, respectively:

	1867.	1868.	1869.
July	$27,079,103 38	$24,734,656 14	$16,989,649 92
August	38,043,340 81	17,848,051 29	13,900,385 70
September	33,714,718 66	13,183,606 99	9,760,796 29
October	26,414,430 29	14,486,636 44	10,092,335 24

Of the amount collected in 1867 there was from income $43,463,655 45; in 1868 $17,733,714 04, and in 1869 $8,365,817 68.

I herewith present, also, the collections from the several sources of revenue during the first quarter of the present fiscal year in comparison with those of like character during the corresponding period of the fiscal year 1868.

The monthly abstract of the collector of the 5th district of North Carolina for August, 1868, and of the collector of the 3d district of Louisiana for September, have not been received, and the collections in their districts for the months stated are not included in the receipts for 1869.

	July, August, and September of fiscal year 1868.	July, August, and September of fiscal year 1869.
SPIRITS.		
Spirits, distilled from whatever materials	$3,726,352 03	$6,021,629 14
Spirits in bond July 20, 1868, tax of four dollars per barrel		1,071,898 56
Distilleries, per diem tax		572 00
Distillers, special tax	65,270 42	66,479 78
Rectifiers, special tax	29,456 88	73,573 24
Compounders of liquors, special tax		7,348 95
Dealers, retail liquor, special tax	1,217,999 22	1,007,971 61
Dealers, wholesale liquor, special tax	254,842 43	215,969 81
Total	5,293,920 98	8,465,443 09
TOBACCO.		
Cigars, cheroots, and cigarettes	$654,163 21	$847,306 24
Snuff and snuff flour sold for use	172,566 59	142,859 55
Tobacco, chewing, &c.	3,724,423 85	2,709,251 40
Tobacco, smoking, all stems, &c.; fine cut shorts, &c.	454,957 18	465,610 73
Dealers in leaf tobacco, special tax		16,634 15

Collections of revenue, &c.—Continued.

	July, August, and September of fiscal year 1868.	July, August, and September of fiscal year 1869.
TOBACCO—Continued		
Dealers in manufactured tobacco, special tax		$69,431 13
Manufacturers of tobacco and cigars, special tax	$23,695 64	24,580 46
Total	5,029,806 47	4,295,673 66
FERMENTED LIQUORS.		
Fermented liquors	$1,619,615 92	$1,722,018 36
Brewers, special tax	96,877 02	68,583 52
Total	1,716,492 94	1,790,601 88
GROSS RECEIPTS.		
Canals, ferries, ships, barges, &c., and steamboats	$134,124 58	$100,894 10
Express companies	146,398 89	159,282 47
Insurance companies	293,019 14	292,992 06
Railroads, stage coaches, &c	873,100 33	827,325 57
All other collections from gross receipts	129,570 99	134,262 31
Total	1,576,213 93	1,514,756 51
SALES.		
Brokers	$91,319 87	$93,989 09
Dealers	795,498 25	759,052 28
Manufacturers of articles not otherwise specifically taxed		849,729 99
All other collections from sales	37,384 93	36,741 47
Total	924,203 05	1,739,512 83
INCOME.		
Income over $1,000	$14,631,978 77	$8,189,870 65
Bank dividends, profits, &c	1,021,994 38	1,166,446 99
Railroad companies' dividends and undistributed profits	664,455 65	966,164 59
All other collections from income	552,433 38	650,637 19
Total	16,870,862 18	10,973,119 42
Banks and bankers, special tax, and tax on capital, circulation, and deposits	$1,090,661 26	$886,078 06
Special taxes not before enumerated	4,053,221 87	2,969,427 27
Legacies	320,277 97	278,590 36
Successions	230,730 38	254,065 55
Articles in schedule A	497,900 34	300,842 69
Passports	14,695 00	8,665 00
Gas	318,076 70	341,127 72
Sources not otherwise herein specially enumerated, including cotton and manufactured articles	11,866,928 49	874,430 98
Penalties, &c	250,150 69	306,402 45
Stamps, other than those for spirits, tobacco, and fermented liquors	3,122,970 23	3,393,471 73
Salaries of United States officers and employees	220,850 53	228,689 55
Grand total	$53,397,963 01	$38,620,898 75

The principal cause of the reduction in the aggregate receipts of 1869 below those of 1868, as shown above, is the repeal of the tax upon manufactures.

The sum of $5,359,492 80 was received in the fiscal year 1869 from the tax of 50 cents per gallon upon spirits in bond July 20, and withdrawn therefrom after that date. The sum of $662,136 34 was either collected prior to the act of July 20, 1868, and at the rate of $2 per gallon, or from spirits distilled after that date and removed from warehouse at 50 cents per gallon. Of the spirits in bond at the passage of the act in July last, 14,676,298 gallons were remaining on the 1st of November. This by the requirements of law must all be withdrawn on or before the 20th day of April next, and with the tax of 50 cents per gallon and $4 per barrel of forty proof gallons will yield a revenue of $8,805,779.

The assessment of the annual list, including income, special taxes and schedule A, was made earlier in 1868 than in 1867, and more of the collections of the former year than of the latter were made prior to the month of July and appear in the receipts of the last fiscal year.

The receipts from snuff and tobacco were smaller in 1869 because of the reduction from 40 cents to 32 cents upon chewing tobacco and snuff by the act of July last, and because of the anticipated use of stamps and the subjection to tax in January next of unstamped stock on hand on which one tax may have already been paid.

The increase from cigars is due in part to the tax imposed upon imported cigars by the act of July. Under this act dealers in leaf tobacco pay a special tax of $25 and two dollars per thousand on their sales in excess of $10,000 per annum. By the former law they were taxed as dealers and paid $1 per thousand on sales above $25,000.

Dealers in manufactured tobacco were first taxed as such in July; prior to that time the payment of special tax as dealers covered sales of tobacco, snuff, and cigars, as well as merchandise.

Manufacturers' sales were made liable by the act of March, 1868, and the tax is returned and paid quarterly. The first return was in July following.

The tax upon rectifiers and wholesale liquor dealers is now very largely increased, and the receipts from the various forms of stamps for spirits, aside from that denoting the payment of tax, will be of no inconsiderable amount.

From a careful consideration of the above, and of other data which the proper limits of my report will not allow me to present, I confidently believe that the receipts for the present fiscal year will reach the sum of $145,000,000.

STAMPS AND THEIR MANUFACTURE.

All adhesive revenue stamps are manufactured by Messrs. Butler & Carpenter, of Philadelphia, for 20 cents per thousand. This price includes the cost of packing in a manner suitable for transportation, and of delivery to an agent of the government in that city upon the requisitions of this office in favor of purchasers and others ordering stamps in different parts of the country.

The number of stamps covered by these requisitions during the last three years is as follows:

	1866.	1867.	1868.
General stamps	162,814,377	140,592,294	118,696,255
Stamps for proprietary articles	236,192,746	233,300,300	248,840,077

The American Phototype Company, of New York city, imprint internal revenue stamps upon checks, drafts, receipts, and other instruments furnished them by the parties who desire such stamps. The cost of these stamps to the government is 12½ cents per thousand; all additional cost, which in no case is to exceed one cent for each impression containing not more than six stamps, is paid to the company by the parties who order the stamps. Messrs. Butler & Carpenter also print similar stamps from steel plates at the same cost to the government as that of the adhesive stamps. The extra expense is arranged between them and the purchasers, subject to the decision of the Commissioner in case of dissatisfaction with the rates charged.

Stamps imprinted upon instruments are not kept on hand for general sale, like adhesive stamps, but are printed only upon order and prepayment by purchasers; and no stamp is imprinted upon any particular form of instrument until the Commissioner has decided concerning the propriety of such imprinting, and the extent of the liability of the instrument.

The number of stamps imprinted by the American Phototype Company was, during the fiscal years—

1866	20,541,690
1867	15,469,504
1868	21,133,556

The stamps for use upon packages of distilled spirits are manufactured by the Note-printing Bureau of the Treasury Department, as were the cigar stamps required by the amendatory act of March 3, 1865.

The number of stamps in their various forms for distilled spirits ordered from the Note-printing Bureau is 839,000 tax-paid stamps; 2,000,000 rectifiers' stamps; 2,000,000 wholesale dealers' stamps; 1,000,000 stock-on-hand stamps; 2,000,000 warehouse stamps.

At the date of this report (November 20) there had been sent to collectors tax-paid stamps 460,800; rectifiers' stamps, 284,400; wholesale dealers' stamps, 245,600; stock-on-hand stamps, 433,600; warehouse stamps, 304,000.

The stamps for tobacco, snuff, and cigars, under the act of July 20, 1868, are furnished by the Continental Bank Note Company, of New York, at prices varying with the kinds and amounts required. Their use is to be commenced on the 23d of the present month.

Stamps are printed upon tin-foil wrappers for ounce and half-ounce packages of fine-cut chewing tobacco, by Mr. Henry Skidmore, of New York, the only printer upon tin-foil in the United States, at a charge of 14 cents per thousand.

All stamps made outside the Treasury building are prepared under written contracts and the direct inspection of an agent of this bureau. The performance of the work in accordance with the terms of the contracts is duly secured in each case; in that of Butler & Carpenter by a deposit of United States securities with the United States Treasurer, and in other cases by bonds with approved sureties.

UNITED STATES COURTS AND ATTORNEYS.

It is the duty of district attorneys, under the act of March, 1867, to make report to this office, at the close of every term of court, of suits brought and the condition of all suits or proceedings in which the United States is a party. The times and character of these reports prevent the distribution of the suits through different fiscal years with positive accuracy, but the following statements are believed to be measurably correct for the year 1868:

Number of suits brought in federal courts	5,305
Of these the number of proceedings *in rem* was	2,294
Number of indictments found and filed	1,981
Number of other proceedings *in personam*	1,030
Judgments recovered in proceedings for forfeiture	1,261
Convictions on indictment, some including more than one person	749
Number of acquittals	219
Number of suits decided in favor of United States	2,532
Number of suits decided against United States	382
Number of suits settled or dismissed	624
Number of suits pending July 1, 1868	2,905
Amount of judgments recovered in suits *in personam*	$741,797 47
Amount collected from judgments and paid into courts	127,810 94
Proceeds of forfeitures paid into courts	1,136,150 73

With the exception of a division of the southern judicial district of New York, and the formation of the eastern as a new judicial district, the federal courts remain as they were before the outbreak of the rebellion. The proceedings growing out of the organization of the national banks and the issue of national currency would alone have almost clogged the already scarcely adequate judicial machinery in some localities; and since revenue cases and proceedings in bankruptcy have been added, the calendars have been so enlarged that in the principal business centres a speedy determination of a contested cause has been hardly expected.

Considerable relief was formerly obtained through terms which were held by judges from adjoining districts, whose own dockets were comparatively light. Payment by the government of expenses incurred by a judge while sitting outside his own district is now prohibited, and judges naturally decline to undertake extra labor at increased cost to themselves. Although the old system may have been liable to some abuses, I respectfully submit that the advantages to the government far outweighed the pecuniary loss, and that, unless some radical change in the organization of the courts be made, it will be wise to return to the system under which judges were willing to relieve each other.

As stated in my last report, the statutes should be amended so as to require the clerks of courts, as well as the attorneys and marshals, to report to this office, that among other things it may learn of the distribution of the proceeds of every suit. The fee-bill of district attorneys, I believe, should be modified so as to give larger compensation than now for the faithful prosecution of criminal proceedings. It is through these, and the imprisonment of offenders, rather than from penalties and forfeitures, that the laws can be successfully vindicated and the revenue more fully collected.

COMPROMISES.

The power of compromise has been exercised with great care, and only upon the recommendation of the local revenue officers or district attorneys, and the approval of the Secretary of the Treasury. No alleged violation by distillers has been compromised except upon the opinion of the government attorney that the offence was technical, or could not be proved to the jury.

The number of cases compromised during the year was 536.

From these there was received as tax	$419,043 57
Assessed penalties, fixed by law	142,003 56
In lieu of fines, penalties, and forfeitures	592,027 68
Total	1,154,027 61

By the statute of July last, in every case where a compromise is made, it is provided that there shall be placed on file in the office of the Commissioner the opinion of the solicitor of internal revenue, or officer acting as such, with his reasons therefor, and after a suit or proceeding in court has been commenced, it can be compromised only with the recommendation also of the Attorney General.

DISTILLED SPIRITS—OPERATIONS OF THE NEW LAW.

The remodelling of distilleries to conform to the law and the regulations, and the erection of distillery warehouses, have been the occasion of great expense and delay to their proprietors, while the survey of distilleries, the procurement and distribution of stamps, the preparation of forms and regulations, and the greatly increased correspondence consequent upon the inauguration of the new law, have imposed an immense labor upon this office and upon the local officers of the district where distilleries are situated. The nature and extent of this work will be best exhibited by a brief reference to some of the most important requirements of the statute.

Every distillery, whether intended for use or otherwise, must be registered with the assessor of its district. Its owner must file with that officer notice of its location, description and boundaries, its mashing, fermenting, and distilling capacity, and its fermenting period, together with the number, kinds, and contents of the stills, boilers, tubs, and cisterns employed. An accurate plan of the distillery and its apparatus, showing the relative location of every still, boiler, doubler, worm-tub, cistern, pipe-valve, and other parts of the machinery, must be displayed upon the premises, and a copy filed with the assessor. With the aid of a person skilful and competent for such purpose, the assessor is required to make a survey of every distillery, and to estimate and determine its true producing capacity, for the purpose of assessment in case of deficient returns. Copies of all the papers above referred to are sent to this office, where a full and complete record is kept of every distillery.

A warehouse must be established for every distillery, and, under the direction and control of the collector of the district, placed in charge of a storekeeper appointed by the Secretary of the Treasury. A bond in the penal sum of double the tax upon the possible production of the distillery for fifteen days must be given by the distiller, with at least two sureties approved by the assessor, conditioned, among other things, to a faithful compliance with all the provisions of the law.

The number of distilleries registered and thus far reported to this office, including those not intended for present use and those for the distillation of fruit, is 1,990.

The plans of 316 distilleries, other than of fruit, have been received and filed, as in accordance with the law and regulations, and others have been returned for correction. Of these, 64 are in Pennsylvania, 51 in Ohio, 41 in New York, 35 in Illinois, 26 in Kentucky, 16 in Indiana, 14 in Virginia, 10 in Tennessee, 10 in Missouri, 10 in Maryland, 7 in Massachusetts, 7 in Wisconsin, 6 in Louisiana, 6 in Iowa, 3 in West Virginia, 2 in Connecticut, and 1 in each of the States of Alabama, Arkansas, Delaware, Minnesota, New Hampshire, New Jersey, and 1 in Utah, and 1 in Montana.

No plans have been received from the Pacific coast, although distilleries there have probably been put in operation.

Distillery warehouses have been established to the number of 459.

From the reports of the storekeepers it appears that 204 distilleries are in operation, with an aggregate daily producing capacity of 227,758 gallons.

The number of Class B warehouses existing on the 1st day of July last was 779. Their number was gradually and rapidly reduced until the 1st instant, when the number was 172, containing manufactured tobacco and most of the spirits distilled prior to the act of July 20 and still in warehouse.

The statute now in operation contains many improvements upon that of 1866, is fuller and more definite in its exactions, places the distilleries and their operations more completely in the hands of the government, and is more rigorous in its punishment of offenders, but its successful operation after all must depend upon the vigilance and fidelity of the local officers. The corruption of storekeepers, gaugers, and assistant assessors, even when assessors and collectors are above suspicion, will always open sources of ruin to honest tax-payers and loss to the treasury, which neither the wisest legislation nor the most stringent regulations of the department can close.

Since the date of the present statute, however, there has been a large reduction in the number of illicit stills in most parts of the country. Those properly registered and authorized have paid, it is believed, a greater proportion of their liability than under the previous law, and the receipts have been in marked and favorable contrast to those of the corresponding time last year.

SPIRIT METERS.

It will be remembered that the joint resolution of February 3, 1868, providing for the appointment of a commission to examine and test spirit meters, further provided that, until the report of the commission and additional legislation upon the subject, all work on the construction of meters under direction of the department should be suspended. Although their price should be fixed by a committee of three—one named by the Secretary of the Treasury, one by the Commissioner of Internal Revenue, and one by the manufacturer.

When I had concluded, in accordance with the recommendation of the commission, to adopt and prescribe the Tice meters, it seemed advisable, for similar reasons, that the prices of meters of different sizes should be properly determined; and after considerable delay in finding suitable persons whose engagements would allow their rendering the service, Messrs. W. T. Duvall, of Georgetown, D. C., Levi J. Knowles, of Warren, Massachusetts, and William P. Trowbridge, of New York city, all skilful and competent machinists, were selected for that purpose. This committee made its report on the 8th day of September, and on the 16th day of the same month Mr. Tice was directed to proceed with the manufacture and attachment.

Under the joint resolution of February 3, he had discharged his employees, closed his manufactory, and when his meter was again adopted he was delayed by the necessity of reorganizing his business and procuring competent workmen.

For the purpose of bringing the meters to as early use as possible, I directed that they should be first attached in New York city, the place of their manufacture, and in Brooklyn, and instructed the collectors of the eighth and ninth districts to notify their distillers that meters were ready for attachment, and subsequently gave like notice to the collectors in the other districts. On the 19th of November meters had been placed in 11 distilleries, and their attachment to others is being prosecuted as rapidly as circumstances, including the opposition of distillers, will allow. I am advised that several distilleries have been closed by their proprietors to prevent the application of meters.

The revenue officers and the manufacturer have been earnestly urged to complete the work in New York and Brooklyn at the earliest moment, that it may be prosecuted in other districts of the country.

I am advised that Mr. Tice now has about 125 workmen employed in his factory, and others engaged in the attachment of meters at distilleries.

All meters are attached under the immediate direction of a government officer, by whom the accuracy of each instrument is tested.

DIRECT TAX.

Under the authority of the 14th section of the act of July 28, 1866, the Secretary of the Treasury suspended, until January 1, 1868, the collection of the direct tax in the States heretofore in insurrection, and a like extension until January 1, 1869, was authorized by the joint resolution of July 23, 1868.

The loyal States, with the single exception of Delaware, assumed the amounts apportioned them, and paid the same from their treasuries. After several years of delay, the State of Delaware continuing to refuse such assumption and payment, the assessment and collection of the tax were commenced by the officers of internal revenue, and are now nearly completed. Indeed, the full assessment of $74,683 33, the tax assigned, has been made, and $64,924 42 have been collected.

The total amount of tax apportioned to the 11 insurrectionary States was $5,153,981 28. Of this there have been collected $2,270,608 23, at an expense of $243,451 47, inclusive of expenses of sales, and exclusive of salaries of commissioners.

The total amount reported to this office as proceeds of sales in the

States of Virginia, South Carolina, Florida, Tennessee, and Arkansas, is $450,419 73. Of this the sum of $128,029 88 consists of lands purchased by the commissioners on behalf of the government when the same were sold for taxes.

Purchases of lands to the cost value of $77,561 18 were made in South Carolina. A part of the lands so purchased has been leased, and a part, by order of the President, resold for educational purposes. The unsold tracts in South Carolina, not under lease, have passed into the custody of the Freedmen's Bureau by force of the act relating to this subject passed July 16, 1866.

The uncollected tax of the insurrectionary States, amounting to nearly $3,000,000, is a lien upon all the real estate upon which the same is assessable. Every parcel in each State is charged with such distributive share of that State's apportionment as shall be determined by its comparative value on the 1st day of April, 1862, and in making assessments the law provides that due regard shall be had to the valuation made under State authority at the period nearest that date.

Since that time estates have been sold and resold; they have been divided and subdivided. Some have received costly improvements, and from others has been swept away all that was valuable. In ordinary times the assessment made upon a comparative valuation so remote would be greatly unequal; but when the immense changes, directly and indirectly brought by the war, are considered, it seems to me that the collection of this tax upon the present statutory basis cannot be further prosecuted without very great inequality and very just complaint.

The further postponement of this subject can relieve it of none of its embarrassments, and landholders and purchasers are alike entitled to its early solution. Unless it is deemed wise, in view of the difficulties suggested, and of the impoverished condition of the south, to abate its uncollected portion altogether, I would recommend the passage of a law allowing its assumption by the several States within a definite period, coupled with a reasonable premium for such assumption, and authorizing and directing the internal revenue officers, in case of non-payment by the State, to proceed with the assessment and collection upon a new basis of taxation.

CHANGES OF STATUTES.

Next to frequent changes of officers there is nothing so prejudicial to the personal convenience and interests of tax-payers, and so productive of loss to the revenue, as frequent changes of the statutes.

The gradual increase of the expenses of the government from 1861 to 1865, and their gradual reduction during the last two years, have secured the passage of at least one revenue bill at every session of the national Congress, and within a period of six years more than twenty-five such bills have passed both houses and received the approval of the President. The pendency of a measure has furnished frequent opportunities for numerous

can now be well determined; if, indeed, a proper regard to the rapid reduction of the debt and the value of the public securities in the markets of the world has not already fixed it at its present amount, and I believe that no advantage can possibly accrue from a material change in the objects of taxation. From several hundreds if not thousands of sources the number has been reduced to a comparatively few, all of which contribute their allotted share without embarrassment, and the masses of the country are not only unburdened, but, except through the complaints of others, are seldom even reminded of the existence of the revenue laws.

The recent act relative to distilled spirits, tobacco, snuff, and cigars, has been in force for so brief a period that but few modifications which ts operations may prove necessary can now be recommended with confidence. I would respectfully suggest, therefore, that the general codification of the revenue laws, begun at the last session of Congress, be postponed a year, that this statute may be more thoroughly tested, and that a single act then be passed embracing all that is valuable in existing laws, and of such character as to insure it against the necessity of amendments for several years.

Some legislation, however, in addition to that recommended in my report last year, and not covered by the act of July last, is, I think, advisable at the present time.

LIMITATION OF COMMISSIONERS' AUTHORITY TO REFUND TAXES ERRONEOUSLY COLLECTED.

The authority vested in the Commissioner of Internal Revenue to refund taxes erroneously collected has been the means of preventing much expensive litigation, and has afforded speedy and inexpensive relief to many persons who have been compelled to pay more than was legally due. While a withdrawal of this authority would be productive of great hardship in many cases, I am satisfied that a statutory limitation of the time within which such claims must be presented would tend to prevent much abuse. When the legality of an assessment is not seriously questioned at the time it is made, the evidence in its support is very apt to disappear with a change in the officers of the district; and it is not then difficult for a skilful attorney to present reasons in support of a claim for refunding such as are hard to be set aside. Different persons succeeding one another in the office of Commissioner will naturally have different views as to the interpretation of portions of the statutes, and he whose claim has been once rejected may present it anew, after a change of officers, with reasonable hope of better success. I would recommend that no claim be allowed unless it is presented within fifteen months from the time when the tax was paid.

STAMPS UPON TAX-PAID TOBACCO AND SNUFF.

It having been found practically impossible to prepare and furnish to

shall be sold or offered for sale except at retail, from stamped wooden packages, unless put up in the prescribed form of package and duly stamped. It was believed that, by the close of the calendar year, the stock on the market, when the use of stamps should begin, would be so nearly exhausted that it would not be burdensome to impose a second tax upon the small remnant unconsumed. The short interval between the 23d day of November and the 1st day of January will not give the intended opportunity for the consumption of unstamped tobacco, and Congress will probably see fit to enlarge it. I have been urged to recommend that provision be made for issuing stamps without charge, to be affixed to all such tobacco as may be in the hands of dealers on the appointed day. Evasions of the law will be comparatively easy so long as tobacco may be sold without stamps, and prominent manufacturers believe that the advantage to the revenue of the early termination of these opportunities will more than compensate for the expense and inconvenience attending it. I fear, however, that if this method were adopted, it would be impossible to prevent the misuse of the free stamps upon tobacco properly taxable, and prefer, therefore, a postponement to a day later than the 1st day of January.

BANKERS' AND BROKERS' SALES.

I have heretofore in my annual reports expressed the opinion that the attempt to collect taxes by means of stamps upon instruments having no permanent value for purposes of evidence would prove a failure. Certainty rather than severity of punishment must be relied on to support the sanction of penal statutes. When both the maker and receiver of an instrument believe that the paper will never come under the eye of a revenue officer, it matters little what penalty is denounced for the omission to affix a stamp. If the writing is of such a character that its invalidity as an instrument of evidence is of slight consequence, evasions of the tax will naturally result. To no one of the various stamp taxes now imposed do these considerations apply with greater force than to the memoranda required of brokers when making sales of coin and securities. These memoranda are in no sense evidences of title. In fact, they are only passed in obedience to the statute requirement, and are soon thrown aside and destroyed. If stamps have been affixed they can easily be removed, and it is hardly necessary to make an attempt to efface the cancellation marks before placing them upon another memoranda. So little scrutiny is bestowed upon these papers as they pass from brokers, that specimens have been presented of stamps which had been issued by gentlemen of the highest respectability while bearing plainly the marks of two and even three successive cancellations. During the fiscal year 1866, when the tax upon sales of this description was paid monthly to the collectors, the receipts from this source were in excess of $2,500,000. In August, 1866, the tax was reduced from one-twentieth to one-hundredth of one per cent., and made payable by stamps; but at the same time such changes were made in the terms of the statute as to render subject many sales which had before escaped taxation, and thus to some extent to counteract the effect of the reduction in rate. Since that time the sales of stamps have been scarcely larger than before, and I am satisfied that a return to the former method would secure a more thorough enforcement of the law and yield much richer results.

LIFE TABLES.

the British laws imposing similar taxes, are embodied tables for determining such values by reference to the expectancy of life at different periods, but our statute is silent upon the subject. When it became necessary to furnish assessors with a standard by which to regulate their assessments, they were referred by this office to the Carlisle tables of mortality as those which were believed to be generally accepted as most accurate in their results. Other tables have been adopted for a similar use by the courts of some of the States, and tax-payers have claimed the right to have their liability measured by these instead of those used by the assessor.

The controversies which thus arise do not merely involve the relative rights of the government and the tax-payer, but in many cases the interest of the life tenant demands the use of one standard, while the remainder man is benefited by the adoption of another. It is evident that so important a matter should be made clear by the terms of the law, and I would therefore recommend either that the proper tables be incorporated in the statutes, or that distinct authority be given the Commissioner of Internal Revenue to prescribe such as he shall deem appropriate.

COMPENSATION OF ACTING COLLECTORS.

By the third section of the act regulating the tenure of offices, passed March 2, 1867, it is provided that, in case no appointment is made to a vacant office during the session of the Senate, "the office shall remain in abeyance without any salary, fees, or emoluments attached thereto," and "the powers and duties belonging to such office shall be exercised by such other officer as may by law exercise such powers and duties in case of a vacancy in such office."

Under the statutes relating to internal revenue, a collector appoints his deputies and pays them out of his commissions, and, when a vacancy occurs in the office of collector, the duties of the office devolve upon one of his deputies. It follows that when a vacancy in the office of collector of internal revenue is not filled during a session of the Senate, a deputy collector must act as collector, while no provision is made for compensating him for discharging the duties of either office. At the adjournment of Congress on the 3d of March, 1867, there were 69 vacancies in the office of collector. Deputies of the retiring collectors remained in charge of their respective offices until new appointments were made, and they have not received compensation for their services. I recommend that some provision be made for paying them proper salaries, and also to meet similar cases that may occur hereafter.

Much inconvenience and delay are now experienced in paying the subordinate officers in a district whenever a vacancy occurs in the office of collector, as the deputy who acts as collector is not authorized to act as disbursing agent.

I recommend either that the official bond of a collector be made to cover his liabilities as disbursing agent, or, if that is not deemed advisable, that the bond given by the collector in the capacity of disbursing agent be made available upon the default of his deputy acting in like capacity, as the official bond of the collector now is for the acts of all his deputies.

TAX OF NATIONAL BANKS TO BE RETURNED AND PAID TO REVENUE OFFICERS.

The 110th section of the act of June 30, 1864, imposing a tax upon the capital, circulation, and deposits of persons and corporations engaged in the business of banking, has never had application to the banks organized under the national currency act, such banks paying a like tax directly to the Treasurer of the United States. As nearly all the State banks which were in existence when the tax was imposed have been converted into national banks or have closed up their business, the amounts reported to this office from this source have shrunk to a very small amount, although the actual revenue has probably increased.

While those banks which are affected by the operation of the revenue law are required to pay their taxes at the end of each month, the national banks pay only semi-annually. This discrimination was adopted when the policy of the government required that every inducement should be presented for the conversion of State into national associations, and it was thought that this comparative infrequency of returns by the latter would prove such inducement. Now that the national banking system has so completely superseded all others, the reason for the distinction fails, and a mere suggestion seems enough to show that the revenue law should be made alike applicable to all who are engaged in the same kinds of business.

SALES OF FORFEITED GOODS BY COLLECTORS.

The act of July, 1866, provided a summary process for the sale by collectors, without the decree of forfeiture, of goods seized for violation of the revenue laws, where the aggregate value of such goods should not exceed $300. Ample checks are thrown around the exercise of this authority for the protection of the innocent, and I believe that no serious complaint of its abuse has ever reached this office. The customs laws have long contained a similar provision, and I am informed that its working has given general satisfaction. The statute in its terms now only applies to goods forfeited under the acts of 1866 and those of an earlier date, and it should be so amended as to apply to forfeiture for violations of any revenue law.

The expenses attendant upon sales made in this way are so small when compared with the costs which accrue before property can be sold under decree of a United States court, that it would, in my judgment, be wise if the same method of procedure be authorized in the case of goods of much higher aggregate value.

SUPERVISORS.

The act providing for the appointment of supervisors of the revenue requires that each shall be assigned to a district composed of one or more *judicial* districts. The services of these officers will be principally devoted to matters having little reference to the boundaries of judicial districts, and a much more convenient arrangement can be made if this particular provision is repealed. In each of the States of Pennsylvania and Ohio the amount of work has been thought to be such as to require the services of two supervisors, but the line between the two judicial districts in neither case coincides with the boundaries of collection districts. Two collection districts in the former State, and four in the latter, are thus placed severally under the jurisdiction of two supervisors.

Again, the proper supervision of the revenues in the five districts of New Jersey hardly furnishes employment for one officer, while it is not convenient to attach the whole State either to the districts including the city of New York, or to that covering the city of Philadelphia. Violations of the revenue law in the northern portion of the State will ordinarily be found connected with transactions in the one city, while in the southern part the connection will be with the other. In general terms the same may be said of many other parts of the country, and I would therefore recommend that the law be so changed that each supervisor may be assigned to a district including such collection districts as may be determined by the Commissioner of Internal Revenue.

REVENUE STAMPS UPON RECEIPTS.

The written instruments subject to stamp duty are, with few exceptions, prepared by persons familiar with the requirements of law, and at places where stamps of the proper denomination are kept, and when necessary may be attached without inconvenience. Among these exceptions receipts for money or the payment of debts exceeding $20 are the most prominent. These are often given under circumstances when compliance with the law would be exceedingly inconvenient if not impossible, and by and to people ignorant of the obligations which the law imposes. It thus often happens that a person innocently issuing an unstamped receipt may be put in peril of prosecution, while a person innocently receiving it may find, too late, that the courts refuse to recognize it, and that he is wronged without remedy.

I am convinced that there is no form of taxation which, producing so much annoyance to the tax-payer, yields so little revenue to the government, and I recommend that receipts be stricken from the schedule of instruments subject to stamp duty.

CIVIL SERVICE.

In my last annual report I presented the distinctive features of the civil service of Great Britain and of several countries of the continent, together with the reasons which, after a study of their superior workings, had convinced me of the pressing necessity of a change for the better in the service of our own country. My experience and observation since that time have deepened my convictions that justice to honest tax-payers and due regard to our national reputation alike demand the elevation of the revenue service above individual preferences and the fluctuations of parties. The antagonism between the legislative and the executive departments of the government, which has so sadly damaged the service for the past two years, may, I know, be regarded as exceptional, and the harmony to prevail hereafter be urged as a full corrective to existing evils; but until there is a positive change in the method of making appointments, importunity will secure recommendations upon which bad appointments must inevitably be made, and from which the public will suffer. A dishonest gauger or assistant assessor, in many localities, may, undetected, do more wrong to the government than lies within the power of an assistant treasurer or a foreign minister; yet these offices, through the skilful management of the applicants and their associates, are often devolved upon men of small ability and less integrity—in the very toils of corrupt distillers. I have known a distinguished clergyman advocating, from the purest motives, the appointment to office of one whom I knew as a leader among illicit whiskey operators. He was cheated by those who, two or three removes from him, had carefully studied the lines of sympathy and friendship, and did not hesitate to use the sacred office of the Christian ministry for personal emolument, through frauds upon the treasury. Without a service which shall insure appointment during good behavior, from comparative fitness, and which shall protect vigilant officers from the malicious attacks of the felons whom they obstruct or pursue, bad men, pressed for place because of their political service or their personal necessities, will prostitute positions they secure for enriching themselves at the cost of the treasury, and the guilty, in and out of office, will seek to blind the appointing authorities and the public, and cheat justice of her rights by assaulting the character of the officers whom they fear.

I fully admit that the spirit of our people is somewhat averse to the permanent service I so strongly recommend; that political aid from those in public positions is exacted by all political parties, and that rotation in office is the long-established practice under local as well as under the general government; but, unless free institutions are to prove failures, ballots must be cast from honest convictions rather than the hope of political preferment or the fear of political displeasure. The inevitable tendency of such practice is the demoralization of our institutions and the degradation of official position—good men in all parties relaxing their interest in public affairs when place-hunting instead of principle is the controlling power, and men of well-earned and established reputation refusing to imperil it in places which have been desecrated by incompetency or fraud. The principles of Mr. Jenckes's bill, reported to the House of Representatives from the Joint Committee on Retrenchment, passed into law, would prove of immense public advantage.

CONSOLIDATION OF COLLECTION DISTRICTS.

Under the act of July 1, 1862, the then loyal States, with the exception of Kentucky and Missouri, were divided into collection districts of the same number, and in most cases with the same boundaries, as the congressional districts. Several of the larger cities of the country—Boston, New York, Brooklyn, Philadelphia, Baltimore, and Cincinnati—comprising or forming parts of more than one congressional district, were thus thrown into more than one collection district. So many intricate questions were constantly arising under the laws as they existed prior to their recent amendments, that I have heretofore believed it impossible for a single officer to discharge properly the duties of assessor in either of these cities. The tax upon manufactures, under which the most puzzling doubts have arisen, has now been repealed; the sections of the statute imposing taxes upon incomes, legacies, and successions, have been almost unchanged for several years, and, except as to a small number of occupations, the same may be said of the sections relating to special taxes and taxes upon sales and gross receipts. The frequent changes in the laws necessary heretofore, through the varying wants of the treasury, have increased the labors of assessors. Doubtful questions will disappear, as the laws hereafter shall be but slightly modified. I am satisfied that the several cities above named can shortly be consolidated into single districts, with a saving of expense to the treasury and of convenience to the public. The present divided jurisdiction leaves many an open door for confusion and evasion; a tax-payer upon one side of a street finds himself assessed, while his neighbor, equally liable, on the other side, goes free; complaint follows inequality of taxation; business gravitates to that district where it is likely to fare best, unless other local advantages are sufficiently great to overbalance those connected with the revenue.

For example, if the officers in one district are lenient in their administration of the law concerning distilleries, it will follow that there distillers will multiply. Increased official vigilance in one district has but the effect of reducing the revenue from its own, while increasing that from the neighboring, district. The upright and energetic officer sees his labor result in a transfer to his dishonest or inefficient colleague of the official emoluments which might have been his own if he had failed to interfere with violations of law. The increased number of distillers, though paying but a tithe of what they should, swells the revenues of the negligent district, and all stimulus to honest effort is well nigh destroyed.

There are other considerations which bear with almost equal weight in favor of the proposition that each single business community should form but a single collection district. Collectors would not so often as now lose sight of delinquent tax-payers through their simple removal from one place to another in the same city. Many tax-payers are residents of one district, manufacturers in a second, and dealers in a third, and the different aspects of the same transaction are thus passed upon by three different officers, neither of whom has, unless accidentally, any knowledge of the action of the others. If a fraud is committed, it is so distributed between the districts that proof becomes difficult and justice remains unsatisfied.

The enforcement of the penal provisions of the statutes is also weakened by the subdivision of power and by the barrier presented to a collector's authority by the district line. The holder of illicit property escapes a forfeiture by crossing a street; and it has been decided by the courts that a rescue is not punishable unless it is consummated in the district where the proceeding began.

The advantages of the proposed consolidation have been already recognized by the statute provision for the appointment of superintendents of drawback, and for placing export bonded warehouses, without regard to their actual location, under the supervision of a single collector.

The cities of New York and Philadelphia are of such magnitude, however, that I should not deem it feasible to include either in a single collection district, unless authority were granted by legislation for the employment of a grade of officers between the assessor and the present assistant assessors. Five deputy assessors in New York and Brooklyn, inclusive, under the direction of the single assessor, would supply the place of eight assessors whose offices would be abolished. For the district of Philadelphia, which is now divided into five districts, I presume that two intermediate officers would be found sufficient. Assistant assessors are now appointed by the Secretary of the Treasury; the proposed deputy assessors would with propriety be appointed by the President, with the concurrence of the Senate.

By the proposed arrangement, the offices of eight collectors in New York, and four in Philadelphia, would be abolished. If experience should demonstrate the need of one or more intermediate officers between the collector and the present deputy collectors, as in the case of the proposed deputy assessors, temporary provision can be made for the employment of such officers without additional legislation.

As the unsettled liabilities of tax-payers under former laws are fast being adjusted, it will be found advantageous, in some sections of the country, to unite districts outside of the large cities. In this way, and in this way alone, can the cost of the service be reduced in a degree commensurate with the reduction of taxation.

THE OFFICE OF COMMISSIONER—A SEPARATE DEPARTMENT.

ment, with the Commissioner as its head, instead of continuing it, as it has hitherto been, a bureau of the Treasury Department. My experience long ago convinced me that such a change would be productive of great benefit to the service; but the subject could so readily be made to assume personal and partisan aspects, that I have hitherto refrained from its advocacy. Judging from the past, the passage of no general revenue law can be expected until near the close of the approaching session; and as the change, if made, will thus coincide with the incoming of a new administration, the question can now be considered solely in the light of its administrative merits.

The erection of this office into a separate department would conduce to a more vigorous and thorough enforcement of the law in the first place by greatly simplifying the work in the office of the Commissioner.

So vast is the volume of business flowing through the Treasury Department that it is manifestly impossible for the Secretary to make himself familiar with all its details; and the same may be said of the Commissioner and the business of his office. Experienced officers and clerks in this bureau, devoting their entire attention to special portions of the law, are necessarily better informed than others can be of their particular requirements, and the peculiar conditions of business or trade to which they are applicable. When the Commissioner has to determine upon proper regulations to be established, or orders to be issued, he does so after full consultation with those of his subordinates who are most familiar with the subject-matter in all its connections. His own lack of acquaintance with details is thus corrected, and a safe and prudent conclusion is probably reached. Any changes made in their subseqnent revision by the Secretary are likely to be productive of injury rather than advantage, for it is practically impossible for those here employed to confer as freely with the Secretary as they do with the Commissioner; and in such revisions the benefit of their experience is in a large measure lost.

Under the present relations of the two offices, so many questions pass from one to the other that the Secretary is constantly compelled to adopt the opinions of his own immediate subordinates, instead of forming a personal judgment of his own, and thus the carefully reached conclusions of the Commissioner may be overruled by clerks without legal and public responsibility.

The separation would prevent the necessity for the joint action of the two officers, which is often attended with considerable delay, even when promptness is an indispensable element of success. It would locate responsibility which is now divided, and clothe the Commissioner with more than a seeming authority.

The benefits of the proposed change would arise especially, however, from its rendering more direct and single the responsibility of the local officers. One applies to the Secretary for instructions, while another, called to act perhaps in the same case, takes direction from the Commissioner. Those inclined to disregard his directions find a plausible pretext in some assumed difference of opinion between him and the Secretary. Those who are striving for the same end find themselves working at cross purposes, while the consequent confusion encourages the wrong-doer and disheartens the upright.

Objection has been made to the proposed separation on the ground that the customs revenue has been successfully managed without it; but it should be borne in mind that the entire responsibility of the execution of the customs laws is vested in the Secretary of the Treasury, the Commissioner of Customs under the law acting only as an accounting officer, or discharging such functions as may be devolved upon him by the

The laws relating to internal duties and customs are framed in many particulars with reference to each other. The official regulations under them, especially those covering the storage and movement of bonded property, are oftentimes not dissimilar.

The Treasury Department within a recent period has been enlarged, not alone as other executive departments have been, by the immense increase of its former varieties of business, but by the addition of several bureaus, either of which, a few years ago, would have been regarded as sufficient for an independent department. It is too large now, and its interests are too complex and diversified for the supervision of a single officer.

I believe the public interest would be best subserved by the erection of a new department, which should embrace the collection of all the national revenues except those derived from the sale of the public lands.

I am, sir, with great respect, your obedient servant,

E. A. ROLLINS,
Commissioner.

Hon. H. McCULLOCH,
Secretary of the Treasury.

APPENDIX A.

In the annual report of the Register reference was made to certain statements which were to be presented at a future time.

Since that report was completed the following statements have been prepared:

1st. A statement showing the tonnage of the Atlantic and Gulf coasts. of the Pacific coast, of the Northern Lakes, and of the Western Rivers, by States; and showing separately the tonnage of sailing vessels, steam vessels, barges, and canal boats.

The tonnage of the country has never before been presented in the statistics of our commercial marine, under any of the above classifications.

2nd. A statement showing the tonnage in the cod and mackerel fisheries by States.

3d. A statement showing the tonnage in the whale fisheries, by custom districts.

The number of vessels of each class, and the total number of vessels in the country, is also stated for the first time.

N. L. JEFFRIES, *Register.*

States.	No. of vessels.	Tonnage.	No. of vessels.	Tonnage.	No. of vessels.	Tonnage.	No. of vessels.	Tonnage.	No. of vessels.	Tonnage.
THE ATLANTIC AND GULF COASTS.										
Maine	3,036	360,579.24	46	18,146.73					3,082	378,725.97
New Hampshire	79	13,395.24	4	452.32					83	13,847.56
Massachusetts	2,852	446,257.63	78	31,680.19					2,930	477,937.82
Rhode Island	194	19,195.80	29	28,055.66					223	47,251.46
Connecticut	713	58,109.25	64	36,165.35	2	171.52	5	540.96	784	94,987.08
New York	2,984	647,857.36	742	359,841.84	304	54,582.03	898	88,393.82	4,928	1,150,675.05
New Jersey	816	64,288.55	60	16,821.67	64	10,083.84	64	6,488.82	1,004	97,682.88
Pennsylvania	717	206,076.29	132	33,250.22	13	11,935.28	457	49,223.36	1,319	300,485.15
Delaware	166	11,880.19	26	12,829.09	6	539.45			198	25,248.73
Maryland	1,566	97,831.77	103	39,831.85	21	3,076.48	18	1,306.53	1,708	142,046.63
District of Columbia	126	5,189.62	27	4,540.68	9	798.92	275	17,736.84	437	28,266.06
Virginia	814	26,840.41	58	5,409.07	15	1,271.47	23	2,051.36	910	35,572.31
North Carolina	291	13,256.15	21	3,064.53	1	28.23			313	16,348.91
South Carolina	180	9,691.03	31	5,148.33					211	14,839.36
Georgia	17	2,472.98	2	782.59					19	3,255.57
Florida	239	15,280.47	30	6,007.87					269	21,288.34
Alabama	90	11,757.47	57	15,777.60	86	4,026.55			233	31,561.62
Mississippi	50	1,276.73	3	41.55	4	109.92			57	1,428.20
Louisiana	476	44,265.78	41	27,120.09					517	71,385.87
Texas	196	12,211.08	36	8,763.14	10	1,166.43			242	22,140.65
Total	15,602	2,067,713.04	1,590	653,730.37	535	87,790.12	1,740	165,741.69	19,467	2,974,975.22
THE PACIFIC COAST.										
California	647	98,372.89	98	40,059.89	30	3,240.54			775	141,673.32
Oregon	22	815.32	31	8,188.80					53	9,004.12
Washington Territory	63	14,187.62	13	1,647.29					76	15,834.91
Total	732	113,375.83	142	49,895.98	30	3,240.54			904	166,512.35
THE NORTHERN LAKES.										
Vermont	24	1,315.14	6	3,256.17			4	275.75	34	4,847.06
New York	415	74,145.70	169	56,277.23	174	20,432.28	1,865	173,664.08	2,643	324,519.29

	Col. 1	Col. 2	Col. 3	Col. 4	Col. 5	Col. 6	Col. 7	Col. 8	Col. 9	Col. 10
Illinois	357	67,357.96	88	10,848.53	4	1,842.93	227	20,704.29	676	100,753.71
Wisconsin	204	29,688.11	35	10,938.90	.....	.....	.....	.....	239	40,627.01
Total	1,855	293,977.85	624	144,117.15	232	36,146.44	2,654	221,362.88	5,365	695,604.32
THE WESTERN RIVERS.										
Louisiana	.....	.....	230	52,025.24	33	3,303.43	.....	.....	263	55,328.67
Mississippi	.....	.....	15	2,396.33	.....	.....	.....	.....	15	2,396.33
Tennessee	.....	.....	63	13,412.83	.....	.....	.....	.....	63	13,412.83
Kentucky	.....	.....	75	22,818.05	14	4,554.82	.....	.....	89	27,372.87
Missouri	.....	.....	210	82,876.60	98	29,246.58	.....	.....	308	112,123.18
Iowa	.....	.....	28	3,258.87	28	1,743.42	.....	.....	56	5,002.29
Minnesota	.....	.....	58	9,774.41	87	9,207.60	.....	.....	145	18,982.01
Illinois	.....	.....	72	16,024.01	99	11,299.64	.....	.....	171	27,323.65
Indiana	.....	.....	26	5,293.88	.....	.....	.....	.....	26	5,293.88
Ohio	.....	.....	165	69,311.24	70	7,388.29	255	22,014.92	490	98,714.45
West Virginia	.....	.....	124	20,717.74	20	1,397.68	.....	.....	144	22,115.42
Pennsylvania	.....	.....	197	53,762.19	385	38,023.88	30	1,362.88	612	93,152.03
Total	.....	.....	1,263	351,671.39	834	106,168.34	285	23,377.88	2,382	481,217.61

SUMMARY.

	Col. 1	Col. 2	Col. 3	Col. 4	Col. 5	Col. 6	Col. 7	Col. 8	Col. 9	Col. 10
The Atlantic and Gulf Coasts	15,602	2,067,713.04	1,590	653,730.37	535	87,790.12	1,740	165,741.69	19,467	2,974,975.22
The Pacific Coast	732	113,375.83	142	49,895.98	30	3,240.54	.....	.....	904	166,512.35
The Northern Lakes	1,855	293,977.85	624	144,117.15	232	36,146.44	2,654	221,362.88	5,365	695,604.32
The Western Rivers	.....	.....	1,263	351,671.39	834	106,168.34	285	23,377.88	2,382	481,217.61
The United States	18,189	2,475,066.72	3,619	1,199,414.89	1,631	233,345.44	4,679	410,482.45	28,118	4,318,309.50

TREASURY DEPARTMENT, *Register's Office. December 4, 1868.*

N. L. JEFFRIES, *Register.*

1590
142
624
1263
3639

Statement showing the number and tonnage of vessels of the United States employed in the whale fishery on the 30th day of June, 1868.

Customs districts.	Vessels.	Tonnage.
Newburyport, Mass	3	287.62
Salem and Beverly, Mass	5	784.79
Barnstable, Mass	59	5,390.98
Nantucket, Mass	5	816.16
Edgartown, Mass	7	2,206.89
New Bedford, Mass	215	55,850.56
New London, Conn	18	2,922.34
Sag Harbor, N. Y	6	1,140.81
San Francisco, Cal	10	1,942.40
Total	328	71,342.55

N. L. JEFFRIES, *Register.*

TREASURY DEPARTMENT, *Register's Office, December* 4, 1868.

Statement showing the number and tonnage of vessels of the United States employed in the cod and mackerel fisheries on the 30th day of June, 1868.

States.	Enrolled vessels above 20 tons.		Licensed vessels under 20 tons.		Total.	
	Vessels.	Tonnage.	Vessels.	Tonnage.	Vessels.	Tonnage.
Maine	357	17,038.45	398	5,067.69	755	22,106.14
New Hampshire	7	67.55	13	146.11	20	213.66
Massachusetts	1,009	54,036.54	196	2,084.56	1,205	56,121.10
Rhode Island	1	31.71	22	242.47	23	274.18
Connecticut	72	2,899.39	68	929.92	140	3,829.31
New York	21	689.28	51	594.28	72	1,283.56
Total	1,467	74,762.92	748	9,065.03	2,215	83,827.95

N. L. JEFFRIES, *Register.*

TREASURY DEPARTMENT, *Register's Office. December* 4, 1868.

APPENDIX B.

TREASURY DEPARTMENT, *December* 1, 1868.

SIR: I have the honor to submit to you herewith a statistical chart illustrative of the progress of ship-building in the United States from A. D. 1817 to 1868. The four lines upon the chart show the ship-building of the entire country, of the Atlantic, Gulf, and Pacific coasts, of the New England States, and of the Western Lakes and Rivers. The statistics of the past give the number of ships, barks, brigs, schooners, sloops, canal-boats, and barges and the tonnage built each year in the several customs districts. The lines representing the tonnage built in the United States, and on the coast, include sea-going vessels, river steamers, canal boats and barges.

In speaking of the sea-going ship-building of the country, I shall therefore refer to the tonnage statistics of the New England States, which is composed almost exclusively of sailing vessels designed for ocean commerce. Besides, during the last 30 years (1839 to 1868) 83 per cent. of the class of vessels usually engaged in foreign trade and 58 per cent. of the entire sea-going sailing vessels of the United States have been built in the New England States.

In presenting a chart like this, of some national interest, I have thought proper to offer the following verification of its results, founded upon a comparison with other reliable statistics.

It is evident that since the formation of the government, American ship-building must have increased at about the same rate as the growth of American commerce. There have been wide differences in these developments from year to year, and even in successive periods of five or ten years, but in long periods we should find a substantial agreement. This is seen to be the case.

The tonnage of American vessels entered at sea-ports of the United States from foreign countries rose from 22,532,917 tons during the 20 years from 1828 to 1848, to 49,562,920 tons during the 20 years from 1848 to 1868, an increase of 120 per cent. During the same two periods of 20 years the ship-building of New England rose from 1,316,896 tons to 2,999,137 tons, an increase of 128 per cent.

This difference of only eight per cent. in the two rates of increase is accounted for by the relative increase, during the last five years, in the building of small vessels designed only for the home trade, and by the falling off in the building of large vessels designed for the foreign trade.

The chart shows that previous to the year 1845 there was a gradual increase of our ocean ship-building, that since that time it has fluctuated frequently and widely, and that during the last ten years it has been greatly depressed. The discovery of gold in California in 1848, and the speculative period which followed, stimulated the ship-building interest far beyond the legitimate demands of commerce. It ran up to its culmination in 1855, when it fell off rapidly, and the commercial revulsion of 1857 depressed it to a lower point in 1859 than it had touched since 1845. Before any material reaction had taken place, the war broke out, and within two years the depredations of rebel cruisers well-nigh drove the American flag from the commerce of the seas.

In 1862 the ship-building of the coast was less than it had been during any year since A. D. 1844, and there has been but little improvement since. The depression of our ocean ship-building is due, almost exclusively, to the great falling off in the building of large vessels designed for the foreign trade. This fact is shown by the following tabular statement:

Statement showing the number of schooners and the number of ships and barks built in the United States each year from A. D. 1855 to A. D. 1868.

[The Atlantic, Gulf, and Pacific coasts.]

Year.	No. of ships and barks.	No. of schooners.
1855	373	528
1856	302	438
1857	243	398
1858	118	367
1859	88	276
1860	109	347
1861	105	327
1862	43	167
1863	83	153
1864	106	282
1865	105	350
1866	84	419
1867	81	476
1868	69	458

Thus it is seen that while the building of ships and barks fell from 373 in the year 1855, to 69 in the year 1868, the building of schooners is in about as prosperous a condition as it was from 1855 to 1860.

The increased cost of building vessels, resulting from the burdens of taxation and the exposure of the ship-building interest, from its very nature, to the competition of the cheap labor of foreign countries, still holds the building of vessels designed for the foreign trade in that low condition to which it fell after the outbreak of the rebellion.

The building of brigs, schooners, and sloops designed for the home trade is not affected by foreign competition, from the fact that our navigation laws exclude all foreign vessels from that branch of our commerce.

The falling off in the building of large vessels since the war is further illustrated as follows: During the five years from 1853 to 1858, 65 per cent. of our total sea-going tonnage built on the coast consisted of ships and barks, while during the five years from 1863 to 1868, only 28 per cent. consisted of ships and barks.

During the year 1855—the most prosperous year in the history of American ship-building—there were 305 ships and barks and 173 schooners built in the New England States, the aggregate tonnage built having been 326,429 tons, while during the year ending June 30, 1868, there were 58 ships and barks, and 213 schooners built, the aggregate tonnage having been 98,697 tons. It is ascertained, moreover, that the average tonnage of ships and barks built since the war has fallen off 10 per cent.

The difference between the numerical expressions of tonnage under the "old" and "new" methods of admeasurement does not materially affect these results. Brigs, schooners, and sloops measure numerically less under the "new" than under the "old" admeasurement, while ships, barks, steamboats, and vessels having closed-in spaces above their hulls have their tonnage largely increased.

A very large number of our best ships were destroyed by privateers during the war, and besides, about 10 per cent. of our sea-going vessels are annually lost or abandoned as unfit for service.

While so large a proportion of our sea-going tonnage has gone out of existence, the depression of American ship-building has had its natural effect in the decadence of American shipping in foreign trade.

During the ten years from 1852 to 1862 the aggregate tonnage of American vessels entered at seaports of the United States from foreign countries was 30,225,475 tons, and the aggregate tonnage of foreign vessels entered was 14,699,192 tons, while during the five years from 1863 to 1868 the aggregate tonnage of American vessels entered was 9,299,877 tons, and the aggregate tonnage of foreign vessels entered was 14,116,427 tons—showing that American tonnage in our foreign trade had fallen from 206 to 66 per cent. of foreign tonnage in the same trade. Stated in other terms, during the decade from 1852 to 1862, 67 per cent. of the total tonnage entered from foreign countries was in American vessels, and during the five years from 1863 to 1868 only 39 per cent. of the aggregate tonnage entered from foreign countries was in American vessels, a relative falling off of nearly one-half.

At the same time our statistics indicate a gradual increase in the total tonnage entered from foreign countries; the fact being that while American tonnage in our foreign trade has fallen off, foreign tonnage has greatly increased.

This depression in the building of American sailing vessels for the foreign trade, as well as the decadence of our sailing marine in foreign trade, has not been compensated by the building or employment of American steam vessels.

The condition of our steam marine is in a lower condition even than that of our sailing vessels.

At the present time there are 39 American and 106 foreign steamers plying regularly between the Atlantic and Gulf ports of the United States and foreign ports, of which 8 American and 98 foreign steamers run to ports in Europe.

The number, tonnage, and nationality of steamers in our foreign trade is shown by the following tabular statement:

Statement showing the number, tonnage, and nationality of steamers plying regularly between the Atlantic and Gulf ports of the United States and foreign ports.

Nationality.	To ports in Europe.		To foreign ports, other than ports in Europe.		To all foreign ports.	
	Vessels.	Tons.	Vessels.	Tons.	Vessels.	Tons.
United States	8	11,927	31	30,939	39	42,866
England	68	150,944	5	2,268	73	153,212
France	6	17,548	2	843	8	18,391
North Germany	24	62,504			24	62,504
Mexico			1	205	1	205
Total	106	242,923	39	34,255	145	277,178

The foreign ports, other than ports in Europe to which there are steamers running, are Havana, Vera Cruz, Rio Janeiro, Port au Prince, Balize, St. Johns, New Brunswick; Halifax, and Yarmouth, Nova Scotia.

This list does not include 11 steamers which run to Aspinwall, and connect with the California steamers from Panama.

The building of ocean steamers is also in an exceedingly depressed condition. During the year ending June 30, 1868, there were but six ocean steamers built in the United States whose aggregate tonnage amounted to 14,855 tons. Nearly all the steamers built in this country during the last five years have been intended to meet the demands of our coastwise trade.

The depletion of our forests of ship timber, renders it probable that within the next ten years, we shall be compelled to resort to iron as a ship-building material. The iron ship-building enterprises which sprang up at several points in this country before the war, enjoyed for a while a degree of prosperity, which gave promise of great future success. That interest is now prostrated.

During the year ending June 30, 1868, there were but six iron vessels (all steamers) built in the United States whose aggregate tonnage amounted to 2,801 tons, all of which were built by Messrs. Harlan & Hollingsworth, of Wilmington, Delaware, and were designed for river navigation.

In order to show our relative inferiority in this branch of ship-building, it may be stated that during the year 1867, there were 99 iron sailing vessels built in England, Scotland, and Ireland, whose aggregate tonnage amounted to 59,033 tons, and 224 iron steamers whose aggregate tonnage amounted to 90,823 tons; the iron sailing vessels amounting to 34 per cent. of the total sailing tonnage built, and the iron steamers to 96 per cent. of the total steam tonnage built.

Thus it is seen that the competition of England has had a more disastrous effect upon the building and navigating of ocean steamers, in this country, than upon the building of large sailing vessels for our foreign trade.

In the building of iron vessels, too, England stands to-day unrivalled, while our country abounds in coal and iron, and as the past has clearly proved, we have all the requisite talent in naval architecture, and the skilled labor in the working of iron, which would enable us to produce as good vessels as ever entered into the competition of the commerce of the seas.

Very respectfully, your obedient servant,

JOSEPH NIMMO, Jr.

Hon. Hugh McCulloch,
Secretary of the Treasury.